# Bath Arts WORKSHOP

## COUNTERCULTURE IN THE 1970s

First published in 2021 by
Tangent Books
Unit 5.16 Paintworks
Arnos Vale
Bristol BS4 3EH
www.tangentbooks.co.uk



Art director and cover design: Penny Dale
Design: Sarah Goodwin
Picture editor: Jennie Potter-Barrie
Research and development: Corinne D'Cruz

A British Library CIP record is available.

ISBN 978 1 91434 502 9

Printed and bound in the United Kingdom by
Short Run Press, Exeter, EX2 7LW

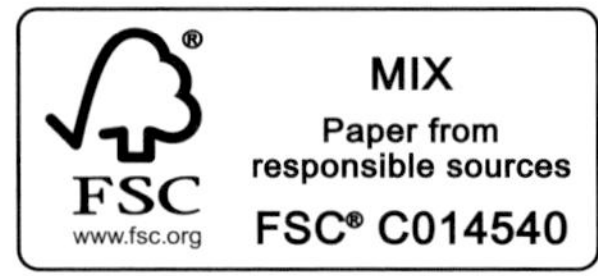

# Bath Arts WORKSHOP

## COUNTERCULTURE IN THE 1970s

BRIAN POPAY  CORINNE D'CRUZ  JENNIE POTTER-BARRIE
PENNY DALE  PHIL SHEPHERD  THORNTON KAY
AND VICTORIA FORBES ADAM

Edited by Victoria Forbes Adam

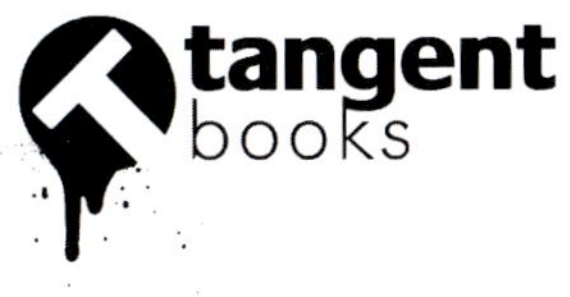

tangent
books

One of the key turning points in my life was the day that a retro-looking tour coach pulled over on a quiet West Country road. I couldn't imagine they were stopping to pick up a hitchhiker (me), so I just stood there. After a moment, Nigel's annoyed voice boomed out from the driver's seat, 'Well come on then, GET IN'. I stepped up to the doorway to see Nigel in the driver's seat with his wild long hair and unruly sheepskin vest sitting behind a dashboard festooned with a cuckoo clock and three 'Normals' in the front passenger seat. I stepped into another world that I never completely came back from.

*~ Jon Kiphart, on his first encounter with Bath Arts Workshop*

# CONTENTS

# MANY THANKS TO ALL WHO HELPED

The idea for this book came from Nigel Leach, lifelong social activist, performer and adventurer extraordinaire. Nigel had realised that Bath Arts Workshop (BAW) had sunk without documentary trace. Its 10-year seminal history was nowhere to be seen and, crucially, the Workshop had no internet profile whatsoever. Nigel got together with Phil Shepherd, the founder of BAW, to discuss writing a book to rectify the situation. After sounding out colleagues and friends, they called a public meeting in Bath in 2017 to brainstorm the idea. More than 100 people turned up, many of whom went on to send us written pieces on their memories of BAW.

At the same time, Nigel and Phil began planning an exhibition in Bath to capture this unique slice of theatrical, ecological and alternative social history. The exhibition, **Brilliant or Bonkers**, ran from June to November 2019 at The Museum of Bath at Work (a building we saved from demolition in the early 70s). It was created by Able Lawrence, Andy Hume, Chris Cooper, Georgina Carless, Nigel Leach, Paul Goddard, Rich Dunnill, Rolande Thomas, Stephanie Mills and Su Fahy, creative artists one and all. Many thanks are due to the family of the late Paul (Nasher) Nachman for providing access to his Super 8 footage of BAW that brought a luminous beauty to the show. The exhibition would not have happened without the initiative and support of Museum Director Stuart Burroughs and the volunteer team.

After the meeting, we created a book group of former BAW members, involving Brian Popay, Corinne D'Cruz, Jennie Potter-Barrie, Penny Dale, Phil Shepherd, Thornton Kay and Tory (Victoria) Forbes Adam. We began interviewing people and compiling a huge mass of documentary, film and photographic material, as well as drawing on Corinne's detailed archive and Penny's college thesis. Natural Theatre gave us access to their photographic records and many hours were spent at the Bath Chronicle's office scouring their files for press clippings.

We thank Mick Banks for his many literary contributions and Louise Osborn for her evocative poem. We are grateful to John Wood for chronicling both his first encounters with BAW, and then how he and others carried forth the spirit of community arts in Walcot and beyond. Thanks also to Steve Henwood of the Bell Inn and Wendy Matthews of Bath Fringe for supporting and encouraging this project.

We owe many thanks to Glyn Davies, architect and co-founder of Comtek. His beautiful architectural drawings and high quality photographs greatly enhanced the book and exhibition. Thank you also to Dave Dyas, John 'the lens' Austin and Roger Perry for many of the photos that helped make this book so captivating.

We thank Jackie Popay, a wonderful creative performer, for her support and contributions; and Rick Knapp, for his ever wry and realistic perspectives. Many thanks also to Ralph Oswick, a stalwart of BAW from start to finish. He was and is a brilliant performer, designer and artist. He contributed wit, writing and comments throughout the project. We were touched by the multitude of written pieces sent in by former BAW members, Bathonians, artists of all hues, and people who happened upon BAW by chance. Their contributions have brought life and meaning to the book.

Our group was voluntary, meeting monthly over a two-year period. We spent months trying to find a 'point of view' that could tell the story, a form that would capture our collective and individual perspectives. Phil wrote the first chapters of the book (along with many other pieces), and as ever brought a sense of the bigger picture, the purpose and values of BAW and the legacy that endured. We all wrote about Workshop life and took on other tasks: Corinne contributed editing, cast a careful eye over the text and brought her organisational skills to budgeting, fundraising and printing. Thornton provided most of the information and resources for the Comtek-related sections of the book; and Brian's writing delightfully captured the anarchy and humour of our performances and working life.

Many thanks to Victoria (Tory) who edited the book with expertise and consideration, working full time for most of 2019/20. And to Jennie who practically lived in our Dropbox account for months on end, creating a visual archive and brilliantly matching images to the text. We are grateful to Jennie and Penny, who both contributed many delightful drawings to the book, and to Penny who coordinated the design process. We couldn't have done it without her artistry and design skills. We thank Bryan Dale for his help with scanning and other practicalities, and our copy editor Jane Baldock whose unerring eye for detail was invaluable. Finally, a massive thank you to our designer Sarah Goodwin for creating such a visually unique and beautiful book.

We are grateful to our anonymous donor whose generosity made this book possible; and our supporters who donated a total of £1,300 on JustGiving. Thank you to all the colleagues, friends and others who were involved in BAW or supported it in so many ways.

The Book Group

# BAW BOOK GROUP MEMBERS

Brian Popay

Corinne D'Cruz

Jennie Potter-Barrie

Penny Dale

Phil Shepherd

Thornton Kay

Victoria (Tory) Forbes Adam


We are identified by our first names at the start of each of our written pieces.
Everyone else is identified by their full name at the start of each of their contributions.

Ralph Oswick is often referred to as Ralph throughout the book.

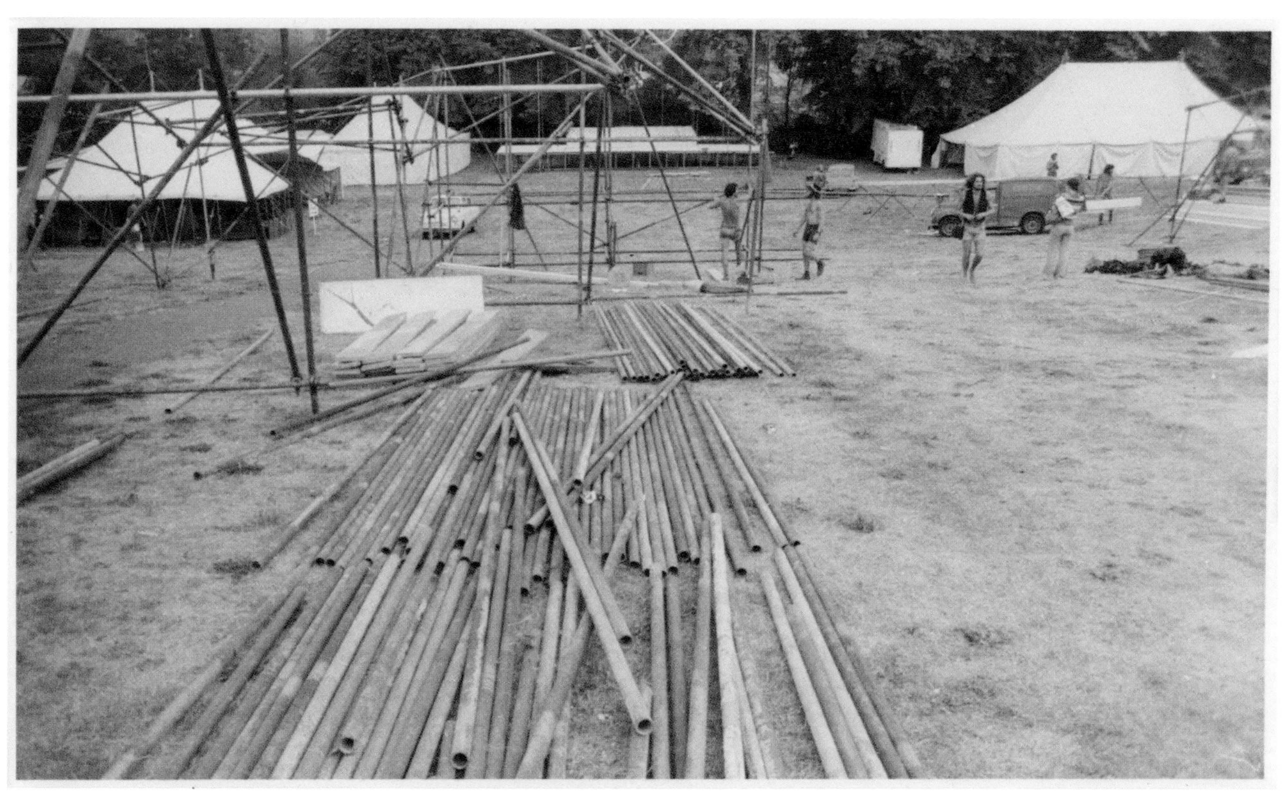

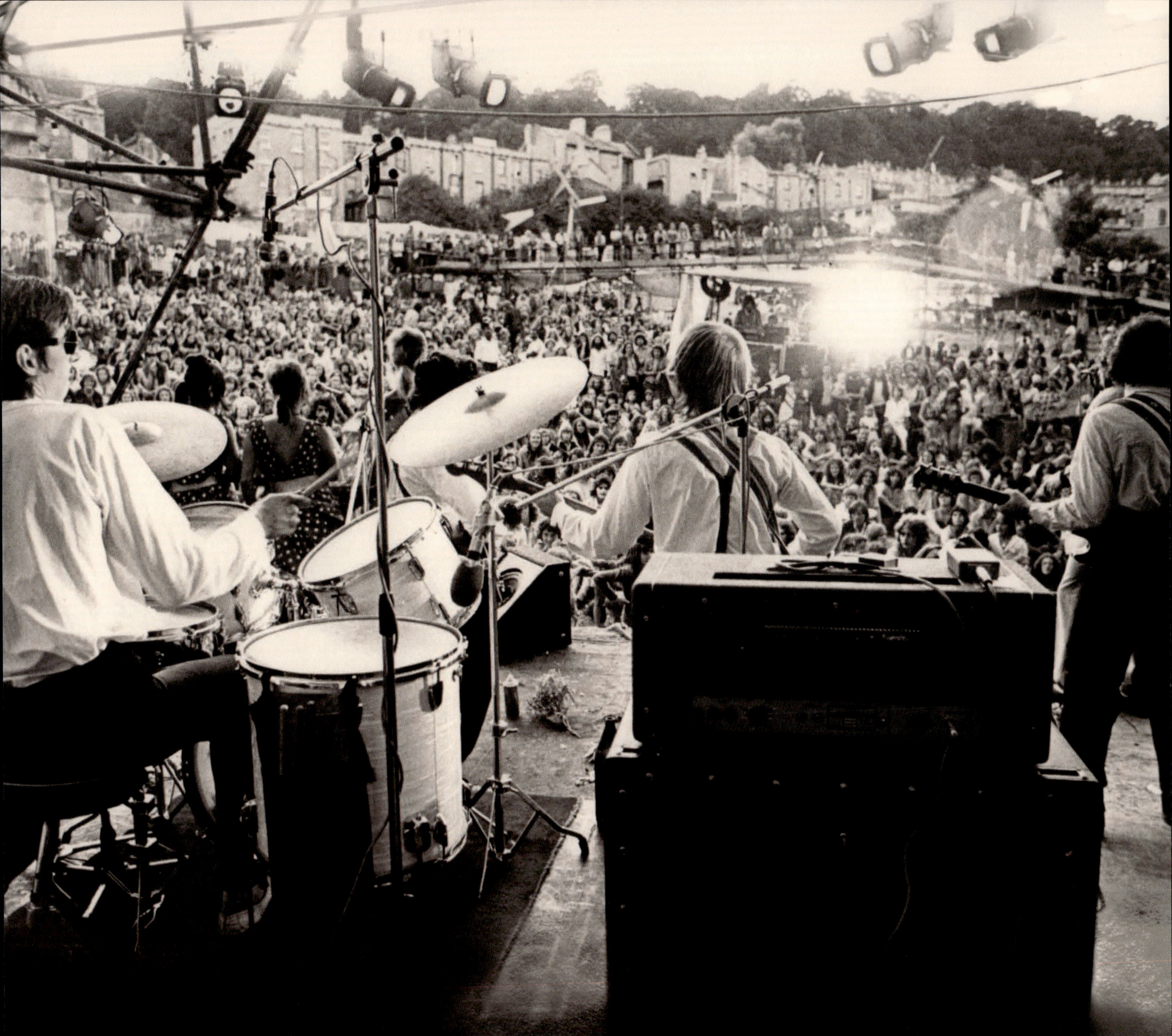

# CHAPTER 1
# INTRODUCTION 1969

In this book we chart the behind-the-scenes story of a unique counterculture that sprang to life in Bath, Somerset during the 10 years between 1969 and 79. It tells the story of how Bath became the setting for a spectacular flowering of creative activity and social enterprise, a noisy and irreverent revolution of artists, musicians, performers, community technologists, entrepreneurs, artisans and radical thinkers, all working with local communities to set up cultural, social and technology initiatives. This was not a perfect flowering and many mistakes were made. There were some disasters and much chaos along the way. But that was the essence of the thing. We were free to experiment and take risks and often the results surpassed our wildest expectations.

Through a collection of first-hand accounts, original photographs and documents, our book is an account of Bath's counterculture in action – the linked stories of Bath Arts Workshop (BAW) and Comtek (Community Technology).

We challenge the assumption that 60s ideals were naïve and unworkable, or an adolescent failure to grow up and take responsibility. We believe that the countercultural expressions of the time amounted to more than just hedonism, lax moral codes and bad fashion! To different degrees we shared a vision of a world in which compassion and generosity came first, along with faith in human creative potential, concern and respect for the environment, and an underlying critique of the class-ridden, consumerist and militaristic culture that prevailed. While not a political movement in the conventional sense, we related closely to other people around the world who were seeking to address the issues and tensions of the time, including growing inequality and discrimination, civil rights, gay and women's rights and the persistent threat of nuclear war.

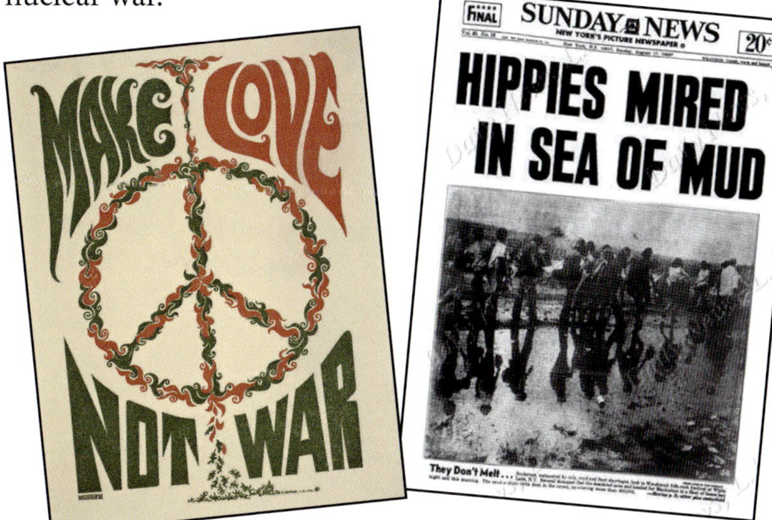

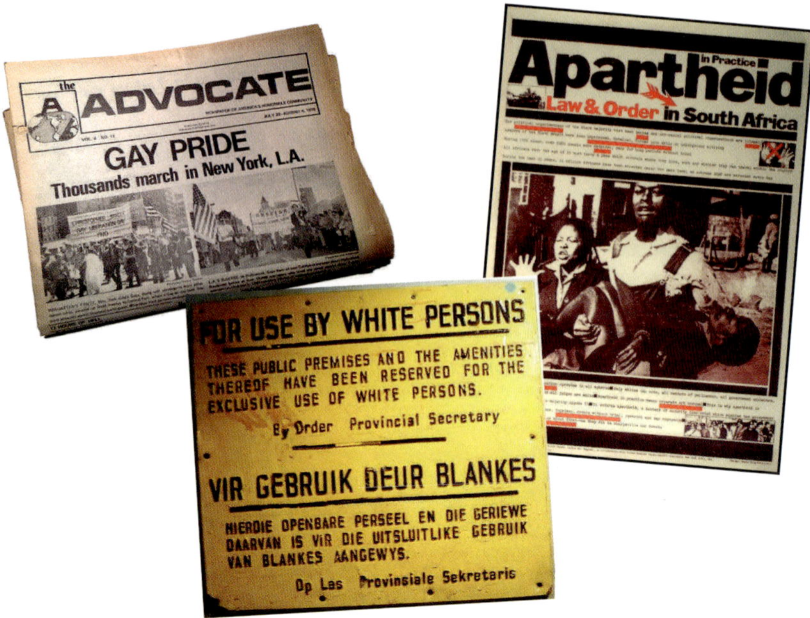


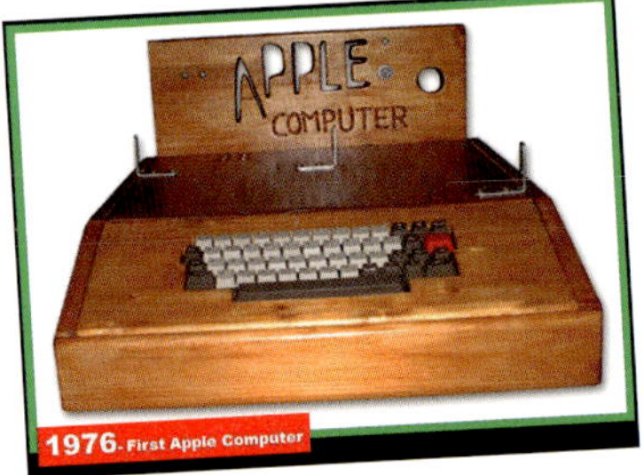


FOR USE BY WHITE PERSONS

THESE PUBLIC PREMISES AND THE AMENITIES
THEREOF HAVE BEEN RESERVED FOR THE
EXCLUSIVE USE OF WHITE PERSONS.

By Order Provincial Secretary

VIR GEBRUIK DEUR BLANKES

NIERDIE OPENBARE PERSEEL EN DIE GERIEWE
DAARVAN IS VIR DIE UITSLUITLIKE GEBRUIK
VAN BLANKES AANGEWYS.

Op Las Provinsiale Sekretaris

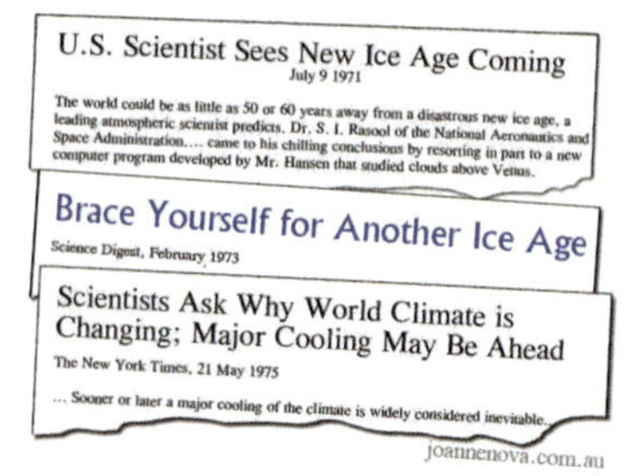


to come. Mainstream indifference to environment problems, such as oil spills, pollution, soil contamination, toxic waste, and wasted resources led to the formation of Friends of the Earth in 1969, and Greenpeace in 1971. The 70s were also an age of rapid tech advance-

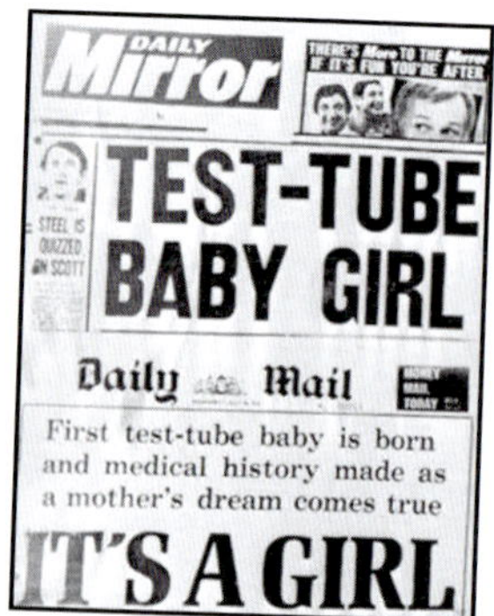


ment, when many of the devices we now take for granted were first designed and manufactured – cell phones, micro-processors, calculators, video games and VCRs – to name a few.

This was a time when suspicion and mistrust of authority were gradually eroding traditional deference, although there was much resistance to change. Economic recession led to power cuts and a three-day week in 1974. Strikes were a constant as wages fell during those years, eventually

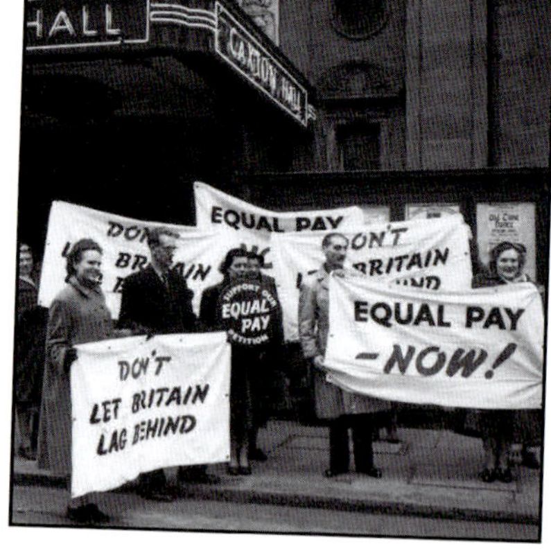


leading to thousands of job losses. Despite the 1970 Equal Pay Act, a woman could not get a mortgage without a male guarantor. Domestic violence and child abuse were commonplace and hidden from view for years

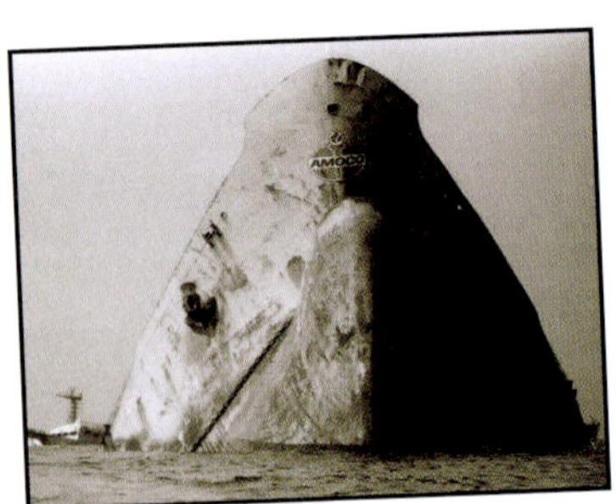

For many of us across the UK, this was a period in which we tried to change the world we had inherited by turning our ideals into reality. Ideals that were informed by attitudes to work, interpersonal politics, the environment, the value of community and a belief in the positive power of creativity. Fifty years on, we ask to what extent the counterculture influenced our lives and wider social attitudes in the long term. We ask whether the ground-breaking ideas, innovations and potential solutions emerging at that time can perhaps resonate with renewed relevance today.

**Phil Shepherd**, who founded the Workshop recalls: It began in the summer of 1969, just before my 21st birthday.

Encouraged by my great friend and collaborator Able Lawrence, I wrote a letter to Bath City Council to see if they would be interested in having an arts workshop set up in the city. I had been struck by the atmosphere of the place after hitchhiking through it some years earlier.  Weaned on Jack Kerouac and be-bop jazz, I was embracing the anarchic positivity and radical ideas of the 1960s with a passion.



**Phil:** My ambition was to create an organisation that would resemble London's Drury Lane Arts Lab, where I had worked until it was forced to close – a space where art and creativity could flourish, where it was possible to take risks and have a lot of fun at the same time, a space where it was OK to fail, and where everyone was welcome. What was brilliant was that I quickly discovered that I was by no means the only one who wanted to go on this adventure; and although there were many who dismissed us as hippies and lay-abouts, and others who found us cliquey, we ended up involving hundreds of people in our work.

My letter to Bath City Council proposed a centre *in which the barriers between arts media are indistinct… in which the interaction between these forms will be given full play*. A

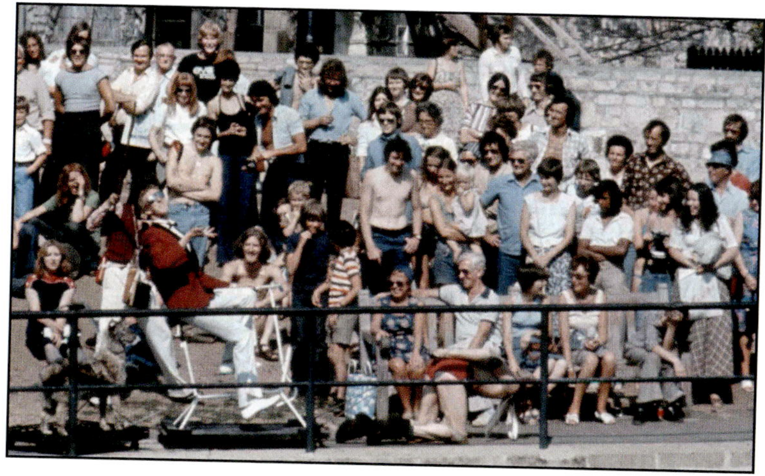

centre in which the opportunity to participate would be given *to as many people as possible… priority being given to setting up a theatre company… to provide a valuable contribution to the life of the community and an ideal outlet for local talent*. To my surprise, Bath City Council responded to my letter suggesting a meeting. With just £40 between us, my friend Ross and I hitched to Bath the following weekend to begin the adventure. We wanted nothing less than to change the world.

Our book tells the story from many perspectives. From those who took a lead role in shaping and delivering the work, to those who took part in our activities; from the fellow travellers exploring their own new ways of living, to those who looked on, not always admiringly! It is a record of a brief moment of freedom, a time when we lived our politics to the full, although we rarely discussed things in these terms. A time when we found a way to celebrate community and creativity and to explore non-consumerist lifestyles. It was a time that influenced many lives and a story that might otherwise remain untold.

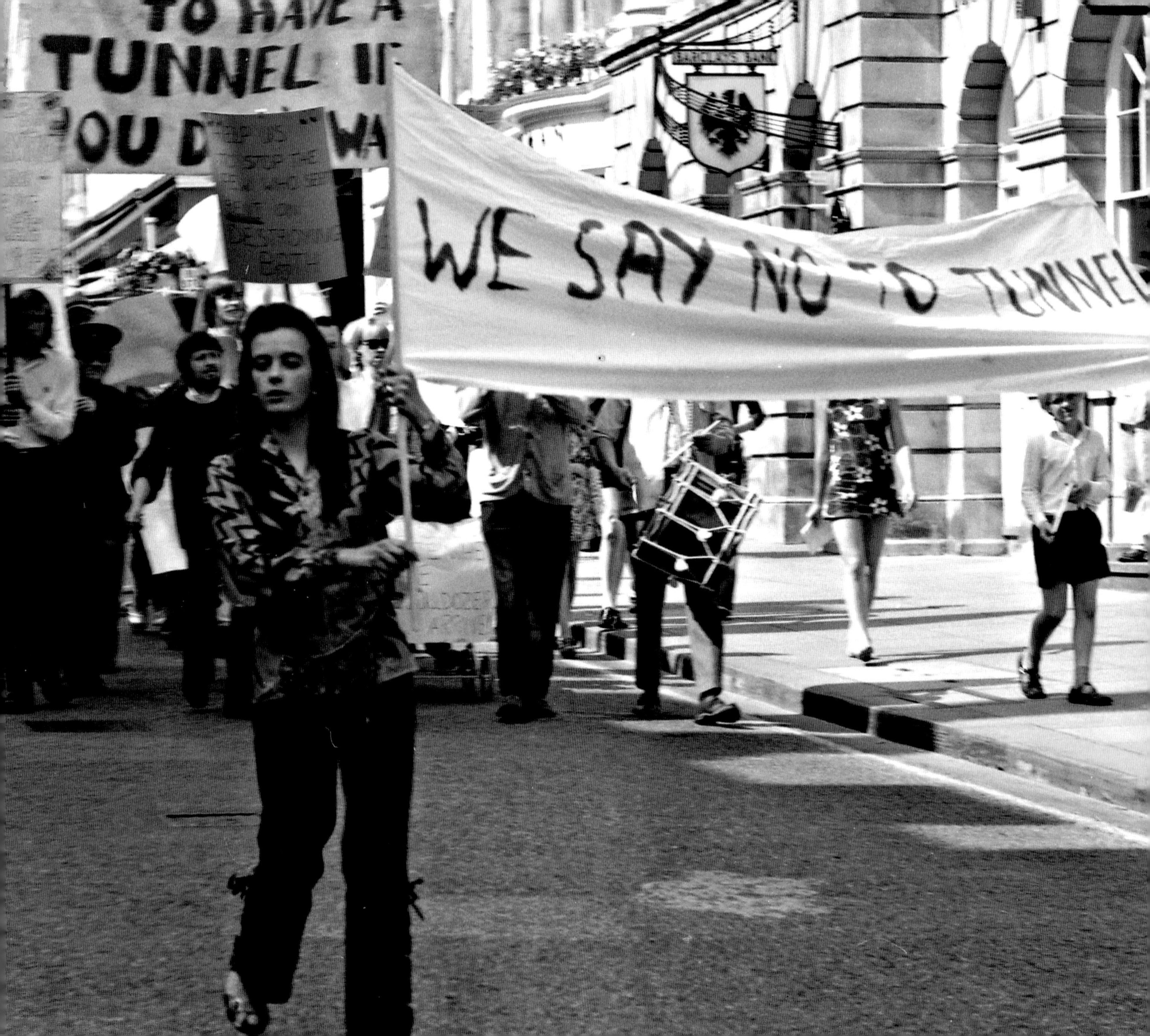

TO HAVE A
TUNNEL IF
YOU D   WA
WE SAY NO TO TUNNEL

# CHAPTER 2

# EARLY DAYS 1970-71

**In which we found our first home and never turned anyone away. We took on printing, street arts and music, and created a unique approach to theatre which would define BAW for the next half century.**

**Phil:** The Workshop found its first proper home in early 1970, on the top two floors of a house at Fountain Buildings at the bottom of Lansdown Hill. On 16 May we held the first of two public meetings in the Crypt Cafe next door, described by Brian Popay as 'a bizarre funereal-themed cafe where guests sat at coffin-shaped tables.

It was about the only place in town where freaks hung out'. My friend Able remembers that 'people came from a variety of sources: local alternative thinkers, university students, wandering beats and hippies. They had a variety of skills and interests, but they were all interested in the idea of getting something new and alternative going in Bath'.

Working at a pace that was to become the norm of the time, within a month of the inaugural meeting we had organised our first event. *A Celebration* was held in Victoria Park on 13 June. Three hundred people showed up.

Richard Coleman was a sociology student at Bath Uni. He'd frequented counterculture centres Indica Bookshop and the London Arts Lab before coming to Bath. He let us use his van for the event.

'I found the University very conservative, so it was exciting to come across BAW and get involved. I loved that connection to the underground culture of the day, and that period remains one of the top 20 experiences in my life.'

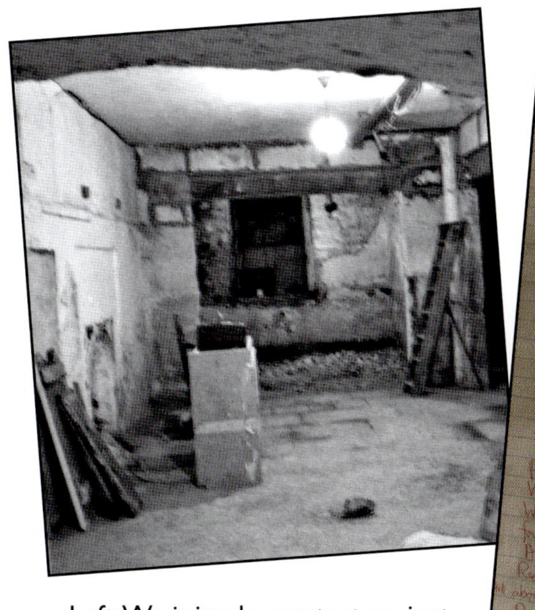

Left: We joined a protest against Buchanan Tunnel (see *Chapter 6*)

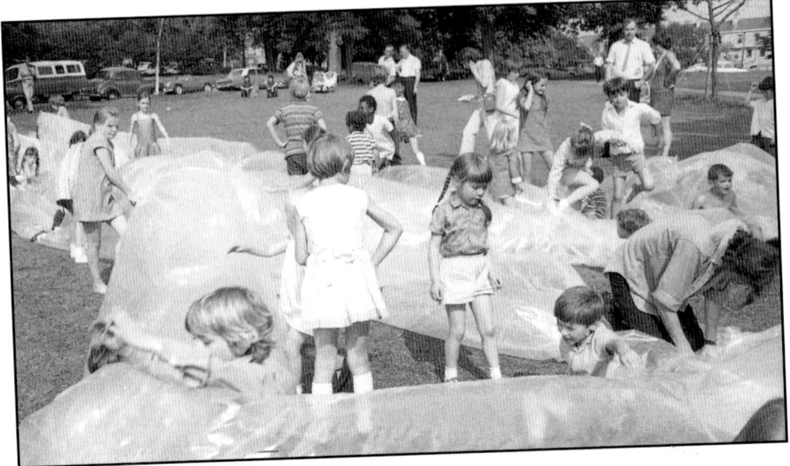

*Absolutely Free* in Victoria Park

**Phil:** A second free event in the park, ***Absolutely Free***, followed on 1 August with inflatables from Pat and Tan Pearson, stories from Paul Cresswell, music from local jazzers Danny Sheppard and Magma, poetry from, among others, Brian Grist and Tony Lopez, painting and more. These were unusual events for that time, in bringing together different art forms in one place, 60s-style happenings really. I remember an excitement and sense of freedom in the atmosphere – something that emerges when you break down barriers and anything can happen. They were the first experiments – prototypes of the festivals to come. Unfortunately a poet used a swear word

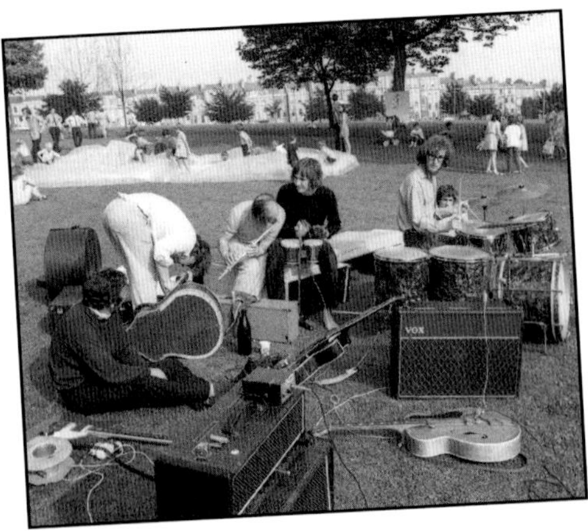

during the event, so feedback in the pages of the Bath Evening Chronicle was mixed!

*We do not want the John Lennon art,* Councillor Evans

*At Hyde Park they are doing it, and it is quite the thing,* Councillor Miss Rawlings

Miss Rawlings was right, of course. The late 60s and early 70s saw a veritable explosion of new work in England. **Corinne D'Cruz** (writing in 2005) described how a culture that embraced street art and community engagement was emerging across the western world.

Some of us came from academic backgrounds, art colleges, drama colleges, universities… some not. Some were more interested in theatricality than others. Some were sculptors or musicians or fine artists. Some could make wonderful soundtracks in a backroom at home – everything seemed to get thrown into the pot and mixed around and things turned out differently from the way they'd been before. There were large and small, visual and verbal, narrative and non-narrative, abstract and naturalistic and any number of intermediaries. And a generous sprinkling of humour. There was no real name for what we were doing. There was a great desire to break down barriers and forge new territory, to 'first-foot' it.
***An Open Letter to Participants at the Internationale Street Arts Konferenz, Münster, 8 June 2005***

**Ralph Oswick** was one of those who travelled to Bath to get involved. He writes: I was working in a hospital mortuary, so it was no surprise that I responded with alacrity and glee to my mate Dave Herschel's suggestion that I came to Bath to work with that strange and wondrous creature the Bath Arts Workshop (BAW). We had studied theatre design at Wimbledon School of Art. It was a fairly classic course but with a strict work ethic and insistence on detail that remains with me today. So I deserted my lifeless charges and went off to be a hippy. A strange kind of hippy in my Pierre Cardin sports jacket and my Harry Palmer glasses. But the trademark of the Arts Workshop was acceptance. It was a remarkably supportive organisation from the outset, a place where people's weaknesses could be assimilated into the wider aspirations of the group and their strengths developed, although we rarely discussed this formally.

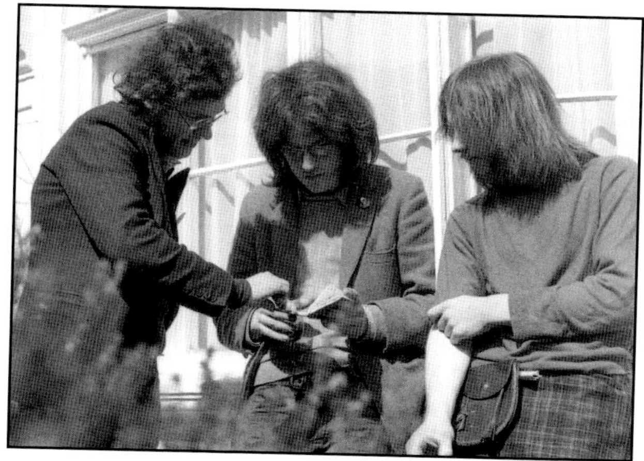

Ralph, Phil, Magnus

**Phil:** These were early days at BAW and we had hardly begun to sense our potential strength. Our resources were minimal although fortunately we had the use of a phone from the very early days thanks to our long-suffering neighbours Sandy and Dave. As more people got involved, we found ourselves invited to run a series of play-schemes at SLAB youth centre at Hanham Common in Bristol. These were arranged through Magnus MacDonald's dad Ian, a GP and local councillor.

It was that summer that Magnus became our live-in chef at Fountain Buildings, building a room for himself out of railway sleepers and orange boxes cantilevered across the top of our precipitous stairwell. None of the rest of us would ever step foot inside it for fear of plummeting to the basement three floors below! Magnus was the first person to get paid any kind of wage by BAW, having negotiated a wage of £1 per week.

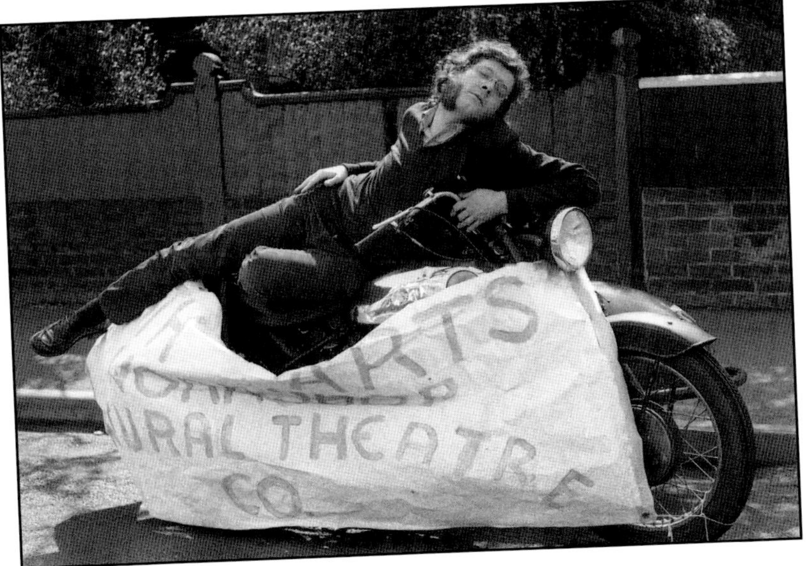


Ralph

**Magnus Macdonald:** Fountain Buildings was great! I remember my interview, applying for a job, coming in, asking for a pound a week, somewhere to sleep and something to eat. That's how I became the cook and learnt how to feed people on a very low budget, getting Jerry to go out busking to raise the money for supplies from the Caribbean shop just up the hill, discovering that spices added to rotten vegetables made them quite palatable, and that's how porridge became a major part of our diet, ending up with a porridge-eating competition some months later! The only reason we needed money was for Natch (Natural Dry Cider), all the rest was hilarity.

**Phil:** We were certainly expert at living on very little, the evening meals being the only form of payment for work done. We took it in turns to do the rounds of local food shops (supermarkets barely existed then) – like the wonderful grocers Cater, Stoffell and Fortts – on the scrounge for ends of bacon, and anything else they might have been thinking of throwing out.

**Ralph:** Having very little money, by the time the community meal came round I would sometimes be shaking with hunger. I once got caught eating a Mars bar and not sharing. The original basement HQ was rather dark and I had gone to the next-door sweet shop in bright sunlight with some scraped-together groats. I thought nobody could see me scoffing it as I came down the stairs but their hungry eyes were used to the gloom and accusing shouts rang out all round. Of course I shared my chocolate.

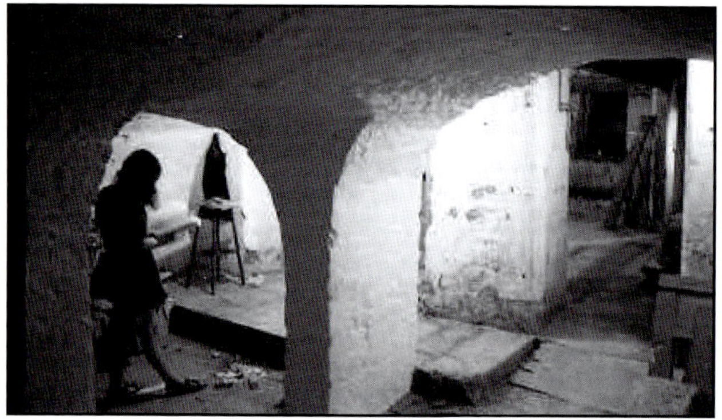
The dark basement

**Corinne** was one of the few Workshop members who was actually from Bath. She got involved while still at school. She writes: I spent more and more time with these hairy Workshop people, some more unkempt than others. I remember celebrating my 18th birthday in May 71 with a roomful of gyrating bodies, manes flowing, in the basement. My parents looked in briefly and engaged in a quick, nervous dance. They were still young then but boy did they look different! My mum with permed hair or 60s wigs, and suits (later put to good use as costumes for our shows) and much shorter skirts than me; and my dad with glossy Brylcreemed hair, suit and tie. Ballroom dancing was their bag, not this new free-form stuff. It's easy to forget but, looking back, the generation gap was much more rigid than it is now.

**Corinne:** I was born and grew up in Bath, the first child of an Anglo-Indian boy with some Portuguese ancestry, who married a West Country girl with German and Scottish antecedents. I was made painfully aware that I was different by the often cruel remarks of my pre-school playmates. Racism was rife in the suburban 50s and 60s, so being the

**Phil:** We were included in the *List of Crash Pads in Great Britain* published by BIT information.[1] This meant we had people turning up every few days asking for a place to stay. We never turned anyone away, with the front bedroom becoming the destination for most unexpected guests. This was mainly down to the late (and much missed) Chris 'Bulldog' Dinmore's good heart, whose room (affectionately known as the 'black hole') was the biggest. Such was the spirit of the times, I don't remember him ever complaining. We had many and various guests, including one whom we recognised in the newspaper years later as one of the Blanket Protesters in Crumlin Road Jail.

We asked nothing of our overnight guests – no ID, no payment, it was all about mutual trust. This trust was never seriously abused. We don't remember having a front door lock and if we did, it didn't work. I used to get fed up however with being woken by the police on their morning rounds, when they seemed to think nothing of walking into my room to enquire if I'd 'seen so-and-

so recently?' Needless to say, I never had. There were no drug busts at Fountain Buildings or at any subsequent BAW buildings or events. We weren't sanctimonious about it, we just didn't want to put the organisation at risk. We had no money anyway, and there were usually many more interesting things to do.

Meanwhile, **Rick Knapp** joined us at Fountain Buildings. Nottingham born, ex-Bath Uni sociology student Rick (who later became a founder director of the BAW Company) was the owner of a Morris Minor ex-Post Office van. So now we had not only a base of sorts but also a practical means of transport. Admittedly it took a good few years for any significant income to be found, but transport and retail became our staple for the following few years, given the lack of revenue support from South West Arts Association or anywhere else.

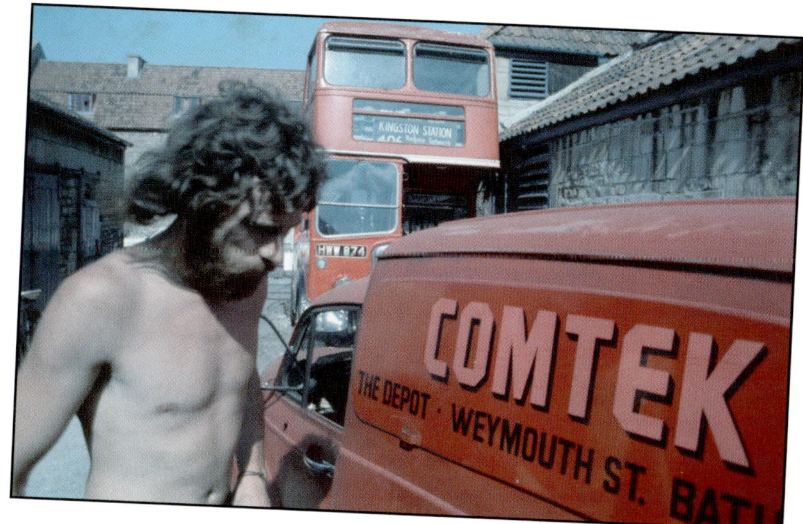


Rick and his van

---

1. A London-based free information service, a local version of whose hand duplicated news-sheets we produced ourselves under the title of *Output Information*. These covered everything from gender politics to home brewing.

**Phil:** Rick always had his head screwed on when it came to money and found it frustrating that, in the early days, the rest of us tended to be so unconcerned on that level. I had heard about the US Yippy movement, who were sort of precursors to the anti-capitalists of later decades. They suggested that work needed to be more like play, an idea I could relate to. They argued that pursuit of a career with finance as a major motivator was anti-life and unhealthy. Not that we were completely unrealistic. Rick and Thornton Kay (who, with Glyn Davies, were later to co-found Comtek) worked hard to generate incomes from promoting benefit music gigs at the YMCA with Tom Browne, and at the University Small Hall.

There was quite a strong connection to Bath Uni in the early days, several of us being students or ex-students at the time, and we were involved in promoting and supporting events on campus from the autumn of 1970 onwards. I remember one of the first occasions, run in conjunction with the University Jazz Society, was with the Mike Westbrook Jazz Band and local jazzers Magma. We provided a light show of sorts based on local film collections. The Uni provided the hall for free on this occasion.

Of course, these were comparatively affluent times (at least up until 1974 when the price of oil quadrupled), which meant we could be less concerned with material survival than our parents had been. It was certainly much easier to draw social security (unemployment benefit) than it ever is now. While there were hidden subsidies too from friends and lovers, those still living at home or with other sources of income, we were all interested in finding new ways of living. Whatever our faults, and we doubtless had many, our default approach was to prioritise the next creative idea, favouring compassion and community benefit above material gain.

## Projects with a vengeance

**Phil:** After agreeing (but rarely actually paying) an extortionate rent, we had begun to use the Fountain Buildings' dark, damp and genuinely Georgian basement as a focus for the work. It was hopelessly inadequate in most ways, but it was available to us and we were undaunted.

**Corinne:** The basement served as our office, meeting and rehearsal space, and through the cold winter of 70/71 we somehow managed to run up a plethora of projects, most of them directly under the BAW umbrella, but some of them collaborations with existing organisations.

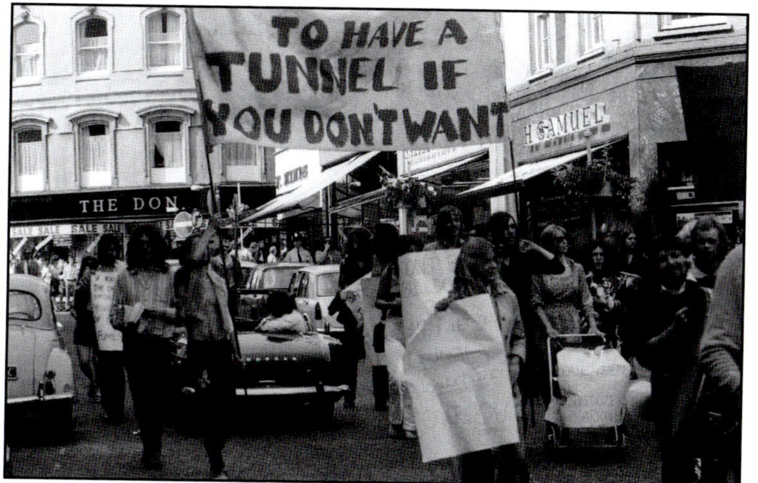


Buchanan Tunnel protest

### Projects included:

- *Output* - a monthly information broadsheet for public distribution which, after the move to the Organ Factory, also offered a telephone help and advice service.
- *Input* - an internal news sheet
- *Genesis* - a magazine
- SPROUT Community Action Group - a collaboration between Bath Youth and Community Office and BAW.
- EAR advisory and counselling service, run in tandem with SPROUT.
- A craft market
- A duplicating service – the inky spills of the Gestetner machine.
- Regular open theatre workshops and a loose formation which gradually evolved into our own theatre company, plus props and costumes that were also available for hire.
- King Kong Workforce – odd jobs, painting and decorating, removals.
- Playschemes and various workshops, discos, creative projects for kids and young people.
- A regular contract with SLAB – a Bristol-based youth project – to lead workshops for kids.
- Jumble sales
- An annual festival of theatre, music, community arts and later alternative technology.
- BAW also lent support and publicity to various groups like the Bath Artists Coop, Bath Claimants and Unemployed Workers' Union, Bath Women's Lib, Tenants' Union, Gay Awareness/Gay Lib and many more.

**Phil:** The only heating was a small fan heater so normal attire was coats and hats but, despite arctic conditions, our energy and enthusiasm carried us through. Help with equipment and occasional small grants came early on from our hero and friend, Phil Garner, the city's Youth and Community Officer.

*Bath Arts Workshop appears to be up against insuperable odds to get people to do something creative,* The Bath Chronicle

**Phil:** King Kong Workforce and transport (and later our shops) grew out of Rick's van and, improbably enough, selling crafts out of the old coal bunker at Fountain

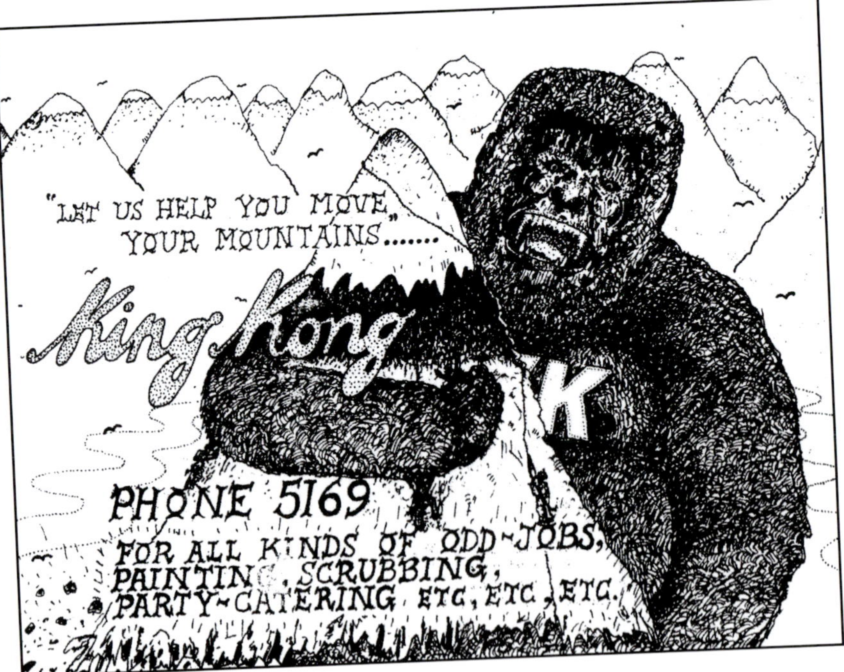


Advert for King Kong in *Genesis* magazine

Buildings. We had glimpsed the building blocks of generative capacity, a way to be independent of grants and subsidies, a way to make our voices heard, unfettered by compromise or other people's agendas. And for a few years, with a huge expending of energy and not a little help from jobs, unemployment benefit and family members, we made it work. We used any surplus income to create theatre, music and art. We were a nascent social enterprise – not that anyone would have recognised the term at the time.

The autumn of 1970 was an ever-accelerating blur of activity – concerts and events, weekly crafts and artwork stalls running wherever we could set up a table, rehearsals for the first theatre show, *The Hassle and Grope Show*, and weekly film shows at our local pub, The Hat & Feather. That is, until the fire officer called a halt to screenings in the pub's upstairs room. After that we ran weekly music gigs with local bands. There was a terrific buzz about those days, everything was possible and we were carried forward on a surge of creative energy and ideas.

## Natural Theatre is born

**Phil:** The ***Natural Theatre Company***, named after Natural Dry Cider (known by every Bathonian as Natch), came together quickly after our first performance, and we decided to stage a new show every Saturday evening in The Hat & Feather.

**Brian:** Our first production, in 1971, was part of a student festival of theatre, a show called *Bewitched, Bothered, and Bewildered* (known as BBB). Soon after came *The Spotty Blelb Show*, a cabaret featuring an oversized youth who achieves enlightenment. *The Respectable Terrace* followed, a melodrama set in Bath. This was followed by the *Lawn Show* featuring an impossibly large piece of Astroturf; and later, *Windows,* a strange stage show in which each cast member was trapped behind their personal window.



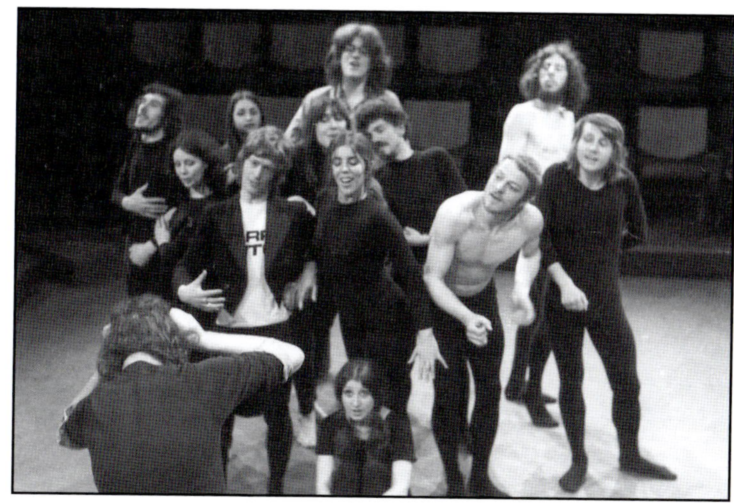

*Bewitched, Bothered and Bewildered*



**Brian:** Our work drew on the idea of 'invisible theatre', a phrase popular at the time. We were often invited to perform alongside a political demonstration. Our response was to adopt an extremist opposing view on the matter, thereby undermining it by its very absurdity. This style of performance we made our own, as we became the objects of our own ridicule, so to speak.

One such occasion was the Festival of Light, a conservative Christian Crusade to restore the morals of the nation. It was led by Lord Longford, Cliff Richard and Mary Whitehouse – well-known figures at the time constantly railing against the younger generation and its immoral ways. Mostly it was anti-sex. The crusade marched through London and culminated in a massive rally at Trafalgar Square. Three male 'actors' from the Naturals mingled amongst the crowd, dressed as Adolf Hitler, a middle-aged dad, and his teenage daughter (Stan Pollard). 'She' handed out her sci-fi erotica cartoons, whereupon 'Dad' angrily snatched them back from the increasingly hostile militant Christians. In the end, 'Adolf Hitler' (Dave Herschel) was picked up by the police and carried off from the square. (The Gay Liberation Front street performers were also there on that memorable day.)

When The Festival of Light came to Bath in September 1971, their rally in front of Bath Abbey was greeted by shouts and jeers from the North Somerset Anarchist group and members of BAW. The protest resulted in a memorable front-page headline in the Chronicle: *We Raised our Voices for Freedom'* – *Bath Abbey Demo by Anarchists.*

**Brian:** At around this time, we invented The Normals. A row of four men, each wearing a complete head covering (a silver lurex stocking), black bowler hat, black dinner suit and white gloves, all of which gave them a rather sinister air. But they could change instantly from scary dominating men to lovable infantile puppies, depending on whether or not they were being threatened themselves. They were

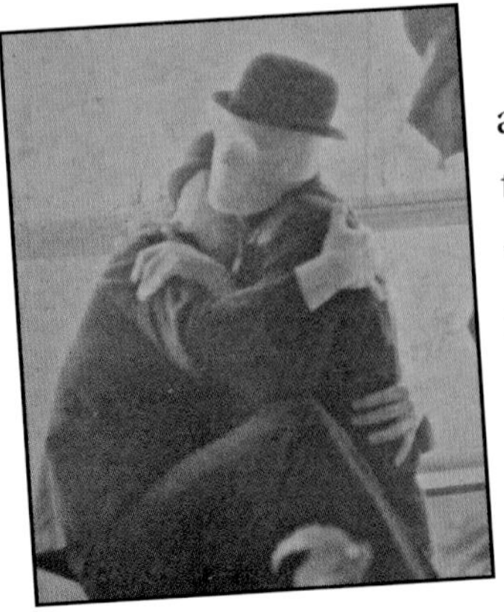

Top/bottom/right:
The Normals

at one moment full of bravado, the next crumbling wimps. They were often wheeled out when we needed an instant authority figure as they could easily double for faceless bureaucrats, men from the ministry, technocrats and so on.

**Jennie:** It was a strict rule that once in costume and in public, we kept in character no matter what. The Normals never spoke and walked in formation. They were vaguely intimidating and vaguely vulnerable. I have sat in

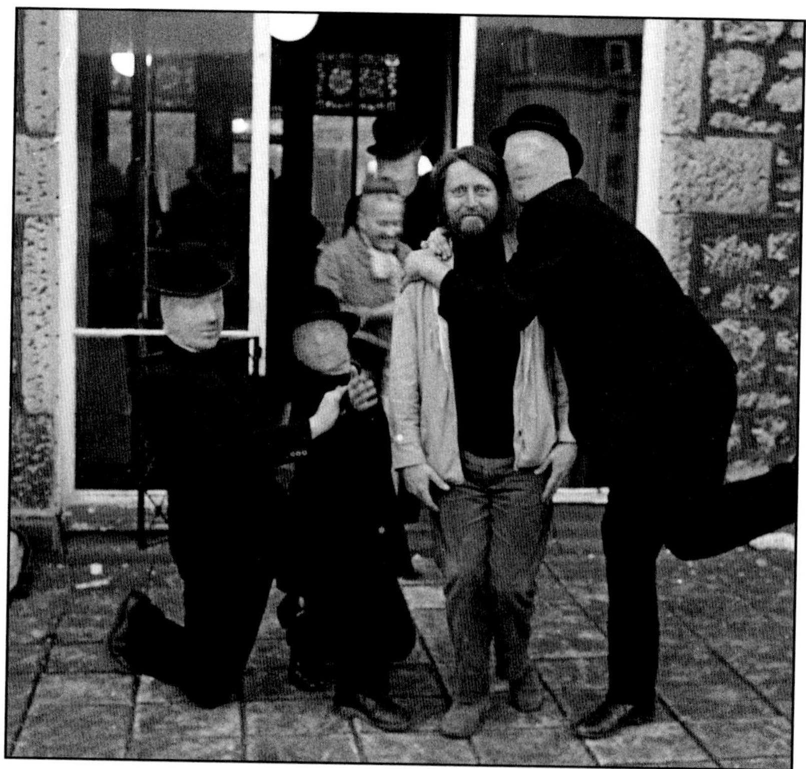

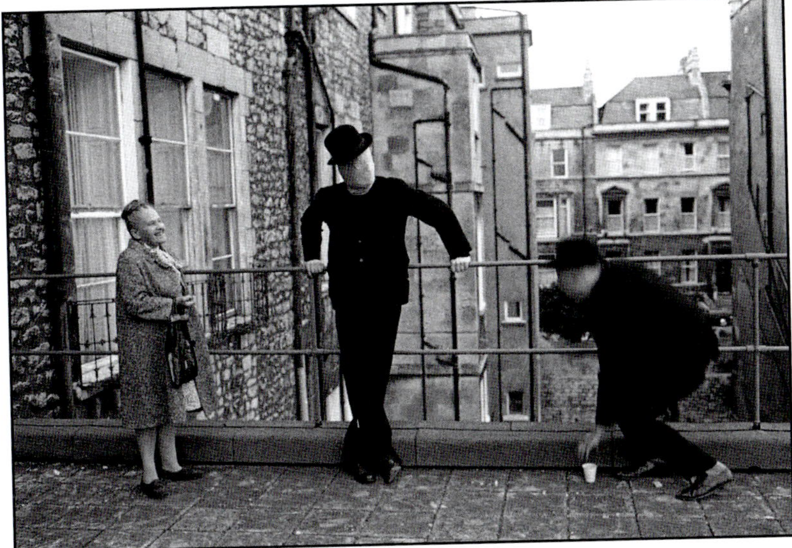

a dressing room and felt the hairs on the back of my neck prickle as my friends changed into their Normals' costumes. Once, after being stopped by the police, they were loaded into a van after refusing to answer questions. They were released without charge once they got round the corner.

## The first festival, 1971

**Phil:** Our first festival ran on the same dates as the Bath Festival in the early summer of 1971. More a string of events under a collective banner then a coherent programme, it was intended to provide an alternative to what we saw as the elitism of the mainstream version. The main children's event in the park unfortunately took place on a soaking wet day, so we hurriedly moved the activities to the Fountain Buildings basement. Astonishingly, quite a few parents and children seemed happy to take their offspring into the damp and semi-gloom of the Georgian cellars. Health and safety? Risk assessments? No such thing in those days, but fortunately no one died, those who attended enjoyed themselves and BAW lived on to see another day.

We were eventually given notice to quit Fountain Buildings when our landlord decided to sell the house. This was probably a good thing, as it was in truth a hazardous environment.

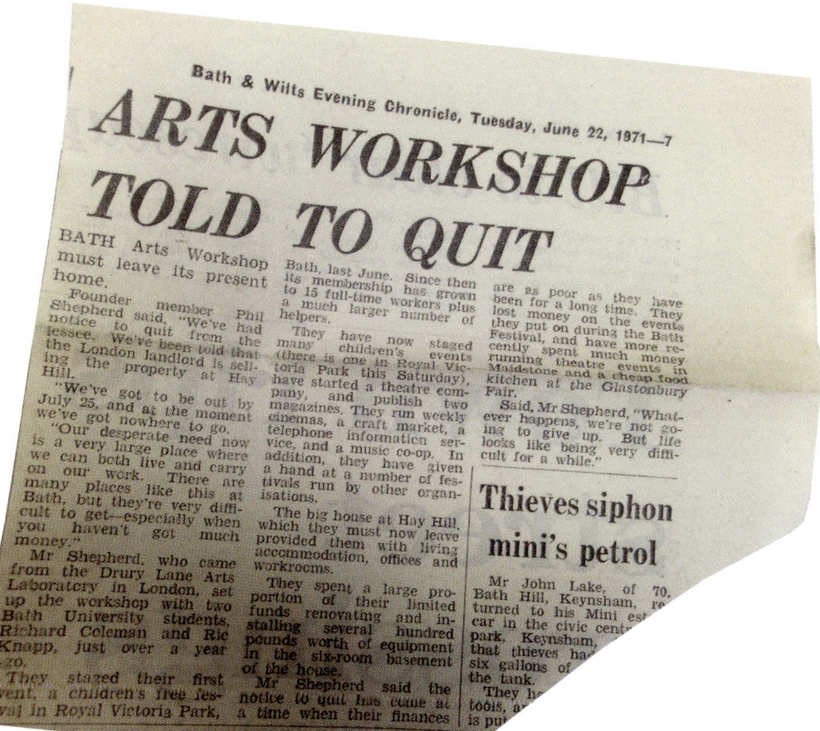

Bath & Wilts Evening Chronicle, Tuesday, June 22, 1971—7

# ARTS WORKSHOP TOLD TO QUIT

BATH Arts Workshop must leave its present home.

Founder member Phil Shepherd said, "We've had notice to quit from the lessee. We've been told that the London landlord is selling the property at Hay Hill.

"We've got to be out by July 25, and at the moment we've got nowhere to go.

"Our desperate need now is a very large place where we can both live and carry on our work. There are many places like this at Bath, but they're very difficult to get—especially when you haven't got much money."

Mr Shepherd, who came from the Drury Lane Arts Laboratory in London, set up the workshop with two Bath University students, Richard Coleman and Ric Knapp, just over a year ago.

They staged their first event, a children's free festival in Royal Victoria Park,

Bath, last June. Since then its membership has grown to 15 full-time workers plus a much larger number of helpers.

They have now staged many children's events (there is one in Royal Victoria Park this Saturday), have started a theatre company, and publish two magazines. They run weekly cinemas, a craft market, a telephone information service, and a music co-op. In addition, they have given a hand at a number of festivals run by other organisations.

The big house at Hay Hill, which they must now leave provided them with living accommodation, offices and workrooms.

They spent a large proportion of their limited funds renovating and installing several hundred pounds worth of equipment in the six-room basement of the house.

Mr Shepherd said the notice to quit has come at a time when their finances

are as poor as they have been for a long time. They lost money on the events they put on during the Bath Festival, and have more recently spent much money running theatre events in Maidstone and a cheap food kitchen at the Glastonbury Fair.

Said, Mr Shepherd, "Whatever happens, we're not going to give up. But life looks like being very difficult for a while."

## Thieves siphon mini's petrol

Mr John Lake, of 70, Bath Hill, Keynsham, returned to his Mini estate car in the civic centre park, Keynsham, that thieves had six gallons of the tank.

They had tools, and is put

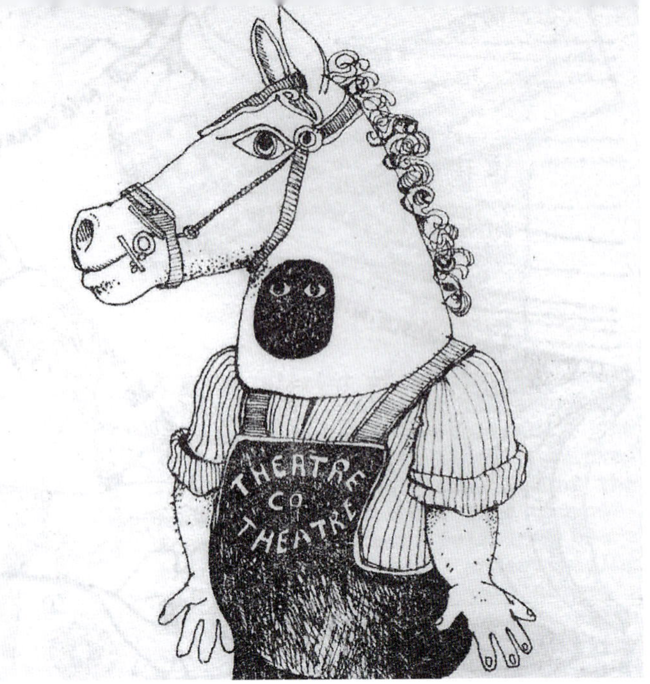





**A**ble Lawrence: We started *Genesis* to circulate information about our new organisation, Bath Arts Workshop, and to connect people with the alternative groups and movements that were beginning to happen in the city. This was before computers, emails, mobile phones etc, so the printed word was the only option. Thus, *Genesis* was born.

We printed it on a Gestetner duplicating machine and used the backs of old cinema posters to make the covers (in those days they were made of thick paper that you could get for free once the film moved on). We produced eight editions, the first in summer 1970, and the last in time for Christmas 1971.

They contained a mix of articles about the problems Bath was facing, as well as poems and stories from mostly alternative-minded people. Each magazine had a short editorial about the Workshop's activities and the often memorable performances by the newly-formed **Natural Theatre Company**.

We published articles on education, housing, community and mental health issues. Space was given to political groupings, ranging from anarchists to Young Liberals. Articles on the permissive society, drug-related issues, and an old people's outing to Longleat, were also among those included.

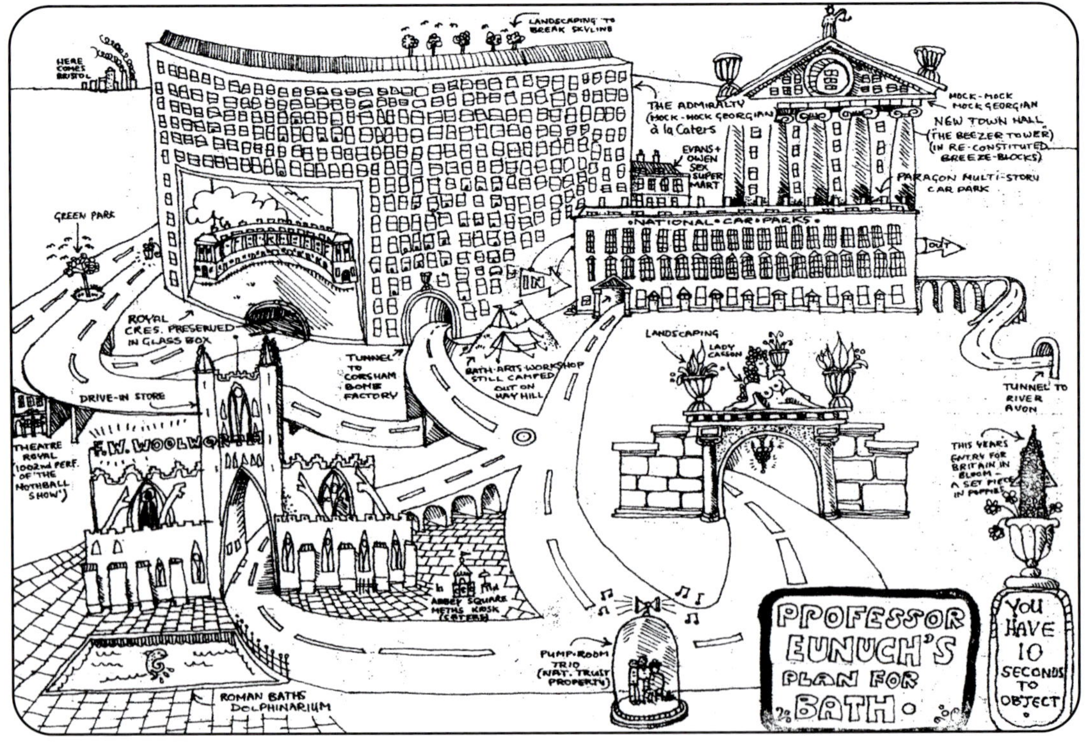

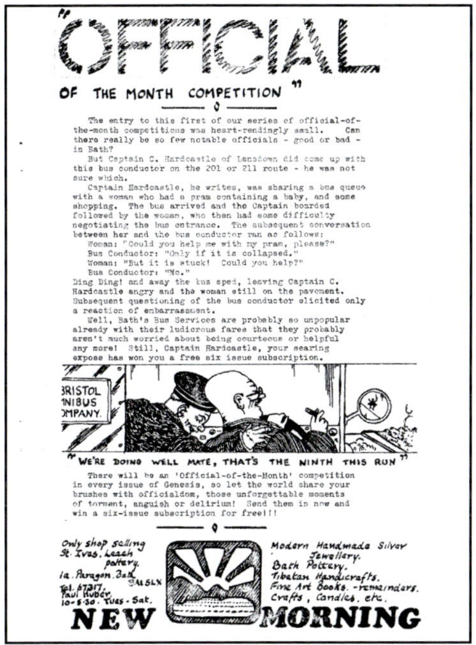

"OFFICIAL

OF THE MONTH COMPETITION "

The entry to this first of our series of official-of-the-month competitions was heart-rendingly small.   Can there really be so few notable officials - good or bad - in Bath?
But Captain C. Hardcastle of Lansdown did come up with this bus conductor on the 201 or 211 route - he was not sure which.
Captain Hardcastle, he writes, was sharing a bus queue with a woman who had a pram containing a baby, and some shopping.  The bus arrived and the Captain boarded followed by the woman, who then had some difficulty negotiating the bus entrance.  The subsequent conversation between her and the bus conductor ran as follows:
Woman: "Could you help me with my pram, please?"
Bus Conductor: "Only if it is collapsed."
Woman: "But it is stuck!  Could you help?"
Bus Conductor: "No."
Ding Ding! and away the bus sped, leaving Captain C. Hardcastle angry and the woman still on the pavement. Subsequent questioning of the bus conductor elicited only a reaction of embarrassment.
Well, Bath's Bus Services are probably so unpopular already with their ludicrous fares that they probably aren't much worried about being courteous or helpful any more!  Still, Captain Hardcastle, your searing expose has won you a free six issue subscription.



There will be an 'Official-of-the-Month' competition in every issue of Genesis, so let the world share your brushes with officialdom, those unforgettable moments of torment, anguish or delirium!  Send them in now and win a six-issue subscription for free!!!

Only shop selling St. Ives. Leach pottery.
1a. Paragon. Bath BA1 5LX
Tel. 67317.
Paul Huber.
10-5.30. Tues - Sat.

Modern Handmade Silver Jewellery.
Bath Pottery.
Tibetan Handicrafts.
Fine Art books. - remainders.
Crafts, Candles. etc.

**NEW MORNING**

At the time, there was much focus on the preservation of Bath's Georgian heritage. Local architects were waging a vociferous campaign against the demolition of Georgian architecture and the infamous Buchanan tunnel scheme (see *Chapter 6*). We published numerous articles, letters and cartoons on this – all deeply critical of the plans which were detrimental to the city we'd all grown to know and love. It is interesting to realise how prescient those articles were, foreseeing the dreadful traffic congestion and pollution problems we are all too aware of today.

There was a lot of encouragement for young people to get involved in the Workshop, and cartoons by young people often featured, as did reports on BAW events and activities aimed at kids and teenagers.



**Able:** Phil and I went to school together, and in our teens we hitchhiked all over the UK (including Bath), as well as driving down to Spain and indulging in many of the more free-thinking activities of the time. I was working in London during the early life of the Workshop but often visited Bath to help out. I wrote and performed in the Naturals' first play – *The Legend of Spotty Blelb* – from which came the Rocky Show.

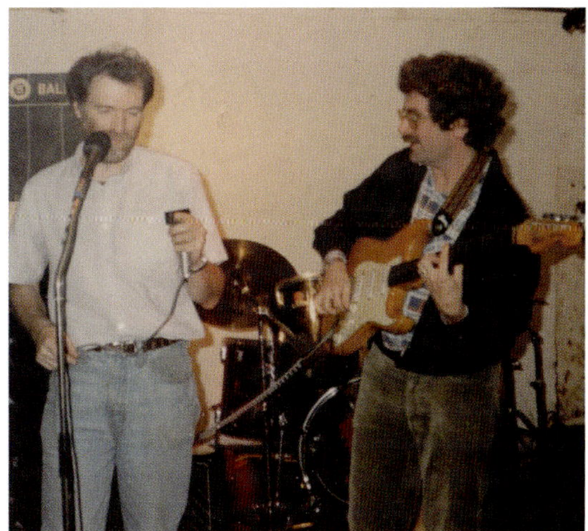

Able and Micky Godwin

I toured several times with early drama outings and sometimes appeared at the Christmas lunches dressed as Father Christmas to help hand round the food.

I started by submitting short stories and articles to the magazine, and from *Genesis 3,* I co-edited it, mostly with the late Dave Herschel. I even wrote a surrealist serial about a mysterious French Count, *Le Comte de Ni'il*, though I have no idea now where this was heading. The story still hangs suspended at the end of Episode four in *Genesis* 7.

At its height up to a thousand copies were distributed, but it was never cost effective so we stopped after Number 7. *Genesis* may not have been an earth shaker, but it definitely reflected the commitment to change and progress that was at the core of those times. I have fond memories of working on it and with the others involved.[2]

---

2. I particularly remember Bob Miles, Kate Greaves, Dave Herschel, Miriam Angell, Rich Coleman, and of course my old friend Phil Shepherd.

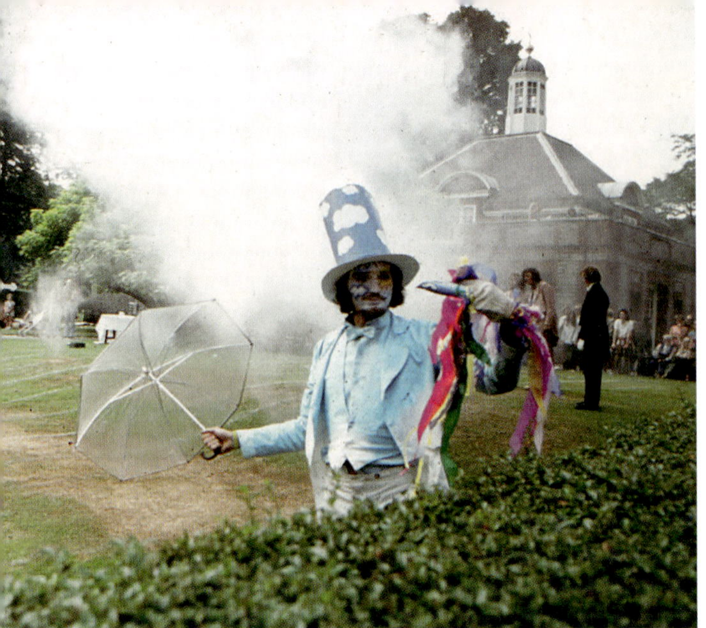

# EXPLODED EYE

**M**itch: Exploded Eye events group was formed in 1972 by the artist Rolande Thomas in Bath. It was a fluid collective involving BAW members, artists, sculptors, dancers, performers, designers, musicians and video artists. It had a strong visual and image-based identity, with performances based in specific locations – the streets, landscapes, buildings. The name came from an 'exploded' picture of the eyes and make-up of my character, the *Blue Sky Man*. Integral to the group was the technical ability and object-making imagination of Rich Dunnill.





**Rolande:** I was involved in amateur dramatics in my teens alongside my art school foundation course at Carmarthen School of Art. During my final year of a diploma course in sculpture at Maidstone Art School, I focused on exploring colour in three dimensions. I moved to Bath in 1970 and became a founder member of the *Natural Theatre Company*, but I soon began to experiment with mixing live performance with my earlier sculptural preoccupation with colour. This merging of theatre, sculpture and performance could be viewed as a logical progression and extension of my creative interests.

Top left: Blue Sky Man. Below: Beaford

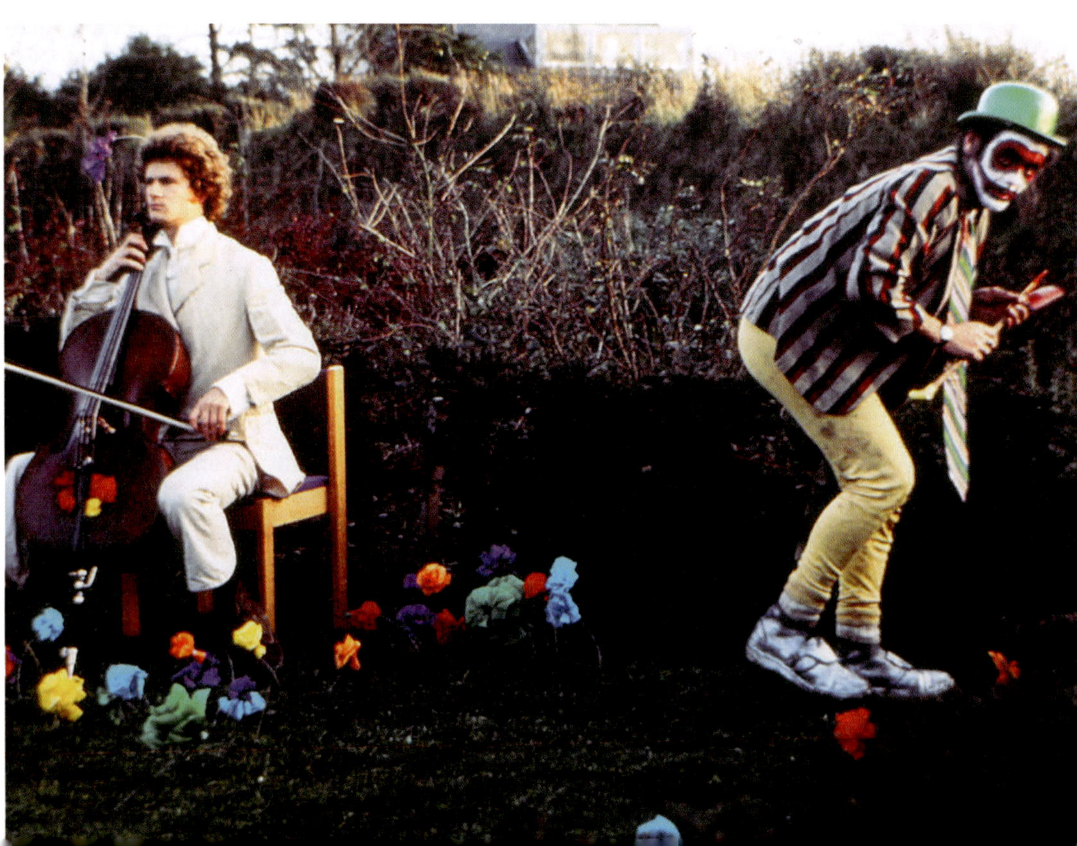

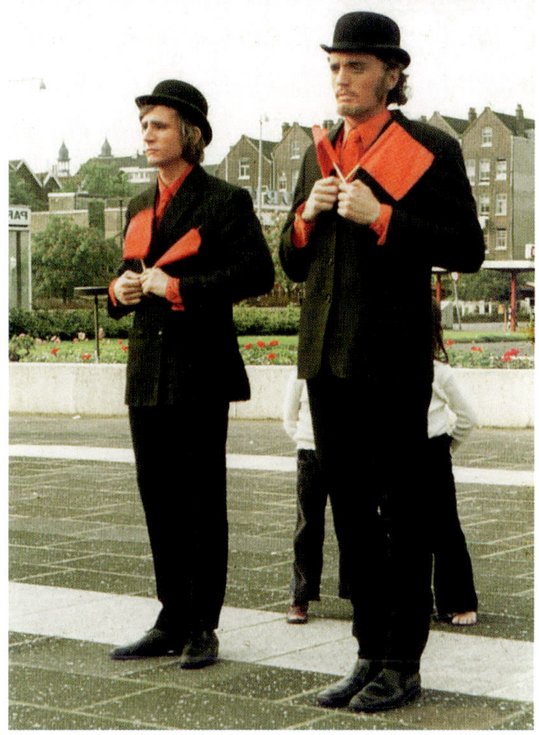

The pin-striped businessmen

**Mitch:** Our first performance was on a Bath street. Two Magritte-like pin-striped, bowler-hatted businessmen with semaphoring flags – Rolande and myself – moved towards each other from opposite ends of the street. Meanwhile in the middle of the street, Ralph and the future puppeteer Andy Hume performed ritualistic activities dressed as workmen in overalls. The ordinary was made extraordinary and the space was transposed from its usual commercial context into an accessible street ballet of living sculpture.

Another piece was *Eat, Sleep, Dream*, specially designed for the Organ Factory as part of BAW's **Another Festival**. Rolande assembled an impressive cast: a mad magician, a cabaret compere, the musical trio **Johnny Rondo Combo** (piano, drums and bass guitar), a nightclub vamp, an airman, and myself as a white blind man with a female muse. Also a waiter and two wrestlers he had managed to find. They presented as a vaudeville act and brought the house down. They left immediately afterwards as they had another gig that evening. All part of the transient nature of performance.

The audience sat at chairs and tables with menus as programmes. Initially, they watched a deliberately tacky cabaret – entertaining and amusing in its own right. In the second half it morphed into dream and nightmare sequences with the oedipal white blind man, food-throwing

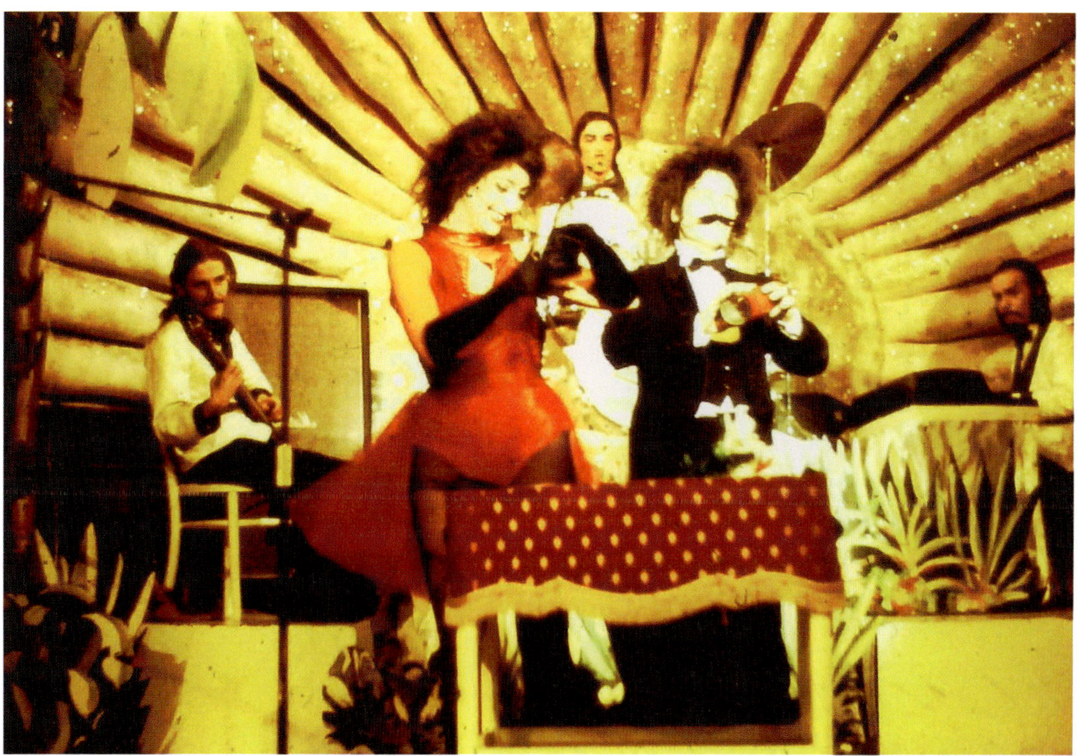

Cabaret

31

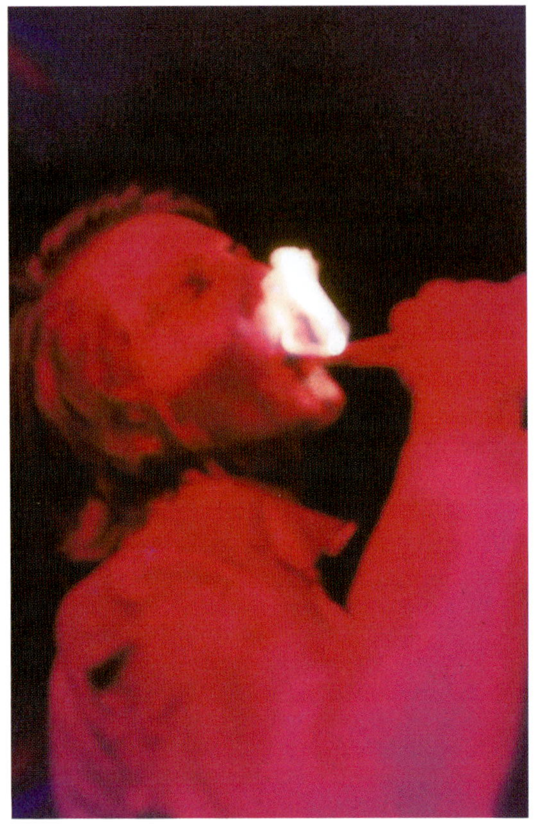

Blazing meal

Exploded Eye shared a platform at the **Birmingham International Performance Festival** with pioneers, visionaries and luminaries of site-specific performance, provocative happenings and performance art. Other companies involved included Welfare State, Matchbox Purveyors, Gasp, Soft Soap, Genesis P-Orridge, and C.O.U.M, Landscapes and Living Spaces and Fine Artistes, as well as Laila and Le Palais des Merveilles and others from Europe. Exploded Eye became part of a movement of performance companies, sometimes catalysed by art college lecturers, and graduates, each with their own unique identity and philosophy.

They expanded, experimented with and transformed the nature of live performance, its settings, locations and environments, and the perceptions and eyes of their audiences in the 1970s.

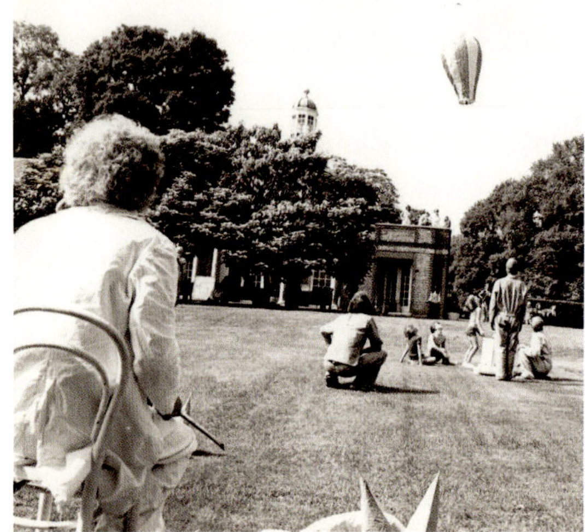

**Mitch:** Other outdoor performances followed. The Serpentine Gallery (1973) hosted my *Blue Sky Man* and Rolande's multi-coloured rainbow tail-coated man. Corinne and Andy Hume were a sepia-coloured Victorian photograph come to life, Ian Spittal was the Green Earth Man with a green hill stomach from which appeared puppet animals. All this combined to create a mysterious, other-worldly, dreamy village green fete, orchestrated by Rolande.

waiters and Rolande as the illuminated man in a costume of lights, eating cotton wool wads of fire in strobe lighting, before the airman and I abseiled down the back of the Organ Factory and launched a multi-coloured hot air balloon into the night sky. The show was later performed at many other venues – Bristol Arts Centre, Albany Empire in Deptford and the Oval House in Kennington.

Below/right: The Serpentine

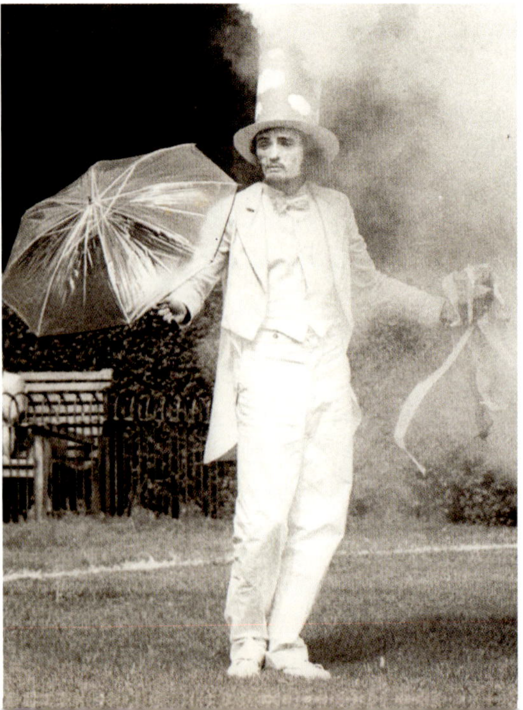

Some of these characters later reappeared in Bath's Parade Gardens during BAW's **Another Festival** in 1973. Also in Parade Gardens we later performed *The White Piece* where a white hunter, a sepulchral gentleman and a veiled cellist performed their Gormengastian rituals.

In May 1975, Rolande and I developed our last project – a video installation *Set Piece for One Performer* at the Serpentine Gallery Video Performance Festival. Rolande was a Samuel Beckett-like character in his bedsit, acting out familiar daily rituals and negotiating

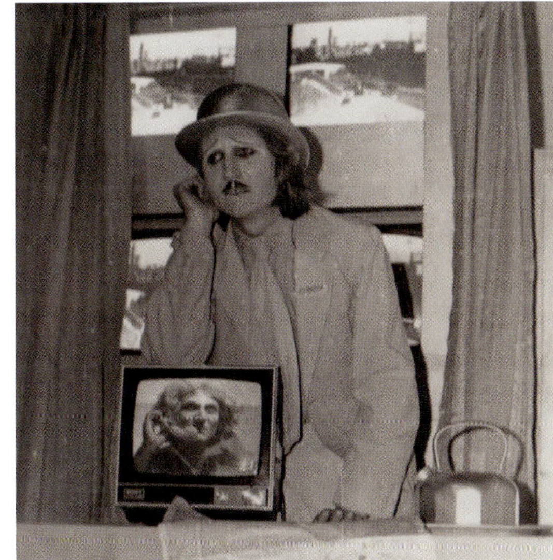
Video show

relationships. We used video monitors as ever-changing window views, as character's heads and also as mutating everyday objects such as a cooker, a cat, a fire and a teapot – the small video screen wittily manipulated to 'pour'. It was an innovative festival celebrating the new medium of video as a live art form with other companies like the **Phantom Captain**. *Set Piece* later toured Scottish art galleries supported by the Scottish Arts Council.

The company had converted spaces into dreamscapes and transported audiences into unfamiliar territories with humour

and theatricality. A re-enchantment of reality. 'The chief thing to know and never forget is that art is dreamland', said John B. Yeats, father of the poet W.B. Yeats. The work with Exploded Eye still resonates and there is always a legacy.

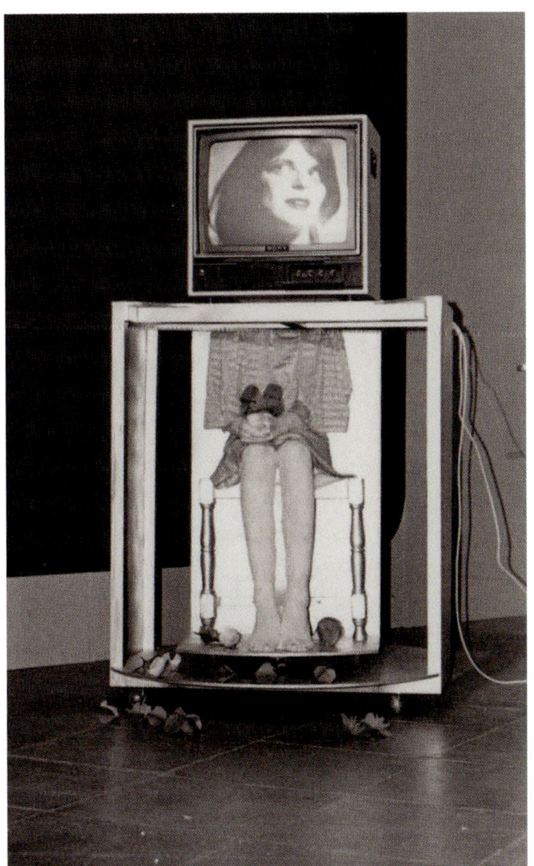

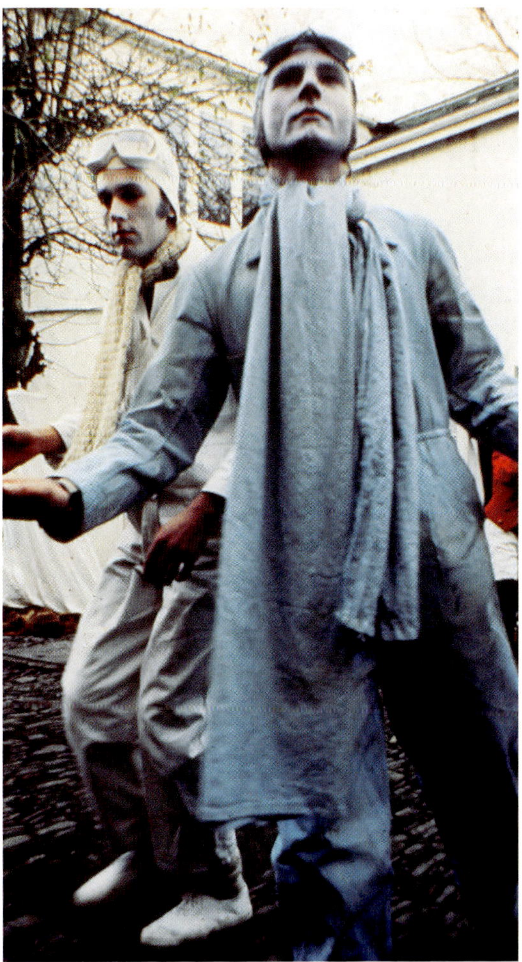
Art is dreamland

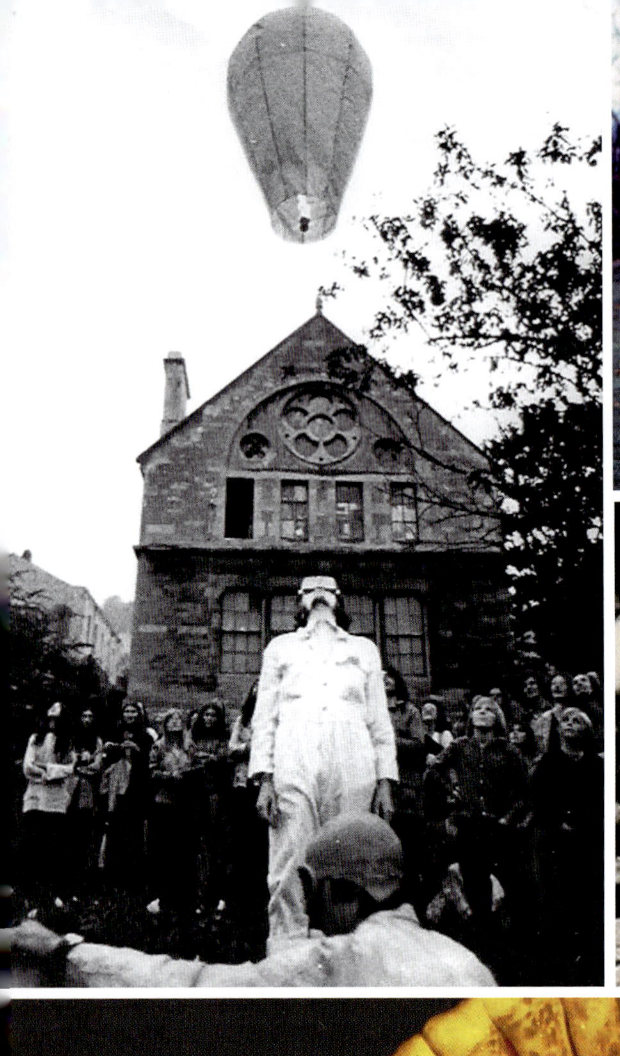
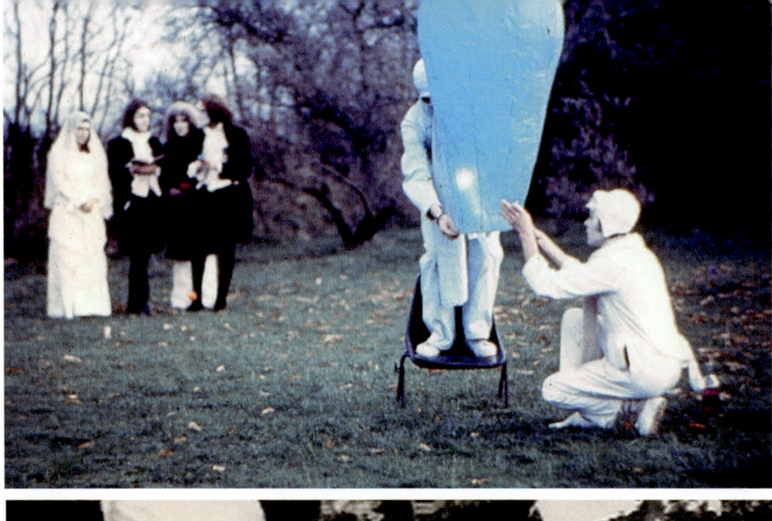
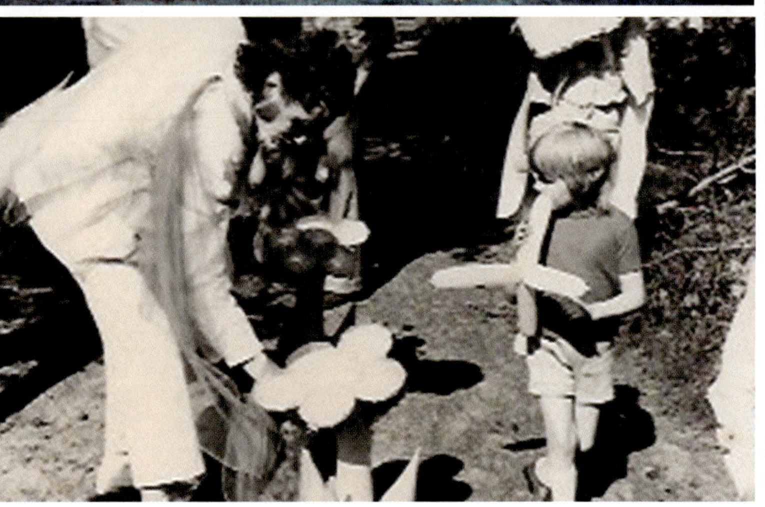
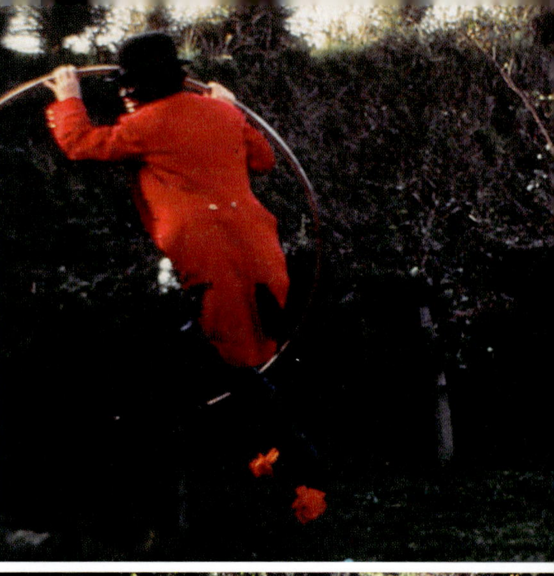
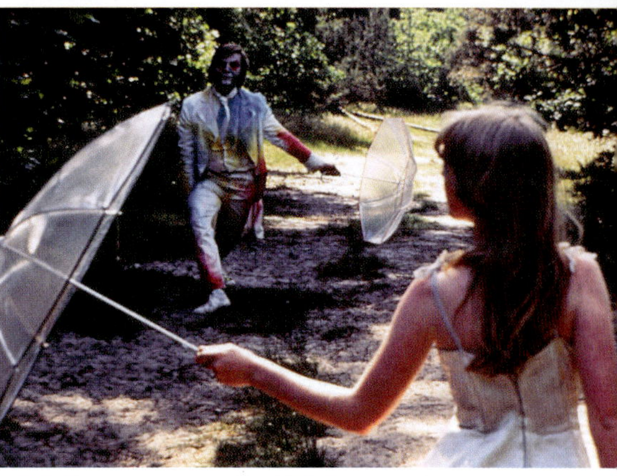
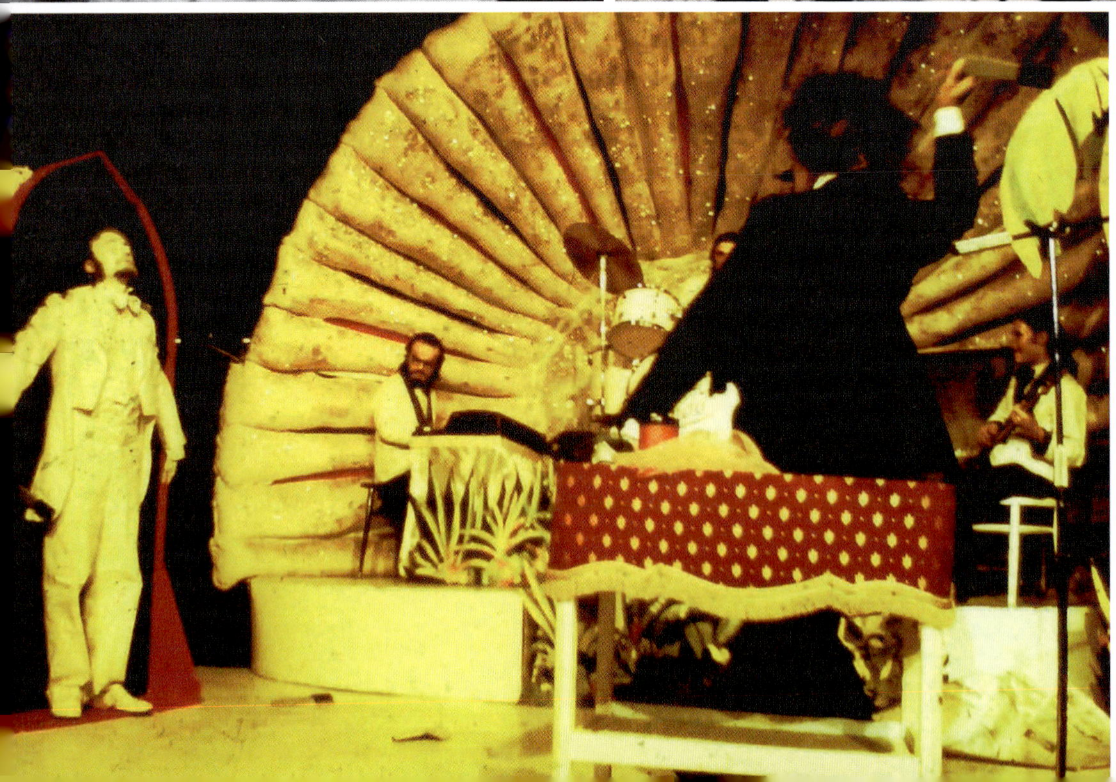
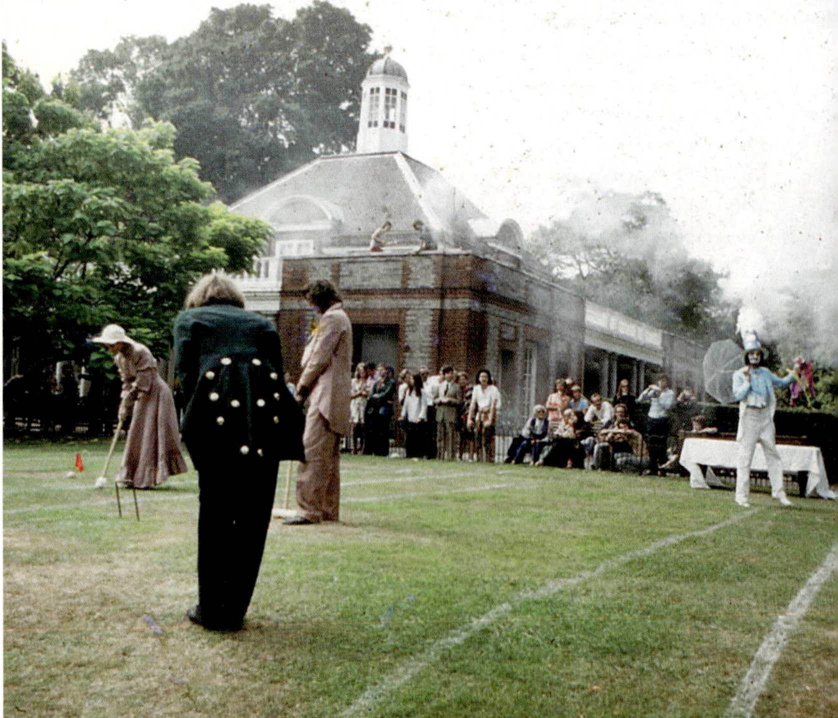

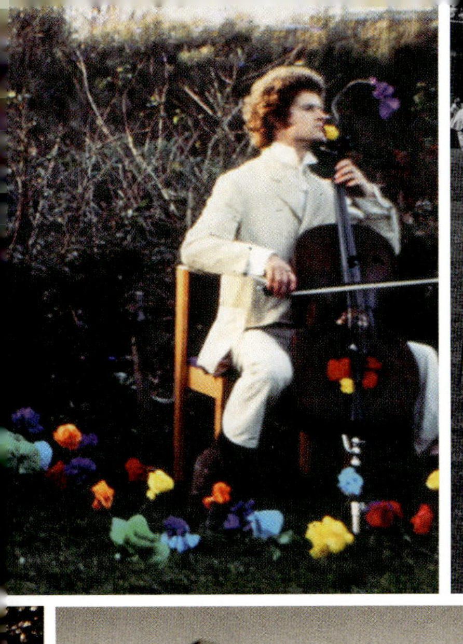
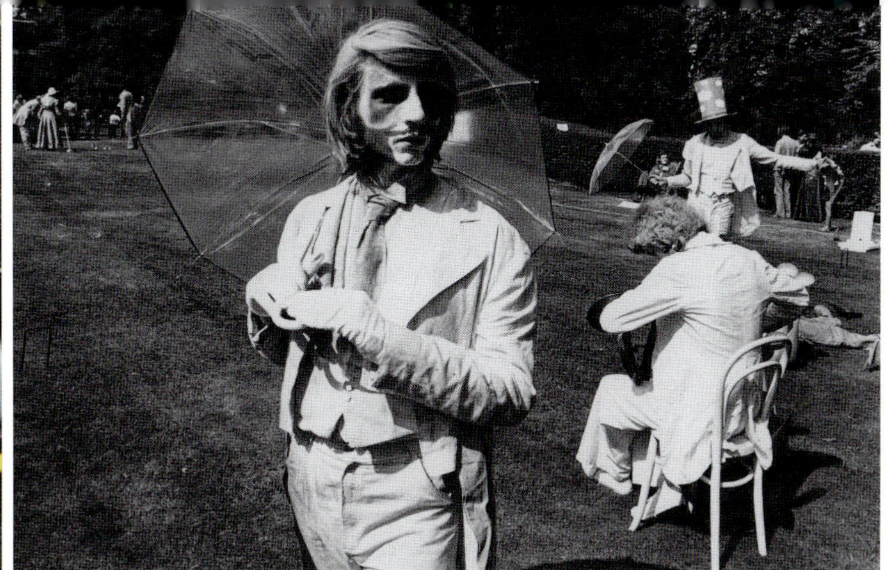
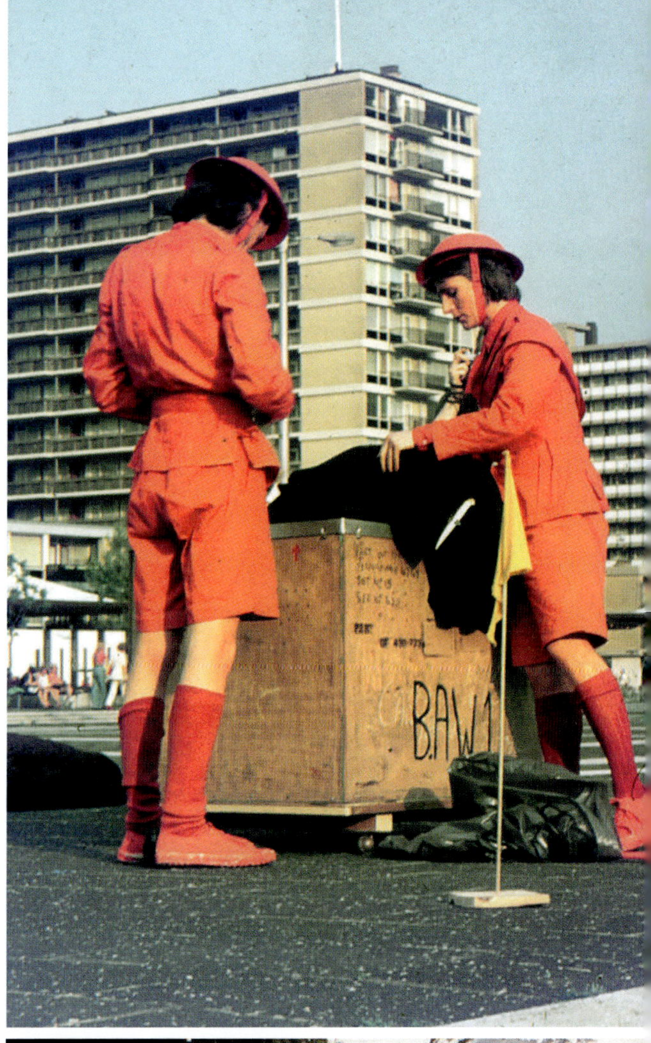
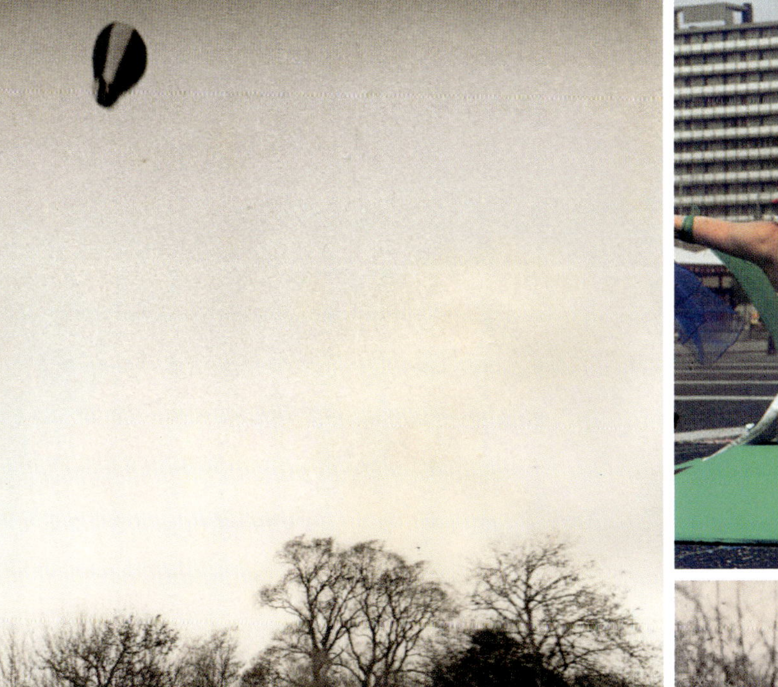
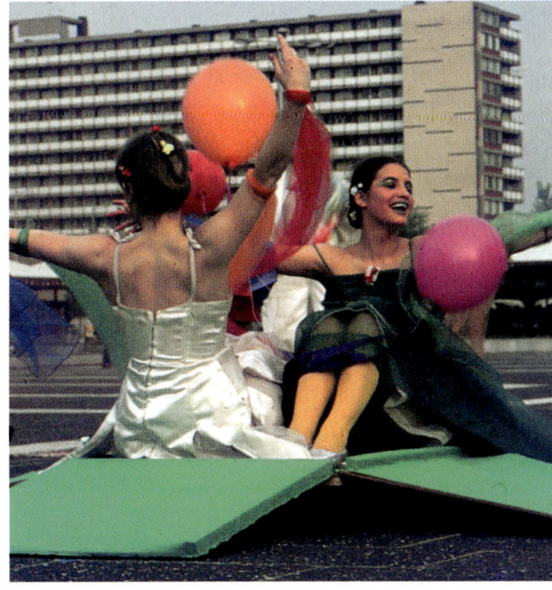
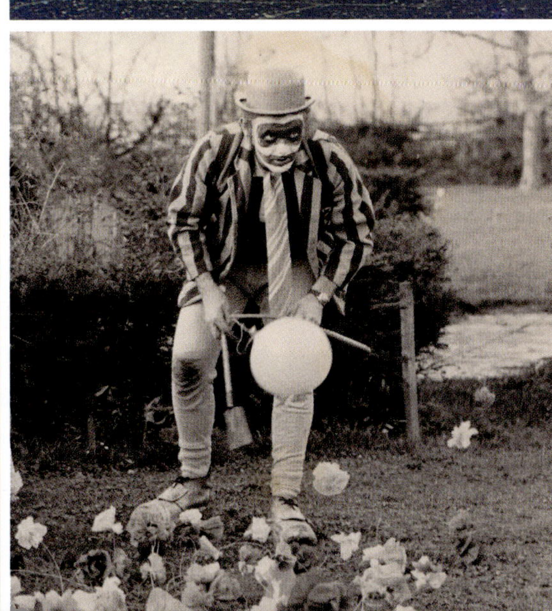
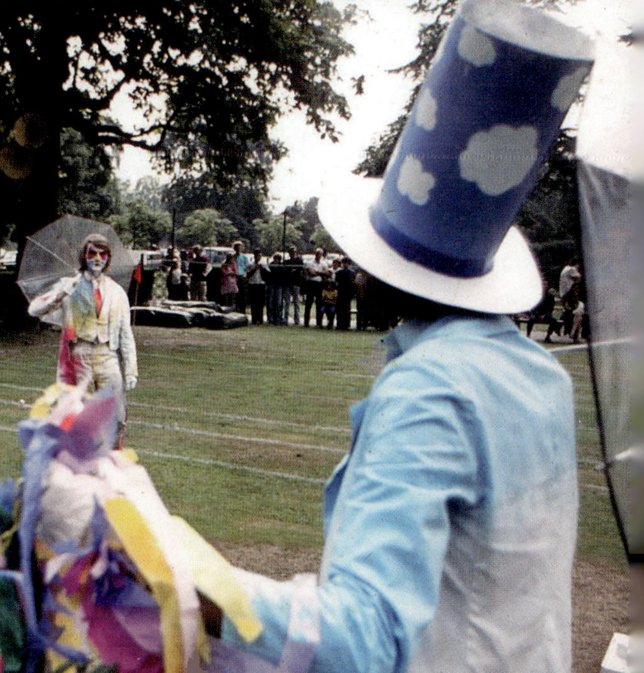

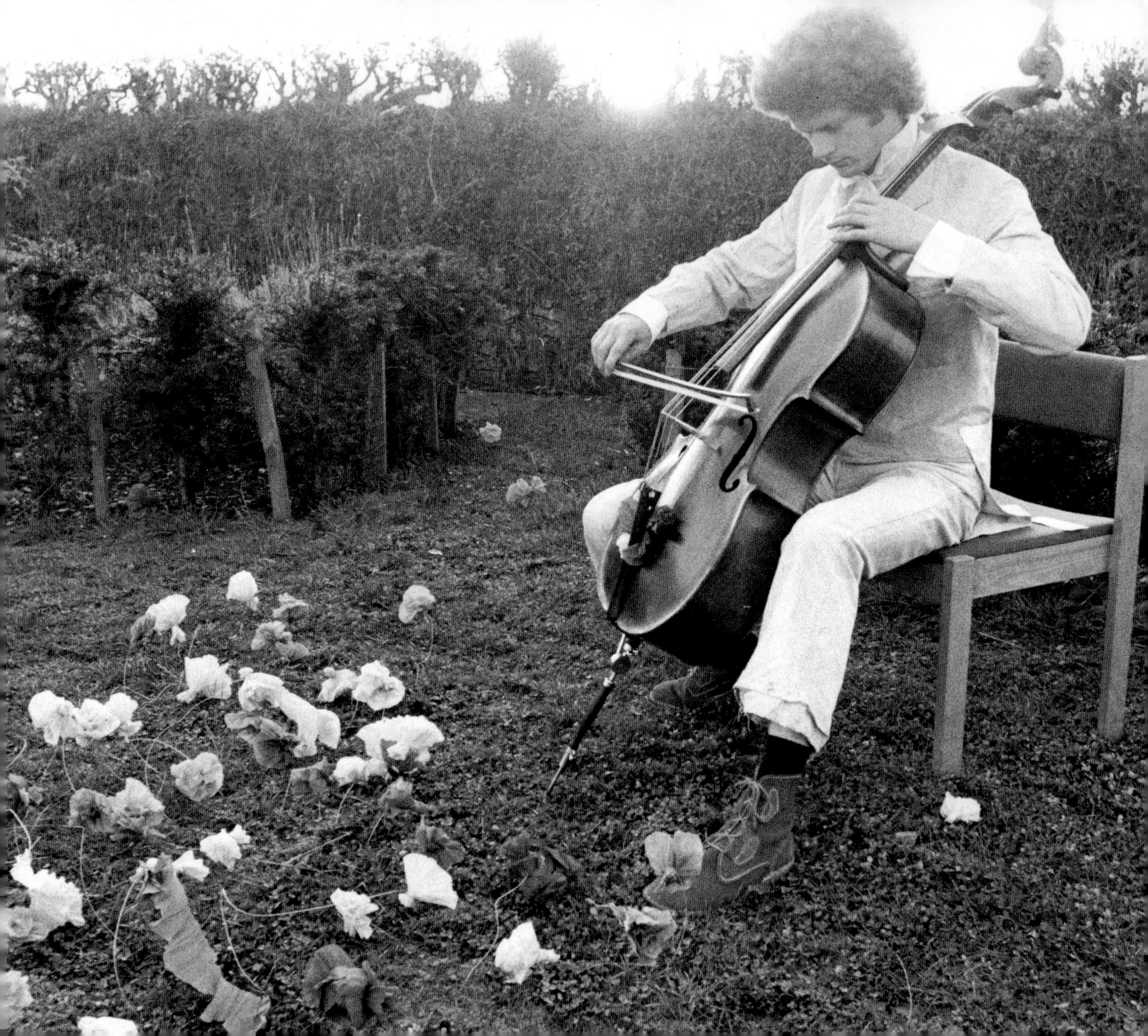

# CHAPTER 3

# EVOLUTION 1971-73

**We were given notice to quit Fountain Buildings but didn't let it foil our plans. We created a theatre in an old Organ Factory and held our first Christmas dinner. We put on mystery coach tours with highwaymen and poets in hedgerows and offended a respectable terrace.**

**Phil:** In the summer of 1971, while most of the crew were serving vats of devastatingly fiery curry at the first Glastonbury Festival, it looked as though we would be really stuck for somewhere to work. After knocking on many doors and lobbying councillors, we managed to secure a new home in a one-time Organ Factory next to the river, which we shared with Bath Canoe Club. The Organ Factory was lovely, around 18m by 6m, with a high ceiling and a mezzanine built across one end, accessed by a widening stair.

The Organ Factory was the dream of a performance and working space we'd been looking for and, moving in on 25 July, we set about cleaning and painting it. We built a set of supposedly flexible (but inordinately heavy) seating units, installed a fire escape (a rope and pulley from a first-floor window) and generally made it usable. After a lot of hard work there were much improved office,

rehearsal, meeting and storage (spaces), making it possible to consolidate and expand our activities.

In those days, hundreds of young people were on the move across the country. There was an impulse to be free of materialist culture and the 'rat race' and to escape the prejudice and deferential ways of post-war society. We were hungry for alternative ways of living. In the Workshop our ethos was to be open to anyone who wanted to get involved.

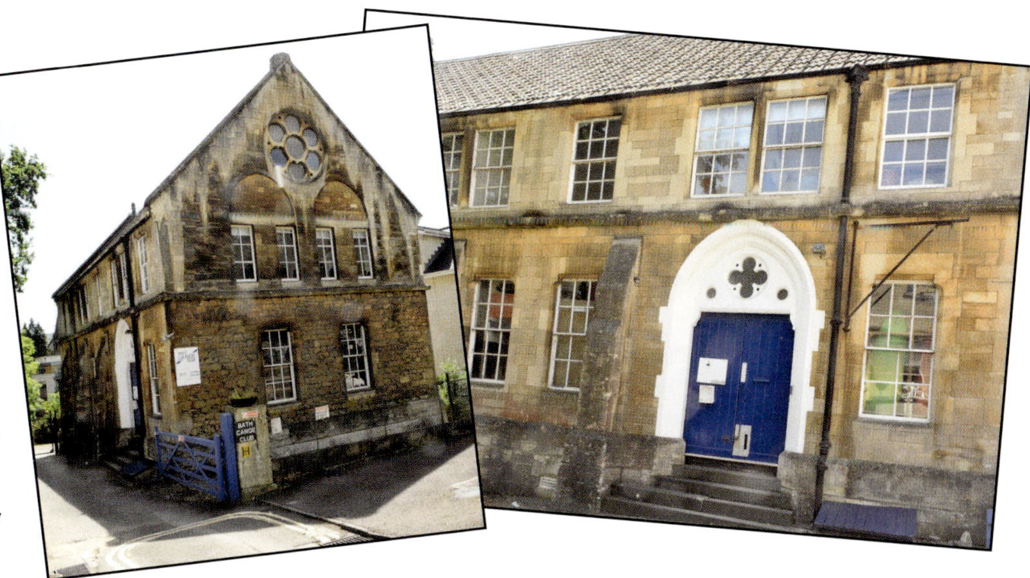

Left: Colin Wood Right: the Organ Factory

**Nigel Leach:** I walked into the Organ Factory in 1972 and asked if I could do anything useful. The answer was 'yes' and I stayed until 1981. I had come from the *Welfare State Theatre Company*, after an amazing four-year experience, but had previously worked in hostels and recognised that a lot of individuals' problems were the result of the imposed culture and norms of our society. I wanted to spend time trying to change that and was to discover just how difficult the task was. However, the experience of freedom following on from periods in the merchant navy, and as a boatman on the River Thames, had prepared me for almost anything that might come my way.

**Jennie Potter-Barrie** also joined up around that time. She writes: Born in 1950, I spent my first 12 years on a council estate in Stockport, Cheshire. It was a life of poverty and simmering undercurrents which could explode into glassy-eyed violence at the drop of a hat or the downing of a pint too many; a society that was stifled by any 'ism' you could name. We had a derogatory word for anyone who was different to us: different in class, colour, religion (not that we really had any) sexuality, ethnicity, nationality. Even different regions of the UK were 'foreign'. People with any kind of disability or difference were fair game for derision. Don't do, don't think, don't aspire, don't tell and don't question. My family moved to Bath from Stockport in 1962. I later fled back to the North to 'drop out and tune in' but found I was doing little to address a gnawing frustration... a need to be with others who were trying to change the way things were. So I moved back to Bath in 1971.

One evening I went to The Hat & Feather to see a show by the *Natural Theatre Company*. I sat in the audience and a man with a great mane of red hair came and sat next to me. Throughout he neither moved nor spoke. He just sat there wearing a plastic pig mask and a plastic policeman's helmet and nothing else. Not a stitch on. I loved it. So funny and so defiant!

My interest roused, I went to another show at the Organ Factory. What I remember most was seeing a woman (maybe dressed as an angel) coming down some stairs in a perfectly observed and hilarious parody of a drunk. I had never before seen a woman breaking the rules so publicly. I was hooked! The next day I joined up and didn't look back. I had found a place where I could be, in a group of people from all different walks of life who wanted to do something positive to challenge the status quo.

That delicious parody of a drunken woman was performed by **Jackie Popay**. She writes: What an amazing time. When you could jump into the abyss of ideas and ideals and make some of your dreams come true. People arrived at BAW by word of mouth. No interviews, no questions, nobody wanting to see your academic achievements. A door was open to you and your zest for life or lack of it. You just arrived and paid a shilling for your communal meal. Most people found someone who shared their thoughts and ideals and someone found you a bed. For me it was the first time I felt free or dared to voice my opinions and believe I could achieve. We were children born in the 50s, keen to escape the predicted life of our parents. There was excitement in the air, a new approach to life.

## Natural Theatre blossoms forth

**Penny Dale:** Natural Theatre was developing apace throughout this period and soon we were beginning to appear not only locally with people like the Play Association and SLAB, but outside Bath – at the Cockpit Theatre in London, at Maidstone Art School, in Newport and, in early 1971, on a summer tour around the south-west's beaches, markets, art centres and festivals. The company was made up of a random group of people – anyone could join in. We developed our ideas in drama sessions and they were transferred and applied to other projects like the theatricalised outings and other events that later became our speciality.

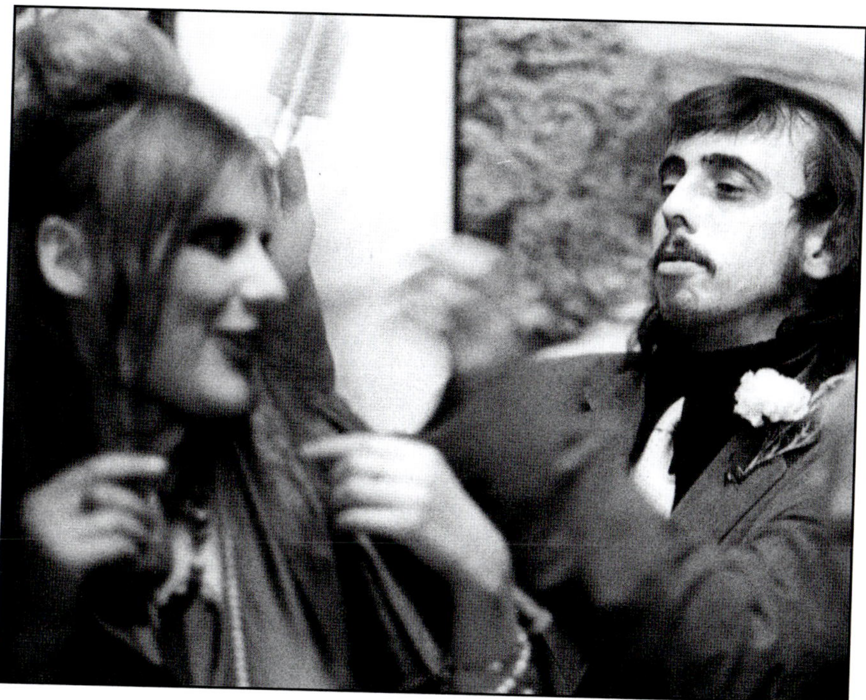

Jackie Popay and Mick Martin

**Penny** joined the Workshop after meeting **Mick Martin**. She writes: I was at an outdoor rock concert with a friend when I met Mick. He and others from the Workshop started dancing with us. They were older than us and made us laugh so much we were captivated. It was one of those rare moments when you feel you've met members of a tribe you've always belonged to.

Mick had moved to Bath after working on the railways in Kent. He immediately fell for the Workshop and joined up. Soon after our first meeting, Mick invited me to go to an evening show, ostensibly to help with props and costumes. I was smitten too with the Workshop but it took me a few months to find my feet in the group. I felt like a young greenhorn in awe of their coolness. Mick had an effortless way with words and brilliant comic timing. Quick-fire exchanges of hilarious improvisation, particularly with Brian and Ralph, accompanied us most of the time. This made the dull parts of life in the Workshop – like long journeys in cold vans – far more bearable. Sad to say Mick died far too young, but his gleeful humour, hard work and versatility exemplified the core values of the group and we miss him still.

**Penny:** In 1972, the theatre company was invited to join the *Cosmic Circus*, an evening extravaganza in London

39

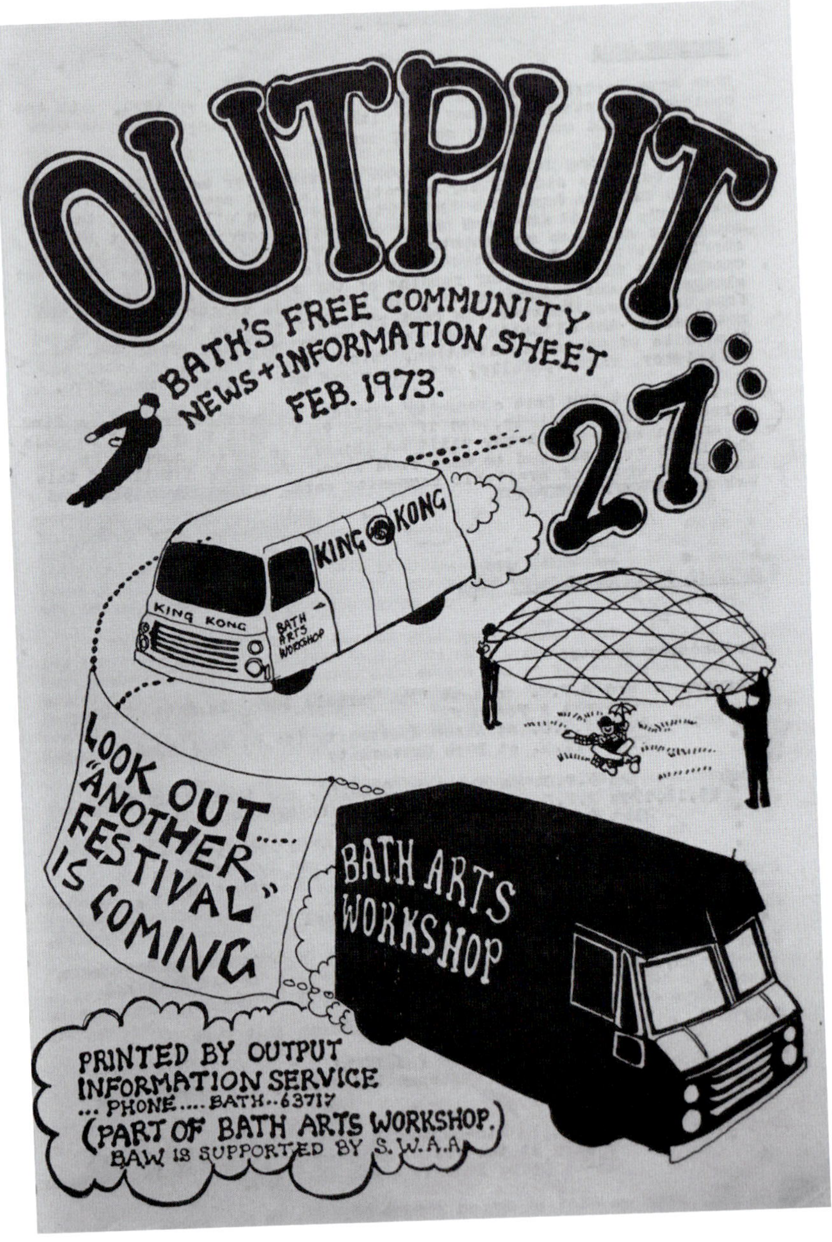



*Output Magazine* front cover

organised by the **Welfare State Theatre Company**. We drove to London in a Morris van bursting at the seams with 11 people, props, a bass drum, and a treadle organ. When we stopped at cafes, the back door was flung open and Ian Spittal, the pianist, played circus tunes, accompanied by others on tambourines, drums and kazoos. We performed this interlude sometimes while waiting for someone to pop into a shop.

Once in London, we went to the space next to the Tower of London. **Welfare State** worked quickly without rehearsal. We were given costumes and instructions and told to join a procession of 'decadent royalty' (fly-infested pig's heads on stakes and offal provided). The show consisted of processions and a fight between the decadent royalty and (symbolic good) giant puppets. **Mike Westbrook** and his jazz band played alongside the event, which ended with a performer in a strait jacket jumping off a high diving board, freeing himself on the way down and landing in a tank of flaming water, followed by fireworks from atop the walls of the tower.

## And everything else

**Penny:** In those early days we established a pattern of work that lasted for years. Alongside our theatrical events and happenings were activities for kids, the lonely and the elderly, as well as our music gigs and discos which raised (some) money for our creative happenings. We generated a huge range of activities, and loads of work was needed to make it happen. We found ourselves involved in many different activities, often taking place on the same day. It was wild and fun and allowed us to use our imagination and express ourselves freely. Our theatre and other activities were completely intertwined. They all grew from our idea that culture and imagination can enrich community life.



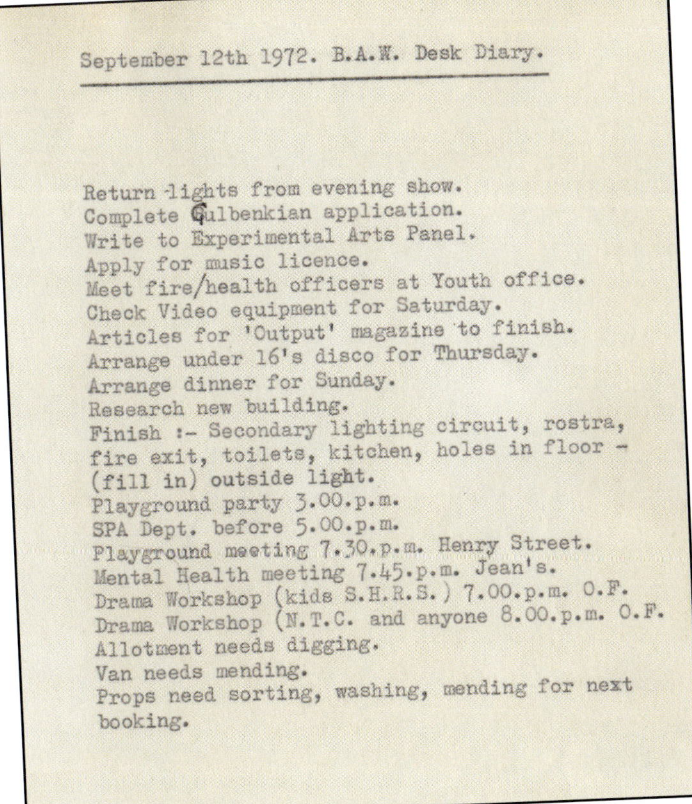

September 12th 1972. B.A.W. Desk Diary.

Return lights from evening show.
Complete Gulbenkian application.
Write to Experimental Arts Panel.
Apply for music licence.
Meet fire/health officers at Youth office.
Check Video equipment for Saturday.
Articles for 'Output' magazine to finish.
Arrange under 16's disco for Thursday.
Arrange dinner for Sunday.
Research new building.
Finish :- Secondary lighting circuit, rostra,
fire exit, toilets, kitchen, holes in floor -
(fill in) outside light.
Playground party 3.00.p.m.
SPA Dept. before 5.00.p.m.
Playground meeting 7.30.p.m. Henry Street.
Mental Health meeting 7.45.p.m. Jean's.
Drama Workshop (kids S.H.R.S.) 7.00.p.m. O.F.
Drama Workshop (N.T.C. and anyone 8.00.p.m. O.F.
Allotment needs digging.
Van needs mending.
Props need sorting, washing, mending for next
booking.

Page from BAW desk diary, September 1972

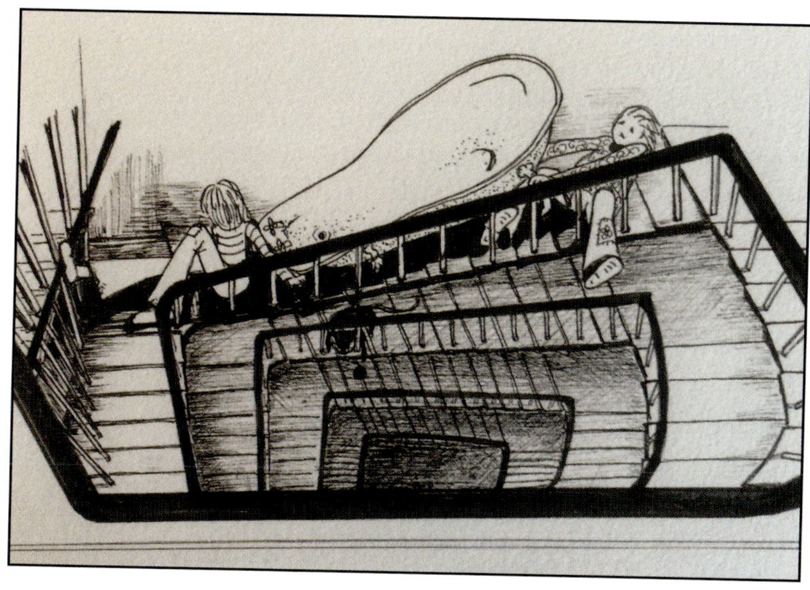

King Kong removals

**Penny:** King Kong Workforce was taking on jobs of all sizes and types – removals, house clearance, painting and decorating, gardening and baby-sitting. The work was mainly to raise money to pay for our meals. But even then, a lot of free or very cheap work was done for pensioners and other people with little cash to spare.

## Kid's play

**Brian:** Kids were involved in the Workshop from start to finish and we knew most of the local ones. In fact they were amongst our most faithful and enthusiastic fans and attended all our events, including the most bizarre and abstract performance art events and poetry readings. They loved it all. Throughout BAW's history we provided art, drama and video workshops for kids, as well as adventure playgrounds, discos and other activities.

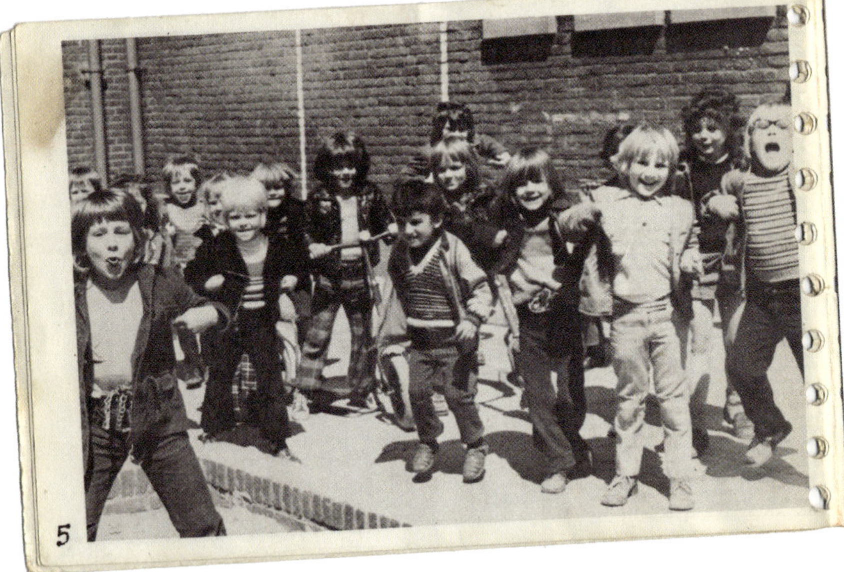

In 1971, Jackie and I set up two youth clubs and an under-16s disco on the Longacre Estate (on the London Road), which evolved into the Longacre Youth Club. We later set up an adventure playground on some disused land next to the Fire Station. The kids could do almost anything they chose as long as it did not harm themselves or others. They were asked to agree to this before coming onto the site.

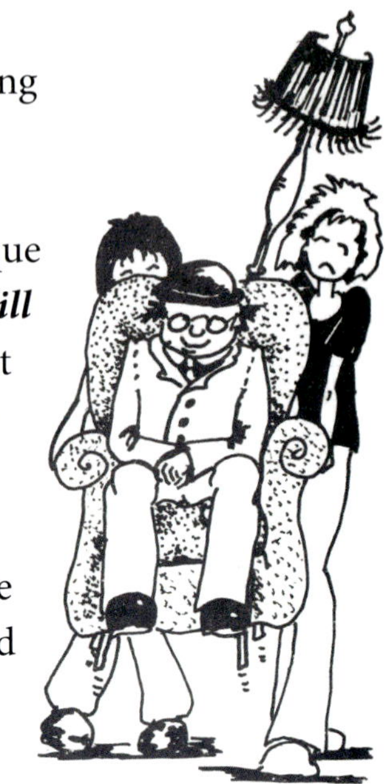

**Penny:** From these activities a unique kids' theatre group – **The Snow Hill Road Show** – was formed later that year by kids living on the Snow Hill Estate (for more on this unforgettable show see *Chapter 4*). They performed plays they wrote and produced themselves – and the results were surprisingly professional and always hilarious. Initially, we realised what they were doing when we found them rehearsing round by the toilets, creating their own version of one of our shows they had seen. Each play they developed had two versions – one without swearing and sex for the adults and one with both for their delighted audience of kids. They had no preconceptions about drama and what kept them going was the same lack of local facilities that had triggered the Workshop itself. They wanted something to do so they did it themselves. We provided rehearsal space, costumes and encouragement.

### A day at the Snow Hill Estate Playscheme, Ron Pritchard

One gloriously sunny day, the air is fresh and as still as possible. We went, about six of us, to Snow Hill with paints, paper, drums, rattles, tumbling mats, costumes and make-up; and with hope that a little spontaneous creativity might break into the shaded sometimes lifeless concrete confines of the estate.

Well it happened beautifully. Within a quarter of an hour, most of the kids were painting the paper, the walls and the bricks in the same streaked-out strokes, were drumming madly, tumbling, laughing, shouting, getting things out of themselves. Some parents gathered inquisitively, chatted together, even joined in. There is shoving to get made-up. One moment children, then Allagazam! Gangsters, clowns, dainty ladies of the most righteous upbringing rush off again to explore their new characters. A parade gets started with a big drum at the front, leading the snake of shaking, dancing, rattling, clapping young human beings en route around the block.

The group running the playscheme soon found the children's parents taking an active part in organising the various activities and this had a considerable part in its success. At the end of the holidays, a final evening 'carnival' was held for everybody who had taken part. There was a barbecue, music, a play by the kids and various entertainments, including a fire eater and acrobatics. The whole scheme was run on the voluntary labour of the organisers and parents, small donations of money, numerous gifts of materials from local firms and a donation from the Freeschool Playgroups Association.

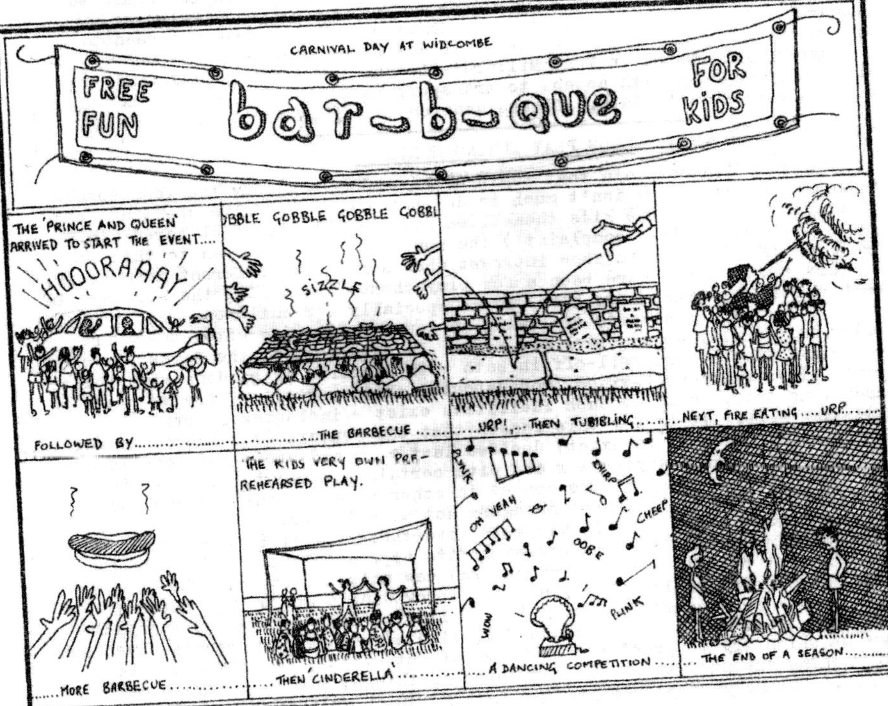


**Penny:** We were creating and living in an organic mix of art, theatre, music and activities for local people. From the outset, we had been working regularly with social and youth services, providing cheap labour and transport, and had organised lots of activities with kids and elderly people. This, combined with our theatrical approach, soon led to the development of extravagant theatricalised events that built on more traditional forms of entertainment for pensioners and others on low incomes. One example was our theatrical coach tour.

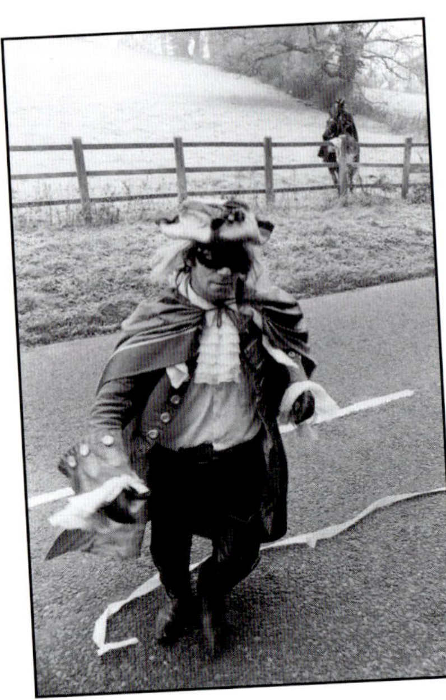

## The Other Outing, 1972

**Penny:** This was a fantastical event for families or lonely individuals who needed a holiday. It was completely free and took weeks to prepare, with help from Social Services and voluntary organisations to identify the participants. It wove together two strands of our lives: working with the local community, and our theatrical approach to all we did.

On a frosty Saturday in November, two 50-seater coaches left Bath, covered in balloons, streamers and confetti. On board was a mixture of people of all ages and occupations from the elderly to tiny babies. Also, the **Mike Westbrook Jazz Band**, **Colin Wood** (a cellist), **Peter Kuttner** (events using colourful food), **Mr Pugh** the radical puppeteer, avant-garde performance artists **Roland and Shirley**, **Exploded Eye** and ourselves, the **Natural Theatre Company**.

Everyone was given a name badge as they boarded, along with a toy watch. When we reached open country, two magnificently-dressed highwaymen were seen galloping across the hill next to the road. They jumped over the bank and stopped the coaches, then held us up at gunpoint before galloping off with our watches.

The coaches pulled into a lay-by outside Wells where two shivering clowns were hitchhiking. Once aboard, they produced bottles of sherry and paper cups. In Wells all the clowns escaped and had to be rounded up from all sorts of unlikely places (e.g. from behind shop counters)

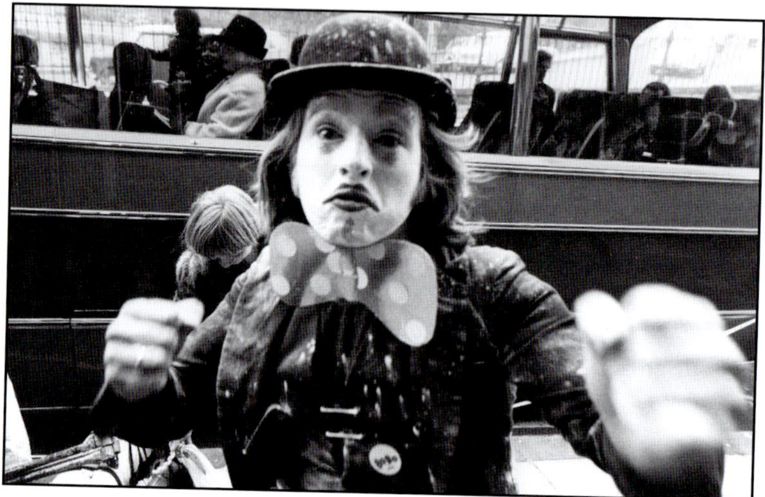

by a wicked ringmaster. There was much shrieking and squawking as the clowns marauded through the Saturday morning crowds. Back on track, we drove through beautiful countryside (stopping en route for lunch and tea with the clowns), then on to a twilight fireworks display and fire-eating in a field.

We stayed the night in Ilfracombe. Supper was courtesy of **Peter Kuttner**: blue soup, orange bread and green spaghetti with purple cheese sauce, followed by a concert. The Normals were the waiters, performing their role with much gesture and flourish and in complete silence. The next day was poetic and serene, starting with a walk along the sea

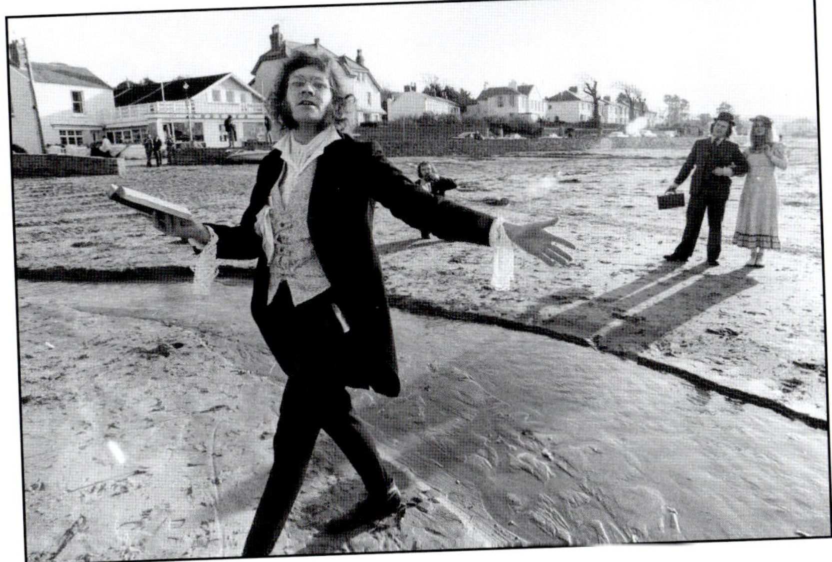

pacing up and down beneath a tree pointing upwards and shouting 'Look up, look up!' whilst Roland (perched precariously up the tree) barked like a dog in reply. This explains a piece of graffiti which later appeared in a Bath pub toilet proclaiming 'Roland Miller is a woof'.

A raucous atmosphere broke through in the evening. In a large back room of a Taunton pub Rocky Ricketts, the aging rock star, and his wife Mavis ran a disco. The evening turned into a huge party with everyone young and old doing the twist to Rocky's old singles.

front where members of **Exploded Eye** dressed as regency poets strolled up and down, intensely melancholy, reciting odes from long paper scrolls. They appeared everywhere, high on the cliffs, on the sea wall, and on a rock in the sea, shouting verse at the indifferent seagulls.

In Beaford, **Exploded Eye** performed a play that ended with several hot air balloons being launched from the garden by brightly coloured airmen. While we ate lunch, **Roland and Shirley** appeared in white costumes onto which were pinned many tiny plastic bags. They contained souvenirs of the places we had visited and things we had done – grass, sand, seaweed, fish (very smelly on the coach), litter, earth, twigs, paper cups, confetti, burst balloons and so on. The climax of the performance seemed to consist of Shirley

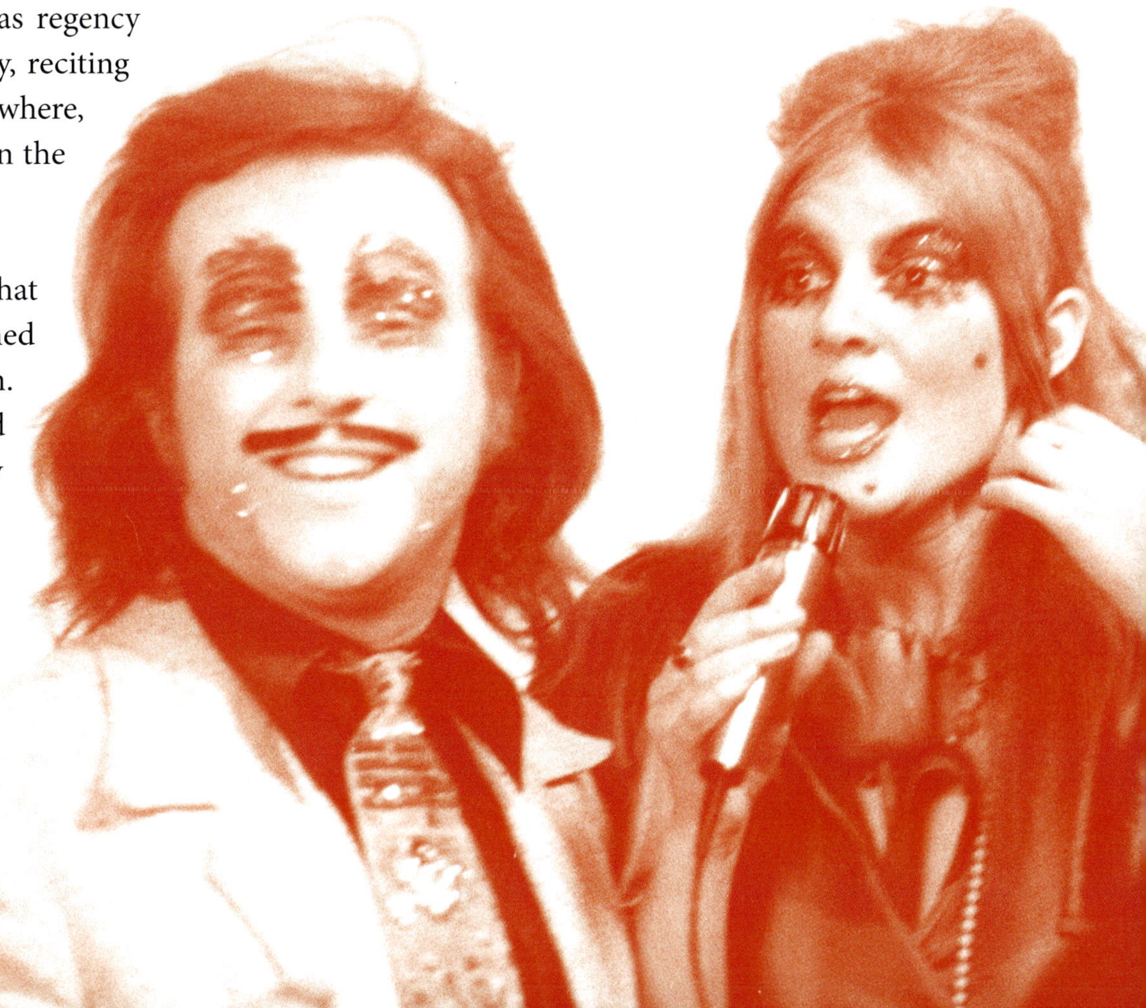

## First free Christmas meal

**Phil:** By December, no one felt like leaving the Workshop – everyone agreed it would be more fun to stay together for the festive season. Then someone hit on the idea of throwing open the doors and inviting others to join in. And so it was.



**Brian:** In 1971, the Organ Factory saw 70 people come to the first of many free 'Christmas meals for the lonely and homeless', an event that became an institution over the years, and is still going on today. I remember driving the Workshop van round Bath streets, inviting those who looked lost or homeless to join our Christmas meal. I delivered them to the venue and watched their astonished faces as they entered the lavishly decorated space.

## Moving on

**Phil:** Life at the Organ Factory was drawing to a close towards the end of 1972. We'd always known our neighbours were unhappy about our presence, and did our best to befriend and win them over. They did have a point. The only road access to the building was past their front doors, and the growing footfall and vehicle traffic were no doubt intrusive. After the chemist at the top of the lane claimed that he'd seen Organ Factory users rifling through his dustbins (supposedly for drugs), we knew that our days were numbered. One of our last performances at the building was a surreal adaptation of *The Respectable Terrace*, a 1951 play for women in one act. It lampooned the small mindedness we felt we had experienced from some of the complainants.

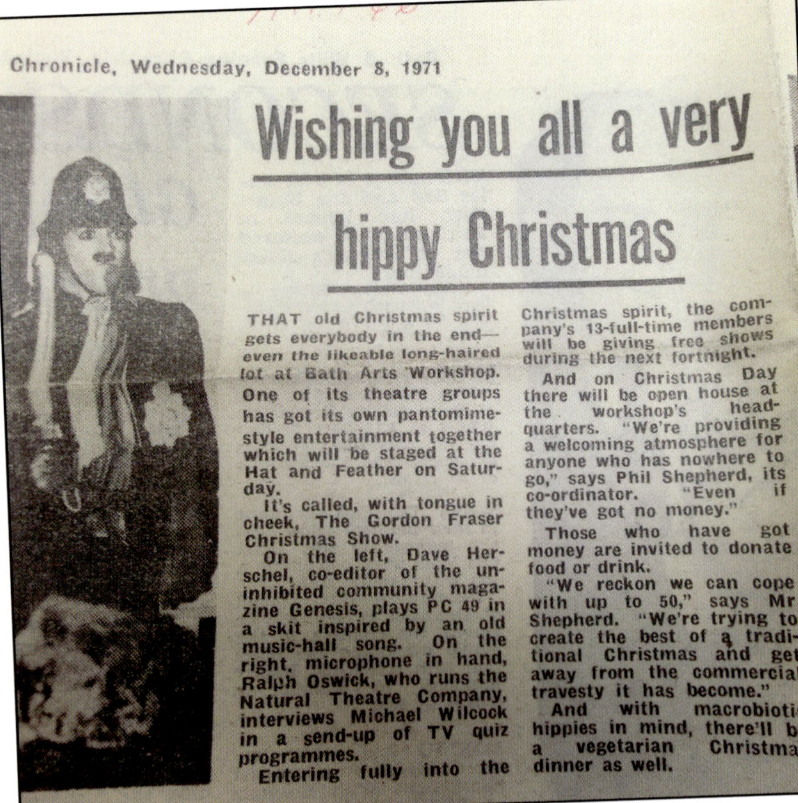

Chronicle, Wednesday, December 8, 1971

# Wishing you all a very hippy Christmas

THAT old Christmas spirit gets everybody in the end—even the likeable long-haired lot at Bath Arts Workshop. One of its theatre groups has got its own pantomime-style entertainment together which will be staged at the Hat and Feather on Saturday.

It's called, with tongue in cheek, The Gordon Fraser Christmas Show.

On the left, Dave Herschel, co-editor of the uninhibited community magazine Genesis, plays PC 49 in a skit inspired by an old music-hall song. On the right, microphone in hand, Ralph Oswick, who runs the Natural Theatre Company, interviews Michael Wilcock in a send-up of TV quiz programmes.

Entering fully into the Christmas spirit, the company's 13-full-time members will be giving free shows during the next fortnight.

And on Christmas Day there will be open house at the workshop's headquarters. "We're providing a welcoming atmosphere for anyone who has nowhere to go," says Phil Shepherd, its co-ordinator. "Even if they've got no money."

Those who have got money are invited to donate food or drink.

"We reckon we can cope with up to 50," says Mr Shepherd. "We're trying to create the best of a traditional Christmas and get away from the commercial travesty it has become."

And with macrobiotic hippies in mind, there'll be a vegetarian Christmas dinner as well.

### *The Respectable Terrace*

**Brian:** The play itself was by Thomas Baden Morris and designed for an amateur dramatics company to put on in their village hall. It was written for an all-female cast, so some amount of cross-dressing was called for. Appropriately enough it was set in a once-fashionable spa town, which of course we immediately translated as Bath. The cast of characters was ideal, including Ralph playing the head of the household, me a lodger with a dark secret, Mick Martin a young sporty thing, Jackie a nosy gossip and so on. We started off following the script but soon found that we were incapable of learning our lines. So we recorded some of the script, and did half the production as a radio play, with the sound emanating from a radio placed centre stage. It all descended into chaos as we kept getting confused by the radio version. In the end, we gave up learning the script entirely and the characters developed their own stage personas in extremis, going into the audience and living out their lives in the real world.

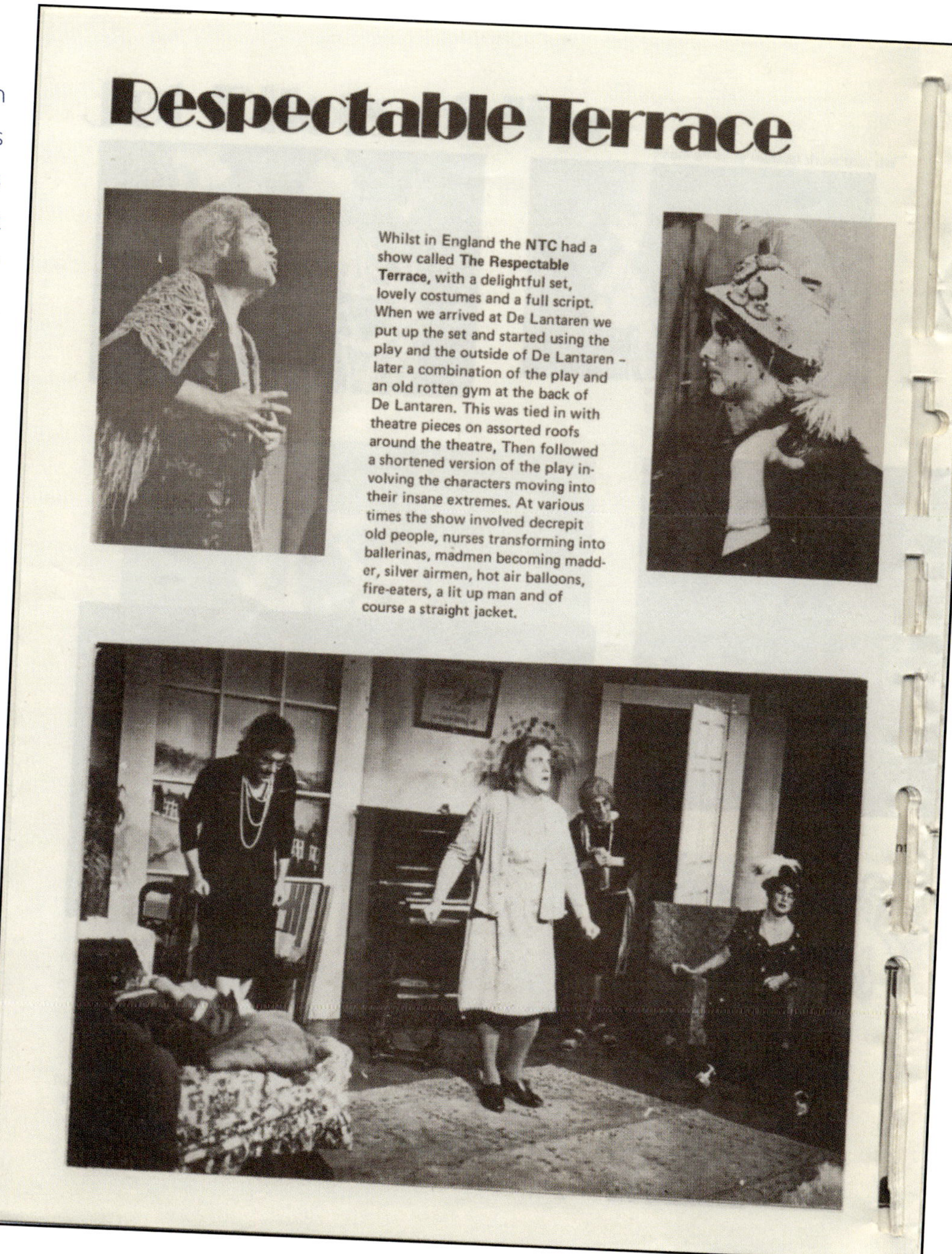


Whilst in England the NTC had a show called **The Respectable Terrace**, with a delightful set, lovely costumes and a full script. When we arrived at De Lantaren we put up the set and started using the play and the outside of De Lantaren – later a combination of the play and an old rotten gym at the back of De Lantaren. This was tied in with theatre pieces on assorted roofs around the theatre, Then followed a shortened version of the play involving the characters moving into their insane extremes. At various times the show involved decrepit old people, nurses transforming into ballerinas, madmen becoming madder, silver airmen, hot air balloons, fire-eaters, a lit up man and of course a straight jacket.

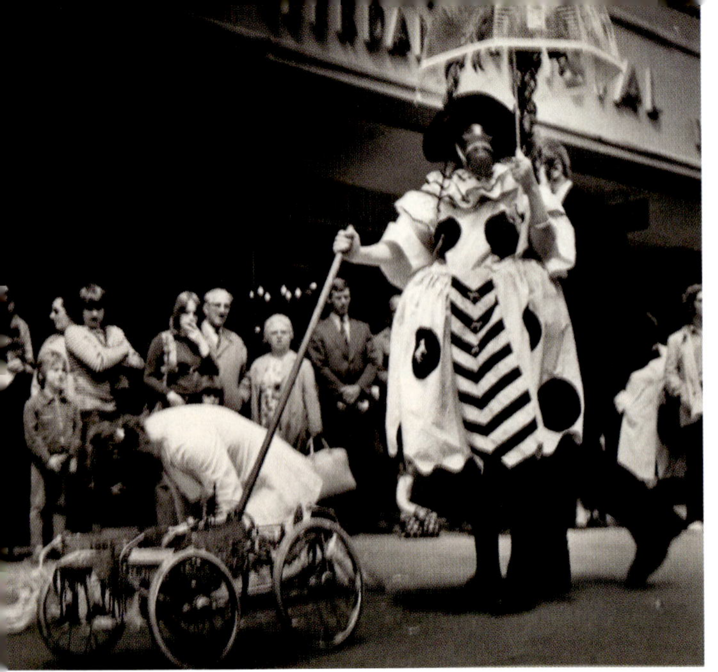



**B**rian: In early summer 1973, we undertook a huge, exciting project. We were invited to a month-long residency in Rotterdam, Netherlands. The whole Workshop caboodle upped sticks along with the theatre company: Andy's puppets, children's entertainers, a DJ and our own Thunderwing Disco,

Exploded Eye and other performance artists, Rocky and the Jets, printmakers, some teenagers and May Branch, an old-age pensioner who had become a close friend. Once in Rotterdam,

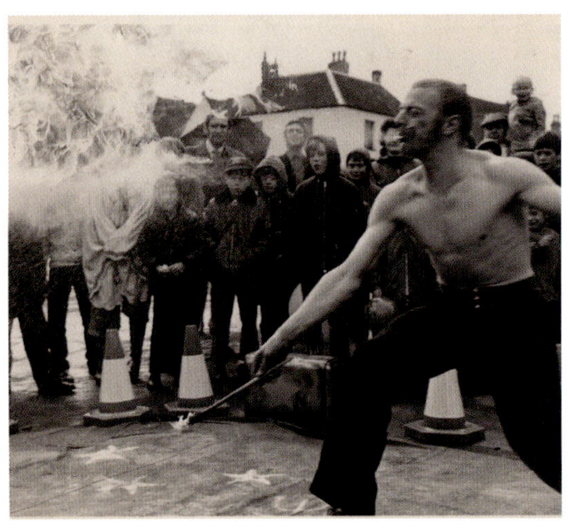

Corin Hardcastle fire-eating

we were based in the *Oude Westen* or Old West. It was an area that was similar to our own in Bath – run down, poor and blighted by council plans to redevelop, so we immediately felt at home there. We spent a month getting involved with local people and

politics, organising mystery tours to the seaside, regenerating old play parks, doing shows, discos and street theatre, workshops for kids and teachers, and painting a playground mural.

Mural in playground

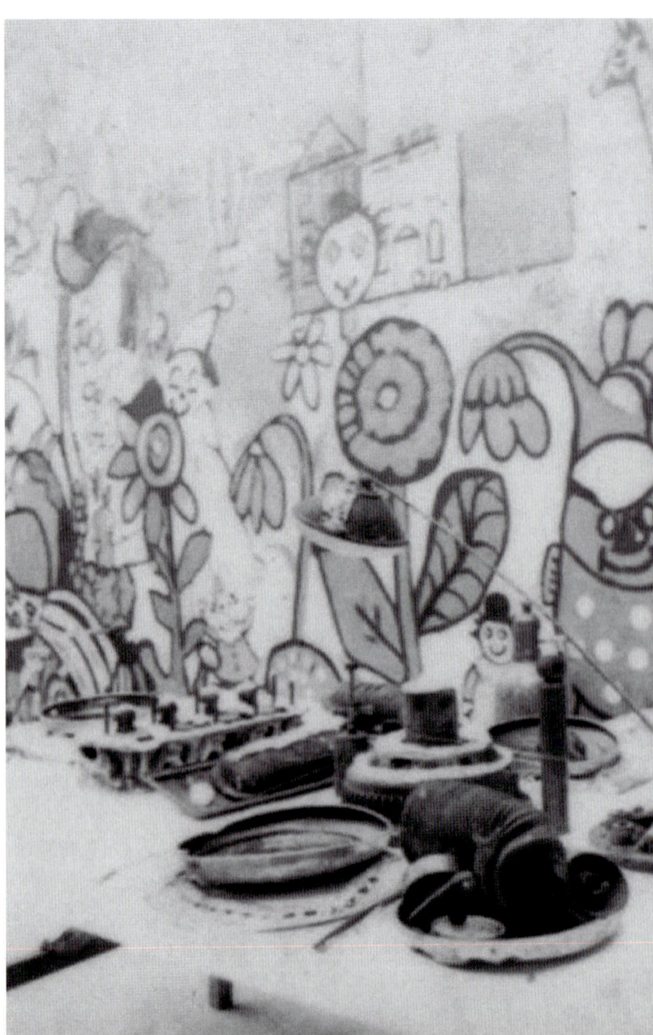

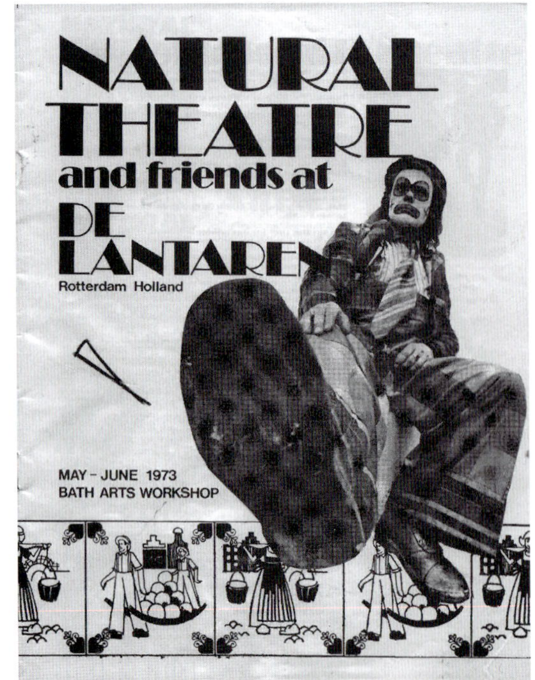

### From Phil's advance notes

If Rotterdam is supposed to be about a working model for an arts workshop principle, then it must attempt to emulate as many of BAW's basic concepts as possible: Breaking down of barriers between work, play, social work, theatre, art, social occasions etc. Maximum cooperation between individuals and groups, maximum sharing of resources, knowledge, workload, love etc. Everyone asked to help with jobs other than their own specific fields.

**Jennie:** Ros Birks and I were dispatched in advance to Rotterdam to organise an entire calendar of events. Going to the Netherlands and organising all that stuff helped me to realise that I could do this. It gave me a feeling of freedom I hadn't had before, a feeling that it was possible to break free of the repressive system I had grown up in.

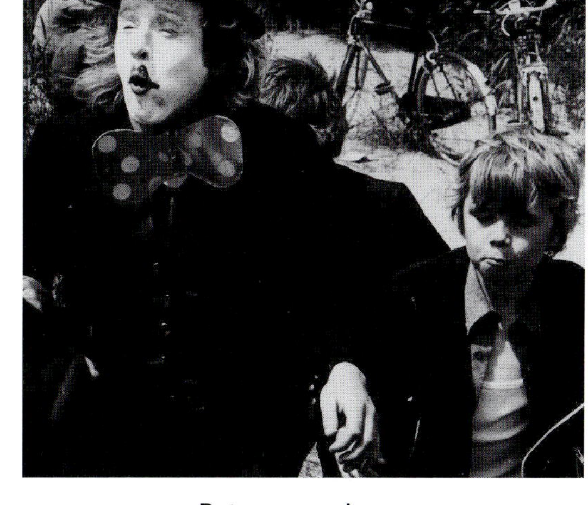

Brian as a clown

### Welcome notes from the advance party

We have put up a lot of info in the coffee bar on the first floor (our office is there)... charts by Ros and Jennie, pics by Corin, maps of Rotterdam and the Old West. The idea of the whole thing is that we work here and in Lijnbaan, a big shopping area with no cars. In the Old West we'll be doing lots in local rather tame playgrounds. Local action group has formed a committee to work with us. Rolande's room for environment is at the back of De Lantaren – big, black, dirty and a bit (very) full of rubbish... could be nice... Placing of props not yet certain but we collect them tomorrow... hope to have clothes racks too.

**Corinne:** We were one big crowd of people, liaising with local community activists to devise/enhance local initiatives as well as performing. The neighbourhood was somewhat deprived, but the many individuals we met were working to make it a better place to live in. Alternative types or council workers, they all seemed to be somehow aligned and welcoming to us. Round the back of the arts centre was a 'headshop' where you could buy Indian clothes, incense and other unspecified herbs.

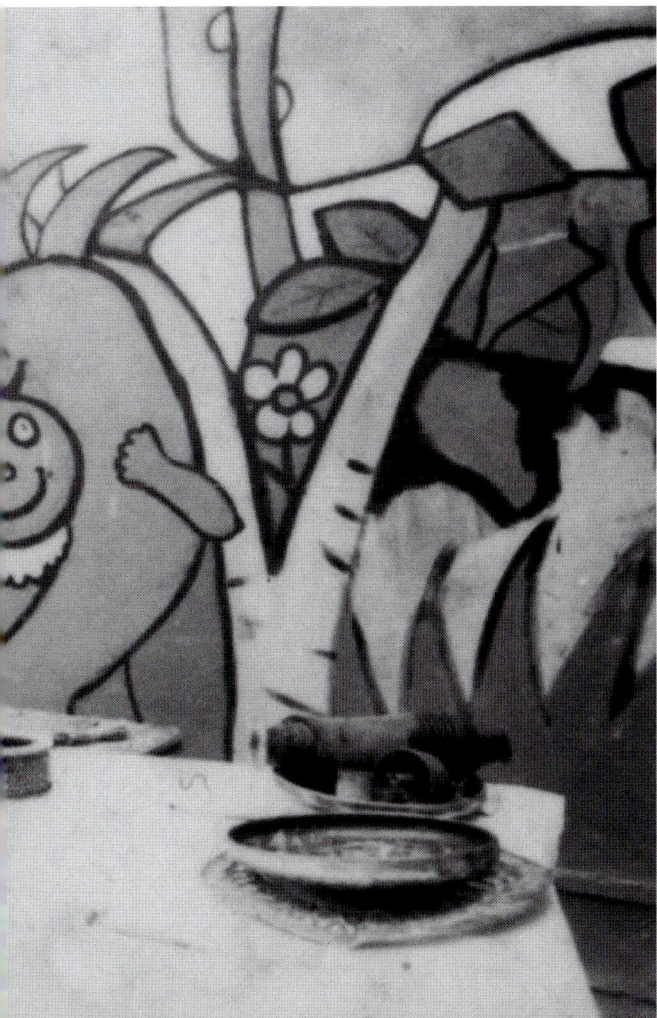

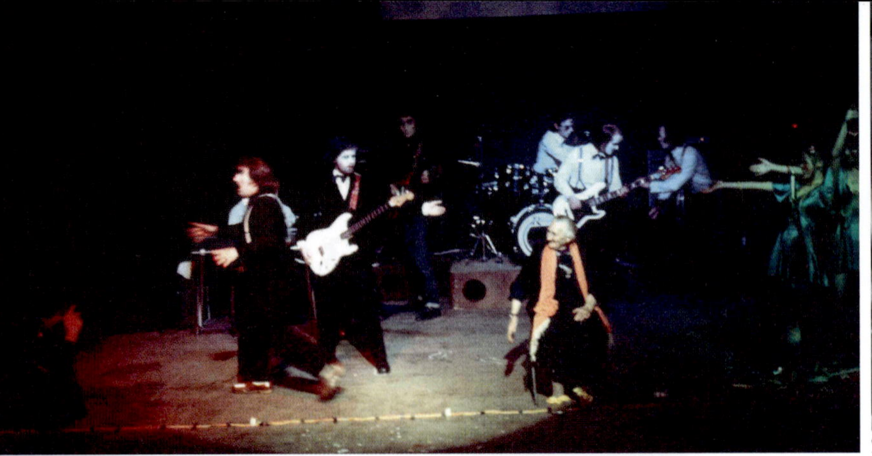

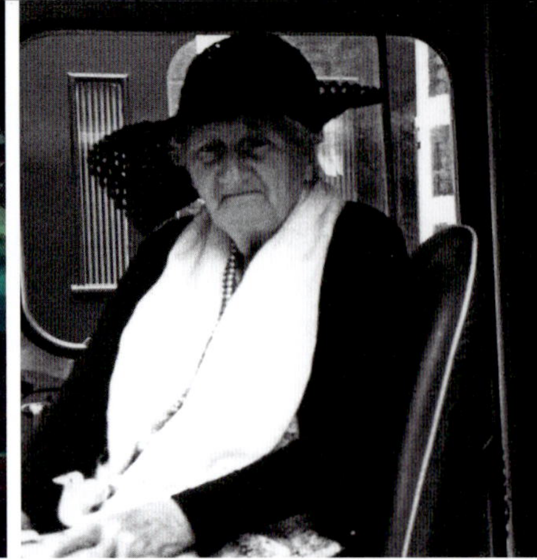

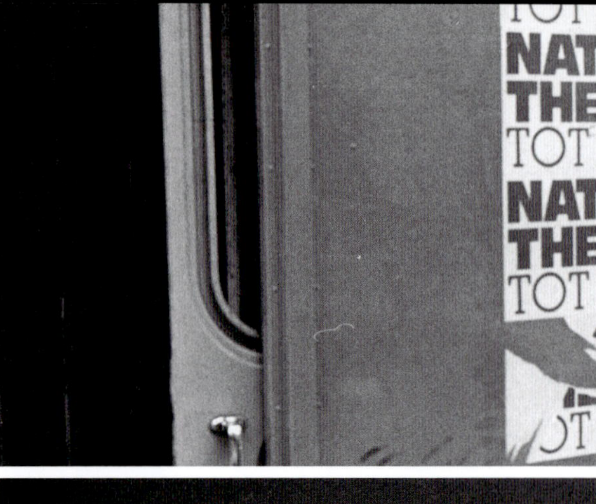


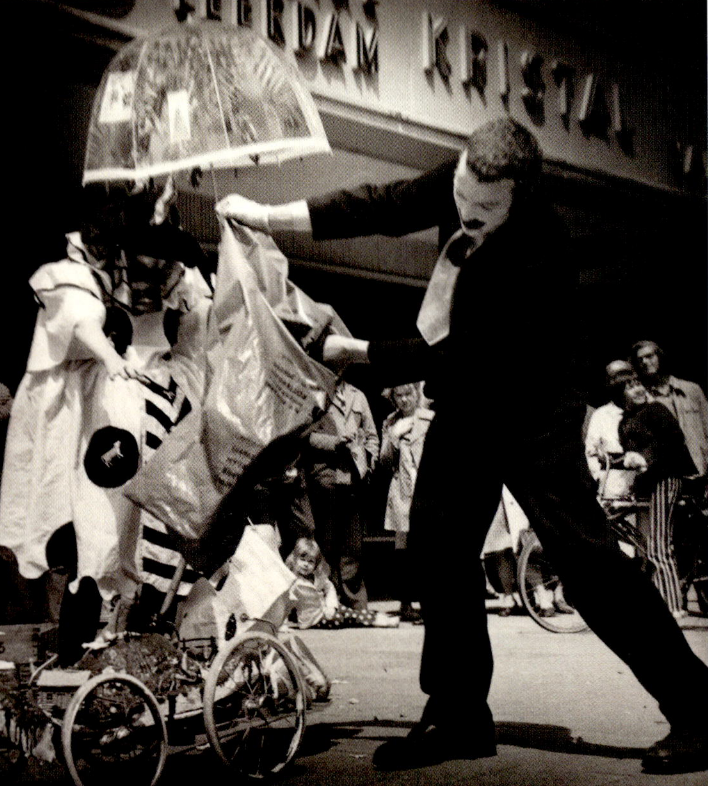

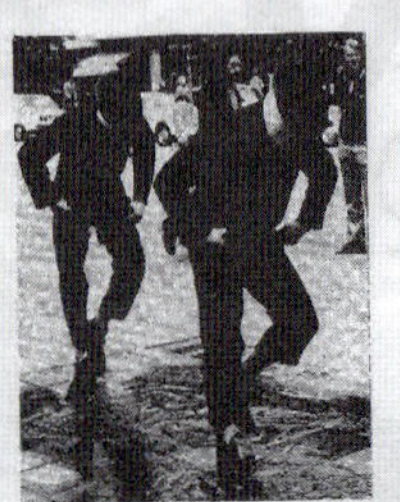

# Timetable

**Mon. May 7th.** Advance party arrive, Committee formed between Local schools, Clubs, Youth organisations etc. to work with Workshop during stay.

**Thurs. May 17th.** First group of 20 people arrive from England.

**Fri. May 18th.** Free introductory Party until 5 am! at the Lantaren, The Old West Cabaret and assorted acts.

**Sat. May 19th.** Sorting show for evening.
20.30. Respectable Terrace (people taken outside blindfold etc.)

**Sun. May 20th.** Children's Workshop, clowns and make-up. Cleaned street.
20.30. Respectable Terrace.

**Mon. May 21st.** Meeting local people, squatting, schools, action group and Club Seven (Kids theatre group).
20.00. Joint rehearsal with HOWK (The Old West Cabaret) followed by party, staff of Lantaren & HOWK.

**Tues. May 22nd.** Lunch time show, workshop for 60 people, 4 groups, trust games.
14.00—16.00. School Workshops, Gafflestraat, Gouvernestraat, Action Group on squatting.
Exploded Eye working in Lijnbaan and central station.
20.30. Respectable Terrace.

**Weds. May 23rd,** 10.30. Workshops at Kindergarten, Josephstraat.
11.00. Interview with Newspaper reporter.
12.15. Details of Outing for 29th. Children's outing to Rockanje.
14.00. Painting of Willems playground with kids.
14.00. Show at Lijnbaan for kids, Normals and Clowns, Shopping Centre. Normals arrested on route.
15.30. People to University to sort details for show next day.
20.30. Respectable Terrace plus 50 kids from local secondary school.

**Thurs. May 24th,** 12.30. Show at University (Medical faculty) Normals and Clowns.
16.00. Painting Playground.
16.00. Ecology official arrives to talk about June 5th.
19.00. Workshop at Club 7 with kids.
19.30. Our House (Ons Huis) local Community Centre, Embroidery Class, Dressmaking and workshop with womens Amateur Dance group.

**Fri. May 25th,** 09.30. Trip to dump for Wood, Tyres, Rope etc.
12.00. Make-up workshop for selves.
14.30. Workshop for evening show (selves).
14.30. Painting Playground.
19.30. Workshop at Our House for older people.
20.30 Respectable Terrace with an audience of over 100.

**Sat. May 26th.** Day Off, trip to Amsterdam.

**Sun. May 27th.** 11.00 Rehearsal for Exploded Eye.
14.30. Puppet show at Lantaren for Kids, Painting and Clowns etc.
16.00. Painting Playground.
20.30. Workshop for Older people.

**Mon. May 28th,** 09.30. King Kong takes Lantaren's magazine to collators.
14.00 Workshop in Gafflestraat school.
14.00. People discuss show at Odeon for June 2nd.
19.00. Workshop for 150 teachers, attempt at more sympathetic approach to children.
23.30 Meeting with HOWK about Odeon June 2nd.

**Tues. May 29th.** Beach outing to Rockanje for 40 kids.
21.30. Respectable Terrace.

**Weds. May 30th,** 10.15. Workshop for 2½ hours at Vanspeykstraat school.
15.00. 3 people to Den Haag to see Ecology film.
19.30. Workshop at Club 7.
20.30. No show owing to Final of European Cup, Workshop for 20 people instead.

**Thurs. May 31st.** King Kong job, moving flat for local resident.

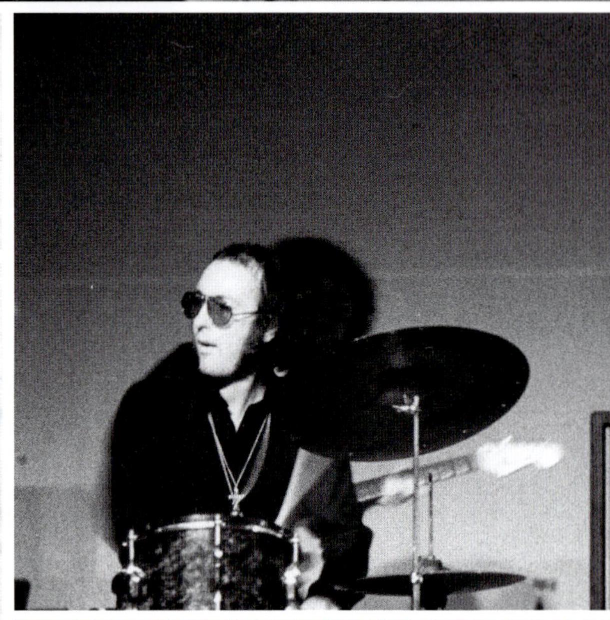

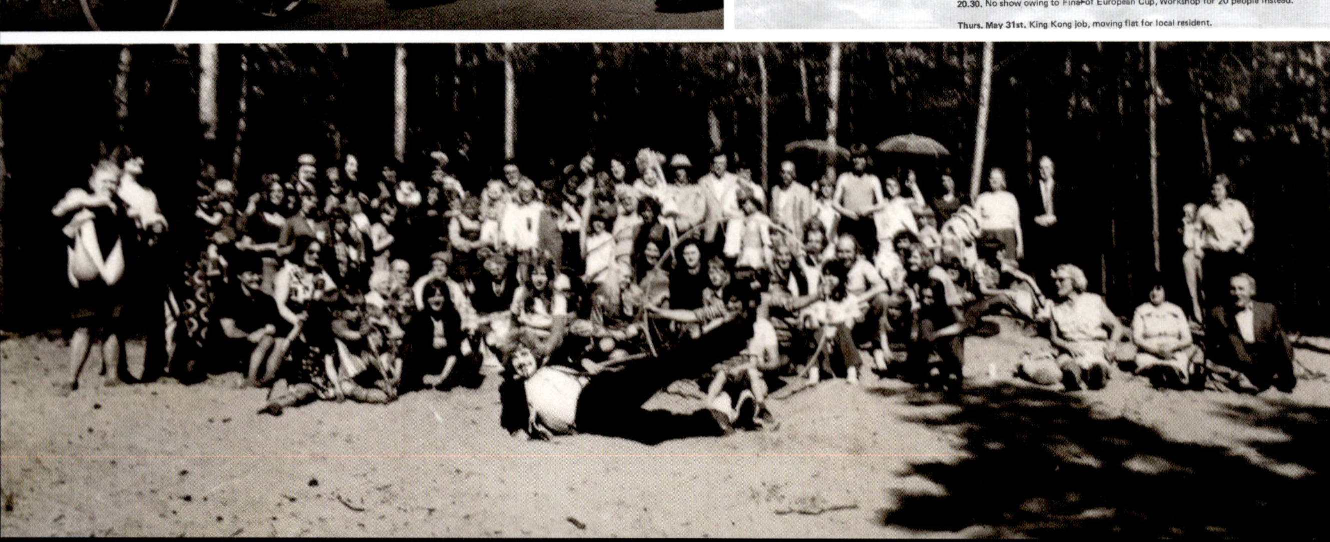

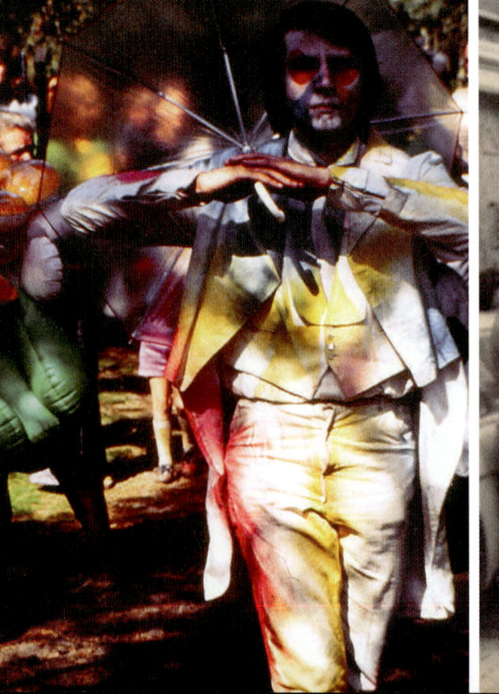

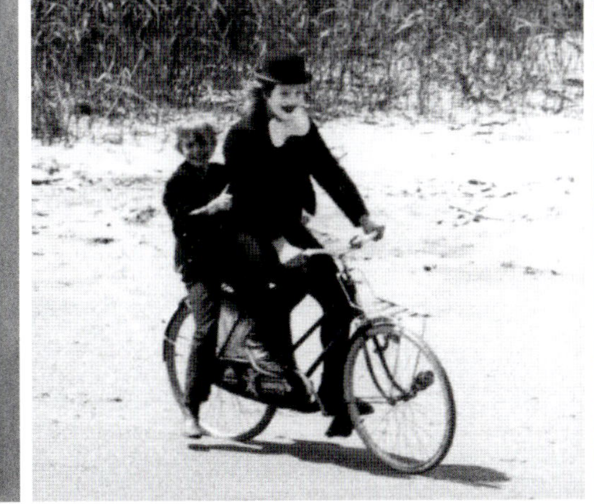

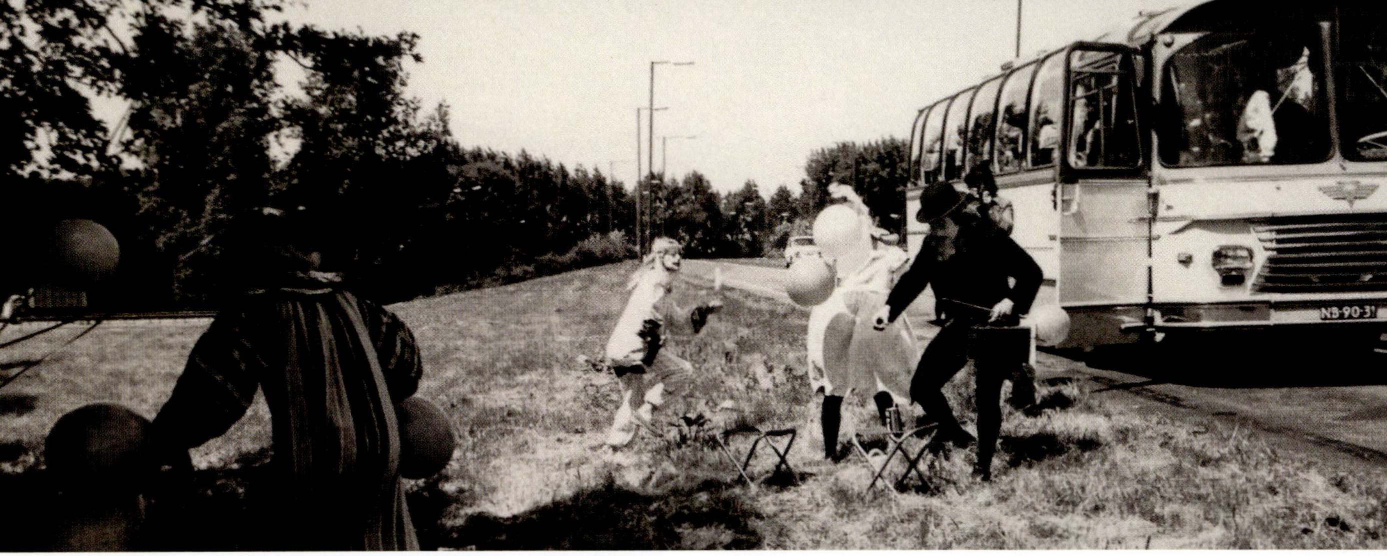

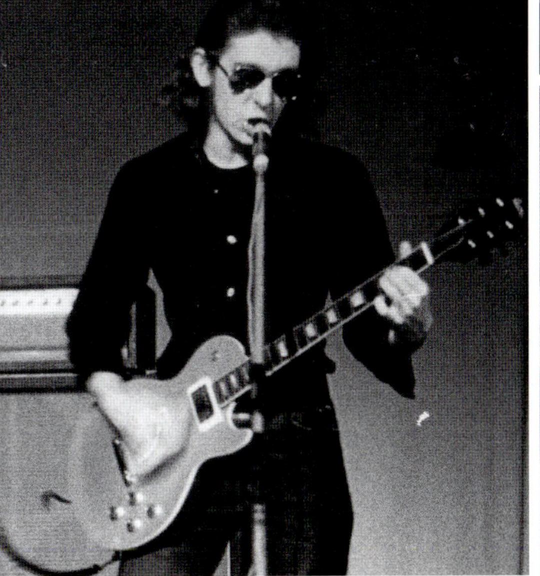

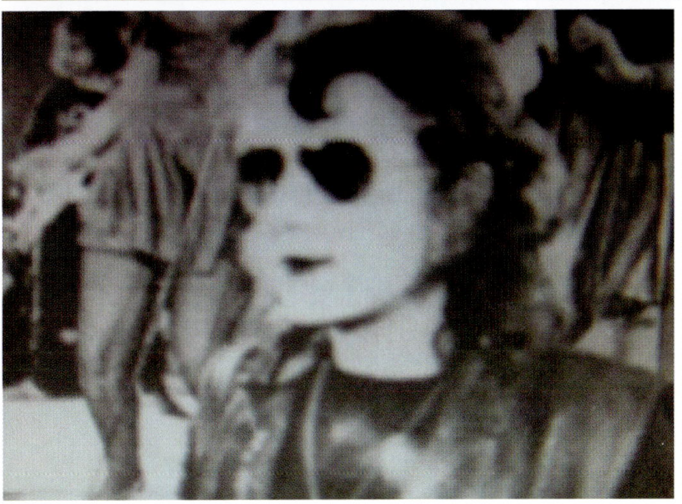

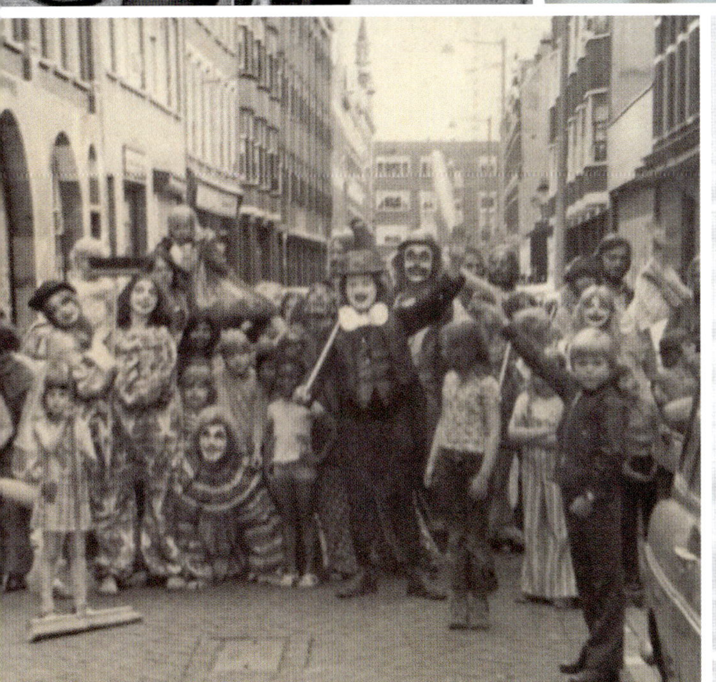

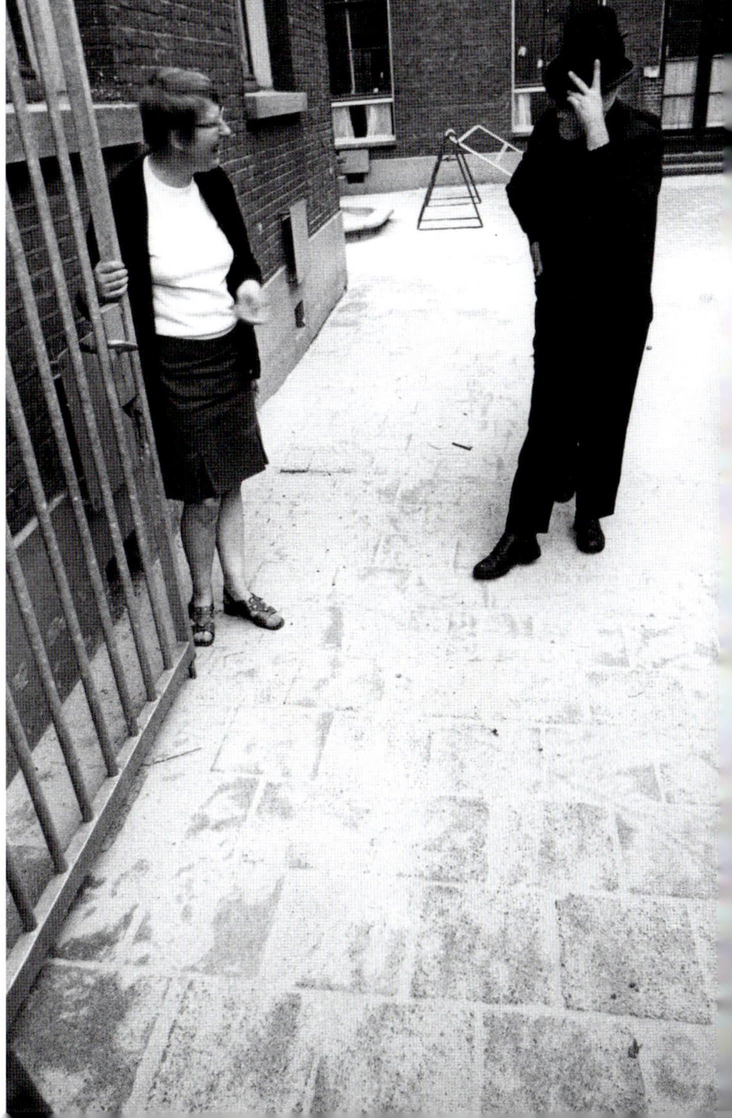

# Timetable

Fri. June 1st, 18.45. Van to Hook of Holland to meet final party arriving from England, collect mattresses on route.
20.30. Respectable Terrace plus Normals leading audience round streets.
22.30. Dark to Light Mission at Exsit Club.

Sat. June 2nd. Late breakfast!
14.00. Video show of work already done.
15.00. Street theatre in Lijnbaan, Normals.
16.00. John & Sue Fox from Welfare State arrive to discuss June 15th Holland Festival.
16.00–18.00. Jets Rehearsal.
20.30. Show at Odeon, Jets, Normals and Clowns.
24.00. Jets at Exsit.

Sun. June 3rd. Day Off?
Kids workshop for collecting street rubbish for painting & collage.

Mon. June 4th 11.30. Video workshop.
Setting up for Ecology Day.
Workshop sorting session.

Tues. June 5th, 10.30. Workshop at school, Gefflestraat.
Ecology Day. 13.00. In Lijnbaan, Puppet show, Cabbages and Hairspray!
14.30. Ecology film in Lantaren.
20.00. Barend Servat, Puppets and lead audience into Environmental display on Ecology.
22.00. Disco in Bar, Party with Jets.

Weds. June 6th, 10.30. Workshops with schools.
14.00. Ecology workshop with kids in theatre.
20.30. Video Workshop with Amateur dance group/keep fit.
20.30. Jets in theatre.
22.00. Video show of Jets in bar.

Thurs. June 7th, Day off?
12.00. Meeting to discuss general situation.
20.30. Video workshop as previous night.

Fri. June 8th, 10.30. School workshop with puppets, Van Speyckstraat.
14.00. Rehearsal with HOWK and NTC for Playground opening.
14.30. Meeting with T.V. officials re Holland Festival.
16.00. Rehearsal for Odeon show.
20.00. Jets and show at Odeon.
20.30. Show and Environment at Lantaren.
24.00. Jets at 'The Flaming Star'.

Sat. June 9th. Football Match NTC v The Beukers.
20.30. Show at the Lantaren.

Sun. June 10th, 08.00. Staff and Workshop leave for Barge trip.

Mon. June 11th. Almost Free!
Preparations for Playground opening and Exhibition.

Tues. June 12th. Opening of Playground Exhibition.
20.30. Combined show with HOWK at Playground.

Weds. June 13th. Rehearsal for afternoon.
12.00. Work with kids in Spangen.
13.00. Street Parade.
14.30. Perform at Centre.
16.00. Puppets.
20.30. Show at Lantaren.
20.30. Jets at Dordrect 'Shiva'.

Thurs. June 14th. Mystery Coach Outing.
23.30. Jets at Milky Way, Amsterdam.

Fri. June 15th. Holland Festival at Schouwberg Plein, plus Solid Gold Cadillac and Welfare State.

Sat. June 16th. Return to England. Hook to Harwich.

**Corinne:** We all slept upstairs at the arts centre, which had a huge attic previously inhabited by pigeons. Andy and I bagged a rather dirty corner which had been partitioned off with a wall and door made of slatted wood with gaps in between. After spending hours cleaning the pigeon shit we could retire with a modicum of privacy in something akin to a wooden prison cell. A stark contrast to the state of the art facilities on the floors below us, but no one minded.

**Phil:** While we were there a lot of advance planning for **Another Festival** in Bath was arranged over the phone. In between rehearsing, performing or running events we were making phone calls, booking equipment and transport, and hustling for materials. The De Lantaren staff didn't seem to mind (arts in the Netherlands were funded to a level we could barely imagine, so a few phone calls didn't even register). People at the other end (in the UK) kept asking us to pop round to check the size of the hall, or the PA equipment, and we had to explain we were in Rotterdam and wouldn't be back for several weeks.

**BAW leaflet:** The last day of our stay and the first day of Welfare State's visit was the first day of the Holland Festival. The Natural Theatre, Exploded Eye, Rocky and the Jets, Thunderwing Disco and Mike Westbrook's Solid Gold Cadillac collaborated with Welfare State on a show for the opening ceremony that was broadcast live on national TV. Sixty people were involved. We had a day for a joint rehearsal for a show that began at 10.30pm

**Mitch:** A climactic moment involved the youngest member of the Workshop, the teenage Pete Smith, as a sacrificial

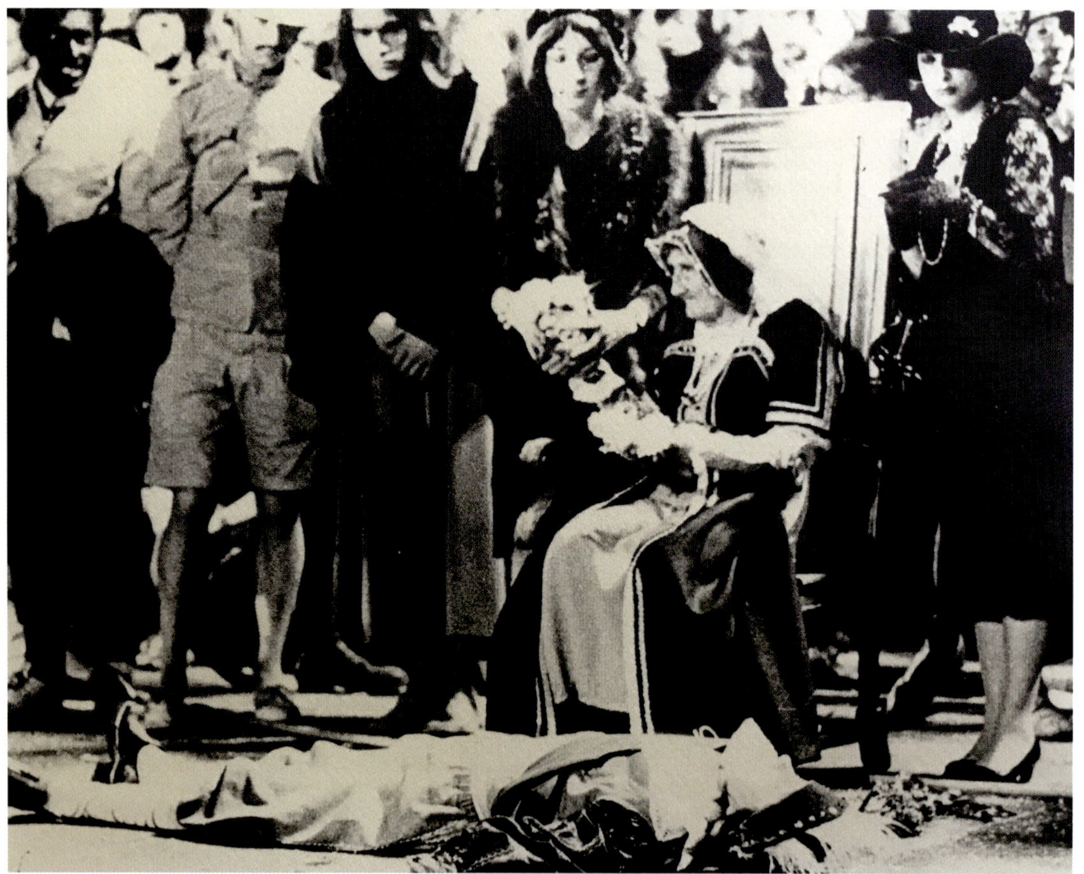

Holland Festival

victim lying prone before the oldest Workshop member, the septuagenarian Queen May, as a catalyst for a rebirth celebration.

**Johnny 'Be Good' Loder (rhythm guitar):** After the theatre show, came

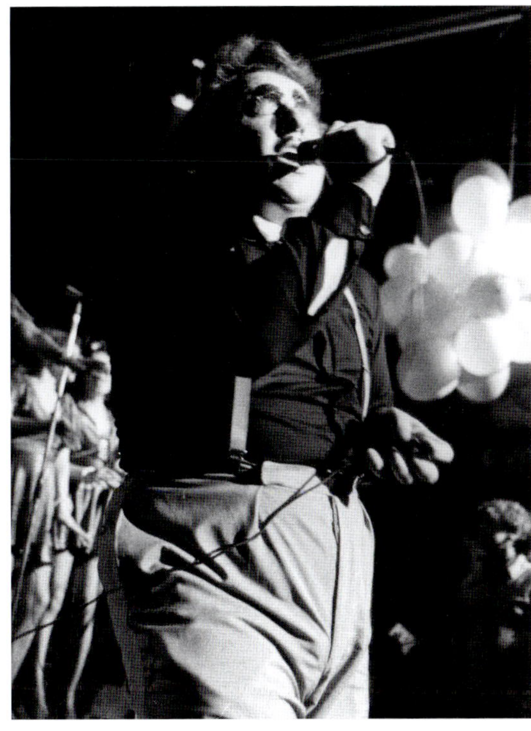

the music. Rocky and the Jets arrived at the city's Theatre Square in two hired limousines with tinted windows and uniformed chauffeurs. We kicked off with *Blue Suede Shoes*. The sound seemed gigantic and in the evening light we could see a huge audience filling the square. Their reaction was fantastic and indeed people were arriving all the time. After seeing the TV coverage, they came along to experience it live. After two encores, the police stopped us playing. Rocky told the crowd that he would keep making records from his prison cell as we escaped to our limos.

**Mitch:** It had been a memorable conglomeration of shows, forums and workshops for a wide range of ages and venues – a dusty old gym, a railway station, a sandy forest, a beach, and the Theatre Square plaza in the heart of the city. The **Natural Theatre Company's** Normals were temporarily arrested and then celebrated their freedom with a programme of unique interactive street arts. Their Fellini-esque clowns were a cavalcade in the square. **Exploded Eye** performed a midnight ballet for taxi drivers at Rotterdam railway station. Community engagement was comprehensive, interactive and led to future collaborations and relationships with the Workshop and the Old West.

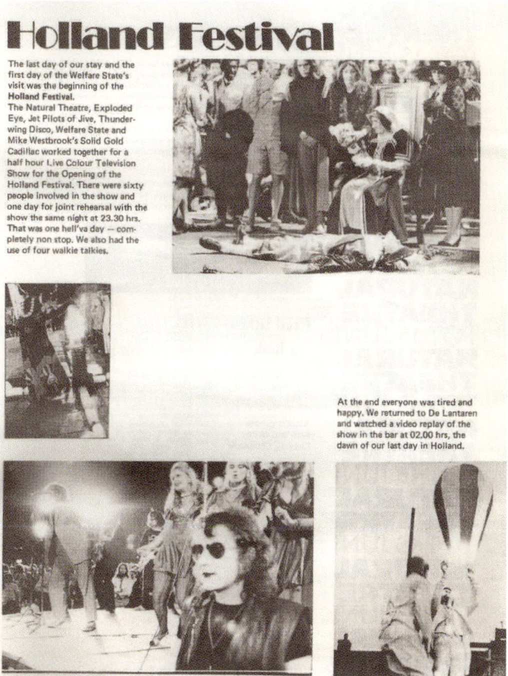

Holland Festival

The last day of our stay and the first day of the Welfare State's visit was the beginning of the Holland Festival.

The Natural Theatre, Exploded Eye, Jet Pilots of Jive, Thunderwing Disco, Welfare State and Mike Westbrook's Solid Gold Cadillac worked together for a half hour Live Colour Television Show for the Opening of the Holland Festival. There were sixty people involved in the show and one day for joint rehearsal with the show the same night at 23.30 hrs. That was one hell'va day — completely non stop. We also had the use of four walkie talkies.

At the end everyone was tired and happy. We returned to De Lantaren and watched a video replay of the show in the bar at 02.00 hrs, the dawn of our last day in Holland.

**Corinne:** At the end of it all, there was an outing for BAW and the people we had worked with during our visit. A barge trip up and down the River Maas, where the only refreshments were bottles and bottles of Dutch beer. I remember that, despite my inebriated state, I persuaded the skipper to let me take the wheel. Happily, he took it back before I hit anything and we survived to see another day dawn.

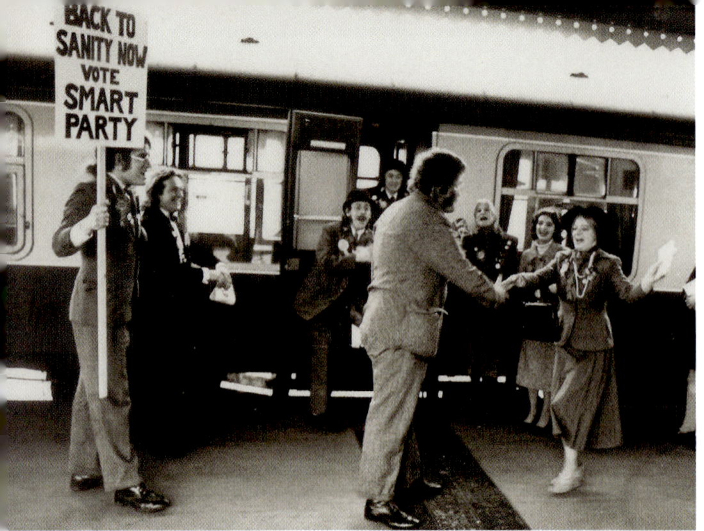

# THE SMART PARTY OF GREAT BRITAIN

**P**enny: The Smart Party developed during 1973. 'Smart Week' was our first event in the spring. Everyone dressed as smartly as possible while carrying out the week's work to test the new attire. By the end of the week, Mick Martin's suit was practically in shreds and covered in mud, since he'd been lugging furniture and equipment throughout. The ploy was partly a reaction to Councillor Plumbridge declaring that we 'Scared everyone to death' because we were so scruffy. We soon developed our Smart personalities and they became adaptable to all sorts of situations, and were able to make points about social and political issues by being absurdly reactionary.

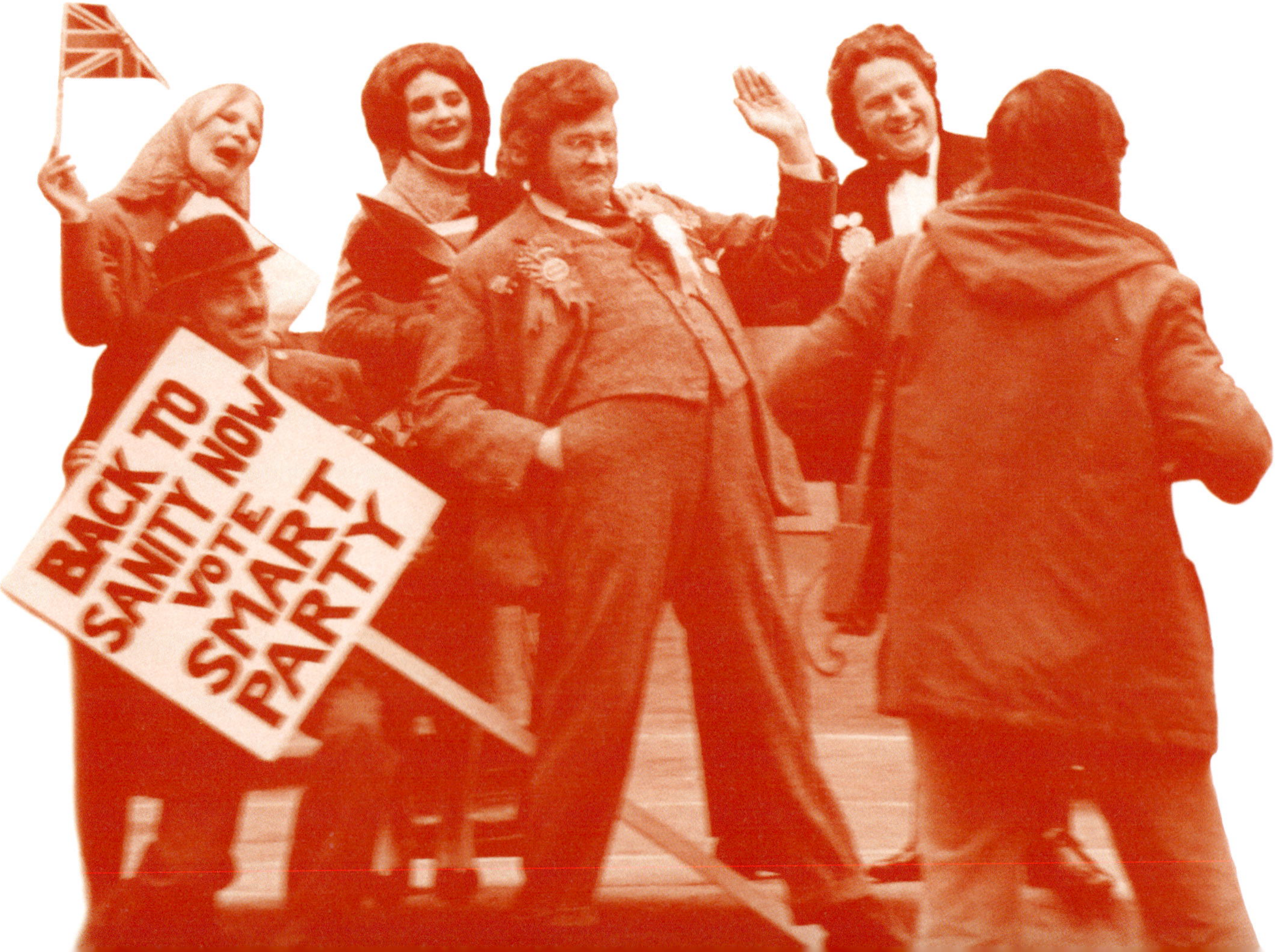

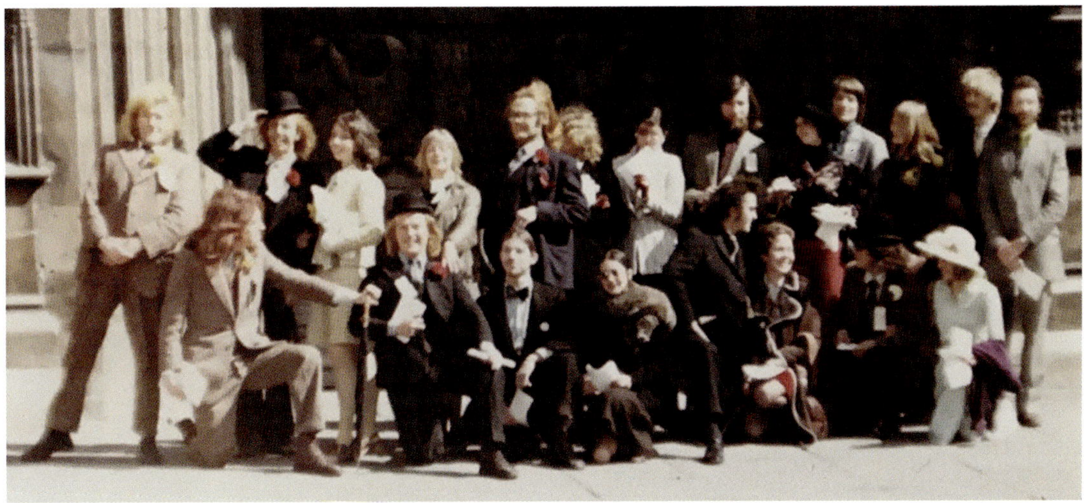

Early Smart Party

**Jennie:** The Smart Party was led by Sir Ralph (pronounced *Rafe*, naturally) Oswick. We encouraged the public to vote for him simply because he was dressed smartly and had a posh accent. We found tweed suits (male and female)

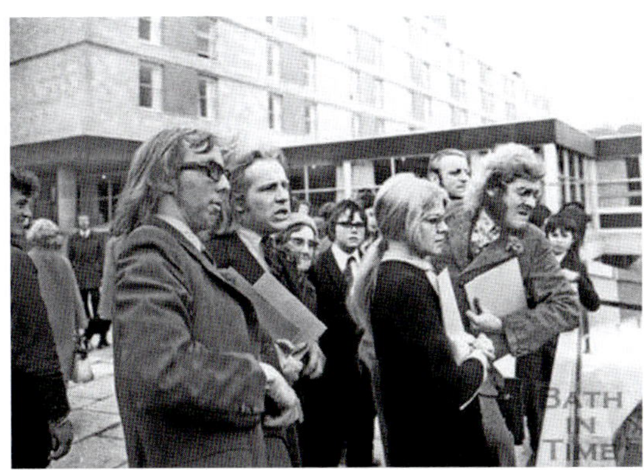

Sir Ralph likens Bath's Hilton Hotel to a cigarette lighter

from the jumble, carried placards saying 'Vote Smart' and generally objected to anything unconventional and endorsed anything Sir Ralph felt was right (and right wing).

## Sports day at the Serpentine

**Penny:** We were booked at the Serpentine Gallery over the 1973 August Bank holiday, so decided to hold a Smart Party sports day on the lawn outside. We hired white linen, china, school benches, tea urns, umpire chair, deck chairs, white coats, tracksuits, a white line marker and hurdles. Each day, a blackboard went up at lunchtime announcing the day's programme. Meanwhile, 'groundsmen' meticulously marked out the track

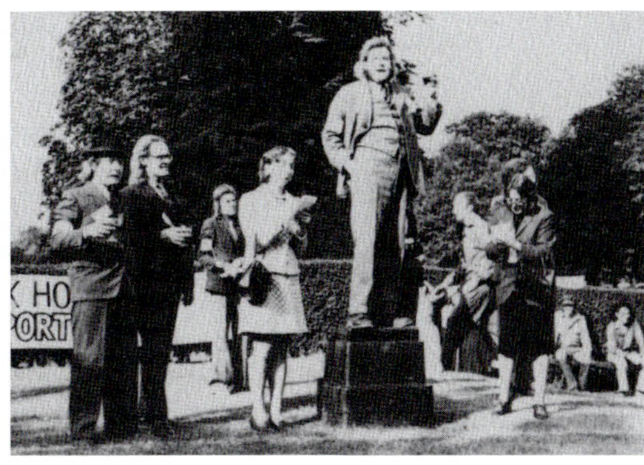

and set up benches for spectators, tea tables, and the Smart Party's own table with wine, deckchairs and a phone. Now and again the Smart Party's own athletes appeared to warm up.

When the events started, huge crowds gathered. Sir Ralph and his entourage presided from their table, drinking wine and talking very loudly. Next to them was a table of toys, sweets and rosettes or prizes. Although they had an air of geniality and benevolence, the

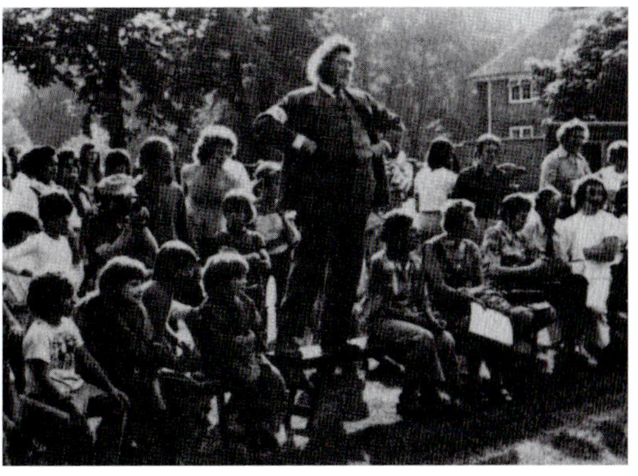

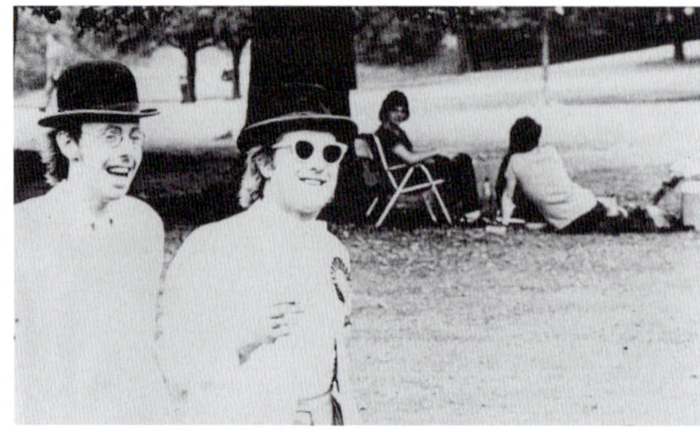

An air of geniality

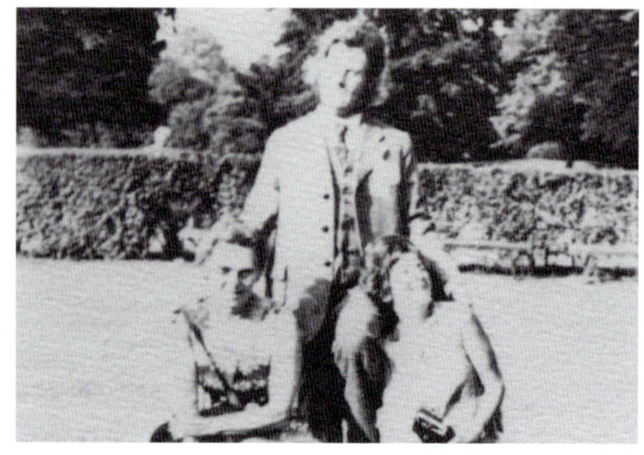

An air of benevolence

Smart's motives soon became apparent: they were obsessed with winning!

The actual sports were organised very professionally by 'officials' in tracksuits. The first few races were played straight. Delighted kids queued up to join in and win prizes. Then came the sack race. Sir Ralph positioned himself half way along the track and climbed into a sack out of sight of the other competitors. As they came level with him, he sent his aides to grab the leading contestants, before jumping onto the track himself and winning by several lengths, often posing for an 'action replay' by his personal photographer. Similarly with the high jump, Sir Ralph halted the proceedings, ordered an attendant to bring a step ladder and mattresses then, after cueing his photographer, stepped off the ladder with a regal salute to win by several feet.

## Outsmarted!

**Penny:** At other times, the Smarts devised their 'intervention' on the spot, possibly in a moment of panic and desperation. I remember one performance when we were invited to perform among the guests at an

Below: Sack race

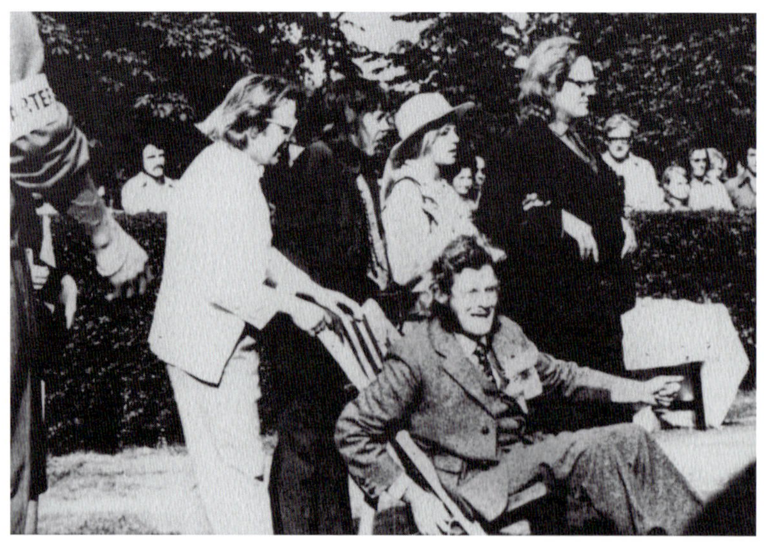

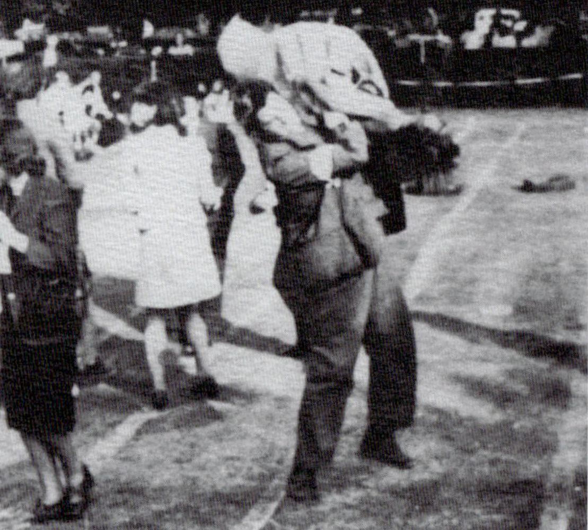

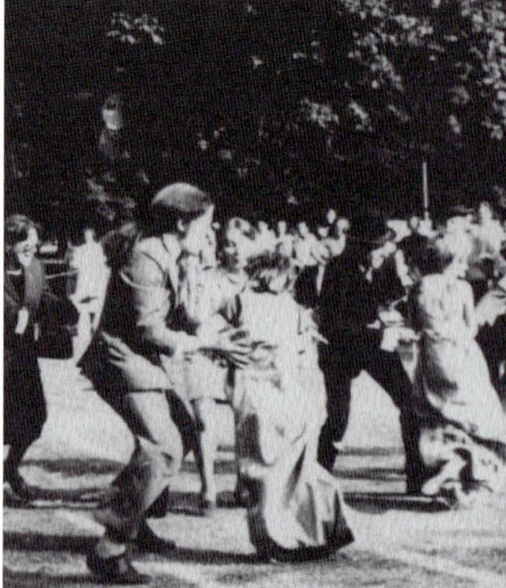

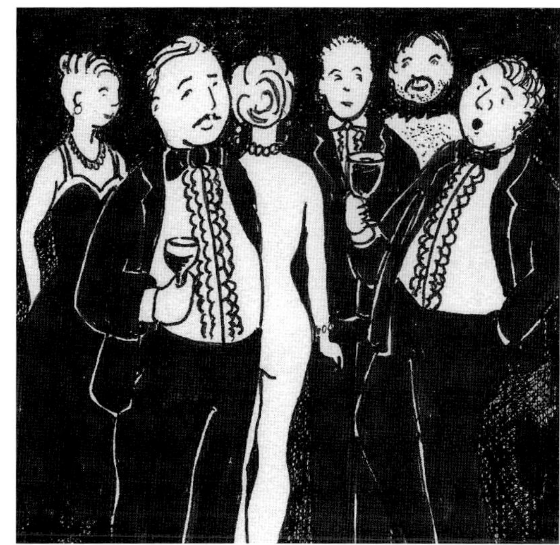

The dark environment
was perfect

Party, with ball gowns, dinner suits and tiaras but once there, we realised our costumes looked completely shabby compared to the expensive attire of the guests. We were outsmarted.

After conferring, we decided to strip off completely and mingle with the crowd naked, albeit with our pearls and make-up on (the men too, faces caked in a thick layer of *Spot-Lite Klear* stage make-up). The dark environment was perfect as we milled about greeting people ostentatiously as if we were old friends. Everyone looked us straight in the eye and tried hard not to look elsewhere. In fact it was a perfect emperor's new clothes experience, as all the guests did a great job of pretending nothing untoward was occurring. The Naturals' version of performance art in action!

architect's party. The venue was a warm, dark and rather swanky basement space. We had planned to be Smart

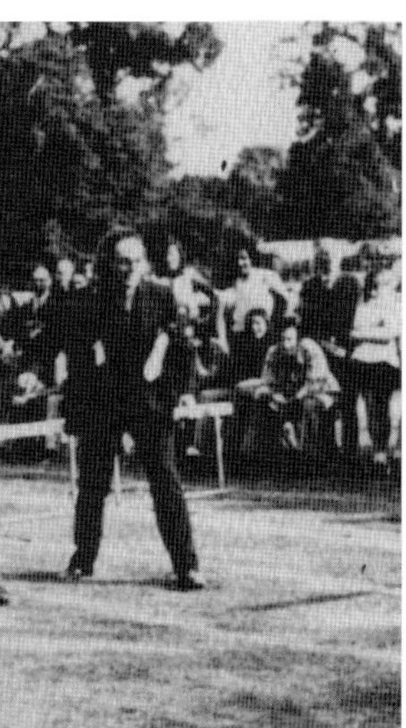

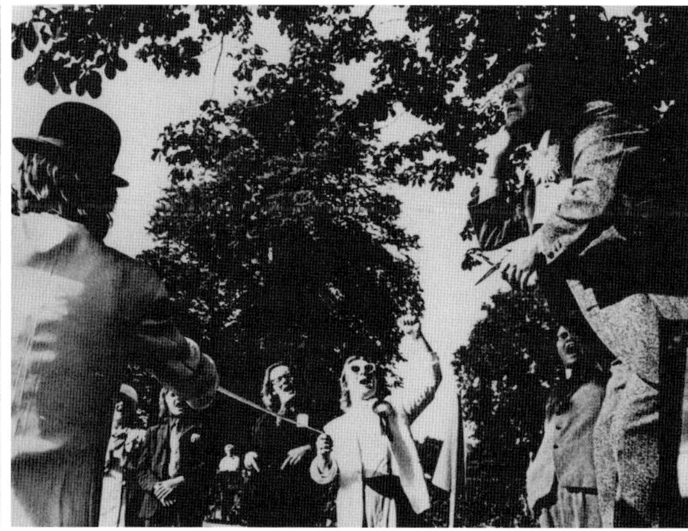

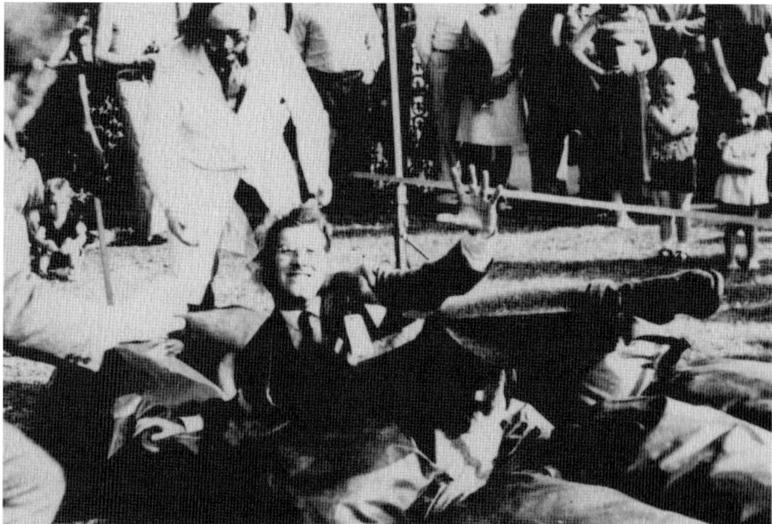

**Phil:** The legendary Paul 'Nasher' Nachman co-founded the short-lived Bath Film Unit in 1972 with the late Paul Callas, later joined by Dave Lascelles, John Austin and Cedric Beatty.[1] After its closure, Nasher went on to set up Workshop Films, through which he recorded many key Workshop and related events of the decade. Nasher's aspiration was to create a regional resource in an era when there was a real appetite for ultra-low budget 'bootlace cinema' at a time when some TV news was still shot on Super 8, with labs in London who would process and print your camera 'rushes' while you waited if your budget allowed.[2] There was a subversive ethos around Super 8 culture – this and its dream-like look appealed to film-makers eschewing the mainstream. Above the door at Workshop Films were displayed the words that said it all: *Embrace the grain*!



Nasher ran courses in film-making techniques at Workshop Films and took on commissions. Even by the end of the decade, it still cost less than £5 per day to hire beautifully-engineered Nizo and Beaulieu cameras, with a Zenon projector available for under a tenner. At those prices it was possible to make feature films on Super 8, and indeed three were produced, including Nasher's best known film (begun in

---

1. The film unit was based at the back of the Cleveland Hotel and was supported by Charlie Ware.
2. Bootlace refers to the narrow gauge of the film stock. Super 8 film is still used today by high-end commercial producers where digital can't create the same look and feel, only these days they have to bike the rushes to Germany to get them processed.

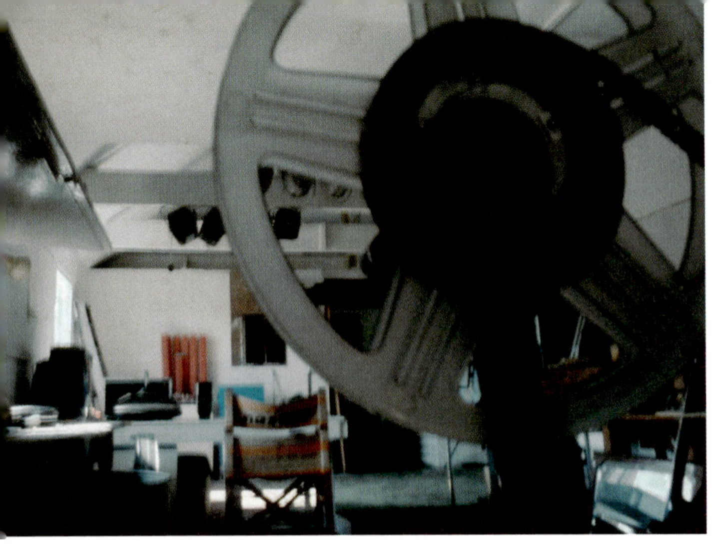

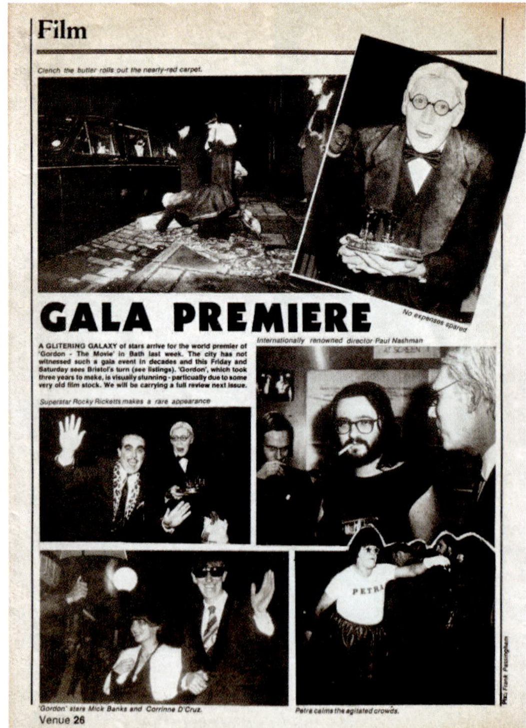

1979), the fabled **Gordon the Movie**. Nasher explained that making a feature grew out of 'my growing frustration with always filming documentary material'. The film deliberately plays on the numerous pitfalls of ultra-low budget Super 8 film making: handheld camera, different film stock, natural (poor) lighting, muffled dialogue and so on. It was described by Bristol's *Venue* magazine as *the cheapest, weirdest feature in the history of film-making… making Herzog's Fitzcarraldo look like a day trip to Margate.*

### Mick Moss

For a while, I was living in the basement under an antique shop just down the road from The Hat & Feather. Nasher had it first and for a while it was the Workshop Films HQ. I took it over and made what had become a damp, smelly, mouldy space into somewhere to live, as well as a small but functioning recording studio, based around Nasher's 4-track Teac Porta-studio. Somehow I'd convinced the Enterprise Allowance Scheme that I was a viable candidate for that Tory launch-pad for budding entrepreneurs. I think you got the dole, plus a couple of quid on top, and they left you alone to fuck up. Perfect for me.

**Phil:** Workshop Films would not have happened without Nasher. It was his energy, his vision, his persistence, not

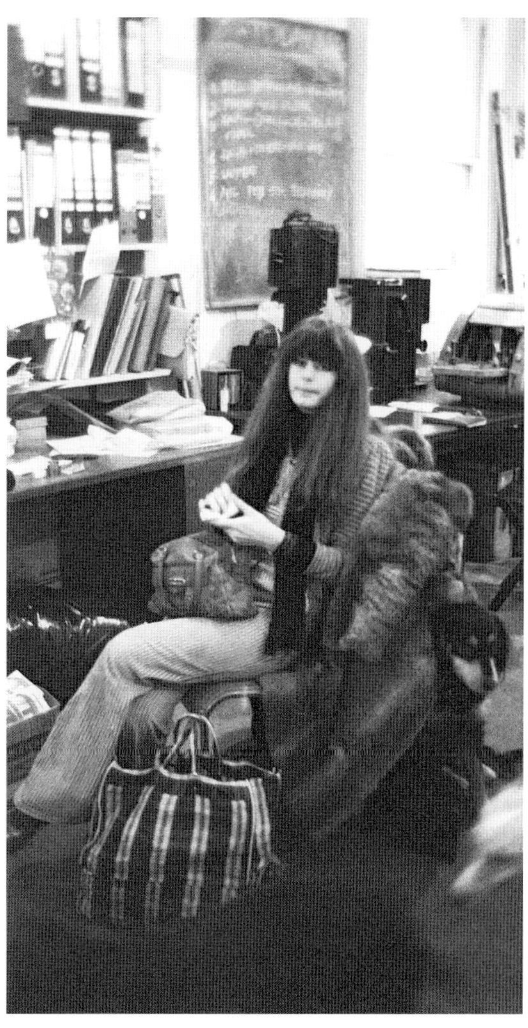

Sophie at Workshop Films

to mention his sense of humour that made it what it was. I had some wonderful film-making experiences with Nasher, among them shooting his film **The Edge** on the coldest night of the year at Severn Beach; and later in the middle of Brazil, filming in defence of local farmers threatened by multi-national companies. It was Nasher who had the original idea of creating a truly democratic public media resource and set about doing just that in Bath. His was the idea that I was able to adopt many years later when I helped establish the Engine Room community media centre in Bridgwater, which is very much alive today.

# OUR DAILY LIVES

**Penny:** We lived closely together, but home life was almost incidental. We started early, ate basic food, mostly out, cooked sometimes, finished work late, often very late, so downtime was rare. But we were close. Close like a family, through constant proximity. There were lots of good times, getting on with things, and other times where tempers frayed with sniping, snapping, sulks and gossip. But there was always lots of laughter, improvised fun arising from intimacy and observations from shared experience. Voices and characters evolved from life on the road and in the shop and office. On tour, we often slept in sleeping bags straight on floors. Floors of people's houses or student union halls or arts centres. Rarely comfortable, but everyone slept after all the activity.

There were loads of drugs in 70s Bath, and people often assumed we were druggy hippies, but we weren't big consumers. We drank quite a bit, mostly in The Hat & Feather, which was our regular evening haunt. An average day in winter, when not on tour, often started with breakfast a bacon roll in a steamed up cafe en route to the shop or office for rehearsal, then working in the shop or on a removal or house clearance and/or a rehearsal. Lunch, a pasty or beans and chips in the pub. Similar activity went on in the afternoon, included things like washing or sorting props and costumes or sewing or designing sets and scenery, or doing graphics and drawings. In the evenings, there might be a communal meal. Few of us had proper kitchens with fridges. So we ate lots of vegetarian stews and curries. Or we'd get a takeaway, or go back to the pub.

When I went to live in River Street, around eight of us shared a no-fridge kitchen and one bathroom. The rooms were large with Georgian proportions and furnished with jumble and purchases from our shop. There was no heating apart from electric bar fires. A huge hot water cylinder fed an enormous enamel bath that was so huge it neutralised the hot water with its cold mass as it filled up. Having a bath in winter was a serious endeavour.

Our clothing was more in tune with today than say, the 80s or 90s. We lived in jeans and T-shirts, with fitted or flared sleeves. Dungarees were popular for both sexes, also all the classic hippy, tie-dye and patchwork fabrics. There were flared cotton 'loon pants' and velvet trousers and jackets and lots of corduroy and cheesecloth. We spent far less time than nowadays refining our hair and make-up. In fact most of our cosmetic skills were used in dressing rooms applying thick layers of Max Factor stage make-up. Costumes were the clothes that took most of our time and attention. We nearly always got changed in communal dressing rooms, sometimes in the back of vans, and there was little self-consciousness. We felt safe together, and whilst there were jibes and pointing and laughing as people transformed into their characters, particularly when the men were squeezing themselves in women's tights I remember – cannot forget actually – getting ready, playing with clothes and make-up and then seriously checking our costumes before going out to perform. We took a lot of care over our 'look'.

Those of us who worked full-time and received wages, were on very low pay for the time. At first, in 1973 around £8 a week rising to £12 pounds in 74. Somehow this was OK. I remember breaking it down to the other friends who wondered how we managed. Our rent was low and reasonable. It was about a third — or quarter later — of the weekly wage. Bills and laundrette costs, clothes and other essentials used another third/quarter. Lots of clothes came from the jumble and furniture from our shop, and we always paid for

what we used — competitive rates of course. As we needed to eat out a lot, almost half went on food... and some beer, and every now and then we'd go out all together on a Friday night and have a curry, and now and again a special evening at the Beaujolais restaurant off Queen's Square, where we'd have *oeuf en cocotte*, followed by *steak au poivre*, staying there late, until the candles burnt down, often spending a quarter of our wages in a few hours, but it was a treat to relish and really set us up from time to time.

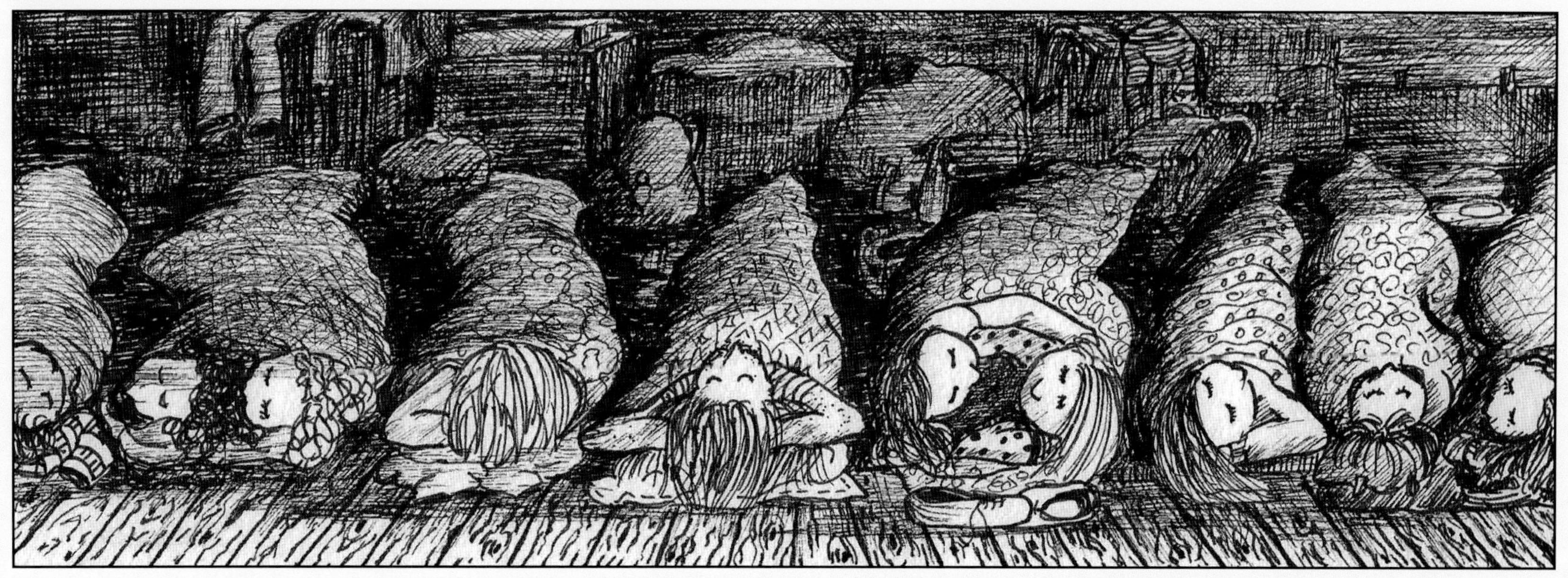

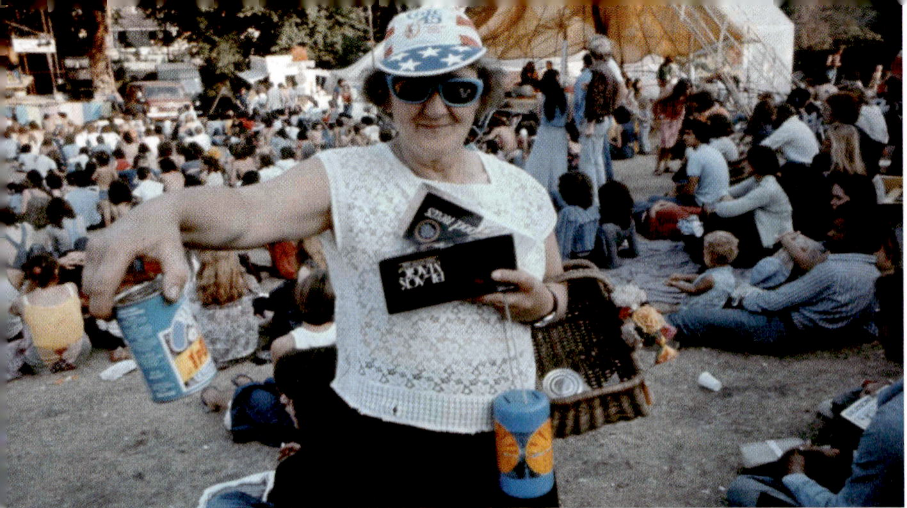
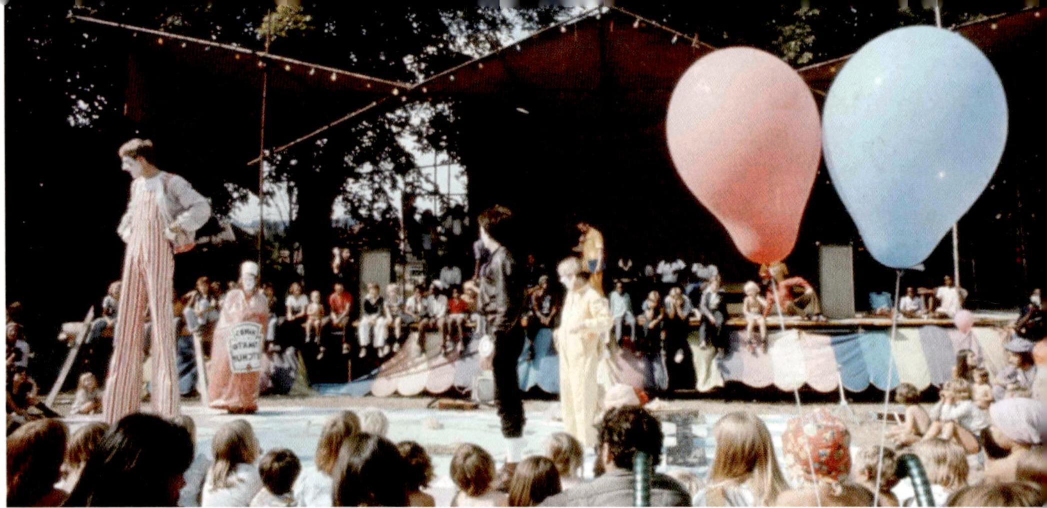
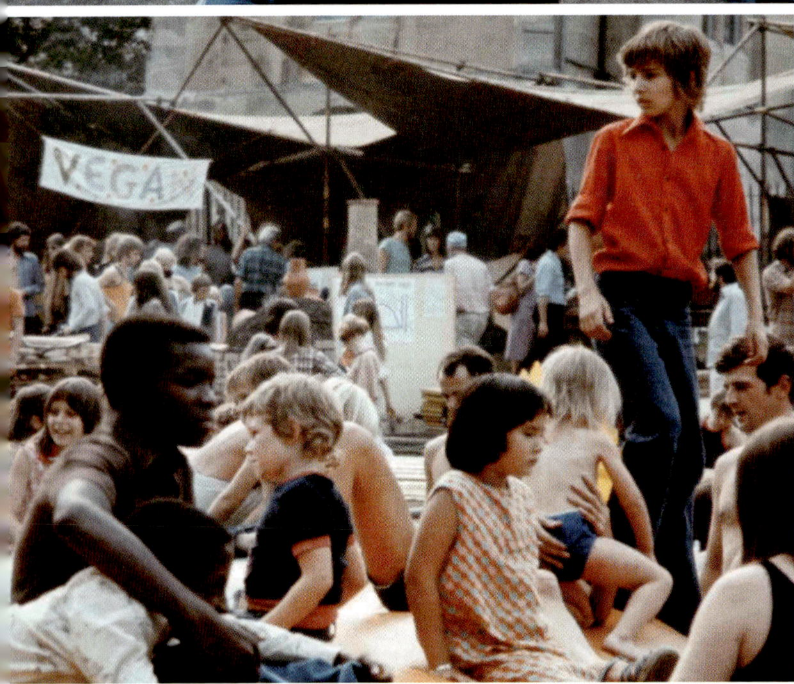
VEGA
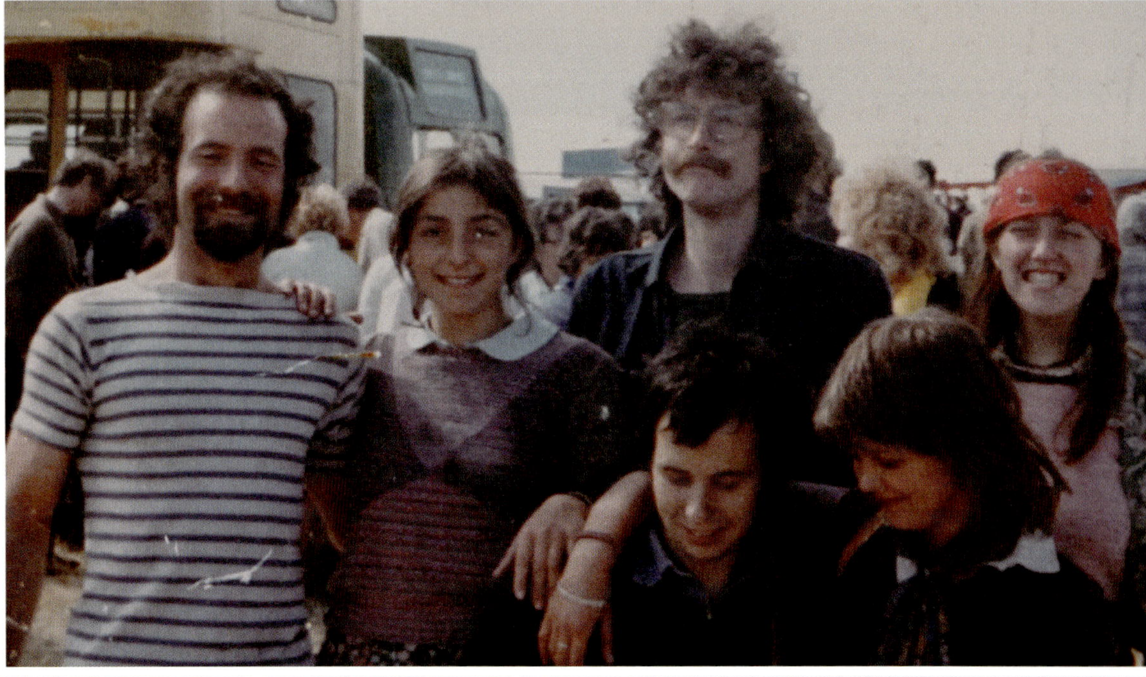
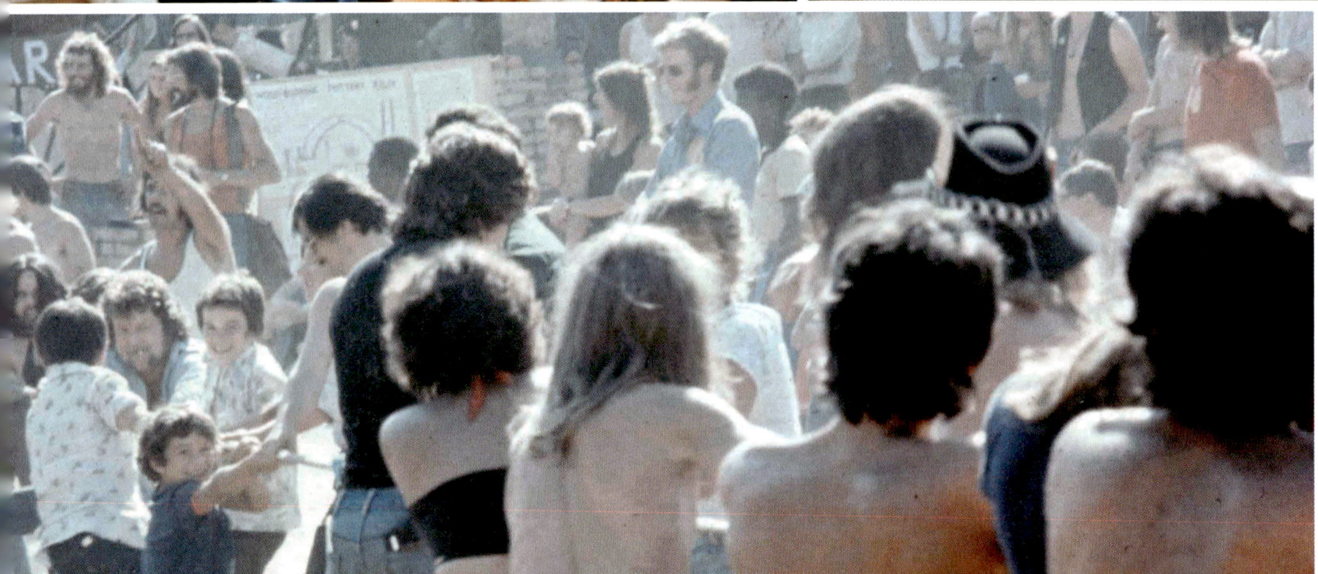
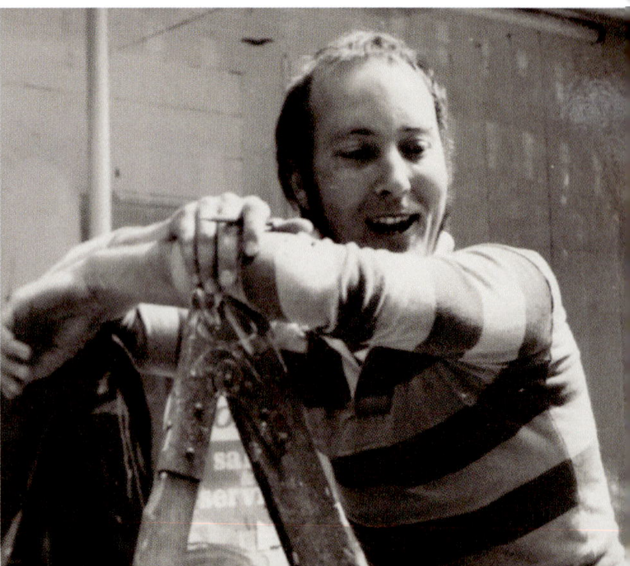

# CHAPTER 4

# SUMMER FESTIVALS UNLEASHED 1972-74

**Bath festivals would never be the same again. Street theatre and music took over the town. There were exploding grapefruits, a Bal Masqué and a solar trumpet. The first Comtek was a joyful mass of people's technology. The city was ours!**

**Phil:** The festivals were our annual opportunity to bring everything together in a glorious outpouring of creativity and experimentation. They were conceived as an alternative to the more conventional annual Bath Festival, and events were planned for all ages. True they had a do-it-yourself quality but this added to the excitement. Those who came to join us in those crazy weeks of freedom included the famed American beat poet Allen Ginsberg, and the artist Peter Blake (who designed the Beatles Sergeant Pepper album). Musicians also flocked aboard, among them Roxy Music, Steeleye Span, Mike Westbrook Jazz Band, and Poly Styrene of X-Ray Spex. Stevie Winwood even played piano in our shop window on one afternoon.

It is difficult to recapture how immersive the festivals were. Reality was suspended and we lived in a world that was carnivalesque and riotous in spirit. The weir became a theatre and the old milk factory a gallery. Upstairs pub rooms were cinemas. An enormous Georgian hotel brimmed with creativity for a whole week. The streets were overrun with outrageous theatricals of every kind. These were the heydays of performance art and its most daring and experimental artists returned year after year to perform in Bath's elegant (and not so elegant) spaces.

In 1973 and 74 we decided to actively involve people living in outlying areas of the town. We invited local groups to organise events and took the festivals to their neighbourhoods. We lacked the resources and experience to fully engage people in those still early days, but the intention was there and we later developed this approach in the Walcot area. Nevertheless, outlying field sites were filled with huge inflatables, food stalls, music and the weird trappings of the newly-emerging community technology. Games, tug-o-wars and tea parties co-existed happily alongside street theatre, poets and avant-garde orchestras.

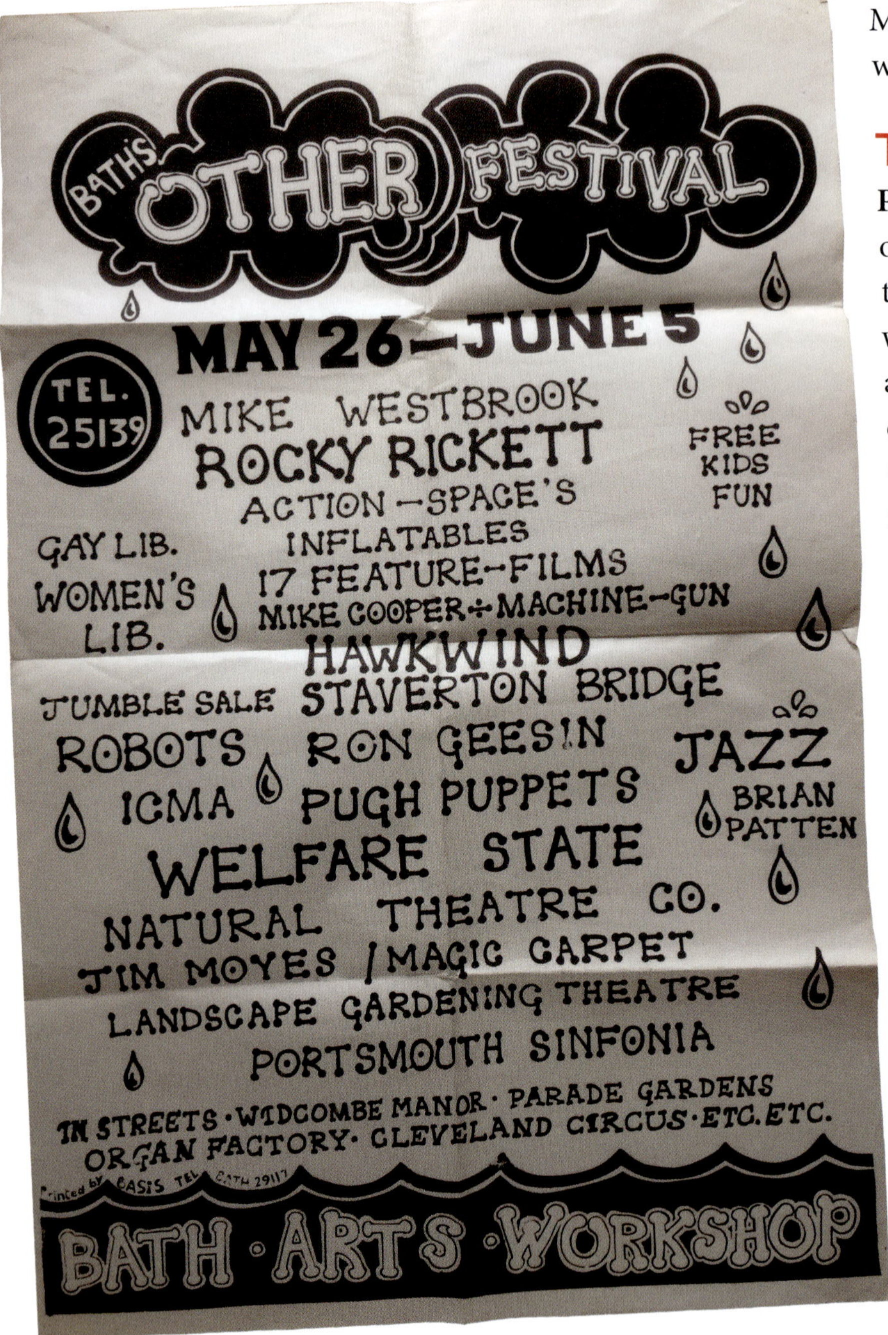


Most of it was free and open to everyone. For those ten days, we lived differently and the city was transformed.

# The Other Festival 1972

**Paul (Nasher) Nachman** of Workshop Films: We wanted our 1972 summer festival to be on a much larger scale than the Victoria Park events of the previous year. Planning was well under way when the millionaire Charlie Ware astonishingly offered the use of a 60-bedroomed hotel in one of Europe's poshest streets – the Cleveland Hotel in Great Pulteney Street. *The Cleveland Circus* thus became a focal point (although only a part of) the festival… loads of small rooms full of weirdness, puppet theatres, an upside-down room, the blue room (everything was blue!)… a cinema complete with projection box, foyer and (melting) ice cream, endless gigs and theatre performances.

The Globs played whenever nothing else was happening, day or night. Magic Muscle, Magma and the saxophonist Lol Coxhill played at every event. The Grand Opening was Rocky Ricketts and the Jet Pilots of Jive with the fabulous Rockettes (our own Workshop band) arriving by helicopter and playing on the hotel balcony (amusingly, the future Lady Mayor lived next door). The last day of the festival was an open-air picnic at Widcombe Manor, where rock merchants Hawkwind were to headline. It got rained off mid-afternoon and the whole shebang moved back to the hotel, where Hawkwind played to a jammed crowd in the Golden Lounge, an enormous gilt and mirrored room… the dates were 26 May to 5 June.

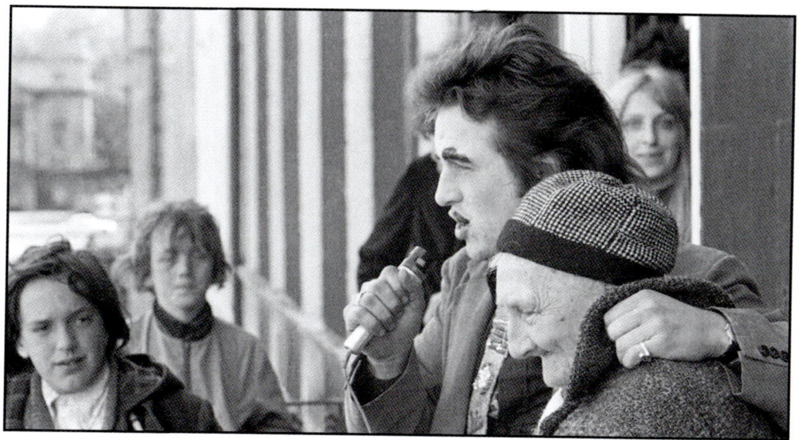

Rocky and May on the balcony of the
Cleveland Hotel

**Nasher (Paul Nachman)** arrived in Bath in 1972 from his home town of Stockport in a leather jacket and Hells Angel style 'original' jeans. He quickly became known for his enthusiasm and his constant flow of creative ideas, not to mention his wicked sense of humour. Nasher straight-away got involved with the Workshop and, with the support of Charlie Ware, became a found-ing member of Bath Film Unit. Sadly Nasher died in 2015, aged 61. He was truly larger than life, much loved for his generosity and humour, and much missed by his family and many friends.

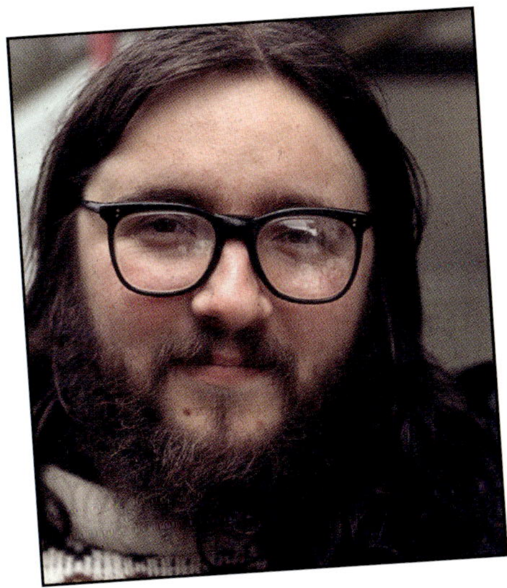

Nasher (Paul Nachman)

**Ralph:** The hotel was in a sort of glorious limbo, it was as fully operational as on the day its former owners had left. There were kitchens still with ham in the freezer, and beautifully furnished lounges including the exquisite Golden Lounge with its gilded pillars and mirrored shutters. Even the bedrooms came with crisp white sheets and bedside lamps and Gideon bibles in the drawers. Spending weeks in residence preparing for the event, we dined nightly on instant mashed potato purloined from the basement larder.

**Charlie Ware** was a true friend to BAW. A devotee of Georgian architecture, he made millions renovating derelict houses in Islington. He came to Bath in the mid-60s where he bought the Cleveland Hotel, the Theatre Royal and his own house in the Royal Crescent. Ralph remembers 'a snappily-dressed long-haired gentlemen' at the back of a festival meeting in 1972. Eventually he spoke up: 'I can lend you a whole empty hotel as a 24-hour venue'. Thus was born the legend of Cleveland Circus. Later, it was the Theatre Royal and his own house for a spoof-posh fundraiser, a helicopter for Rocky and the Jets and much more. He was generous to a fault and a catalyst for some of our boldest adventures.

**Phil:** Before the start, we slept in different rooms every night while we made the building ready, Mick Martin, Ralph and I in a room each, with an early morning call from the operator. Pencils lined up in the kitchen, poised to take the breakfast orders. The lift still worked then, although it was too small to accommodate the heavy dressers and tables we were shifting to the top floor to make space for the events

BATH ARTS WORKSHOP

and installations we planned – more of them with each passing day. Being able to say 'yes' was so brilliant: 'Could I build an upside-down room?' 'Yes Colin.' 'A blue room, a room full of sky?' 'Yes Rolande.' A puppet theatre?' 'Yes Ted.'

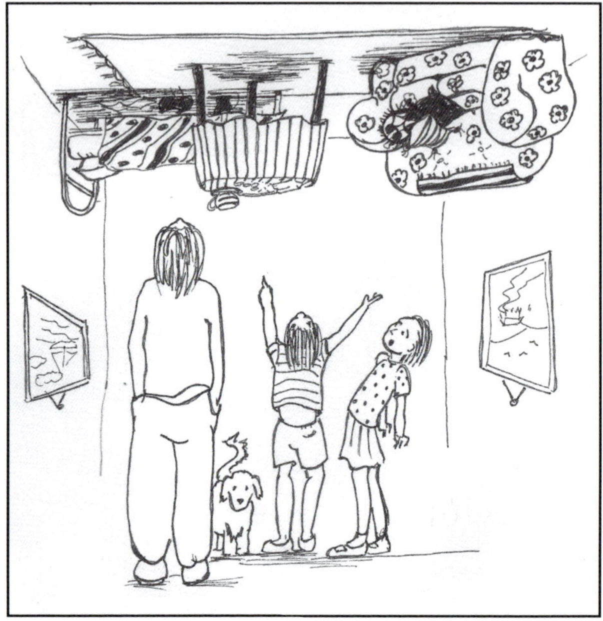

Colin Mansfield built the *Upside Down Room* which was a perfect mirror image. On the ceiling was the couch, the settee, the half-rolled joint on the little table. Everything you'd expect to find in a bedsit but upside down. Rolande did *My Blue Heaven*, the first installation by **Exploded Eye**. You went in and it was like being adrift in the clouds with bird songs (sound tape by Able Lawrence), blue light, and blue-clad performers. These and other room installations (or 'environments' as we called them then) were by members of

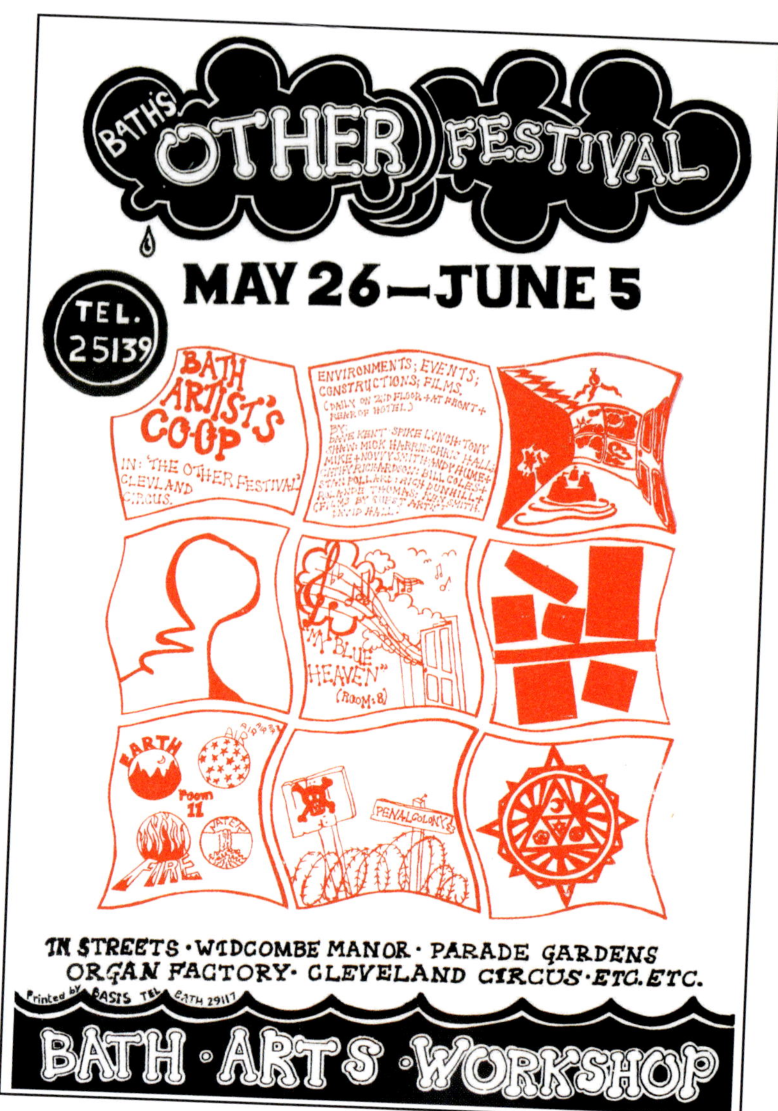


Bath Artists Coop

the Bath Artists Coop who were given the run of the whole second floor of the hotel. Other events were completely unplanned. The art critic John Berger apparently gave a talk in one of the hotel salons, although we knew nothing of this until years later.[1]

---

1. We are grateful to Ivor Morgan who told us about this event.

**Phil:** A surreal atmosphere enveloped the whole period. We were living and breathing the festival, taking part in it and organising it at the same time. Just before the start, I remember meeting with the fire officer to agree the emergency lighting in the basement. Candles in jam jars filled with sand were agreed! About a week in, Ted Milton (of *Mr Pugh's Puppets*) offered me a glass of red wine. It went straight to my head and I realised it was the first alcohol I'd touched since the festival began. People may have thought of us as a hedonistic bunch, but we were far, far too busy to party, too caught up in the bonkers whirlwind we'd created together.

## Snow Hill Road Show meets Hawkwind

Meanwhile, Shaun Smith of the Road Show remembers rehearsing for their first performance in the Cleveland Hotel to the sounds of a rehearsal by the deafeningly loud rock band Hawkwind. The Road Show had emerged out of BAW playschemes and drama workshops for kids from the Snow Hill Estate on the London Road.

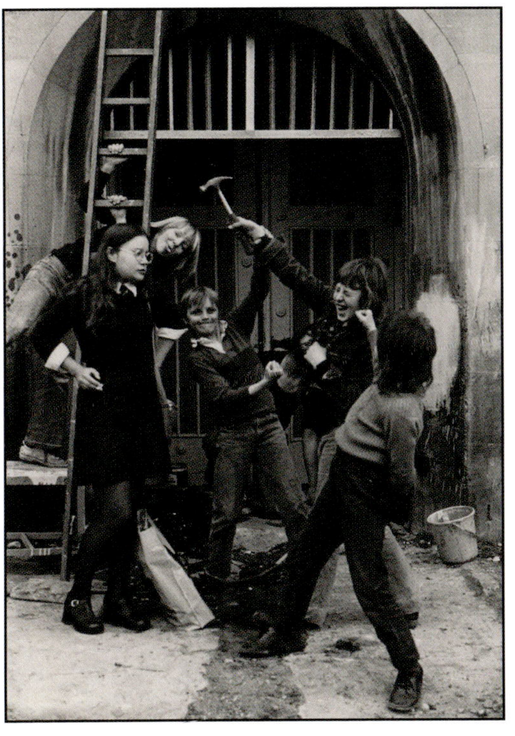

Some members of
Snow Hill Road Show

WIDCOMBE PICNIC.

11.00 a.m. Sunday June 4th – 1.00a.m.Monday June 5th.

ARRANGED BY BATH ARTS WORKSHOP, AS A FINAL EVENT OF THE 1972 'OTHER FESTIVAL'.

|  |  |
| --- | --- |
| 11.00a.m. | Bath's very own STEEL BAND from Burlington Street (Gate) |
| 11.00a.m. | GORRILLA FOOT – Rock & Roll from Corsham (5) |
| 12.00 midday | BRISTOL STREET THEATRE (4) |
| 12.15 p.m. | SMOOTH LOSER – Great New Group! (5) |
| 1.00p.m. | BATH DRAMA CLUB presents 'The Man with a load of mis-cheif (2) |
| 1.30.p.m. | ACTION SPACE INFLATABLES provide fun for everyone(6) |
| 2.00.p.m. | STAVERTON BRIDGE-Traditional Folk Music from Devon (5) |
| 3.15.p.m. | NATURAL THEATRE COMPANY)- Noisy! Crude! Rude!9(4) |
| 3.45 p.m. | DRAGBLOD – Hobbit Music (5) |
| 4.30.p.m. | SHIT – that legiondary group! (5) |
| 5.15.p.m. | WARM PITH, Street Theatre from Bristol presents 'Thats no way to Die!'(5) |
| 5.15 p.m. | BURNT TULIP THEATRE. A new theatre group based at Bath University.(5) |
| 5.30.p.m. | Folk songs from JERRY SIMON.(1) |
| 5.45 p.m. | The Music of MIKE GODWIN & PAUL SKINNER (1) |
| 6.00.p.m. | Free Music from BREAD & CHEESE (5). |
| 6.30.approx. | Two theatre groups combined- ICMA – from London's Oval House and the famous LANDSCAPES & LIVING SPACES. |
| 6.45 p.m. | Poets on the main stage. |
| 6.45 p.m. | More from STAVERTON BRIDGE (2) |
| 7.30.p.m. | Sitar & Tabla Music from Jim Noyes & Kesh Satho (5) |
| 8.30.p.m. | FROG DOE ( who used to be Something Musical)From The Wilds of Cornwall (5) |
| 9.30.p.m. | Electronic Music from HAWKWIND.(5) |
| 10.45 p.m. | MIKE WESTBROOK&& GEORGE CHAN have spent two days working at the 'CLEVLAND CIRCUS: with local musicians, and what they have been doing, You will see to-night.(5) |
| 11.45p.m. | A Lyrical Interlude with RON GEESON (5) |
| AND AT 12.30p.m. | TO FINISH OFF! Sitar Music from KENNETH WELLS.(5) |

Refreshments will be available, and have kindly been provided
BATH ARTS WORKSHOP,BEAU NOSH Inc.

**Ralph** adds: My mum was staying in one of the bedrooms during the festival and famously one night at 2am, she marched into the room occupied by Hawkwind in her winceyette nightie and told them to keep the noise down as she was trying to sleep. They shut up immediately.

## Finale

**Phil:** As it turned out, the Widcombe event was rained off in the late afternoon, and we brought Hawkwind back to play at the hotel. Just before midnight, I was standing on the street gazing at the extraordinary sight of the huge building ablaze with light in every room. It was a 20th century Noah's Ark, crammed to the rafters with people, laughter and creativity. 'Are you the organiser here?' I turned to see a policeman. 'We had a phone call, it appears there's a bomb in the building and it's going to go off at midnight.'

We looked at the building: The sound of Hawkwind in full flood pumped from one of the lounges, the Mike Westbrook Jazz Orchestra from another. 'What do you think we should do?' I asked, 'Um, let people know' he said doubtfully. We tried, the policeman and I, but got no further than the jam-packed lobby. A few people we managed to speak to stepped outside, but making ourselves heard above the music was almost impossible. We realised after a few attempts that midnight had passed and nothing had happened. The policeman left without comment.

Widcombe picnic programme

**Georgina Carless** remembers those early festival days: I was about 14 and still at school when I first encountered BAW. Looking back, I have impressions rather than distinct moments. They were very heady days when riffs from the music festivals on Bath Recreation Ground could be heard resonating around the hills of Bath and amazing sunsets filled the sky and warmed the stone of the then blackened Bath buildings. I remember the Widcombe picnic with the beauty of the place and so many drifts of exotic people. So glorious, bucolic and magical – laid back and theatrical somehow – reflecting my memory of those days. There was an organic sense of something happening and burgeoning in every corner of Bath, and The Cleveland Hotel was one of the venues. The upside down room, the blue room, performances, bands and events all taking place simultaneously, the building incredibly run down and in some parts still hotel-like, were ready to be possessed by the creativity that was everywhere.

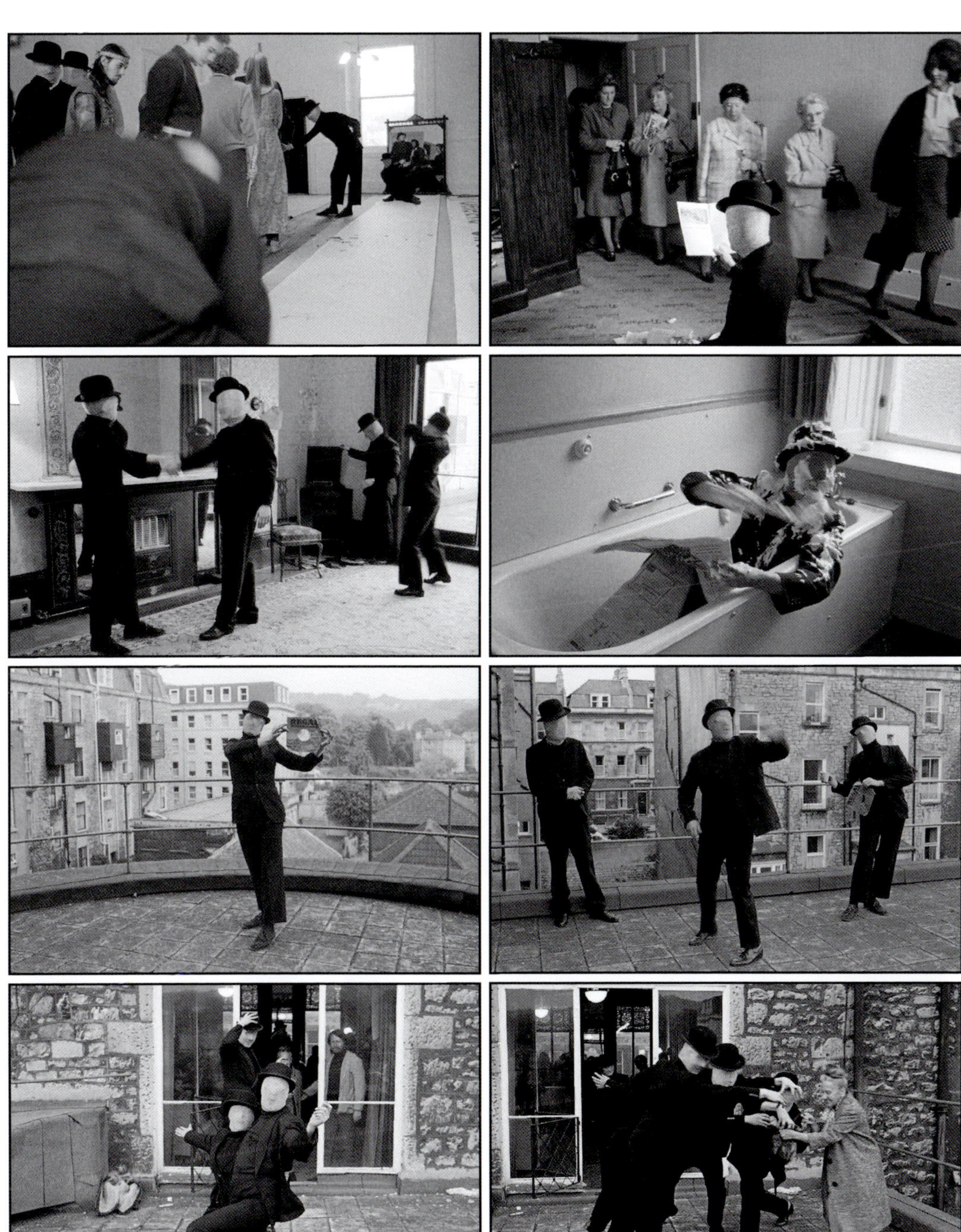

# Another Festival 1973

**Phil:** The festivals were definitely not about playing to a cultural elite and we set out to make them as inclusive as possible. For example, we chose to run them when sixth formers were not in the middle of exams (unlike the main Bath Festival dates). In 1973, filled with confidence and enthusiasm, we decided to build something city wide – to engage with everyone rather than patrons of the Georgian city of high culture. Initially, we thought we'd use church halls or pitch marquees to house our events, but someone came up with the brilliant idea of building our own structures – domes! We had the expertise on hand with the nascent Comtek technologists (and their yard in Weymouth Street), plus Earthstar Structures working nearby.

We figured we could blag the materials – one way or another we knew it could be done.

And so it was. Two domes were built, one on Lymore Fields in Twerton, and the other off the London Road in Kensington Meadows. They were built from steel scaffold tubes and fittings into a hexagrammic gridshell, intended to house up to 100 people at a time, and were impressive to look at, quite unlike anything seen in Bath before. Each dome was covered with a lightweight, fire-retardant

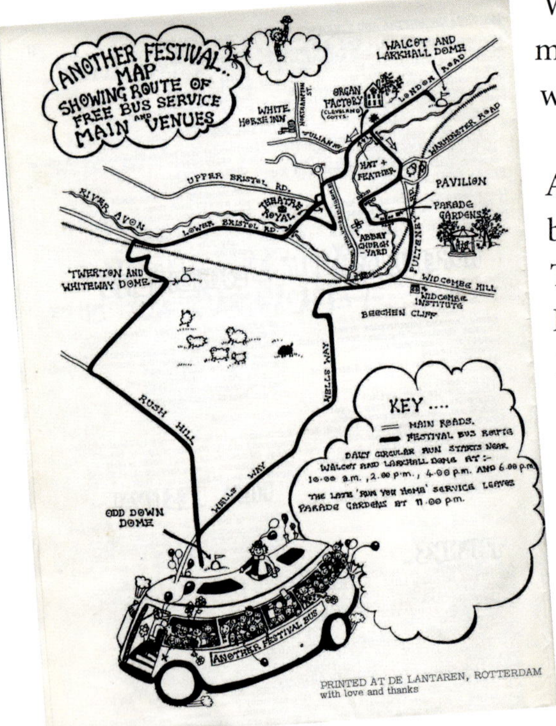


Shuttle service

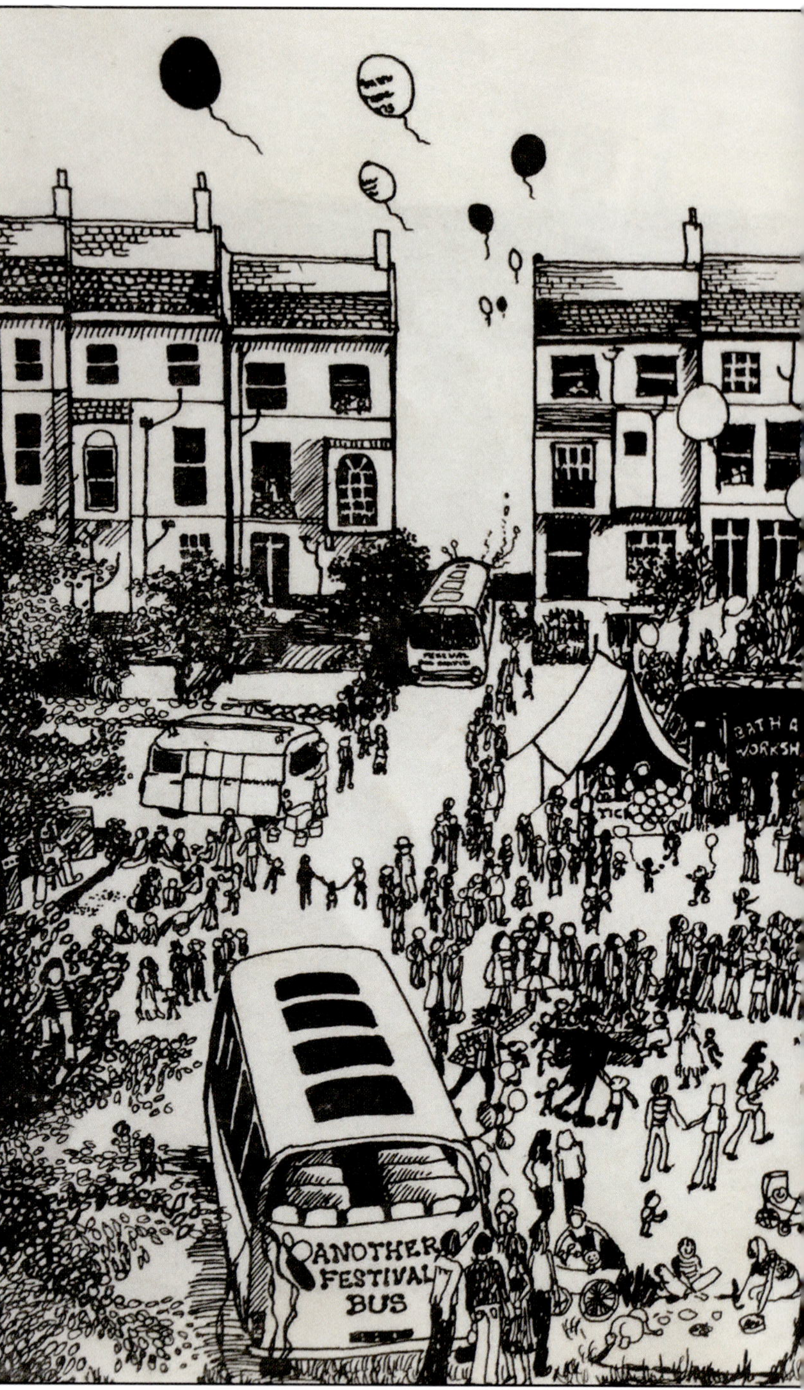

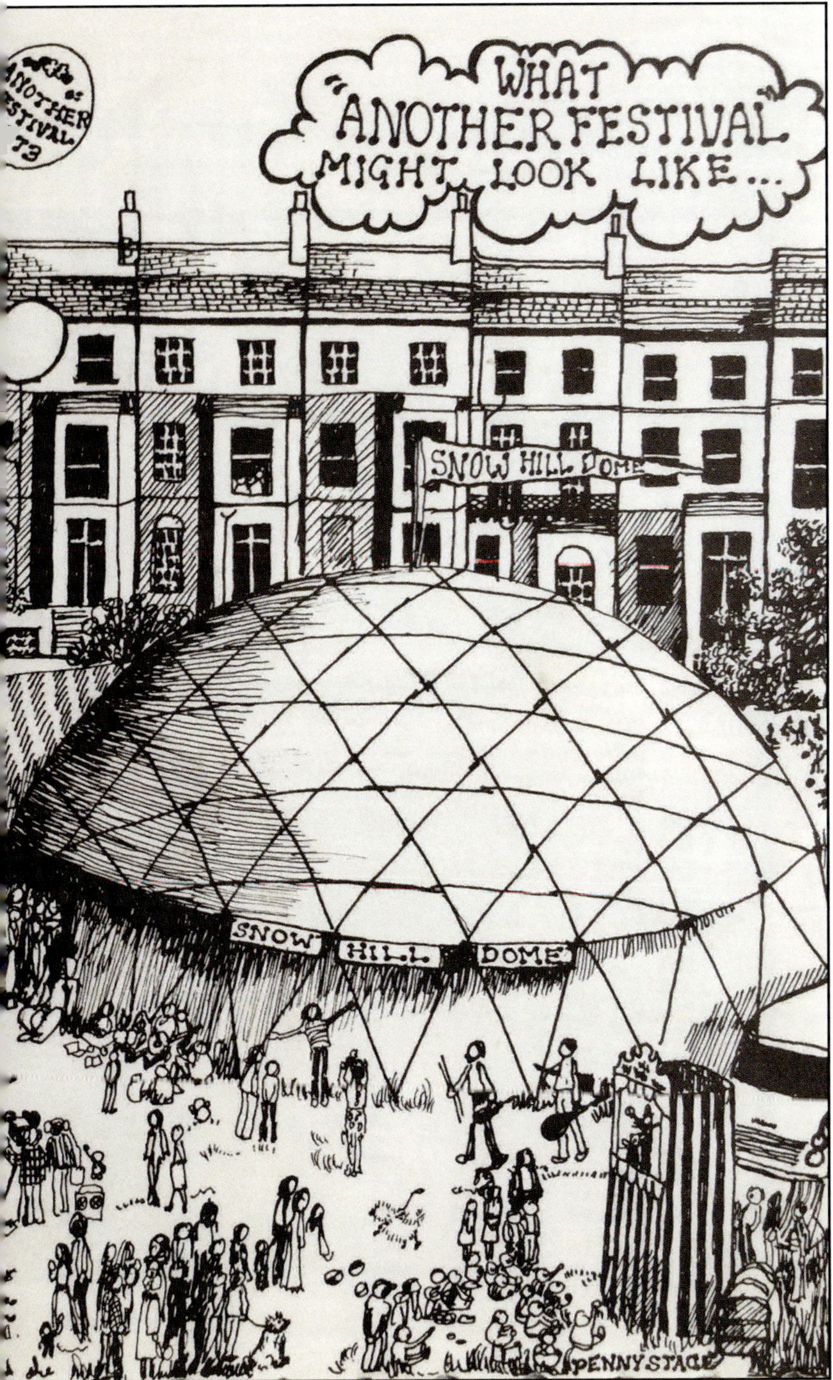


Mylar film shell, silver in colour and helpfully donated free of charge in large quantities, but annoyingly prone to rattling loudly against the steel in anything but the slightest breeze. It also tore easily so a lot of gaffer tape was used on running repairs. A third site, in Odd Down, was based at the Rugby Club building and field. We put on a free coach service to shuttle people to and from the different sites and to events in the town centre.

From humble beginnings in the Fountain Buildings basement two years before, we were set to stage a festival on an epic scale. A festival staged on three sites and in the town centre, to run for 10 days from 27 July to 5 August.

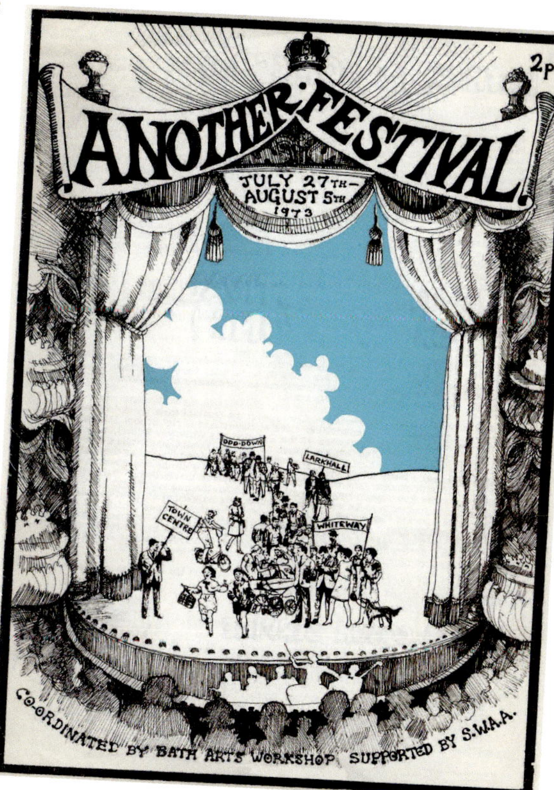


### Theatre Royal

**Phil:** Meanwhile Charlie Ware (he who loaned us Cleveland Hotel) had, to our amazement, become the new owner of the Theatre Royal and offered to let us use it for the festival. So that year, the old theatre with its plush red velvet seats and gilt balconies, was transformed into a steaming, heaving morass

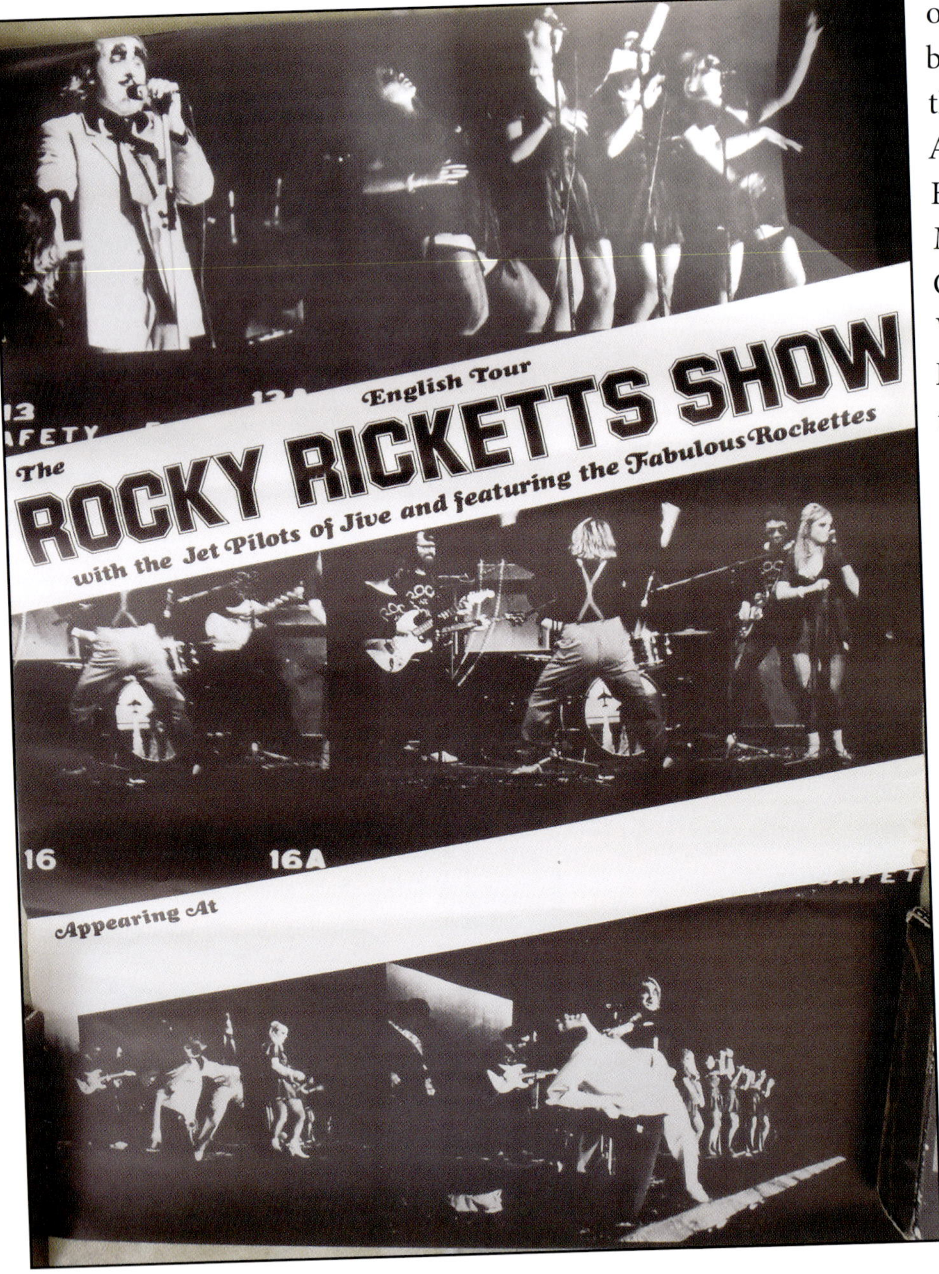

Rocky Ricketts and the Jet Pilots of Jive

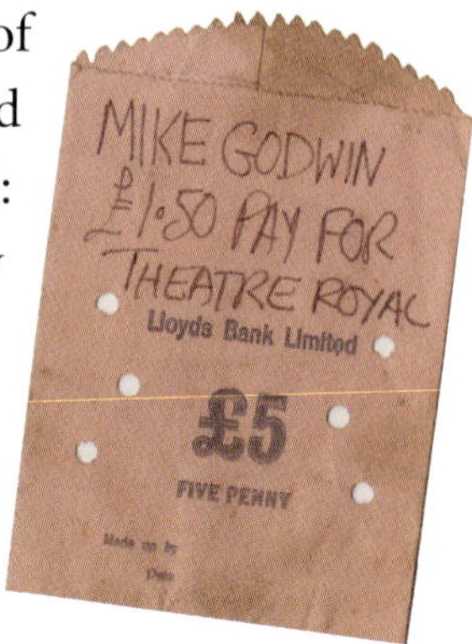

of music and people. Dozens of bands were booked and in the end those who played there included: Albion Country Band with Ashley Hutchings and Martin Carthy, Bees Make Honey, Brinsley Schwartz, Charlie and the Wide Boys, Chilli Willi, Keith Christmas, Pete Brown, Pink Fairies, Shakin' Stevens and the Sunsets, Mike Westbrook's Solid Gold Cadillac, and of course our own Rocky Ricketts and Jet Pilots of Jive, featuring the fabulous Rockettes. **Ralph adds:** Also featuring that year, in that bastion of straight-ness awaiting renovation, were off beat choirs, community variety shows, a bird impersonator and the poet Allen Ginsberg.

**Corinne:** Aside from the Theatre Royal, loads of other musicians and bands performed in the different venues across the city, both indoors and out. The experimental musical group Henry Cow was one such, as was sitarist Manesh Chandra and his Indian classical music band. The Jamaican band the Cymaron, a brass band and numerous folk musicians joined the throng, along with our own Thunderwing Disco and other DJs spinning their discs at the various sites.

### The city was ours

**Tory:** And then there was theatre – daring, hilarious and in weird places. In festival season the entire city

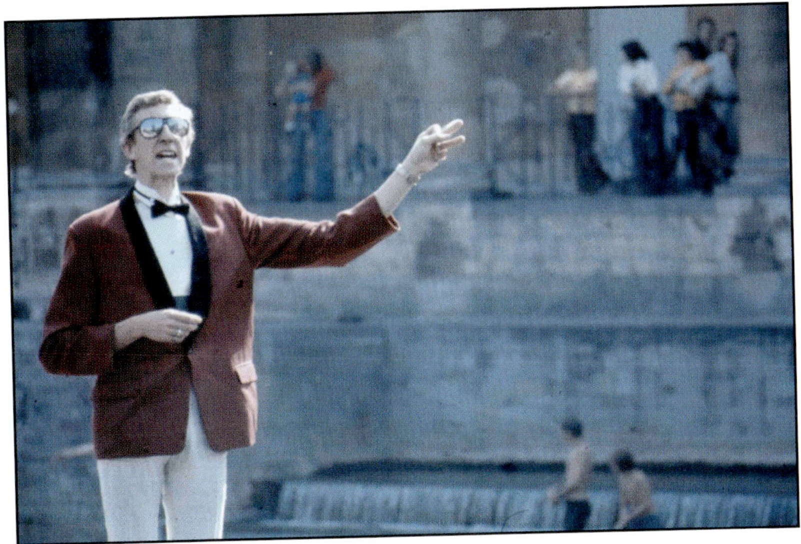

Peter Slim at Pulteney Weir

of Bath was transformed into a huge beautiful theatrical arena, full of unexpected locations where anything could happen. Performers of all persuasions found a space for experimentation and the freedom to try out new ideas. One much-used venue was Parade Gardens, a Victorian park with a bandstand, steps and abundant shrubbery. In the centre of town, it overlooked the weir and the River Avon, offering a ready-made audience of unsuspecting tourists and Bathonians as well as keen festival-goers.

**David Gale** of *Lumiere & Son* remembers a performance there by *John Bull Puncture Repair Kit*. He writes: One of the most ingenious pieces I saw was *Film Crew*. In this year's version, the crew comprised a director, the star Peter Slim, a cameraman, stuntman and best boy. The boom mike was a loofah suspended from a bamboo cane, the tripod had

mannequin's legs and the camera was artfully constructed from two round biscuit tins fixed to a box. Further equipped with a quantity of exotic props – distinguished by the great unlikelihood of their ever being found together in a situation that it was possible to imagine – the film crew was in a position to: a) claim that it was making a film; b) point out that scenes in films are generally shot out of order; and c) select any location that struck them as promising.



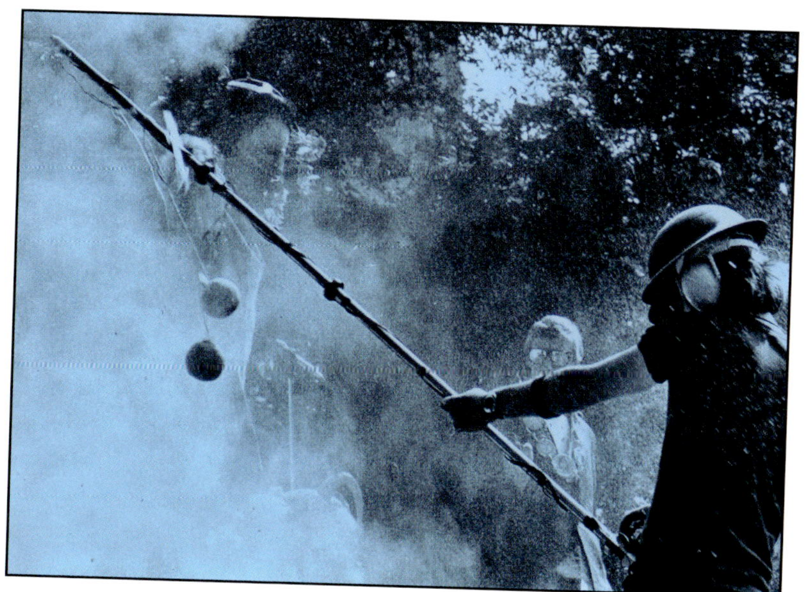

Exploding grapefruits

**David Gale:** They could go anywhere. They could shoot close-ups which bunched them. They could set up a long shot with the crew on one side of the park and the actors in the middle distance. In case the spectators focused too much on the crew, the director, invariably a petulant creature in jodhpurs, used the megaphone to bark at the hapless cast. The spectators were thereby stitched into the wide picture and could stand as close or as far from the scene as they wished. It was big, it was detailed, it went on for hours and was unceasingly inventive.

Who can forget the towering beanpole Mick Banks as the movie star Peter Slim, sporting a dashing white panama and a glistening shirt cut from cardboard, languidly descending the steps into Parade Gardens over and over, attempting each time to synchronise his passing by a gigantic ornamental urn with the props man who, hidden on its far side, would lunge forward extending a stick bearing a banana on a string so that the fruit would appear in the periphery of the star's vision, startling him.

Either the star or the props man would mistime the encounter, leading to endless retakes. The director, I recall, yelled apoplectically at his charges '*You go down the steps, you see the banana, it startles you and you brush it away! You brush it away!*'

**Lumiere & Son** had themselves heard about the BAW festivals 'that welcome displays of oddness' from Neil Hornick of **Phantom Captain**. In 1973, Lumiere came from London to perform *The Duke and His Fools,* a piece that David Gale described as 'an erratic passeggiata featuring a foppish 18th century lord, a wan and distracted Pierrette and a convulsing polka-dotted clown who made noises like a chicken'. The troupe wandered up and down Walcot Street and randomly about the town.

**Mitch:** *Exploded Eye* were also to be found in Parade Gardens with their *White Piece,* in which a white hunter, a sepulchral gentleman, a maid/nurse, and a veiled cellist performed their Gormengastian rituals.

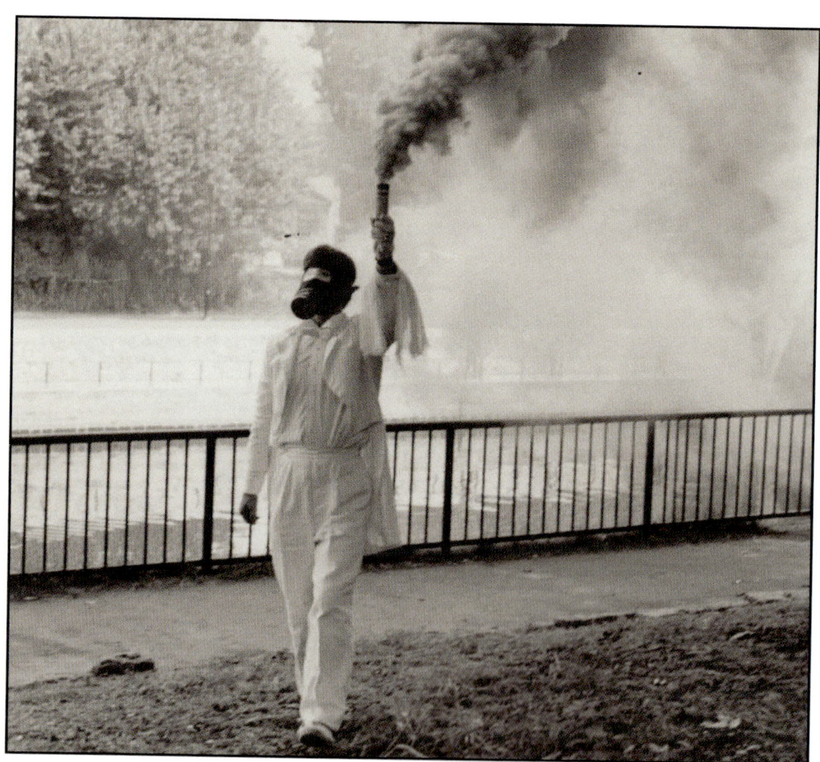

Exploded Eye in Parade Gardens

Another *Exploded Eye* piece involved characters in an impromptu and hastily put-together walkabout to fulfil their performance schedule in Parade Gardens. The performers were Paul Goddard, Corinne and Mick Martin.

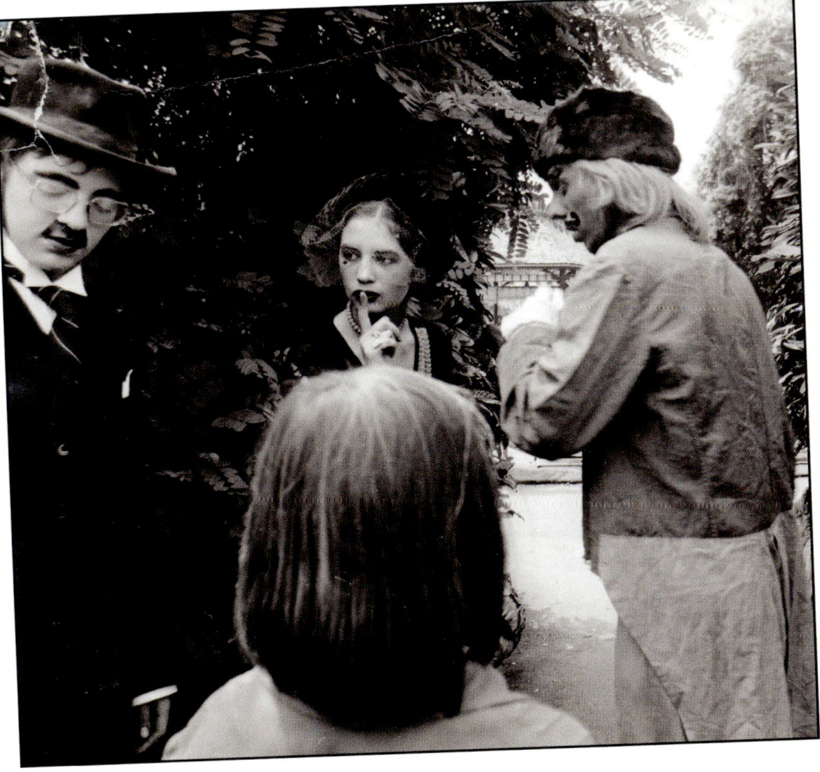

**Performers included:**
Amazing Black & White Mime Show
Exploded Eye
Gasp Theatre
Kipper Kids
Hull Truck
John Bull Puncture Repair Kit
Kilvert's Diaries
Landscapes and Living Spaces
Lumiere & Son
Magic of Kovari
Paul Hansard's Puppets
Monad Theatre
Phantom Captain
Mr Pugh's Puppets
Professor Crump
Strider Dance Company
And of course our own Natural Theatre Company, performing daily everywhere.

Lots of people just turned up and joined in. **Paul Goddard** (*Professor Crump*) writes: During those years, I was at the Chelsea School of Art creating sculptures which I integrated into performance pieces. I felt my course was slightly restrictive and unsupportive of the emerging performance art scene. Luckily, a lecturer suggested I might find like-minded artistes in Bath who put on an annual alternative festival.

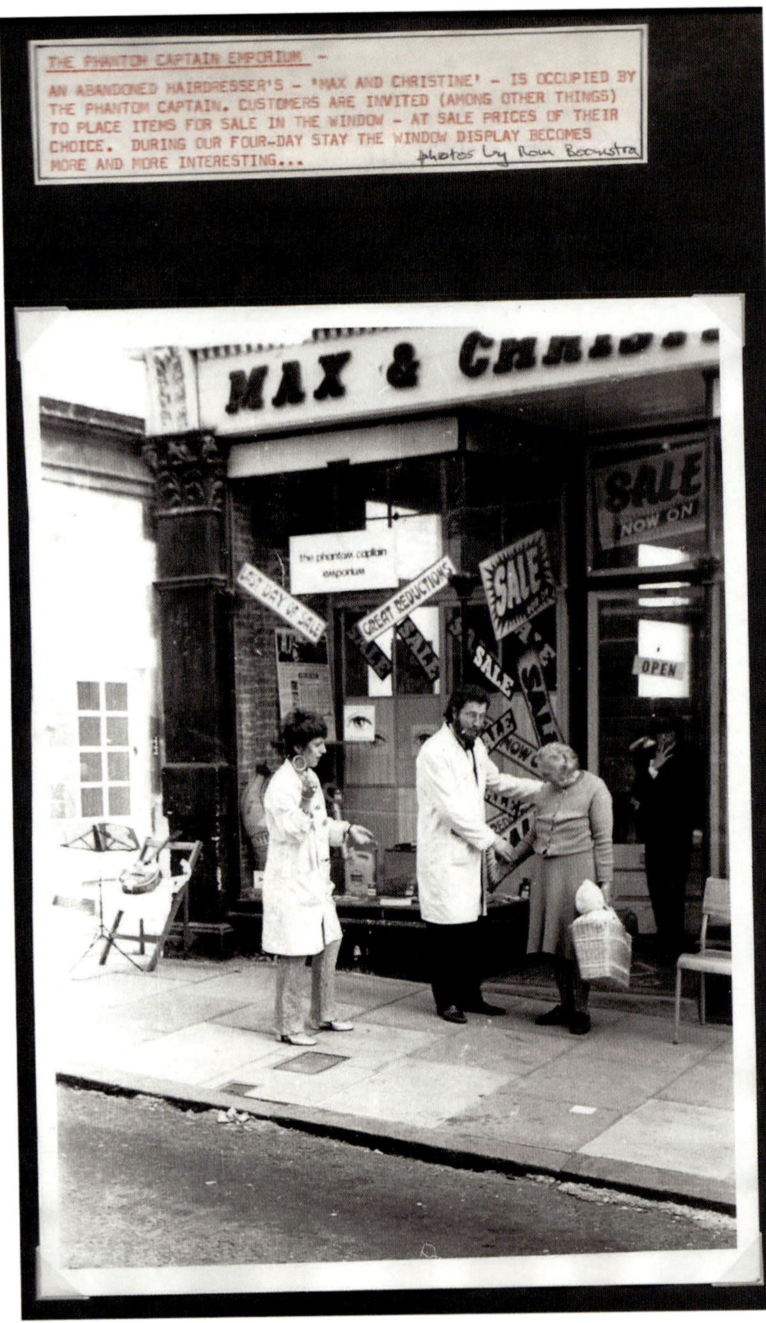



Phantom Captain and May Branch outside BAW shop

**Paul:** In 1973, I entered the offices of the Bath Arts Workshop and was immediately put into service. Each day was different, either helping with equipment, dressing up as a clown, walking in some mad parade, or jumping onstage as one of Rocky Ricketts' crazed fans. I had nowhere to stay so it was suggested I squat in a disused dairy, which was being used as an exhibition space for the kinetic sculptures of the artist *Charles Byrd* and I duly became its caretaker. It was a crazy creative time and all suggestions were welcome. I fondly remember helping Ted Milton, of *Mr Pugh's Puppet Show*, to pack his equipment into matching ex-army canvas suitcases, each a different colour and each numbered differently. His shows were very inspirational, as was the comic timing and professionalism of the emerging *Natural Theatre Company*.

## But was it art?

**David Gale** describes one unexpected display in our Walcot shop window by *The Kipper Kids*: One sunny morning I was walking down Walcot Street and, as I passed the shop, I saw that one of the windows was filled with torn-up paper right up to the ceiling. I drew level and studied it closely. At first it seemed that what you saw was what you got. Then I noticed some movement. The paper scraps were shifting about. I bent down to improve my sightline and saw a length of knob with two hairy bollocks beneath it. It was rather like those episodes in folklore where a person is going down a lane and sees a sprite in a hedgerow but it is gone in a trice. The knob receded. I walked on, greatly uplifted. The shadow cabinet had taken the reins, we had occupied the streets – the city was ours!

## Fun for all

**Phil:** Alongside theatre and music, poetry, puppetry, film and artistry of all kinds, each day's programme was jam-packed with a huge array of events and activities. During the planning stages we had worked hard contacting local residents and community organisations in the outlying areas and they responded brilliantly. We provided equipment, transport and small amounts of funding, but loads of the events were organised and run by local people.

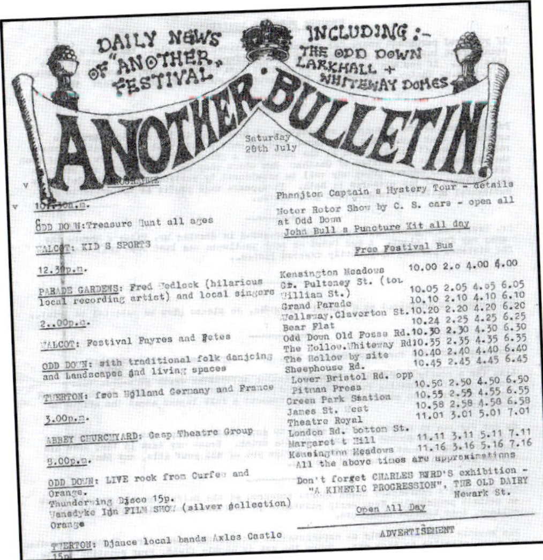

### Extract from Auntie Rozzie's gossip sheet, 1973

Work going ahead in the three areas; Chris Last/Chris Pouncett/Nigel in Twerton have already contacted over 40 people (vicars, teachers, shop-owners etc). Jackie to start Keep Fit classes for Snow Hill ladies at Organ Factory. Festival symbol for posters and letter-heading a SPOTTY BOWLER… Possible events… Rock and Roll revival night, amateur night, Pavilion: Gay Lib, Women's Lib discos, organ recital, reggae night; suggestions still welcome for performers; next festival meeting Saturday Feb 10, Organ Factory. Bring Sandwiches. Help needed to distribute leaflets and put up posters.

**On the festival programme:**

Grand Opening Procession

Old Tyme music hall

Coach outings for pensioners

Kids' outings to the seaside

Adventure playgrounds and painting classes

Inflatables

Kids' talent contests

Video and 'instant' TV

Fancy dress competitions

Funny football matches & sports days

Girls' football matches

Painting competitions

Ceilidhs

Magicians

Dog shows

Salvation Army open-air church services

Country walks & Keep Fit classes

Jumble sales

Model plane exhibitions

Chess, bridge, draughts and poker evenings

Baby mornings and old folks' evenings

Picnic on the last day

### Behind the scenes

**Phil:** The logistics were mind-boggling, with probably three dozen of us working at full tilt to ensure the smooth running of the multi-media programmes, half a dozen sites and a myriad of indoor venues. Hugh Gunton, Estates Director of Bath City Council gave us the use of two empty shops: the Old Dorchester Cafe opposite the railway station, that became the festival cafe; and the shop next door that we set up as festival HQ and information centre. By a stroke of luck we managed to borrow some radio telephones. At a chance meeting Nigel heard that if we joined Civil Aid we could use theirs. So we did.

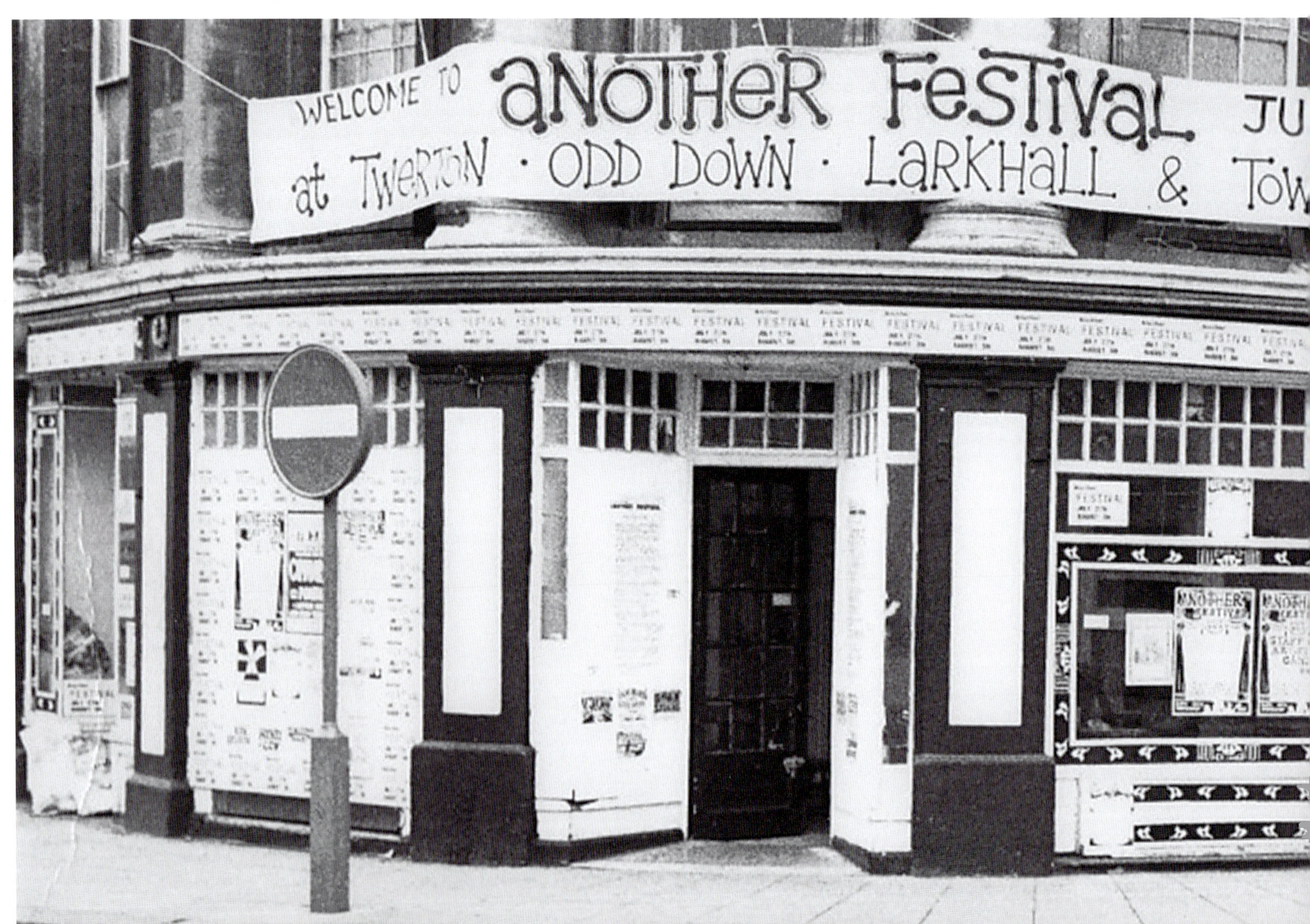

**Magnus Macdonald** took on food and accommodation for the festival, an experience that stood him in good stead when later setting up and running markets at Glastonbury Festivals. He remembers: After scraping most of the mould off the walls, we used the old cafe to feed crew and performers (a couple of hundred people in all). We didn't have much money to pay people but thought at least we could feed them properly. To do it we went out to garner the help of others involved in alternative catering – people like John Potter, then with RIB in South Wales, Harvest Wholefoods and others.

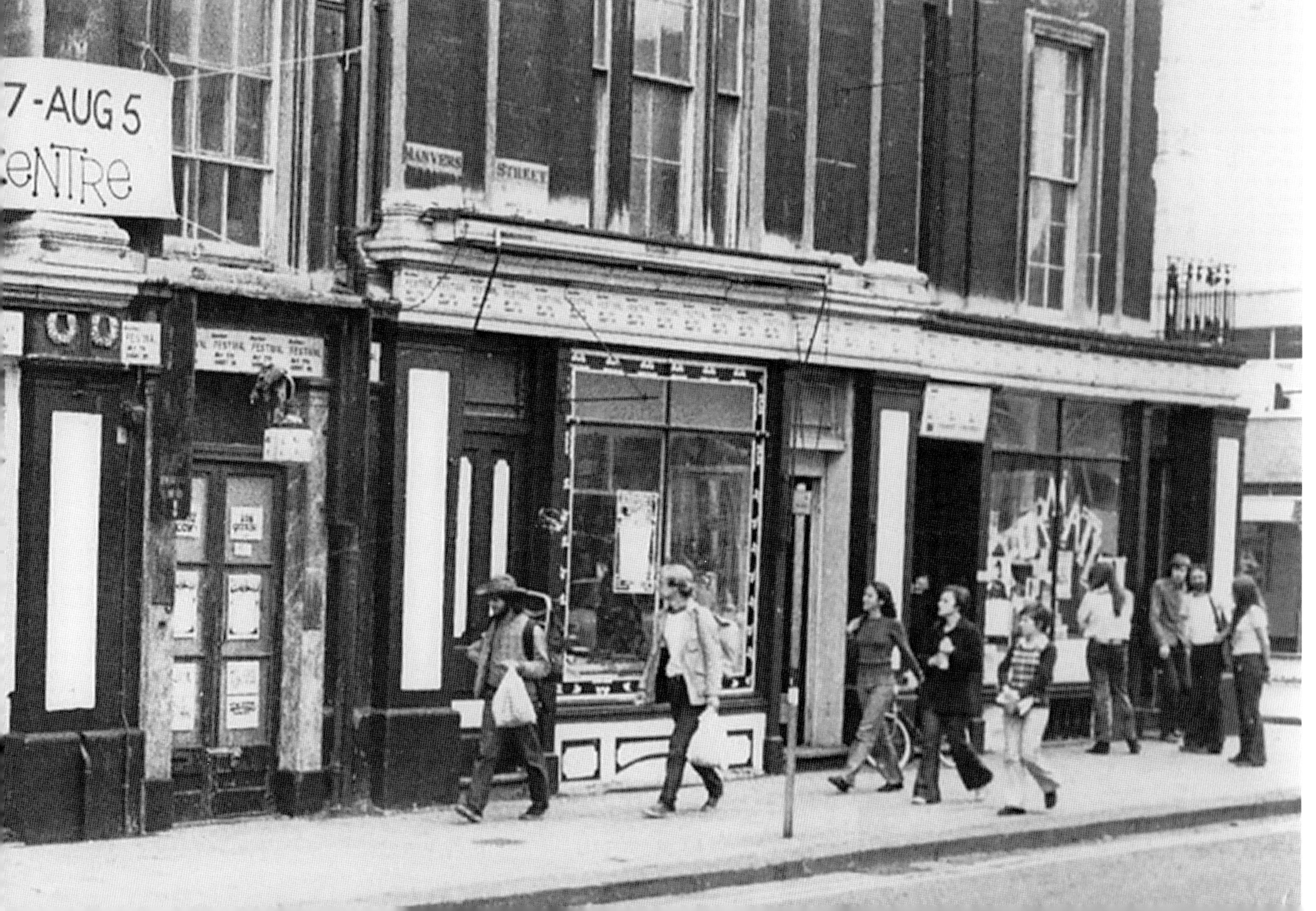

**Magnus:** Things didn't always go according to plan. One afternoon, we put on a tea party at the cafe for a group of kids from Twerton. I was having tea with an official from Civil Aid and trying to have a serious conversation. For some reason the party had been arranged with the boys at one end of the room and the girls at the other. Suddenly, a cake flew across the table and in the next second the air was full of cakes, sandwiches, tin mugs and spoons flying in all directions. The civil servant and I ended up crouched under the table. Evidence of this massive food fight was apparently still visible five years later on the ceiling.

**Tory:** I got my first job with the Workshop that summer. Magnus somehow rooted me out to work at the festival information centre. People rushed in and out all day writing messages in a huge book, to be picked up later by whoever

they were meant for. Or they'd ring in and I would transmit the message. Usually it was about transporting performers and getting equipment from one spot to another. We also greeted arriving artists and performers and directed them to their accommodation.

At about midnight every night, the Workshop staff came in for a planning meeting that often lasted a couple of hours. They were like troops coming in from the battlefields, jostling and telling tales of the day's adventures. Dave Digby seemed to be in charge of the heavy stuff. He wore a leather biker's jacket and khaki trousers (quite rugged) and carried a tiny notebook and pencil that he wrote in constantly. I realised what a massive logistics operation was involved behind the scenes.

Huge amounts of gear had to be moved constantly between various locations. The talk was of PA systems, scaffolding towers, lighting rigs, tarpaulins, festoon lighting, trestle tables, stacking chairs, catering equipment, flatbed trucks, two ton truck, half-ton van. Most of the stuff had to be begged or borrowed, often by the following day by Workshop members who were simultaneously performing or running events themselves. I was bedazzled by the scale of the thing, most of which Phil Shepherd seemed to hold in his head from the top down to the minor detail. It was fascinating and unfathomable and I barely left the premises for the whole ten days.

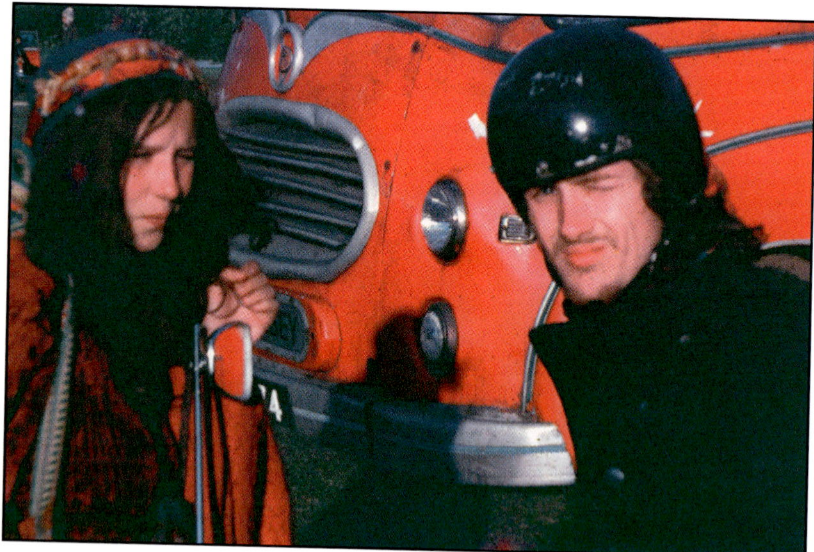

Dave Digby and friend

## Festival day

**Phil:** For those of us working on it, a festival day could comprise an almost unreal combination of activities. Jumping into the spacious driving seat of one of the old Commer walk-through vans, barefoot in tee-shirt and jeans, such a great feeling of empowerment and endless possibility, we felt we could take anything on. On one day, I remember driving a group of children to one of the domes for the morning Snow Hill Road Show, collecting a donated sofa for the shop on the way back, a lunchtime plate of egg and chips in The Hat & Feather, then down to Kensington Meadows to help set up a pensioners' tea party. Then back in the van to the Guildhall to return tables and chairs, round the back of the Cleveland Hotel to load up the Workshop Music PA system, and on up to Odd Down to rehearse for an NTC evening show.



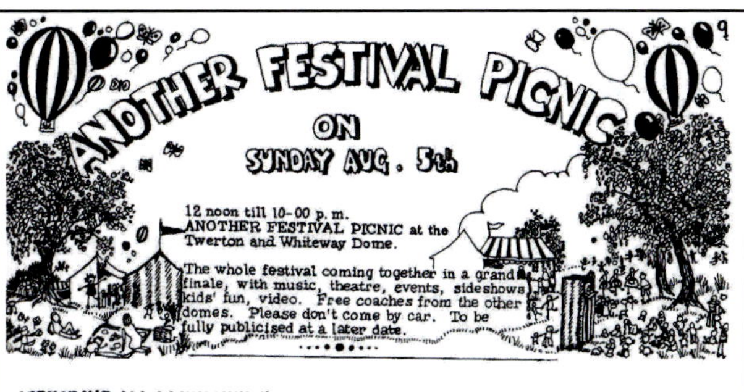

ANOTHER FESTIVAL PICNIC

ON SUNDAY AUG. 5th

12 noon till 10-00 p. m.
ANOTHER FESTIVAL PICNIC at the Twerton and Whiteway Dome.

The whole festival coming together in a grand finale, with music, theatre, events, sideshows, kids' fun, video. Free coaches from the other domes. Please don't come by car. To be fully publicised at a later date.

APPEARING ALL WEEK THESE:-

ARTISTS

GABRIELI BRASS ENSEMBLE

We are very lucky to have this leading ensemble to play for us; they play a wide range of classical brass instruments.
Wednesday August 1st - 7-30 p. m.
Theatre Royal

ANOTHER PROJECT

Any group or individual is welcome to contribute to this project, which is an exhibition to assist the individual in understanding and improving the city in which he lives. If you wish to help please contact Bath Arts Workshop. The exhibition is at the Technical College, beneath the new Theatre building, and will be open throughout the festival.

SHAKING STEVENS AND THE SUNSETS

'A Working Class Hero' is an act not to be missed.
Rock 'n Roll is NOW'
Monday July 30th - 7-30 p. m.
Theatre Royal

KILVERT'S DIARIES

An event to recreate the rural atmosphere of England in the 1880's, as captured by Kilvert's Diaries - first performance outside London, given by William Plomer, editor of the diaries, and directed by Patrick Garland.
Tuesday July 31st - 7-30 p. m.
Friends' Meeting House, York Street

WILLIE BARRETT

Comes to us courtesy of Community Music, a non-profit making music agency based in London. Willie's recent single on the Track label is entitled 'Murder Man'

TRADITIONAL FOLK GROUPS

Several beautifully costumed traditional folk dance/yodelling song troupes invited from Holland, Germany and France as part of the Twin Cities celebrations

MR PUGH

Not only a very lively puppet show, but also a chance for you to see how it all works and to make your own puppets!
Monday July 30th - 1-00 p. m. Odd Down
Tuesday July 31st - 7-30 p. m. Theatre Royal
Thursday August 2nd - 2-00 p. m. Twerton
Saturday August 4th - 2-00 p. m. Organ Factory

SHIRLEY AND DOLLY COLLINS

Two of the best traditional English folk singers
Thursday August 2nd - 7-30 p. m.
Theatre Royal

ALBION COUNTRY BAND

A traditional electric folk band, an offspring of Fairport Convention and Steeleye Span
Thursday August 2nd - 7-30 p. m.
Theatre Royal

BATH PEOPLE'S ORCHESTRA AND OPERA GROUPS

(Local people are invited to join the orchestra and opera group and can do so by contacting Bath Arts Workshop) The programme features two short operas: 'The Foolish Old Man Who Removed The Mountains' and 'Cinderella' together with extracts from 'All Hail John MacLean'. Words and music by Ivan Hume Carter (words of John MacLean's speech by John MacLean) Cinderella to be played by Patsy Harrison
Saturday August 4th - 2-30 p. m.
Theatre Royal

**Phil:** It felt like endless summer that year, one task flowed to another, and once all the public shows were done, late evening we'd gather back at HQ for the daily debrief, before getting together somewhere and having a drink to unwind. Seamless days and nights.

**Corinne:** All of this was done on a minuscule budget. BAW's grant aid that year was £5,200 from the Arts Council and South West Arts, £1,430 from the Calouste Gulbenkian Foundation, and the princely sum of £50 from Bath City Council, with self-generated income roughly matching the total grant income. This funded the entire programme of annual activities not just the festival. Without the hundreds of hours of volunteer help, local business support, and the fact that BAW staff were taking a pittance of a wage if at all (around £8 when there was enough money), none of it would have been possible. Nevertheless, there were those who believed we shouldn't have been funded at all, with one councillor exclaiming *'they should do it in their spare time'*. The trouble was we didn't have any.

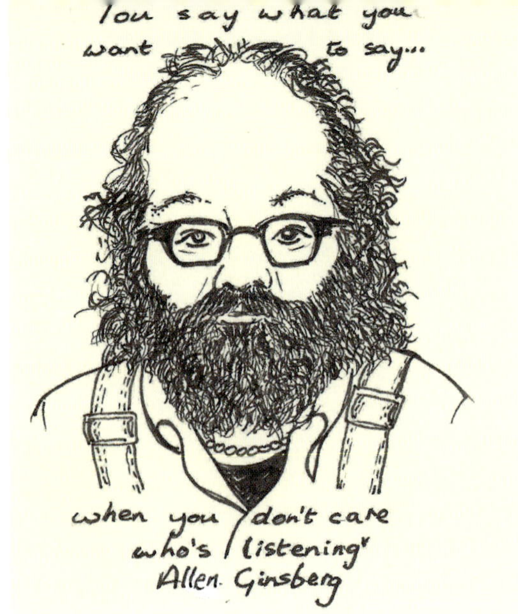



# ALLEN GINSBERG IN A TWERTON DOME AND ELSEWHERE

**M**itch: One evening I went to a poetry recital by the poet Allen Ginsberg in Rotterdam. He was a prolific poet of the Beat Generation, celebrated for his epic poem *Howl*. After the performance, my friend Dave Digby suggested I invite him to appear at our festival and he agreed. When the time came, we drove to London to pick up Ginsberg from Barry Miles' flat.[2] Ginsberg was on crutches at the time having broken his leg. After picking up some fish and chips we drove off to Bath with him and his companion, the poet Harry Fainlight. In the car, Ginsberg chanted Blake poems with hand-operated harmonium accompaniment. It felt magical as we arrived in Bath with Ginsberg's words echoing in our ears amid the beauty of the hills, like the refrain from Blake's *Nurse's Song* from *Songs of Innocence*.

We took him to the festival information centre opposite the railway station. Then came a radio telephone announcement that a magician booked for Twerton hadn't turned up. Ginsberg volunteered to step in despite having literally just arrived. So we went to Twerton where he performed his Blakean *Songs of Innocence* and Tibetan Buddhist chants to an audience of kids from the local estate who initially responded with playful tugs of his beard and Tarzan-like calls, before falling silent.

Phil witnessed the scene from a different vantage point: As Ginsberg read and chanted, the wind was building outside the dome; a sea-borne storm was on the way in. The flimsy metallic material covering the dome began to flap about noisily and a tear appeared in the roof. Grabbing some gaffer tape, I climbed to the top of the dome to fix it. Looking down, I could see Allen, cross-legged directly below me, in full recital. The sight of him chanting to these Somerset teenagers, so moved to silence by his presence, is an image I will never forget. The wind continued to build, with the hail and rain stinging my face and arms, I remember thinking 'Life gets no better than this.'

**Mitch:** After a well-received free appearance the next day in Parade Gardens, Ginsberg's third and final performance was at the Theatre Royal on a billing with the **Mike Westbrook Jazz Band**. Mike had decided to perform a musical

---

2. Miles was a 60s counterculture activist who established the Indica gallery and bookshop in London where John Lennon met Yoko Ono, whose show was being hosted there. He co-founded *International Times* (IT), Britain's first underground newspaper, with John 'Hoppy' Hopkins and money from Paul McCartney.

happening instead of a traditional concert. There was mock bowing and conducting, while musicians such as George Khan and Phil Minton played snatches of music among the audience and in the boxes at the side. In response some people walked out or complained vociferously, although some were amused and engaged. To avoid further ructions, we decided to offer free entrance to anyone from Mike's event to the Ginsberg recital. When he appeared, there was an unsettled air in the theatre, with some latent hostility in the atmosphere. When Ginsberg mentioned the word 'improvisation' early on, someone in the audience yelled sarcastically, 'improvisation, oh, you don't say'. Ginsberg, unfazed, immediately replied with an extempore song 'Yes, we're improvising!' It was a turning point in a performance that had started tentatively. He was beginning to win over the sceptics.

Ginsberg began to weave a spell. He was backed on guitars by two local musicians Pete Kilgour and Johnny 'Be Good' Loder, part of a thriving local music scene, aided and abetted by BAW's Workshop Music. Pete and John sat cross-legged either side of Ginsberg and his hand-operated harmonium, backing him with, in Ginsberg's words, 'all the chords of *The House of the Rising Sun*' and their own embellishments. He went on to transmit a performance of William Blake *Songs of Innocence and Experience*, Tibetan Buddhist chants, and a panegyric to Gay Liberation that prompted an ecstatic dance in one of the boxes from our favourite hairdresser.

Included was an epic poem that encompassed Ginsberg's America, the second law of thermodynamics, the ecology of the world and Kerouac ('Jack, buried underground now'), capital cities and our city of Bath. The reaction of the audience became ecstatic. Ovations. The concert had begun inauspiciously and ended tri-

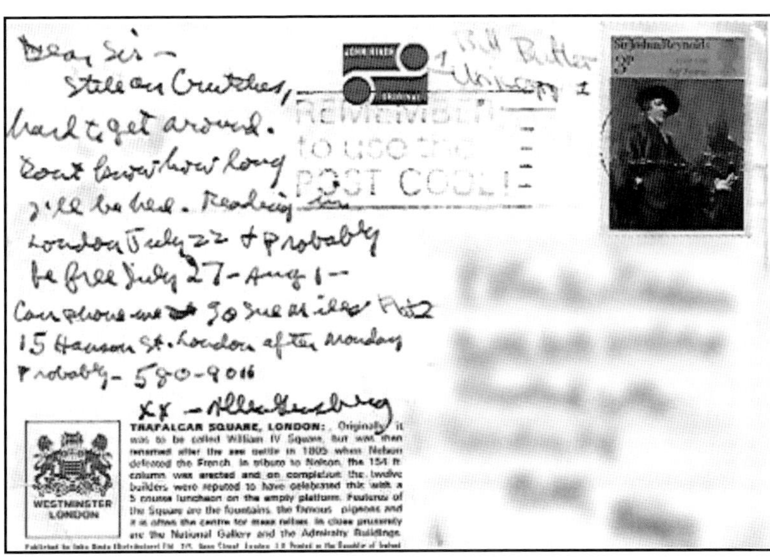

umphantly. In the words of Van Morrison, 'Poetic champions compose'.

The next day, he left from Bath railway station with tickets we provided. We thanked him for his generosity. As in the Joni Mitchell song, 'He played real good for free'. He brought some angelic dharma magic to **Another Festival** as well as having his beard tugged on a local housing estate.

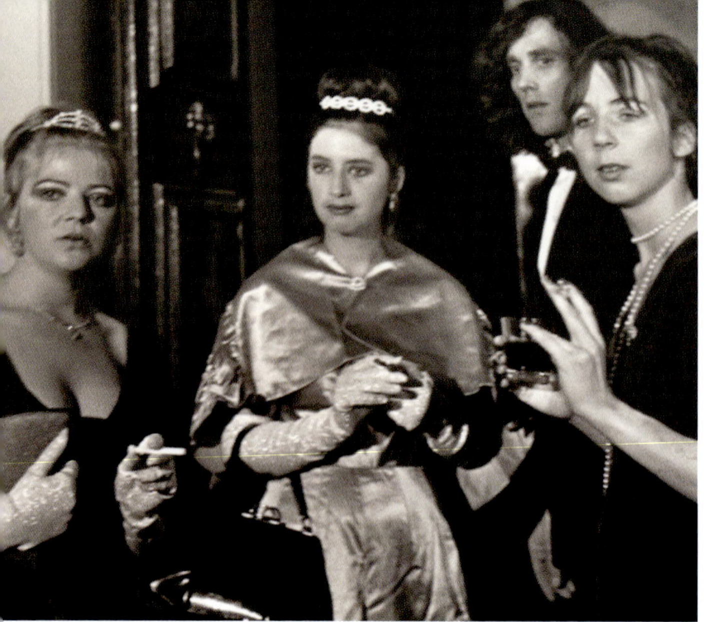



## BIAFRA LUXURY PRODUCTS EVENT AND BAL MASQUÉ

**Corinne:** In the run-up to the *Last Festival* (1974) I needed to raise money for the Twerton site so I asked Charlie Ware if he would lend us his house in the Royal Crescent for a society ball. The evening, presented by the *Natural Theatre Company*, was a spoof corporate event and product launch, held by a fake company Biafra Luxury Products.[3]

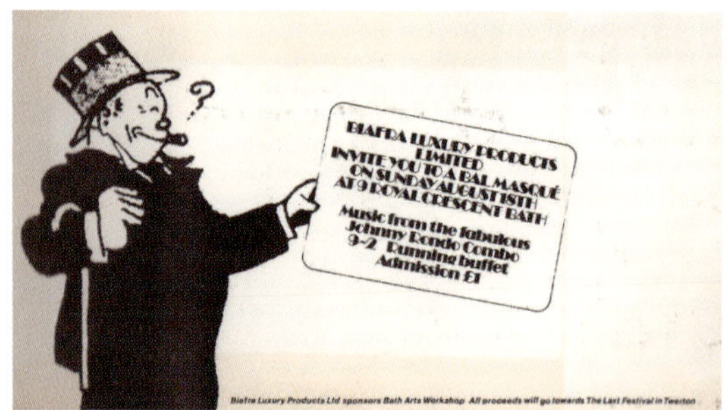

The products themselves were dozens and dozens of extremely attractive but completely useless left-foot shoes, recently donated to our charity shop. They were displayed ostentatiously on racks near the impressive entrance hall. The event was hosted by our own bigot of the business world, Sir Ralph Oswick, along with his friends and hangers on – all tiaras, diamonds and dinner suits. There was a buffet (budget £20) and a bar run by Heriot and Jenny from The Hat & Feather. Gordon, the pianist from our shop, a man with a chequered and indecipherable history, gave a rollicking rendition of the old pub song *The Laughing Policeman* while the guests were entertained by Sir Ralph and his friends. More salubrious music came from local singer Felicity Haze, who teamed up with the delightful musical group the *Johnny Rondo Combo*.

My younger sister Yvonne, with her brilliant singing voice, performed a

Felicity Haze with Johnny Rondo Combo

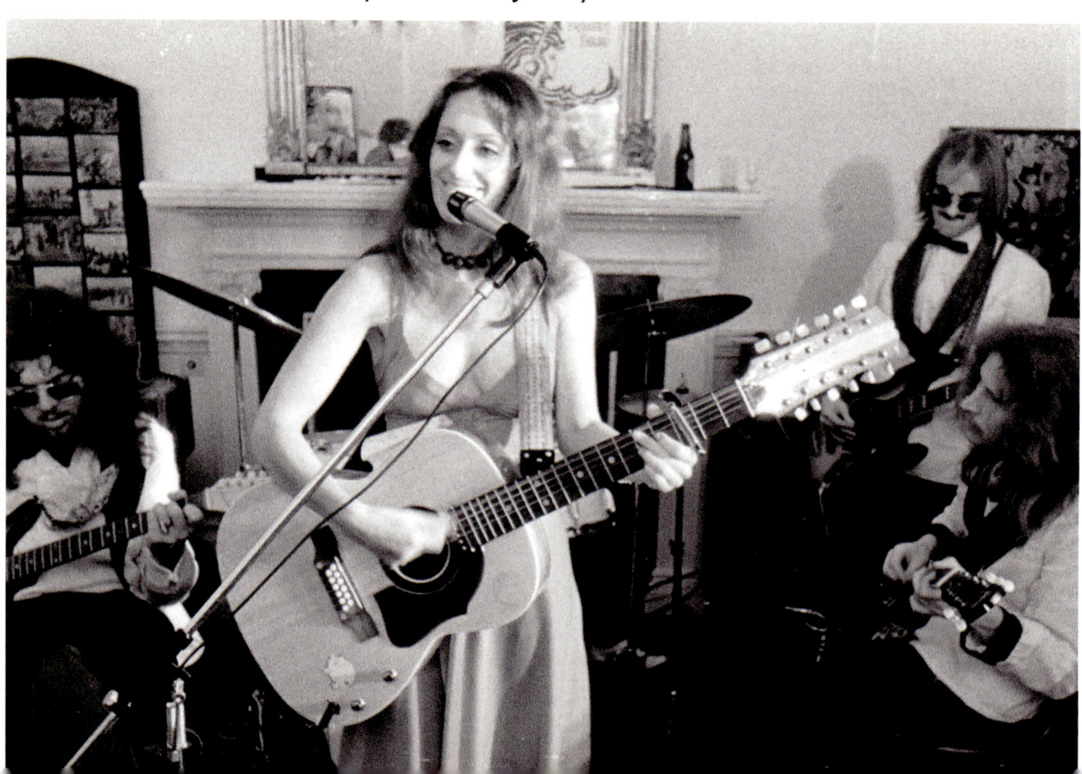

song or two with her friend Marie, who later morphed into the singer/songwriter Poly Styrene, fronting the band X-Ray Spex. She was one of the first icons of punk rock, a tiny bundle of energy exploding over the stage, with her signature tune *Oh Bondage Up Yours!* that opened with the spoken line *Some people think little girls should be seen and not heard*, before launching into a kind of punk feminist anthem.[4] I think even Bryan Ferry of Roxy Music was there as a bemused guest.



**Jennie** adds The Dance of the Four Veils: Sometimes we just wanted to have a laugh and be impetuous. So when it was suggested to Sarah and I that we could surprise everyone with a 'Dance of the Seven Veils' next to the shoe display, we grinned and said 'fine,

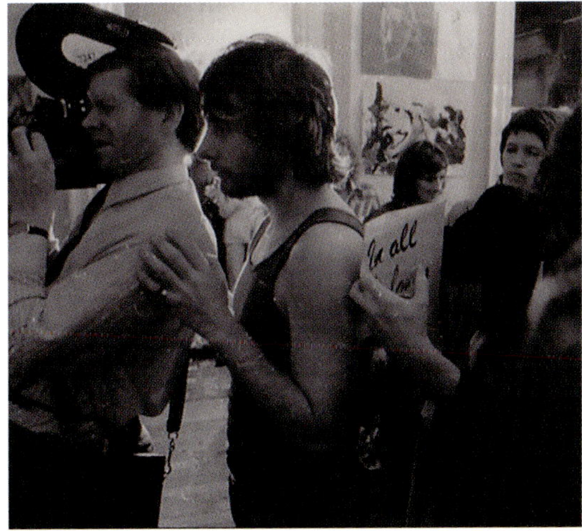

Film crew

but only after the film crew have left'. We only had four veils and decided that two each was enough. We waited upstairs, clad only in those veils, for the signal that the film crew had left and descended... the lift opened and we started our dance, only to find the crew were still in the doorway. It took them about two minutes to start filming again. That film has been aired twice but I never saw it. I was too busy making sure my mum was nowhere near a telly.

**Corinne:** The tickets were designed for free by local graphic designer Carl Willson. They cost £1 and went like hot cakes – everyone wanted to see inside Charlie Ware's house. And it was typical of the way we put things together; there was so much creative enthusiasm, dynamism and talent around, both inside and outside BAW itself. There were so many people you could call upon and most of them helped for free.

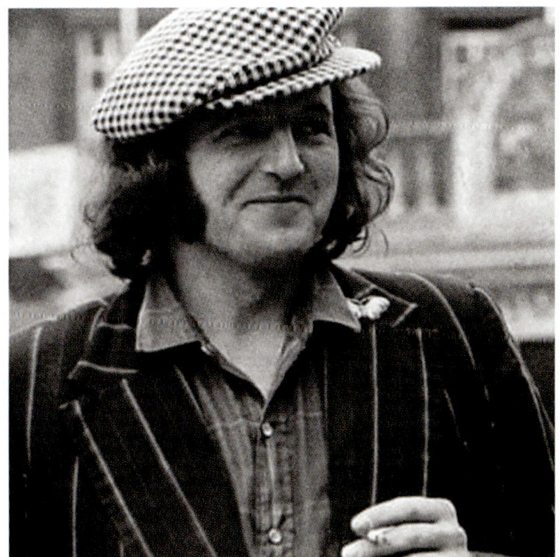

Charlie Ware

3. In 1967, armed conflict erupted between the Nigerian government and the secessionist state of Biafra. Nigerian troops imposed a blockade on Biafra which led to mass starvation. Our event title obliquely referred to the smug indifference of the corporate world.
4. Marianne Joan Elliott-Said (Poly Styrene) sadly died in 2011.

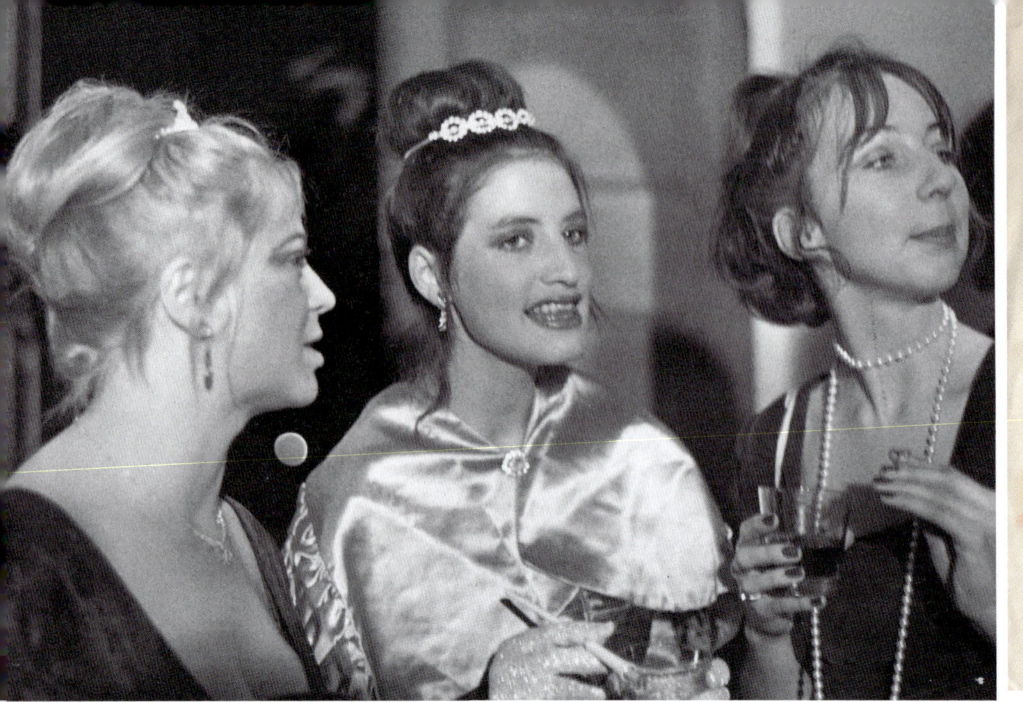

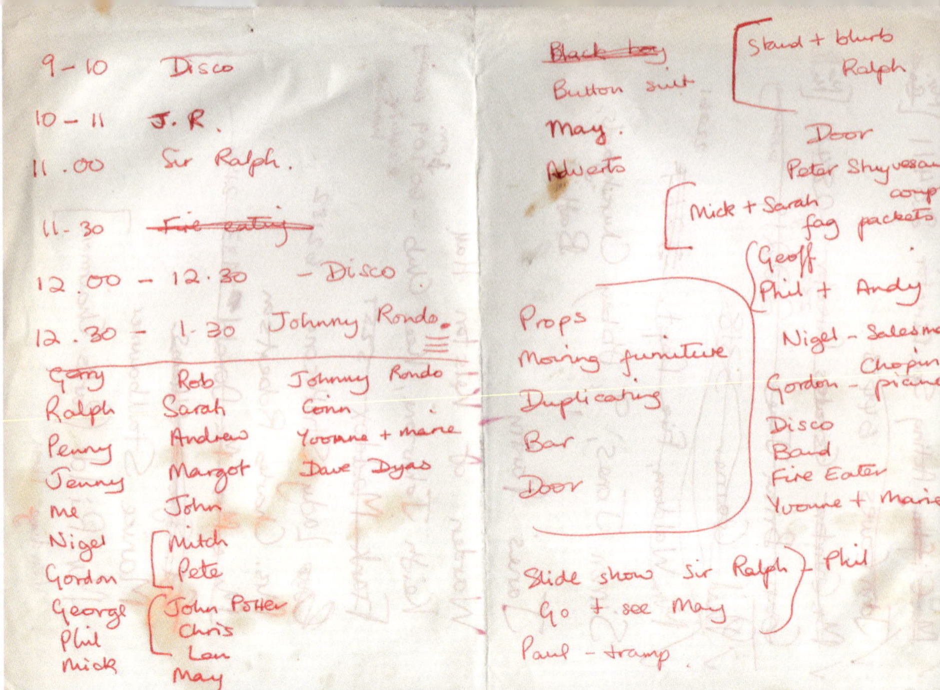


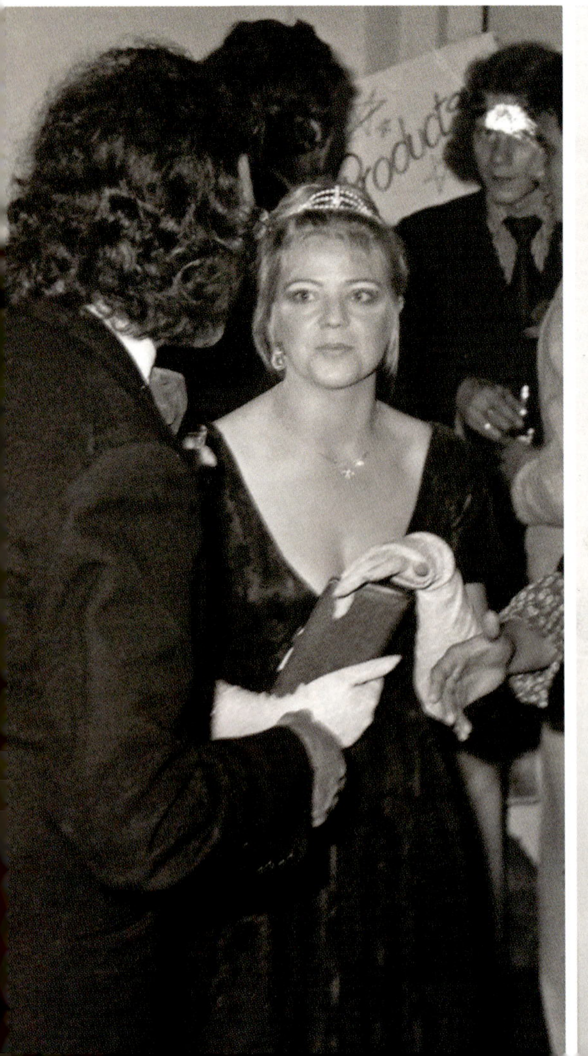

# Biafra Beano at the Royal Crescent

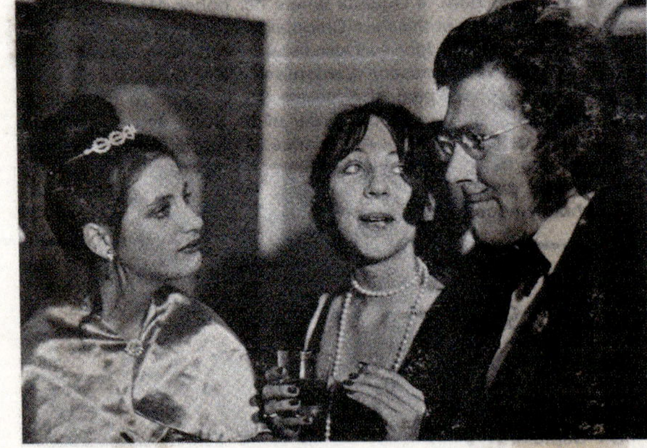

On Sunday, 25th August, Bath saw the high spot of the social scene. Biafra Luxury Products Ltd., those well known patrons of the arts who are currently sponsoring Bath Arts Workshop and The Last Festival, held a private reception for shareholders and customers at Mr. Charles Ware's in the Royal Crescent. Everybody was there, including the B.B.C., who had received a tip off that Sir Ralph Oswick, leader of the Smart Party of Gt. Britain and South Africa would attend, in his capacity as Chairman of the Board of Directors.

In fact Sir Ralph was on his way to Washington for his forthcoming impeachment, but his son, the Right Honourable Ralph Oswick Jnr. stood in for him.

A rather inconguous note was the presence of Hughie "the Shark" Leach, over from America. Usually reliable sources have it that it was Sharkie Leach who fixed the impeachment for Sir Ralph. Sharkie was doing a grand trade in pairs of two left foot shoes—the latest from the Biafra Products range. Remarkable restraint was shown by Ralph Oswick, Jnr. (*right*), when he learnt that while he had been interviewed by B.B.C. correspondant Robin Knight, Mr. Leach had sold his car to one of the guests.

Among the ladies at the party were Miss Penelope Stace (*centre*), Miss Jennifer Harrison-Smythe, and Miss Clorinda Cruise (*left*), who were all seen dancing at one stage or another, with much sought after Oswick aides Mr. Philip Shepherd and Mr. Andrew Hume, to music provided by the Johnny Rondo Combo.

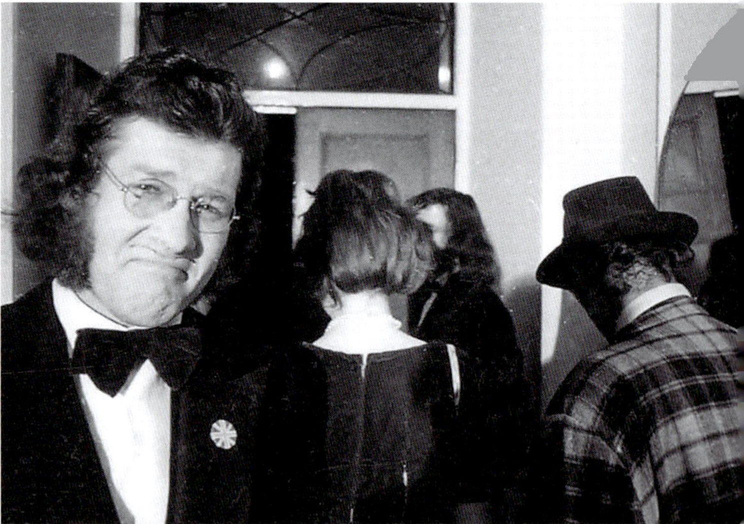

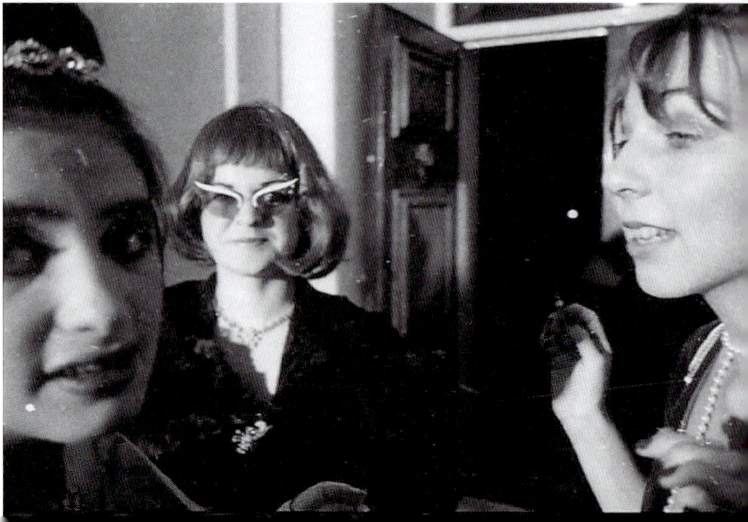

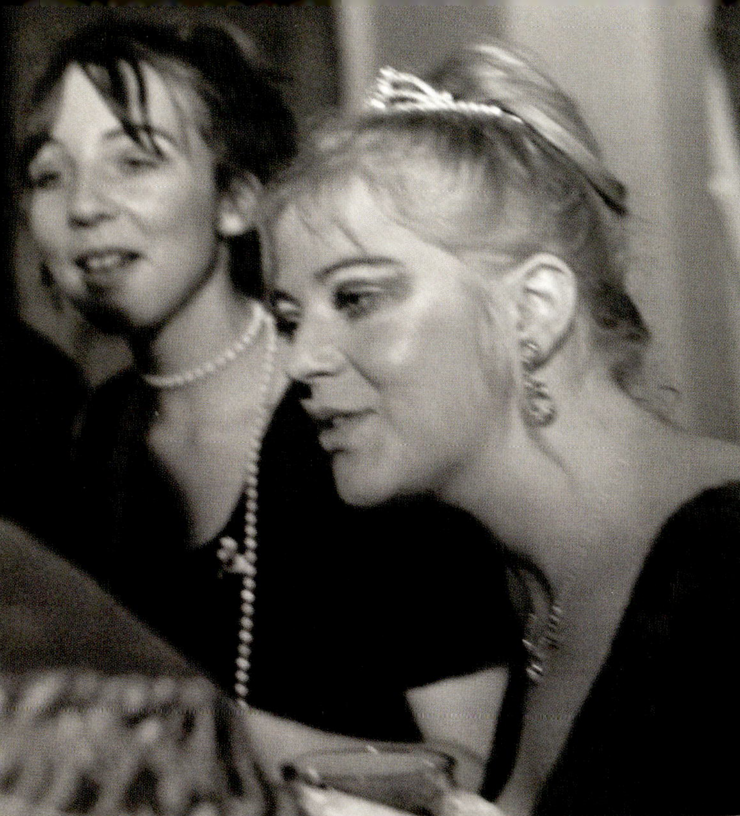

## BIAFRA LUXURY PRODUCTS LTD
### (incorporating "Yours By Arrangement")

Dear Colleages, Friends, Shareholders and Customers,

We have great pleasure in welcoming you to Biafra Luxury Products 3rd annual Promotional Progress Reception. We hope this evening will give you a long awaited chance to meet or perhaps even speak to our directors, planners, designers and administrators in an informal andd relaxed setting. Remember, every thing you see here tonight can be purchased, and our sales representatives will be on call in case you feel in the midst of the jolity the urge to do some serious buying.

The Chairman of the Board would like to express his gratitude both to "The Last Festival Old Folks Social and Welfare & Adventure Playground Trust" for allowing us to donate a handsome sum to their charity (and so relieving us of a considerable tax burden) and to Mr Charles Tupper-Ware, without whom this party (and a million others in homes all over the country) would not have been possible.

### Timetable of Events

9pm-10    Pierre le Roi Discotheque
10-11     The Sound of the Jonny Rondo Combo
11pm      The Chairmans Speech.Progress Report

12-12.30 Disco
12.30-1.30 Jonny Rondo Combo

B.B.C. in attendance
Launching of the new Biafra Eco-Shoe
Refreshments
Remember; BIAFRA means LUXURY ONLY YOU CAN AFFORD

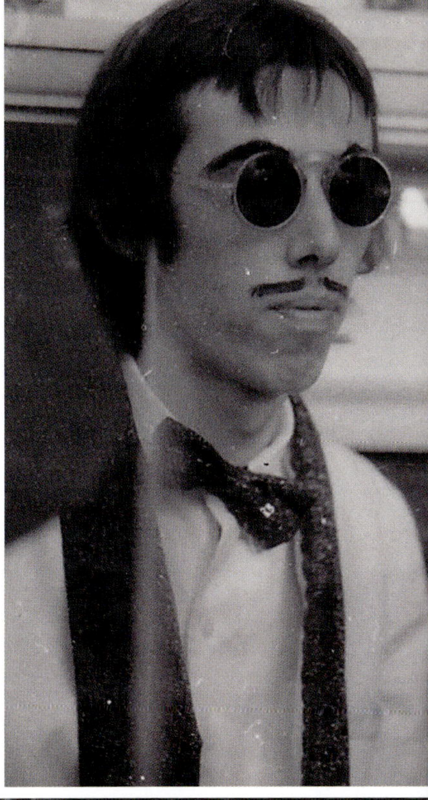

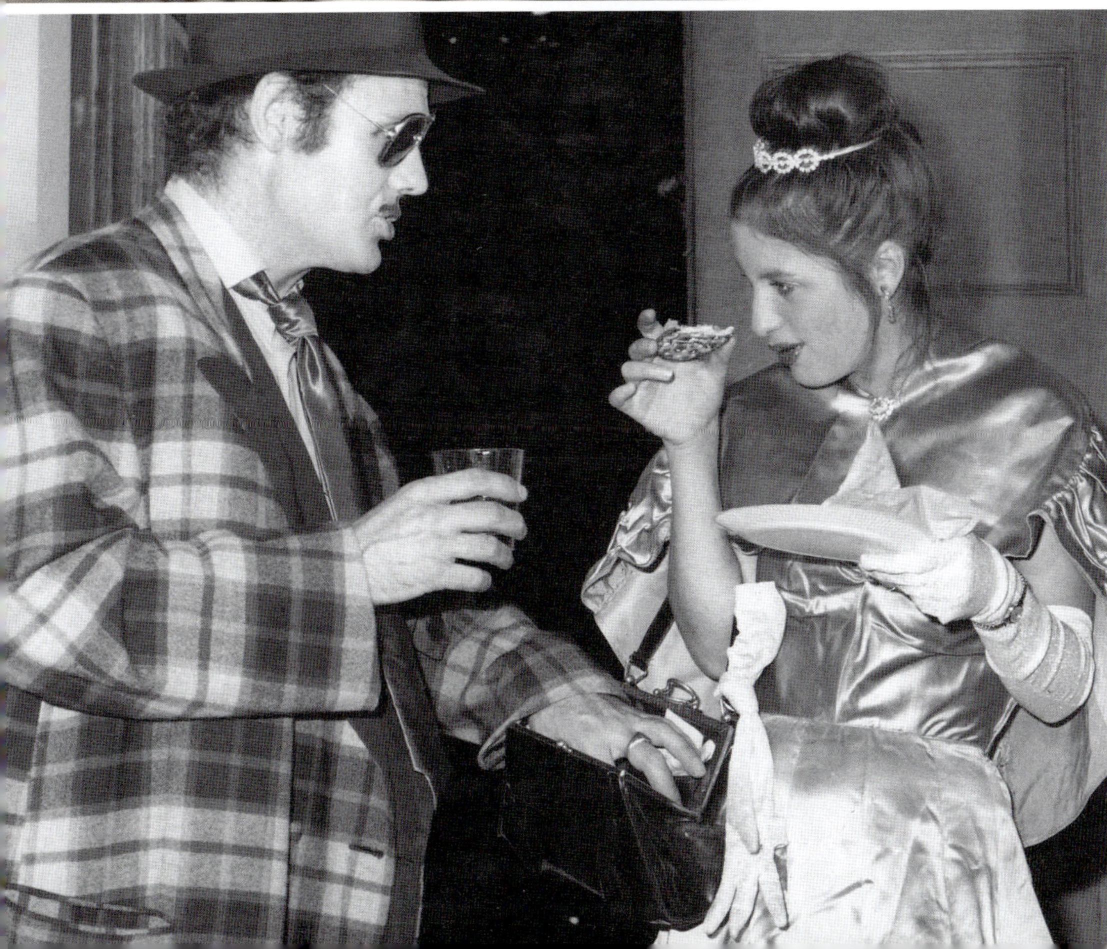

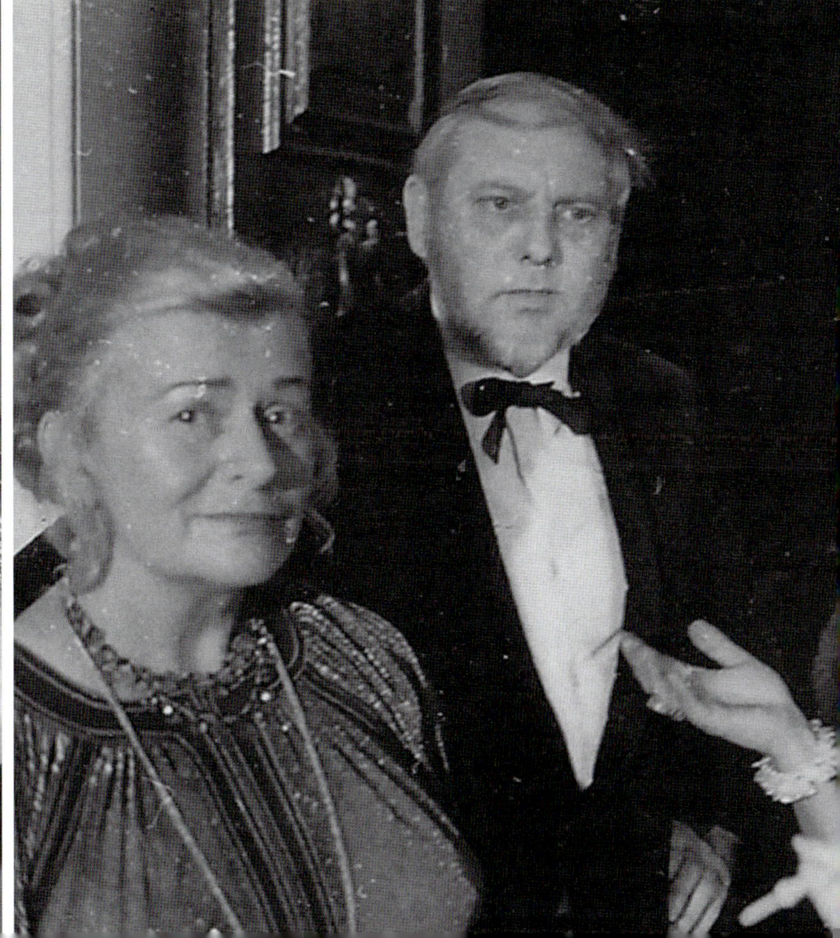

# The Last Festival 1974

**Corinne:** And so to *The Last Festival* which ran from 23 August to 1 September. It definitely *wasn't* the last and we never intended it to be. It was a tongue-in-cheek title echoing the gloom of the times, the oil crises (and resulting high prices) and miners' strikes, 3-day weeks and power cuts, failing infrastructure and economic policies. So let's have a last fling before it's too late! And we did.

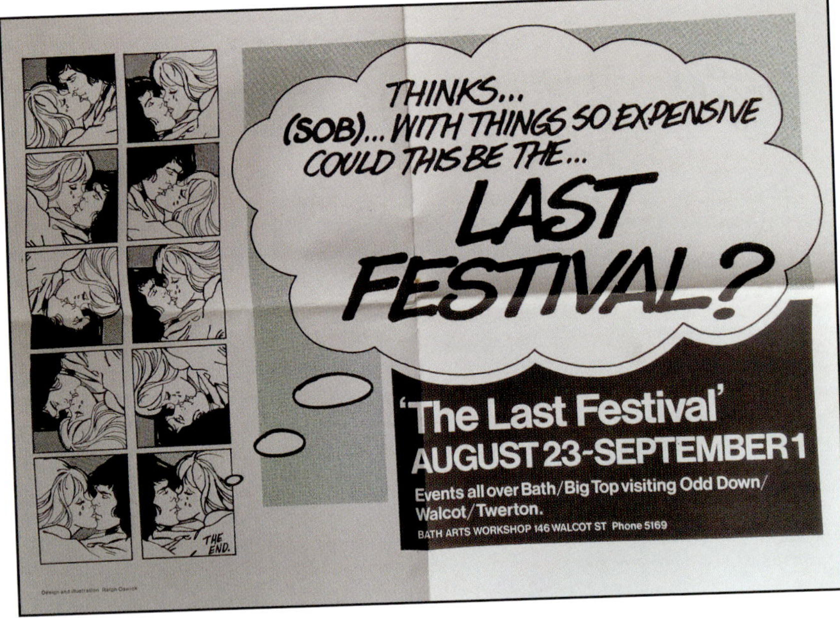


**John Wood** had recently arrived in Bath and chanced upon the festival: I'd never seen anything like it. It happened over 10 days on different sites, in town, in Victoria Park, and in Kensington Meadows (Walcot), Odd Down and Twerton. It gathered fringe theatre, music, art, community and alternative technology and allied trades from all over the wider counterculture. Friendly people turned up in old

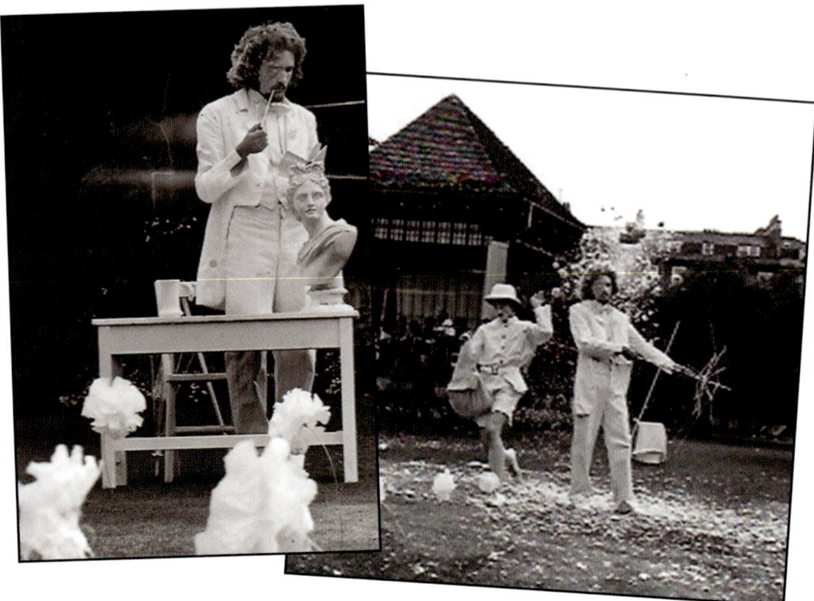

Exploded Eye at Parade Gardens

vans and buses to perform and contribute. The whole thing was wide-ranging and alive with enthusiasm and optimism. It was lovely. I have a memory of an artist in Victoria Park who painted on water, not with water, on it. I still don't know how he did it.

### *Last Post Festival News*, 25 August

A Welfare State Theatre show in Parade Gardens: Quiet. Then obsessive shipbuilding and a tranquil flute. Salt and saplings in a gradual build. Merciless drummers and anonymous pirates riding in a direct phalanx. Brief and bloody sack of ship. Conquerors and vanquished shipmen march off to the beat of the demon drums. (Can anyone make head or tail of this because I certainly can't?) Bob Jones, Festival Transport.

**John Wood:** I remember beat-up vans going round coordinating the various sites, linked by radio telephones (this was long before mobile phones existed). All led by Phil Shepherd who seemed to us like the king of Walcot Street with his indefatigable energy and long red hair. He was everywhere. I came across him at one point in a suit and tie, dressed he said to talk to the city council.

In those days, we'd never seen anyone with long hair in a suit. But, and this is what stunned me at the time, none of it happened in some half-assed anarchic way, but it was all really well organised. Everywhere else that I'd experienced hippy culture, the revolution was always going to start tomorrow, man, after we'd rolled another joint. That clinched it for me. Clearly I'd arrived somewhere special.

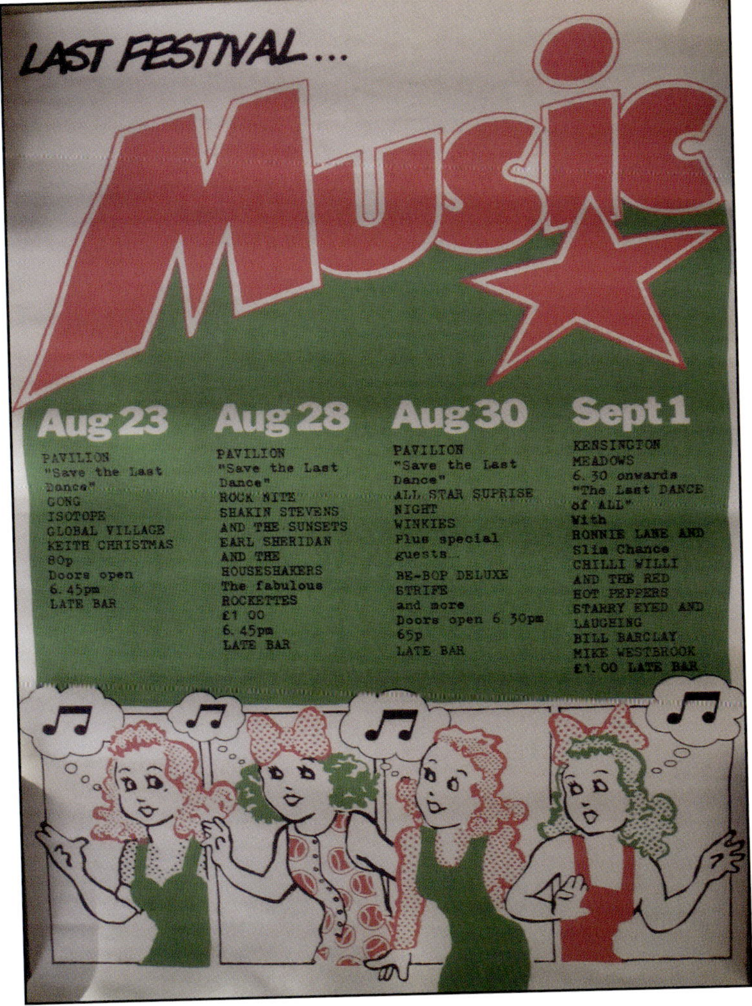


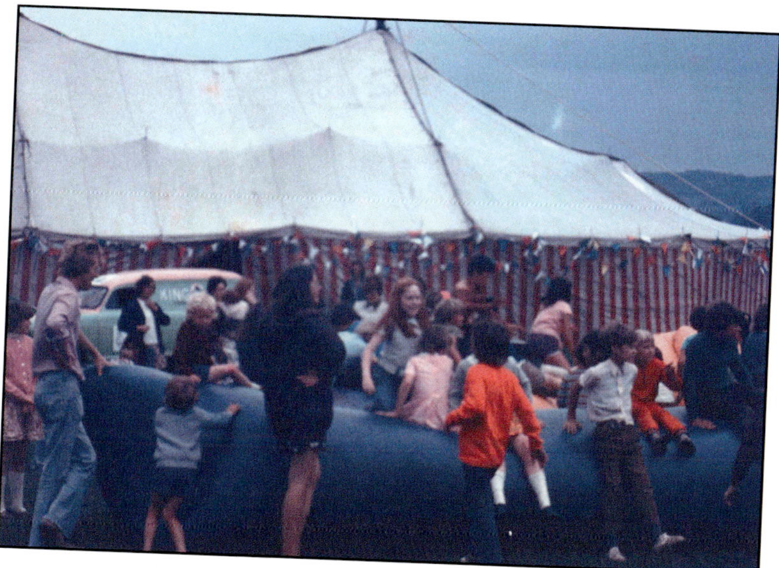
The big top in Twerton

**Corinne:** The festival took place on the same sites as in 1973 but in sequence rather than simultaneously. We borrowed *Welfare State's* enormous big top circus tent and, with their help, pitched it on each site for three days, then struck it and moved on to the next. Although there were still events in the city centre, the idea was to increase community involvement by focusing on each area in turn, with grand processions from one site to the next.

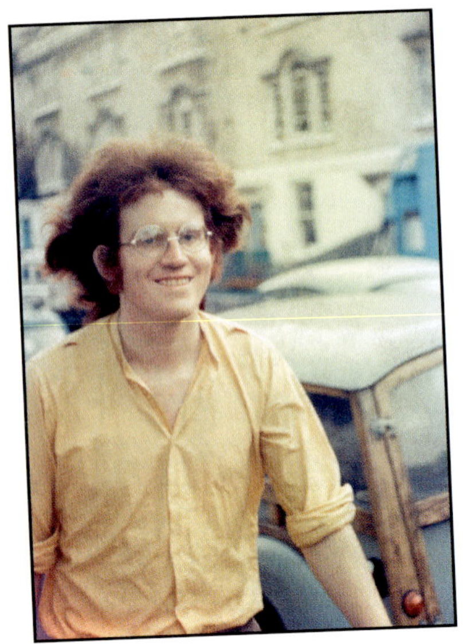

Phil living
the dream



## Stephen Cripps

**Phil:** For me the highlight of the festival was *Stephen Cripps'* exhilarating and atavistic performance-sculpture in Kensington Meadows.[5] Cripps had been a student at Bath Academy of Art and for the festival he created a Heath Robinson-like mechanical structure, maybe 12 feet high and as wide again; an intricate assembly of bicycle frames, wheels, kitchen utensils and scrapyard detritus, animated by a maze of gears, wires and pulleys, fly wheels and axles. Cripps sat at the heart of it, a gentle presence astride a stationary bicycle, his pedalling being the engine that brought the

---

5. Stephen Cripps was born in 1953 and died in 1982.

whole to life. Cripps was fused with the machine, alive to every nuance of the whole, lost in its world, his boundaries indistinct. It worked brilliantly, partly the artist's attempt to create a working world apart, partly joyful celebration of the absurdities of life, and partly a timely warning about ceaseless activity without purpose. Children loved it, were quite transfixed by the sheer magic of it. This was genius work and my single best memory of the art we presented in those years.

## Weather problems

**Corinne:** We were thoroughly thwarted by the weather. It rained down in torrents and gusts, 9 days out of 10. We had booked some veteran comedy entertainers like Tommy Trinder and Sandy Powell hoping they would draw in more elderly people. It didn't work at all and the only ones who

Some more objective reporting in the chronicle yesterday. This time it was Sandy Powell who was the hapless victim of workshop's drive to disillusion veteran comics. Once again the audience didn't realise that they werent supposed to be having such a good time and Mr. Powell told us how much he had enjoyed himself. Pity really, that while they were being so fearless and objective they ignored the little speech that Tommy made at the end of his act, although they reviewed the act itself – not forgetting the bit about the tent being rain-soaked and windswept, still, no doubt the Chronicle will be glad to hear that on Thursday they will be spared a long lonely vigil waiting for news to happen because at 3.00 in the afternoon the news will come to them. The intrepid Chronicle reporters will have grandstand seats as Auntie Margaret liberates the Evening Chronicle

braved the rain-soaked field to see Tommy in Twerton were the kids and us. Sandy Powell had the same experience but he was a real trouper and enjoyed his big top shows. Unfortunately, at one performance he fell off the stage while impersonating an old-time magician. Despite his 74 years, he picked himself up and carried on with the show.

### Liberation of *Bath Evening Chronicle*

**Tory:** The wet weather and high winds caused problems with the tent and all our equipment, leading to delays and even cancellations, a situation the **Bath Evening Chronicle** seemed to relish. Several articles described the festival as a flop and a failure. In the end, Aunties Margaret and Joyce (Ralph and Brian) 'liberated' the Chronicle via a symbolic cleansing process that involved drawing a circle of Sanilav toilet cleaner around the front of its premises.

**Corinne:** The Twerton site in particular became a dismal quagmire with vehicles getting stuck in the mud. A couple of BBC people from Bristol arrived unannounced as we were clearing up the site, lost control on the mud and went over a bank. Unhurt, luckily. The hoped-for local audiences didn't turn out in great number. They were probably sensibly huddled round the black and white telly, watching Z-Cars with a packet of crisps containing a twist of salt. But late one night a group of youths did come into the field, where they overturned the portable loos before we managed to stop them. After that, we arranged for people to sleep on site.

**Jennie:** I was sleeping in a coach on Kensington meadows for security. In the middle of the night, someone flung open the door, shouted 'bomb' and threw a ringing alarm clock into the vehicle. Hutch (friend and bouncer extraordinaire) chased him but he escaped into the darkness.

By the end of the festival, the *Festival News* reported: Despite high winds and cloudbursts, the Big Top is still in

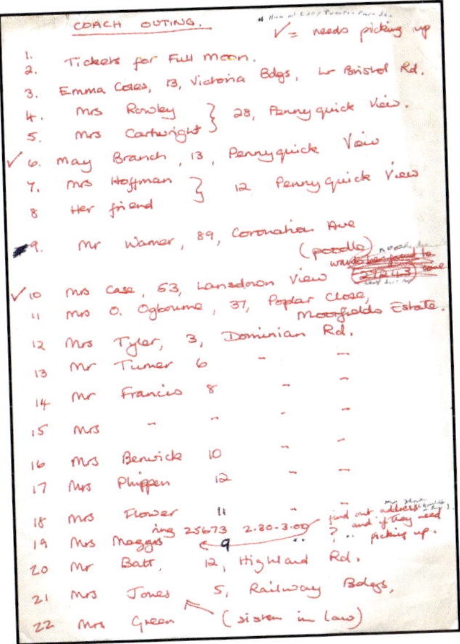

To do list, coach tour

one piece. The show goes on whatever. Most of the daytime events have been well attended with loads of kids getting involved in cooking, building, jumping on inflatables etc. The evening show attendance has been disappointing but the atmosphere in the 'Top' has been warm and friendly. Odd Down's Day started cold and windy but the procession was lovely despite one coach and one van running out of petrol en route. The Walcot organisers, Spike and Helen, organised a coach trip to Weymouth yesterday and had 47 customers, most of them kids. Walcot Rules OK, to quote Spike. It rained all the way to Weymouth but cleared up like magic when the coach arrived. There were a load of stops on the way as the kids rushed to the loos and some were sick. However, at Weymouth they all had a whale of a time.

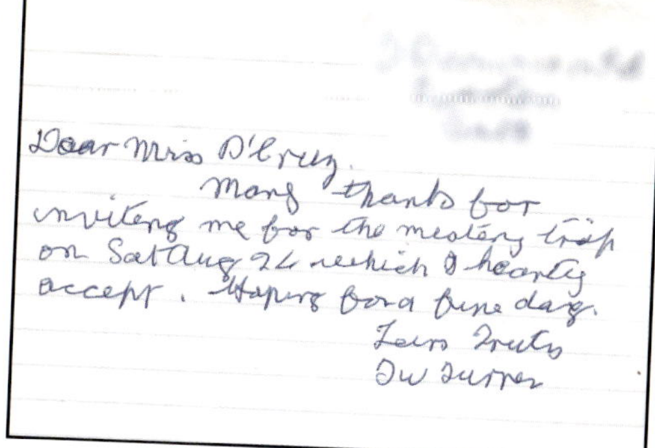

Letter from a guest on a coach trip

91

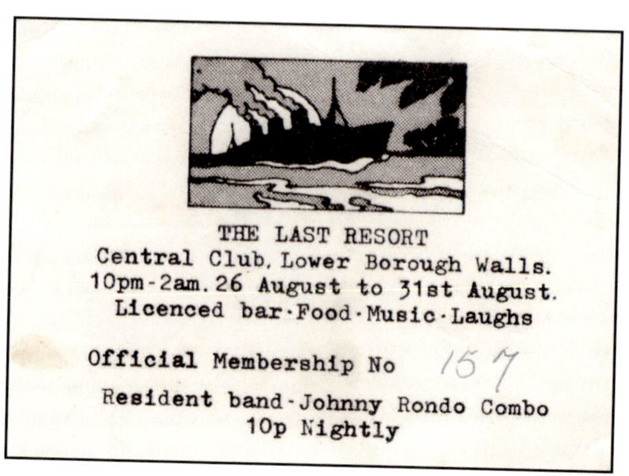



## After hours

**Tory:** For the first time, we ran an after-hours club for festival performers and workers. *The Last Resort* was housed in Bath's Central Club. After our 13-hour days, we flocked down there for food and drinks. There we were, the whole unruly crowd of performers, cooks, ecologists, musicians, engineers, drivers and artists working our guts out to make the festival happen. We were exhausted and euphoric, so coming together late at night was obviously an opportunity for much gossip, flirtation and other after-hours chaos.



### Last Resort Menu

Starters: Fruit juice, Melon, Paté Marguerite.
Mains: Stuffed cabbage, carrots & potatoes or
   Egg, Cheese or Pilchard Salad.
Afters: Fruit salad and fresh cream, pancakes.

**Tory:** The bar stayed open until 1.30am – unheard of in the 70s. This was probably the main reason why the club was soon packed to the gills, with lots of non-festival people piling in after the pubs shut. A firm statement from 'festival management' followed. After that the entrance was closely guarded and we had to show our numbered membership cards to get in. The entrance fee was 10p. Musicians booked to play at the festival often turned up and played there. John Wood remembers one night when Pete Brown (he who wrote *Sunshine Of Your Love* for the band Cream) turned up with his band and played. A great night!

## Comtek 74

**Tory:** In 1974, Comtek (Community Technology) planned the first of three exhibitions to coincide with the festival. It was an impressive display of eco-activism, with a focus on environmentally-friendly solutions to land conservation and food production, renewable energy sources, salvage and construction, housing, medicine and much more. The exhibition aimed to bring together a whole bunch of

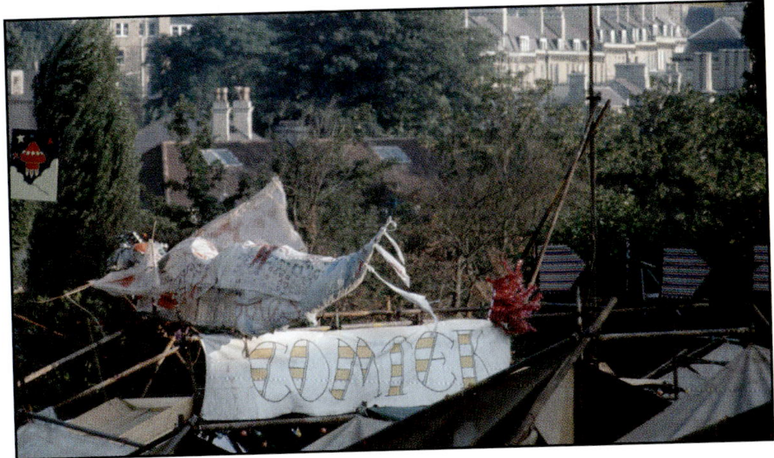

people involved in different aspects of ecology in all its manifestations, and to create a forum for discussion and action. To make it happen, Thornton and Rick toured the UK in an old Fiat 500, eventually drumming up enough support to host 40 exhibitors including Earth Star Structures, Graft On, Harvest Wholefoods, Housing Action, Low Impact Technology, Rational Technology Unit, Street Farmers, Transport 2000 and the Belgian group *Mass Moving*.

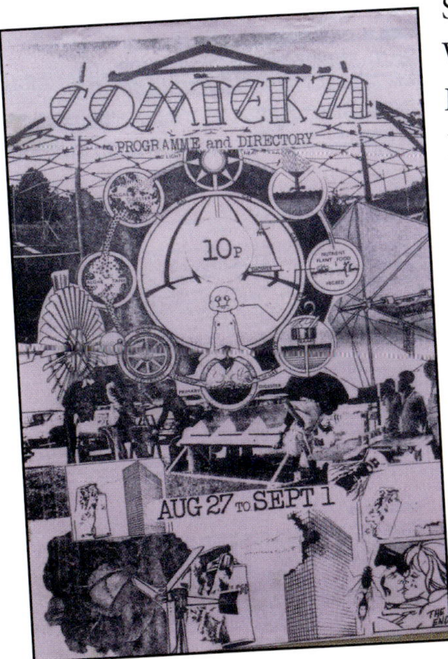

**Rob Llewellyn,** then an alternative shoemaker, came along to join in. He writes: I hitchhiked from Oxford to Bath in the summer of 1974 because I'd heard about a festival of alter-native and low-impact technology in the city. I was fascinated by the concept – my grasp of what was going on was hazy but passionate. I was 18 years old and full of ideas about alternative societies, communes and non-hierarchical political structures.

There were wind turbines and crude partly-wooden structures that could generate electricity without burning fuel. I remember a solar trumpet, a huge construction, built by a group of wild Belgian hippies (see *Mass Moving* below). The horn was powered by water heated in domestic radiators painted black and mounted on a south-facing rack. By 9.30am, the sun had heated the water enough to produce steam, which fed through an enormous horn until it started to blare forth. I think it upset people nearby so, not surprisingly, the Belgians disconnected it for most of the time.

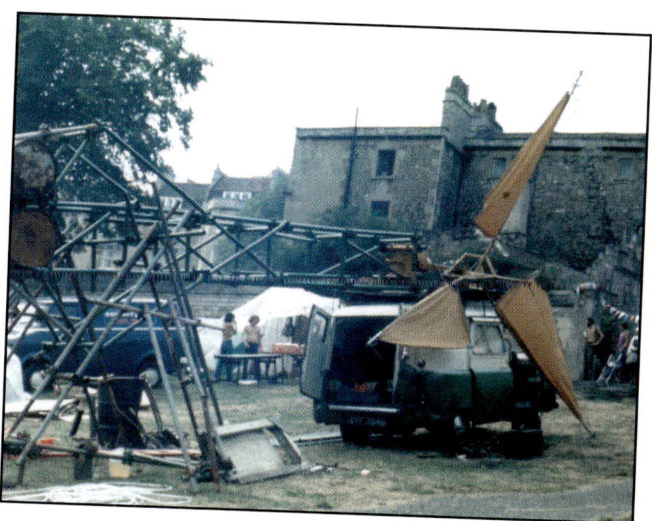

Building a solar trumpet

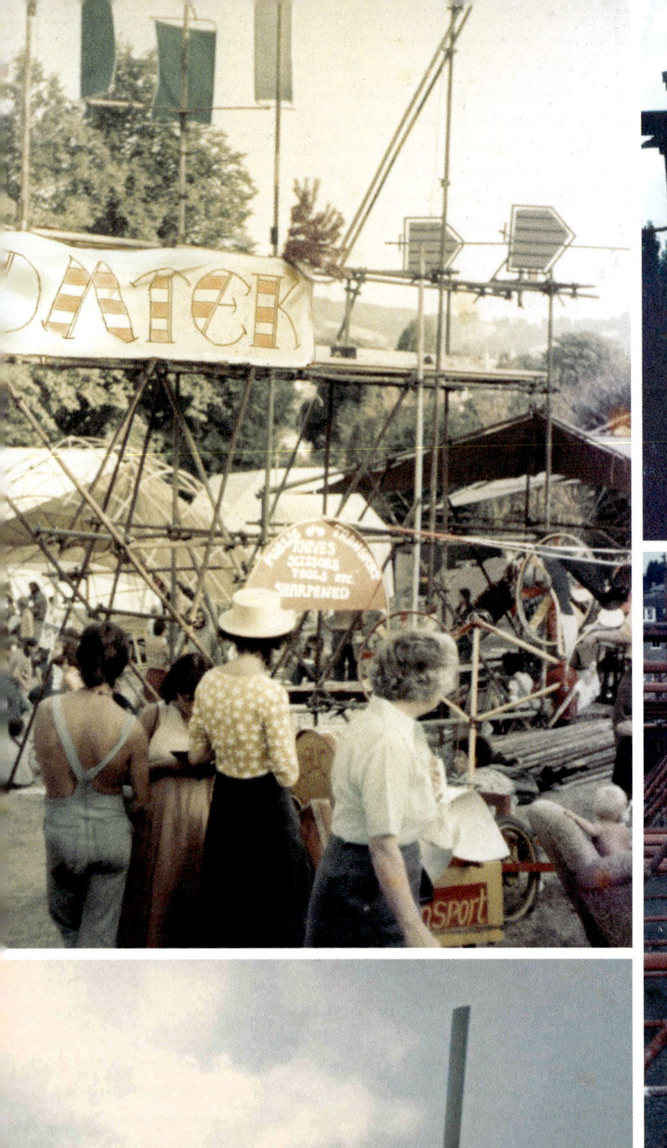

COMTEK
KNIVES
SCISSORS
TOOLS Etc.
SHARPENED


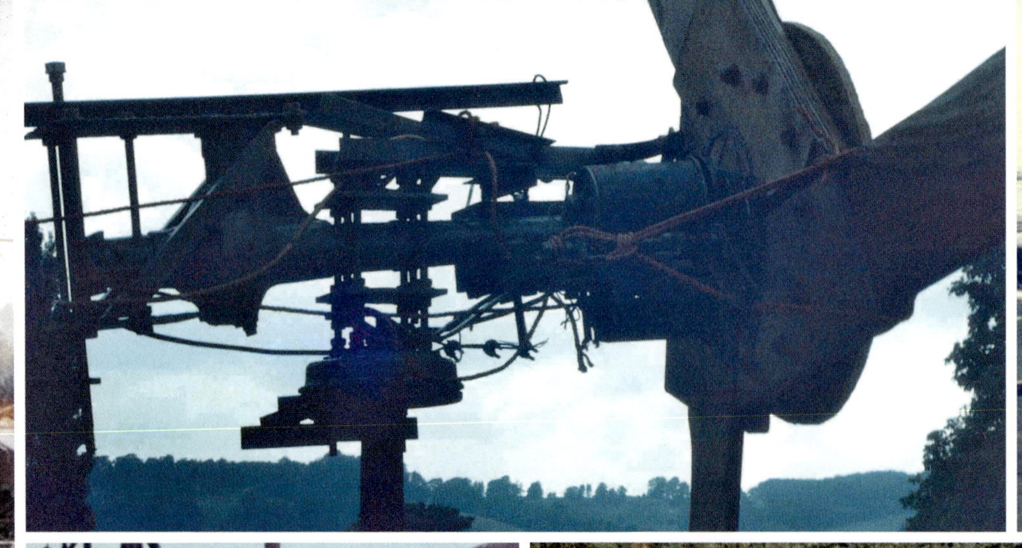

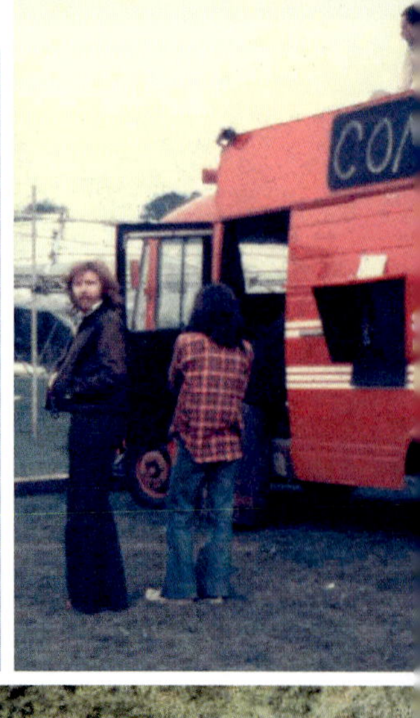

COM


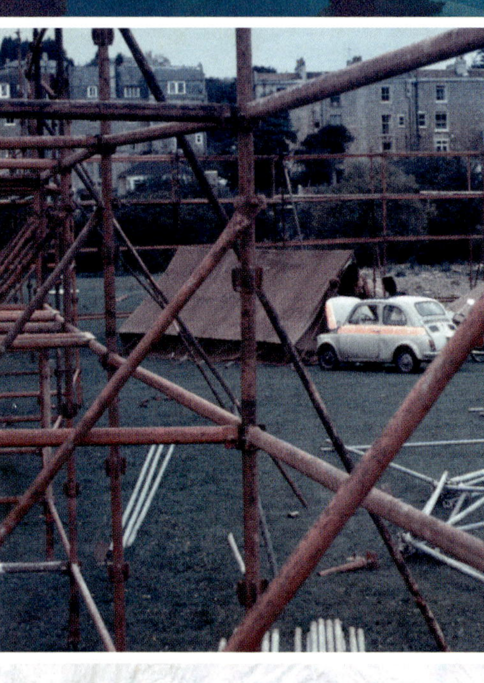

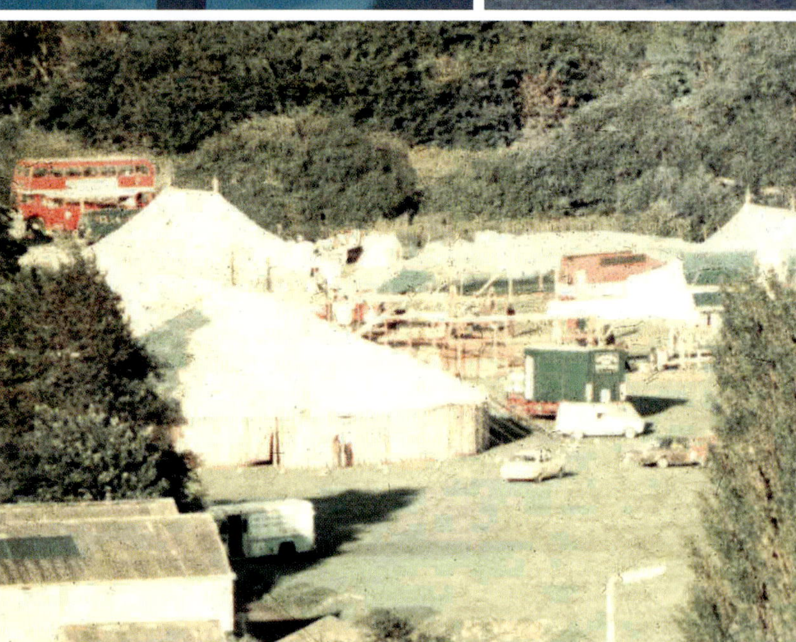

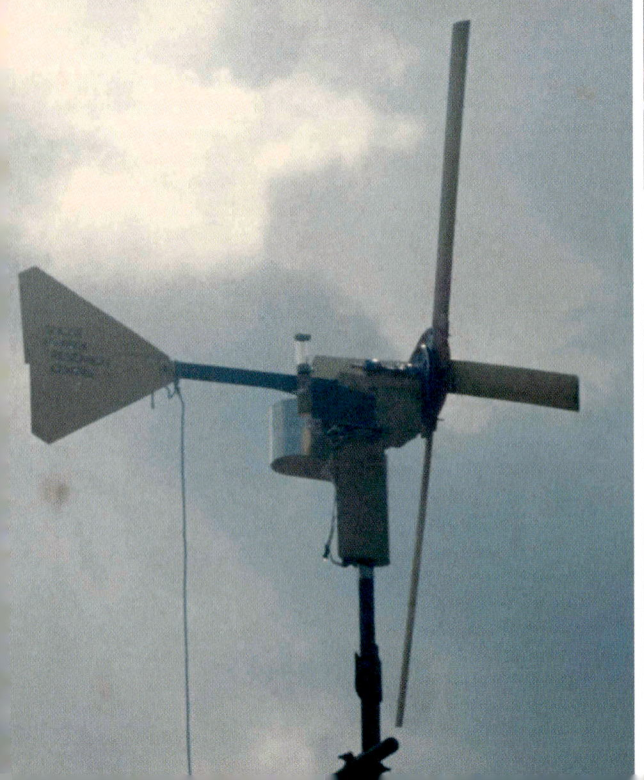

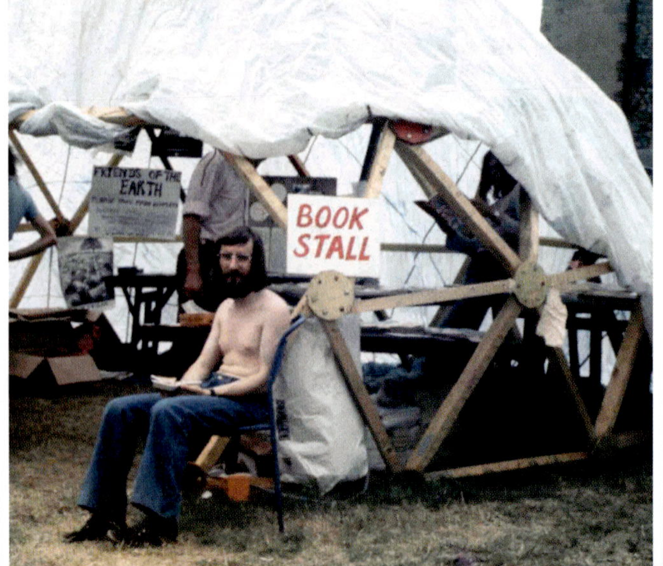

FRIENDS OF THE
EARTH
BOOK
STALL


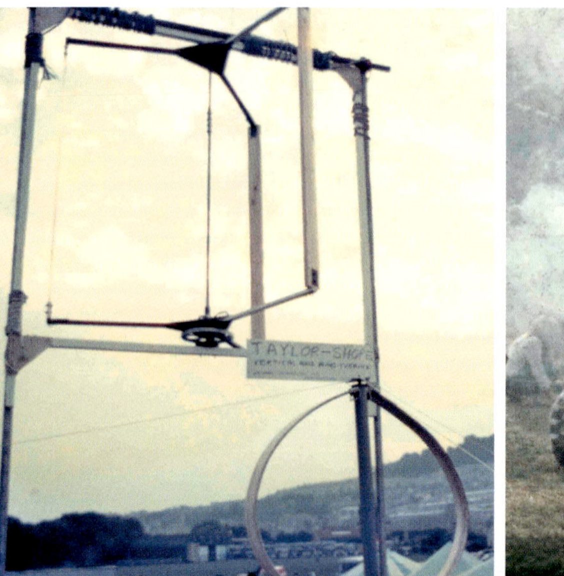

TAYLOR-SHOR

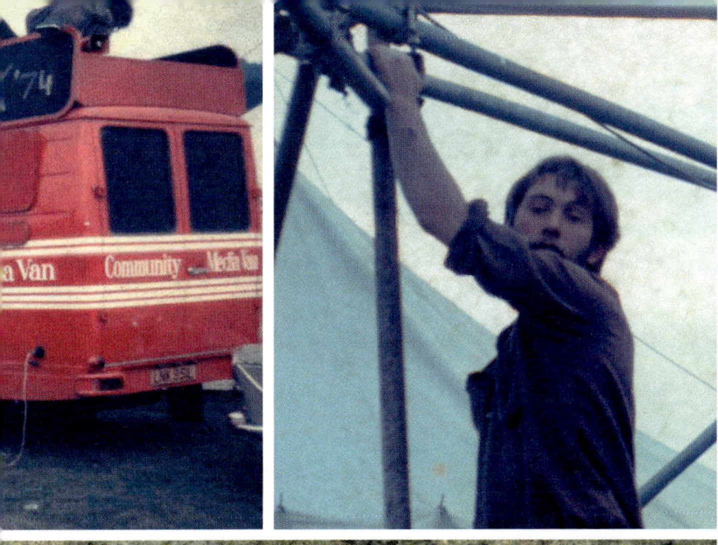

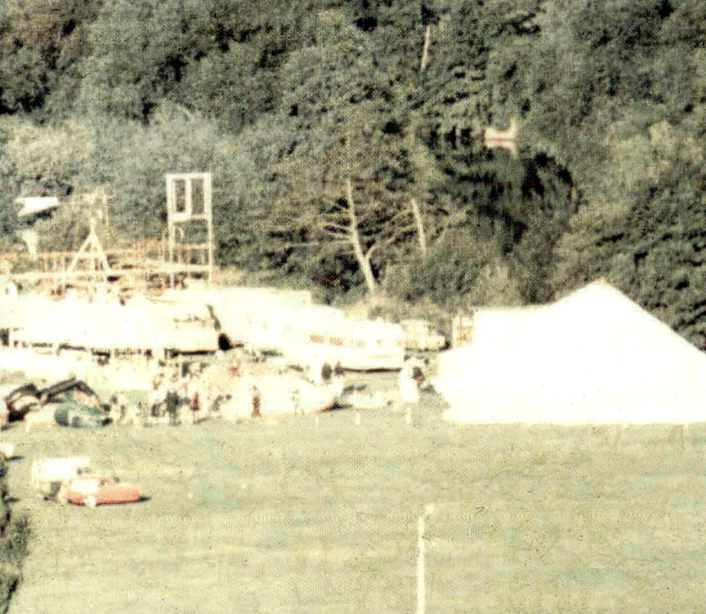

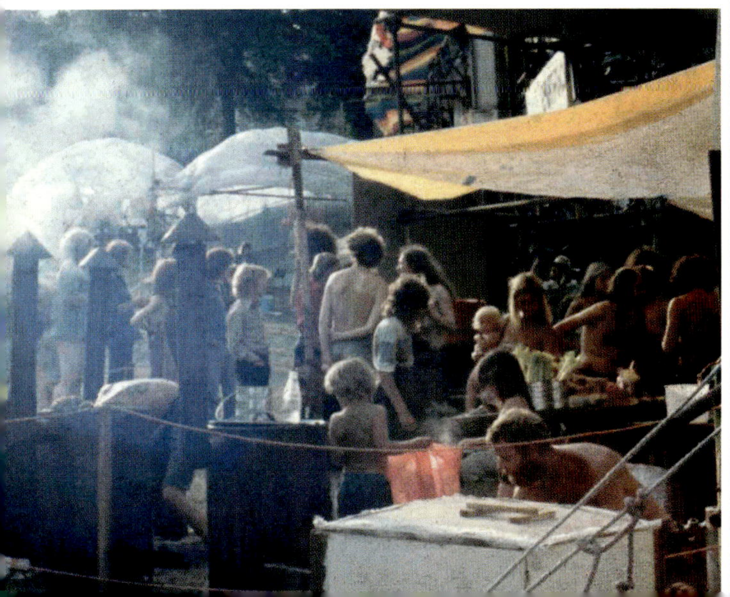

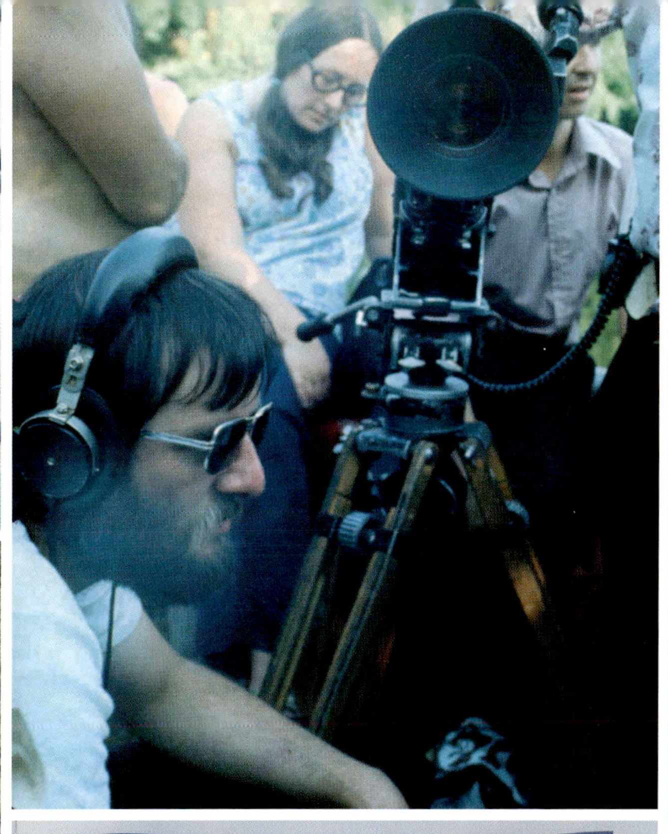

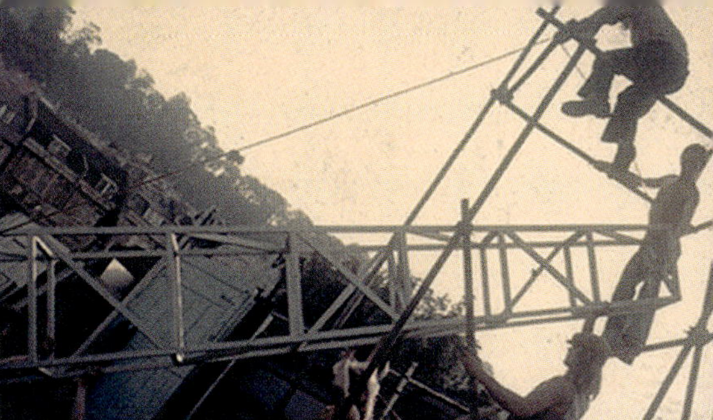

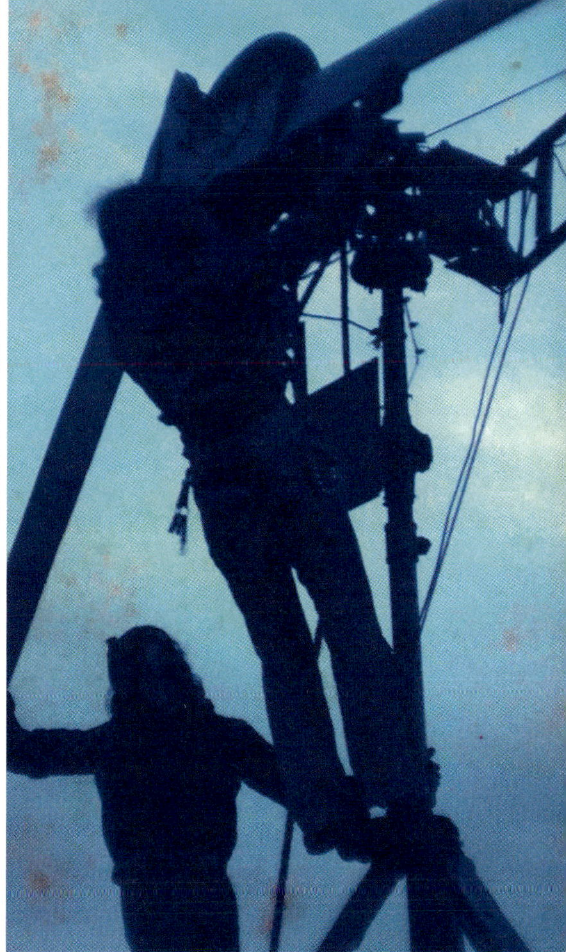

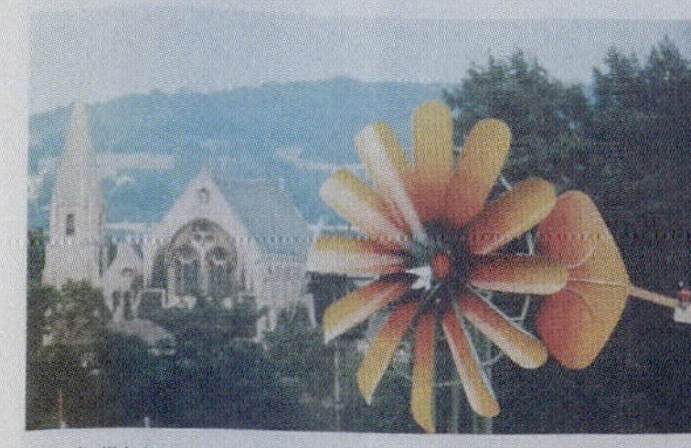

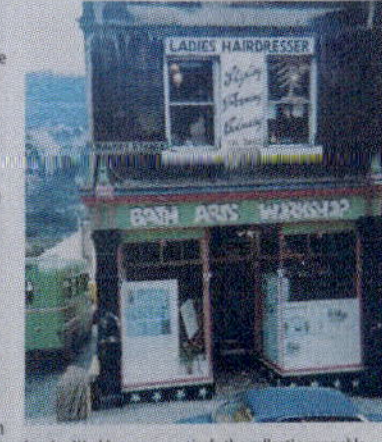

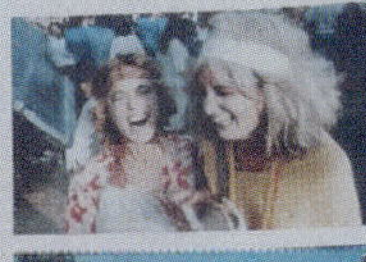

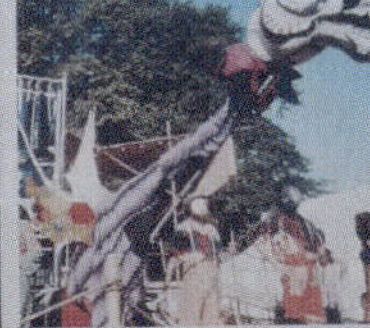

The central article is reproduced below.



# Counterculture of the '70s in Bath

**Destination Walcot**

Bath Fringe likes to think we're still ahead of the game, but there was a time when the city's alternative festivals were in the avant garde in both art & technology, actual world leaders.

The artistic part of the 69-79 festivals included a lot of what was then called Experimental Theatre or Performance Art, most of which would be quite at home in FAB this year, and still more of it would be familiar from green-field festivals (large scale temporary public art) or community events (outdoor circus & theatre, lantern processions).

The next decade brought events in other parts of the city, the Bath Arts Workshop, the Print Shop, The Natural Theatre (celebrating their own 50th anniversary from this summer to next), serious micro-budget film-making, and a community of local adventurous performers and artists whose cultural influence on Bath is difficult to over-state. Also a number of entertaining legends, most of which turn out to have been true.

With the support of Arts Council England and local sponsors, this year's Fringe includes: outdoor theatre directed by Trevor Stuart, here in the early days with the acclaimed Lumière & Son; art and performance in Walcot Chapel (previously better known as Walcot Village Hall) by groups evoking art of the period (ARCC) or who themselves starred in the festivals (the one and only Johnny G), plus FAB events (see Walcot Chapel in the end pages of this guide); The Bell has the milkfloat printing workshop, films of the 1970s events, and performances from successive generations of Walcot faces, on the last day of the Fringe (Sunday June 9).

There will be a symposium on 50 Years of Outdoor Theatre, with key groups of the era, at the Museum of Bath at Work on Saturday September 28th. More details on www.bathfringe.co.uk nearer the time.

**9th June – 31st August, open 10.30am - 5pm, every day.**

## Exhibition and workshops created by Bath Arts Workshop History Group

*Museum of Work at Bath, (MOB@W), 348, Julian Rd. Bath, BA1 2RH.*

Bath Arts Workshop was founded in 1969 by a group of young people who sought to create spaces for performance and arts inspired events in Bath and the locale. Working co-operatively the collective was able to reduce costs by sharing space and equipment and securing material and resources at a discounted price for community theatre and arts projects. One of the many lasting legacies of the workshop is the Natural Theatre Company, still travelling the world and based here in Bath. Another key element of the Workshop – Comtek (Community Technology) – was concerned with ecological issues, recycling, alternative technology and the future of sustainable living on a local level.

2019 marks the 50th anniversary of the initial set–up of Bath Arts Workshop/Comtek and to celebrate the anniversary The Museum of Work at Bath presents an archive exhibition and workshop programme, with the participation of community energy / climate emergency groups, repair cafes and recycle / reuse projects active in Bath today.

**Sunday 9th June from 2-5pm**

## Opening of the Exhibition

Events, activities, workshops, entertainment, technology and community engagement. Print your own catalogue at the resident Pink Milk Float Mobile Press and enjoy activities such as film screenings, immersive installations, viewing archive posters and ephemera plus the DIY ethos of Bath Arts Workshop in 1969 – 79.

**Saturday 15th June 10am-1pm**

## The Past, Present and Future of Community Energy

Bath & West Community Energy and 10:10 Climate Action speakers join 1970's Comtek founding members to describe how local residents have been actively involved in renewable energy initiatives and explore what we can all do to build a cleaner energy future. Sessions on

- DIY community technology in the 1970s
- Taking Action on Climate Change
- Community involvement in local community energy
- a panel session asking how we can all get involved in reducing our energy demand and achieving 100% clean energy by 2030.

This seminar will be particularly timely following Bath & North East Somerset Council's recent declaration of a Climate Emergency. This free public event will be guest chaired by actor-comedian ROB LLEWELLYN. More details nick.bird@bwce.coop

**Throughout the exhibition from June 29th till August 31st**

## Brilliant but Bonkers Saturdays

Join us for something different happening most Saturdays DIY workshops 'making through sharing', repair cafés, events and film screenings - look out for a re - emergence of the BAW 21st Century White Rabbit Film Club with a programme of 70's Arthouse/ Alternative Films screened at the Museum throughout the exhibition.

Discussions / Events / Workshops will run June-August check on website http://www.bath-at-work.org.uk/ call Museum 01225 318348 follow us on Instagram @ bawhistory – the flowering of the counterculture in Bath, 1969 -1979.

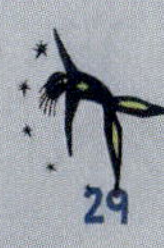

29

Full booking information on page 2

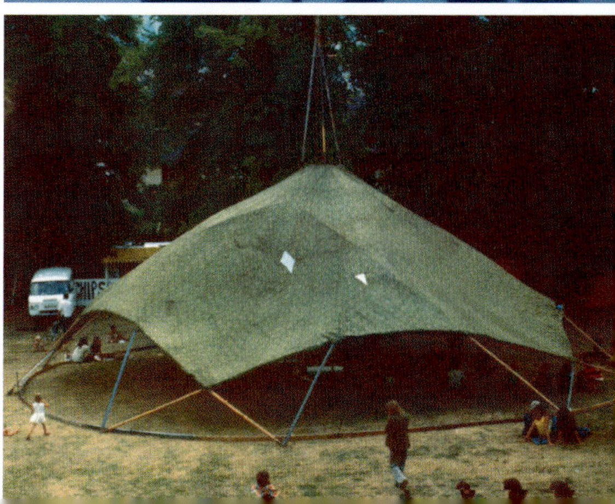

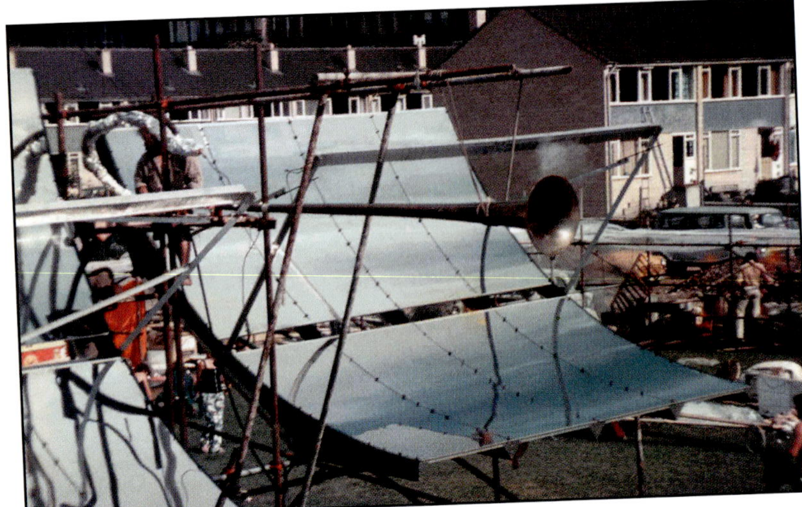

Solar trumpet



**Rob:** I recently flew in a helicopter around the Burbo Bank wind farm extension in Liverpool Bay: 8-megawatt wind turbines with 80-meter blades is an impressive sight. I've lived long enough to see some of the technology – so optimistically on display in a field in Bath in 1974 – make a genuine contribution to the UK's energy needs. Currently 28 per cent of electricity for the whole country is coming from wind.

**Tory:** *Mass Moving* from Belgium was a radical group of artists and engineers whose work comprised projects and short-lived actions. Their goal was to take art out of museums and galleries by 'invading the streets' and to promote the importance of the earth and the concept of the planetary chain. Their absolutely unforgettable event that year involved dumping an old car *completely encased in concrete* in the middle of Southgate shopping precinct. The operation was carried out in the dead of night as a protest against the city's transport policies.[6]

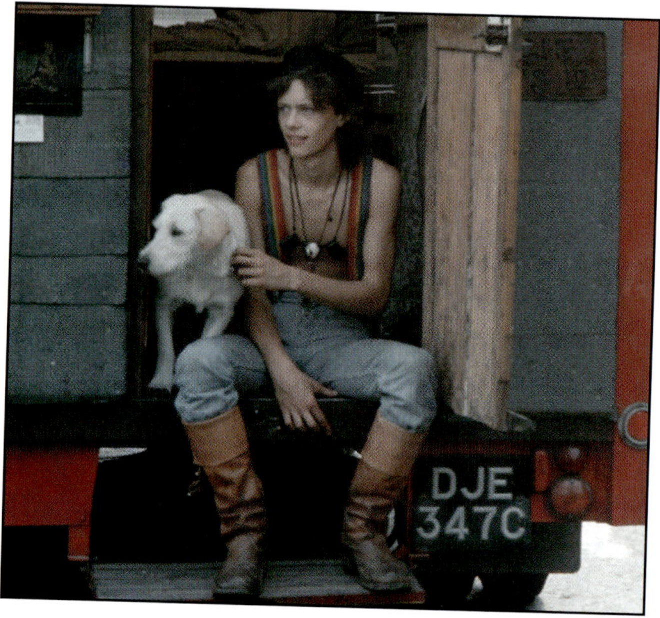



Rob Llewellyn



6. ***Mass Moving*** folded in 1976 with a spectacular *auto-da-fe* destroying their machines and burning drawings, photos, films and posters. More information can be found at www.mementoproduction.be

Back on the field, **Mass Moving**'s enormous solar-powered trumpet 'broke wind' just at the right moment as the police passed by on their way to a perfunctory interrogation of the car-cementing suspects.

**Undercurrents**, the radical science and alternative technology magazine, perhaps best summed up the exhibition: With Britain's first community technology festival, Thornton, Rick and the rest of the Workshop gang managed to assemble that critical mass of attenders needed to set the social chain reaction going. Events began ponderously and it took two days for dampened spirits to be lifted by the realisation that **Comtek 74** had slowly become the joyful mass of people's technology that everyone secretly hoped it would be. (**Undercurrents** 8, October-November 1974)

### Flashbacks

**Jennie:** We were so busy during the festivals that we barely slept. We must have eaten but when? I do remember a vegan woman called Sue who arrived with her toddler, Tom, to sell brown rice and lentils. Brown rice was a new thing then and she showed me how to cook it. We didn't wash much either. I never made it back to the house, and definitely no time to heat up water for a bath. Instead I sometimes took my towel to the public baths at Bog Island. It was about 10p for a huge tub filled with lovely hot water.

So many flashbacks: theatre, music, baby shows, windmills, solar panels, greasy poles, fire eating, big names and small bands, meeting new people and old friends, gaffer tape,

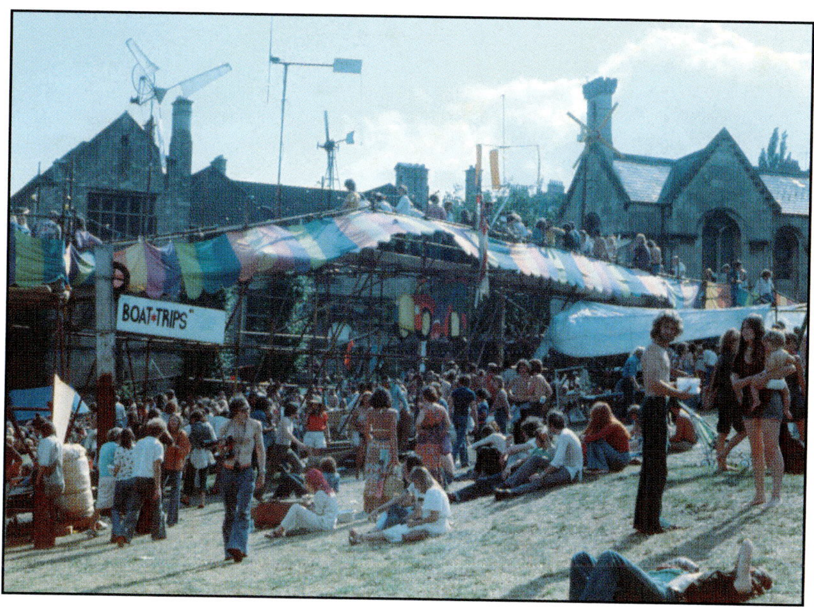

*Spot-Lite Klear* stage make-up, costumes held together with safety pins, scaffolders (bare chests), Hare Krishna chanters in orange robes, clowns, Normals. Sandy Powell's wife as his assistant looking so elegant in an evening gown, last-minute panics, laughter, friendship, sequins and mud!

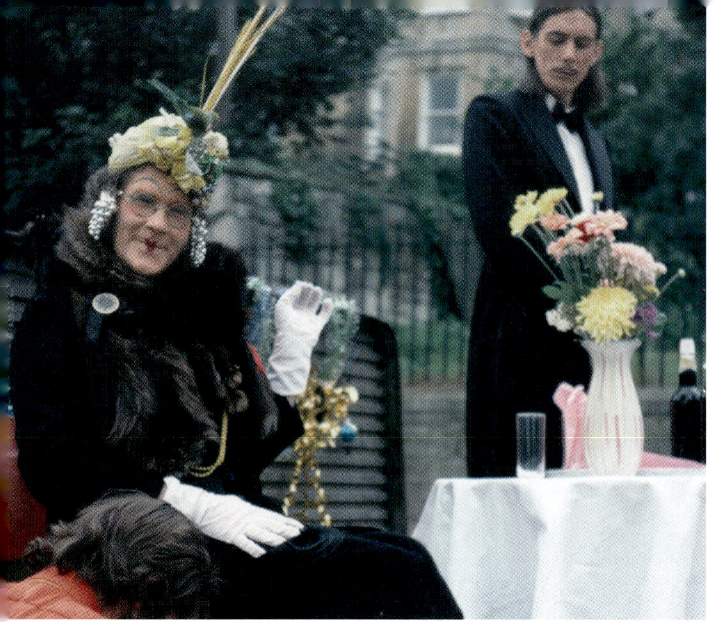



# THE RISE AND RISE OF LADY MARGARET OSWICK

**R**alph Oswick: Lady Margaret began life as a humble auntie in a flowery frock. She emerged from my character in *The Respectable Terrace*, the amateur dramatics play performed by **Natural Theatre** at the Organ Factory in 1972 (see *Chapter 3*). The play was conveniently set in a hotel in Bath and written for women. Our cast was predominantly male so we had to get in touch with our inner woman to act our parts convincingly (which of course we did).

My character, named Margaret, soon developed an independent life and a powerful personality, using the classic **Natural Theatre** trope of mocking the establishment by seeming to be one of them. Thus she drew attention to events

(and herself) by protesting against them. Her hats grew exponentially in line with her popularity and delusions of grandeur.

BAW's first cafe, Auntie Margaret's Teashop, was named in her honour.[7] Margaret personally opened this establishment and subsequently hosted poetry readings whilst perched on an armchair in the shop window. The readings lasted as long as her bottle of Nobility Cream. On one occasion, my mum came in whilst Auntie M was in mid-gargle with this delicious British sherry. A lady asked her what was going on and my mum answered 'I think it's supposed to be some sort of performance.'

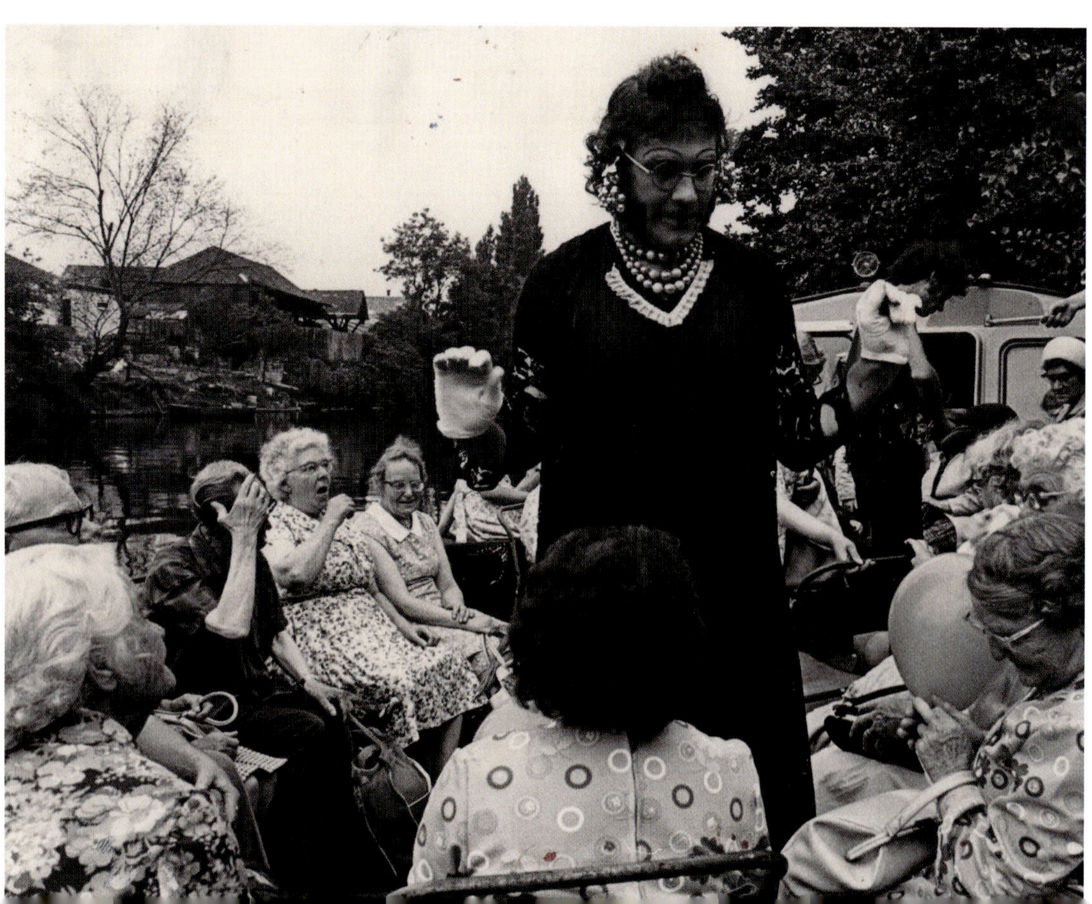

## Love's dream

Auntie Margaret's most famous street performance was done to a scratched 78rpm record of *Love's Dream* by Franz Liszt; it involved her setting up a Christmas crib with cut out figures placed in a circular sun motif drawn on the pavement with Harpic and Trill birdseed. It ended with Auntie M biting off the head of an artificial robin (complete with foaming blood capsule) then placing it in a miniature crib. An Arts Council assessor declared it to be the most moving piece of mime they had ever seen… but of course it was completely meaningless and used props that had randomly appeared in the Workshop jumble (like many of our artistic creations).

Inevitably, Auntie became Lady Margaret Oswick after she graduated from a plastic rain hat to a grander and more extravagant class of millinery purloined from the **Natural Theatre**. Her title was conferred upon her via

7. The teashop was BAW's first shop and cafe. It was at 1A The Paragon, a narrow three-storey building, perched dangerously above a stone staircase that led down to Walcot Street.

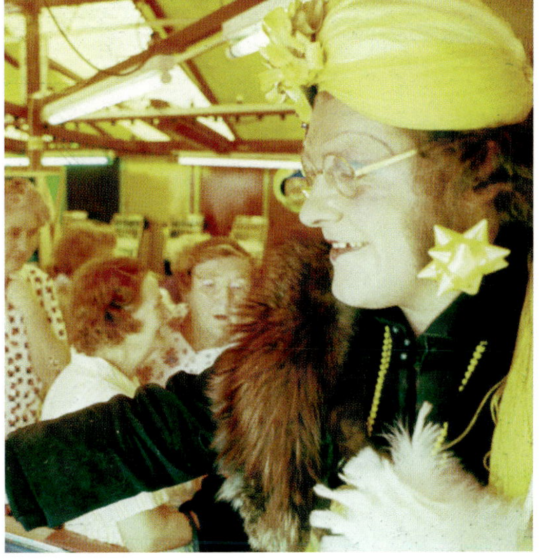

her marriage to Sir Ralph Oswick, bigot and leader of the Smart Party of Great Britain. In later years, they often broadcast together on their Radio 4 show, although strangely in 'real life' they never appeared together. Poor Sir Ralph mysteriously passed away soon after the vet visited their Wiltshire residence to deal with a lame horse.

Lady Margaret went from strength to strength. Accompanied by a retinue of wrinkled retainers she tumbled out of her Rolls Royce to grace a huge variety of events: rock concerts, tea parties, pub discos and garden fetes, where she often enjoyed the inflatables. She took part in processions, illuminated

Christmas lights and held musical soirées, where she delighted audiences with her trilling soprano.

A highlight of her ladyship's long and rarefied career was leading the Queen's Jubilee procession down the Mall in her capacity as honorary royal nanny in 2002, an event that boosted the **Natural Theatre's** audience figures by several million. It was sadly Margaret's first and only appearance alongside the Household Cavalry and the Grenadier Guards. Lady Margaret has now taken semi-retirement but she is willing to grace the odd wedding, funeral or bah mitzvah in return for ready cash.

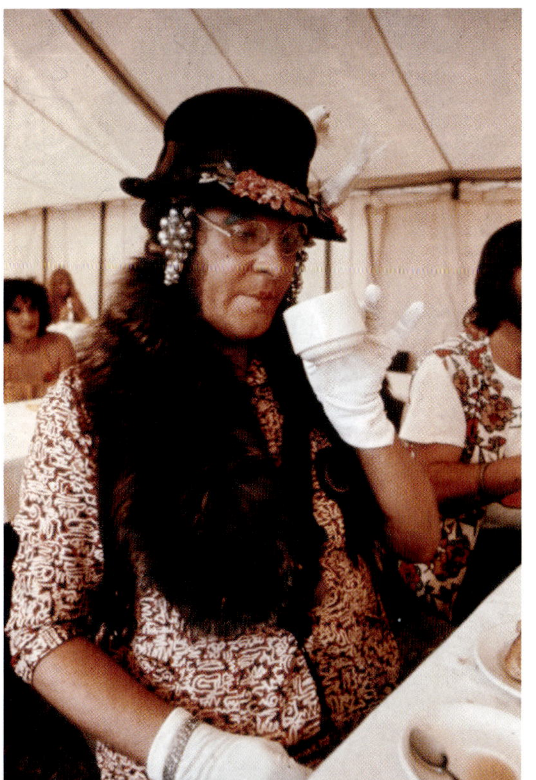

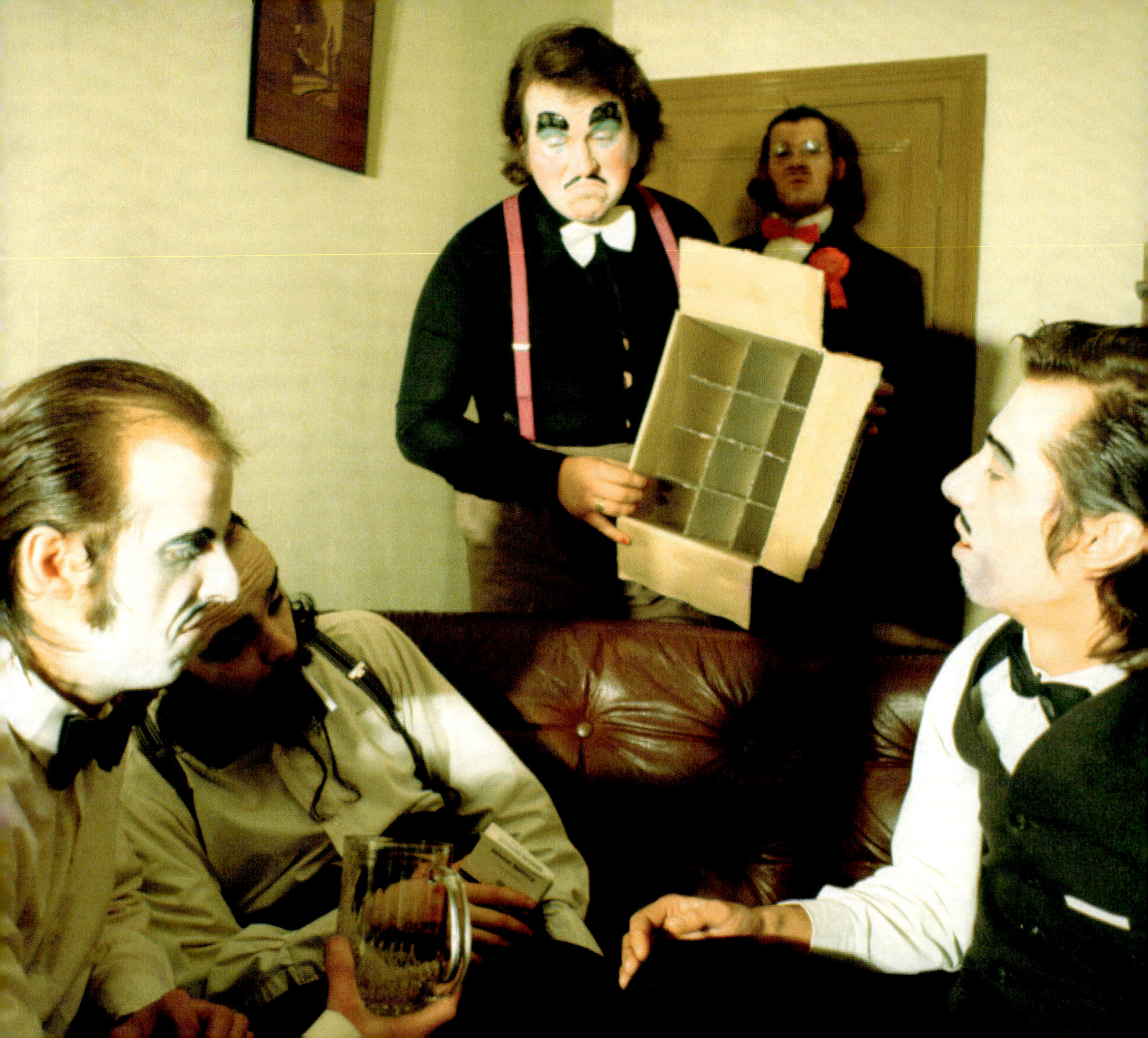

# CHAPTER 5

# THE ROCKY RICKETTS SHOW 1972-78

**An aging 50s rock star made a comeback, with a rock 'n' roll band and his fabulous Rockettes. Manager Vince Pube threw raffle prizes at the audience. The finale was Gloria, featuring Rocky's surreal liberation rap. Make of it what you will!**

**Able Lawrence:** The Rocky show evolved from **Natural Theatre's** first play, *The Legend of Spotty Blelb*, which I had written for them. It was a pseudo-Dickensian story of how a poor young lad's life is transformed by meeting a rock star. That lad was Spotty and the rock star was Rocky Ricketts with his band, The Jet Pilots of Jive.[1] From early on, the band used to appear during the play, with Brian Popay as Rocky. Over time, he became the front man in a full-blown rock and roll extravaganza that involved most of the musicians in Bath.

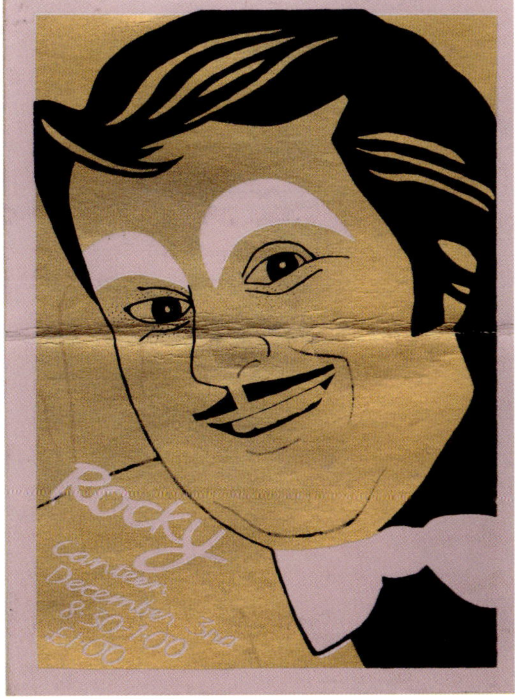


Above: A rare artefact found by Rocky's mum in his sock drawer
L to R: Snakehips Sidebotham, Dave Holland, Rocky, Vince Pube, Sticks Kaminsky

**Brian:** The premise was simple. Rocky, now past the first flush of youth, was having yet another comeback. In the fallow times between the peaks and troughs in rock and roll, he was forced back into his day job as a greengrocer in South Acton, a fantasy based on the real life shop next door to where I was born. Most of Rocky's back story was based around my own. Rocky had seen the green-haired rocker Wee Willie Harris at the Chiswick Empire, something that I, aged 10, had done. He lived in a council house as I had done. In fact, Rocky was a version of me writ larger than life.

---

1. The name was coined by the late John Loder, a Jets Pilots guitar player.

**Micky Godwin:** Someone had the idea of putting the band together and I eagerly signed up as guitarist Brian Damage. The original line up included Johnny (Be Good) Loder and later Pete Allerhand on guitar, Ian Spittal (or Pete Kilgour) on bass, with Chris Hall and later Colin Mansfield as the drummers. Dave Holland played Wurlitzer piano. The ensemble was completed by the fabulous Rockettes as backing singers (of whom more below). Phil was often the

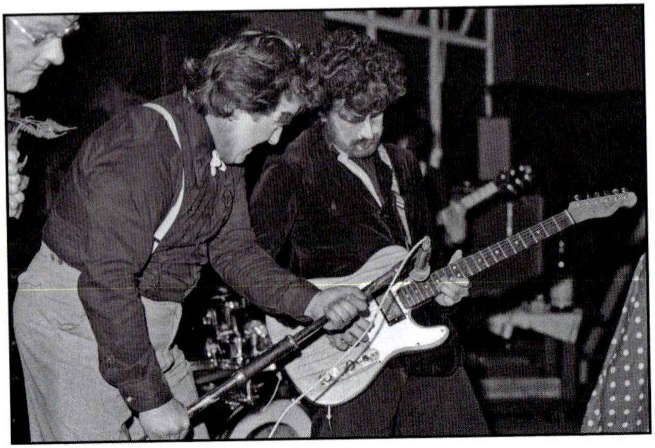

Brian Damage

hippy promoter, on occasion appearing naked but for his mane of auburn hair.

**Micky:** Rocky needed a build up before he came onstage, so my job was to lead the band through a tune (often *Walk, Don't Run*). Vince Pube, Rocky's manager, circulated throughout, flicking dandruff off the Jet Pilots' shoulders with a feather duster, disinfecting Rocky's microphone and generally fussing about. The Rockettes then flounced in with much palaver and shrieking, removing their fur coats and getting

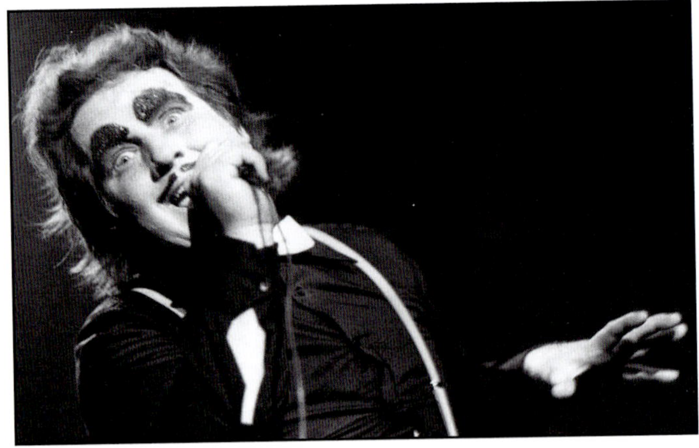

### The entourage
Rocky Ricketts – Brian Popay
Vince Pube, manager – Ralph Oswick
Hippy promoter or bodyguard – Phil Shepherd
Peter Slim, movie star – Mick Banks
Rocky's mum – May Branch (aged 73)
Spider, Teddy-boy bouncer – Paul Lawrence
  and the Fabulous Rockettes (*see below*)

### The band
Brian Damage, guitar – Micky Godwin
Johnny (Be Good) Loder, guitar
Pete Allerhand, guitar
Snakehips Sidebotham, bass guitar – Ian Spittal
Sticks Kaminsky, drums – Colin Mansfield
  (sometimes Chris Hall)
Dave Holland on Wurlitzer piano

### ...and later
Frank Aust, lead guitar
Manny Elias, drums (later drummer with Tears for Fears)
Richard Malandrone, guitar, bass guitar

ready to swoon at the sight of Rocky. The legend himself then burst onto the stage in a blaze of sound and light (looking like Arthur Lowe in a wig wearing Kiss make-up according to one reviewer), and we launched into an old favourite like *Be-Bop-a-Lula*. There were many theatricals throughout, culminating in the finale, a frenetic version of *Gloria*.

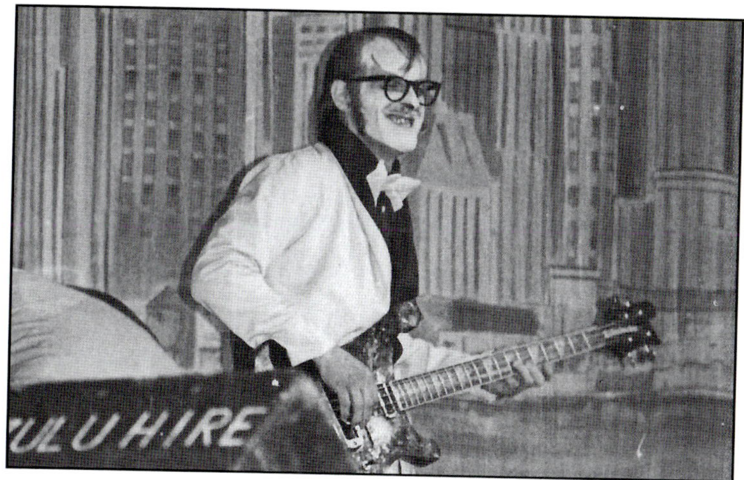

Ian (Snakehips Sidebottom) Spittal

**Ralph:** Vince Pube was Rocky's stage manager and exotic dancer. He of the ludicrously greased quiff and permanently pursed lips, wielder of feather duster and air freshener. Probably offstage he did Rocky's washing and many other menial tasks, but onstage he was definitely in charge. He also handled the 'merch', a revolving sales stand in the foyer, selling tacky mementos like Rocky's old tissues, and the famous Tinkle Tampons (Lil-lets with bells), 'make periods fun again'. Vince took a cut from all Rocky's gigs, but also owned a profitable fibre-glass curtain warehouse in Penge and a mock-Tudor house in Southend where he relaxed between tours.

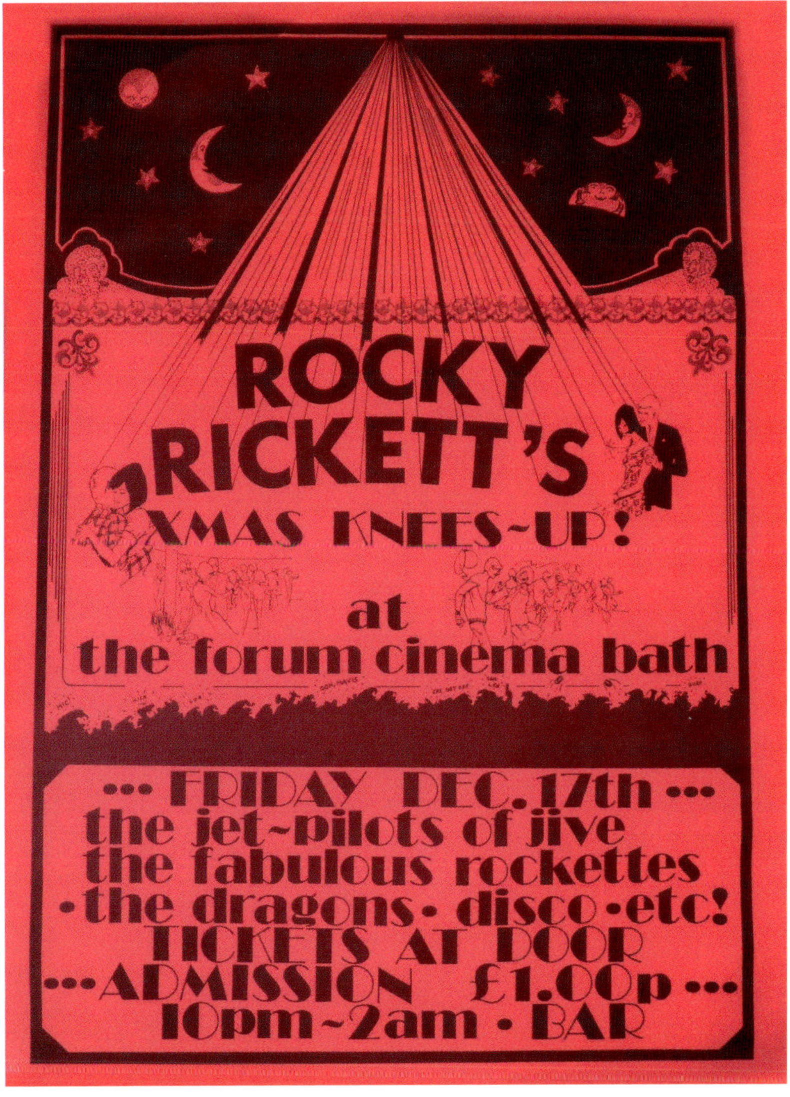


**Tory:** Before I joined the Workshop, we locals often went up to Bath Uni to drink in the (cheap) student bar and see bands play. One night, I stumbled into the main hall where Rocky and the Jets were playing. I was amazed when they burst onto the stage in an explosion of rock and roll. Rocky

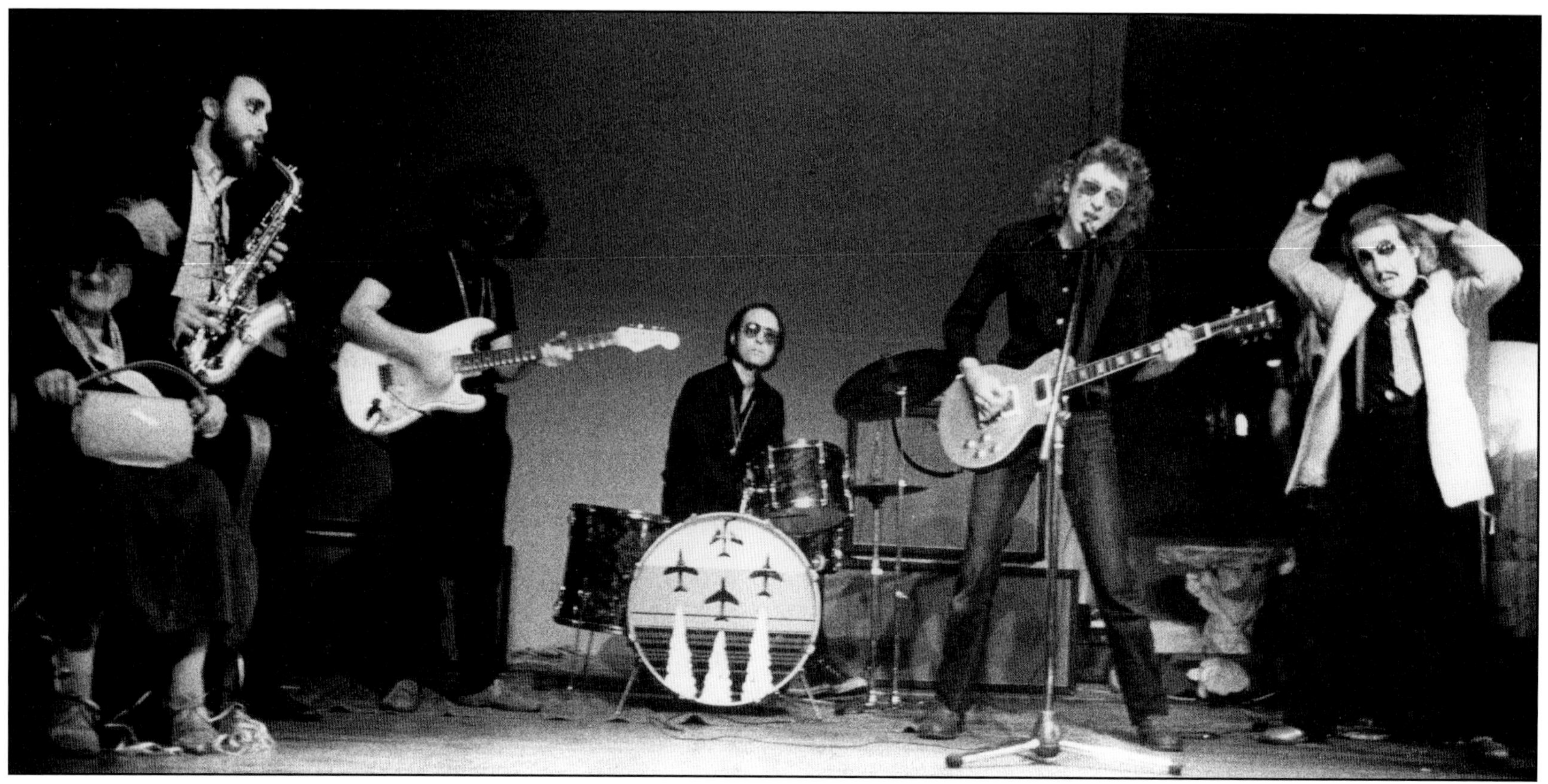

and the musicians wore white make-up and their brows were thickly painted black. Their clothes were mainly black and they wore dark glasses. Their greasy locks hung to their shoulders, they were cool and exciting and so fantastically theatrical and over the top. There was glitter and light everywhere. What a brilliant idea – an aging sleazy rock star makes a comeback – it poked fun at the narcissistic ways of the rock bands of the time, as well as being a fantastically high energy show.

Above, Rocky's mum (far left) with the band

When the Rockettes came onstage I couldn't believe my eyes. They flounced on wearing cheap fur coats and red polka-dot dresses with full skirts and pointy false boobs. They had massively backcombed beehives and were plastered with extreme make-up – huge glittery red lips and thick turquoise eye shadow. Their lower lashes were clownishly painted-on thick black lines. They shrieked and had fag packets tucked into their bras and stockings and swigged from bottles of beer. They were flagrantly sexy and raucous but – most thrilling of all – they were girls like me showing off and acting outrageously in the midst of a full-blown rock and roll show.

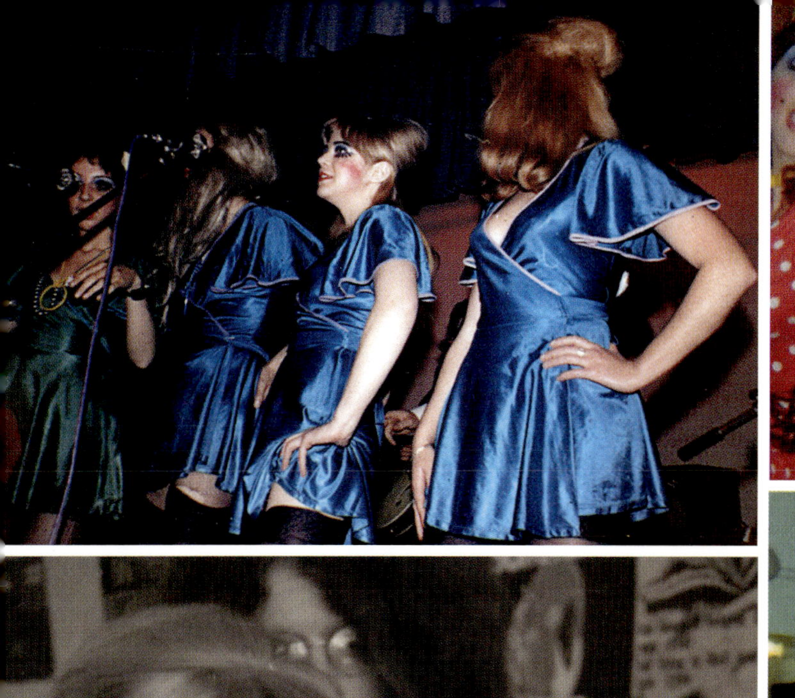
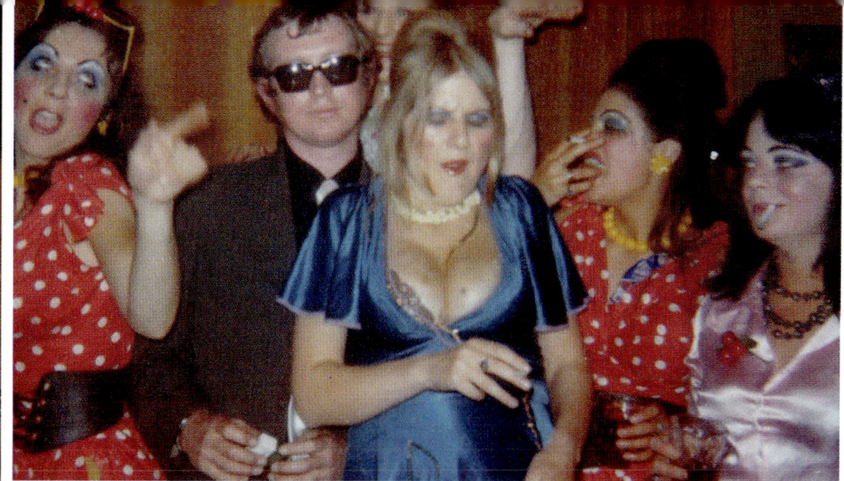
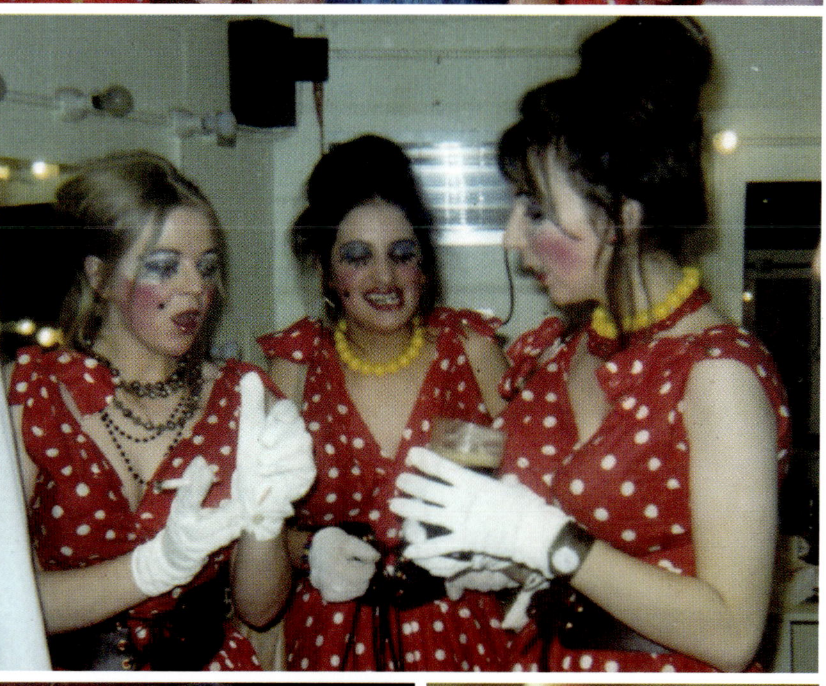
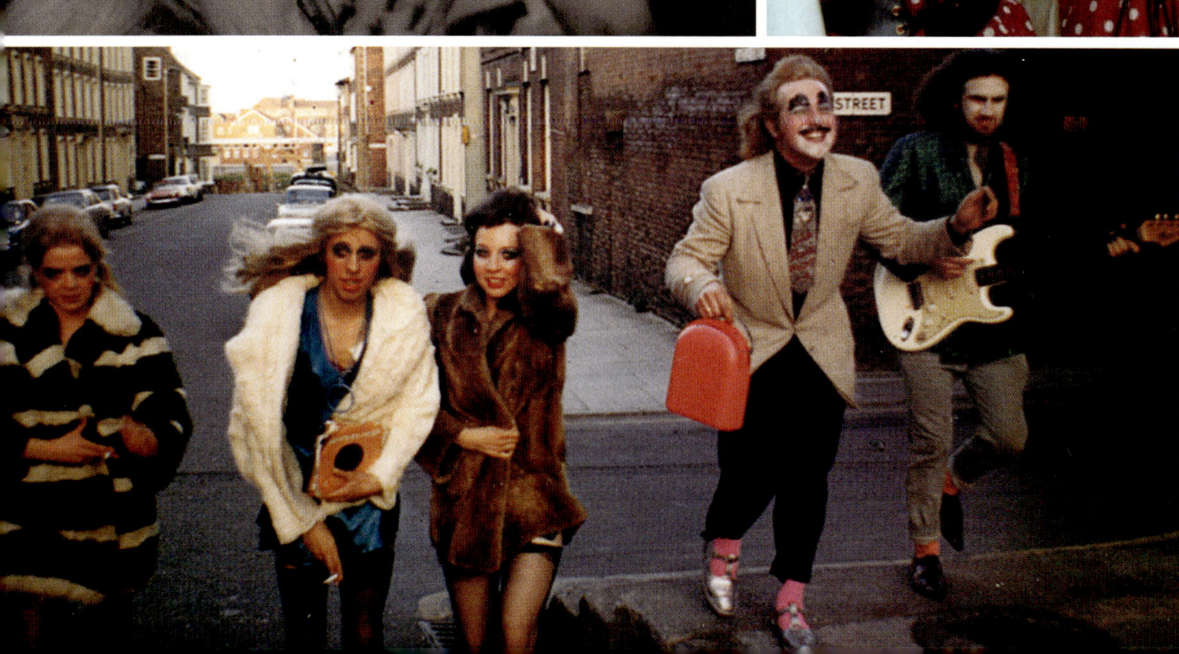
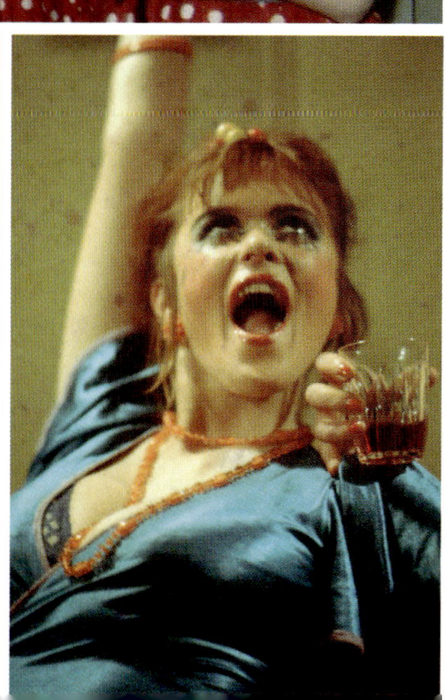
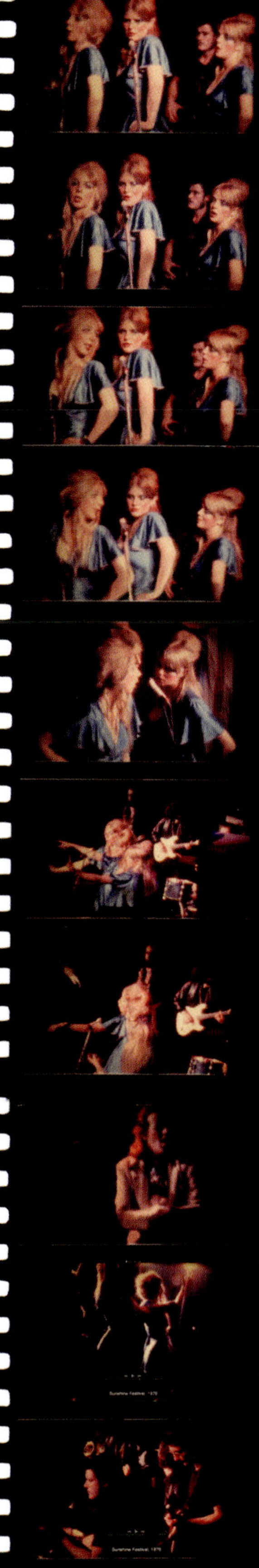

**Jennie:** The Rockettes' original outfits were shiny turquoise mini dresses from Etam with a pink trim, which we later wore for the second half of the show. But my favourites were the red and white polka-dotted rock 'n' roll dresses. Penny and I spent an evening making foam cones to go inside the tops to give us pointy boobs. We wore stiff net petticoats beneath our full skirts, wide silver belts, and bright yellow plastic stud earrings and bead necklaces. The look was completed with black fishnet stockings, suspenders and stilettos from the jumble that we sprayed with silver paint.

There were so many shows and I loved, loved doing them. Getting ready the dressing room was total chaos. Every surface was littered with tubes of *Spot-Lite Klear*, thick stage make-up of orange hue, plus glitter (that spilled everywhere), sticks of red and white face paint, and deep blue for our eyeshadow. And cheap hair spray applied until our beehives were stiffened nests of tangled hair. Once I grabbed the hairspray and smothered my hair, before realising it was the silver spray paint. I had to carry on regardless knowing that the hot stage lights were doing a grand job of hardening the paint. It took hours of pain-staking detangling with a comb and solvent to get it out.

Upon leaving the dressing room, we all stayed in character until we got back. I remember so clearly the moment before going out onto the stage – the sheer joy of knowing that everyone would have a great time. A moment when the mind went blank... then we stepped out and were different people.

**Micky:** The Rocky Show quickly got gigs in and around Bath and Bristol. In 1972, Rocky arrived by helicopter (courtesy of Charlie Ware) to his performance at Widcombe Manor during **The Other Festival**. The following year at **Another Festival** we played in one of the festival geodesic domes, and with saxophonist **Lol Coxhill** to a packed crowd at the Theatre Royal. At the time, we

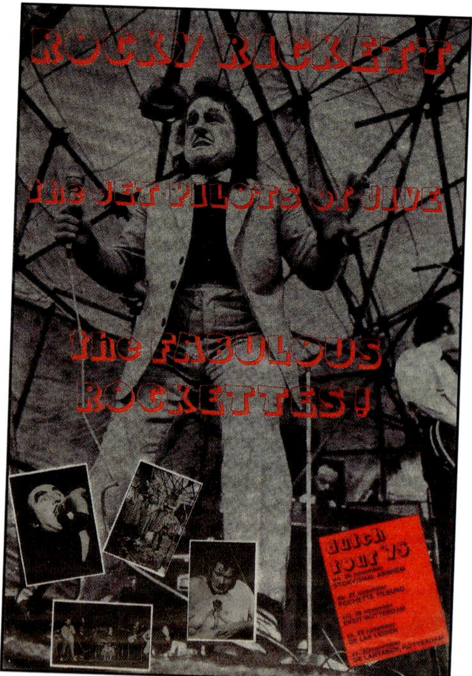

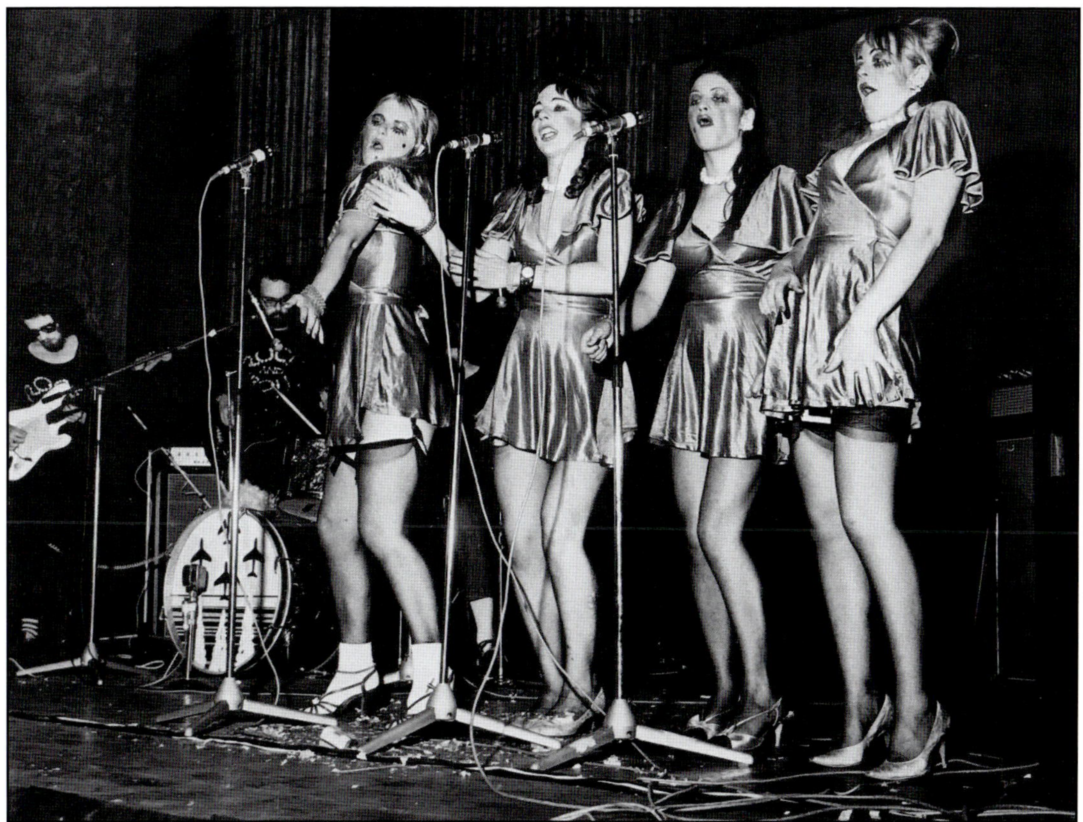

had developed links with the De Lantaren arts centre in Rotterdam and while there in 1973, we played our first open-air concert which was broadcast live on TV. Rocky's 73-year-old mum appeared onstage in that show, as she often did in those early days. We toured frequently in the Netherlands after that. At one gig in the far-out and groovy Melkweg club in Amsterdam, a stoned audience fled in terror from a show involving strobes and naval distress flares.

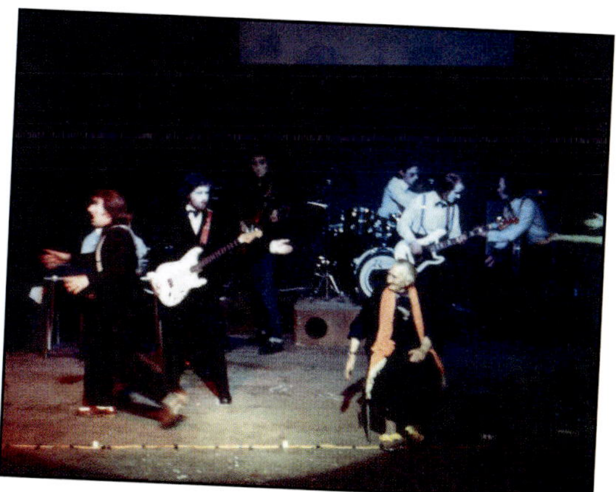

**Rocky's playlist**
Be-Bop-A-Lula
Blue Suede Shoes
Chapel of Love (Rockettes)
Dream Lover
20 Flight Rock
Hound Dog
Love Potion No. 9
Poison Ivy
Get your Kicks on Route A46
(not 66!)
Shakin' All Over
Sisters (Rockettes)
Something Else
That's Alright Mama
The Wanderer
Walk Don't Run
Willie & the Hand Jive
You Really Got Me
Gloria (always the final number)

**Jets' intro numbers**
Telstar
Walk, don't run
Wipe Out

Above: Theatre Royal
Left: Rocky's mum (May)
at De Lantaren

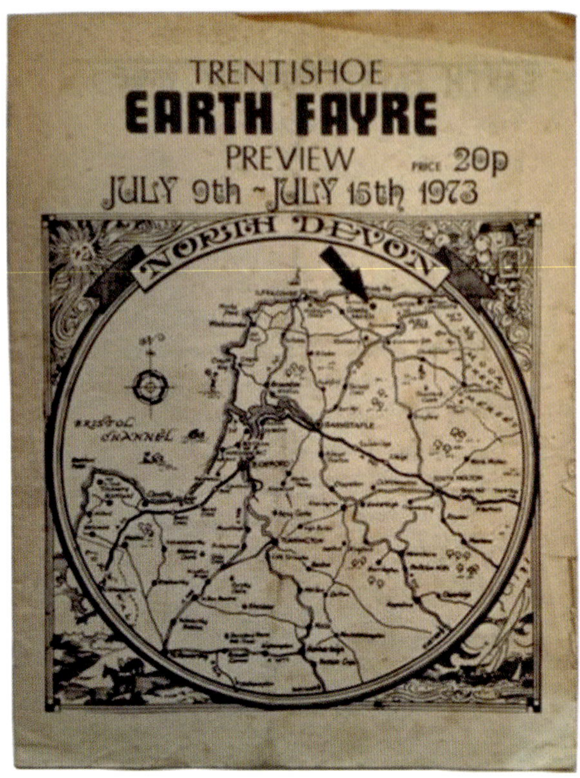



**Pink Fairies roadie, Boss Goodman** wrote about the gig on a free festival website (possibly tripping): The Bath Arts Workshop supplied us with a show called Rocking Ricky & the Ricochets and the something and something who I couldn't begin to describe… but they did bring on three dancing, gum-chewing, going-to-be rock girls who were dynamite… [we] followed these three polka-dotted wonders off the stage, over the wall, across a field, past a hot dog van, and eventually to their truck where we peered through the windows… [At which point Ralph appeared and chased them away].

**Corinne:** As the show progressed and developed, we added more stage effects and theatrics to the songs and the production took on a more surreal tone. Mick Banks painted

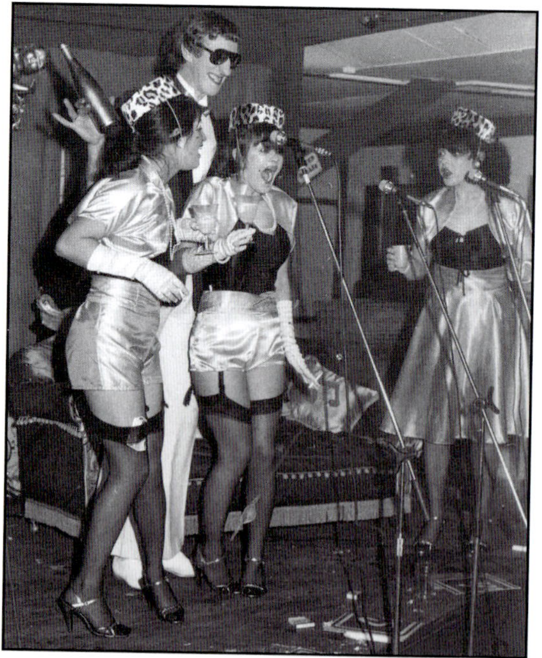

New outfits and champagne

**Micky:** At Trentishoe Free Festival in Devon (1973), we appeared on the bill with then-famed bands like Chilli Willi, Hawkwind and The Pink Fairies. When Rocky exploded into *Blue Suede Shoes,* the whole crowd went wild. I got so carried away that I broke a string during a solo in *Dream Lover* (at the point where the ghost of Eddie Cochran appeared). The show ground to a halt while I went to change the string. A poet took to the stage during this interval, until Rocky barged him off the stage and crashed into an extended version of *Gloria.* Later, a complaint was made about the noise which eventually resulted in the police escorting Rocky off the field as he called out to his fans to write to him in prison.

hula hoops fluorescent pink and made invisible harnesses so that the Rockettes could gyrate without dropping them. He designed and made an enormous fluorescent champagne bottle which he flew in for *Love Potion No 9*. It poured out a stream of polystyrene granules which showed up remarkably well under UV lighting, (obviously we'd never use those now!) During *Dream Lover* he flew in winged, guitar-strumming cherubs that Ralph had fashioned out of large baby dolls. By then, little Frankie Aust had joined as a guitarist. He was so tiny that Rocky could pick him up and spin him round while he carried on playing guitar riffs.

> **Corinne:** In the mid-70s, we made new Rockette outfits. I visited that wonderful theatrical supplier, Borovick's of Soho, and found some bright yellow, black polka dot, shiny, UV-sensitive material to replace the red ones. For the second half, I designed bright pink satin boleros with circular wraparound skirts that we flung off at some point to reveal pink satin shorts worn over black lace corsets that I'd found in a mail offer in the *News of the World*. All topped off with pink satin pillbox hats trimmed with fake leopard-skin velvet. I trimmed Rocky's jacket lapels with the leftover leopard-skin, too.

**Ralph:** Mid-show, Vince ran a raffle that involved various desirable luxury prizes including a 'candlelit dinner for two' – two candles, a packet of frozen burgers and some hard-boiled eggs. Once I forgot to boil the eggs and I didn't bother after that, especially at local Bath gigs. Boys in the front row became adept at catching them and lobbing them back at Vince with obvious results. Mick's impossibly

debonair movie star, Peter Slim, appeared onstage to pluck the raffle tickets from a bag and hand out prizes to unsuspecting winners, but more often Vince simply chucked them directly into the audience.

**Mick Banks:** During this phase, Ralph hit on a brilliant fix that gave the show further instant, if at times surreal, razzamatazz. He discovered a theatrical costumiers with a large selection of lurid stage backcloths, deliverable direct to the venue by British Road Services. As a result the Jets found themselves playing on the Champs-Elysées or in the middle of Times Square after dark, or on the deck of Sinbad's pirate ship, or half way up a beanstalk, depending on the vagaries of what was available on the day of dispatch.

Before the show and during the interval, Pete King and Chris Peecock ran a disco kitted out in extravagant female regalia.

> **Chris Peecock:** touring with the Rocky Ricketts show was … indescribable. I couldn't believe my luck. I was swanning around the UK, Germany and the Netherlands performing in awful tacky drag as DJ before the main show, and actually getting paid for it.

**Tory:** It's hard to describe how powerful a character Rocky was. I remember watching Brian before the show and sensing a build-up of intense energy and concentration – he seemed to withdraw from himself and visibly become another person. By the time he was ready he spoke, breathed

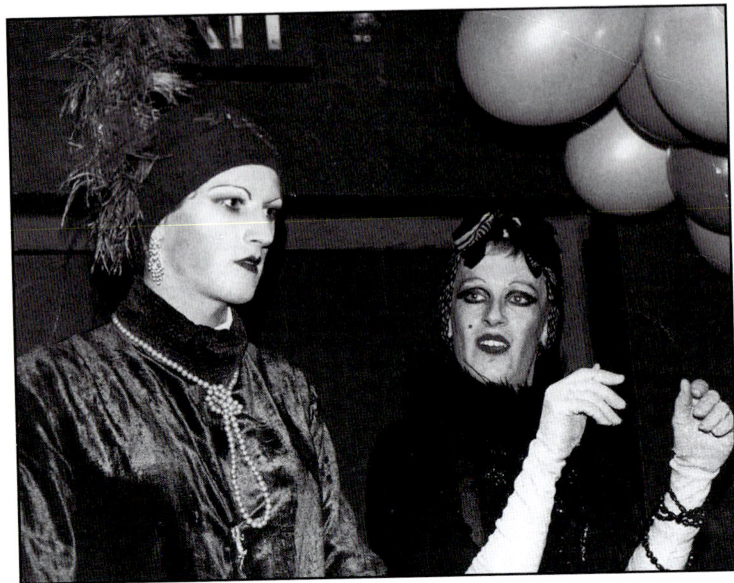

Pete and Chris

and was Rocky. Once onstage, this energy was maintained throughout, along with his vicious satirical improvisations between songs, often targeted at the audience and the vanities and delusions of the druggy/mystical aspects of hippie culture.

The real madness always reached its peak with *Gloria*, which Rocky dubbed a 'social comment' number. It built up to a frenzied climax, involving strobe lights and a long instrumental section. Rocky often ripped Vince's shirt to shreds and he (Vince) ended up 'vomiting' blood and collapsing onstage while the Rockettes also flailed about on the floor, having taken their dresses off and undergone an onstage freak out. On occasion Vince even crowd-surfed, hovering sweaty and bare-chested above the audience.

One (unknown) journalist reviewed Rocky's album, recorded live at Bath Pavilion. He wrote: During *Gloria*, Rocky attempted to 'liberate' the audience by asking them to strip, led by Vince, who promptly got shot for being ugly, all to a pleasant backing session from the band, who eventually remembered they were supposed to be playing *Gloria*. The encore was Led Zeppelin's *Communication Breakdown*, but after six bars Rocky stopped the band saying, 'Next year, next year it's progressive'.

### The album – *Rocky, Live at the Pav*

**Brian:** Our album was recorded live on New Year's Eve 1975 at the Pavilion, and labelled 'stereo enhanced to mono'. Only 200 copies were ever made but in the meantime the album attained cult status, so much so that in 2007 a CD was made to ensure its longevity. Recording was by Dave Lord (Avon Recording Services) and the album was released on the Crescent Label in early 1976.

**Tory:** The show was gloriously chaotic but the musicians and the band were great – without their solid musical base the show wouldn't have worked so effectively (or at all). Yvonne Hellin was a Rockette for a while. She had a great singing voice and brought some real class to the backing vocals. We Rockettes practised in between shows, to get the timing and sound of the backing *bob-she-wop-bops* right. Here is *Bath Chronicle* journalist Simon Kinnersley reviewing **Live at the Pav**: 'The problem of transferring the spirit of the show to a record is obvious but on the whole it works well, thanks largely to Rocky's personality, with his raw asides and dry

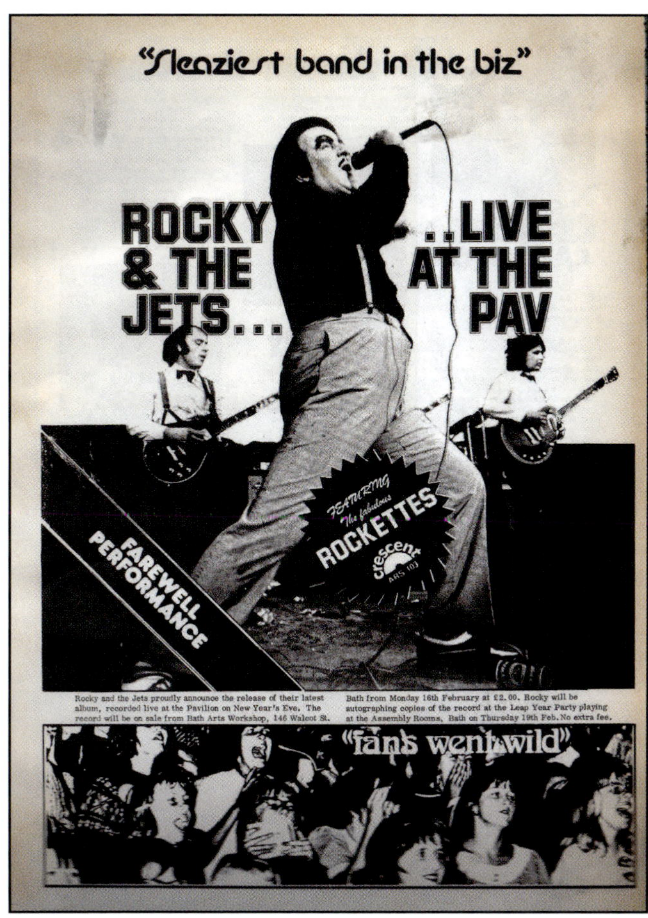



Rocky and the Jets proudly announce the release of their latest album, recorded live at the Pavilion on New Year's Eve. The record will be on sale from Bath Arts Workshop, 146 Walcot St. Bath from Monday 16th February at £2.00. Rocky will be autographing copies of the record at the Leap Year Party playing at the Assembly Rooms, Bath on Thursday 19th Feb. No extra fee.

humour. And when all's said and done he's a pretty useful singer. The opener *Poison Ivy* is a gas, with Rocky jerking off the lyrics menacingly, murky guitar battering away and sharp vocal bursts from the Rockettes'. And then on to *Gloria*: 'Suddenly it picks up… and unexpectedly it reaches a great high, with an acidic liberation rap from Rocky and some really spiteful guitar underneath winding up to some

head battering chords at the end… As far as I can tell… apart from the unlikely screams at the beginning (of the album) there's been no over-dubbing, leaving it how it should be – ruff 'n' raw![2]

The Rocky Show played on through the years, Bridgwater, Bristol Poly and The Granary in Bristol, Chippenham, Exeter, Oxford Poly, The Roundhouse and Dingwalls Club in Camden, once at the Institute of Contemporary Arts, and all over the Netherlands. But the Bath gigs were always the best. Our local fans had lived through the evolution of the band, they'd seen Rocky arrive by helicopter in 1972, they'd rocked in the aisles at the Theatre Royal, and we'd played at every one of our summer festivals, culminating in a massive concert on the Walcot burial field in 1976. In Bath we knew

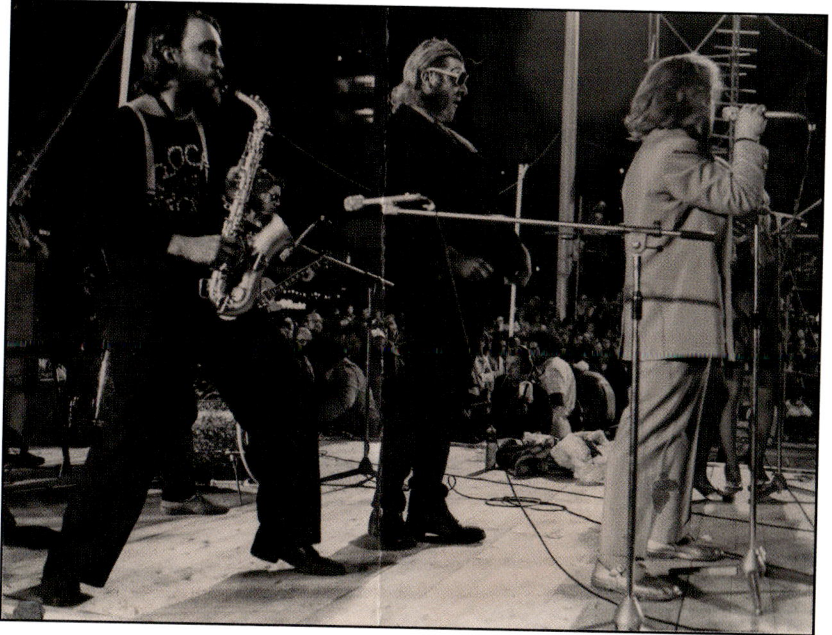

2. Simon Kinnersley, *Bath & West Evening Chronicle*, 12 February 1976

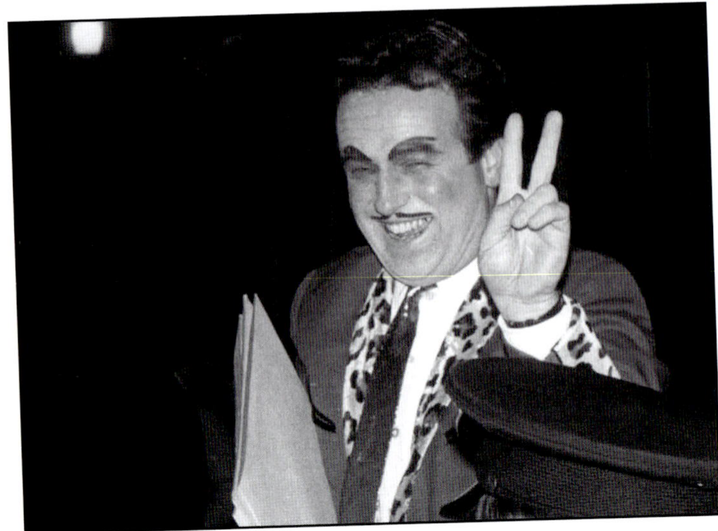

our audience well and there was a sense of everyone playing along with the fantasy of a comeback, the intense hype of Rocky's arrival, the squawking flirty Rockettes, the hysteria surrounding the ridiculously cheap glamour, the cheering fans. It was a kind of collective parodic performance in which everyone played their part. The show came to an end when Rocky finally retired in 1979 and went to live with his mum in Slough. His alter-ego, Brian, for a short time fronted a psychedelic rock band **P.G. Trips**, before going on to found his own street theatre company **Fine Artistes**.

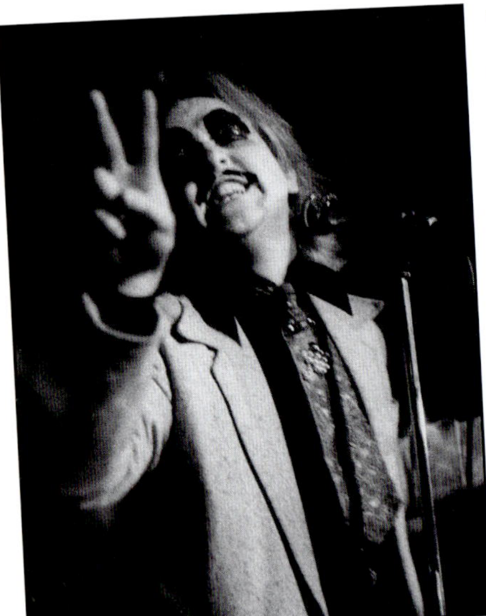

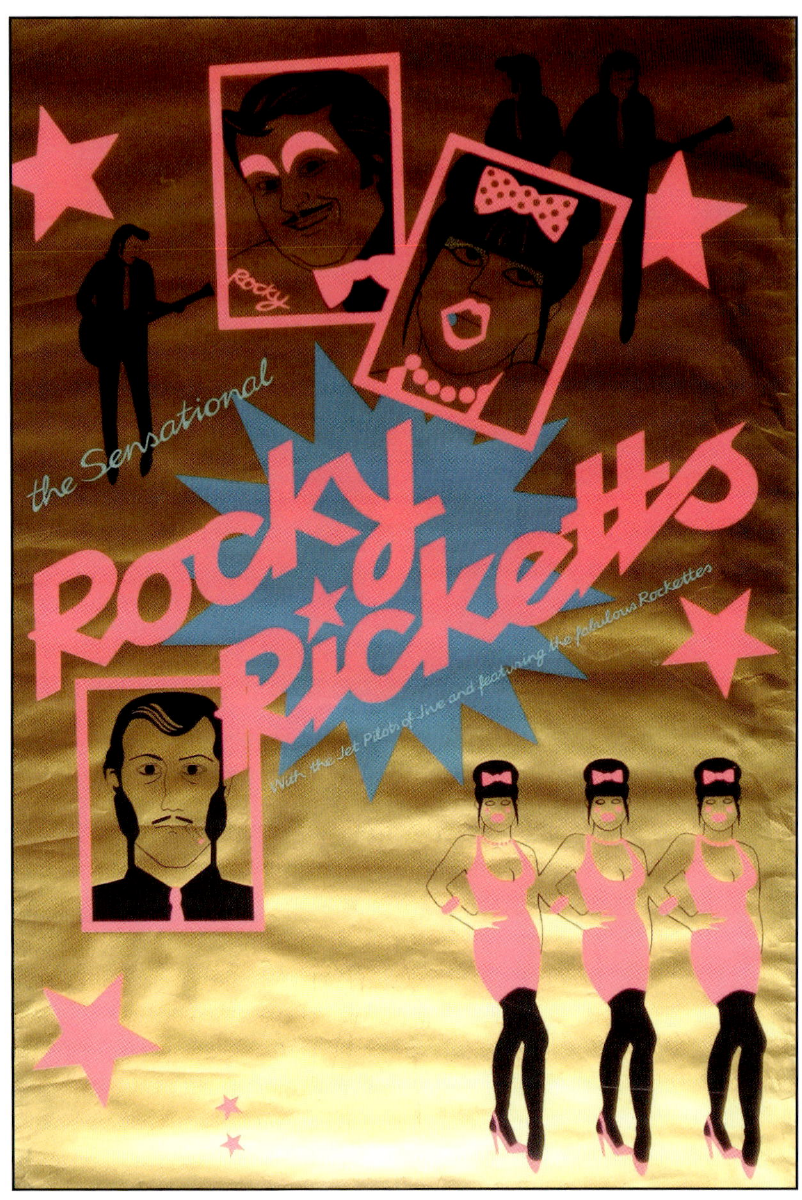


Another rare artefact found by Rocky's mum in the bottom of his shoe tidy.

## Flaming Star Club, Rotterdam[3]

One of the most bizarre gigs we ever played was on the docks in Rotterdam in 1973. We accepted the offer to play because the fee was much higher than usual. When we arrived at the club the owner, a 15-stone giant of a man, greeted us with a massive Alsatian on a heavy metal chain. His opening gambit was 'We have many bands here and if we don't like them we throw them into the river, ha ha!'

The club was a kind of cellar at ground level, housed in a storage space with a road above it. The entrance was painted off-white and appeared to have blood stains on the walls. Once inside we were greeted by a surreal scene: the club was roughly square-shaped, with the bar in the middle, staffed by a mean-looking character with a scar across one cheek. The walls were decorated with large black and white photos of Elvis, Buddy Holly, Eddie Cochrane etc. A woman drummer occupied an alcove on a high platform, drumming along to whatever rock and roll record was playing on the juke

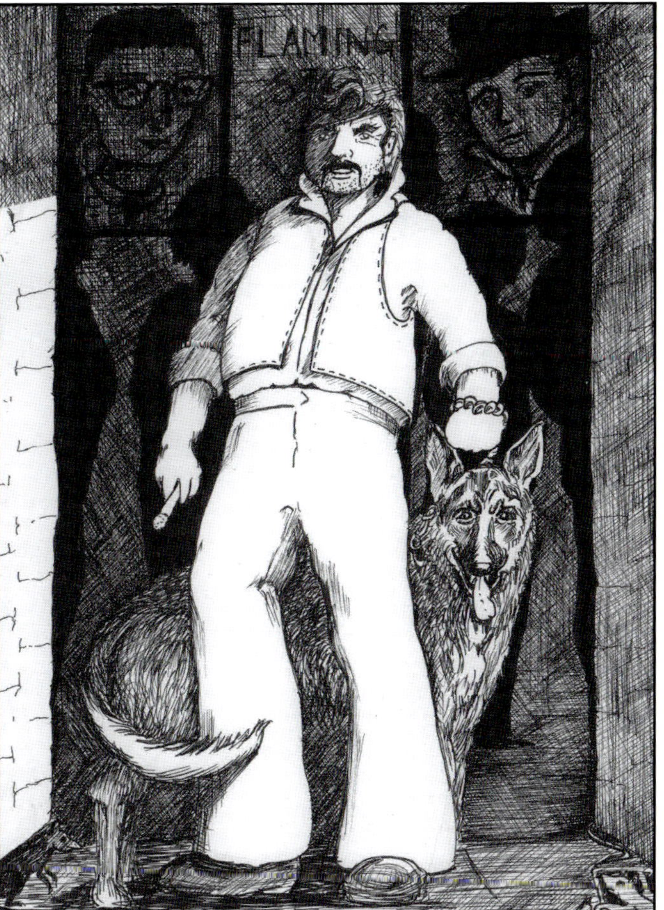



box, creating a beat-heavy sound that filled the air in a very weird way.

We changed in a minute room where the owner kept a freezer cabinet, before heading onto the stage that would have comfortably taken a solo act, but was tiny for a band with nine people plus drum kit and amps. It was crazy! As the room started to fill up, our 'bodyguards' – Phil Shep, Phil Oates, Nasher and Dave Digby stood resolute and expressionless in their leathers and sunglasses, before a distinctly intimidating crowd of men and women who eyed us with suspicion.

The response wasn't ecstatic but the club owner loved us, thank God. Trays of beers appeared and he applauded every number with gusto. We were all pretty tense and uncomfortable and were glad to reach the end of the show in one piece. As we were leaving, the owner gave us a huge wad of Dutch guilders – it was by far the biggest fee we were ever paid.

---

3. Writing by Jennie and John Loder.

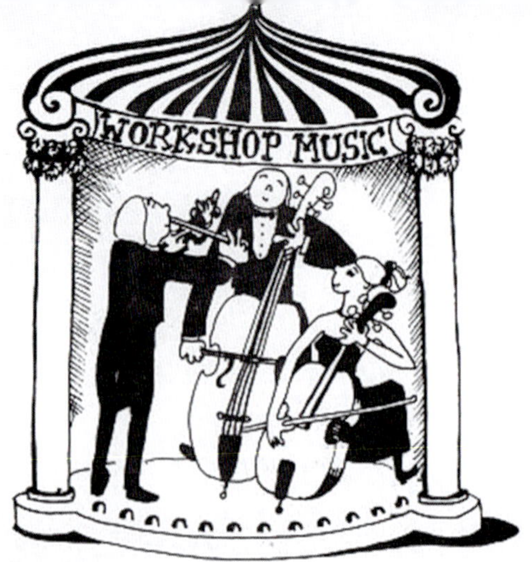


# WORKSHOP MUSIC 1972-77

**R**ick Knapp: We created Workshop Music in the early days of BAW, putting on rock concerts and gigs to fund our other activities, albeit with varying success. By 1973, we had somehow managed to raise enough cash to buy a 200-watt Carlsboro PA system and some decent Shure microphones and these were used for just about everything, including the early Rocky and the Jets gigs. We also hired out equipment to local bands and DJs. We did some local gigs which usually involved musicians living in Bath. Guitarist Pete Kilgour was always ready to do a gig, as were Ian Spittal and Colin Mansfield (Jet Pilots band members). We put on gigs with them and the band Drusilla and eventually the Rocky Ricketts show; but not having any money it was difficult to do much, although we used The Hat & Feather and Langridge Village Hall on Lansdown a lot.

**Rick:** In those early days I used to transport and set up the 200-watt Carlsboro PA. At one early Rocky gig, I also had a tape loop Watkins copycat with me. I think it was a village hall somewhere – in Freshford maybe. Suddenly I realised there was a natural reverb in the hall that fed Rocky's vocals into the Watkins and tuned it to the same reverb. The whole place went into 'wap-wap' mode. Gratifyingly, the audience responded enthusiastically.

Nicky Millican was one of our first promoters. She had some good contacts and was influential lining up the bands for Cleveland Circus, with Global Village Trucking Company and Hawkwind being the main ones. We also put on some big concerts in 1974. Sarah Acheson (then in her early 20s) stage-managed Cockney Rebel and Bebop Delux at Bath Pavilion, as well as a celebrated Roxy Music gig at the Theatre Royal (which Charlie Ware still owned at the time). Other big-name bands booked by Workshop Music were Motorhead and AC/DC.

**Phil adds:** We organised these big concerts with very little experience and

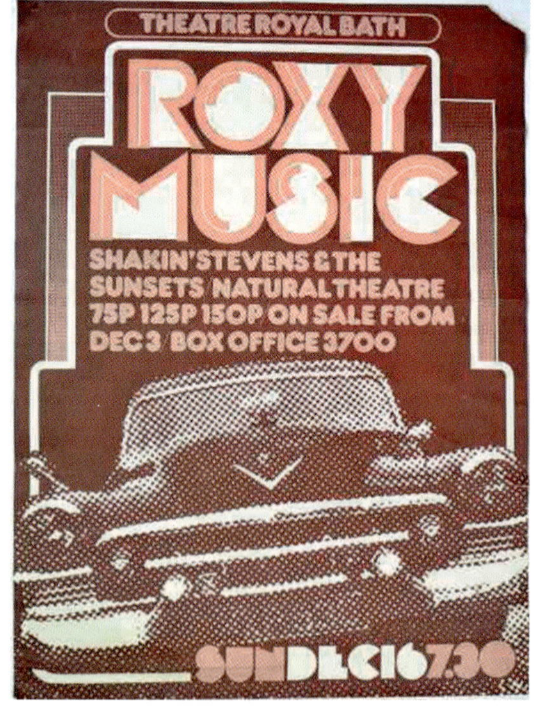

virtually no cash so inevitably our plans went awry sometimes. In 1974,we booked Captain Beefheart to play at Colston Hall, Bristol. In those days, bands tended to arrive onstage hours later than advertised, and audiences were equally used to waiting. On that night, the band called just before they were due onstage to say they wouldn't play until paid in full. We managed to cajole the box office into giving us the £600 fee (far more than we could ever get our hands on in those days) and hotfooted it to Beefheart's motel in Rick's van. We silently counted the cash out in their darkened room and the concert went ahead.

### Surprise skills

**Penny:** Our music promotion (and in fact all our activities) presented opportunities to learn new skills and gain experience in unexpected areas. I was at a BAW meeting when someone asked, 'Who's going to do the electrics for the shows and the festival?' It turned out to be me. Starting one gig at a time, learning about lighting and sound equipment, I graduated to doing a whole tour of the Netherlands, arriving at new venues every day, including the famous Milky Way club in Amsterdam. This involved meeting the technician in each venue, adding our lights to theirs, sorting sound and playback and sourcing dry ice, all in an afternoon. Then for the performance, doing all the cues from an unfamiliar box backstage each night. I remember the lighting dimmers at the Milky Way were brown Bakelite, Frankenstein-like electrical devices, with antique winding handles, instead of the usual sliding dimmer controls.

For a couple of the festivals, I co-ordinated all the power, lighting and electrics with the help of a brilliant co-worker, Phil Robinson. He did all the sums for the amps, volts and watts to make sure nothing shorted or blew up. For the 1974 *Last Festival,* Phil and I towed a massive Perkins 30 KVA, three-phase generator from one big top site to another and wired up power leads to stages and the lighting tower. We used mattocks to dig in the armoured cable for the generator, hammered in a huge metal earth stake and started it up with a great roar and chuff of diesel fumes. We set up equipment and dimmers high above the rehearsing bands on the scaffold lighting tower. We worked out lighting plans. Then in the evening shows, switched and faded lights up and down and pointed follow spots onto the amazing live performers. Taking it all down again in the rain and dark was not so much fun. But it was surprising to find I could do such things, and I was only 19 at the time.

### Passing shows

**Penny:** Booking and managing rock concerts was one element of the whole (mainly a lot of hard grind) but another wonderful strand of our musical life arose from doing Rocky show gigs, which gave us the opportunity to cross paths with all sorts of amazing bands and musicians. Often, we only realised in retrospect how close we were to future rock stars. My very first gig was a Rocky show at Chippenham Neeld Hall. We shared backstage with an unusual, even more glittery and startling band than our own. It turned out to be Roxy Music. They were new to us, and everyone else that Saturday night – but not for long. They were touring their sell-out first album, released in June 1972. We worked in iconic London venues like the Roundhouse in Chalk Farm and the Rainbow in Finsbury Park, supporting bands like Hawkwind. We did the Rocky show on a wind-blown clifftop site in Devon and at the Trentishoe Festival, with the Pink Fairies.

The **Natural Theatre Company** was often booked to provide a theatrical element to music and other gigs. In the summer of 1974, the Rockettes spent an evening working with Ronnie Lane (of the Small Faces) when his touring, big top *Passing Show* stopped at a nearby town. On that occasion, we Rockettes introduced Ronnie and the band to our favourite drink which was port and lemon (they said they loved it!). We worked in the audience as Normals at an Arthur Brown gig and again with Roxy Music at the Theatre Royal in Bath, where the Rocky Show also shared the bill with Shakin' Stevens and the Sunsets.

Often, musicians played in vans on the way to gigs for our entertainment and joined in at rehearsals for our own shows. *Mike Westbrook* and *Lol Coxhill* were among many brilliant musicians who appeared with us regularly or overlapped at the same events.

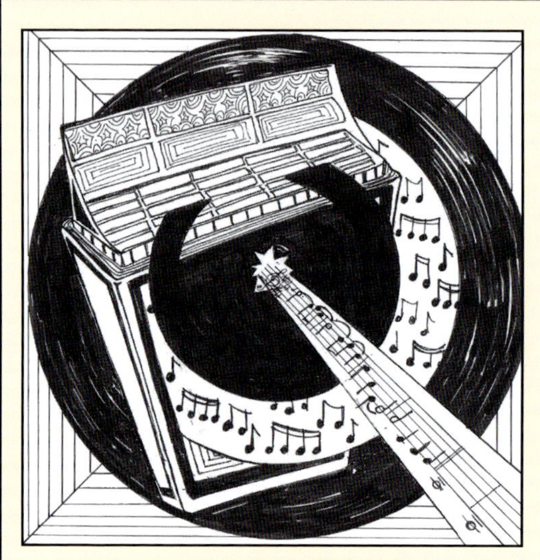

There were loads more 45rpm records or 'singles' in the record charts in those days. Each time they were played on the jukebox, they were logged by the machine. Records repeatedly chosen, or ignored, were retained or deleted by the company who serviced the jukebox, effectively creating a pub playlist.

## Always a soundtrack

**Penny:** There was always a soundtrack to our lives via vinyl records and the jukebox in The Hat & Feather. It's strange to remember now that all our music, apart from at live events and some radio, was listened to via vinyl records. There were no personal playlists on demand in those days, so listening to what you really wanted to hear was rarer. You'd have to wait for a song to be chosen by someone on a jukebox. Buying a whole album was a serious move, equivalent to £20-25 today, and our wages were rock bottom. So we all had favourites we'd saved up for.

I remember leaving home when I was just 18, to go and live in a big shared flat with several others from the Workshop. I took very few things with me, but the most precious were the albums, probably 10 or so, and Joni Mitchell's *Blue* was number one for me at the time. At parties round Bath in the early 1970s the Rolling Stones album, *Let it Bleed,* was bound to be played at some point, but others like Velvet Underground, The Doors, Bob Dylan,

**Songs from The Hat & Feather jukebox, circa 1974**

Alice Cooper - Elected
Argent - Hold Your Head Up
Atomic Rooster - Tomorrow Night
Bachman-Turner Overdrive - You Ain't Seen Nothing Yet
Black Sabbath - Paranoid
David Bowie - Drive in Saturday
         - Jean Genie
         - Life on Mars
Deep Purple - Black Night
Derek & the Dominoes - Layla
Don McLean - American Pie
The Faces - Stay with Me
Focus - Sylvia
Free - Alright Now
Golden Earring - Radar Love
Hawkwind - Silver Machine
Jefferson Airplane - White Rabbit

Jo Jo Gunne - Run Run Run
Lou Reed - Vicious
Ike & Tina Turner - Nutbush City Limits
Mott the Hoople - Roll Away the Stone
         - All the Young Dudes
Pink Floyd - See Emily Play
Rod Stewart - Maggie May
Roxy Music - Virginia Plain
Rolling Stones - Angie
         - Brown Sugar
         - Tumbling Dice
Steppenwolf - Born to be Wild
10cc - Rubber Bullets
Stevie Wonder - Superstition
Whiskey in the Jar - Thin Lizzie
The Who - Won't Get Fooled Again

Neil Young, Frank Zappa, Pink Floyd and John Lennon were ubiquitous, too.

When we were on tour we shared albums we all liked, which narrowed things down a bit. In 1973, we spent a month working at the De Lantaren arts centre in Rotterdam (see *Chapter 3*). While there, we had an off-duty room where we hung out, cooked breakfast and did office stuff. We listened to Roxy music's second album and Lou Reed's *Transformer* many, many times. Maybe it's a testament to the quality of those two records that they created a soundtrack of those times – one which is still strongly evocative today.

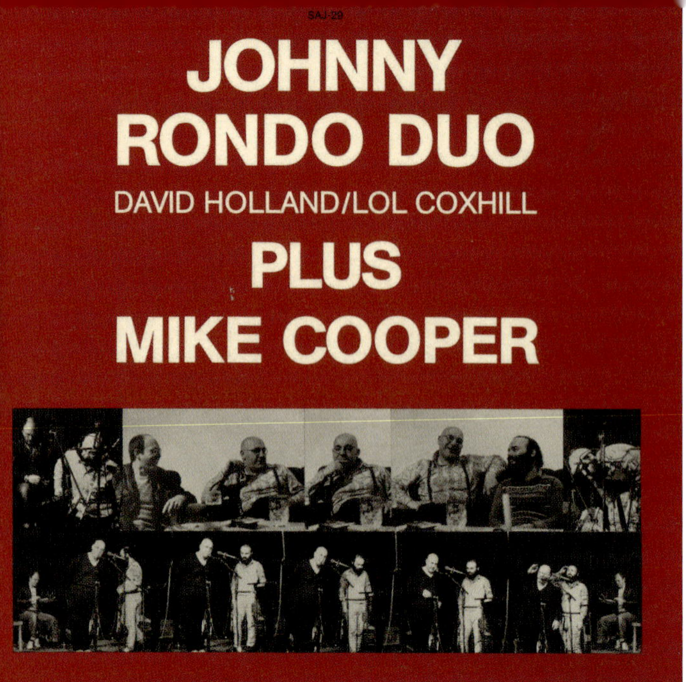



# THE JOHNNY RONDO COMBO BY DAVE HOLLAND

Music flourished during the 70s in Bath and a large number of musicians played together in different combinations. I was in the first cabaret for **Exploded Eye**. I played my Wurlitzer electric piano and the other musicians were Ian Spittal on bass guitar and Colin Mansfield on drums. All of us also played in the Rocky Show. We were the Jet Pilots of Jive, and on occasion we all took on non-musical roles with the Naturals.

I remember one item in the cabaret was an old song called *Hard Hearted Hannah, the Vamp of Savannah*, performed by Caroline Maynard. I changed most of the lyrics to fit the show: '*I'm pleased to meet ya, I'd like to eat ya…*' (She sings to a love who she wants to consume by eating him). Ian made a palm tree out of two sections of plywood, one for the trunk and one for the foliage. We wore adapted white waiters' jackets, with silver Lurex lapels, cuffs and bow ties. Fixed to the back of the tree was a UV light, which accentuated the appearance of our jackets and teeth.

We were the **Johnny Rondo Combo** (I borrowed the name Johnny Rondo from an old cowboy film). The stage wear and palm tree conjured up an image of ocean liners and travel to exotic places, possibly imaginary ones. Continuing into a life independent of **Exploded Eye**, we added guitarist Pete Allerhand, recently returned from another European country. We also accompanied a singer called Felicity Haze, including one very memorable gig at the Longleat restaurant.

**Dave:** I had started visiting Bath in 1971 when I came to see Welfare State perform an outdoor show in the Abbey Churchyard. I worked with them until 1973, based in the north of England. That year, the saxophonist Lol Coxhill also joined and we collaborated on the music. So it seemed natural to invite Lol to play with the Johnny Rondo Combo. We did art college dances, including Cheltenham, and Pete arranged a booking at the Chateau Impney near Droitwich.

I made a discovery one day when listening to the Pump Room Trio, who played 'palm court' music to accompany conversation and the consumption of tea and cakes at the Pump Room next to the Roman baths. Although the trio (piano, violin and cello) played selections of light classical music, I was surprised to notice one day 'Oh, now they are playing *Summer Holiday*'. This gave me the idea that if the music sounded right on the instruments, you could play anything at all.

Over time, I set about composing pieces to suit this idea. In Bath I wrote the *Caucasian Splinter Mystery*. Later in London I wrote *Russian Dance*, which has elements of Hungarian gypsy music, as well as the South American music often called Inca. Whilst in Bath, I remember looking at titles in the JRC repertoire: *Let's Go Away for a While, Do you know the way to San Jose, Western Intrigue, The Somnambulist's Dream, The Waves of Copacabana*, and realised that many reflected the idea of exotic travel referred to above.

This idiosyncratic repertoire was never going to be mainstream anything. However, the concept of world music came about, Latin American music came into vogue and decades after I derived inspiration from the Pump Room Trio, lounge music became a thing, with a kitsch flavour and a strong sense of irony. I pursued this interest further, honing the material, improvising around it and inventing hybrid styles.

Another influence in Bath was the incomparable Gordon Robbins. No one could fail to be delighted by Gordon's generosity of spirit during his cider-fuelled excursions on the piano, for example at the Curfew pub in Cleveland Buildings. His magnificent party piece

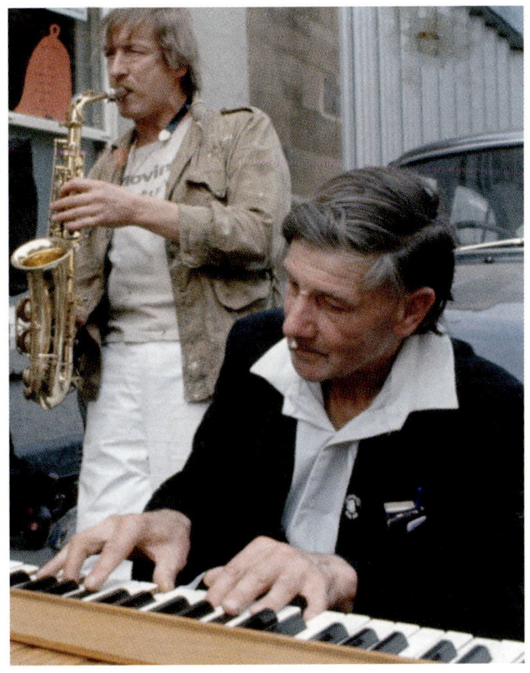

The incomparable Gordon Robbins

was *The Laughing Policeman* but his repertoire was extensive. Lapses of memory never halted the onward flow. Sometimes he would dither about on a few notes and chords whilst deciding what to play next.

In the summer of 1976 during the BAW festival, I recorded an impromptu performance Gordon did in the window of 146 Walcot Street, with **Lol Coxhill** joining him on saxophone, and the barely audible **Colin Wood** on cello. Two summers running, I also performed with Lol at Ladymead House on a bill with Captain Headlam, wowing the elderly lady residents with his concertina, hooter, sea shanties, and bits of business and scurrying about. Colin joined us, too. Other festival venues we did included Parade Gardens, and the Royal Mineral Baths.

At the end of that summer, I moved to London and the **Johnny Rondo Trio** was officially born, Lol, Colin and I making our debut London concert playing 'reading music' at West Norwood public library, followed by the Oval House Theatre Club in Kennington. Included in our repertoire were three tunes Gordon Robbins had played: *My Heart Belongs to Daddy, Bei Mir Bist du Schön* and *The Sun Has Got his Hat on*, alongside tunes from the Bath version of the Combo.

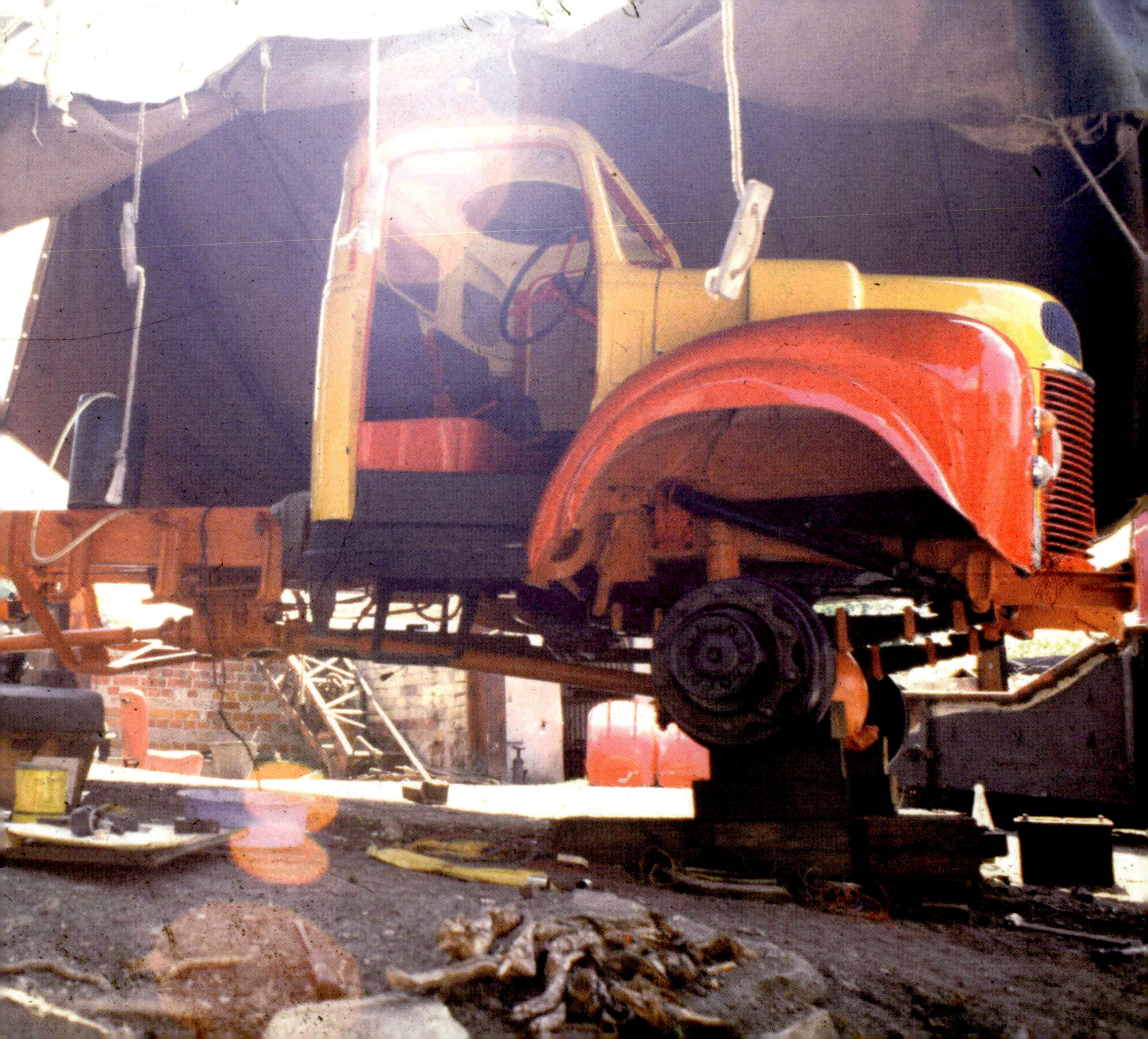

# CHAPTER 6

# COMTEK 1973-79

**The limits of untrammelled economic growth became clear and we became eco-activists and cycling pioneers. We saved Georgian buildings from demolition, reclaimed building materials and explored renewable energy.**

**Thornton:** Glyn Davies and I founded Bath Community Design Workshop in 1973 as an architectural offshoot to Bath Arts Workshop. We began by helping to stop the unwarranted demolition of some fine old buildings. In 1974, we set up an office upstairs at 1a The Paragon and Rick Knapp joined us.[1] Shortly afterwards, we shortened the name to Community Technology and then Comtek.

**Thornton** on life before Bath: 1950s London bomb sites, demolitions, rag and bone men, scrap paper dealing; 1960s toshing and selling sunk Thames dinghies. Culture: Dostoyevsky, ICA, Matisse, Hendrix, Cream, folk, rock. Holiday jobs: dustman, laundry, theatre and film, building (my passion). But after two years in architecture at university, it turned out I lacked the social niceties (wrong family background, chucked out for 'not being a professional man', meritocracy hah). I found myself in Bath, aged 20 in 1970, thinking about what to do. I met Phil… a kindred spirit, cultural nomad, who had the germ of an idea to create an arts hub, which he called Bath Arts Workshop.

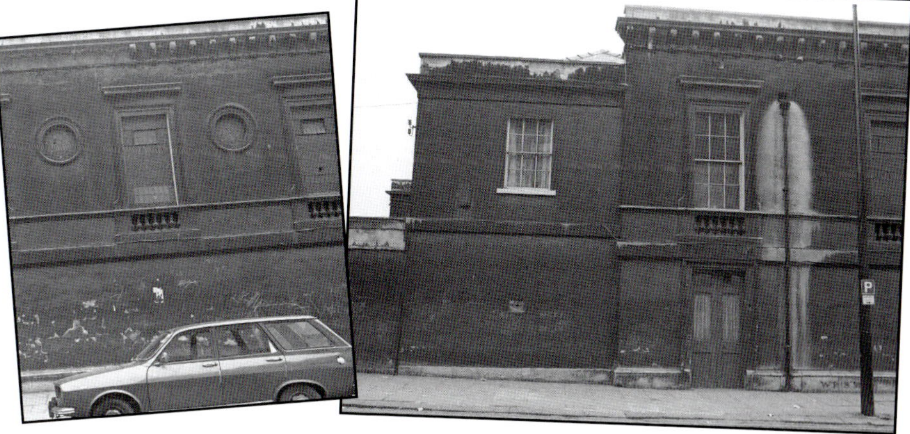

The buildings were black with soot

---

1. Rick had been involved in BAW since 1970 and he held the lease on 1a The Paragon. At the time, it housed our first Workshop shop on the ground floor, which later became Auntie Margaret's Teashop.

**Glyn Davies** arrived via a different path. He had taken on his first post-graduate job for Wiltshire County architect's department in Trowbridge when he and his wife Yve first saw Bath. He writes: Even though the buildings were black with soot, the architecture and its setting made such an impression that we decided to settle here. We became increasingly concerned about the number of historic buildings that were being demolished. Local campaigners against the demolitions included BAW, who had a distinctive way of drawing attention to the issues, through street theatre and other events designed to involve the public, often staged in disused buildings. The campaign to repair and reuse old buildings, instead of replacing them, was an area where I could contribute and I joined Thornton at the Design Workshop that soon became Comtek.

During this early period, we supported the community use of empty buildings and developed Architectural Aid to assist people who were bringing derelict buildings back into use. We provided practical advice and helped with planning permission applications, building regulations and local authority improvement grants. Reclaimed building materials were used, not only for cost reasons, but also to match the original buildings.

## Comtek depot

**Thornton:** On 2 August 1974, Rick Knapp and Phil Shepherd signed a three-year lease for a range of run-down buildings previously occupied by the former seed merchants, Woodbridge's that, by 1974, was owned by the kindly Roy Harper of Harper Furnishings. The buildings spanned the riverside at the end of Weymouth and Bedford

Right: Weymouth Street depot

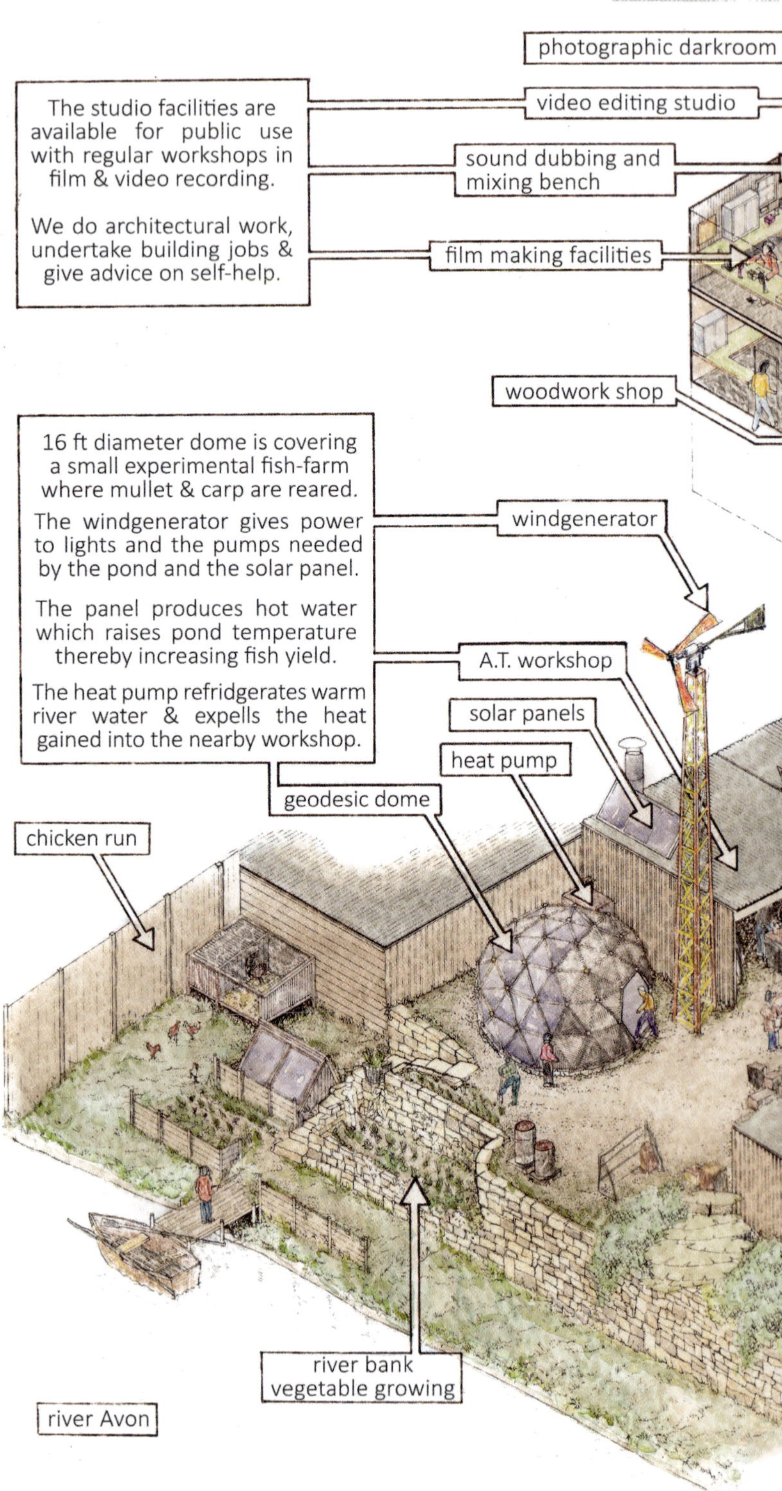

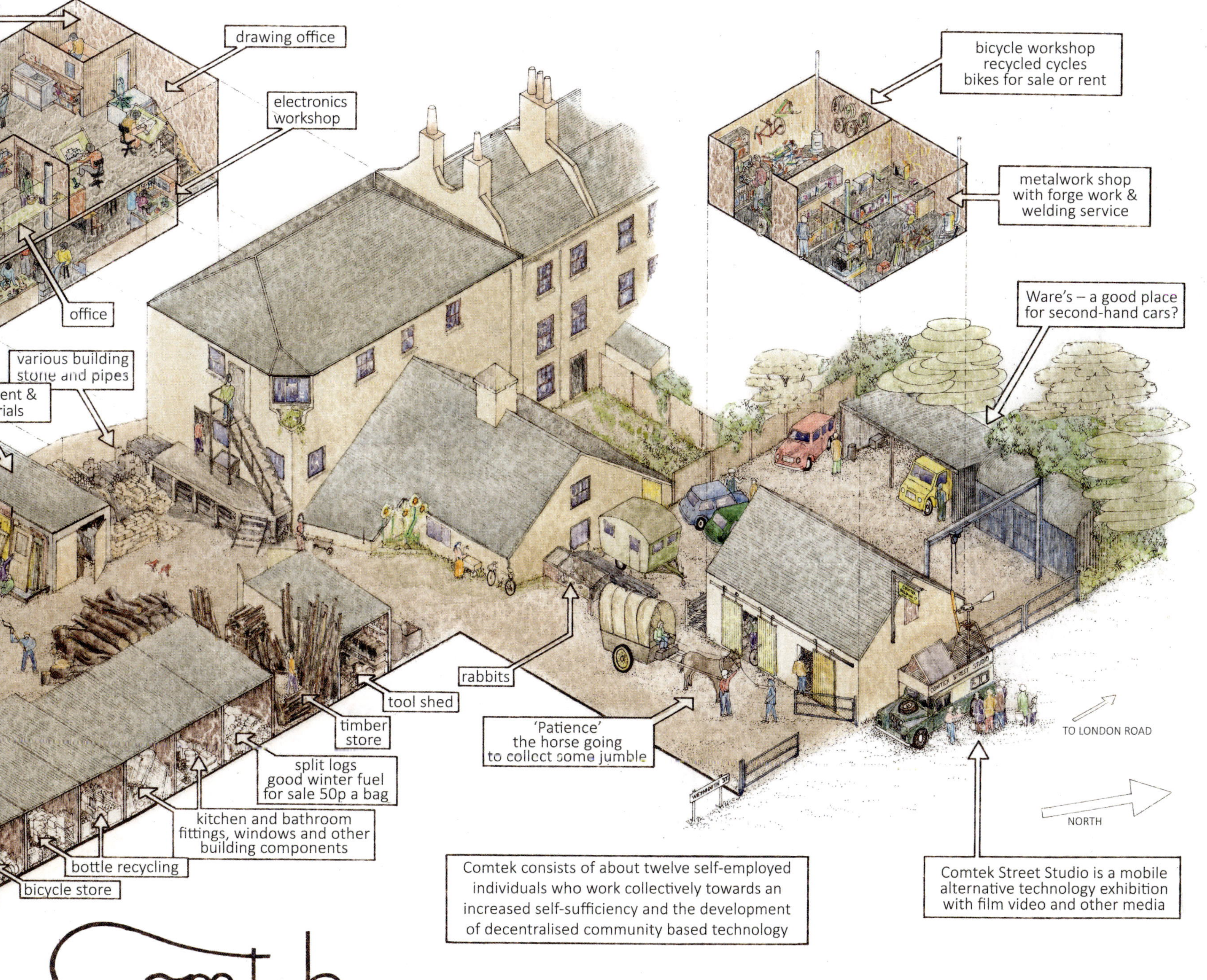
drawing office
electronics workshop
office
various building stone and pipes
ent & rials
bicycle workshop recycled cycles bikes for sale or rent
metalwork shop with forge work & welding service
Ware's – a good place for second-hand cars?
rabbits
tool shed
timber store
split logs good winter fuel for sale 50p a bag
kitchen and bathroom fittings, windows and other building components
bottle recycling
bicycle store
'Patience' the horse going to collect some jumble
Comtek consists of about twelve self-employed individuals who work collectively towards an increased self-sufficiency and the development of decentralised community based technology
TO LONDON ROAD
NORTH
Comtek Street Studio is a mobile alternative technology exhibition with film video and other media
Comtek  Community  Technology  Bath Arts Workshop  PHONE 6371
DRAWN BY : GLYN DAVIES Dip.Arch.
SCALE: AN EIGHTH OF AN INCH EQUALS ONE FOOT FEB 1976

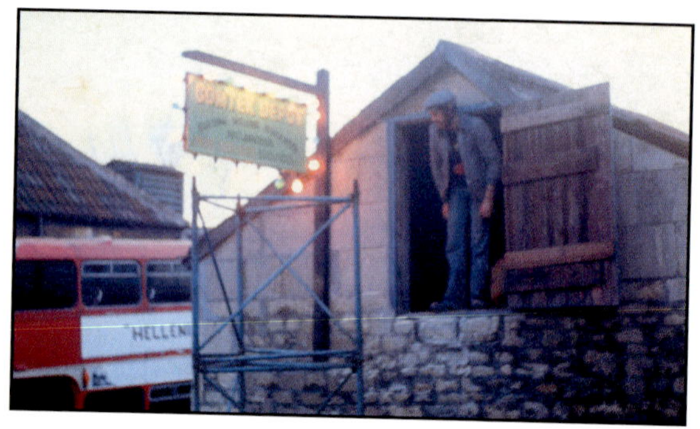

Weymouth Street depot

Streets in Bath, and these became the new premises for our proposed *Comtek Collective*. Our work and areas of expertise encompassed domes, architecture, planning, media, film & TV, a housing coop, building, stage management, events, Comtek festival exhibitions and Civil Aid.

**Comtek Collective:** The pilot project (that went on to become Comtek) would consist of a building large enough to accommodate… woodworking, metalworking, printing, electrical, building, crafts and clothes… also sound recording, films, TV, photography, printing and a design office and transport department. *Thornton Kay, June 1973.*

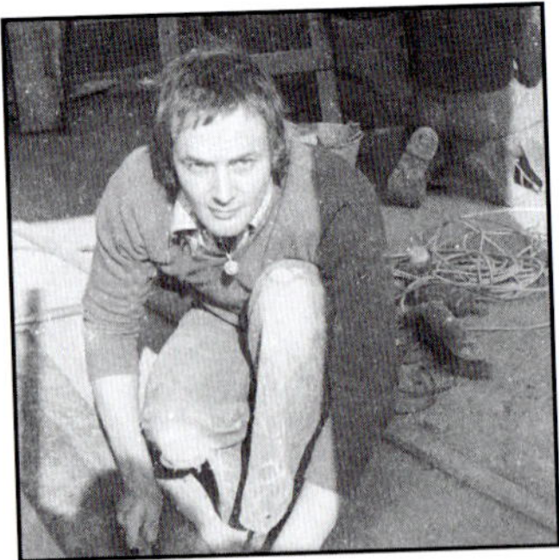 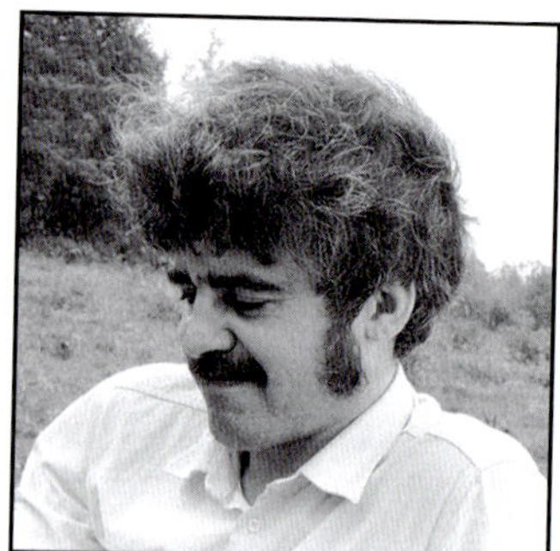

Thornton and Glyn

The Collective quickly expanded to involve a wide circle of people, including Brian Ford, Dave Rappaport, Hugo

Grimes, Jenny Hiles (now Caccia), John Potter, Ken Heraty, Nick Allen, Pat Jannaway, Paul Nachman (Nasher), Rich Cooper, Thom Brajkovich and Tim Gardner. We were helped by Bath City Council, especially the chief executive David Beeton and estates manager Hugh Gunton, among others.[2] Our longstanding friend and ally Charlie Ware was also involved. After going bankrupt in 1974, he rented cheap space at the Comtek depot where he started what became the world famous Morris Minor Centre.

**Jennie** remembers: For me the depot was a magical place! There were wind and solar things and domes where Brian Ford grew vegetables. He brought us a cauliflower one day and I made a cauliflower cheese, so sorry I didn't wash it properly Brian, even more sorry for the caterpillar. I'm sure I even remember a fish pond. There was a blacksmith's forge, the real thing with Patrick Jannaway, Hugo Grimes and Rich Cooper toiling away amidst sparks and smoke and steam. Rick Knapp being grumpy and Thornton being enigmatic. Old trucks and spare parts everywhere and, of course, John and his bikes, old bikes being given a new lease of life. It was a higgledy-piggledy place of wonder, but very solid and real amidst a jumble of wood, metal and rope.

**Glyn:** We used the depot for the storage and resale of building materials, along with facilities to develop and promote the use of renewable energy through community and DIY

---

2. Others who supported Comtek included Carl Jaeger, Cyril Beazer, Cyril Howe, David Brain, John Davis, Russell Frears and Wessex Water.

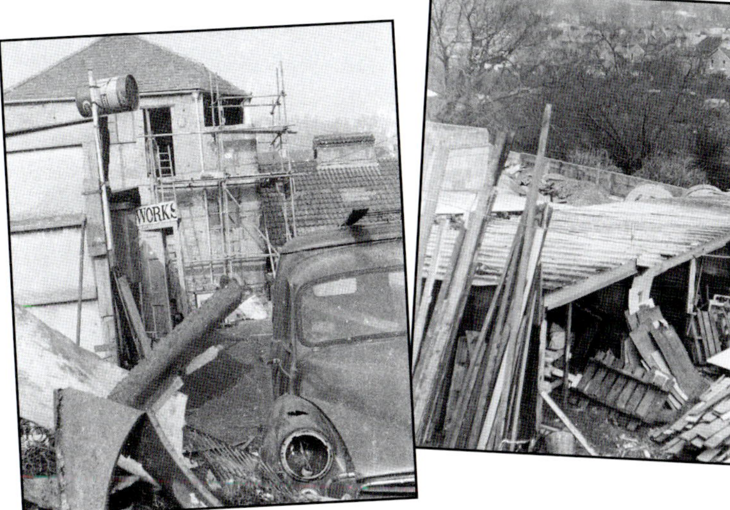

methods. At the time, there was limited awareness of climate change, despite new images of earth from the moon which highlighted the finite resources of the planet. The depot also served as HQ for our architectural work and support for campaigns against the demolition of historic buildings. We encouraged people with a cross-section of skills to take up self-employment and pool their resources through an informal cooperative that helped the participants to achieve their potential and also enabled larger projects to be carried out by acting together – a social synergy.

## Bath community video

**Glyn:** Early in 1973, Comtek and BAW began exploring the use of community television with a video project coordinated by Peter Mitchelson (Mitch). We initially borrowed equipment from Bristol Channel local cable TV. Finally in December 1973, after raising money from jumble sales, we bought a set of second-hand video equipment for

£375. We moved our studio-based, heavy mains equipment around in a wheelbarrow with an extremely long extension lead that we hoped to plug into the supply of a helpful neighbour or shopkeeper.

During the winter of 1974-75, we converted a space in the depot into a drawing office with a photographic dark room and a film editing studio. When it opened in May 1975, we were able to include video editing facilities thanks to an Arts Council grant. Video was used to benefit the community in three main areas: regular editions of *Walcot News* replayed in various local venues including schools and colleges; drama workshops with children; and as an added dimension to performances by the **Natural Theatre Company**. Bath Community Video Television (BCVTV) was now established with a permanent studio and portable equipment.

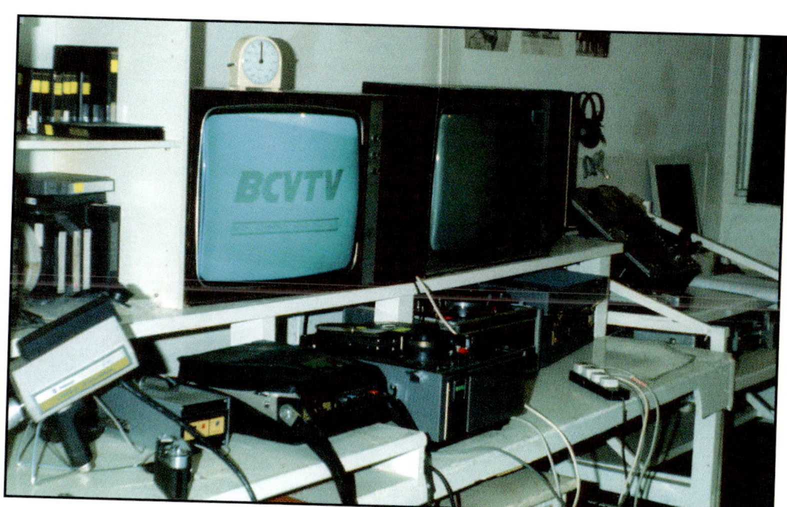


Video studio at the depot

## Renewable energy

**Brian Ford:** I arrived in spring 1975. I'd finished an architecture course and spent a year working in a small practice in Gloucestershire. I had heard about the *Comtek 74* exhibition of alternative technologies that was part of BAW's summer festival. It sounded right up my street so I set off for Bath to join in with *Comtek 75*. Once in Bath, Nick Moore and I organised a series of weekend workshops to promote a DIY approach to domestic-scale renewable energy projects. These included making a small wind machine, erected next to the dome at the depot, and a solar

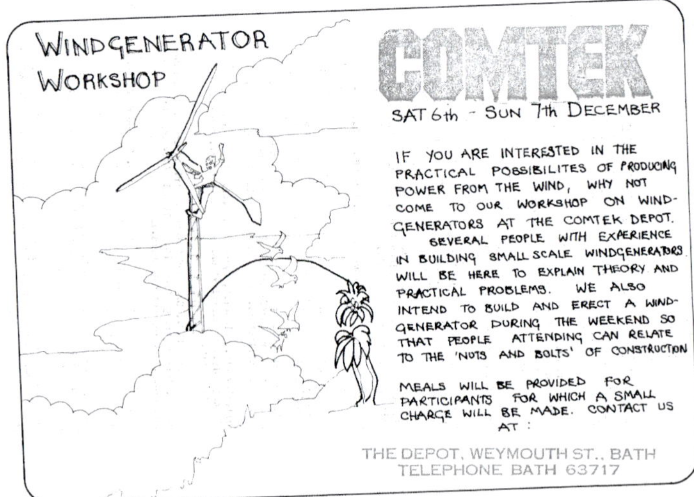


water heating system. Nick and I started designing and installing solar water heating systems and doing building work for people we'd met at the festival. Eventually Kevin McCartney and I wrote a DIY solar heating book, which was published in 1978 and then translated into four European languages.

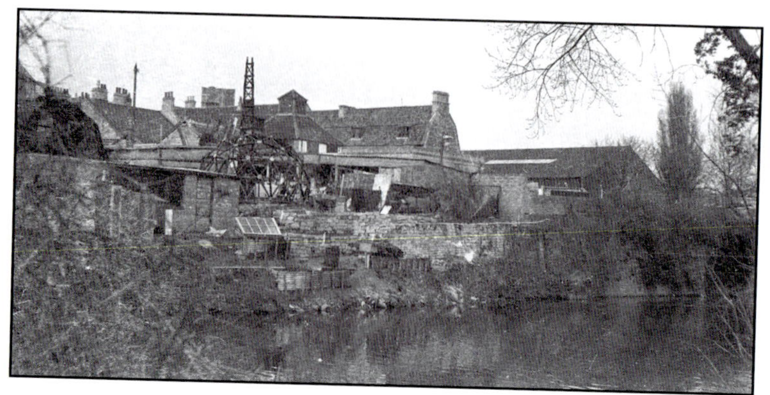

View of the depot from across the river

## The forge

**Rich Cooper:** In 1973, I was training to be a teacher in Bath but had kept in touch with friends from my home town in Surrey who were interested in alternative technologies, bicycles etc. One Christmas we were camping in the woods at Box Hill, exploring the mines and checking out the railway tunnel, when we had a visit from Thornton. He told us about plans for the *Comtek 74* exhibition. We duly loaded our double-decker bus and went along to join in. I camped

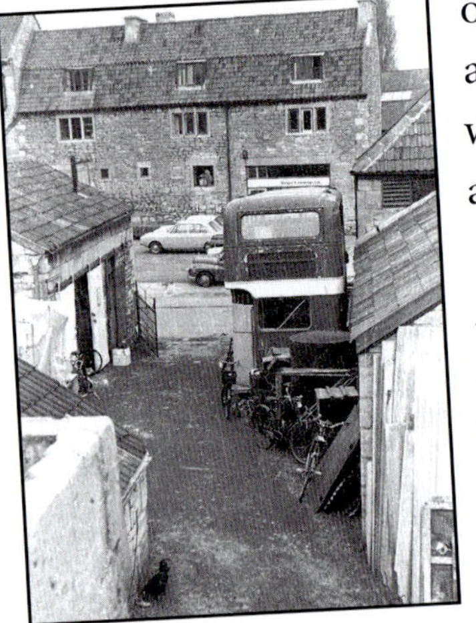

out on Kensington Meadows along with the gang (that was when I first saw Hampton Row across the river. I still live there).

Among my friends who moved to Bath was Patrick Jannaway. He had done a proper blacksmith's

Rich's double-decker bus

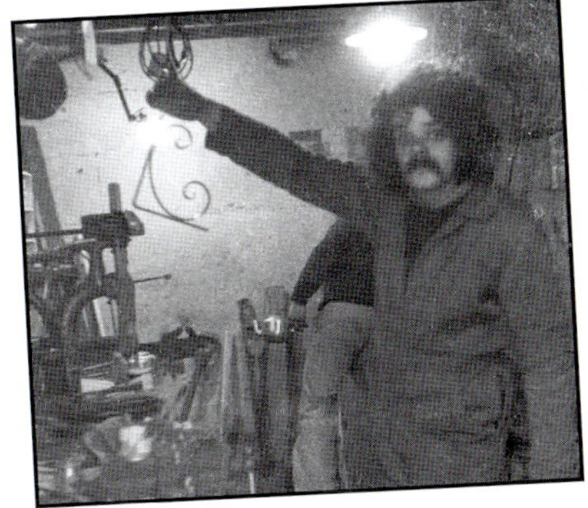

Pat Jannaway

apprenticeship and wanted to set up a workshop with like-minded people. When I finished my course, I joined Pat in an old stable building at the depot and started my career in metalwork. John Potter was kicking his bicycles about at the other end of the stable. It seemed that Comtek was the practical branch of BAW. Nominally a collective, it was run by Rick Knapp really, with Thornton playing his part.

The hot summer of 1976 saw us create a mobile stage structure for Tower Hamlets (Phil was working there at the time), probably the most coherent thing we did as a group. Another involvement with BAW was with Civil Aid (Bath Branch) led by Nigel Leach.[3] We loaded some catering equipment, including Soyer Boilers (developed for Crimean War field kitchens) into our double-decker and off we went to Watchfield, a free festival on an old airfield in Oxfordshire. Here we set up a frcc food kitchen, with firewood chopped largely by Hells Angels.

I feel fortunate indeed to have fallen in with these people, they have been my friends and comrades most of my adult life and I still haven't had to get a proper job.

---

3. For more on the adventures of Bath Civil Aid, see Chapter 7.

## John Potter and his bikes

**John:** We put a small advert in the *Bath Evening Chronicle* and got a free van full of bikes. When another advert was similarly successful, a larger storage area was needed. Half a garage changed to a whole ex-stable at Comtek. At this

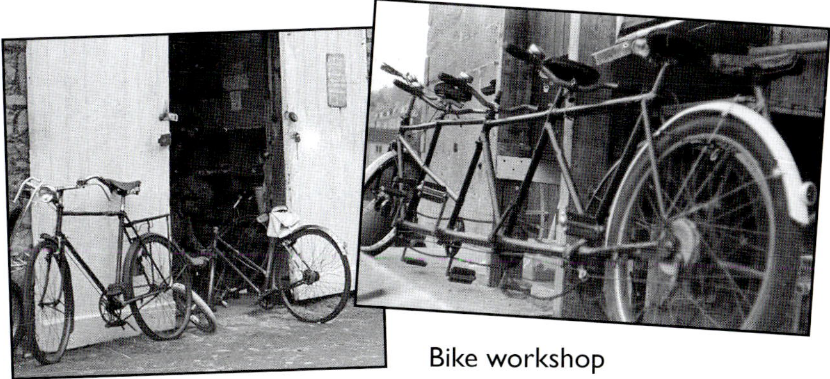

Bike workshop

time, people started making enquiries about all the old bikes and a couple were soon sold. To make space for a bit of a workshop, the contents of the stable were moved outside each day, where they sometimes caused a blockage. Two or three times a week, a lorry driver in a hurry would

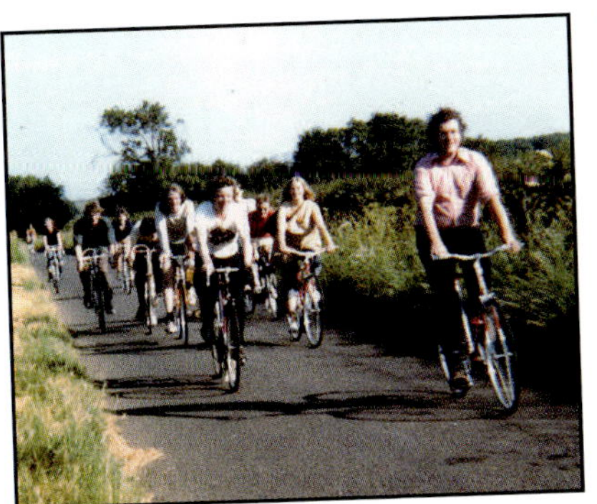

Off to the Mead
Tea Gardens

complain to Rick Knapp. The reply was always, 'It's John's fucking bikes'. Many bikes were brought back to long life. At weekends, anything going was lent or hired and crowds of us would head up to the madness of the Mead Tea Gardens. Over the long summers, bike rides developed going deep into the countryside. All sorts of people joined, always with time for tea.

One day, I went along to the decorating shop for some basic needs. A rather grumpy man sitting with the racing paper asked 'do you want this shop?' Very soon after, when a 200 quid overdraft had been spent on beer and paint, *John's Bikes* opened.

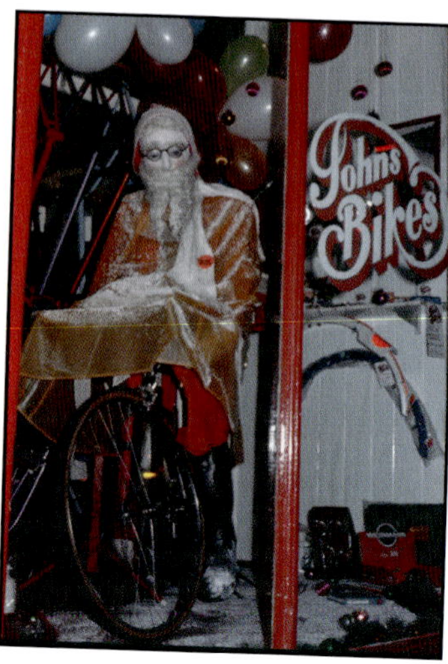

John's Bikes

I soon arranged for a van-load of bikes and people to join the **London to Brighton Bike Ride**. During the 1975 *Walcot Festival,* I met Robert Stredder and together we planned the 1976 ride with a goal of a few hundred cyclists: It rained, a group of us were thrown out of a pub in Ditchling and everyone had a brilliant day. From the 400 that year, the numbers went up and up and it became the biggest bike ride in the world.

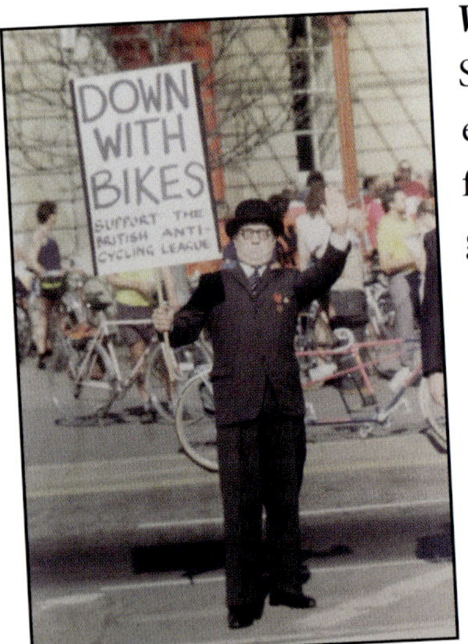

A bit of mad
street theatre

There were all sorts of events, tours and rides, involving all of Bath Arts Workshop – from driving support vans to making thousands of sandwiches or even roasting pigs. The **Natural Theatre Company** would join in. Not only would a bit of mad street theatre be very, very funny but it also diverted attention from the rain and the long, steep hills. We had frequent use of fraudulent mileages – there really was little chance of getting a non-cyclist to do over 75 miles, unless you told them it was 59!

## Domes and other structures

**Glyn:** We were all interested in domes. As a student I'd been to a lecture by Buckminster Fuller, who developed the geodesic dome after working with members of the Bauhaus Architects. They had helped build the first geodesic dome in Germany in 1924. Fuller was a proponent of the concept of synergy, a system that transcends the sum of its parts.

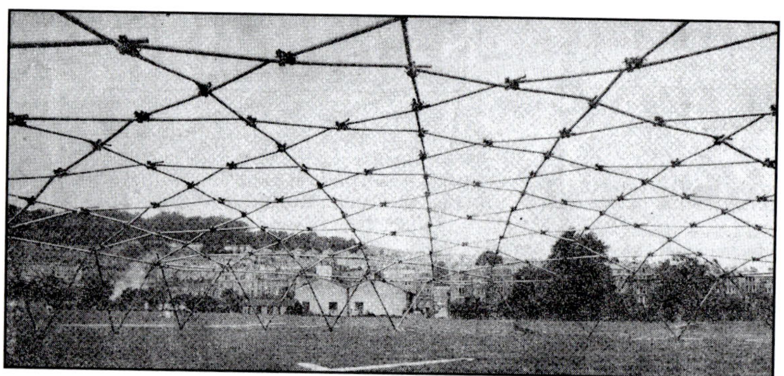
1974 dome

The **Comtek 74** festival dome was built by Thornton and me, along with Francis Leonard, who built the first Glastonbury pyramid stage. He invented the tri-strut, a method of using straight scaffolding poles to create a self-supporting domed structure. The tri-strut is useful because it is simple to construct for temporary spans of about 30 metres, but ultimately it isn't structurally efficient. Each straight tube rests on the centre of another which can cause the tubes to bend. Eventually, hire companies became reluctant to hire out the poles which had a tendency to be returned slightly bent out of shape.

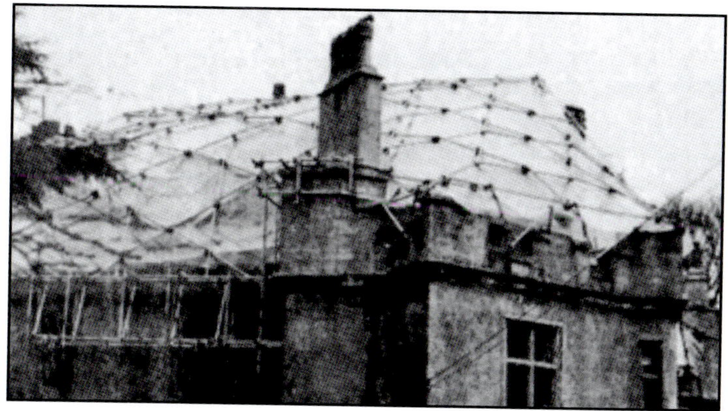

Francis Leonard built a canopy to protect
Charlie Ware's house, Battlefields, during repairs,
*Architectural Design 4, 1973*

## It came together then it changed

**Thornton:** In 1976, Comtek's activities included building material reclamation, weekend Comtek workshops on alternative technologies, a building cooperative, bike repairs, a design studio, fish farming, a forge, hydroponic food production, mechanics, woodworking, video and film production and wine bottle reclamation. But the organisational structure, which was a loose cooperative run by consensus on egalitarian lines, began to creak.

In an article written at the time, Glyn presciently captured the fault lines:

Inevitably, some people can earn more money more efficiently than others, and those that do can find themselves subsidising the others. This situation, and the fact that some people at Comtek are paid a wage from the Workshop, raises questions about financial equality and levels of commitment, and a consequent re-examining of basic ideologies. Naturally, personalities occasionally come into conflict. In fact throughout the history of the Workshop, much of its energy has come from interaction and abrasion between personalities. But by spring 76 the gulf between grant subsidies and earning money from jobs was widening. Half of Comtek has decided to help the Workshop with its new project at the former Riverside Day Nursery where there is scope for alternative technology, renovation and food production alongside the nursery. The other half, including the three founders, will continue working independently from the Workshop. ***Where do we go from here? Development of Comtek, Glyn Davies, April 1976***

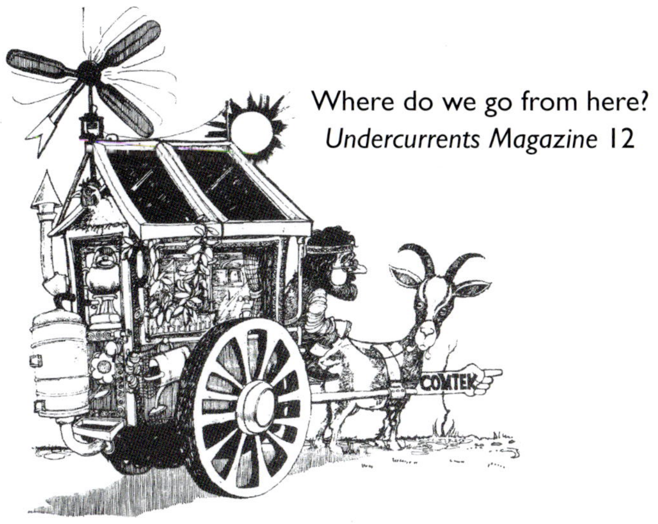


Where do we go from here?
*Undercurrents Magazine* 12

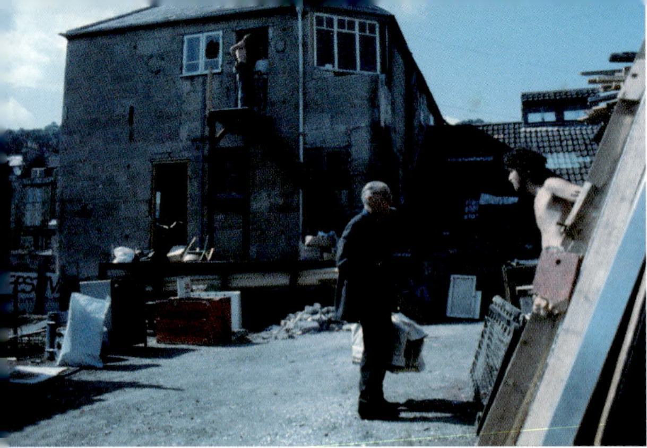
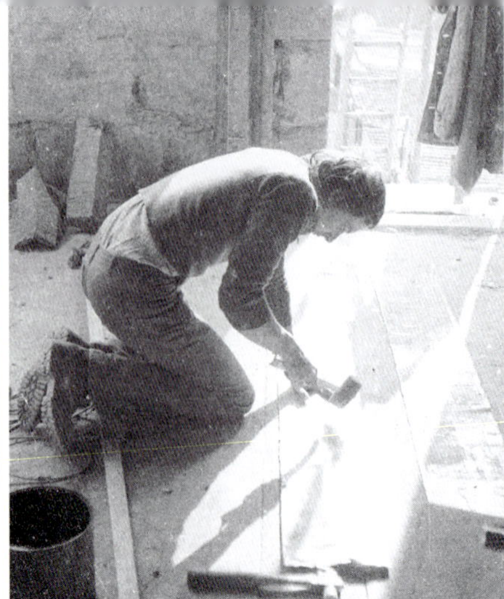
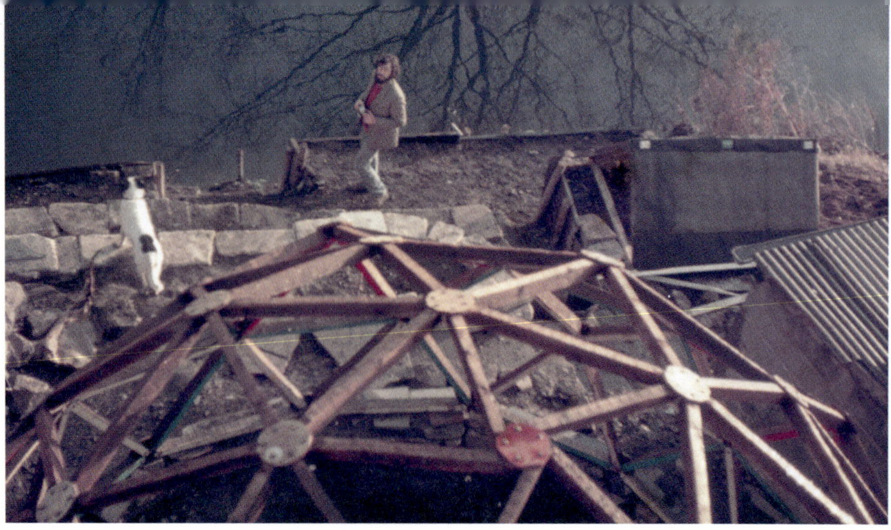
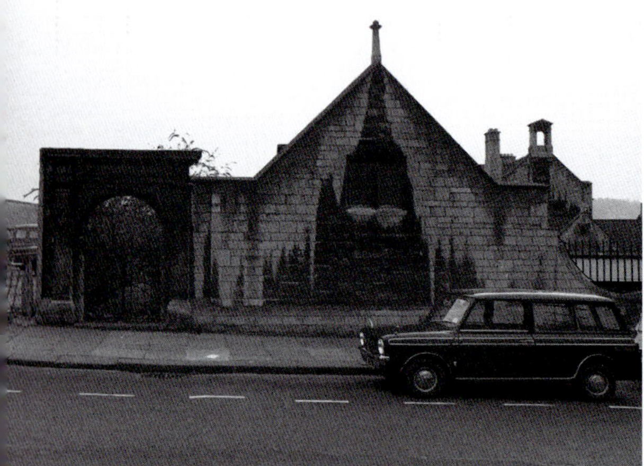
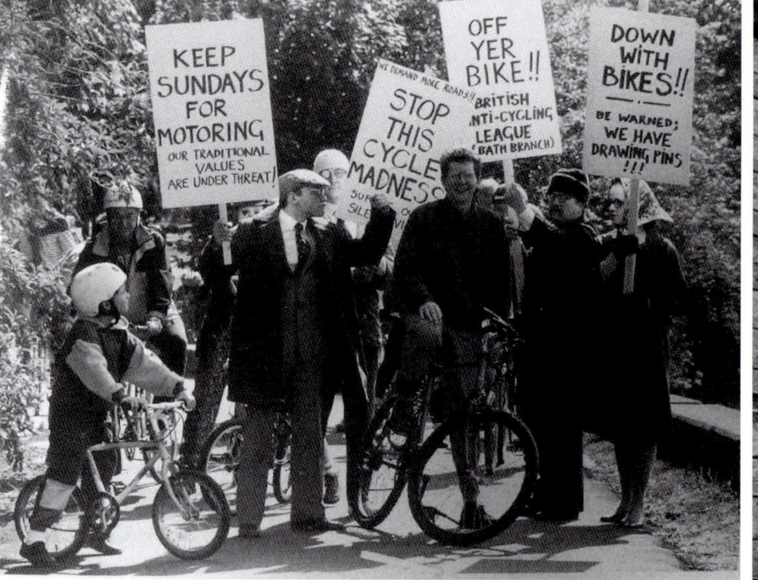

KEEP
SUNDAYS
FOR
MOTORING
OUR TRADITIONAL
VALUES
ARE UNDER THREAT!
OFF
YER
BIKE!!
STOP
THIS
CYCLE
MADNESS
DOWN
WITH
BIKES!!
BE WARNED;
WE HAVE
DRAWING PINS
!!!
BRITISH
ANTI-CYCLING
LEAGUE
(BATH BRANCH)

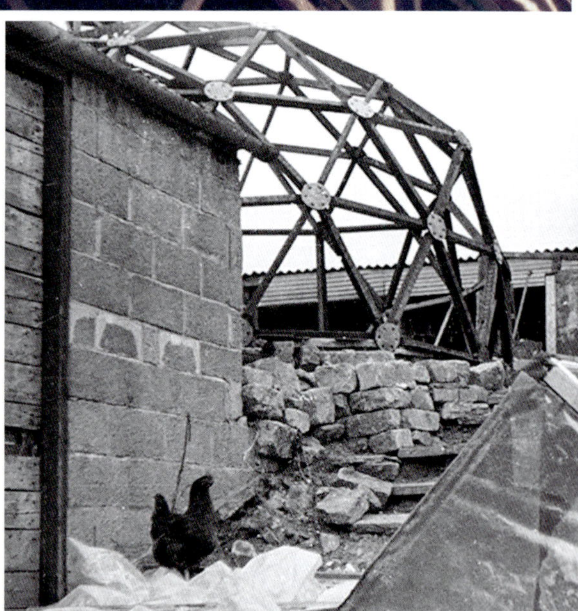
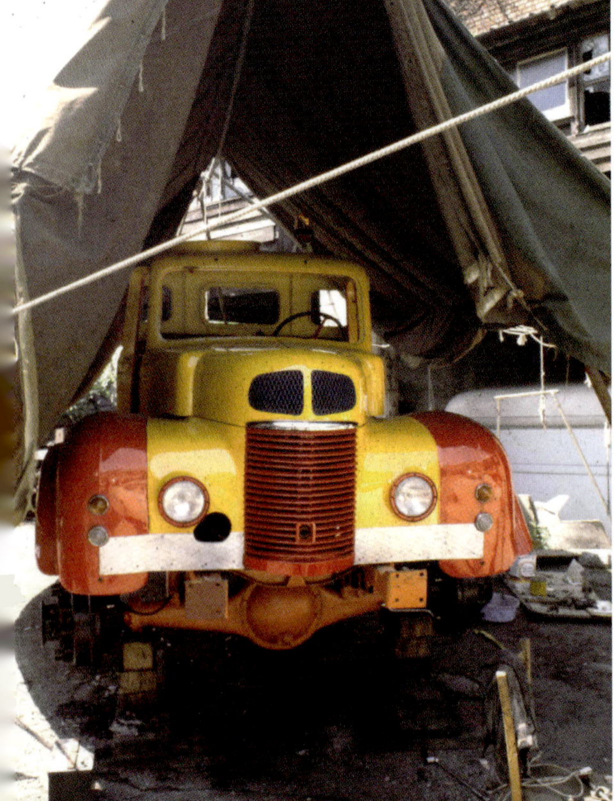
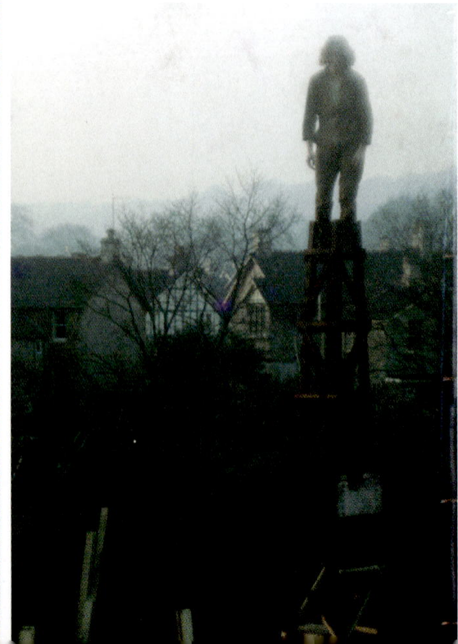
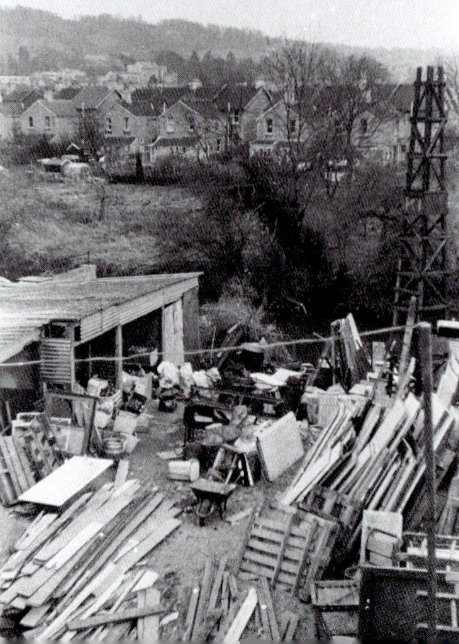
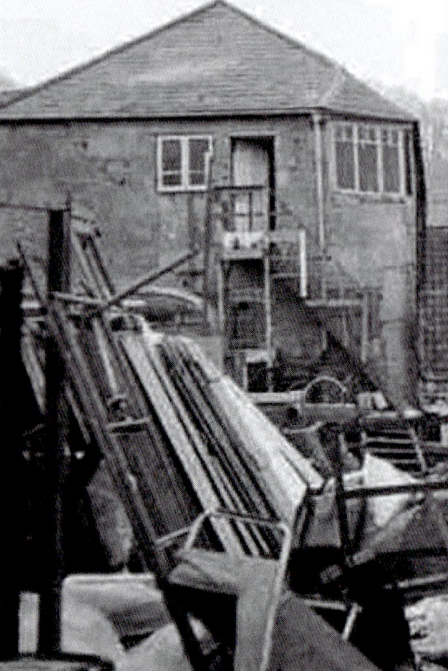

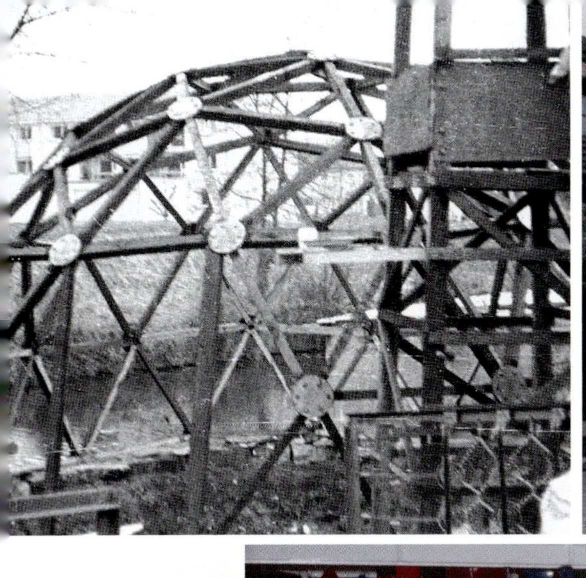
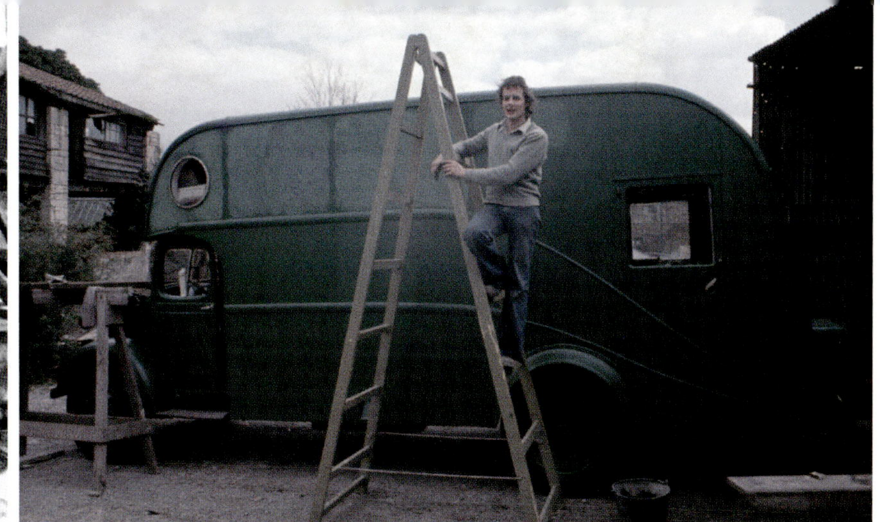
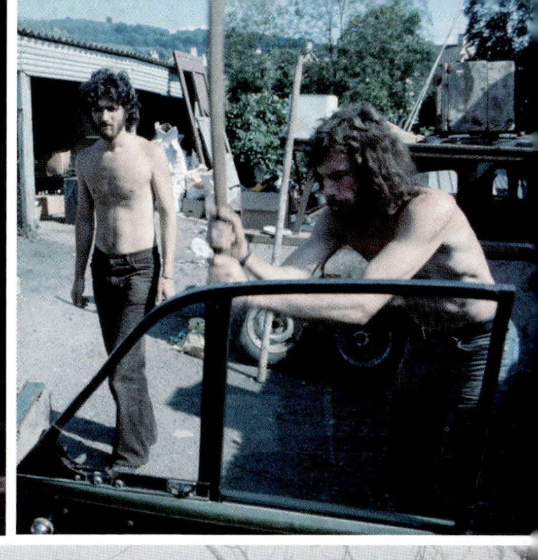
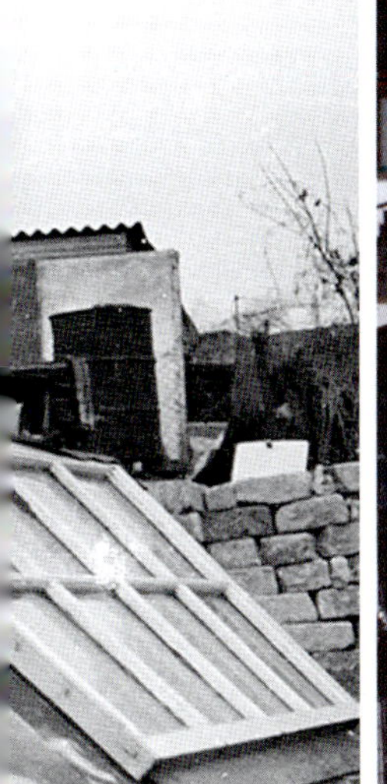
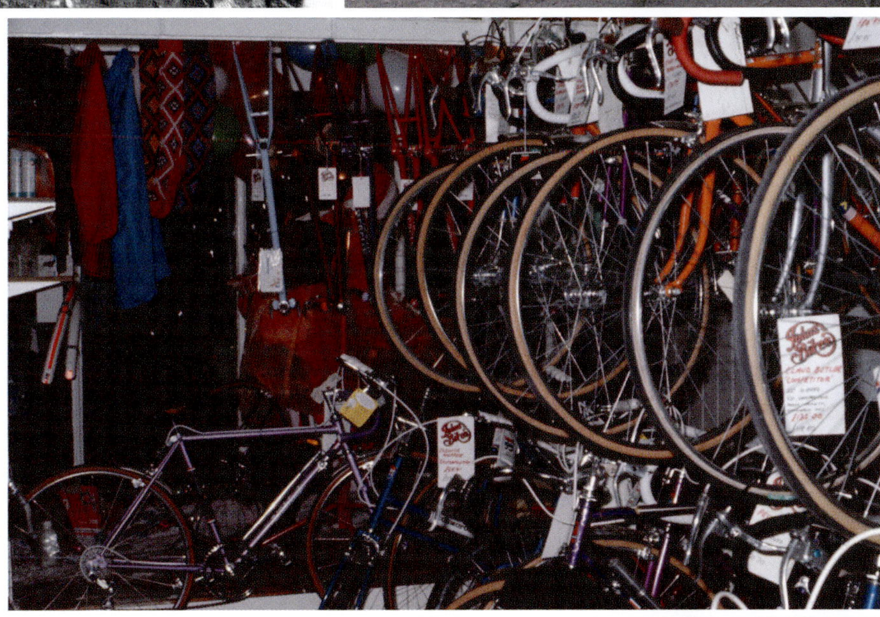
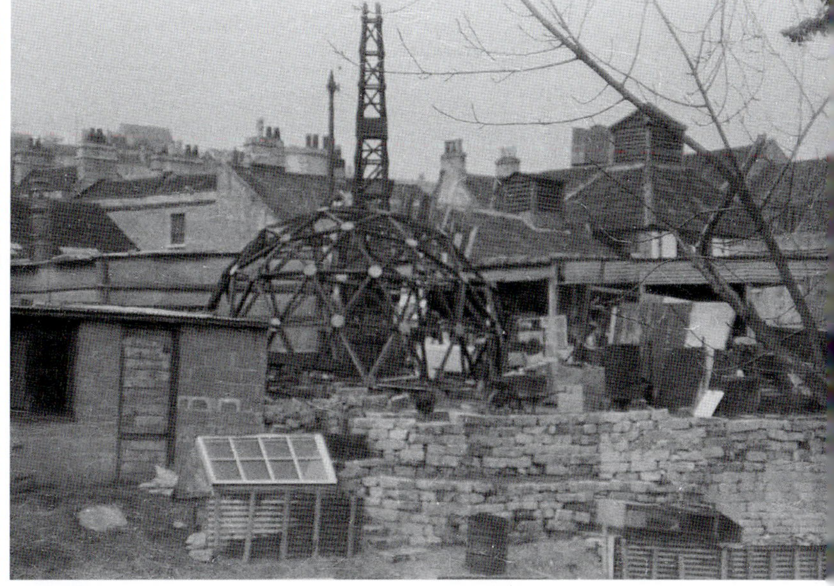
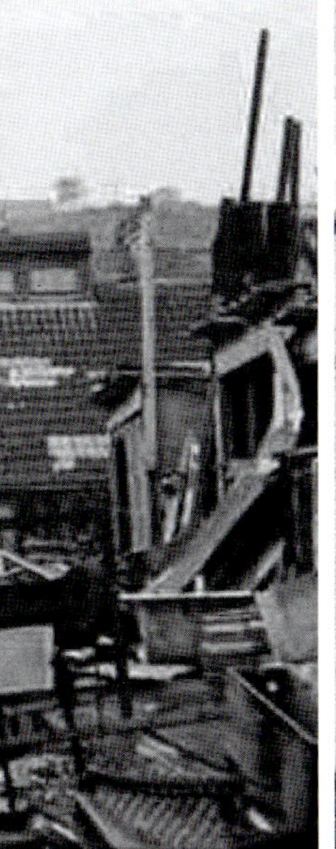
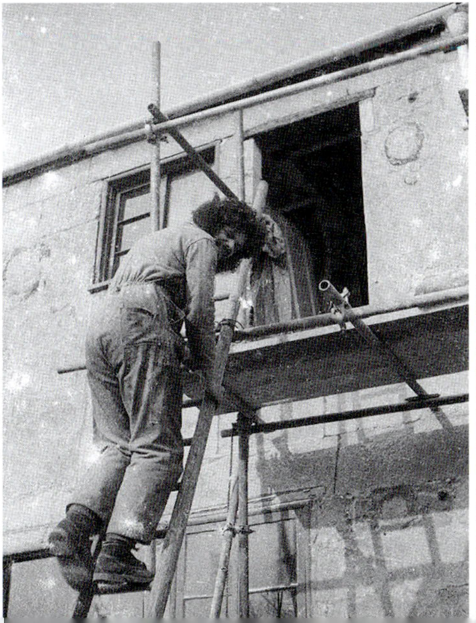
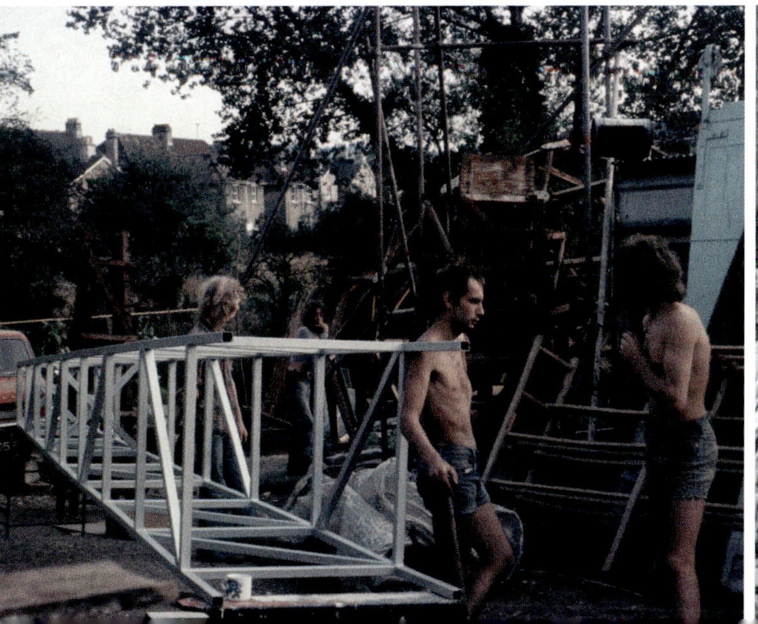
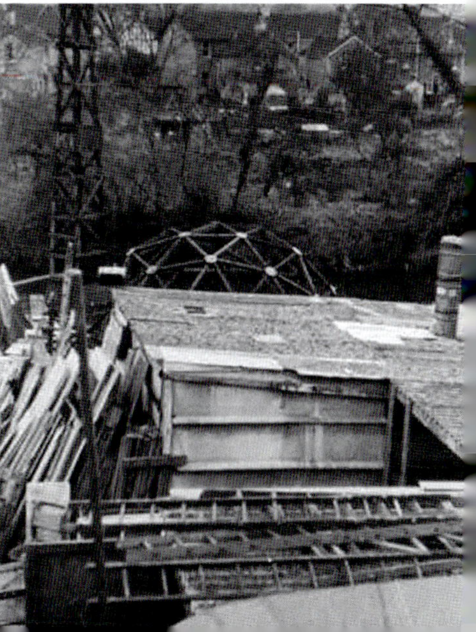

## Walcot Reclamation

**Thornton:** In October 1976, Rick Knapp won the contract for Comtek to clear the builders' stores and workshops of Hayward & Wooster's yard, a large area of land and Victorian workshops along the River Avon, fronted by the Georgian house at 108 Walcot Street.[4] The property had been compulsorily purchased by the city council in 1970.

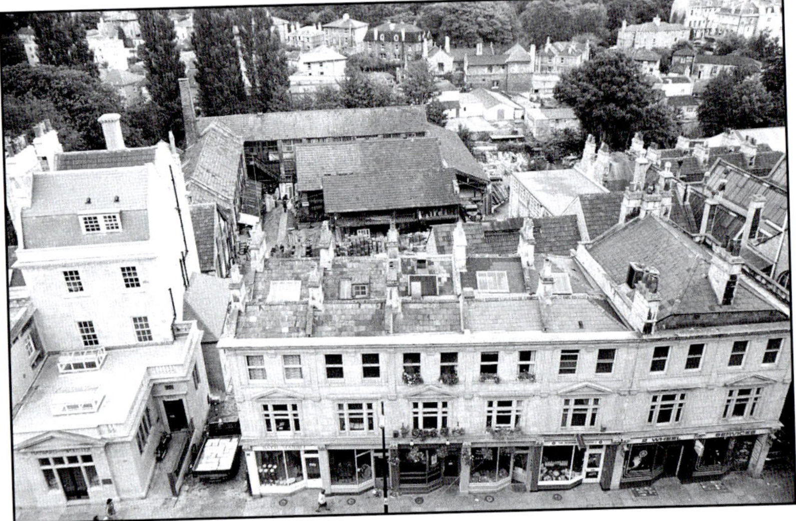

Street entrance to Walcot Reclamation

The work was undertaken by Rick, Rich Cooper, Simon Chippindale and me the following February. Rick initially negotiated a short-term lease and Walcot Reclamation (known locally as 'the yard') was officially born. We came up with the name because it had a double meaning: that the business was reclaiming building materials, and that the

group was reclaiming the Walcot area which, due to blight and recession, had become an area of run-down empty buildings and bankrupt businesses.

Walcot Reclamation started opening on Saturday mornings to sell architectural salvage cleared from the yard and the former Comtek depot. Rick and Paul Ridout also rescued items from ongoing Bath demolitions, especially marble fireplaces and cast iron grates. At the time, builders converting Georgian houses into flats usually smashed them up with sledge hammers. They'd take the bits down to the scrapyard and exchange them for some extra cash for the workers on a Friday afternoon. We began offering higher than scrap prices if the builders would carefully remove these historic

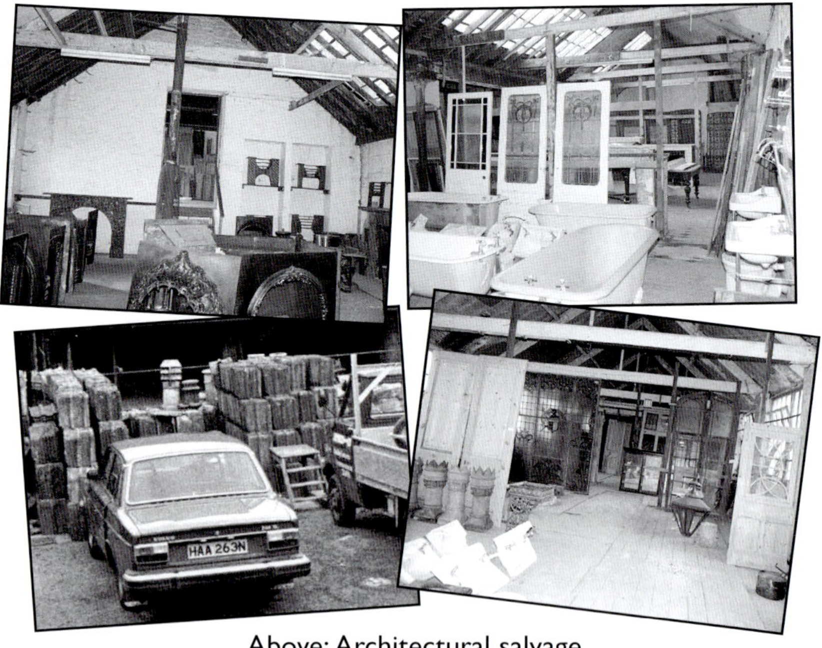

Above: Architectural salvage
Right: Drawing of Walcot Reclamation

---

4. The former poet laureate Robert Southey had lived in the house. Like much of Walcot, the yard, buildings and surrounding land had been blighted for years by the proposed Buchanan Tunnel scheme (*see next section*).

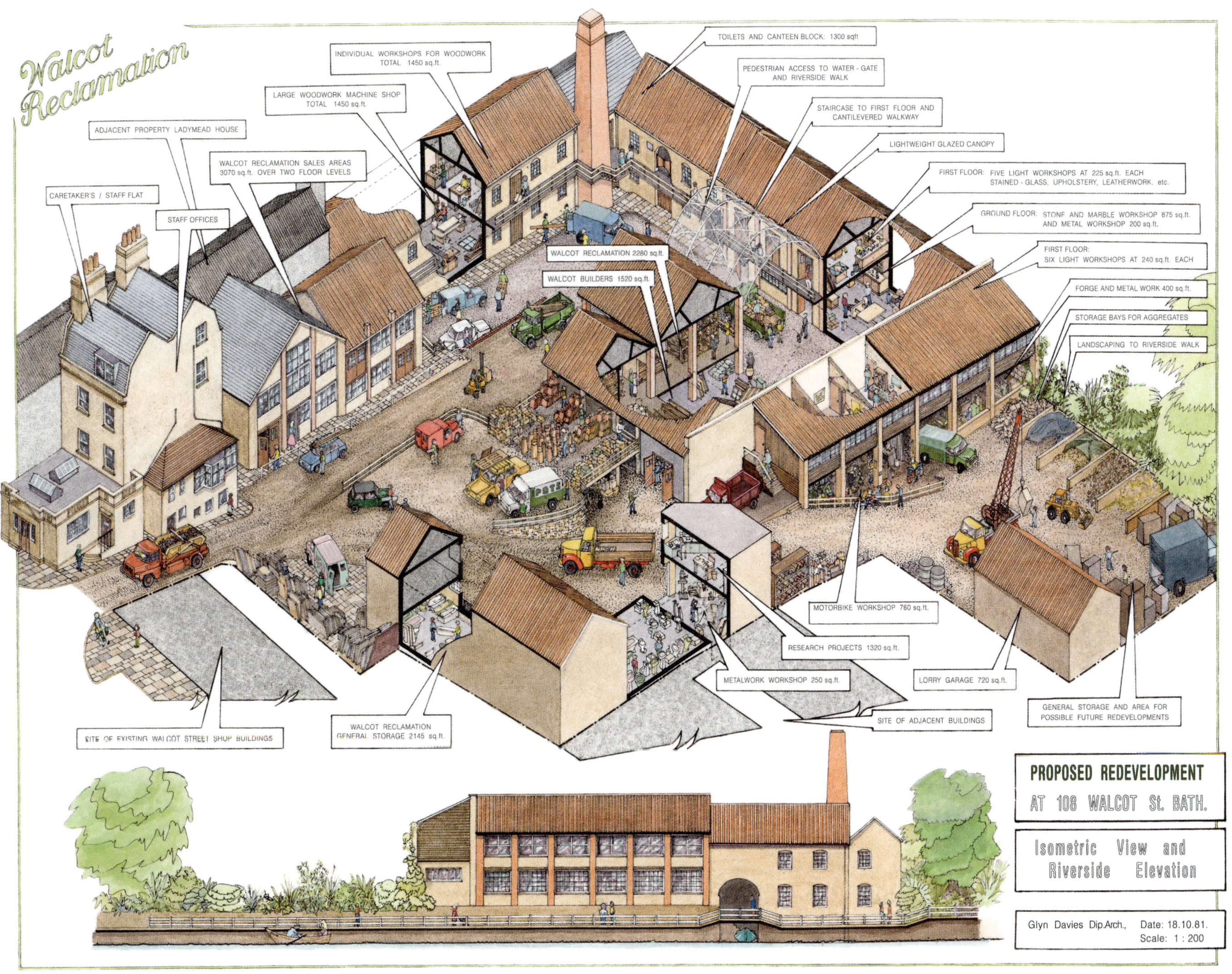
Walcot Reclamation
TOILETS AND CANTEEN BLOCK: 1300 sqft
INDIVIDUAL WORKSHOPS FOR WOODWORK TOTAL  1450 sq.ft.
PEDESTRIAN ACCESS TO WATER - GATE AND RIVERSIDE WALK
LARGE WOODWORK MACHINE SHOP TOTAL  1450 sq.ft.
STAIRCASE TO FIRST FLOOR AND CANTILEVERED WALKWAY
ADJACENT PROPERTY LADYMEAD HOUSE
LIGHTWEIGHT GLAZED CANOPY
WALCOT RECLAMATION SALES AREAS 3070 sq.ft. OVER TWO FLOOR LEVELS
FIRST FLOOR: FIVE LIGHT WORKSHOPS AT 225 sq.ft. EACH STAINED - GLASS, UPHOLSTERY, LEATHERWORK,  etc.
CARETAKER'S / STAFF FLAT
GROUND FLOOR: STONE AND MARBLE WORKSHOP 875 sq.ft. AND METAL WORKSHOP 200 sq.ft.
STAFF OFFICES
WALCOT RECLAMATION 2280 sq.ft.
FIRST FLOOR: SIX LIGHT WORKSHOPS AT 240 sq.ft. EACH
WALCOT BUILDERS 1520 sq.ft.
FORGE AND METAL WORK 400 sq.ft.
STORAGE BAYS FOR AGGREGATES
LANDSCAPING TO RIVERSIDE WALK
MOTORBIKE WORKSHOP 760 sq.ft.
RESEARCH PROJECTS 1320 sq.ft.
METALWORK WORKSHOP 250 sq.ft.
LORRY GARAGE 720 sq.ft.
SITE OF ADJACENT BUILDINGS
GENERAL STORAGE AND AREA FOR POSSIBLE FUTURE REDEVELOPMENTS
SITE OF EXISTING WALCOT STREET SHOP BUILDINGS
WALCOT RECLAMATION GENERAL STORAGE 2145 sq.ft.
PROPOSED REDEVELOPMENT AT 108 WALCOT St. BATH.
Isometric View and Riverside Elevation
Glyn Davies Dip.Arch.,    Date: 18.10.81.    Scale: 1 : 200

pieces and so began to create a market for architectural salvage at the yard.

**Thornton:** I found some old 'producer gas' manuals from WWII, which were then used by Simon Chippindale and Robin Hunt to convert a car to run on wood.[5] Rob Llewellyn, an itinerant shoemaker, subsequently of *Red Dwarf*, *Scrapheap Challenge* and *Fully Charged* TV programmes, was one of a number of people who converted

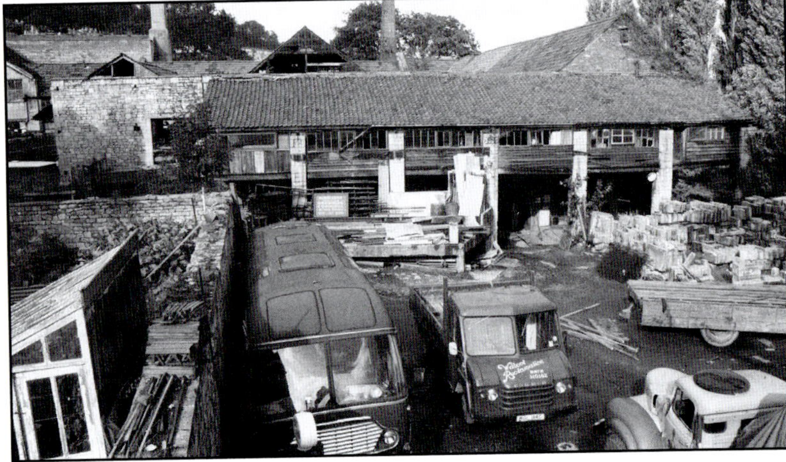

an assortment of trucks, coaches and ambulances into live-ins, the precursor of the tiny home, with plans to travel the world wood-fuelled. Glyn and I also helped Luton Futures, a planned Luton version of Comtek.

Comtek had been an informal cooperative. Walcot Reclamation and Walcot Builders became limited companies owned by Rick and me where, like Mondragon, no-one

---

5. Producer gas is a fuel generated from 'gasified' wood.

earned more than three times the lowest paid. We created workshops that were used for supporting local artists and craftspeople. We also supported Schumacher's global Intermediate Technology Development Group at the yard.

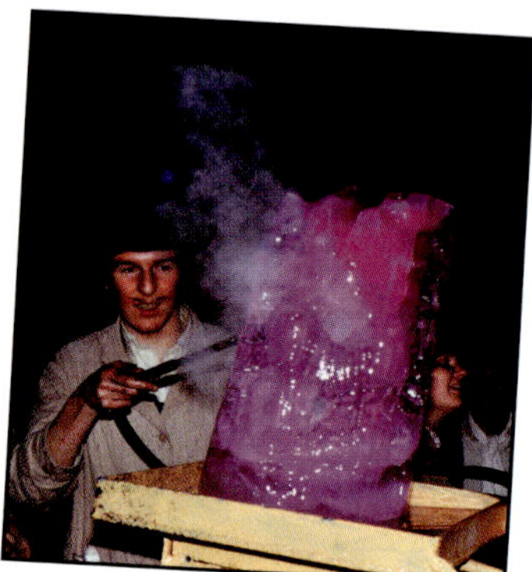

Tom creating a
steam sculpture

**Tom Costello:** I managed to get a workshop at Walcot Reclamation. At that time, the yard was a great hub for a multitude of skilled artisans. I was employed to repair fireplaces but I also used the space to make my own steam sculptures, which I toured with the Natural Theatre Company.

To reduce the shortage of housing, Walcot Builders helped bring many unoccupied privately-owned houses in Bath back into use with government mini housing association grants (mini-HAGS) via Solon Housing in Bristol. This had started in 1974, when Bath Housing Coop was formed with Brian Popay as chair, Rick as treasurer and me as manager, employing a few Comtek building teams. Over a four-year period, more than a hundred run-down Bath properties had simple kitchen and bathroom upgrades, rewiring and basic structural repairs, with decoration and fittings made by tenants, often reusing reclaimed building materials. By 1979, Walcot Reclamation and Walcot Builders were employing around a hundred people. From counterculture to mainstream in ten years!

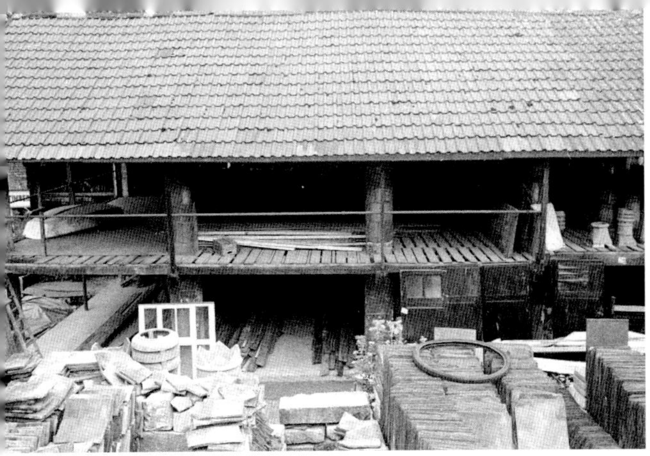

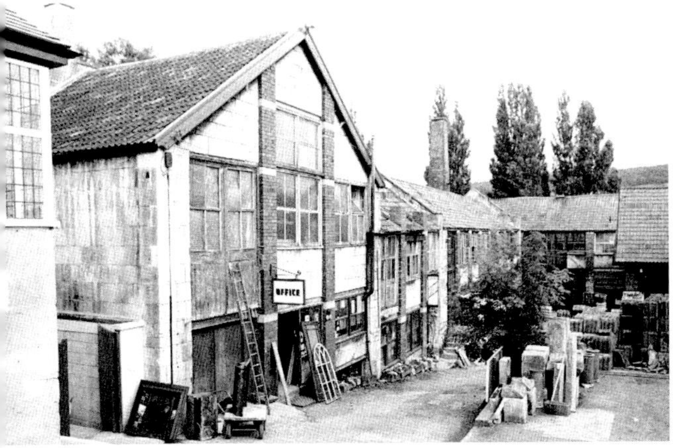

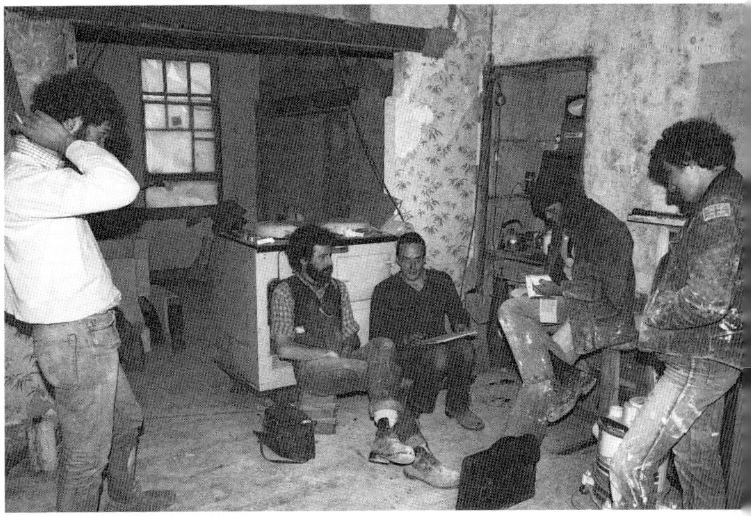

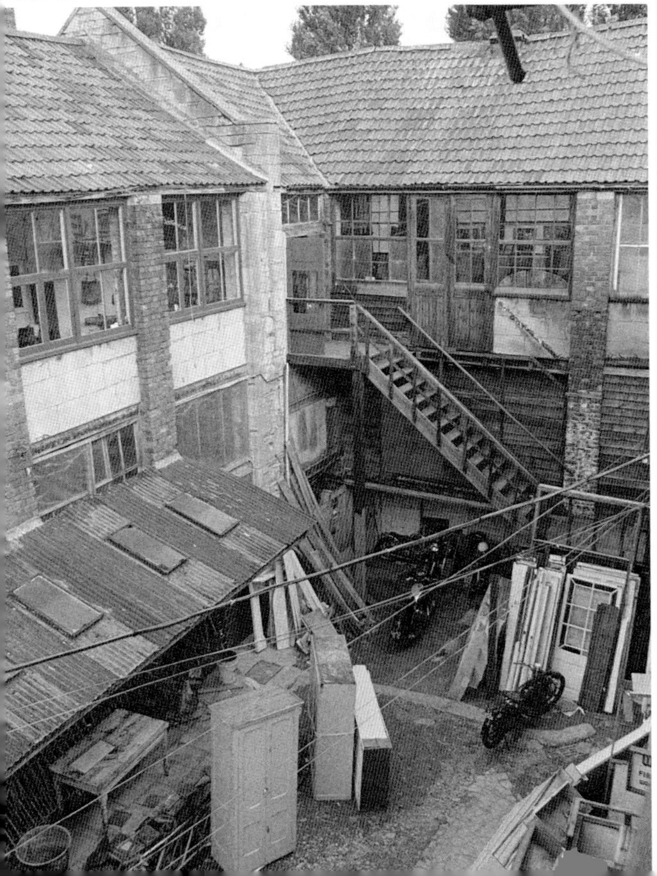

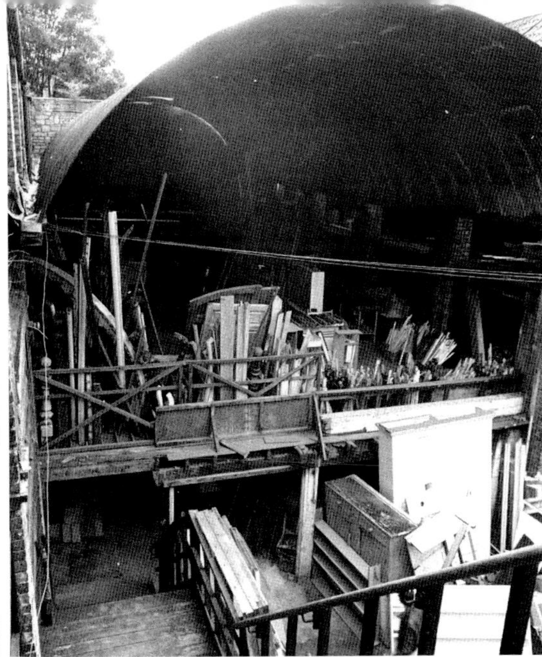
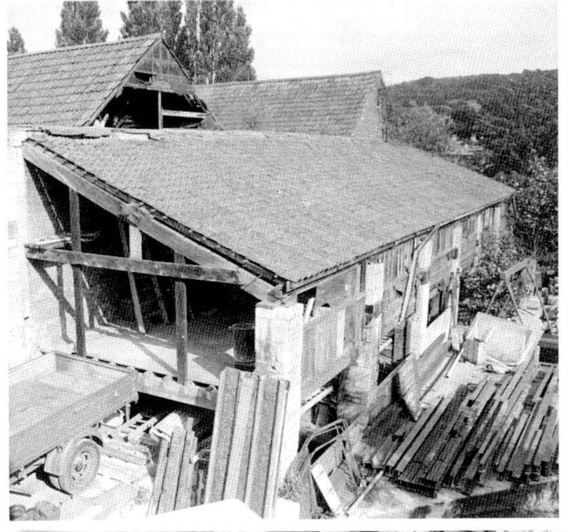
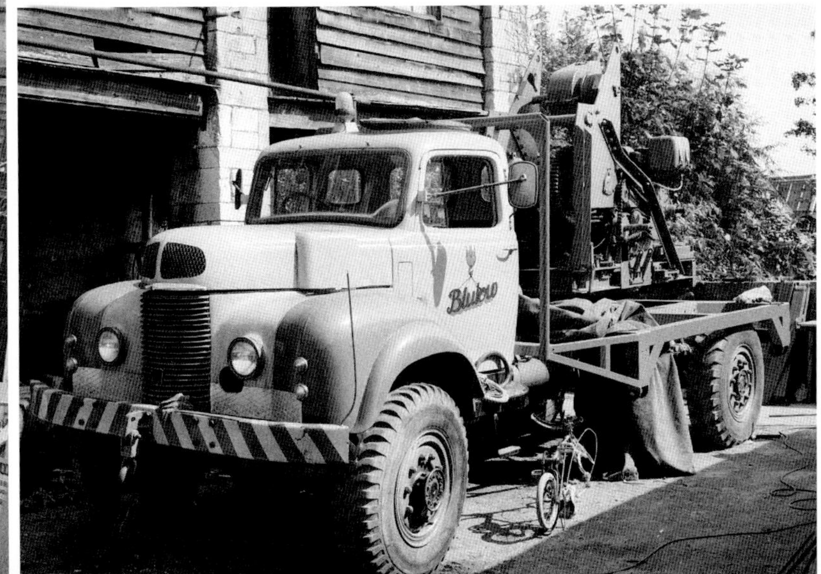
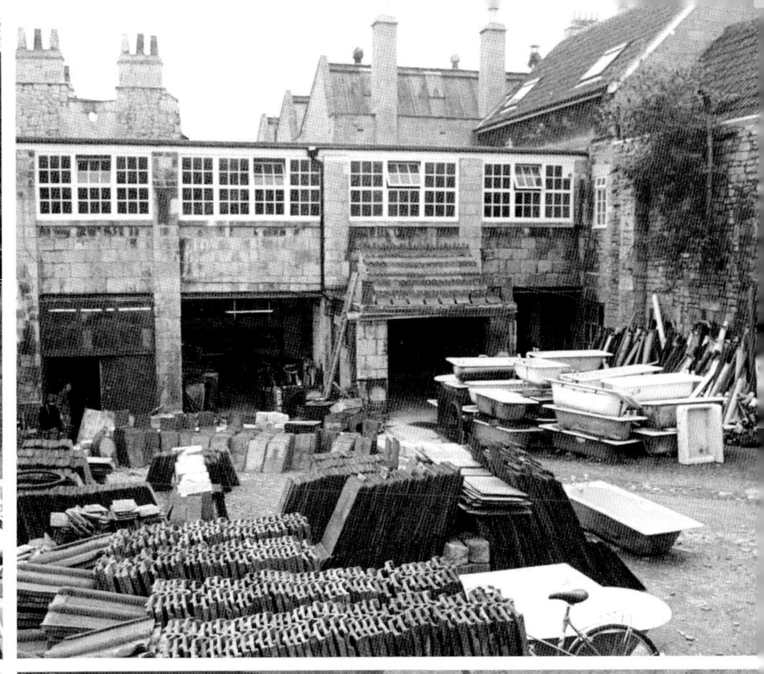
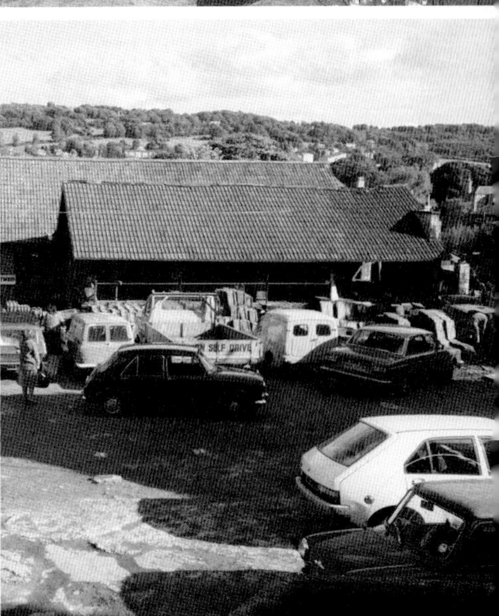

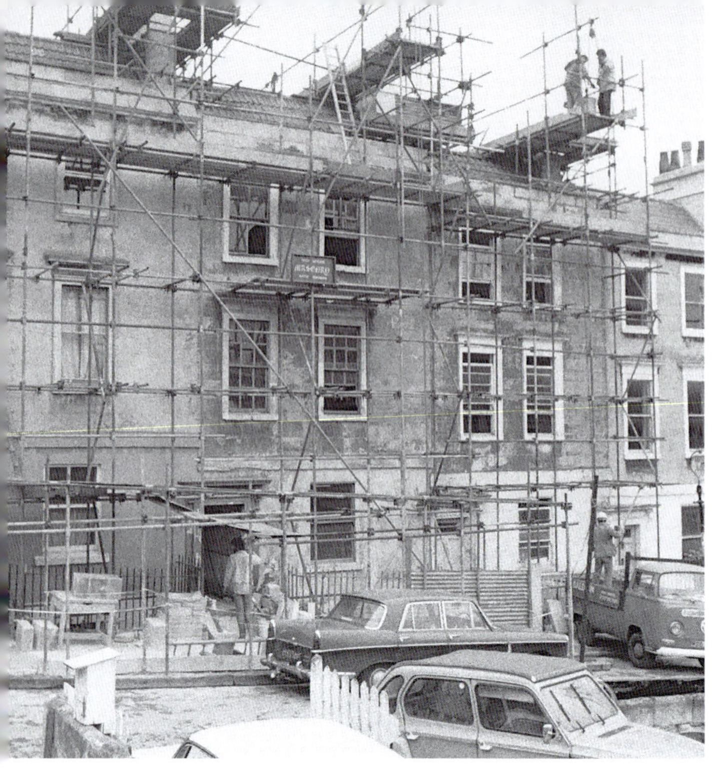



**Glyn Davies:** From the early 70s, Comtek ran campaigns to save historic Georgian buildings from demolition or redevelopment for commercial purposes. We used our architectural skills and building expertise to produce building plans and alternative proposals for uses beneficial to the local community. We soon realised that our video project could be incredibly useful for these campaigns. In the 70s, there were no mobile phones, computers or social media. The immediacy of video had much more impact than today and, screened in the intimacy of a club, pub or local meeting, it became a powerful tool for involving local people in issues that directly affected their lives. We found we could also play our community videos to council officials, and this was a good way of exerting pressure to achieve our goals.

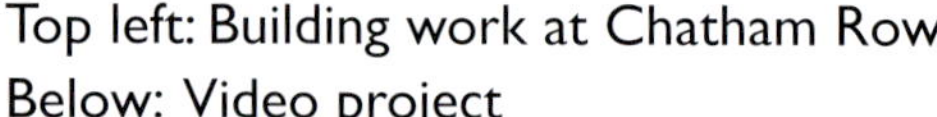

Top left: Building work at Chatham Row
Below: Video project

### The Sack of Bath

**Glyn:** Our protests occurred against the background of a massive wave of slum clearances in the 1960s and early 70s. These destroyed old housing stock and replaced them with blocks of flats and tower blocks. Much-needed housing resulted in many cases, but the situation in Bath was very different. The city council seemed oblivious to the grace and beauty of the town's unique Georgian architecture. It embarked on numerous schemes to demolish thousands of historic buildings and replace them with monolithic blocks now recognised as totally inappropriate for Bath.[6] Fortunately the government recognised the need to stop this carnage and from the early 70s, laws were passed to protect buildings of architectural value.[7]

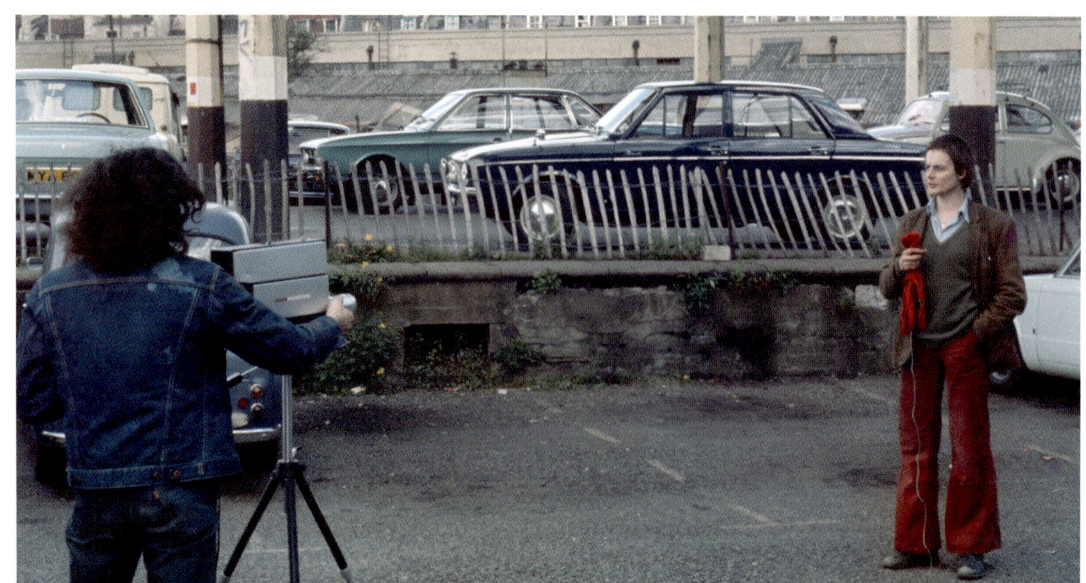

## The Royal Tennis Court

**Glyn:** One of our first campaigns, in 1973, followed the demolition of a Georgian riding school in Julian Road by the city council. The building had become unsafe after the wind-bracing was removed from the roof. Spurred into action, we decided to campaign to

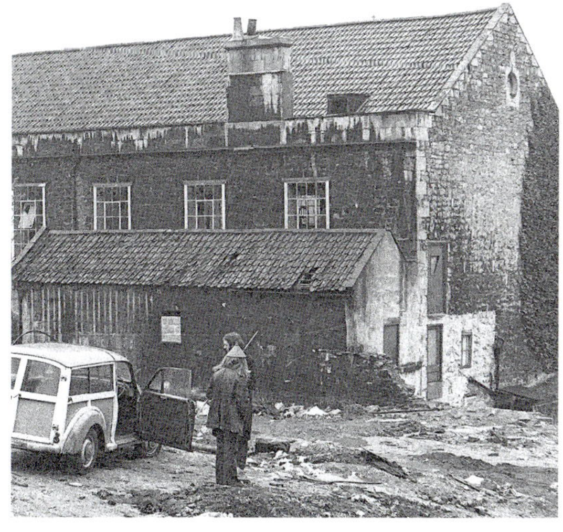

The Royal Tennis Court
in 1973

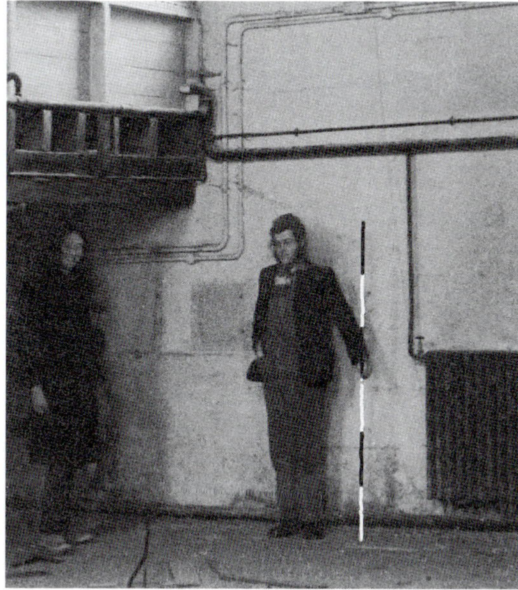

Ralph with survey rod

save the next-door building, Britain's only Georgian Royal Tennis Court, built in 1777, in Morford Street.[8] The city council planned to demolish the building despite its Grade II listing.

We carried out a survey of the building and prepared drawings showing alternative uses, such as conversion to community use. We made a video about the historic importance of the building and presented our own proposals along with local people's views on all of this. The video was shown to the Estates Committee, who were discussing the issue at the time. Others were involved in pressuring the council, but we felt that watching video footage of local people expressing their views had a powerful impact on committee members. In the end, the building was saved and became the Museum of Bath at Work. Forty-seven years later (in the summer of 2019), it housed an exhibition, **Brilliant or Bonkers**, about the work of BAW and Comtek in the 1970s.

---

6. Adam Fergusson's 1973 book *The Sack of Bath* drew national attention to the issues with dramatic photographs of the destruction.

7. The Town and Country Planning Act of 1947 required historic buildings to be listed. Further Acts in 1953, 62, 68 and 72 added greater measures of protection and some made grants available for restoration.

8. The only other 18th-century court in the world is in Bordeaux.

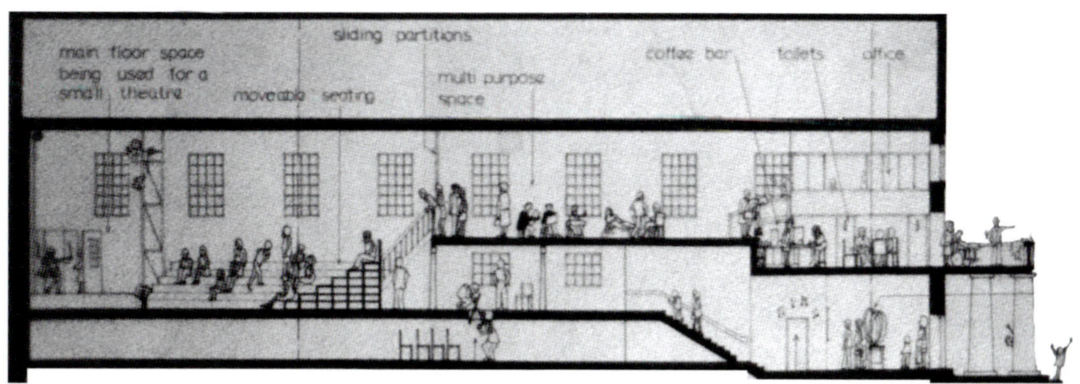


Part of a Comtek drawing showing uses for the tennis court

The writer **Alan Bennett** lamented the destruction of Bath in his 2016 book *Keeping On Keeping On:* When I first came [to Bath] in the 1960s they had just set about demolishing streets and streets of early nineteenth-century housing, the service quarters for the grander buildings in the town. They were said to be of no architectural interest or significance, with no notion that they were part of an architectural whole... And so it has gone on since, with acres of indifferent modern buildings all carefully constructed in [often reconstituted] Bath stone as if that was all that was necessary to bind the city together.

## Walcot Village Hall

**Glyn:** The 1974 Village Hall campaign had a huge impact on community life. The building was an old mortuary chapel that stood at the top of a burial field off Walcot Street.[9] It had been out of use for years and was in a sorry state of disrepair. The leaded light windows were smashed and it was boarded up by its council owners. In May, Comtek and BAW held a one-day event on the burial field, with music, theatre and other activities to raise funds for the chapel and convert it for use as a village hall.

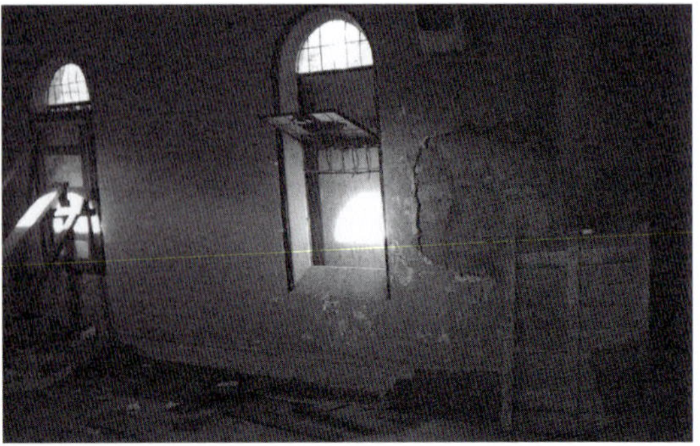

Dilapidated interior

Our video team ran workshops to make your own TV programme and recorded the events as an edition of *Walcot TV News* that was replayed in various places in the local area over the next few weeks. This helped to increase donations by extending and prolonging the appeal. Comtek carried out a survey of the chapel and we produced drawings with a schedule of repairs for volunteers who did the work free of charge. With BAW and others we set

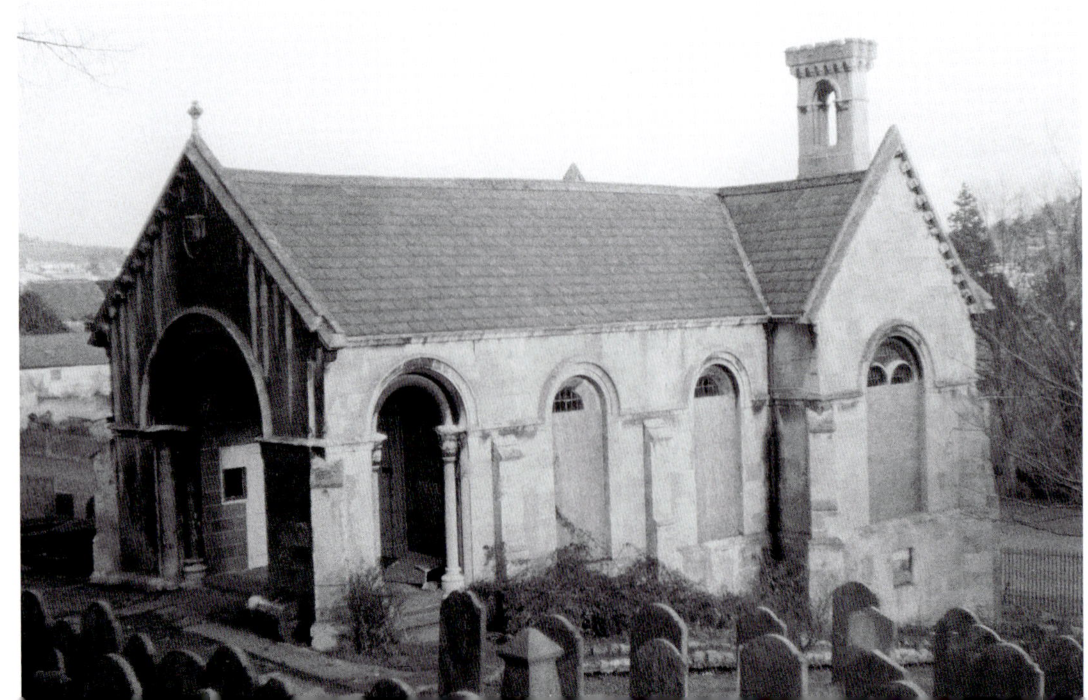

Walcot mortuary chapel, 1974

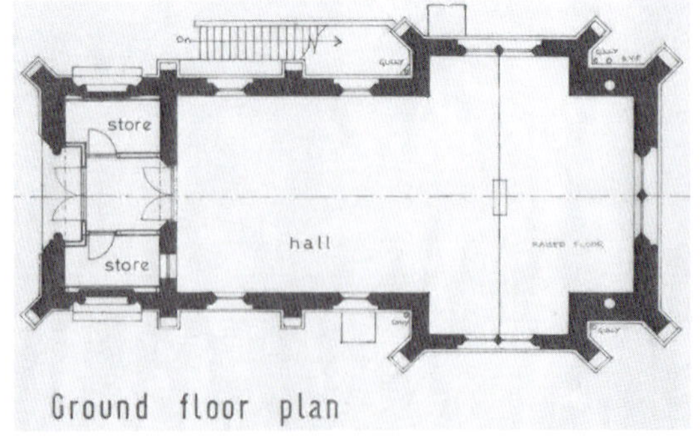


Plan to convert to village hall

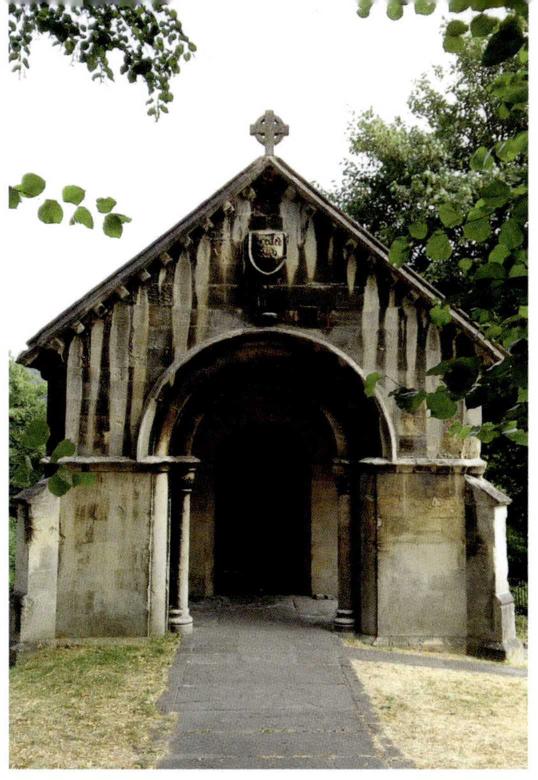

Walcot Village Hall now

## And other buildings

**Glyn:** Comtek was also involved in a campaign to save Chatham Row, a graceful terrace of 12 Georgian houses that runs from Walcot Street down to the river. It was given an initial Grade II listing in 1950. Despite this, in 1967 the council's fire department almost unbelievably used the grandest house (at the bottom of the row) to test the fire resistance of Georgian buildings by setting it alight! By 1973, the houses were essentially being left to rot pending construction of the Buchanan tunnel which, if it had gone ahead, would have resulted in the whole row being destroyed.

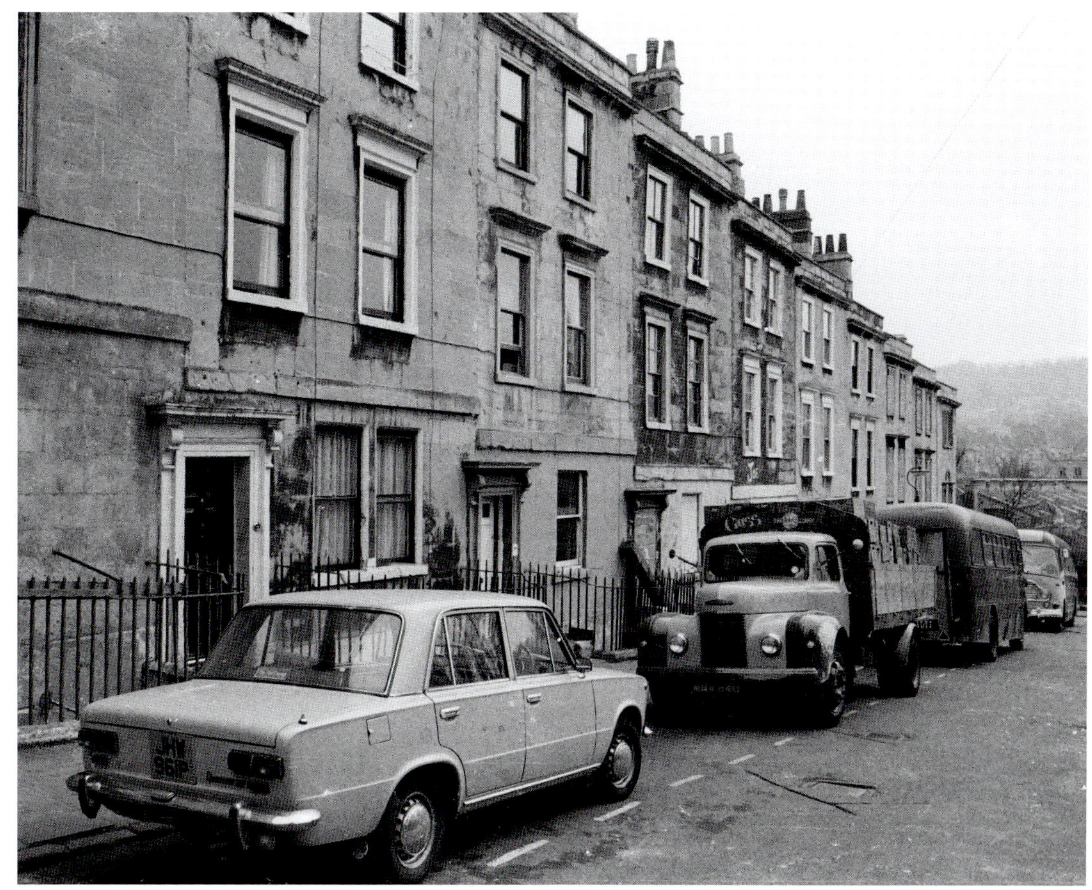

Chatham Row, semi-derelict in 1974

up a committee to get the repairs done and run the building, and a charter was drawn up to protect its future use. The newly-restored Walcot Village Hall opened its doors to the public the following year (1975). Since then, it has been used for thousands of community events – theatre, music, exhibitions, jumble sales, rehearsals, meetings, and an infinite array of other activities. It lives on to this day.

---

9. The burial field was cleared in 1924 to create space for public use, although some gravestones were relocated to the small graveyard surrounding the chapel, which was itself later deconsecrated.

### Buchanan Tunnel Scheme

The tunnel scheme emerged in 1965. Its purpose was ostensibly to regulate traffic flows to and from London to the east and Bristol to the west. If built, it would have resulted in the demolition of swathes of Georgian buildings in the Walcot area. While the scheme was under consideration, the whole area was blighted and neglected for years, leading to the deterioration of many buildings, and an increase in empty houses. Opposition to the scheme was nevertheless gathering momentum in the early 70s and, by 1975, the Save Bath Campaign was attracting national interest and support. The tunnel scheme had been abandoned by 1976.

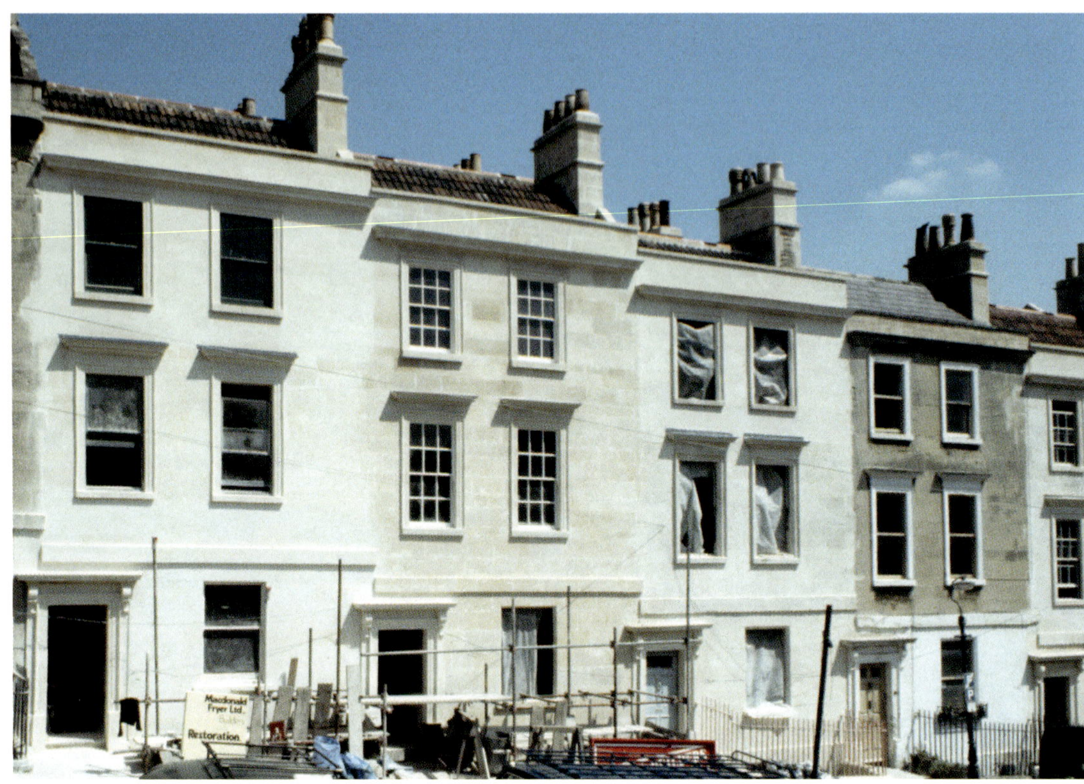

Building work almost finished, Chatham Row 1982

**Glyn:** In 1973, our video team recorded and played videos of squatters being evicted from the steadily deteriorating houses in Chatham Row to draw attention to the reality of homelessness and the numerous empty houses. Meanwhile, the broader anti-tunnel campaign had continued apace and in 1976, the city council established a Conservation Study Team, a move that marked a dramatic policy shift and recognition of the need to protect Bath's architectural heritage. With renewed enthusiasm, we at Comtek supported the owners of five of the houses to combine resources and form a group renovation scheme. Comtek's architects, including the late Dougal Hunter, applied for central government and city council grants. In 1980, Historic Building Grants from both bodies were awarded to the renovation group. Most of the building work was done by the owners with Comtek's help.

Finally, when the redundant Green Park Station, owned by the city council, was up for redevelopment in 1974, we began thinking about a useful purpose for it. From 1974, we used video recordings of the building and various proposals to stimulate public interest and discussion. Thom Brajkovich,

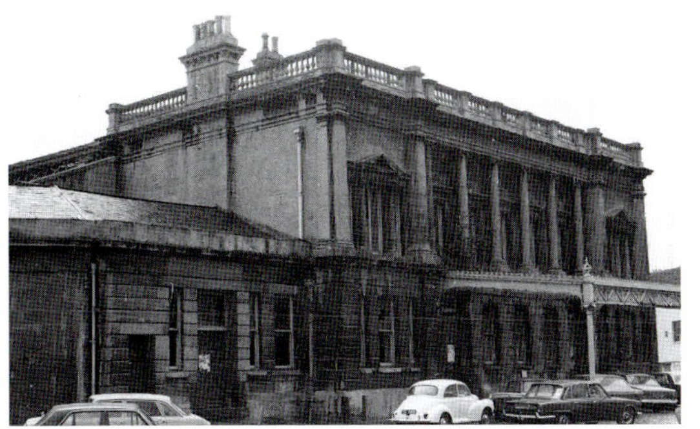

Green Park Station, 1974

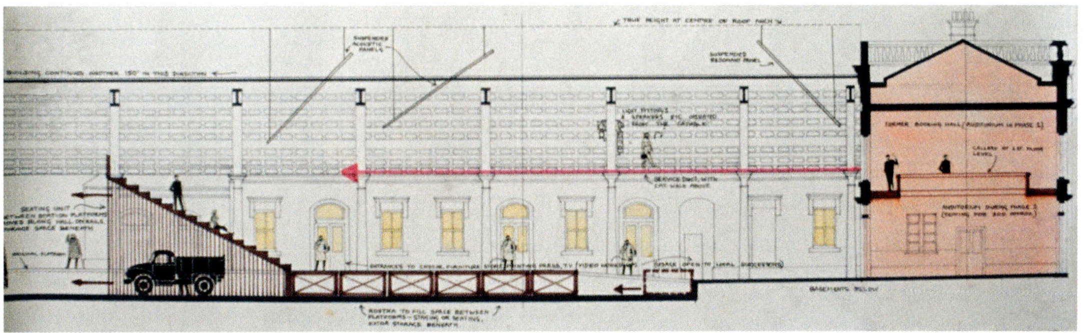

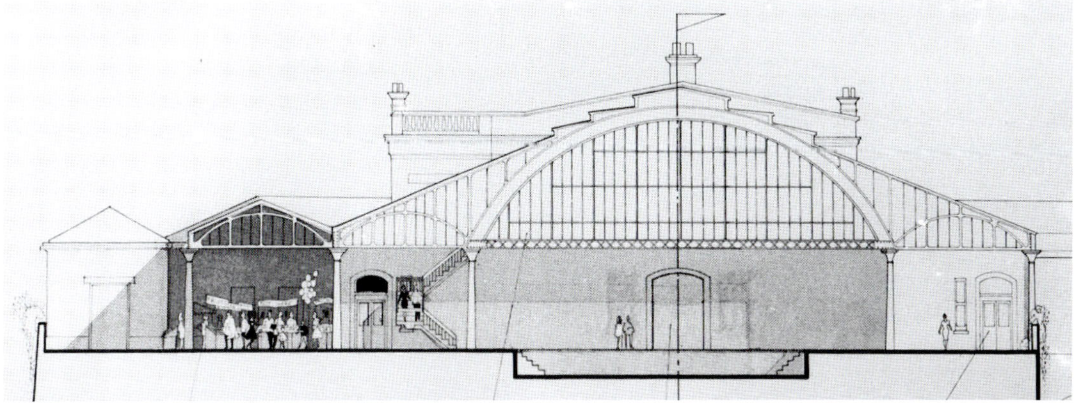

an American architect working with Comtek, prepared plans adapting the buildings for various community uses, including a flexible auditorium in the train shed. The plans were submitted in cooperation with a developer proposing housing on the rest of the site. Our proposals were voted favourite by the public. Eventually Sainsbury's developed the site and it was re-opened in 1982. Today, about half the train shed is available for events and a farmers' market, and there are community facilities in the platform buildings, including cafes, shops, stalls, and meeting rooms.

Comtek drawing showing market and restaurant (top) and flexible use of restaurant area (above)

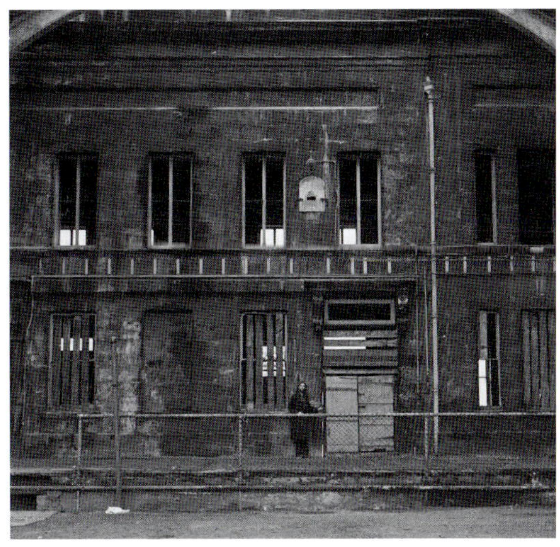

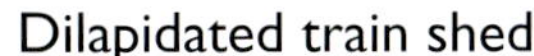

Dilapidated train shed

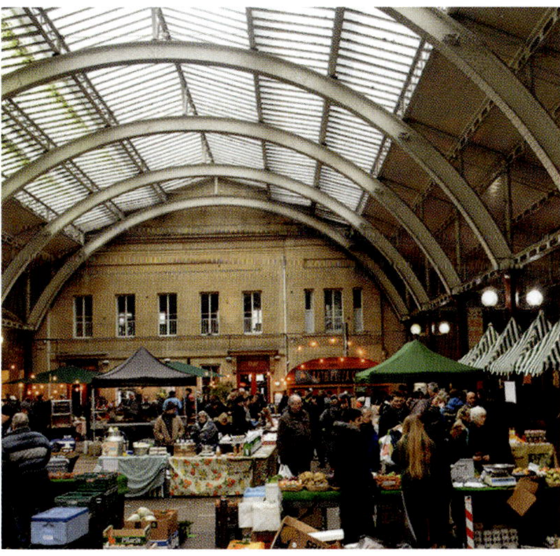

Farmers market in train shed 2019

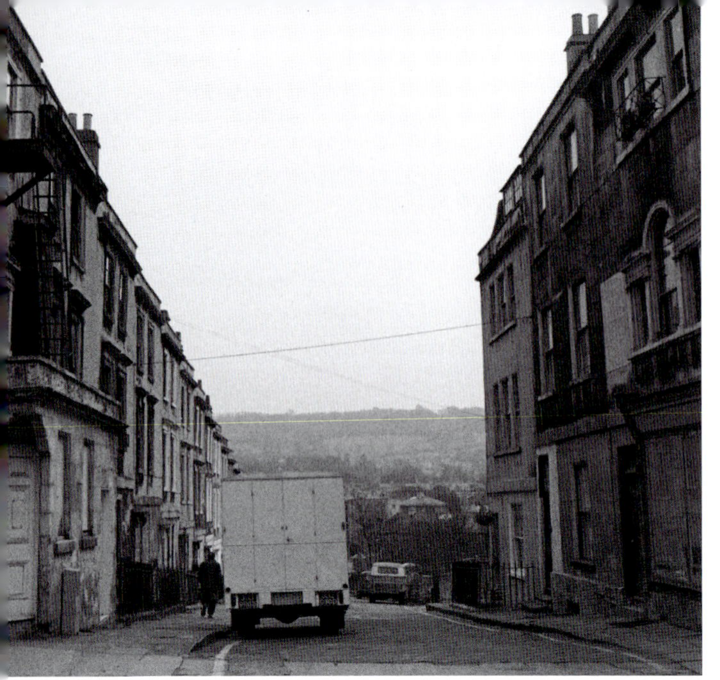

# ALTERNATIVE HOUSING ON THE RIVER BANK

The impact of blighting in Walcot, and the resulting lack of housing, affected local people in various ways, some of whom created their own solutions.

**Simon Chippindale**, a resident of Walcot, remembers: Our friends Fritz and Princess needed a home (they were both too young and outlandish to rent), so Fritz built a shack out of wood and corrugated iron on the river bank at the end of the Row. Number 12 had been derelict for years and sometimes in the night rotten timbers came crashing down inside. This made Princess nervous and soon they moved out. But they had seen the possibility of housing on that land. The river bank had never been used as it flooded every November, but after the new weir was built, flooding was greatly reduced.

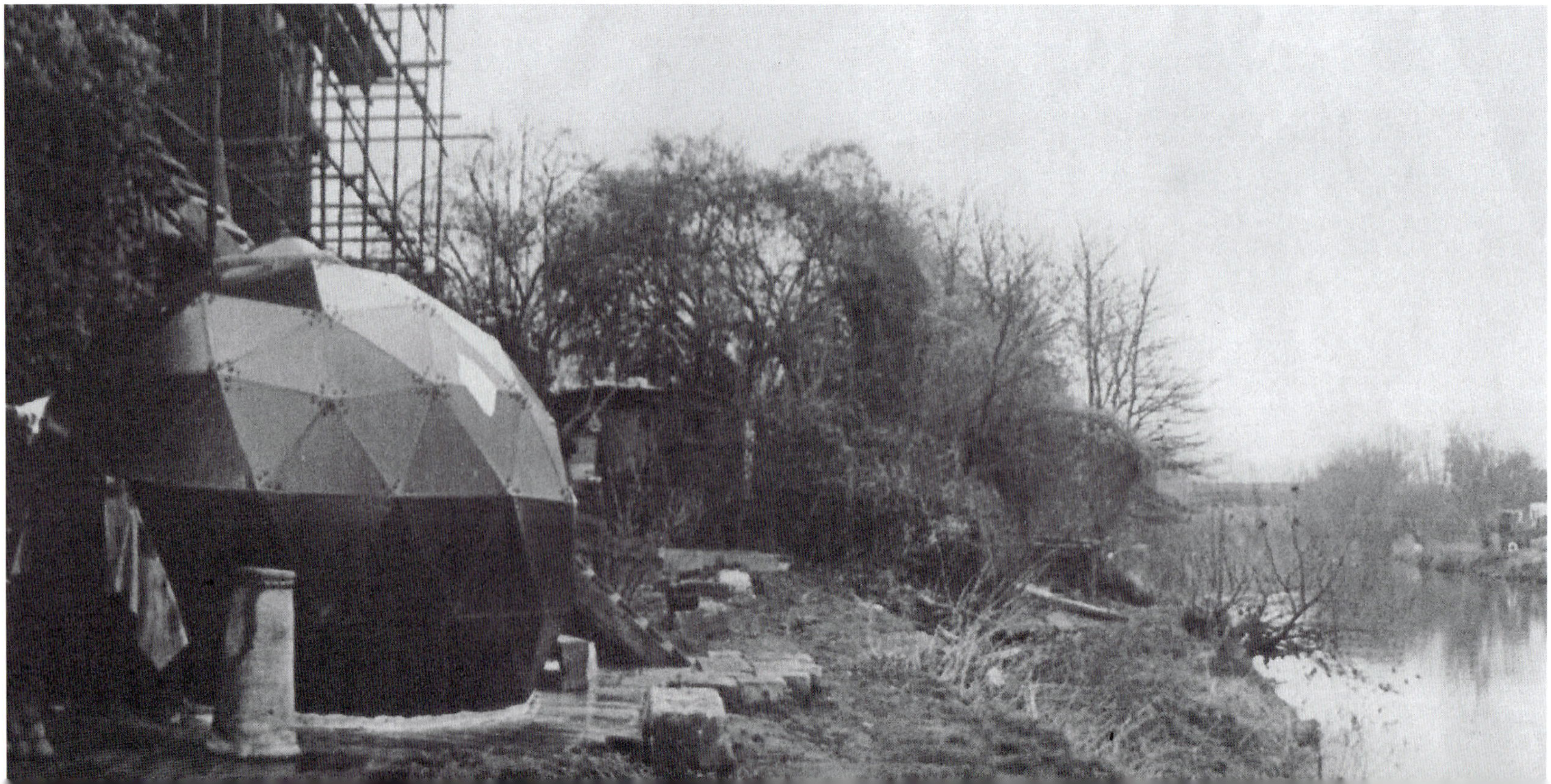

Someone, I never found out who, cut triangles from half-inch sound insulation boards saved from the Cleveland Hotel. They were intending to build a Buckminster Fuller (geodesic) dome at the **Other Festival** that year (1972) at Widcombe Manor. My partner Pauline found the unused pile of triangles and I carried out the job of constructing a dome on the river bank.

Canadian Pete built another low shack from scrap wood but then got worried about flooding and built a second house on stilts closer to the river. Dick Cunliffe, Tim Cutting and I became residents, fortunately with the generous support of those living in Chatham Row at the time. One afternoon, when not much was happening, Tim suggested that three of us put our names into a hat and swap all our worldly goods except clothes. It only took a minute (I missed my record collection and comfy bed, but what's done is done).

Taking our lead from Tim, as we did because he never told anyone what to do, we had a very tolerant village where anyone was welcome to come

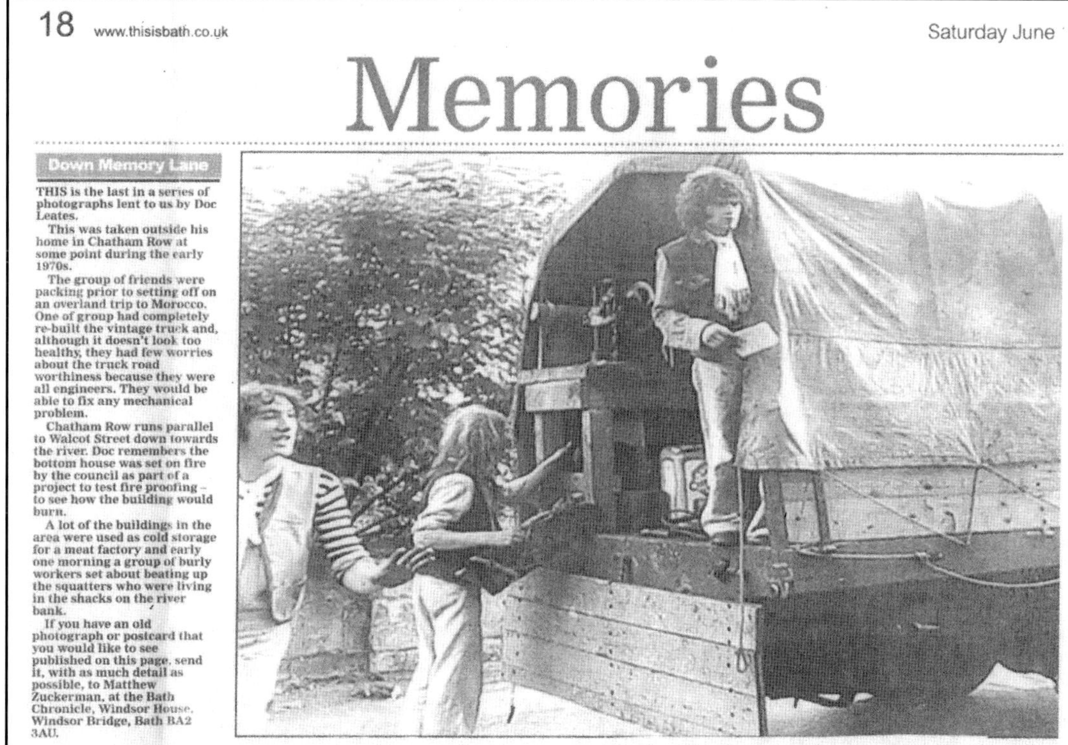

18    www.thisisbath.co.uk      Saturday June

# Memories

**Down Memory Lane**

THIS is the last in a series of photographs lent to us by Doc Leates.

This was taken outside his home in Chatham Row at some point during the early 1970s.

The group of friends were packing prior to setting off on an overland trip to Morocco. One of group had completely re-built the vintage truck and, although it doesn't look too healthy, they had few worries about the truck road worthiness because they were all engineers. They would be able to fix any mechanical problem.

Chatham Row runs parallel to Walcot Street down towards the river. Doc remembers the bottom house was set on fire by the council as part of a project to test fire proofing – to see how the building would burn.

A lot of the buildings in the area were used as cold storage for a meat factory and early one morning a group of burly workers set about beating up the squatters who were living in the shacks on the river bank.

If you have an old photograph or postcard that you would like to see published on this page, send it, with as much detail as possible, to Matthew Zuckerman, at the Bath Chronicle, Windsor House, Windsor Bridge, Bath BA2 3AU.

and do anything, which in the end was its downfall. Some of the hipper schoolkids discovered us and soon learned to prefer lazing around on the riverbank to afternoon lessons. For a while, everyone was happy but when the school authorities found out, they had to exercise their duty of care and put a stop to such sybaritic behaviour. Which led to a highly illegal raid by ice factory thugs armed with axes and sledgehammers, in the early hours of a rainy Tuesday morning, backed up by a squad of police. An interesting exercise in defensive tactics. By the end of the morning, one house had been demolished and it was clear that the river bank's days were numbered.

# HOW WE LIVED THEN

**Tory:** What did we think about love and sex in those years and how did we relate to one another? At the time we didn't think much about national politics, but our lives were definitely affected by the dramatic social and legal changes that were permanently uprooting centuries-old ideas about men and women. In 1967, the contraceptive pill freed women to be sexually active for the first time without getting pregnant, and the Equal Pay Act was passed in 1970.[1] From the late 60s, a strong feminist movement emerged, and 'the personal is political' captured the idea that power dynamics play out within our personal lives.

In those heady days of possibility, we in the Workshop had definitely embraced the spirit of the 60s revolution with its simpler promise of sexual freedom and equality. We imagined living and working together and promoting these principles in our work. From the outset, we supported Women's and Gay Liberation groups (as they were then known). But feminism itself was somehow never part of the core. Our style was more rooted in practical action and brazen theatrical humour – poking fun at authority rather than addressing gender or political issues.

This was provincial England in the 70s and BAW inevitably mirrored society to a degree. Around two thirds of our members were men. There was an age gap, too. The men were in their mid-20s, whereas many of us women were 18 or younger when we joined in. We longed for change but were perhaps initially less confident or concrete on how to achieve it. In the early years, the men were the most prominent initiators, experimental performers and eco-activists. Of course, our projects could never have happened without the talents and work of us women, but at times our contributions were unseen or undervalued. As the years rolled by, we gained more recognition.

There was always much camaraderie – a sense of common purpose, of mucking in, the pleasure in belonging to a riotous alternative tribe. We were all insiders and anyone was free to have a go.

Kate Greaves and Pat Richardson put the core admin in place in the early days. Jackie Popay was a true artist, continually inventing her own theatre. Corinne was a key performer, organiser, costume designer and seamstress. Penny, aged 19, took on the electrics and lighting at our festivals and concerts. Jennie had barely arrived when she went to Rotterdam to organise a month-long community arts and theatre programme, along with

---

1. Gender equality remains a distant goal 50 years later. It is striking that Barbara Castle, the politician who played such a major role in achieving the Equal Pay Act, has seemingly disappeared from our political history.

Ros Birks. There was always some massive task to throw ourselves into and we found ways to learn new skills. And everyone in BAW was paid the same wages from start to finish, so there was equality on that front.

Sexual stereotypes were rife across the board in those days and Workshop humour sometimes shaded into sexism, publicly and privately, in a way that diminished our bodies and intelligence. Dodgy jokes appeared in Workshop newsletters, 'the Rockettes had a set-to when they were all trying to talk to the same man' was one such. Typical of the times and 'ironic', but sexist all the same.

The Rocky Show itself was a bizarre conglomeration of gender parodies that drew on every sexual stereotype of the era: the Rockettes were either dim-witted or scarily sexual. Rocky was a vain and fading B-list singer, struggling to keep up with the virility of the psychedelic era. The vanities and vagaries of masculinity were no exception, whether on- or offstage. Men performing as women were a constant in our world and we took it completely for granted. Male nudity also played its part in our theatrics, in its own way subversive. A man's naked body is all too fragile, masculine power unmasked one might say, a taboo that is still firmly in place.

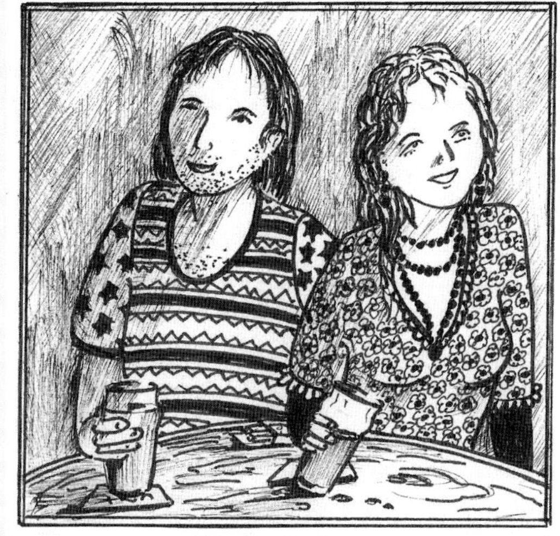

We were the first generation to live in shared houses and experiment with 'free love'. It was easier for the men – suddenly the rules changed and plentiful sex was possible. We women wanted to join in and be free (and we were), but were still shy about our own sexuality. And we dealt with the consequences of unprotected sex on our own – we didn't talk much about that.

On the other hand, we lived so closely together. We were free to be clumsy and imperfect together in a kind of intimate solidarity. There was no on-line porn with its preponderance of contempt for women and its dull obliteration of female sexuality. Our womanly bodies were not yet commodified – there was less pressure to sanitise and glamorise every inch of our flesh or display ourselves on social media. Our unruly female bodies had more room to breathe, unremarked by ourselves or other people. Or so it seems now.

Love, companionship and casual sex were part of life and intermingled with our working lives. There was an acceptance of human foibles that felt real and reassuring and this helped us develop our skills and resilience. Twenty years on, I was dragging a flipchart across a dust-blown town in Haiti before a human rights workshop. There was a power cut and the vans had broken down. I remember thinking, 'Bath Arts Workshop taught me how to do this'.

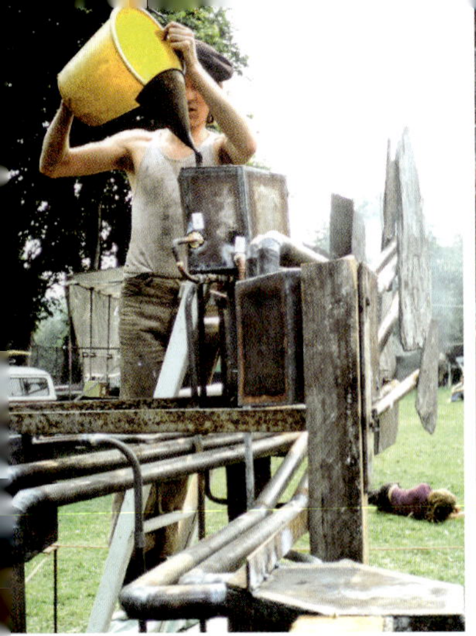
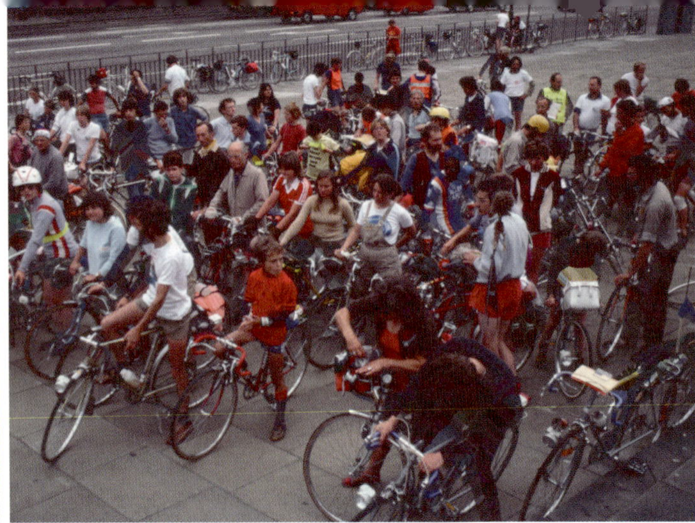
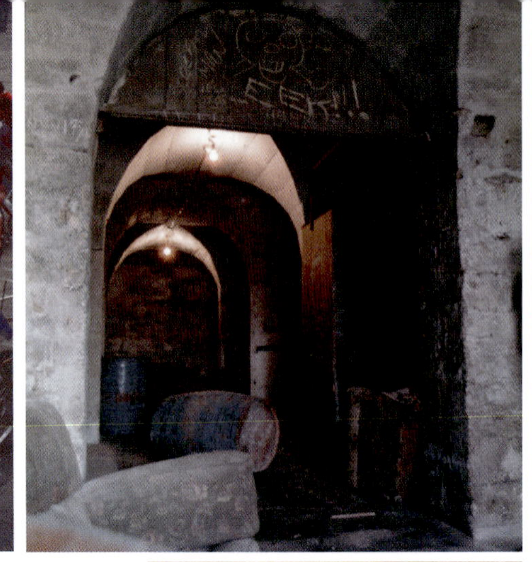
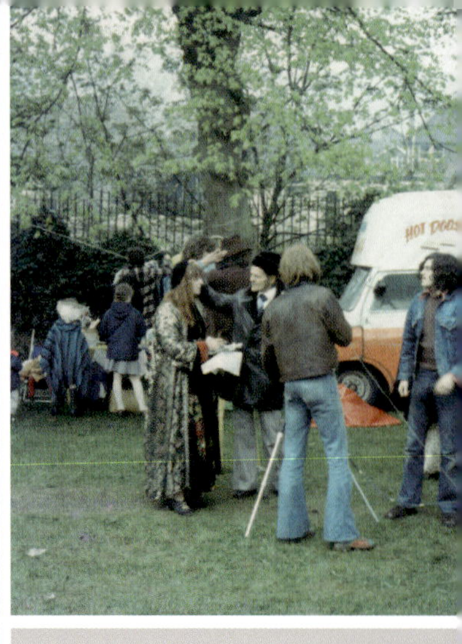
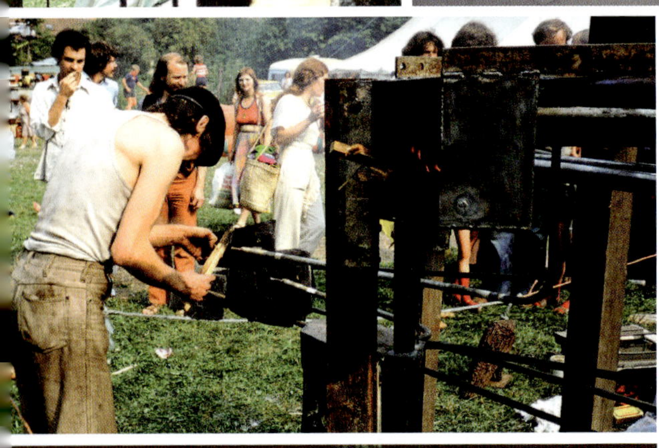
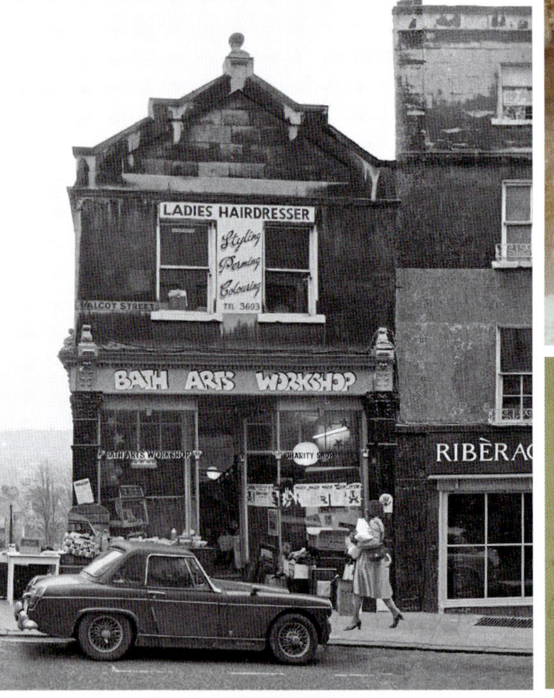

LADIES HAIRDRESSER
Styling
Perming
Colouring
TEL 3693
WALCOT STREET
BATH ARTS WORKSHOP
BATH ARTS WORKSHOP
CHARITY SHOP
RIBERAC

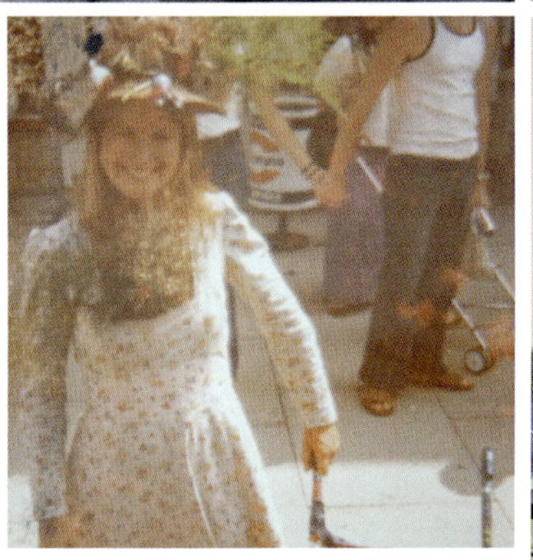
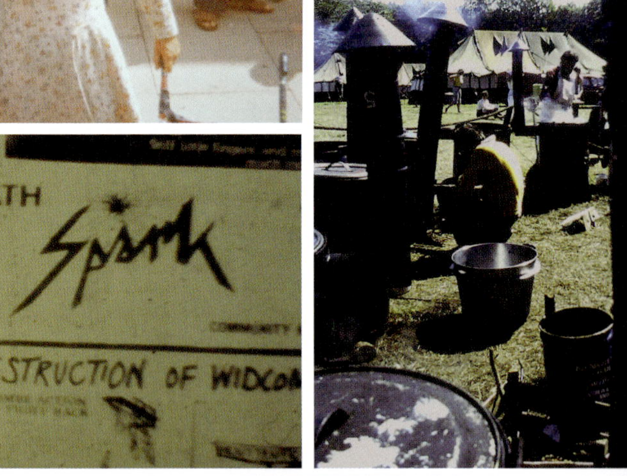

BATH
Spark
DESTRUCTION OF WIDCO

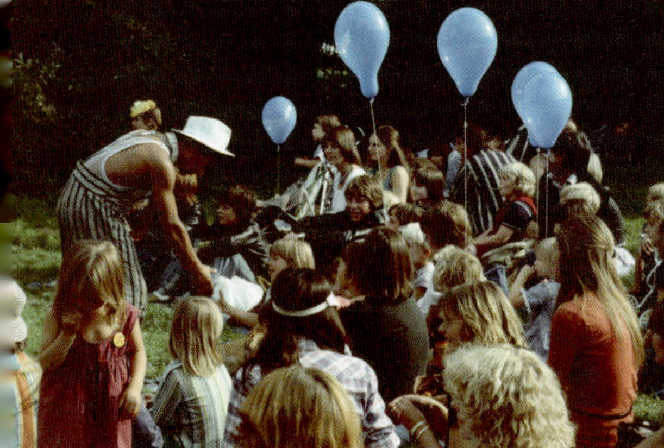
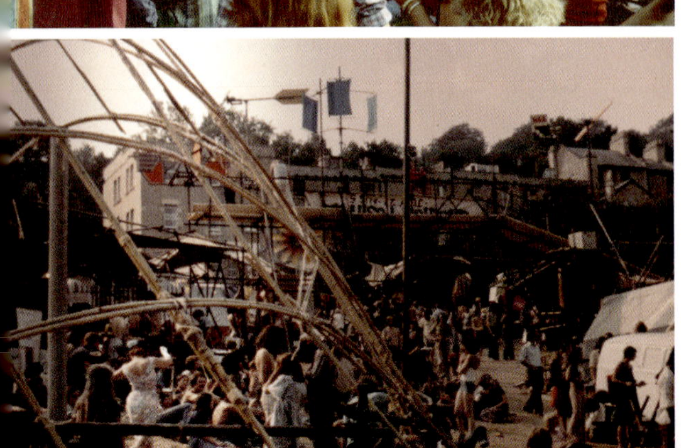
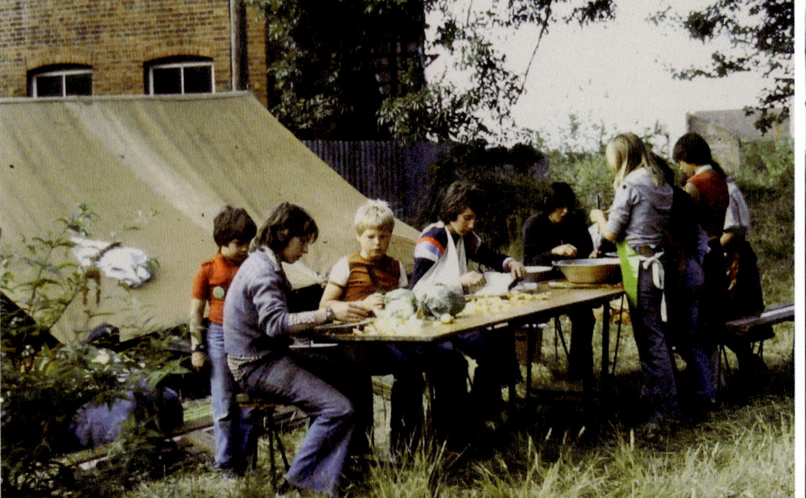
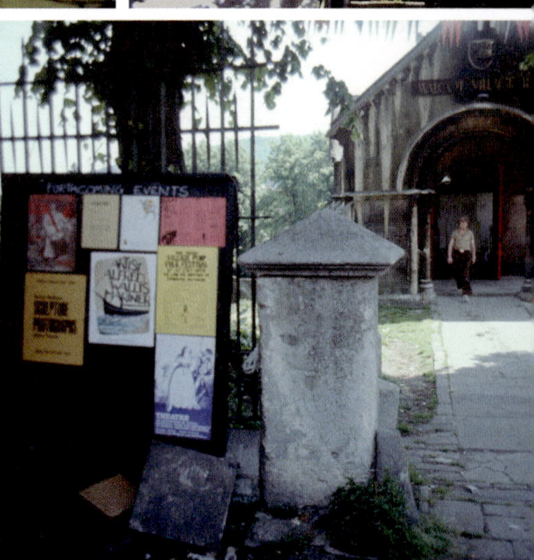

FORTHCOMING EVENTS

# CHAPTER 7
# THE WALCOT YEARS
# 1974-79

**In which our velvet-trousered evolution came of age. We ran a second-hand shop and cheap removals in pink and green vans. We joined Civil Aid and served 9,000 cheese rolls for Rock against Racism in Brockwell Park. We made films, supported musicians and served free Christmas meals for 200.**

**Tory:** The Workshop really came together during the Walcot years. Everything we'd worked for had begun to blossom and bear fruit. We relocated to our shop and office at 146 Walcot Street in late 1973. The shop itself, our community transport service and summer adventure playgrounds provided a hub and linked us strongly to the local area. Our small upstairs office was *Natural Theatre* HQ, and a base for Workshop Music. It was 'central admin' for our summer festivals and bookings for the Walcot Village Hall. From 146 we also fundraised for and organised our annual Christmas dinner celebrations for anyone who wanted to join in.

During the same period, Nigel Leach embarked on a major project to expand and develop BAW's activities, finding a home at the Riverside Community Centre where, in 1975, he and others set up a print shop and an alternative truant school, with the latter offering a unique and adventurous curriculum for disillusioned kids. Raising funds and renovating the building involved a lot of work, but once up and running the centre became an important local hub, providing useful practical services and a venue for community groups to host their own community and social events. Nigel was also the instigator of our encounter with Civil Aid, a move that led us into undreamed-of adventures including mass catering and theatrical survival events (more to be revealed below).

By late 1974, Comtek was well established at its Weymouth Street depot, so we were more geographically spread out. But we were always inter-linked and collaborated on many projects, especially the festivals. Arguments and disagreements were inevitably part of daily life but, despite the conflicts, our commitment remained firm: to encourage creativity and a spirit of 'anyone can join in'. There was always theatricality and fun to be found in our work as well as immense practicality. And beneath it, an unspoken sense of purpose – to be less materialistic and to respect the planet.

# A shop in Walcot Street

**Penny:** We were given notice to leave the Organ Factory at the end of 1972 but remained there until the autumn of 1973. During the first part of that year, we had spent a month in Rotterdam working with communities in the Old West neighbourhood. We came straight back to preparing the massive ***Another Festival*** that summer. During the festival, we used the Organ Factory for performances, rehearsals and storage.

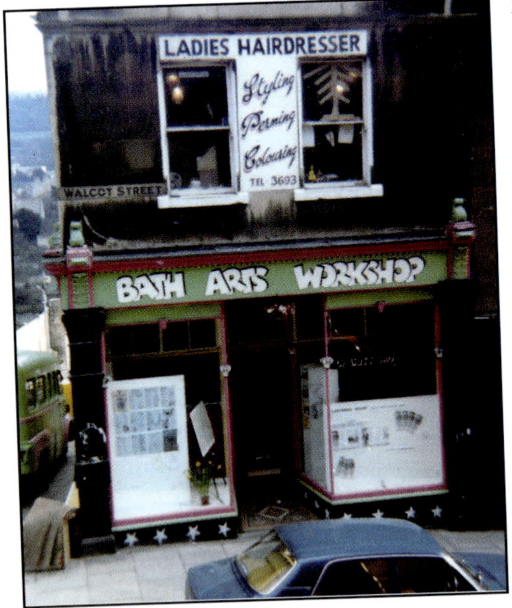

The repainted shop front

In the meantime, Bath City Council let us take over Max and Christine's empty hairdresser's shop at 146 Walcot Street. It was a moment of transformation for the Workshop. We lost a permanent performance space of our own, but gained a shop and office in the heart of Walcot, along with two big display windows to do as we wished with. Once we had the keys to the shop, we cleared the downstairs area and painted the shopfront in our garish Workshop colours, bright pink and green. Upstairs became our new office with just enough space for paperwork and meetings, plus storage of more valuable equipment – film editing, video, disco paraphernalia and so on.

**Brian:** The shop opened in autumn 1973. We sold all sorts there: donated items, cash and carry domestic goods, second-hand furniture and jumble clothes. King Kong Community Transport had its heyday during these years. We picked up donations from houses all over Bath in a variety of vehicles ranging from small vans and two-ton lorries, to a large flat-bed truck, as well as offering low-price removals to the social services department of the council. At times, we offered unlikely items for sale such as a V8 Rover car. This happened at the height of the mid-70s oil crisis.

**Sarah Acheson:** The purpose of the shop was to raise money for community projects run by BAW and also to recycle furniture, clothes etc for the local community. It meant we had a visible and accessible presence in Walcot, and a wage for those of us who worked there. There were lots of regular shoppers, browsers and people who came in for a chat.

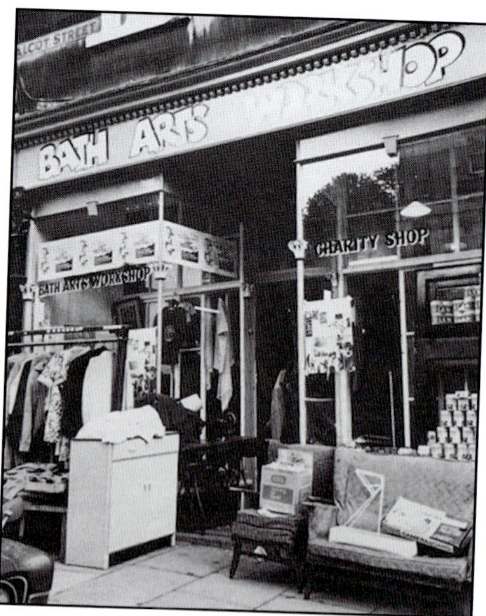

Stock on the pavement

The stock often spilled out onto the pavement – getting stuff in and out was worse when we had done well with donations and the piles of furniture threatened to injure customers and staff alike.

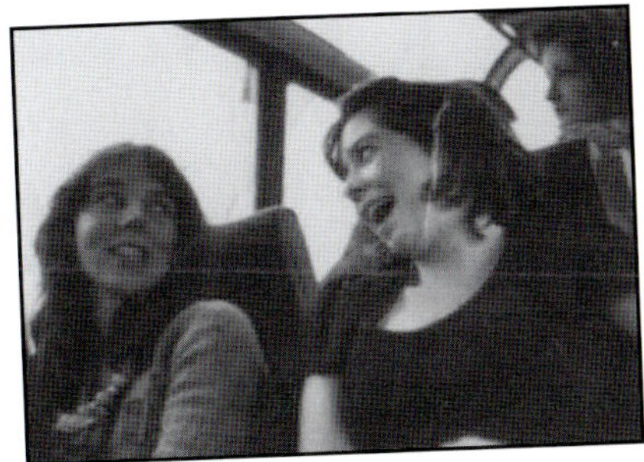

Sarah (right) with Penny



**Brian:** Working in the shop was a job that Mick Martin and I had hilarious fun doing. On one occasion I recall, two gents had unwittingly bought the same large wooden table. No amount of negotiation could persuade either to give up the table to the other. So Mick simply sawed the table in half and grandly presented one half to each! **Ralph adds:** Another time when Mick was on shop duty, we heard the horrendous sound of breaking china. We'd put a box of odd saucers on sale, something like five for 10p. An antique dealer came in and asked for a trade price. Mick said he'd rather smash the lot than reduce them any further – and there he was tap dancing in the box of crockery with the ashen-faced trader looking on aghast.

We were helped by Kitty Sutton, who had appeared from Odd Down on the outskirts of town and ended up working full-time in the shop. Gordon Robbins was also part of our crew. He was a man of no fixed abode and an accomplished pub piano player, who sometimes serenaded the customers with highlights from his repertoire. His songs were interspersed with a cackling laugh.

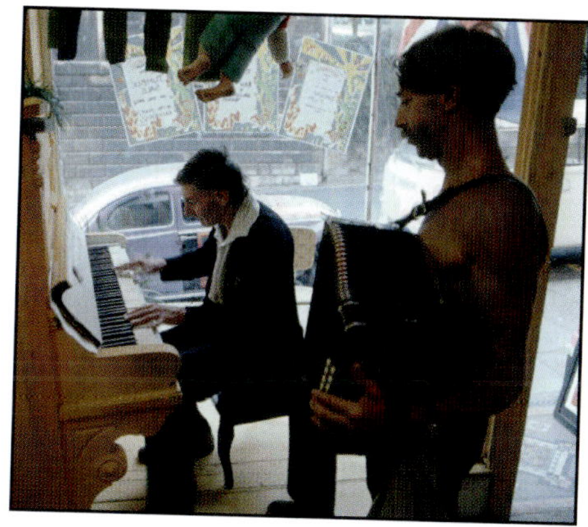

Gordon in the shop with Captain Headlam

### Mary Gouldbourne (then Mary Kiss)



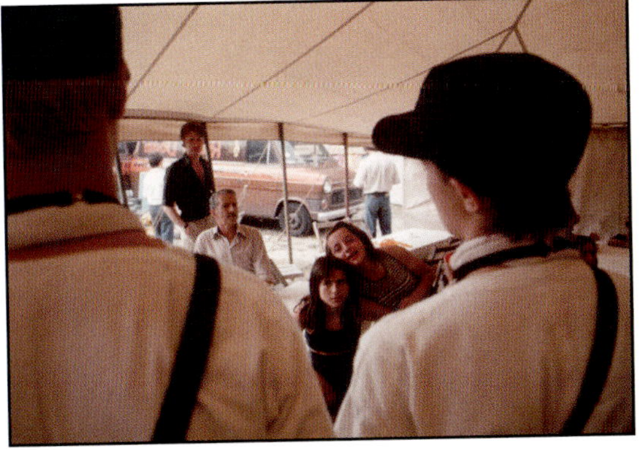

Mary and Marie Edwards checking out Lumiere & Son

We were lucky kids. Ralph could be caustic and hysterical but that was always what I found amusing about him. Walcot Street is in dire need of something real like that again. The world needs more arts workshops and less phone/coffee and designer crap.

## Art in the windows

**Brian:** We often used our shop windows to stage impromptu exhibitions and window displays that occurred unannounced. Here our art-school skills found an outlet for expression. Once we turned the place into a high-class antique shop that was constantly closed, but which had a window full of wares. They included a stripped-down upholstered chair presented as a desirable antique valued at £1000, and the archaeological remains of a box of washing powder suitably 'distressed' and priced at over £500, and said to have been discovered during excavations of the Roman Baths. All this subterfuge aimed to highlight the way that Bath was slowly becoming more trendy and gentrified.

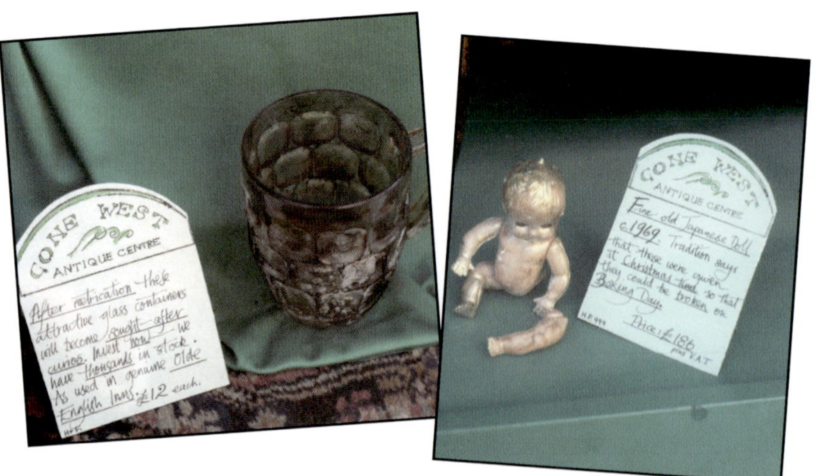

A Charles Byrd machine

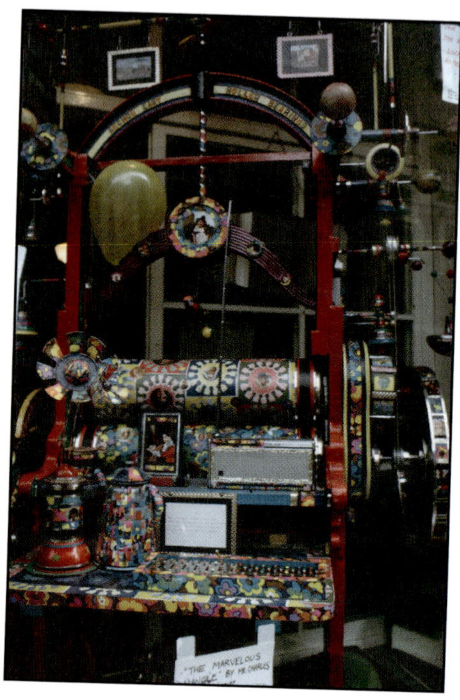

On another occasion, we covered the shop windows with brick wallpaper. We left a couple of panels out so that passers-by could peer through. Those who did were confronted with the sight of an old lady sitting alone in her flat. She was May Branch, a 73-year-old pensioner and a great friend. Through the other window, a man was slowly changing into a woman, representing two sad sides of a 'secret Bath'. Or we featured other artists providing a sort of free art gallery. One such was a Welshman called *Charles Byrd*, now aged 100 and still working.

## King Kong Community Transport

**Sarah:** Meanwhile King Kong was going strong – we filled our Walcot shop with furniture, china and bric-a-brac from house clearances. I was the King Kong coordinator for a while in 1974-75. We offered a commercial rate and a community rate for people on low incomes, with one subsidising the other – another simple but genius idea from BAW. Prior to doing this, I hadn't realised vital stuff, like some pianos having iron frames and being extremely difficult to get out of attic flats. We operated on a shoestring and seemed to have frequent crises, such as wildly under-paid staff not always being reliable, old vans breaking down, MOT licences failing and 'O' licenses running out when you weren't looking. Also, shockingly, some people weren't 100 per cent honest about how much furniture they needed removing, resulting in delays for the next customer and irate phone calls. Overall though, many people on low incomes had an affordable service and it helped keep our vans on the road. David 'Napoleon' Shopper was indispensable to King Kong in those days (and like everyone else he also took part in **Natural Theatre** when the need arose). He could drive any vehicle and often helped me out when other drivers let me down.

**A pensioner:** Don't call it King Kong. Call it the service that cares.

**Mick Banks:** And in the vernacular 'what goes up must come down' we collected things, heavy varnished things. These ended up in the shop where some were sold, some incorporated into performances and others into ingenious window displays. For the Queen's Silver Jubilee in 1977, Ralph constructed a whole window of Union Jack furniture with the Royal Train running in and out of drawers and cupboards. These had previously been salvaged, meticulously painted and adapted for a stage show that Corinne and I had written and performed. The chain of recycling was infinite.

## Ladymead House social group

**Sarah:** Around this time, the Workshop ran a day club for the remaining residents of Ladymead House in Walcot Street, before the building was sold and redeveloped as flats. I understood them to be elderly, institutionalised 'fallen women', some with a degree of learning difficulties. There had previously been a regime where the women who lived there had little involvement in the outside world and were able to make few choices about their daily lives. Their situation was a hangover from a radically different approach to the welfare and rights of powerless women, and the partial 'opening up' of their home was one of the many examples of social change in the 70s.

What I experienced in the day club and our outings was the sheer joy of sharing simple activities with people who have been deprived of so much in life. We would have a piano player and sing songs or do craft – all of us enthusiastic, but with not much in the way of skill, especially me. One memorable outing was to the Roman Baths, where the guide struggled to be heard over the euphoria of people who hadn't had to walk there in a crocodile. I was pregnant for part of the time there, and then went back with my baby (Daisy, now 42) who was the subject of great interest. What I have realised over the years since, is that many of the women would have lost their own babies, not being considered fit to bring them up. It was a pleasure to share that time with them.

## Walcot Village Hall

**Tory:** A few yards down from our shop was the Village Hall. Formerly a mortuary chapel, it had been refurbished thanks to Comtek's architects, and was open in time for the **Walcot Festival** in 1975. From then on, it became a wonderful venue for BAW and a vast range of other groups and individuals, despite being freezing and ill-equipped. It was totally unheated so winter rehearsals took place huddled around Hector, a roaring calor gas heater. Performers had to change in the dark and musty crypt before trudging up the path to the front entrance.

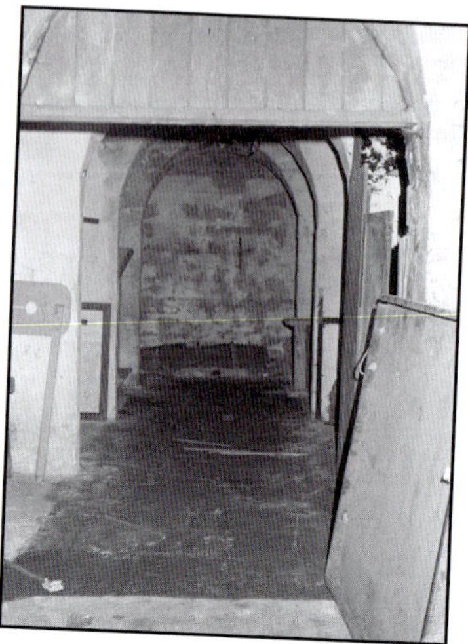

The crypt



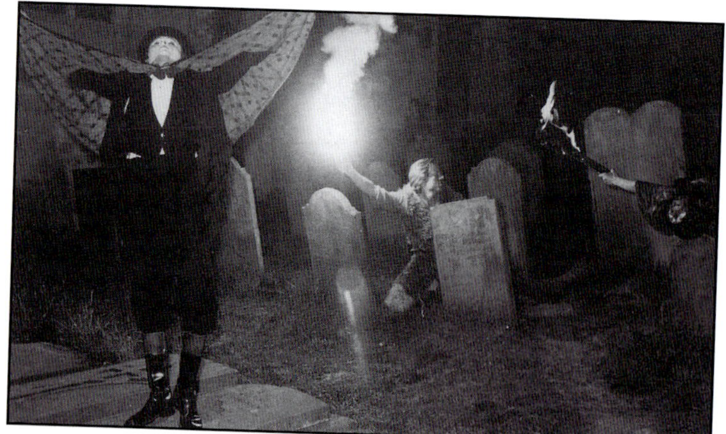

Hammer Horror



The hall was managed by a committee of BAW members, local people and a councillor. It was used for hundreds of performances by visiting artists – **Exploded Eye**, **Landscapes and Living Spaces**, **Lumiere & Son** and many more. The Naturals performed there often. It was essential to our Walcot festivals and in 1978 the site of the riotous Beano Club (see *Chapter 9*). At different times, it hosted a vegetable market, jumble sales, kids' workshops and a rehearsal space for theatre groups and bands. In 1976, Corinne managed to get the Village Hall accepted onto the Arts Centres Grid.[1] This meant we could offer decent fees to performers, as well as booking groups like **The People Show** for the first time.

## Andy's Puppets

By 1975, **Andrew Hume (Andy)** had made and was running a self-supporting Punch & Judy show that was used at many BAW events, tours in the Netherlands, at our summer festivals and at schools, fetes and children's parties.

**Andy:** As with most people I got involved in most Workshop activities, from cooking at the Organ Factory in the early days, and later with Civil Aid and the Christmas dinners. Most enjoyable was working with **Natural Theatre** and I did stints as a clown, a Normal, Smart Party etc. I also worked

---

1. The Grid was a South West Arts Association initiative that subsidised regional venues to book national touring groups.

**Goings on**

(April to June 1977)

| | |
|---|---|
| Abrakadabra, clown and puppet troupe | Grand & Not So Grand – an evening of Opera |
| Adrian Hedley mime artist shows and classes | Dames Nellie Tesco & Clara Boot, with Chas Ambler |
| Andy's Puppets | on piano |
| Art Exhibition | Janet Tamblin's Magic Lantern Show |
| Brog Puppets | Landscapes and Living Spaces (Roland Miller & Shirley |
| Chamber music concert | Cameron) |
| Contemporary dance classes for adults and children | Lumiere & Son |
| Cycles Dance Company | Mr Pugh's Puppets |
| Cycling exhibition for National Bike Week | Professor Crump |
| & a bike ride and picnic | Road Poets – readings at the Village Hall |
| | Wakefield Tricycle Company |

with Mitch and Rolande of **Exploded Eye** in the early days of the theatrical coach tours.

**Andy:** I hitchhiked from London in 1971 and was heading for Ireland when, by chance, my lift ended in The Paragon, Bath. Impressed with the architecture and it being early evening, I headed to The Hat & Feather, there meeting some BAW members. Needless to say I didn't continue my journey as I found the whole enterprise inspiring

At some point, after we'd moved into the shop at 146, I was asked to look after the accounts for BAW, which were quite comprehensive by then as the organisation had grown considerably in a relatively short time. I ran a reggae disco for a while for the kids at Snow Hill, helped collect jumble for the shop, did community decorating, helped with festivals

and looked after the flat and then house in Rivers Street, where a number of BAW members lived. I left in 1979 to open a puppet theatre in Bath, plus family commitments. Like a lot of people, I think the Workshop had a profound influence on my life.

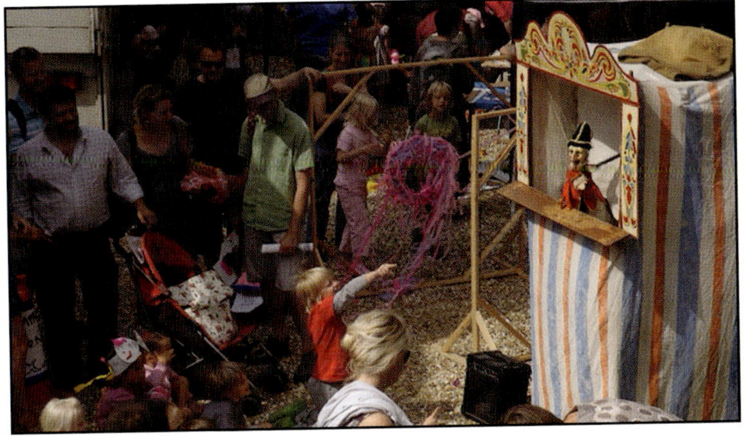

Punch & Judy

153

### Curt Smith (of Tears for Fears)

I consider myself lucky that in a world of conformity and structure I grew up in the formative years of the Bath Arts Workshop. The relief I found at the adventure playground, where abstract creativity was a thing to be embraced not stifled. That painting, singing, making crafts, even climbing trees and getting caked in dirt were also valuable learning experiences and paths to growth. I first experienced the power of live music at the Walcot Festival and attended religiously every year. I considered these people my family and still look back with gratitude on those years.

My first band rehearsal was at the Walcot Village Hall. Our first recordings were at Crescent Studios next door. My role models were Jackie, Brian and Ralph. I wanted to be Rocky Ricketts. Luckily I got close and will be eternally grateful!

## Adventure playground

**Louise Osborn (then White):** Children and teenagers were always part of Workshop life. Over the years, we ran many drama and video workshops, did stints at residential holiday homes for children from inner cities, and ran youth

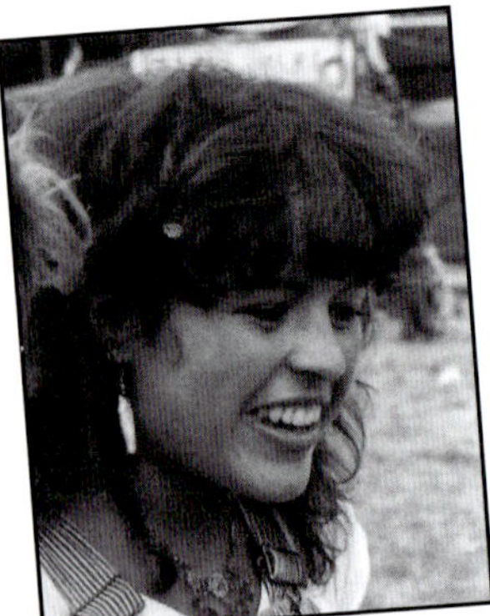

clubs and adventure playgrounds in the Walcot area. I was 23 when the Workshop asked me to run the 1978 summer playground on a piece of wasteland at the bottom of the burial field. I had no training but this was a time before you had to 'qualify' for everything. The Council gave us some funds and resources – an old green wooden trailer hut with a little stove (around which we huddled when it rained); three big blokes on Community Service Orders; an assistant play worker (Adrian Hall); spades and pick axes, hammers and nails, some old theatre sets, ropes, and several telegraph poles and large pieces of timber.

Louise: I had dropped out of college and arrived in Bath by chance in 1976. I set up a vintage clothes stall in Walcot Street indoor market and met Yvonne Hellin (a Rockette at the time). She took me to a Rockette 'audition' in the Village Hall and the rest was history. I joined the band and became a full time member of BAW and the Natural Theatre.

The blokes on community service were brilliant. Tattooed and muscular, I remember them with their shirts off, swinging pick axes and heaving around telegraph poles. With some of the older kids, they dug a massive, makeshift

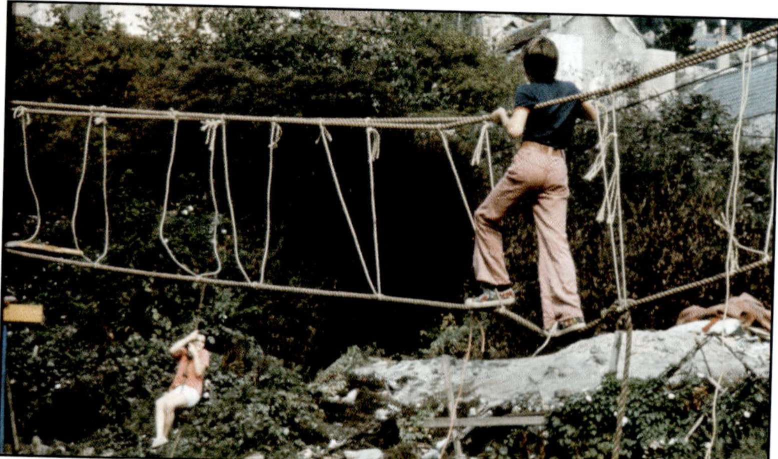

Adventure playground

muddy 'swimming pool', across which a treacherous aerial runway stretched from pole to tree. There were climbing structures, hiding places and loads of mud. The kids got stuck in with hammers and nails to help construct a climbable and habitable city from the old theatre sets. We painted it in brilliant colours. On rainy days, we played cards and board games and painted. But mostly we were outdoors. We had sand and water play. We cooked and made fires and often got very dirty. We made up stories and plays, and acted them out with painted faces and make-shift costumes. We also spent a lot of time hanging out and chatting. Probably feeling and going through a bit of boredom before finding the next thing to do. Kids were often left on their own to form bonds and find friends.

Nobody did anything bad and miraculously no one got seriously hurt. I think we had a first-aid kit supplied by the council, which we kept in a box under one of the trailer benches. There was a real sense of pushing the boundaries of adventure, whilst having adults around to talk to, get support from and imaginatively play with.

As I remember it, it was mostly a long hot summer and about 20-25 kids came every day. There were lots of kids from the Snow Hill Estate, and some little girls who arrived in pretty dresses and patent shoes – I remember them getting stuck into the sand and water (and being embraced by the older children). I have very little memory of contact with any parents. I don't remember the site being inspected and health and safety wasn't an issue. We went on bus trips in an old coach (no seat belts of course) visiting stately homes and other play sites. We had lots of picnics and so many laughs! It was a significant opportunity for me – being given that responsibility and the freedom to forge those relationships and explore the boundaries of my own imagination.

### Tessa Beeching – Memories of a kid in Walcot Street

Mum arrived in Bath first. I arrived with my grandparents at Easter 1974 and started school at Parkside Infants a few days later. While there I made friends with some of the children who lived in and near Walcot St and was introduced to the lovely people at Bath Arts Workshop. Jackie and Brian Popay were lovely to me and Ralph Oswick put up with me very well too. As well as all the families on Walcot St and Chatham Row.

The other joy was the adventure playground. I remember Louise and Adrian helped us. We came up with a list of what we wanted to build and then made it. We had dens in the trees. A zip wire, climbing frames the lot. I decided I wanted a swimming pool so we dug it out for what seemed like days. Then a cement mixer appeared and it was lined and for a glorious very short time it was a beautiful shining pearl of clean water until it turned into a glorious mud hole. It has flats on it now, nowhere to have it now.

I had my seventh birthday party in Walcot Village Hall. Not many kids came but most of the Natural Theatre Company did – all dressed up. It was a wonderful day only slightly marred by my teacher breaking her tooth on the birthday cake, which looked great but was hard as a rock.

## Riverside: Printshop and truant school

**Nigel Leach:** Our move to the Walcot Street shop inevitably limited our capacity to develop in-house creative activities but I was still keen to pursue the idea of a permanent community arts base in Walcot. In the summer of 1975, I worked with a friend, Meg Roberton, to do just that. The Council offered us a single-storey concrete building at minimal cost that became Riverside Community Centre.[2] We raised funds for the renovation that included painting, cutting and refitting 300 panes of glass and finding some minimal furnishing. The centre opened in May 1976. Louise Ingham, then a student at Bath Academy of Art, set up a basic community print shop, and we established a mums and toddlers group, discos, and music evenings organised by a local Afro/Caribbean group. We also used fibre-glass moulds to construct two boats and bought a cheap outboard motor.

Even before it was opened, some local children used to hang about at the centre, either excluded from or not wanting to go to school. Teachers Dick Phillips and Paul Mitton then set up a truant school for them.[3] The classes, while happening at set times, bore little resemblance to their rejected schooling. Trips were arranged to the Welsh Mountains for children with no experience of camping. Lessons both in school and out included foraging, building large kites, orienteering/ map reading and on at least one occasion learning to steer and manage a narrowboat. Meanwhile, the government's Commission for Employment and Skills was persuaded to

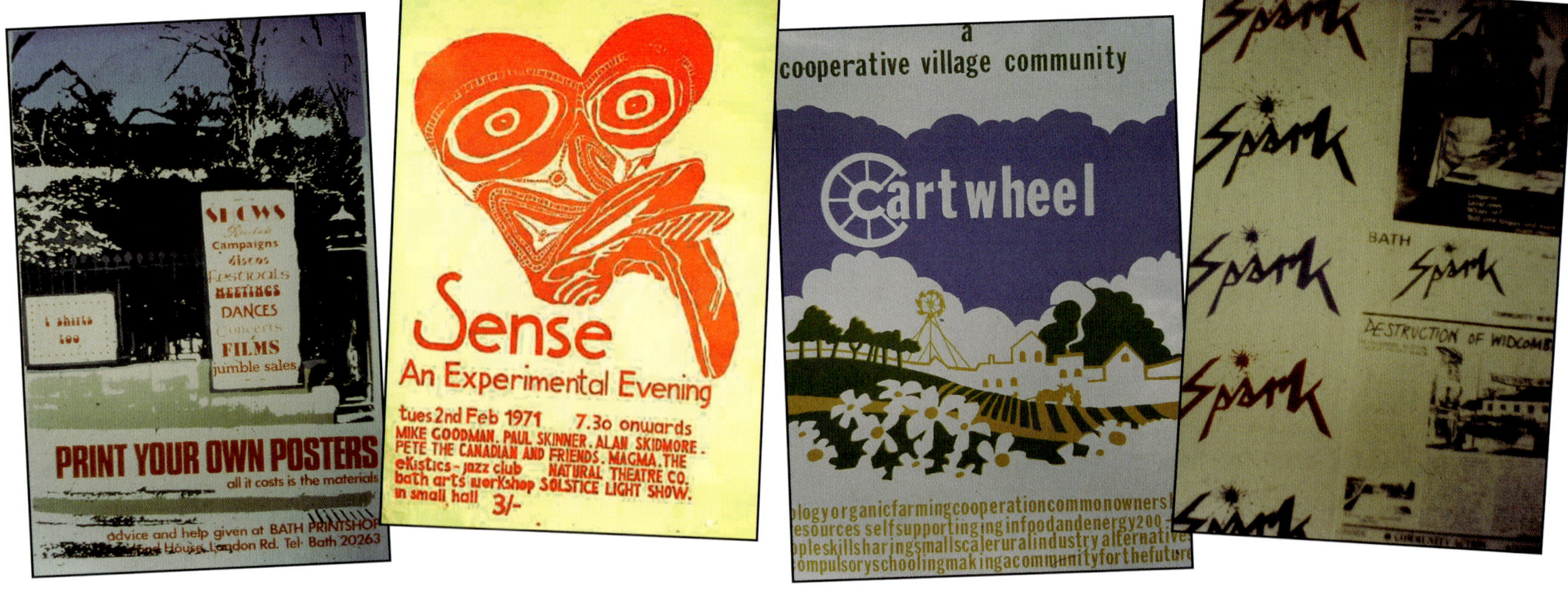

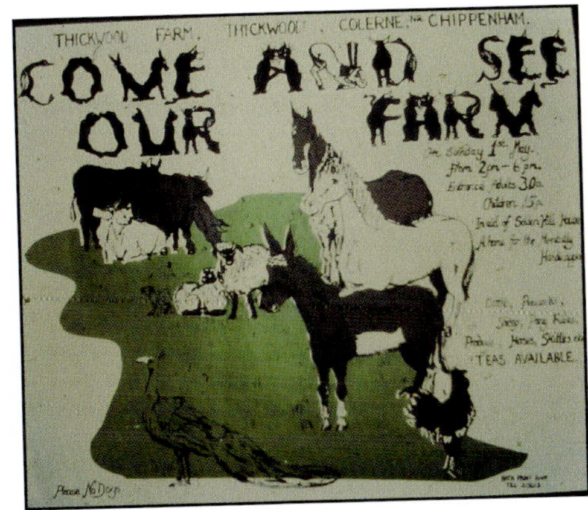


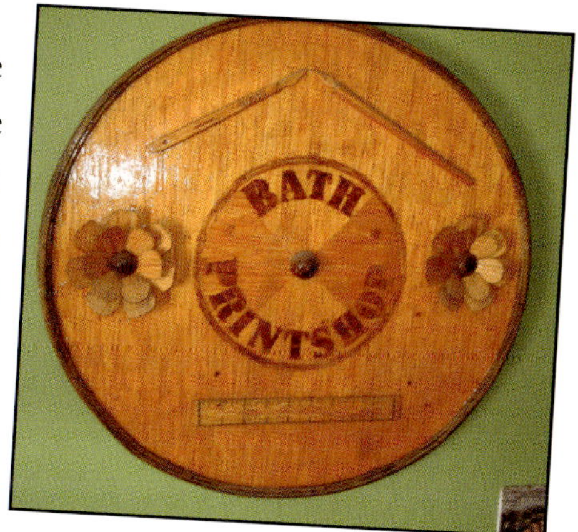


fund four members of staff.

We were plagued with odd incidents of vandalism and complaints from across the river about noise etc. On Christmas Day 1976, some local children came down and started larking about. By the end of the day, most of the window panes were broken, mostly for fun rather than malice. But this led another group to break in and attempt to burn the building down. Several door frames and partitions were wrecked and much of the inside was smoke-blackened. We couldn't afford the repairs so in the end we found alternative premises for the truant school and the Printshop and regretfully abandoned the building in spring 1977.

The Printshop moved into a two-room basement below the Women's Aid Shop. We started off with basic equipment but soon expanded, acquiring a Litho press, process camera and a duplicator. We moved again in late 1978 to the ground floor of Longacre Hall, where there was far more space and light. By then, we were screen printing a community newspaper *Bath Spark*

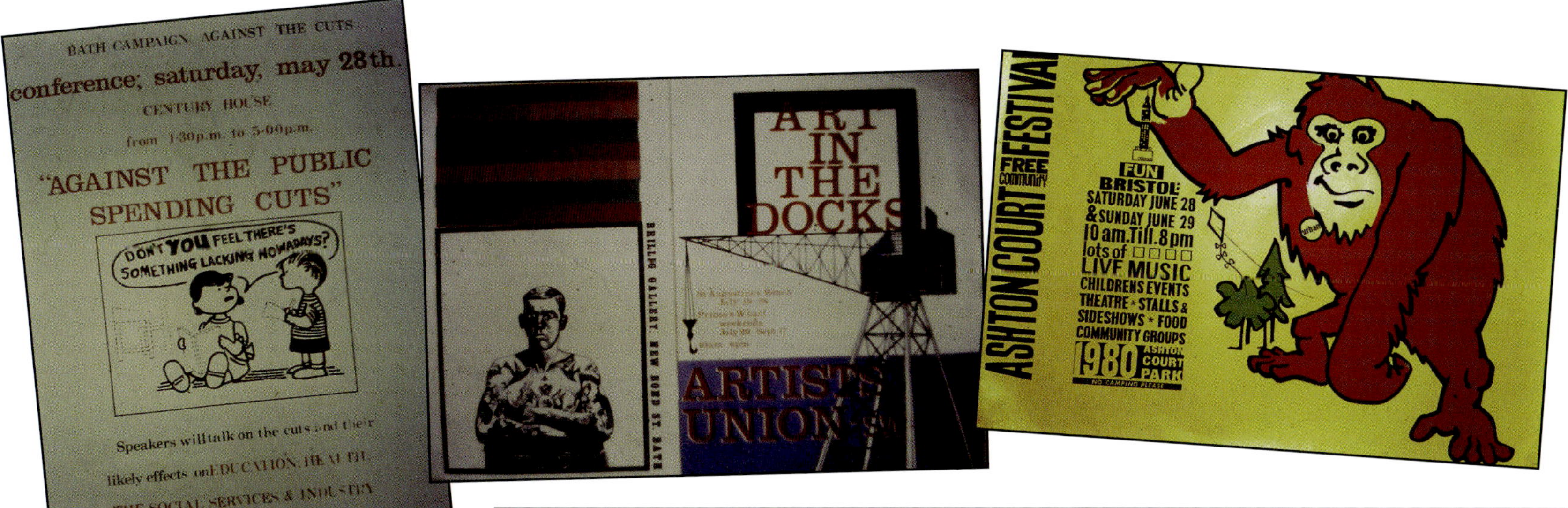


2. The building was in York Place off the London Road.
3. Both Dick and Paul have since passed away.

and printing a wide range of materials from artists' posters to self-published books, pamphlets and magazines for groups as far away as Brighton, Exeter and Gloucester. We also did print jobs for local businesses, although our main focus was on supporting community initiatives. For a while, we were self-supporting and by early 79 we were paying wages for two staff members. Two others were there on government employment schemes as well as many volunteers. It lasted until 1983, when we sadly had to close it down.

## Civil Aid ahoy!

**Tory:** Our six-year involvement with the national voluntary organisation Civil Aid was one of the most unexpected and radically adventurous things we did.[4] On the face of it totally outside our ken, it meshed surprisingly well with our 'anything is possible' approach, as well as providing much heavy-duty catering and other equipment of great practical use for the huge outdoor events that were so much part of our lives. Thus we got involved in mass catering at festivals and protest marches, and even survival events adding, as ever, a theatrical twist to the proceedings.

**Nigel Leach** was instigator-in-chief and field commander and he takes up the story: Our initial encounter with Civil Aid was in 1973. At a chance meeting someone told us that we could borrow their radio telephones for *Another Festival* (not a mobile in sight in those days and no internet). Brilliant idea since there were three sites and a central HQ near the railway station. We'd have to join Civil Aid to do it though. So we did. And as the Bath City branch of

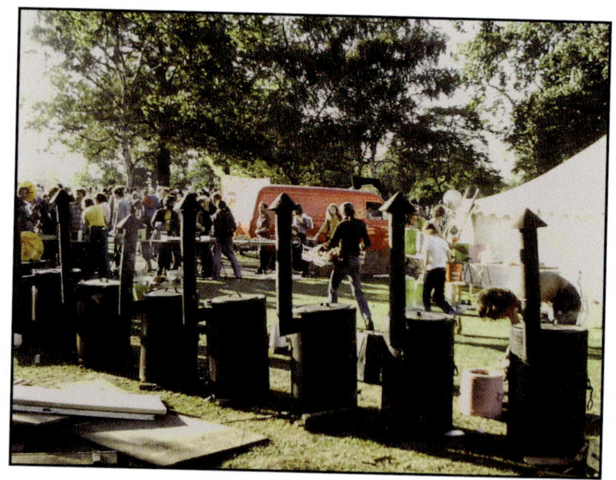

4. Civil Aid was a national voluntary organisation set up by the government to replace the defunct Civil Defence Corps. Civil Aid trained its members to fill auxiliary emergency roles in the event of a disaster – rescue, field kitchens, first aid etc.

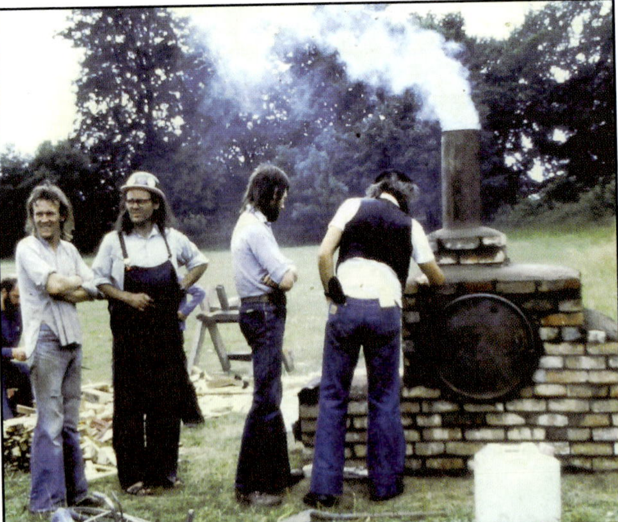

Brick-built oven

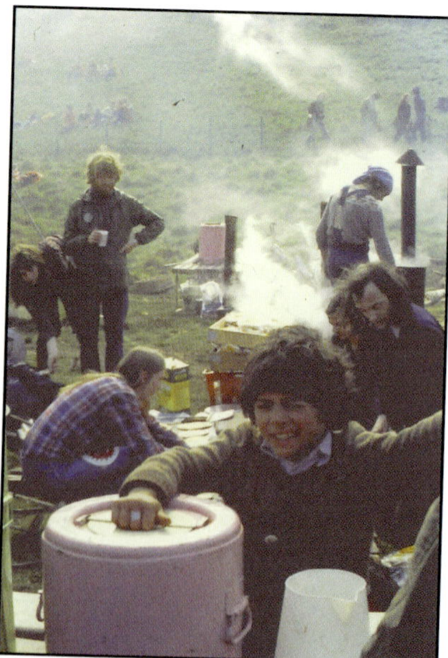

that organisation, we later took possession of a vast load of Civil Aid field kitchen equipment that was stored in the Bath registry office.

## On the march

**Nigel:** Our first assignment was a canal dig in Droitwich in October 1973. We pushed an old pram with a thermal tea urn, cups, milk, sugar and warm doughnuts along a muddy canal bank and gave them out free to the participants, some of them knee-deep in mud. They had a whip round at the end of the day and with that we were able to buy some more equipment, including our first Soyer boiler.

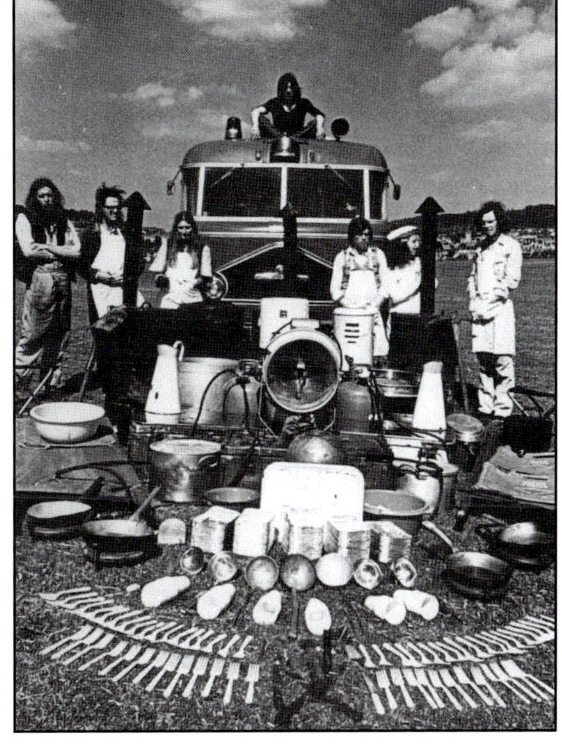
The crew

### The Soyer boiler

Nigel: The focal point of our operations was always the Soyer boiler invented by a French chef, Alexis Soyer, during the Crimean War. It became a standard British Army and Civil Defence cooking aid through to the late 50s. A single boiler could provide soup, stew, curry etc. for 100 people. At peak operations we had 10 of these and, with our six tea and coffee urns, could provide an endless supply of tea and coffee, hot water for babies' bottles, handwashing in the kitchen and even hot water for rum punch when the weather was inclement.

**Nigel:** We felt we could tackle anything after that and in the next years took part in some 25 events for up to 10,000 people a day, travelling hundreds of miles to provide food at anti-nuclear and anti-racism events. We catered for a Rock against Racism rally one Sunday in Brockwell Park, London where we sold 9000 cheese rolls, 7000 teas and coffees and a mountain of salad. Later, we provided food over several days for a Campaign for Nuclear Disarmament (CND) march from Aldermaston to London. It was a logistical challenge. Our first stop was to serve breakfast in Reading. While we did that, our van went to collect milk and set up a mid-morning tea break further along the road. Then it returned to collect the breakfast stuff and clear up. The pattern continued over nearly 40 miles. The evening meal was in a public hall in Acton. The marchers went upstairs to leave their stuff and when they returned, they were greeted by a piano and player, and tables for four with menus and candles… and pudding!

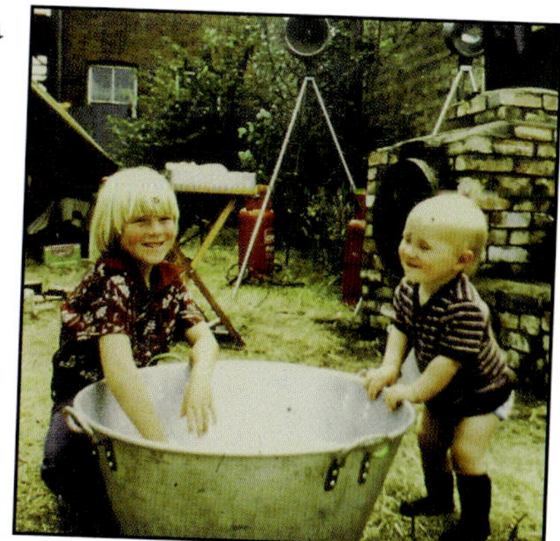
More crew

## Secret garden

Bath Civil Aid went on to cater for a 1979 conference of the Association of Community Artists (ACA) in Newcastle. **Chris Foster**, then an ACA member, met Nigel and Bath Civil Aid at that event. Chris writes: About 60 of us were sitting in a freezing, redundant industrial building with barely any facilities, when the door flew open and a rather wild-looking fellow burst in and bellowed, 'Right you lot if you want dinner you'd better get outside and help prepare it'. Outside was a large van being unloaded by teenagers from a truant school. There were Soyer boilers, huge cooking pots, folding tables and bags of ingredients. People were sent to scavenge wood while others chopped and peeled. About 90 minutes later, we all feasted on hot veggie curry. Hot meals continued throughout the weekend and on Sunday cakes were baked in an oven built from materials found on site. I learned that the van had come from Bath and had driven over the Pennines in a blizzard and been dug out of snow drifts. That wild man was Nigel and his group was Bath City Civil Aid. Forty years later, we are still firm friends.

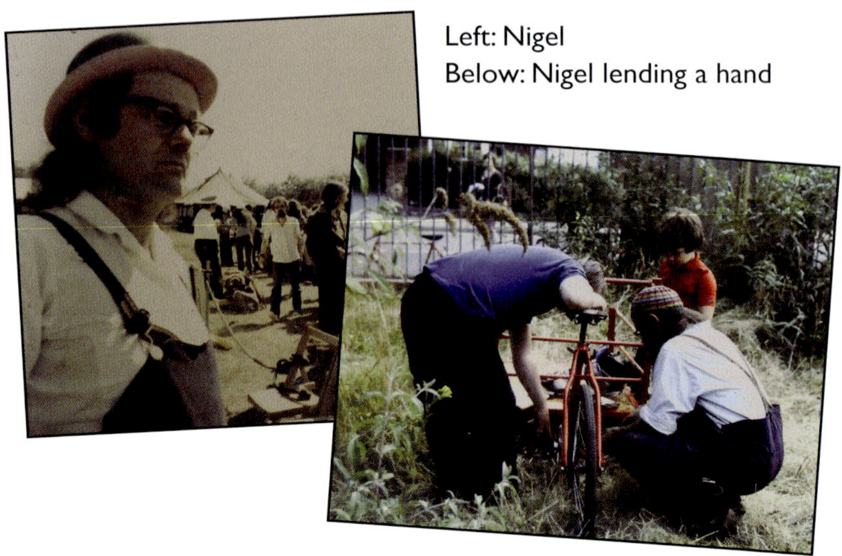

Left: Nigel
Below: Nigel lending a hand

We later invited Bath Civil Aid to come to Leiston, Suffolk to cater for a community festival featuring circus skills, shadow puppet workshops, folk music workshops, a community bike ride and a Mad Hatter's Tea Party. The Civil Aid crew fed the festival workers but also created a wonderful *Secret Garden Cafe* each evening in a secluded, overgrown walled garden. Word spread about the magical

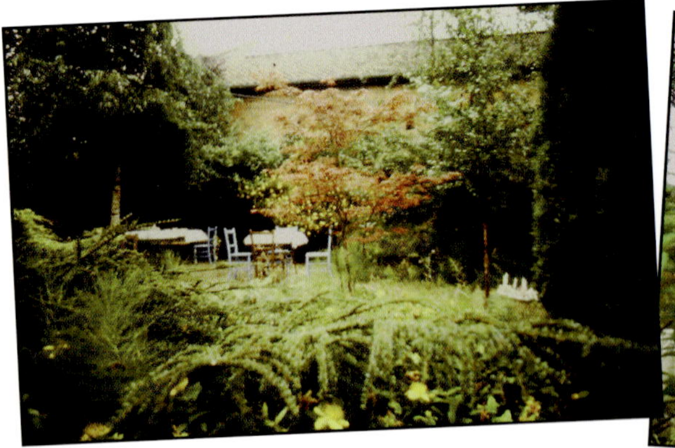

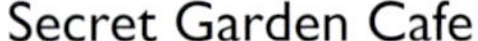

Secret Garden Cafe

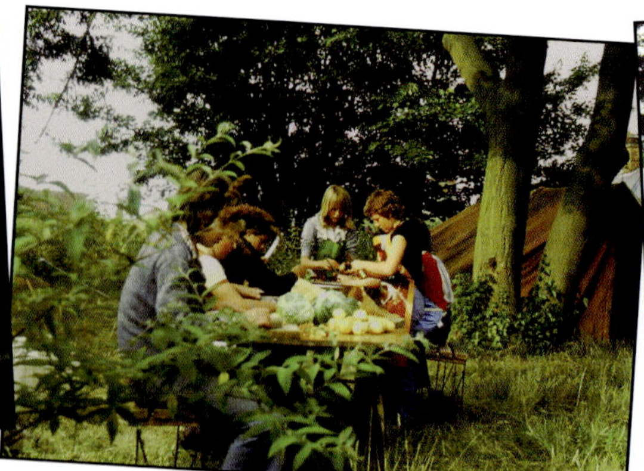

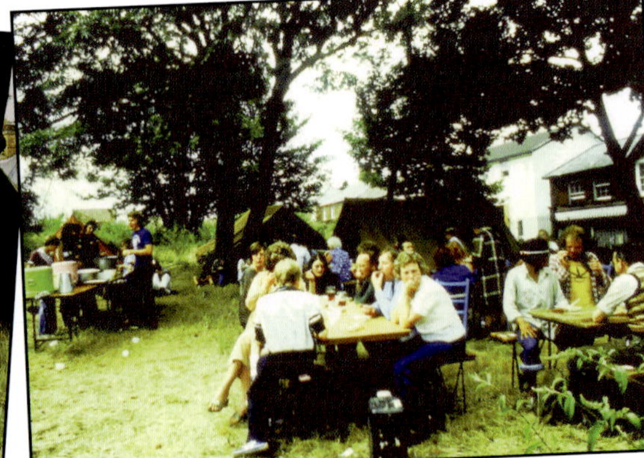

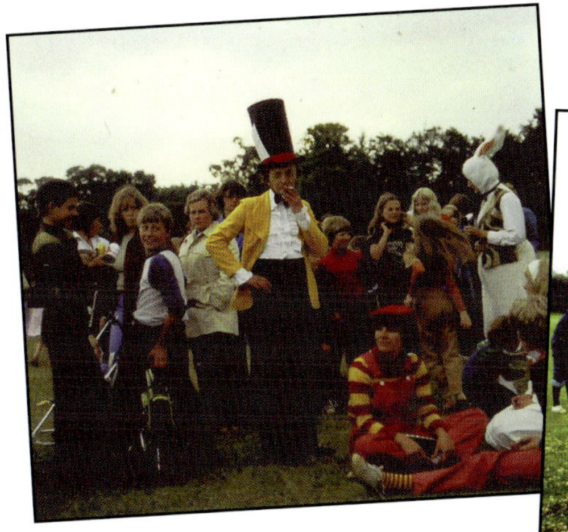

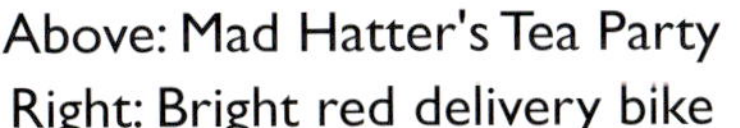

Above: Mad Hatter's Tea Party
Right: Bright red delivery bike

The participants, drawn from fire, ambulance and Civil Aid groups (including one unsuspecting participant who arrived in a skirt and heels) arrived at a Bath car park one late November evening, only to be given a poem that, when deciphered, directed them to the  Walcot Village Hall. Once there, they were loaded into the back of a lorry in pitch darkness and driven to an old army camp staffed by officials in white coats with torches.

Reveille was at dawn the following morning. Our participants were treated like prisoners and forced to forage for food (it was pretty much boiled snails or nothing that season, although eventually they were given some porridge). After supper that evening, flashes and loud noises came from the woods and the participants were told to go and investigate. They returned with a Gaelic-only speaker with a shamrock on his helmet. The participants eventually 'discovered' he was a pilot on a training flight that had crashed in the woods, who needed help with injured passengers. Search parties were organised but the searchers stepped on some of the 'victims' and missed others completely. They got to bed about 2am and the second day had to be cancelled as everyone was so exhausted.

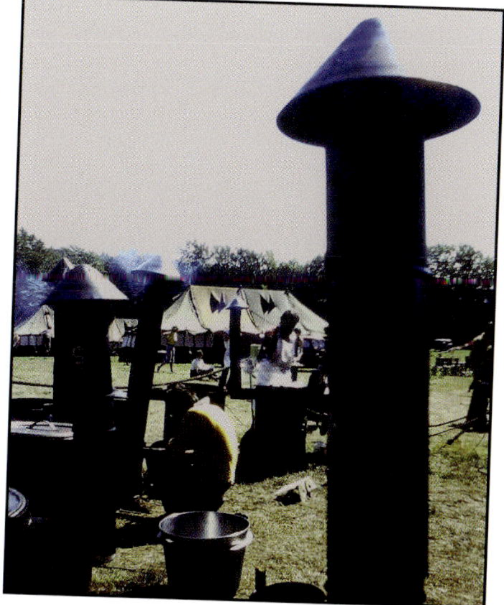

environment and theatrical presentation of food and drink – and after a few days, queues could be seen forming every evening. Then there was the Mad Hatter's Tea Party, bright blue sandwiches, green orange squash, all accompanied by Nigel dressed as a clown, charging round the field hosing people down with water from a stirrup pump mounted on his bright red delivery bike. They were great days.

## Operation Auntie

**Nigel:** At one point we Bath Civil Aiders were invited to join a training exercise in Bristol. It involved breakfast followed by a two-hour exercise centred on rescuing a victim down a steep slope, then lunch. This was much too easy and not at all what we had in mind, so we decided to run our own 'survival' event devised with the help of the ***Natural Theatre Company*** in late 1974.

**Brian:** Similar activities took place with us acting as participants on Ron Pope's farm in an out of the way place in St Catherine's Valley. Ron was an ex-army survival expert and we spent a weekend in his woods, making shelters from bits of trees and gathering food from whatever was to hand. We made fish traps to entice trout from the stream and tried to imagine that the social order had broken down. Finally on the last day, Ron unexpectedly, and very much out of character, blew the stream up with plastic explosives and we all had fresh trout for tea!

## Money matters

**Tory:** Money was never plentiful and throughout its history BAW engaged in its own forms of social entrepreneurship to raise funds for its arts and other activities. These included our shops and cafes, craft markets, transport, removals and other community services, jumble sales, rock concerts, discos, and theatrical events of all kinds. Some projects, adventure playgrounds, Riverside, the Printshop and the truant school among them, received support in kind and workers via the various government employment and community service schemes that existed at the time. Comtek was largely self-funding through its architectural, artisanal and reclamation activities (see *Chapter 6*). Civil Aid was also self-supporting, charging for expenses, travel costs and services supplied. Much of the labour was carried out by volunteers in exchange for free food and time off, from what were usually 24/7 operations, to listen to the music at festivals, join the protest or participate in whatever was going on.

By 1976, BAW and the ***Natural Theatre Company*** were receiving regular grants from the Arts Council of Great Britain for theatre and community arts activities.[5] The details are hazy but we remember weekly wages of about £8, going up to £12, and then a big jump to £40 a week by about 1978.[6] We survived quite happily on this – rents were cheap, we didn't need cars in Bath (we had our vans for travel), and we mostly wore second-hand clothes. We received a grant to buy a smart new Mercedes van in 1977 for the theatre company. This was a massive change as it had proper seats and a bulkhead so we didn't slide about at the back or collide with our props and costumes. That van saw an end to extremely frequent breakdowns on motorways and endless waiting for tow trucks and garage repairs.

A disadvantage of the new regime was having to account for the arts subsidies we received. Sometimes we ran out of funds and temporarily suspended our wages. We survived by taking on other jobs or signing on for unemployment benefit (the welfare state still functioned then). In May 1978, we had a cash flow crisis and the Arts Council

---

5. The first actual grant came at the end of 1971 – £1,250 from South West Arts, for *Genesis*, NTC and community projects. Grants from the Arts Council started around 1972/73, although it was not until later that we began to be paid wages.

6. Grants in 1977 were £19,500 from the Arts Council for wages, video project, local projects, exhibitions, film club, Walcot Jubilee festival, murals etc. Plus £13,250 from the Arts Council Experimental Drama Panel for the NTC. Bath City Council chipped in £300 for improvements to the Village Hall. In 1979/80 the total grant for BAW and NTC was £27,000.

suspended our grants until our accounts had been audited. We managed to do this, and grants resumed until 4 November 1981, when the Workshop closed for a variety of reasons (see *Chapter 10*). Many of the other initiatives survived for several more years, a testament perhaps to their relevance and utility: The Printshop closed in the early 1980s, Walcot Reclamation continued to operate until 1989 and the ***Natural Theatre Company*** remains active to this day.

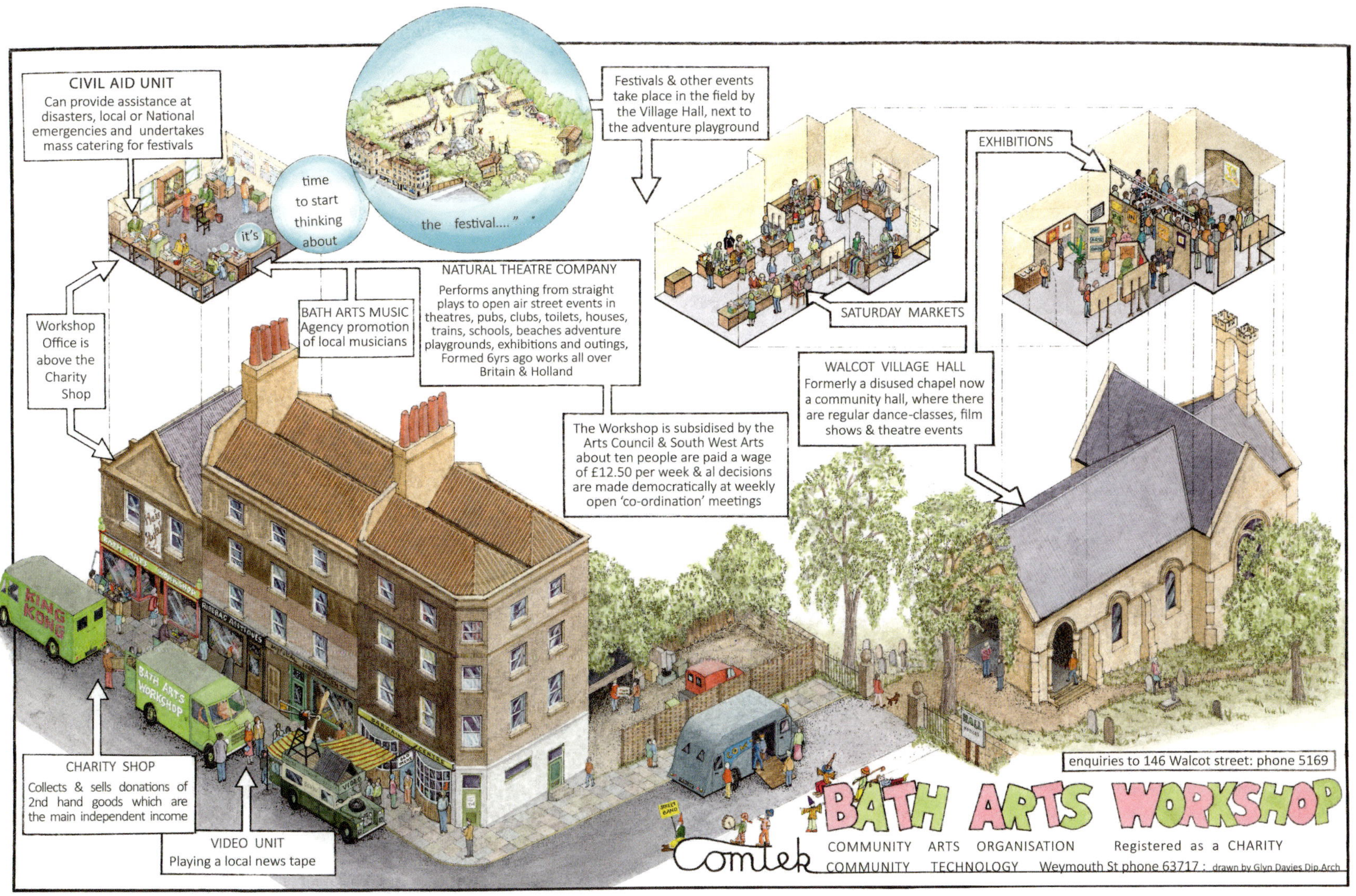

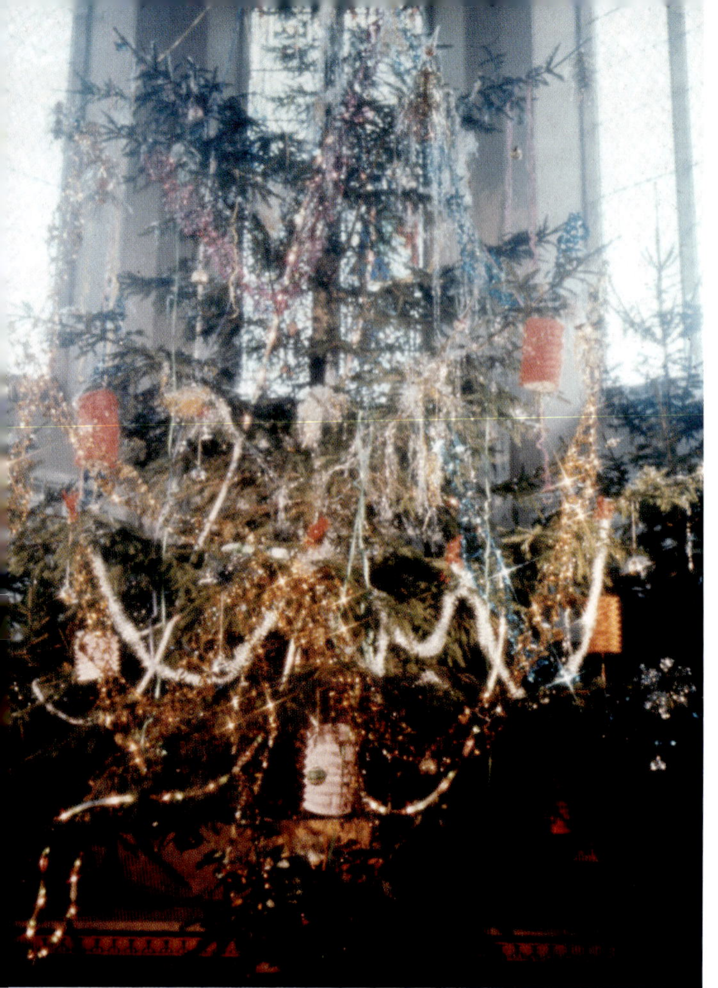

# CHRISTMAS PARTY FOR ALL 1973-79

In this case, the focus was on people who needed to escape the isolation that Christmas often brings, and those with no cash to spare. Our guests were mostly elderly and living alone (known then as old-age pensioners), or on the streets. We got to know them as the years passed and had help from social services to identify individuals who might want to attend. But anyone was welcome

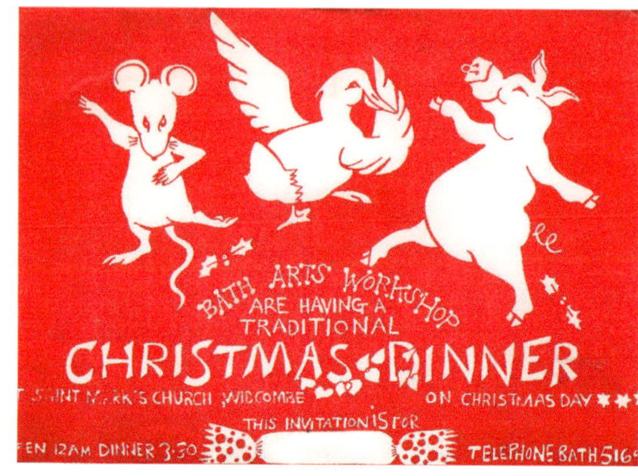


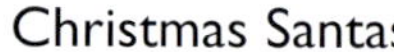

Christmas Santas

and some families and kids joined in as did many friends who turned up to help. On Christmas morning, we drove

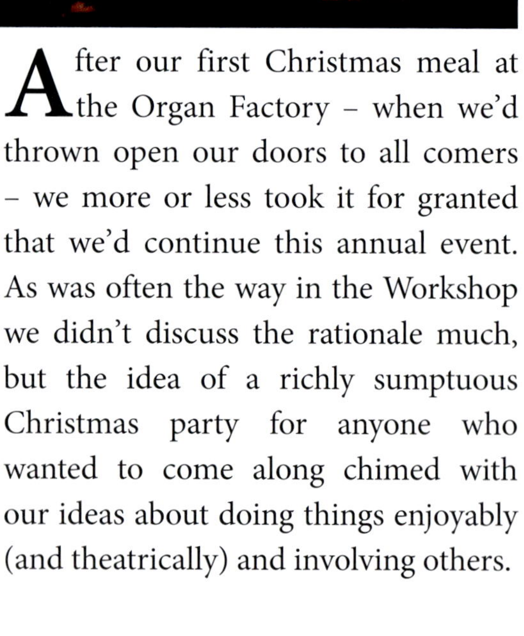

After our first Christmas meal at the Organ Factory – when we'd thrown open our doors to all comers – we more or less took it for granted that we'd continue this annual event. As was often the way in the Workshop we didn't discuss the rationale much, but the idea of a richly sumptuous Christmas party for anyone who wanted to come along chimed with our ideas about doing things enjoyably (and theatrically) and involving others.

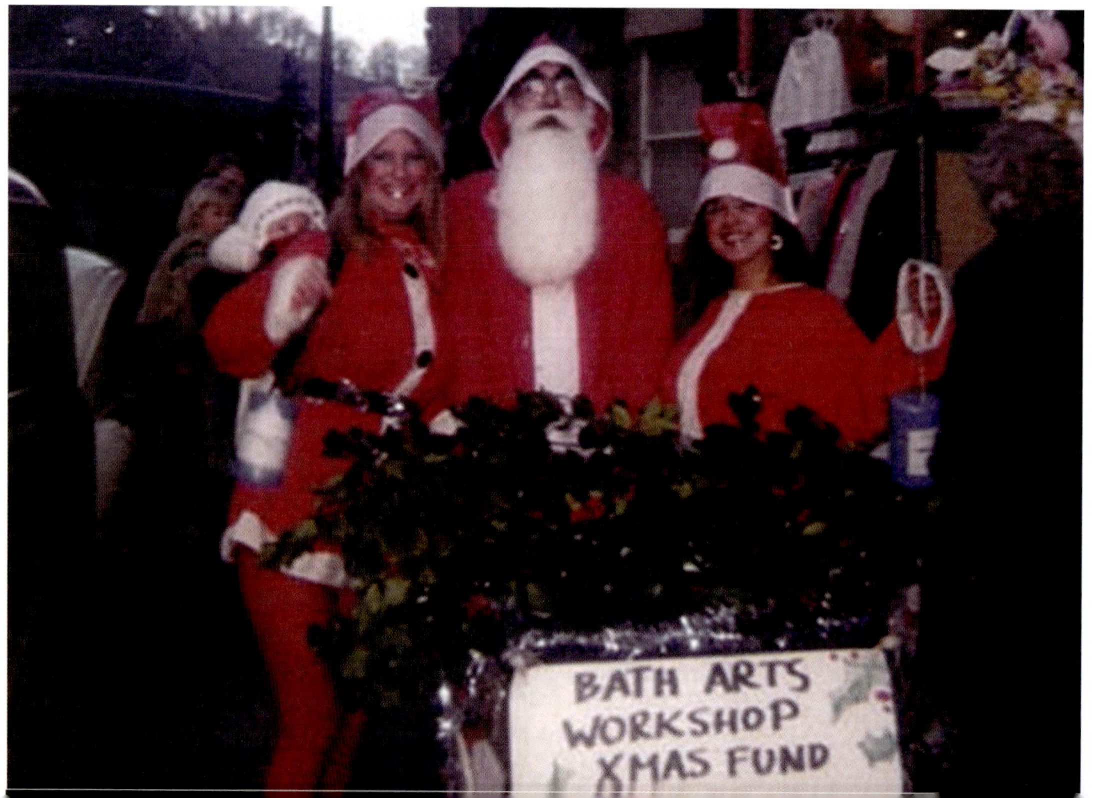

our vans round Bath looking for people with nowhere to go. We invited those we found and, if they were up for it, gave them a lift to our dinner.

Up to 200 people attended the festivities which were totally free. They took months to organise, and involved virtually everyone in the Workshop, as well as bringing together many volunteers and business supporters, and many private cars that were put into service for transport on the day. We spent much time raising funds and

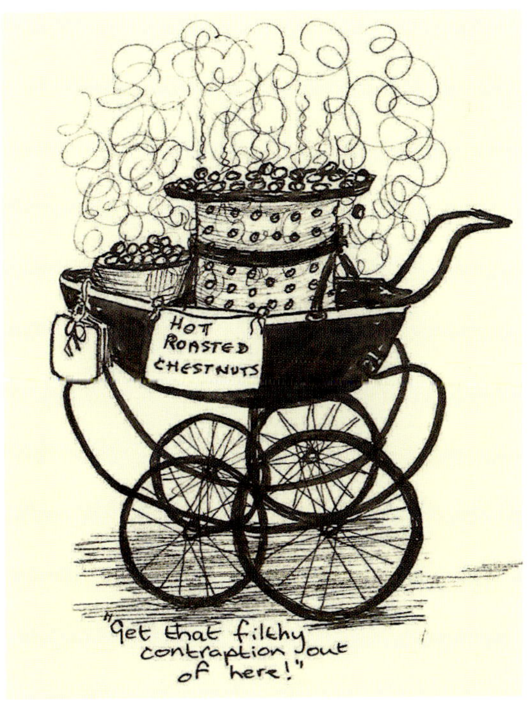


provisions (we had no budget for this event which cost the equivalent of £5-8,000 in today's money). We ran jumble sales in various outdoor markets and did loads of street and pub collections. We sold hot roasted chestnuts around the town centre and outside The Hat & Feather – often kitted out in glittery make-up and Santa/Santarette outfits.

**Rich Cooper** built the brazier for the chestnuts which was mounted on an old pram frame. It was prone to billowing smoke before the embers got hot. One night while outside Nero's Club on George Street, the owner Mr Benny (known to Bathonians as a man of considerable bulk and a powerful personality) came out in a fury and ordered us to 'get that filthy contraption away from here'.

John Potter (of John's Bike's fame) was head chef, with Chris Last his right-hand man. In the run up to Christmas, John usually set up a massive aluminium bowl full of Christmas pudding mix in Kingsmead Square. For 10p passers-by could stir it with a giant wooden spoon. As Christmas drew

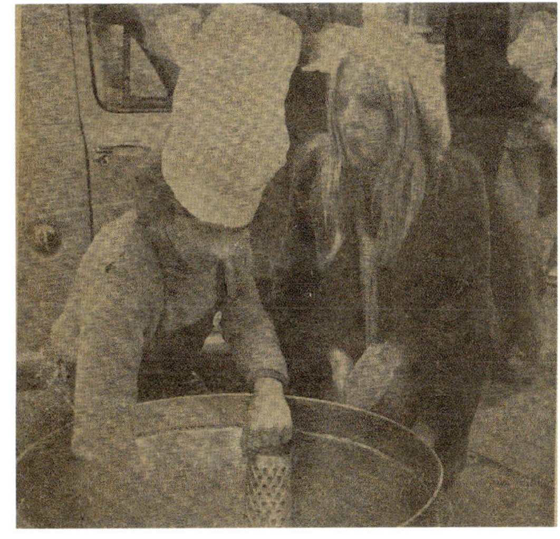

nigh, we approached food shops, pubs and off-licences for donations. They were extremely generous – the turkeys came from local butcher Stanley Gibson, who always erred on the side of generosity – and M&S regularly allowed us to collect its date-expired goods on Christmas Eve, but dozens of others contributed. Pub landlords and off-licences were equally generous, donating a plentiful supply of sherry, whisky, wine and beer, which was all most enthusiastically received.

There was nothing institutional or municipal about our Christmas meals. As Mick Banks said, when our guests climbed aboard the van, 'they might be greeted by over-solicitous vicars in

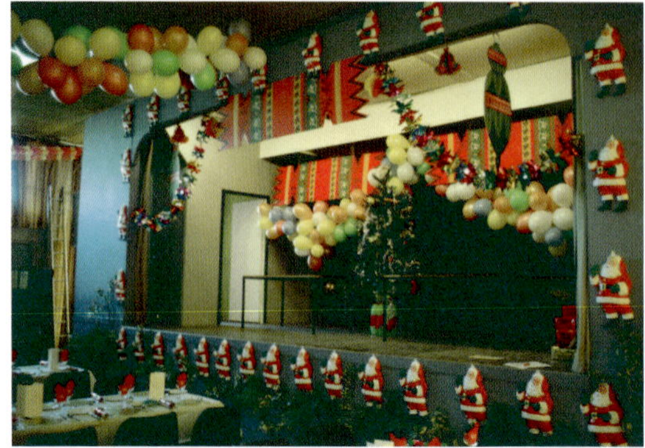

paper hats or a Rockette, the driver a blustering, pipe-smoking Smart Party member'. The decorations at the venue were lavish and beautiful. The tree was magnificent, the room garlanded with hundreds of balloons, and the entire scene glowed with colour from our stage lights. Again quoting Mick, 'it was surrealism with its best party clothes on'.

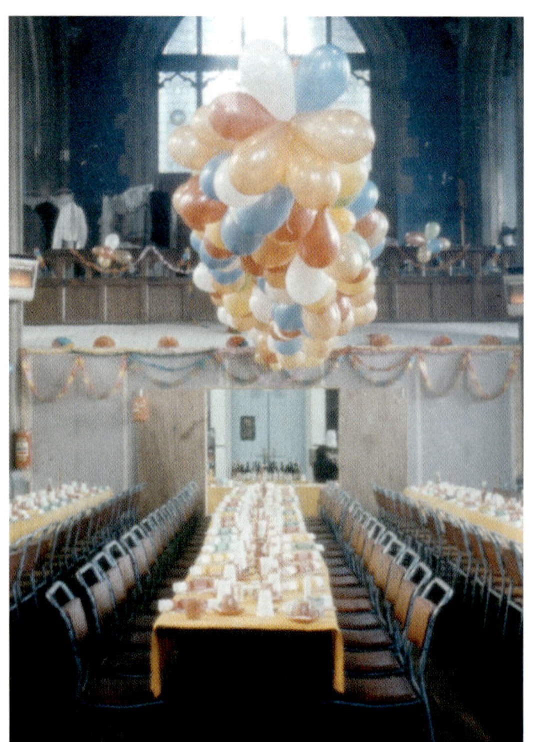

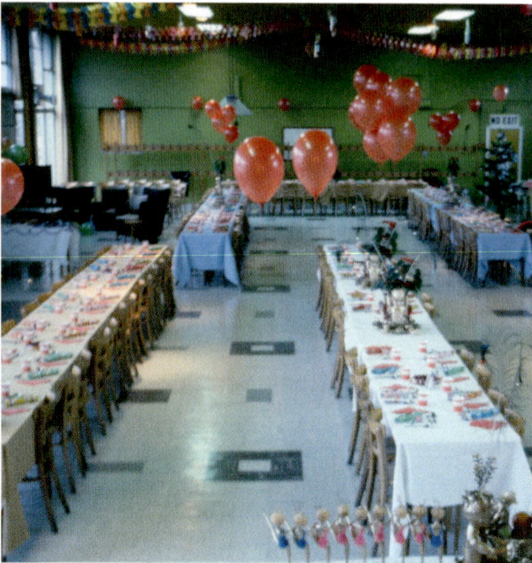



**Jennie:** Let's have theatre, a choir, a magnificent tree, decorations, balloons and presents for all. Let's have tables set with crisp white linen, sparkling cutlery and glasses. Smartly dressed waiters and waitresses, 'Wine madam, or something else perhaps?' A hearty roast dinner with all the trimmings followed by Christmas pudding and mince pies with brandy butter. Entertainment, a little ballroom dancing, cups of tea, cakes and a raffle, before being delivered back to your door with a present.

The dinners were held at St Mark's Church in Widcombe three times. We used the Civil Aid Soyer Boilers (set up outside) to boil up vast quantities of

Brussels sprouts and carrots plus shed loads of potatoes, which were later roasted in ovens at the church. Potter, Chris and their kitchen crew had to be there at dawn to light the boilers and get the whole thing going, which was indeed a massive operation. One year, we cooked the turkeys at the church, using ovens from Cleveland Hotel that

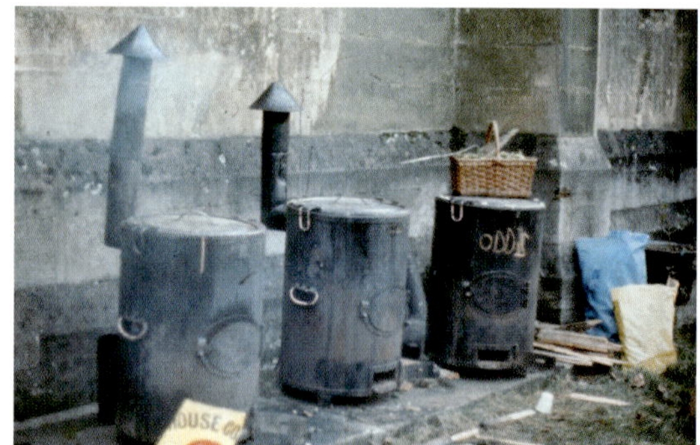

Soyer boilers at St Mark's

166

were plumbed in by the Gas Board. Another year, they were cooked the night before, in our various houses and flats. We carved them at the church then served them onto very hot plates, adding the veg and boiling hot gravy, using a large catering calor gas stove in the side chapel to get everything hot for serving. There were difficulties with lighting the boilers, and adhering to the cooking times, so there were often delays, but somewhat haphazardly it always worked out and dinner was eventually served.

**Corinne:** At the 1977 Christmas dinner, John Potter and his immaculately attired waiters did a magnificent ceremonial parade around the tables, each carrying on high an enormous golden roasted bird.

In 1974, for the first time the engineering firm Stothert & Pitt agreed to lend the Workshop their works canteen, which had an efficient modern kitchen equipped to serve hundreds of meals daily. Things were far more punctual that year and we returned three times more. Their loan of the canteen was

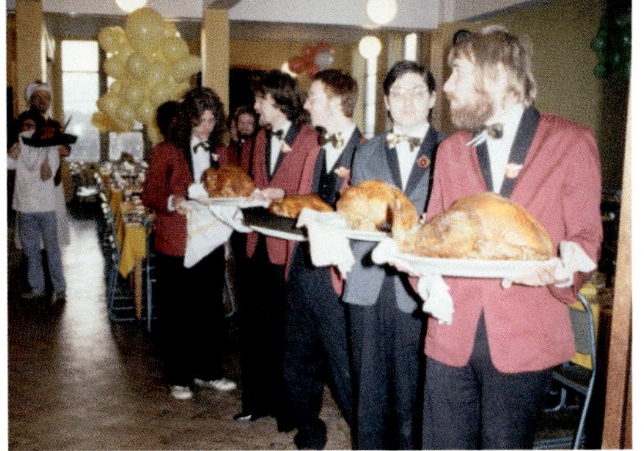

Turkey parade

much appreciated by all of us at BAW and the guests who came to the lunch.

**Sonny Hayes,** the magician writes: We met the Bath Arts Workshop people at the Melkweg Club in Amsterdam and they invited us to their Christmas party in 1975. A splendid feast of bacchanalian excesses, if pensioners can be bacchanalian? What was most impressive was the lack of patronising in the Workshop's approach to the community, rather it was based on fun

and empathy. For this 20-something hedonist, I had had virtually no contact with the 'aged' but this was a party for pensioners, the highly respectable and the less so, a mixture.

I talked to a lady who had become suicidal when she lost her sense of taste and smell, another heartbroken, who had lost her lover and husband in the same year. The interaction was hardly casual and it was soon clear that many of these seniors had the same financial concerns as the young people serving them. Overall, there was jollity and an affirmation of togetherness. I know we performed but remember nothing of the performance. I do remember the party.

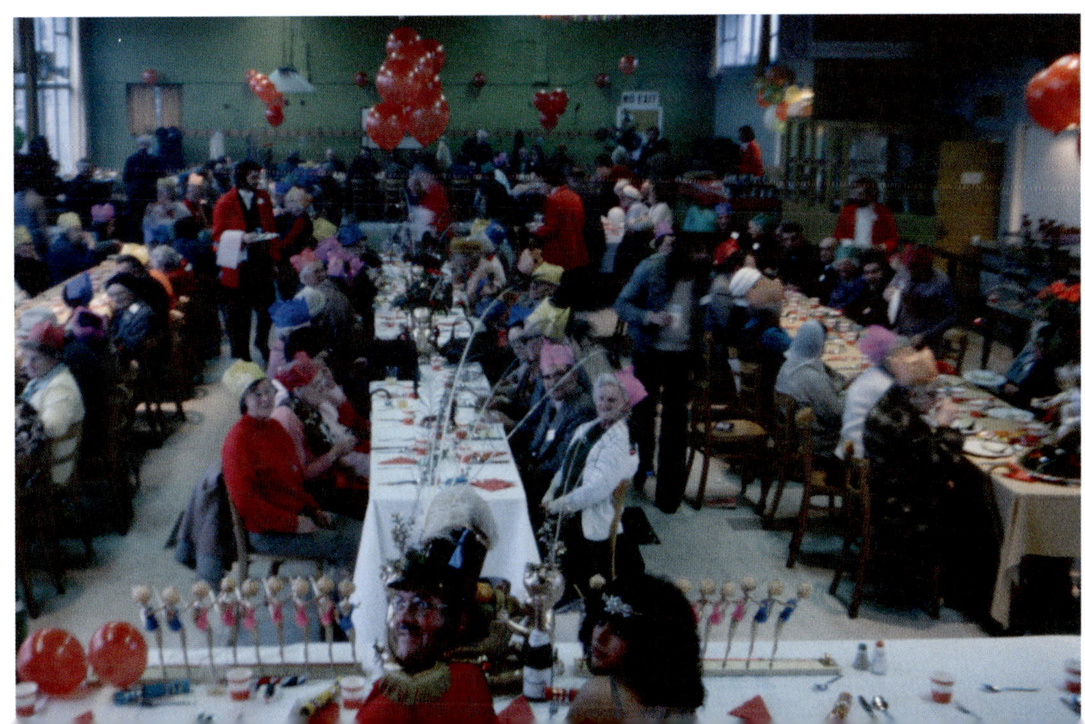

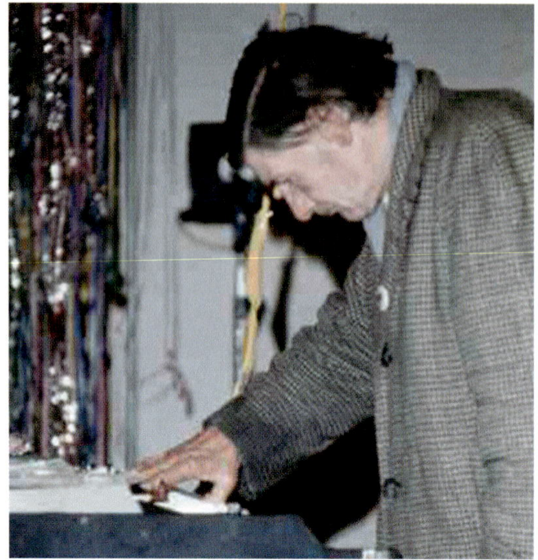

Live entertainment was always part of the program. Captain Headlam came with his accordion and Gordon played the piano. **Sonny Hayes** performed his magic show one year and **Theatre Slapstique** another. One year, **Dusty Lane** (son of Kitty who worked in our shop) performed. He was a glamorous female impersonator with an extravagant auburn wig and an opulent silken gown bedecked with lace. For several years, the Vicar of South Stoke (Tory's father) and the church choir appeared in the early evening to sing Christmas carols, lending a peaceful air to the celebrations.

**A letter from Mrs Mills** (of Walcot Street): Ladies and gentlemen it gives me great pleasure in thanking the Bath Arts Workshop, all of them, for our Christmas dinners and parties they've given us year after year. Also the donors and shops for their kindness. If only they could see the senior citizens' faces light up when they see the beautiful tables and decorations, it is a great delight… We would also like to thank the Vicar of South Stoke and the choir for the carols.

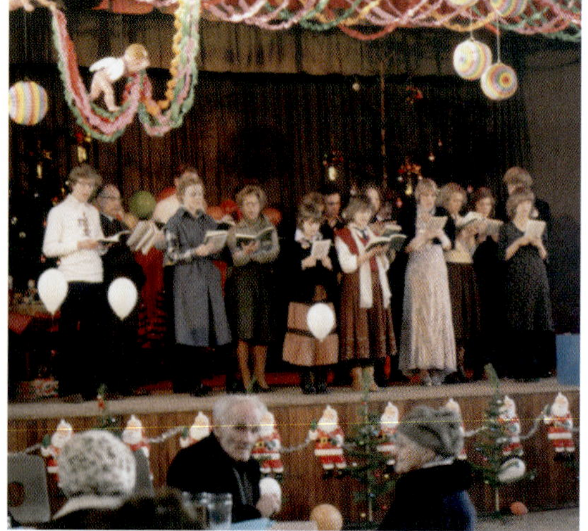

Of course we Workshop members weren't 'staff' in the usual sense of the word. We dressed up in our fine costumes, had lunch and joined in the activities, sipping from the abundant supply of alcoholic drinks, although Thornton recalls being totally abstemious year after year as he was always driving one of the vans. It was always a good laugh and made Christmas worthwhile somehow.

The last Workshop Christmas was in 1981 at Stothert & Pitt. In 1982, it was taken over by Bath Council of Open Churches, (later Bath Churches Together), and is now run independently by a committee of volunteers.[7]

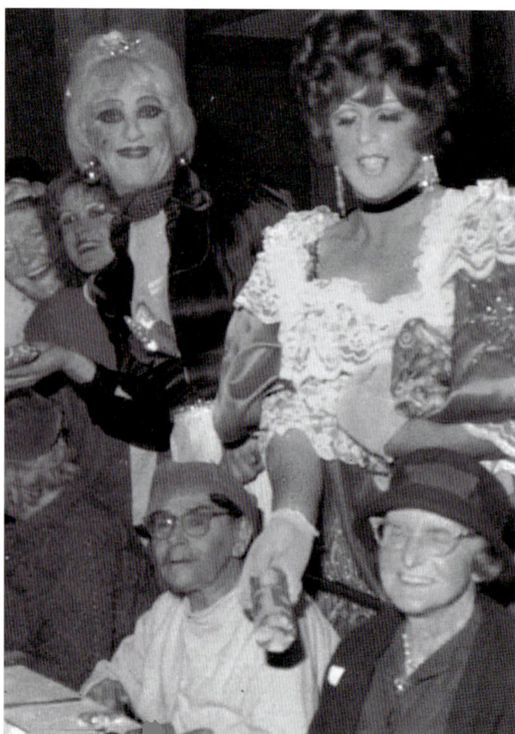

Top: Gordon played the piano
Right: Dusty Lane (Bruce Sutton)
Top right: The choir

7. Information is available here:
http://www.bathopenchristmas.com

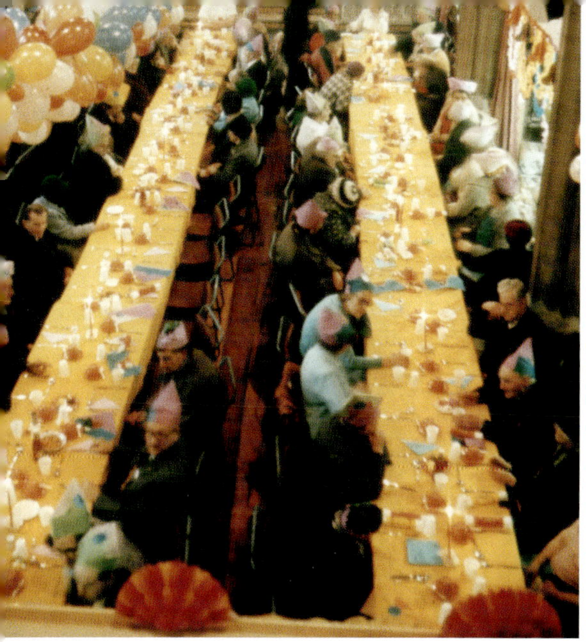

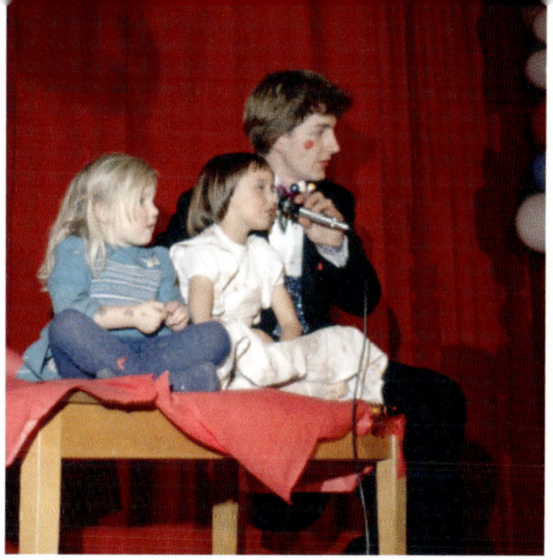

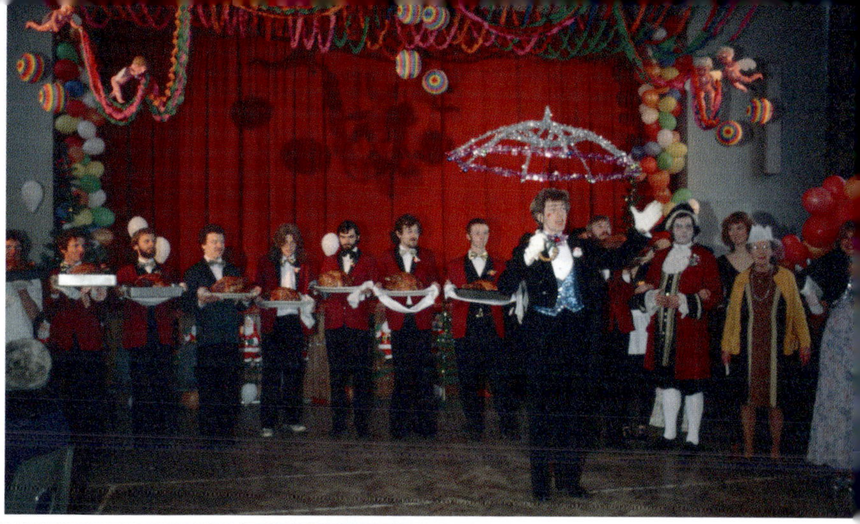

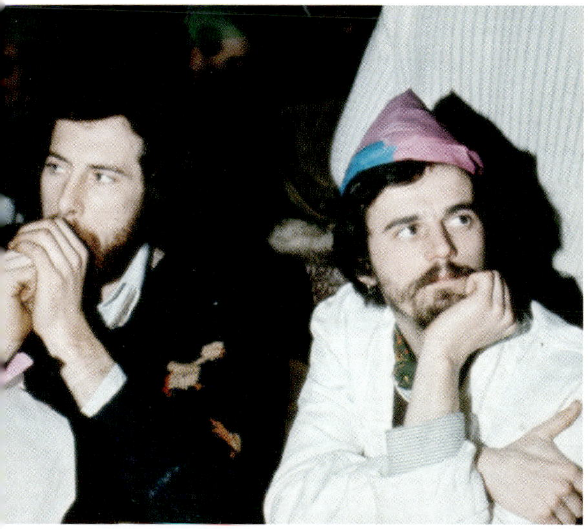

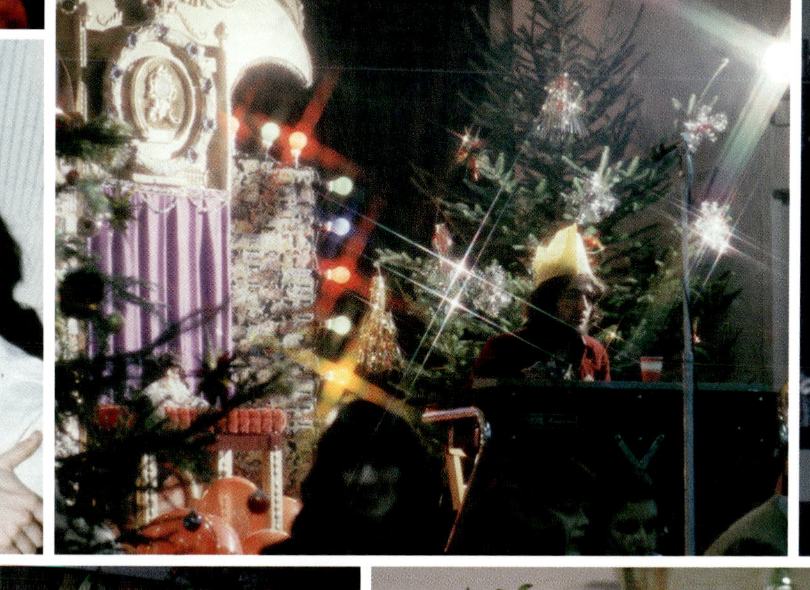
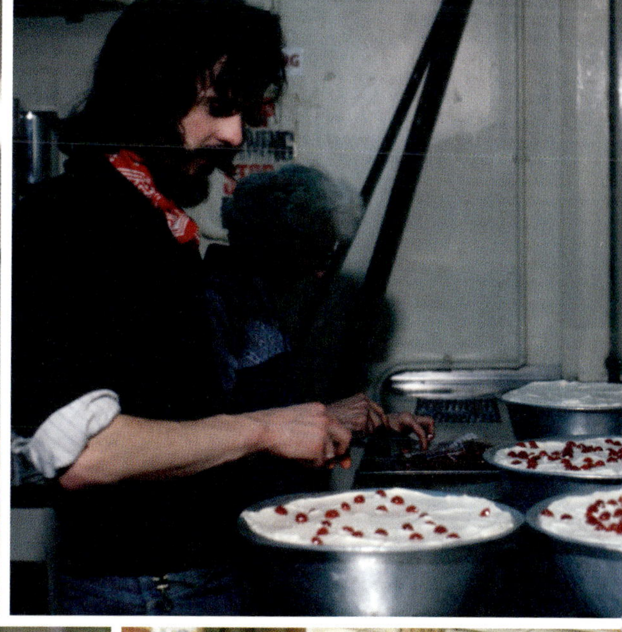
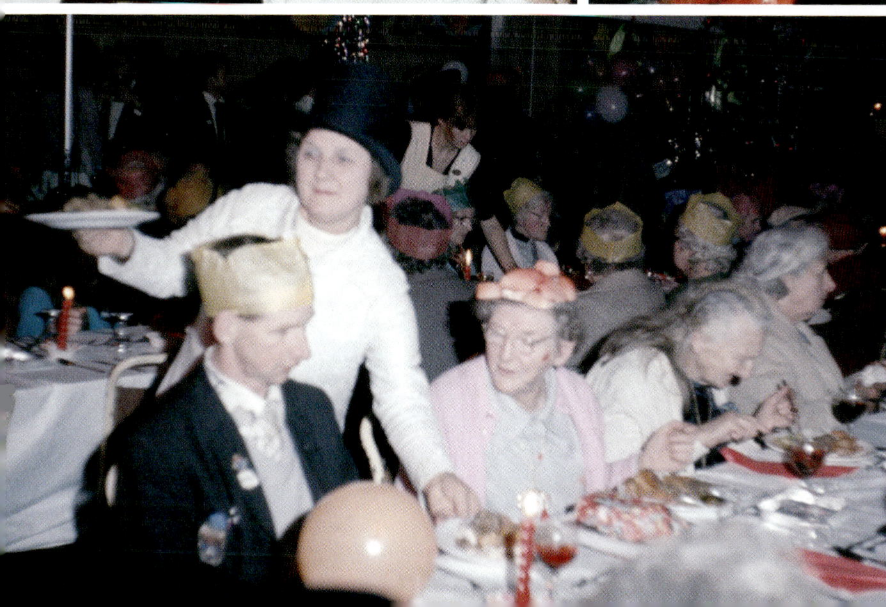
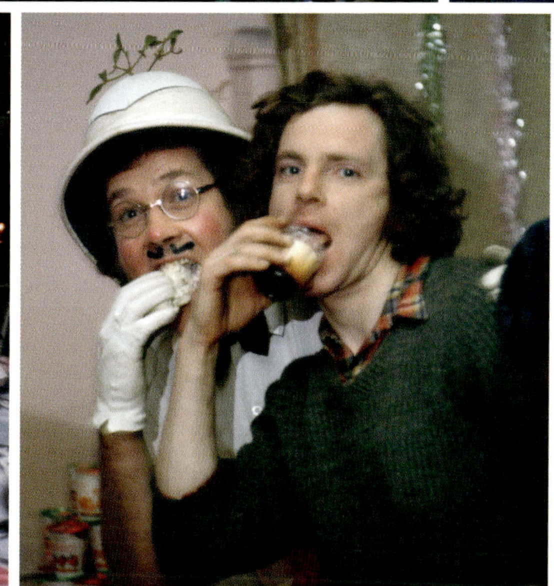
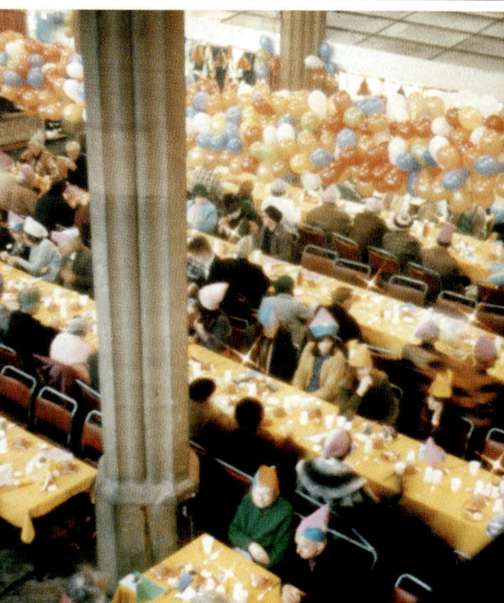

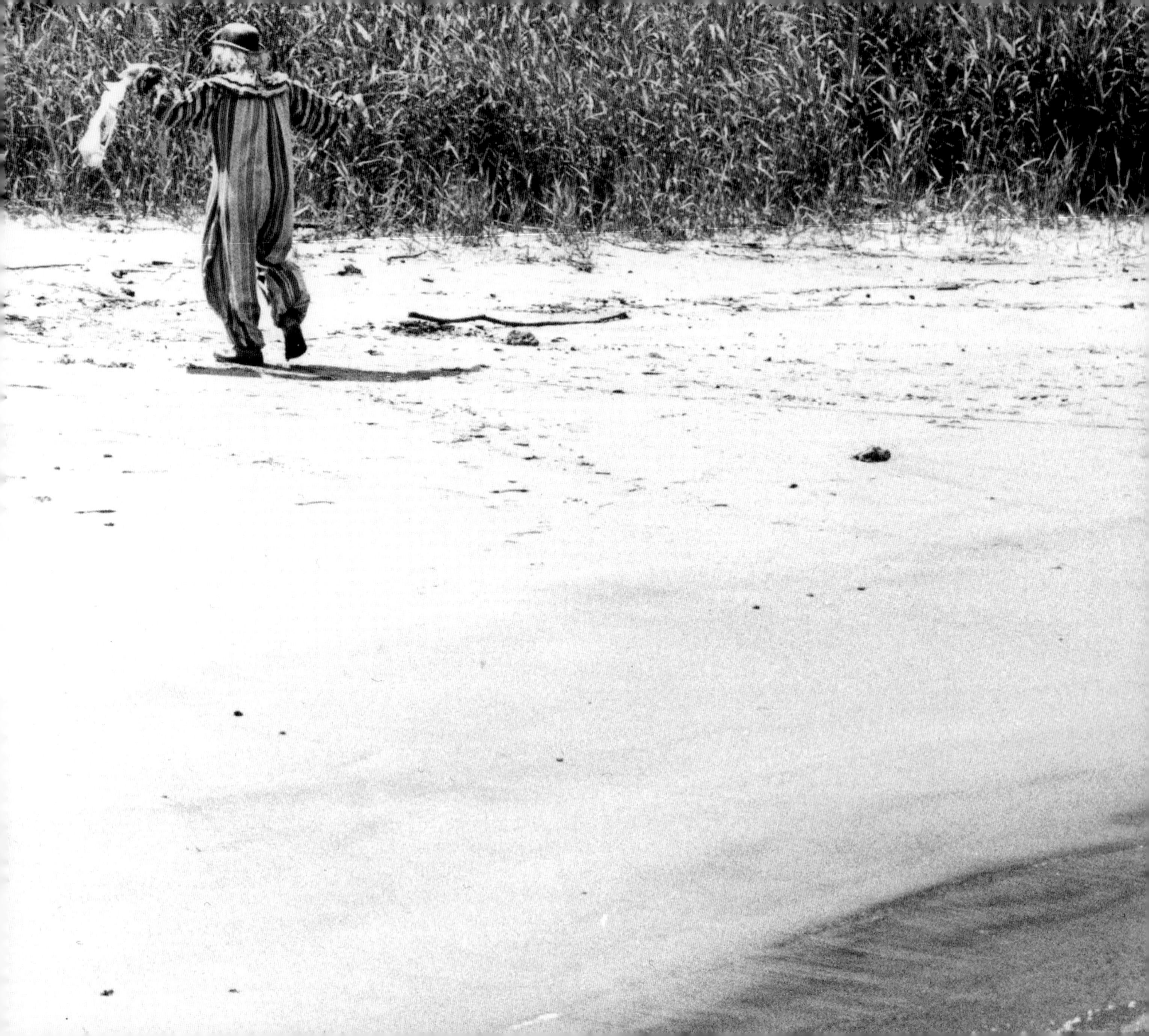

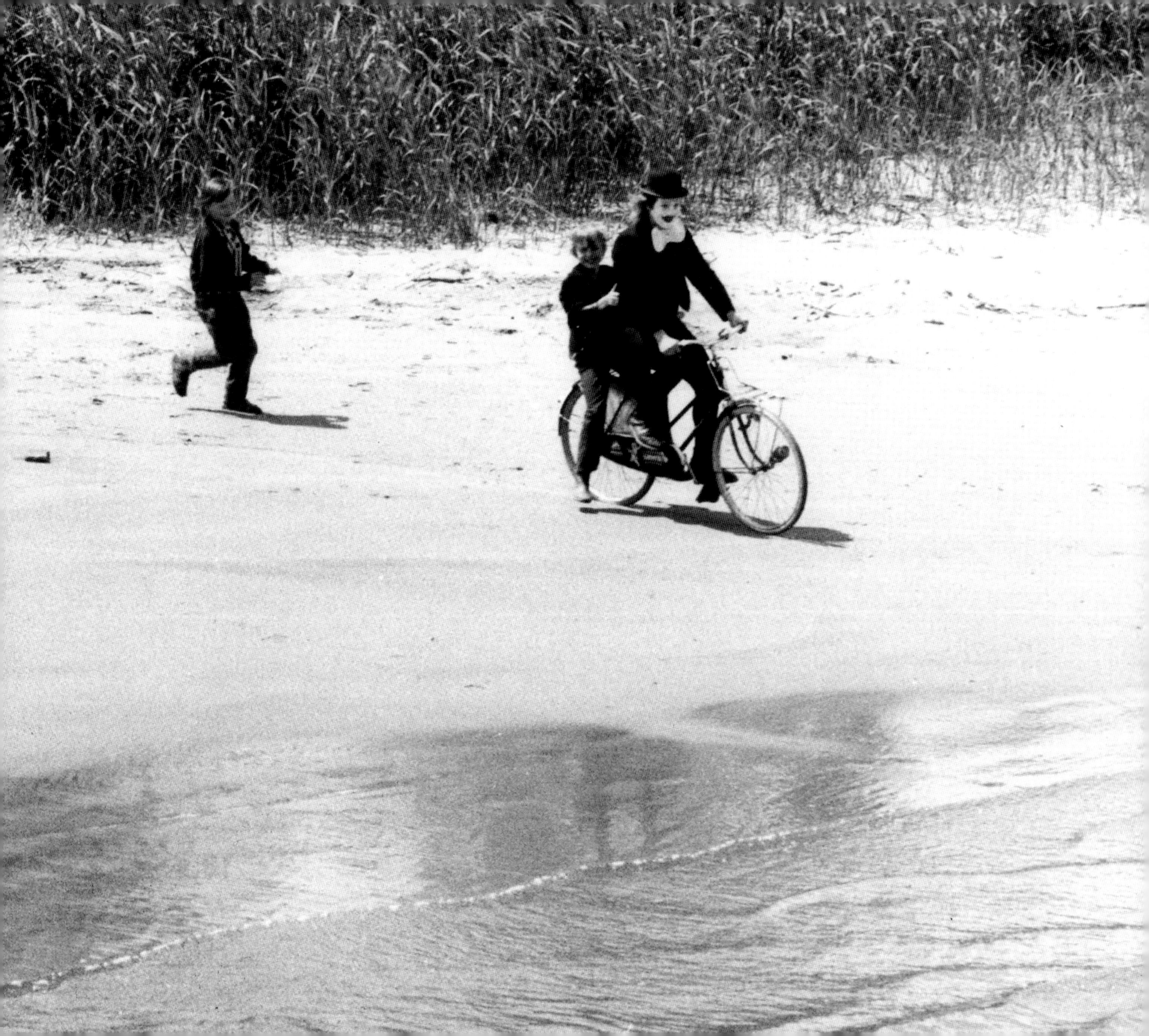

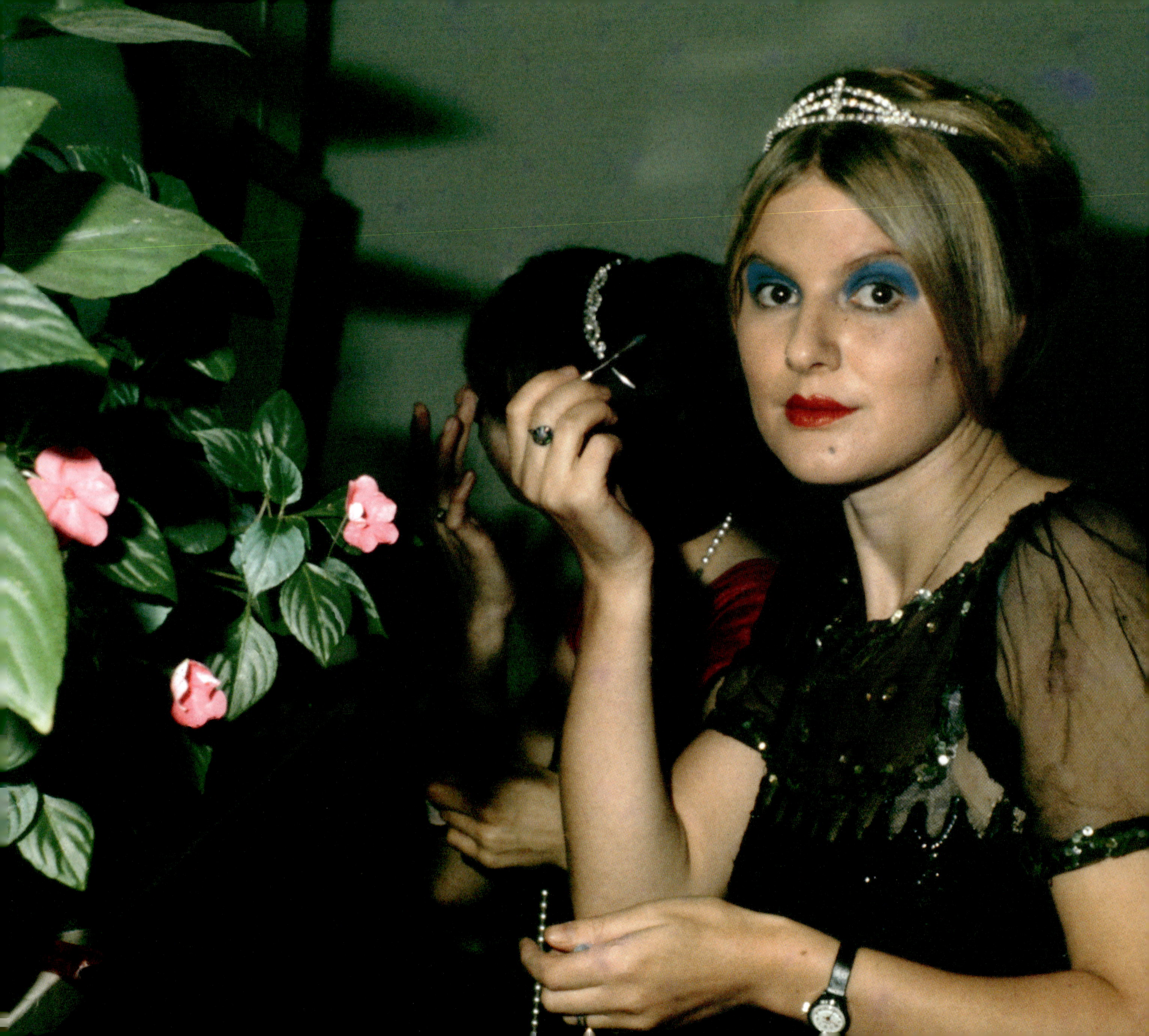

# CHAPTER 8

# WHAT THE NATURALS DID 1974-79

**In which the Natural Theatre Company became a phenomenon. We spent more time on our visuals than on rehearsals and came to life in the streets. We upstaged the Duke of Gloucester and got too close for comfort to the Dublin police.**

## In the street

**B**rian: The Natural Theatre Company was a phenomenon in its own right and it cut through everything we did. Every task in the Workshop was carried out with a sense of theatricality and humour which had its roots in the ethos of the Naturals. We never took ourselves too seriously – but what we did we took very seriously indeed. Performing in the open air, in streets, parks, shopping centres and at outdoor events of all kinds, was always going to be a major attraction for us and much of our theatre took place outside. Our work demanded an immediate, uninhibited response from

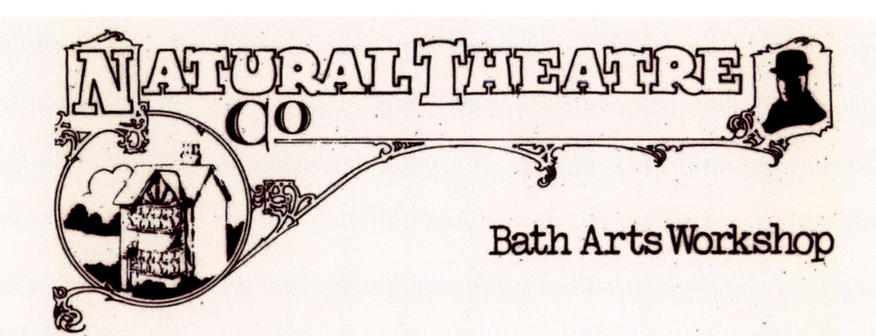


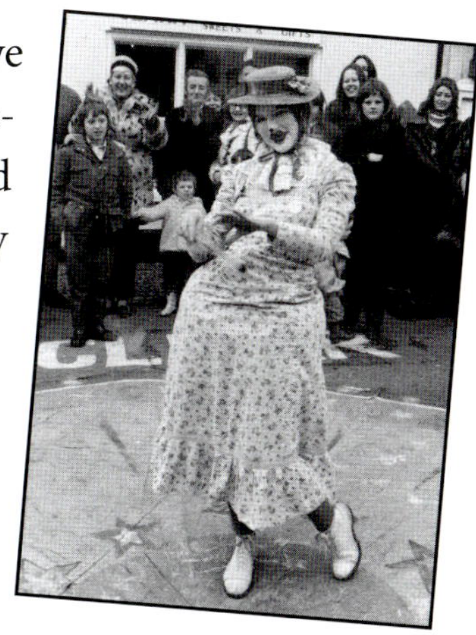

the audience. As we progressed, we found that we liked our work to respond to the environments we found ourselves in and the characters likely (or unlikely) to be found in them.

**Jennie:** Our street theatre often tried to point out the absurdity of reliance on social 'givens' but to do it with humour. One early piece was *Swapping*. Each member of the group took to the streets in different roles – window cleaner, painter and decorator, nun, housewife, drunkard, traffic warden etc. When meeting another player, we swapped props and roles – the housewife handed out parking tickets, the traffic warden climbed a ladder to clean windows and the nun rolled about in the gutter clutching an empty whiskey bottle, much to the consternation of passers-by.

## A Rockette is normalised

**Jennie:** The idea of poking fun at social norms and fixed roles sometimes infiltrated our early indoor shows. On one trip to Rotterdam I was in the advance party with Nigel, Phil and Ralph. We were booked to do an evening show – which didn't exist! The only costumes we had with us were the Normals and the Rockettes (the red spotted dresses). The only character that could speak was the Rockette.

We set up seven office desks one behind the other. The first belonged to a 'secretary' (the Rockette). It was covered with her personal knick knacks, typewriter, telephone etc. She spent the first day chatting on the phone, filing her nails, gaily, dizzily and noisily getting on with business. Throughout the 'week', the Normals arrived after she had left for the day and removed something personal, until only the typewriter remained. Each day, she was a little less lively. By the end of the week (and the show), the Normals arrived to take her away, by then speechless and depersonalised. She had been 'Normalised'.

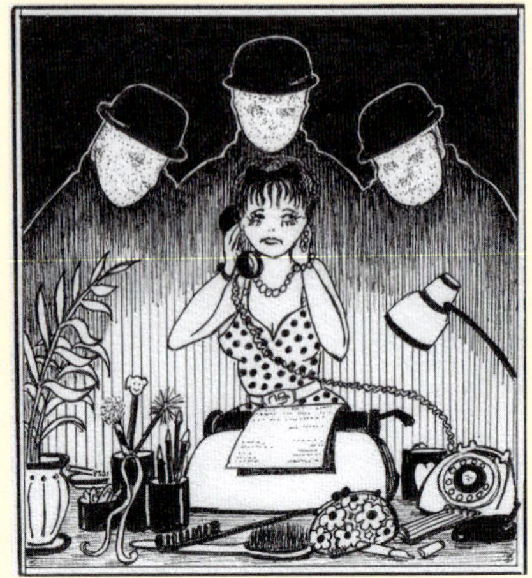

A Rockette is Normalised

## Unusual couple

**Jackie Popay:** My ideas for performances came from the life I was actually living. My eldest daughter Rose was born in 1974. When she was a new-born, I did a piece in the tent at Comtek 74. I was dressed as a woman clown in a billowing dress with a white face and exaggerated cherry-red lips. I sat at a table breastfeeding Rose whilst eating fruit that I plucked from a huge bowl on the table. A few months later Rose, aged about six months, was my little bridegroom kitted out in a miniature morning suit and tails that I made for her. I was playing the daydreaming wife anticipating a perfect future which could all be bought. I remember going shopping and trying out mattresses with my mini husband. He never complained, he just dribbled and said ga-ga.

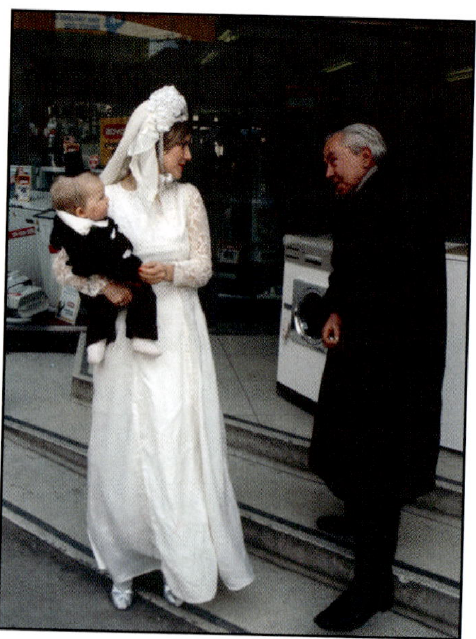

The little bridegroom

# Red carpet

Our characters arrived unannounced at real events when the need arose. One such was a protest at the horrendous, costly refurbishment of Bath's Theatre Royal, and its snobby official opening. The local press reported on the event in detail.

### Before the Duke arrived

(Adapted from *Bath & Wilts Evening Chronicle*)

The Duke of Gloucester came to admire the Theatre Royal's £50,000 interior redecoration last night. The Duke had flown by helicopter to a private home where, according to a rigid and security-conscious official programme, the royal party was invited to partake of scrambled eggs and bacon. There were heavy security precautions in and around the theatre and police reinforcements were tucked away, with plainclothes officers mingling in the crowd.

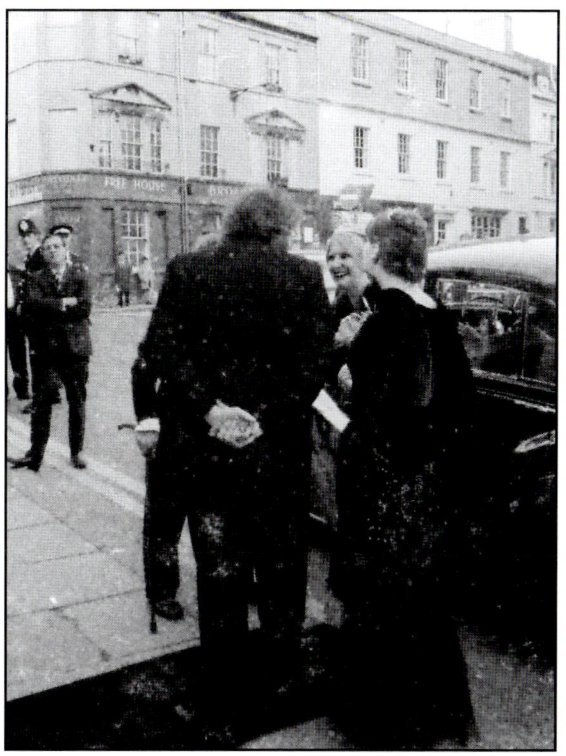

A red carpet was rolled out

The scene was thrown into confusion when at the exact moment the Duke was due to arrive, a limousine drew up. Sir Brian Popay stepped out and rolled a red carpet across the pavement to the theatre entrance. Sir Ralph Oswick appeared along with Ladies Jacqueline and Penelope, all immaculately attired. A flurry ensued among the officials, but the impostors were quickly rumbled despite loudly protesting they had simply forgotten their tickets.

They were escorted from the theatre by the police and the Chief Superintendent hastily kicked the red carpet aside. He later said, 'I knew it was a hoax when I saw one of the VIPs get the red carpet out of the boot!'

# The look

**Ralph Oswick:** I and others in the Naturals department eschewed the agit-prop theatre prevalent at the time. Our approach was that the best way to undermine the enemy, and the funniest, was to look as much like the enemy as possible. We weren't political and yet we were. The fact that we existed was political. That we performed (and even rehearsed) in the streets was political. When we protested the demolitions planned for Bath, it was more for the fun of dressing as bulldozers and attacking the Pump Room than for making a political statement. But intrinsically political nevertheless.

From a group of Dutch Anarchists: The Natural Theatre look the straightest but they are the most fucking far out!

**Ralph:** And so 'the look' was born. The look became an obsession. Hard edged, I think I called it in an Arts Council grant application. We famously spent more time getting every visual detail of our characterisations right than we did rehearsing. In fact, the performance was often the rehearsal. We didn't necessarily know what we were going to do, but the perfectly thought out look gave us confidence to just go out there and do it.

**Brian:** Often our early pieces were inspired by the random donation of a set of costumes. For instance, a set of brass band uniforms given to the shop made it possible for a team of militaristic types to perform a spoof on the government's Protect and Survive strategy, something that was current at the time (what to do in the event of a nuclear bomb attack). The same costumes also kitted out a drumming band that could be wheeled out to processions, shopping malls and housing estates as needed. We adapted these follow my leader formations to many characters and settings, often using quite large groups of people. It was always unpredictable and allowed us to breach many boundaries.

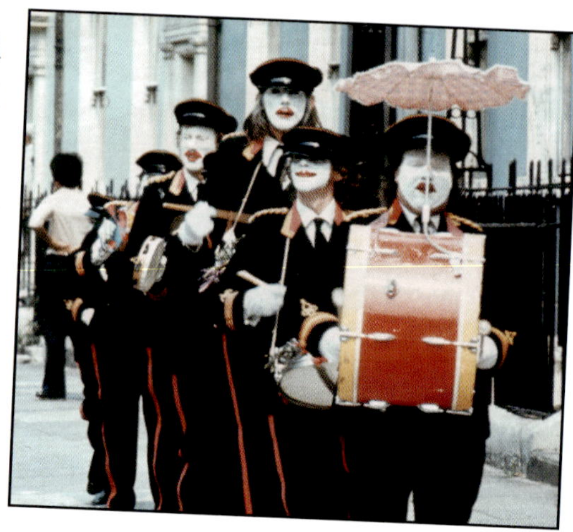

Drumming band

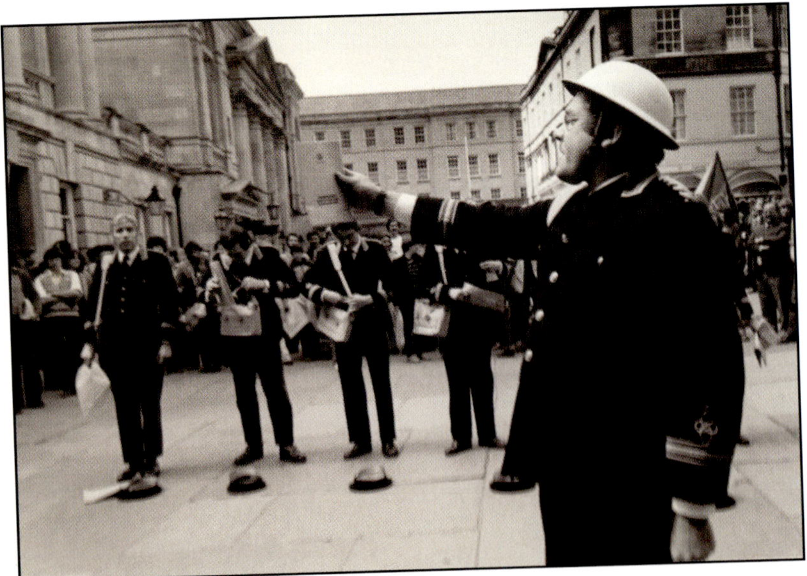

Protect and Survive

**Tory:** In 1974, we took a clown drumming band to the Byker estate in Newcastle. We wore extreme costumes. Mine was a half-face rubber clown mask that covered my forehead and nose (clammy and sweaty even in winter), a shoulderless chiffon ball gown with a large false bottom, a little fur cape and huge silver bunches of grapes earrings. I loved that drumming band... the simple beats and the freedom to march wherever the mood took us. Nasher filmed us zig-zagging in and

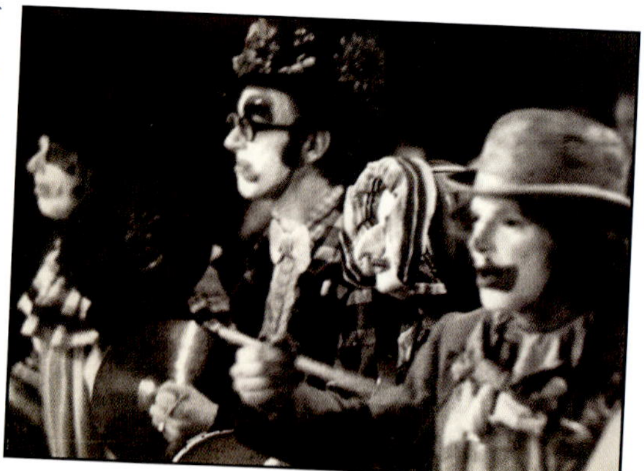

Clown band

## Dirty protest

**Ric Jerrom:** On occasion, we were political – and explicitly so with somewhat shocking consequences. We visited the Dublin Festival for the second time in 1979, where our dressing room was in the Gaiety Theatre. The Tom Stoppard play *Every Good Boy Deserves Favour*, was showing nightly to packed houses. It criticises the former Soviet Union practice of treating political dissidence as a mental illness. The audiences were wild for the play – tumultuous applause and a great mill of them outside on the pavement each evening, not merely enthusing about the play but also (as we saw it) congratulating themselves on living in a civilised country where nothing like the Soviet practices could ever happen.

At the time, about 60 miles away in the notorious H Blocks at The Maze prison in Northern Ireland, IRA prisoners were staging blanket and dirty protests following suspension of their political prisoner status by the British Government in 1972. They had refused to wear prison uniforms and went naked or wrapped in blankets. As the government refused to concede and tensions escalated between guards and prisoners, the latter smashed up their basins and all the cell furniture was removed. The prisoners were not allowed to 'slop out' and in the end

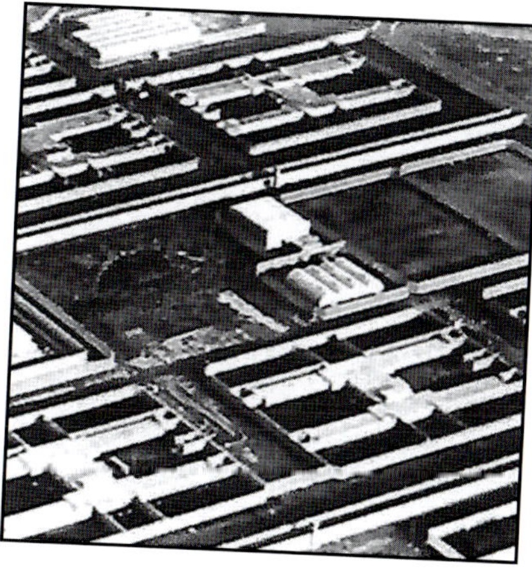

were being held in filthy cells, scattered with excrement and rotting food.

One evening Brian, Pavel Douglas, Tom Costello and I stripped down, smeared dirt on our faces and wrapped ourselves in dirty blankets. Just before the play ended, we positioned ourselves on the traffic island opposite the theatre entrance, about five yards from the kerb. We were brightly lit by harsh white street lights, though with our faces in shadow. The voluble, happy, self-congratulatory crowd swelled out onto the pavement and immediately lapsed into complete silence. But not for long.

Men started shouting and a few women started to cry. After a minute or so, a couple of men crossed the road and shouted 'What the fuck do you think you're doing?' We had agreed to say nothing so kept quiet, but were suddenly surrounded by armed men (we were close to Dublin Castle, HQ of the Garda and Special Branch). They broke up the crowd and shoved us up against the theatre wall, demanding to know what we were doing. They were quite violent so, in the end, I broke our rule and said we were a British street theatre company here for the festival. They took a bit of persuading but we invited them to our dressing room and after that they snarled off, advising us not to try that piece again.

**Ric Jerrom** arrived in Bath in 1974 in a borrowed Land Rover. That night, he met Phil in The Hat & Feather, who persuaded him to drive it at 6am the following morning to support a *Save that Tree* campaign in Walcot Street (the tree was saved). He worked on and off with the Naturals and wrote parts of the script for *Wanton Ways* (see below). And with John Wood the linking script for the televised *Partly Political Broadcast on behalf of the Walcot National Party* for **Walcot Nation Festival** in 1979. The following year he became BAW community arts organiser.

## Abroad

**Corinne:** During the second half of the 70s, the Naturals were in great demand and we toured extensively in the UK and Europe. This was a period when you didn't have to chase gigs, they came to you. Contracts were often verbal

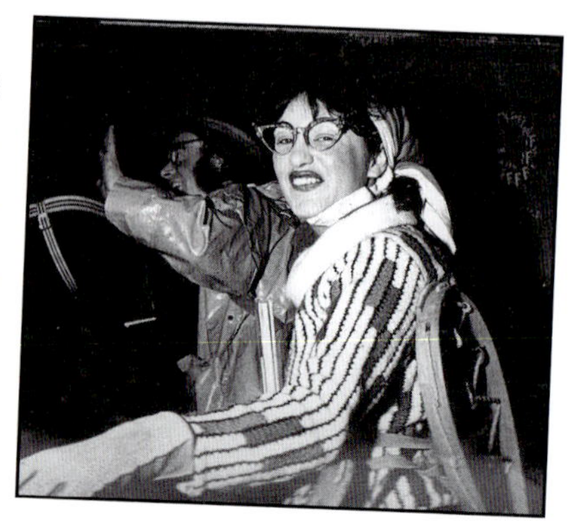

agreements made on the phone and backed up by the odd handwritten letter. We didn't realise it at the time, but the UK was at the forefront of the burgeoning alternative and street theatre movement. The first country to seriously engage with British groups was the Netherlands, with De Lantaren in Rotterdam becoming a second home to the Naturals and other UK theatre groups. Later, we visited the Alstervergnügen Festival in Hamburg and won prizes there for our work in 1977 and 78.

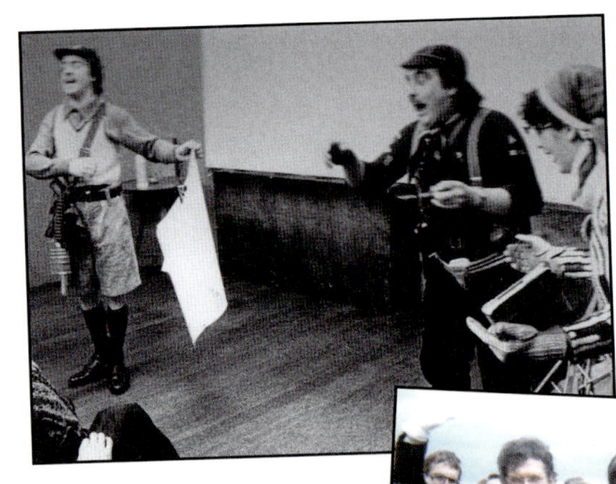

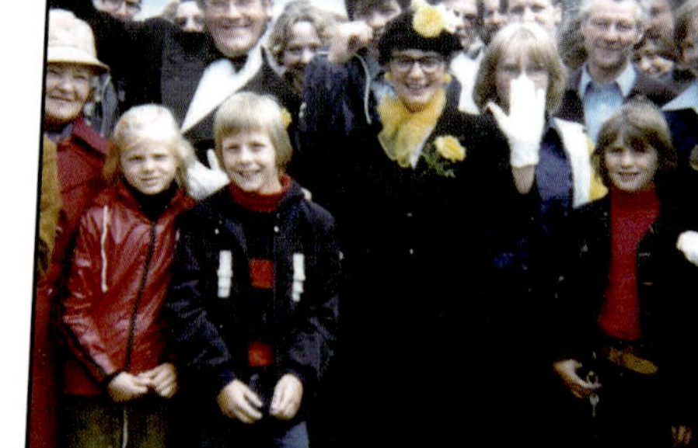

Top and middle:
Sci-fi in Netherlands
Right: Alstervergnügen

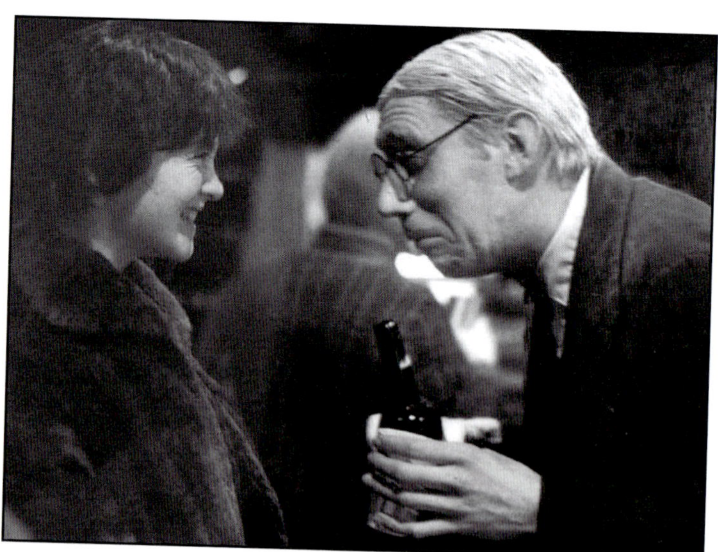

Ric as Clench the butler

## Yellow suitcases and a wedding

**Tory:** In 1977, we developed a new street theatre piece that evolved from a performance involving orange suitcases created by Mick Banks and Corinne during a four-month trip to Australia.[1] Back in Bath, we changed the colour to

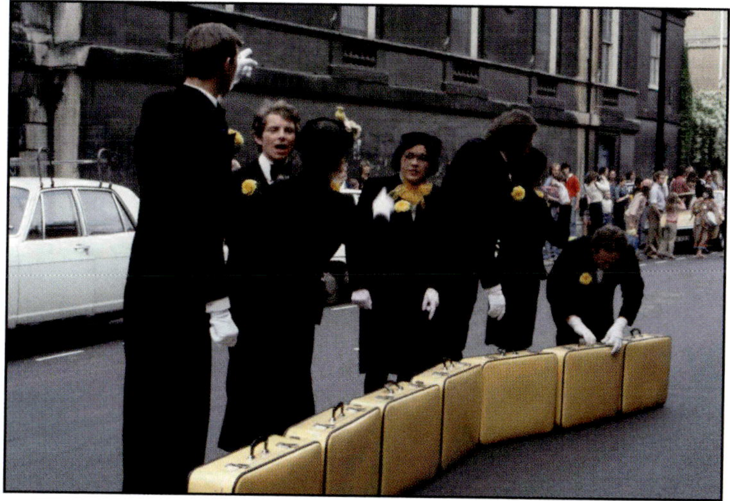

yellow and Mick joined seven identical suitcases together with a simple articulated mechanism. Then, dressed in black suits and linked by our joined-up suitcases, we took to the streets. We were smartly-dressed tourists looking for our hotel, a restaurant, a taxi, which at times we clambered into, before emerging on the other side of the vehicle. We marched onto traffic-laden roads, had loud exchanges with lorry drivers, entered restaurants and toilets and generally created havoc, complaining vociferously about the lack of service or whatever occurred to us in the moment.

---

1. While there, they gave lectures on BAW and John Bull Puncture Repair Kit, as well as various performances and teaching projects. The piece using orange suitcases was created for the exterior of the Sydney Opera House.

**Mick Banks:** The interiors were all custom-built. Mine had a fitted clothes rail with a line of wire coat hangers and a battery-powered burglar alarm. I triggered it periodically, then opened the case to discover that all my clothes had been stolen! We took the piece to the Alstervergnügen Festival in Hamburg, where its blend of synchronised pattern forming and default daftness won great acclaim. In those days, the growing momentum of the Natural Theatre meant we could assemble very large teams. The teams, an admix of full and part-time performers, friends and their partners, have rarely seen the light of day since and the iconography they employed was occasionally on an unprecedented scale. A late example was a team of professors dispatched to clean civic statues in Vienna. Nine at the bottom of the ladder giving advice. One at the top not acting on it!

This astonishing company uses the street in the fullest and funniest manner imaginable… the most popular [scenario] involved a human string of seven harassed commuters… bustling in step through the crowded precinct attached to their seven interlocking bright yellow suitcases… I met various people who had followed them for hours on end… About 200 people descended with them onto the U Bahn. The group, waiting for a train, closed ranks and began snapping away for the family album… The train arrives. They enter it, followed by about 50 grinning admirers, while the rest of us wave them goodbye from the platform.
**Michael Coveney,** *Financial Times,* **22 July 1978**

**Corinne:** Later that year at the Dublin Festival, the Naturals staged an adapted version of *Phil Grimm's Progress* (see *Chapter 9*). In this case, the audience accompanied Phil on his journey from the City of Destruction (earth) to the Celestial City (heaven) via central Dublin and the River Liffey. I was Phil's Good Companion and arrived at Dublin's famous footbridge in a limo to preside over the part where the pilgrims must cast out their worldly goods. We had previously given joke watches and plastic coins to the audience which they threw ceremoniously into the Liffey (admittedly not our 'greenest' moment). We were a little apprehensive about how the irreverent nature of the show might be perceived. We needn't have worried – two nuns followed us the whole way hooting with laughter.

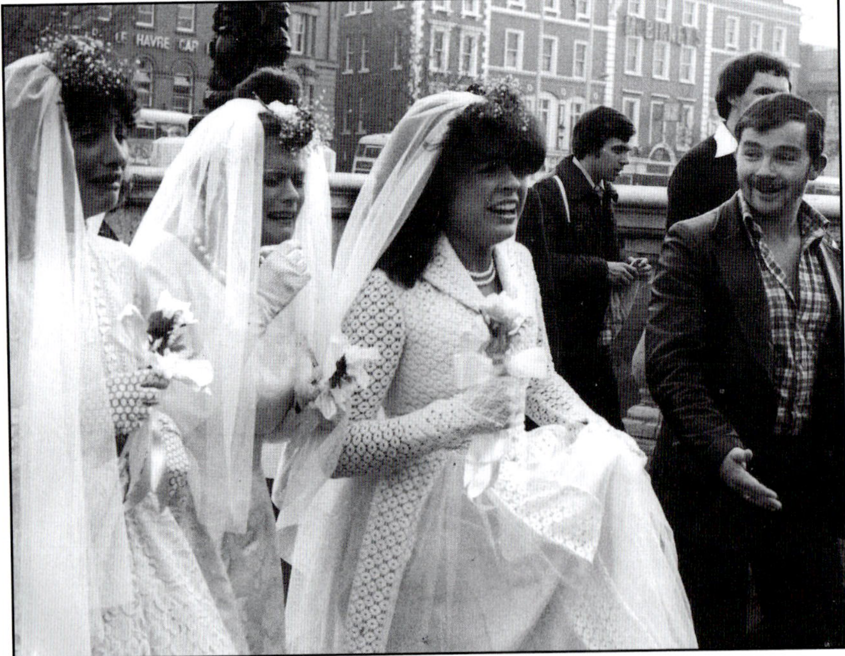

On the same trip, we staged an outdoor wedding where three weeping brides enlisted fathers, friends and family en route to the ceremony.

The triple marriage ceremony… developed into a tumultuous nuptial procession through the backstreet vegetable market… one of the brides pursued a surprised old Dubliner through the streets with a cry of 'Daddy come back' and people almost fell out of windows in their determination to see what was going on.
**Michael Billington, *Guardian*, 1978**

## Indoors

**Tory:** The Naturals did a few indoor shows over the years. One that worked really well was *Windows* in 1975. It was about isolated individuals trapped in a place that was both strange and familiar. Each character stood behind a window frame (they were suspended from the theatre ceiling). I mainly remember Jennie who was seven-months pregnant slowly undressing in her window to reveal her enormous bump, before putting on a nightie and gazing down upon it. And Jackie as a sad woman carefully covering her face with a white clay face mask, peering as it were into an invisible mirror. Brian reproduced his June Ramsey character (from *The Respectable Terrace*), a middle-aged, middle England lady. Did he rub dog food over his clothes which was then licked off by his actual dog Dustbin? The mind boggles. Lady Margaret was the narrator, but he/she walked off half way through after getting tongue-tied. The window frames were beautiful old things borrowed from Comtek.

**Jennie:** Some of our shows were a bit random, albeit visually arresting. In one show in Rotterdam, Tory and I began as peasants in flowing skirts and headscarves, before metamorphosing into hermaphrodites, the look completed by home-made male genitalia. Were we making a point about gender identity? I have no idea.

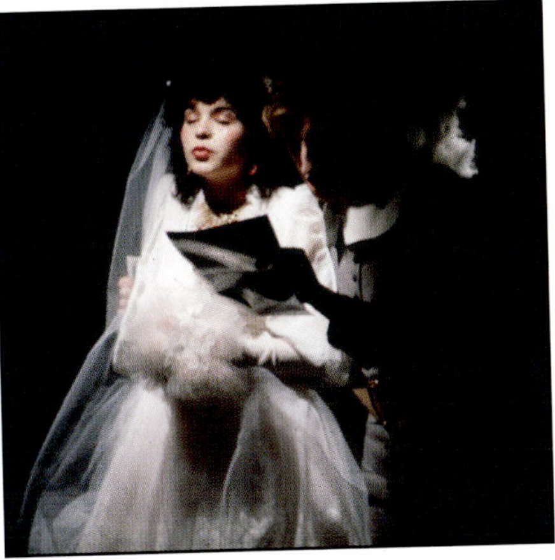

Wanton Ways

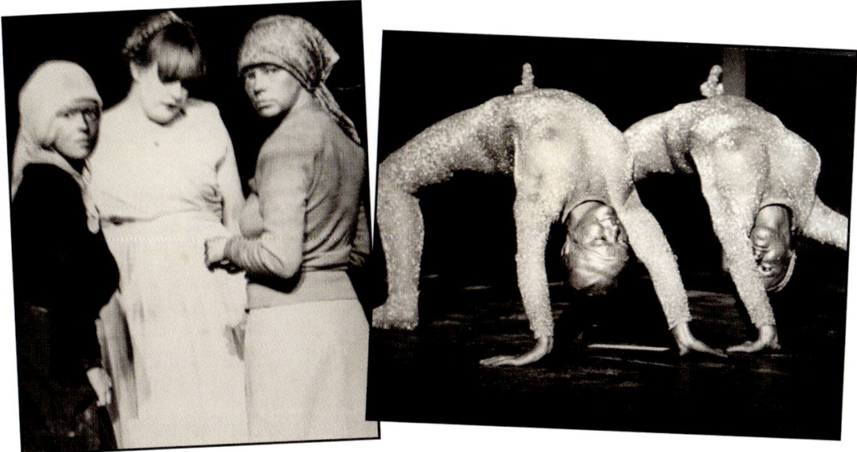

Before and after

We took the show to an arts centre in Boston, Lincolnshire, where a perplexed critic from the local paper wrote a blow-by-blow account of every scene, concluding with the following: 'The play ended with a weird scene looking into the future. The cast walked onstage wearing sunglasses to the sound effects from the film *Close Encounters of the Third Kind*. Although difficult to understand, the play had the audience on the edge of their seats – they simply didn't know what was going to happen next!' *The Standard*, **9 February 1979**

## On the road

**Tory:** Another piece, *Wanton Ways* (1979), involved a bunch of tentatively-linked characters, all trapped but trying to find a way out/forward (a recurring theme perhaps?). Swathes of candy-floss-like industrial waste hung down from the ceiling. We had somehow come by a vanload of this stuff. We called it Mish Mash, and used it constantly as a prop. The cast included Barbara Vaughan as an aviator, Brian as an alchemist (and later a sadistic member of the aristocracy), Ralph as his wife, Mick Banks as a pilgrim, Louise as a bride who ended up in a reality TV show with Mick as presenter, the women becoming nannies caring for violent babies… and so on.

**Jennie:** We spent many hours travelling. In the early days, we were in our old Commer vans with sofas in the back, squeezed in between props and costumes. They constantly broke down so we were used to being stranded on the motorway. Once on the way to Rotterdam (in the coach that time), the windscreen wipers broke as we were driving across the Zeider Zee. A storm was raging, rain was lashing down and the wind whipped the sea. Pete Smith, then a teenager from the Snow Hill Road Show, volunteered to lean out of the window and manually wipe the windscreen – which he did quite effectively. There were lots of early starts and long ferry trips, and we were always hungry as the timetable never seemed to allow much time for meals. We used to pile into Heston services (near London) for breakfast, totally dishevelled on those mornings and ravenous for food of any kind.

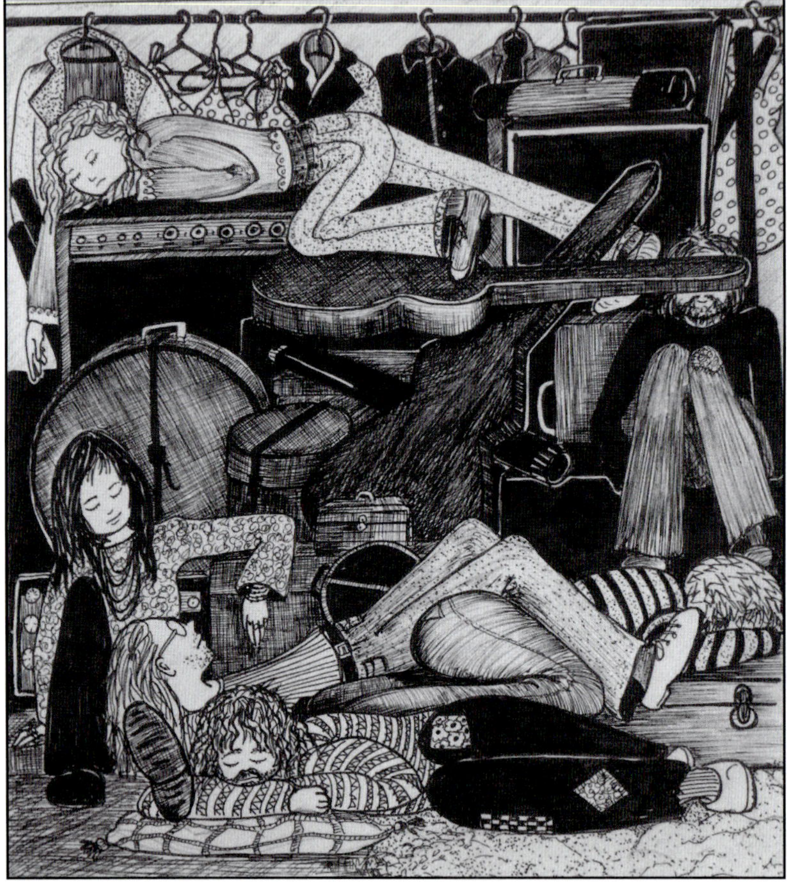

Back of the van going home

**Tory:** Later, we had the far more reliable and comfortable Mercedes with its beautiful B.A.W. lettering on the side. Fewer breakdowns but still very long journeys and lots of lugging heavy gear – we always had so much stuff! We played ridiculous word games and outlandish competitions invented by Ralph, read, and slept when we could. What did we eat? Egg, sausage and chips, bacon sandwiches, and cheese rolls. I liked chips with curry sauce after the pubs closed. Harvest Wholefoods started doing natural yoghurt and honey, which was a new delicacy for us. We drank a lot of tea and roll-ups were common among the smokers. Everywhere was smoke-filled then.

**Mick Banks:** When the gig involved an overnight stay in London, our journey home usually began with a visit to Brian's mum near Shepherd's Bush. After that a trip to the local bakers for London Cheesecake, a pre-war pastry with a white spaghetti-like shredded coconut topping.

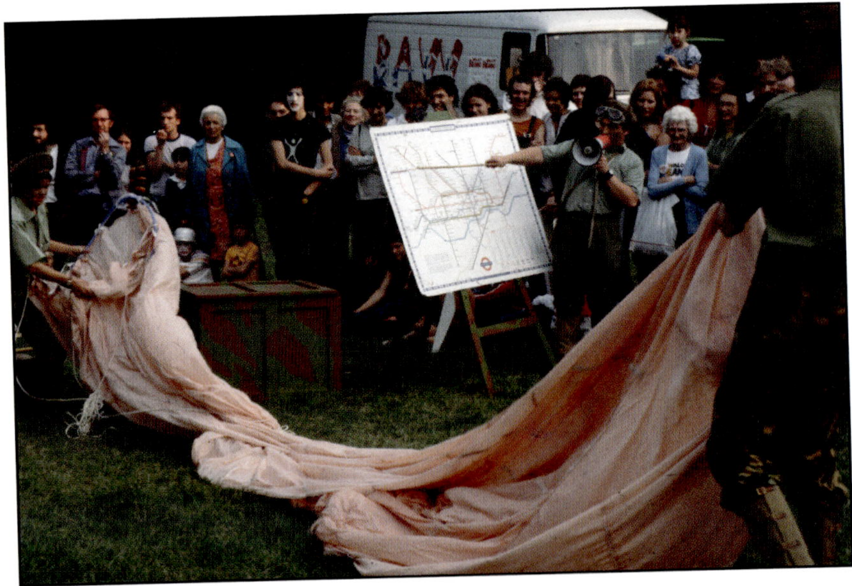

Balloons with our beautiful new van in the background

182

Alternatively, we'd stop off at the Italian ice cream parlour in Acton (Brian's mum worked in the laundry there when he was a boy). And finally out onto the open road. Not the M4 though. Instead we usually took the A4, the old route to Bath and the West Country. The drive home often took us in search of rural idylls along hidden lanes and byways which lasted well into the gloom of a winter's evening. Eventually we arrived in Bath, unloaded our props into the crypt, put the rail of costumes up into the office to be guarded by the mice, and then a mad dash to The Hat & Feather before last orders.

# Back home

## Love unspoken

**Ralph Oswick:** Around the time of the Beano Clubs (see *Chapter 9*), Barbara Vaughan and I devised a modest operatic soirée entitled *Grand & Not So Grand*. We sang duets while Chas Ambler played the piano. Brian was our onstage stage manager, letting off explosions etc. We used to pick on someone and say they were from the Arts Council (once there was a real one) and fire a massive confetti cannon at them. The songs ranged from Olde Tyme Music Hall to Puccini. My character was Dame Nelly Tesco and Barbara's was Dame Clara Boot. When I sang *Love Unspoken* by Strauss, I used to leave the room and possibly even the building to trill forth the echo from afar! We mainly performed in the Village Hall, but also did

a small tour of minor art centres: Folkestone, Grantham, The Oval, Penzance, Sherborne, Walsall, plus a few pubs and outdoor recitals, including one at Corsham Fete.

**Barbara Vaughan** was a talented actress, singer and comedienne, who arrived in Bath in 1977. She sang a show-stopping version of *That Old Black Magic* as the witch, Grizelda Crone, in *Elsie and Norm's Macbeth*, and played a manic Scottish cook in the spoof whodunit *Blood Weekend*. Both shows were performed at the Village Hall and on tour with the group **Dramarama**. Barbara often performed at the Beano and with the Naturals — including a show in which she sang a song while suspended from a harness as the aviator Amelia Earhart.[2]

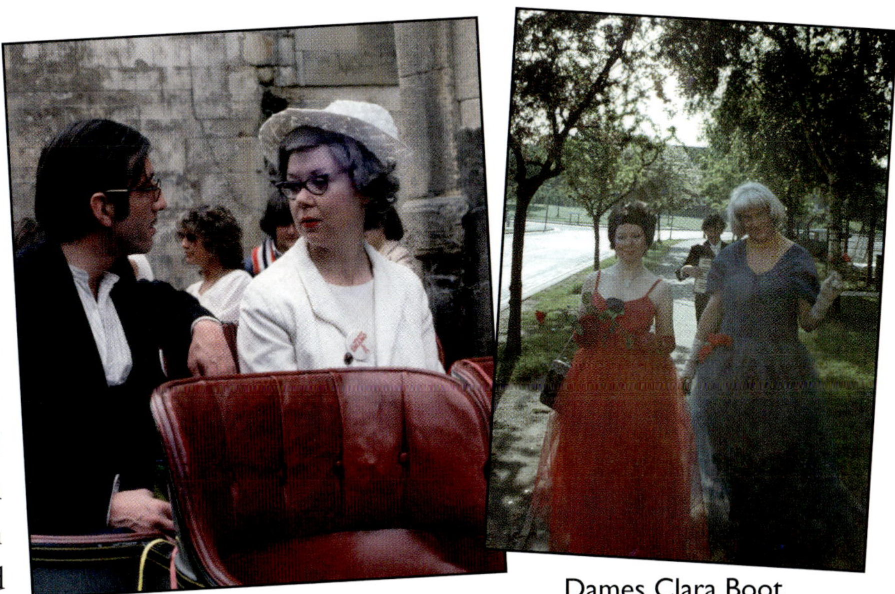

Barbara and Steve Ehrlicher

Dames Clara Boot and Nelly Tesco

---

2. Sadly Barbara had MS and she died in 2006, a few weeks before her 57th birthday.

## Alter-ego

**Chris Peecock:** Day to day life in the shop and office in Walcot Street was often entertaining but the highlights for me were performing with the Naturals. I still think that much of the street performance work in those heady days was truly ground breaking. Our immaculate turnout and the surreal nature of the stereotypes we often portrayed always made us stand out, and the fact that we were always moving. I felt lucky to be able to create characters and use them in so many different scenarios. My female alter-ego, Mary Mingeworthy, was the strongest and longest lived of them. She started off as a local busybody and gossip but soon morphed into many contradictory guises, including DJ and ardent fan of Rocky Ricketts, poet, fortune teller, performance artist and head of a team of cheerleaders. Her most endearing traits were her constant cheeriness, and her enthusiasm and willingness to try almost anything once!

Another character was *Half and Half* (male and female), sometimes appearing as a bride and groom or as a Fred and Ginger tap dancer. I got carried away when I decided to use smoke flares hidden in the heels of my tap shoes – the idea was to perform a sort of dancing Red Arrows, with smoke billowing forth from my shoes. It worked up to a point but I had to cut the performance short when my shoes burst into flames and I burnt my feet. How I suffered for my art. The crowds of course loved it.

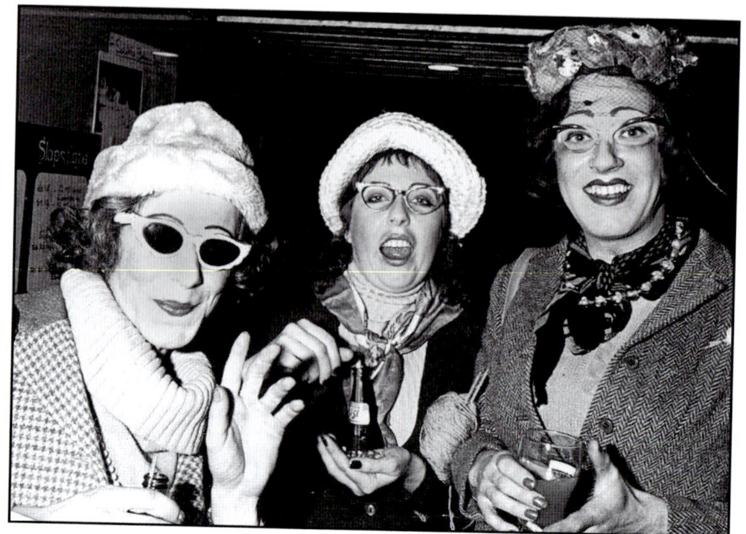

The three gossips (Chris on the right)

My overall favourite moment was a brief appearance in Nasher's epic ***Gordon, the Movie***. A still from my scene appeared on the cover of *Venue* magazine. Fame and fortune at last. Ha!

**Brian:** And so during the first 10 years of Natural Theatre, we refined our work, improved our techniques and experienced a constant turnover of ideas. We had the time, freedom and opportunity to meet and work with so many of the daring inventive theatre groups that emerged during those years. All this meant that for us it was a truly creative period.

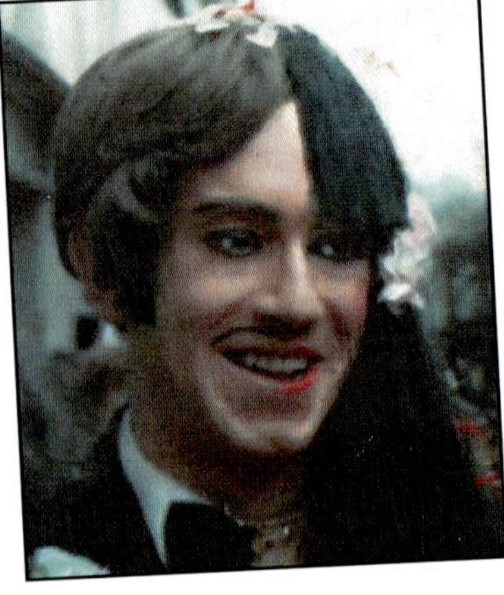

Half and Half

## All in a day's work

**Jackie Popay:** As soon as we got back to Bath, we jumped back into the world of the Workshop. Daily life brimmed with many activities, including part-time jobs when we weren't being paid. I sold hand-made clothes and cakes in the Workshop Shop and ran workshops for teenagers in Warmley. Modelling at the art school and for **Peter Blake**. Organising jumble sales, Christmas dinners, recycling buttons, clubs for children, adventure playgrounds, *Spotty Blelb* and Rocky shows that led many of us towards theatre and the Natural Theatre Company. Travelling to the Netherlands. Organising wonderful festivals. There were theatre workshops, free form music and a myriad of groups with which to identify. I worked for King Kong Workforce, sanding windows, and demolition, then lugging furniture up and down staircases for King Kong Community Transport.

I often worked in the shop on Walcot Street sorting out the jumble, serving and chatting to the customers and the kids who came in all the time. Doing discos in the evenings with Rocky Ricketts (I was his lovely wife Mavis). Or the Rocky show with all the exciting chaos of preparation –

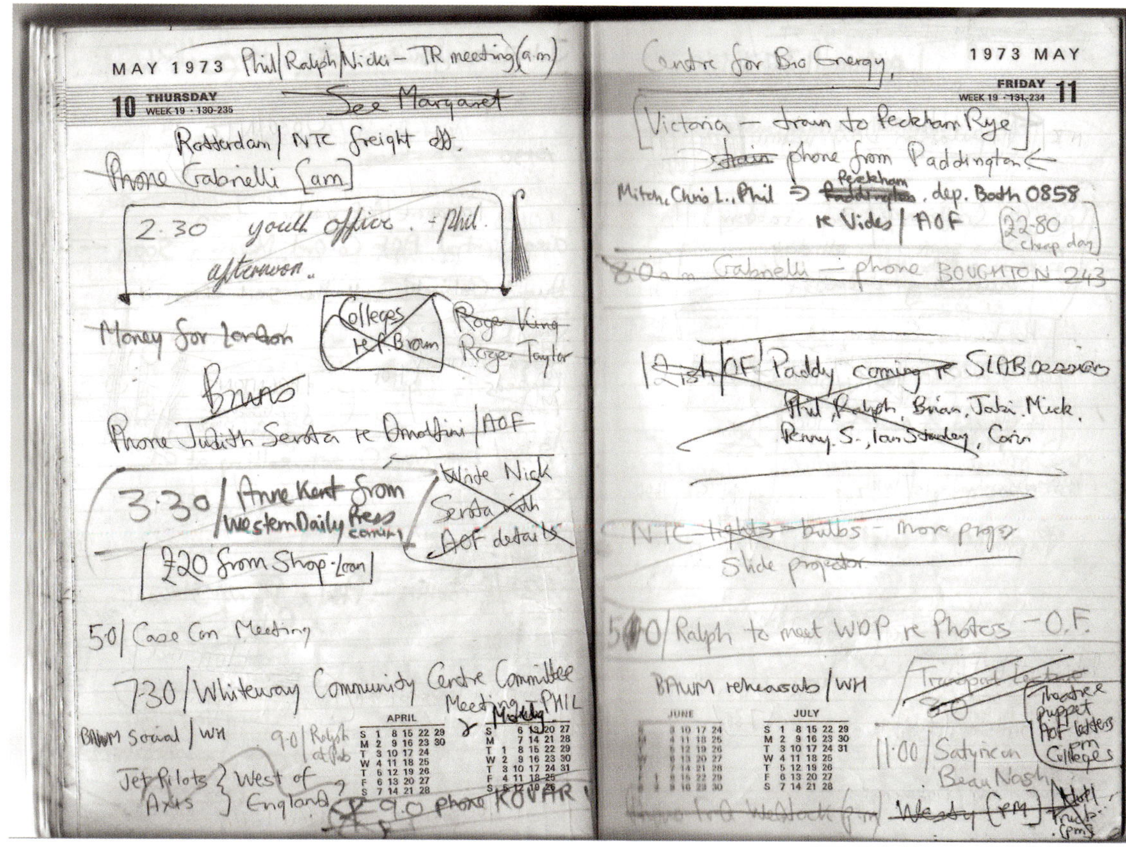

loading the van, sound checks in murky venues, dressing rooms squashed together, silver stilettos, hair spray, make-up and glitter… followed by the wonderful pulsing sound of rock music and flouncing onto the stage in a blaze of light.

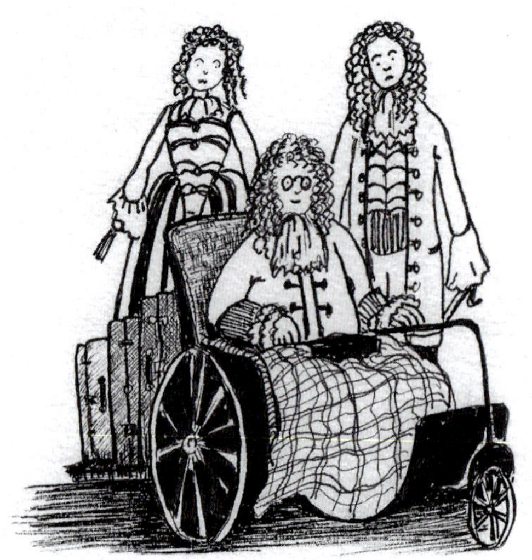

# THE WHEELCHAIR
# AND THE BOX

**R**alph Oswick: Around 1976, we devised one of our strangest and most sensational outdoor performances. It was challenging to perform for many reasons but invariably elicited an extreme response, and much gasping and shrieking from those who chanced upon it. The Wheelchair (as we called it) was mainly performed on the streets of Bath and in Dublin, but also, memorably, in Walsall.



**Ralph:** It is night. A group of knicker-bockered flunkies calved in white stockings, an archbishop and fine ladies with long noses and extravagant make-up, surround a bewigged professor in an ancient Bath Chair. A tartan blanket is swathed about his legs and an assortment of aged leather suitcases are strapped to the back of the chair. As the motley group shuffles forward, the professor begins to display the horrid artefacts he has stowed in assorted caskets in his collection – a plastic shrunken head with bloody blond hair and a false spider set in velvet...

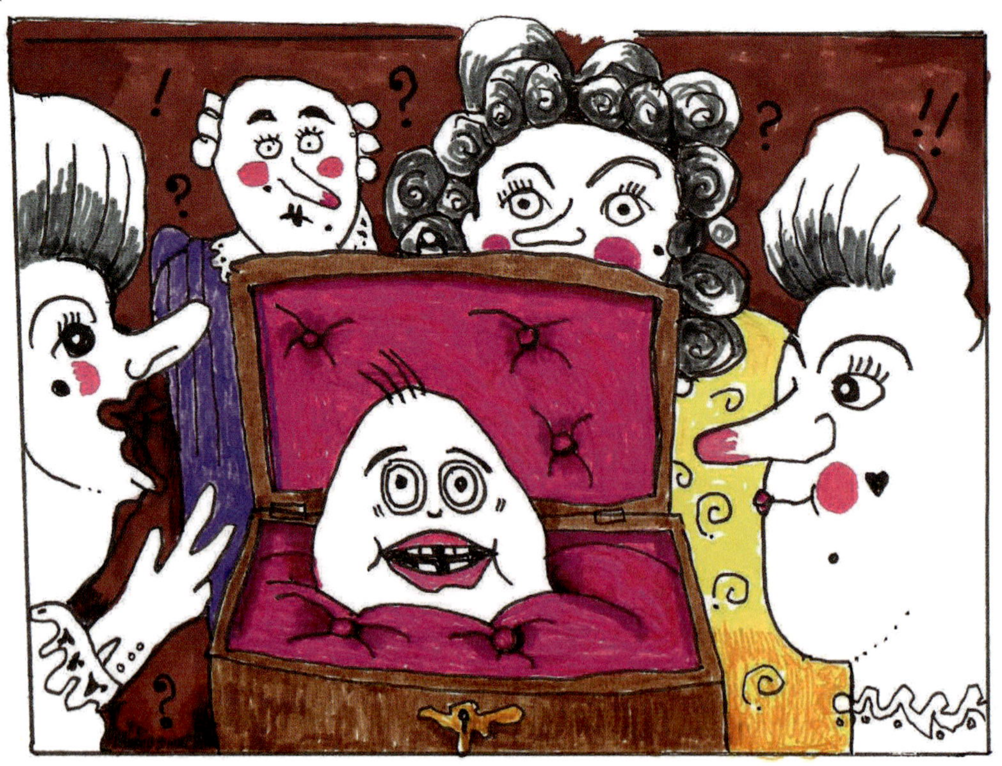

**David Gale:** Finally, all eyes are on the box upon his feet. The professor is by now encircled. Children have been pushed to the front, for surely this will be delightful. There is much hissing, groaning and heavy breathing until, with a cry from the grotesques, the box is opened. There, set in a bed of blue velvet, is a tiny face with two bright eyes and full red lips. It is no bigger than half an orange. A murmur of enchantment ripples through the crowd.

The lips part. A tongue slides out and is withdrawn.

As one, the crowd steps back. There are cries of horror and alarm. Health and Safety issues momentarily arise (their regulation only recently enshrined in 1974), as rugged members of the public spill onto the road, gathering unto them their children. A mesmerised silence descends, broken only by muttered mansplaining (the term was yet to be coined) from those anxious to regain their dignity after shrieking incontinently. Slowly, and with great care, the crowd inches back toward the wheelchair.

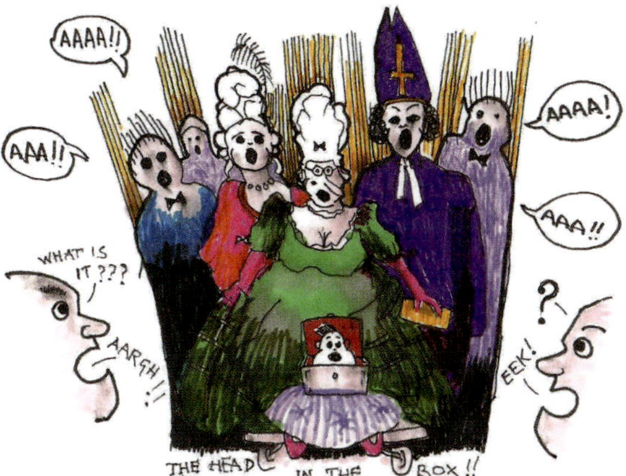


The professor, unperturbed, smiles pleasantly as the mouth puckers and makes kissing noises. Or perhaps puffs upon a borrowed cigarette or samples a crisp. It makes no sound. As the crowd squeals, the lid is lowered and the retinue conveys its grand passenger up the street, leaving a huddle of passers-by enveloped in a cloud of amazement.

**Ralph:** Our face in a box was a version of the old party trick when someone has an upside-down face drawn on their chin. I was the professor (or Georgian lady) in the chair, while the body attached to the face lay prostrate in a rack under the wheelchair, their feet contained in the hollow stack of suitcases. Because of the cases and the crush of auxiliary characters, the

illusion of a grimacing, lip-smacking little face in a box was totally convincing (as well as totally bizarre for the brave and uncomfortable actor ensconced within – usually Andy Hume or Tory).

One woman in a Walsall pub – watching her Guinness sucked into the little creature's mouth through a straw – calmly responded to her friend's squawking inquiry as to what the *eff* it was – with 'Well, it's just one of those… you know… one of THOSE!'

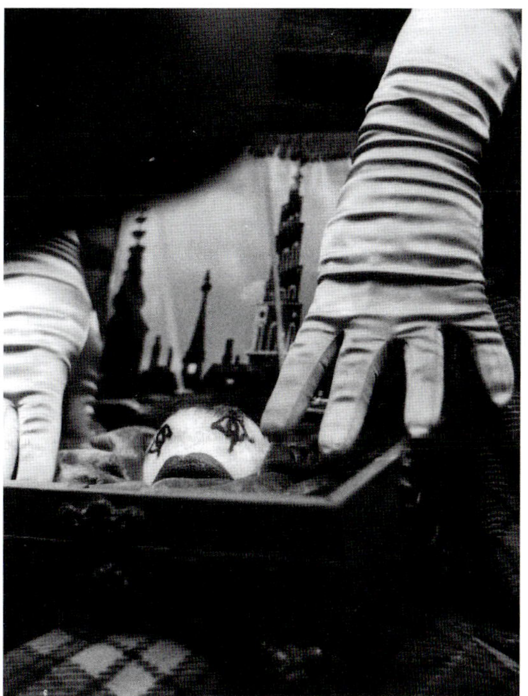

'It's just one of THOSE'

# A YOUNG WOMAN'S WALK IN WALCOT STREET BY LOUISE OSBORN

Shabby shops, before the chic set in,
selling useful things and hippie charms,
carpets, junk and second-hand clothes,
a watery pint and a bacon sarnie.
Greasy spoon cafes, motorbikes and reclamation,
where you could listen to jazz, get your bike tyres fixed,
picnic and play on the old burial ground,
buy roll-ups, a newspaper and launder your dirties,
bid for a sooty Georgian house, at auction, for under ten grand.

And in a rundown shop – once a ladies' hairdressers –
stood the Bath Arts Workshop.

This was in a time of inflation and industrial strife.
Three-day weeks and electrical power cuts,
a time of 'them and us'
when Bowie outed Ziggy and
working-class families first flew to foreign sun.
A time when a generation of girls
living in the shadow of nuclear war,
were surfacing from post-war childhoods
of restraint and perseverance, where we had learned that
we were nothing much to shout about,
and advised to keep small,
remembering that shame filled our pockets.
Now colliding with the Female Eunuch,
Spare Rib, Virago Books and a rising feminist tide,
the spirit of this time was contradictory, exciting, complicated.
A time before everything was commoditised,
a gritty, earthy kind of innocence,
caught between thrift and a new extravagance,
between a casual sexism, racism, homophobia,
and a creeping new wakefulness.
But at least, back then, you could still just fall into things
and discover – by stumbling – your passions.

Bath Arts Workshop – once a ladies' hairdressers –
a collective of art school rebels, theatricals and eco shakers,
Lady Margaret and Rocky Ricketts,
community activists and educators,
cross dressing, confronting, attracting castaways –
paint-smeared children, in t-shirts and tutus,
old ladies, Mrs. Mills and May Branch, Kitty Sutton,
and grey, cackling Gordon Robbins,
in his shiny short-trousered suit, resident fag
and magic pianist fingers.

The misplaced ladies of Ladymead House,
clutching handbags and headscarves,
old Jack with his street piano,
Civil Aid and King Kong Transport.

And me. I washed up there, too, on Walcot Street,
and there I found my tribe.
A young woman, half formed, not yet attached to my own opinion,
it was amongst this ornamental gaggle that I began
to find both feet and voice.
Pulled to the impolite, irreverent, anarchic thrill
of unruly theatre in the street, of counter cultural shocking,
of chaos, community and care.

In a dilapidated shop – once a ladies' hairdressers –
this depot, junk-piled with curiosities and sour smelling clothes.

Wooden stairs to a hot print-filled office, paper piles and industry,
inventive hive, phones ringing, rife with giggling and shouting,
chip papers and inky duplicators, walkie-talkies and fag smoke,
spilling out by hand, ideas and agendas,
festival visions, rotas and touring plans,
littered amongst the strewn wigs, paste jewels, tiaras, dungarees,
frocks, sweat, spare wheels, vicious bitching and greasepaint stench.

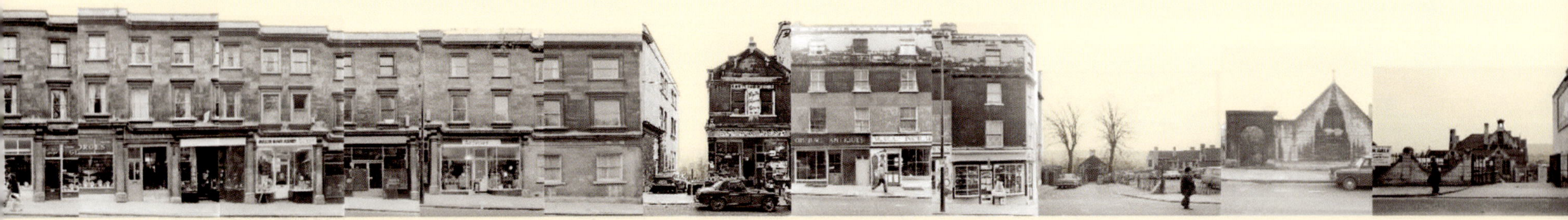

With this tribe I travelled Europe –
strutting the stage with glittered lipstick, gum and fags,
Rockettes, grotesques, and abandoned brides,
posh voices, Smart Party, Keens, and some yellow suitcases
joined together with drainage pipes and an irrepressible charm.
We were 'The Undisputed Masters of the Street'.
Nannies and Normals, white gloves, prams and a mouth in a box.
Faux opera singing, fund raising, piss taking, fun and larks.
From Brighton Pier to Amsterdam,
from Vienna to Dublin, Hamburg to Birmingham and beyond.
Travelling on old sofas in the back of the 'banshee wagon' –
an ancient pink and green bus, painted on a sunny day.
Sleeping on bare wood floors in never-before-visited European cities,
eating chips with mayonnaise (!?!) and exotic foreign foods.

Theatre in theatres, in streets, parks, metros or escalators,
stilts and stripes, rainbows and marching bands.
Clowns and fire-eaters, love affairs and heartbreaks and
all the inevitable pains of belonging.

And, then, back home in Bath,
collecting jumble and tattered furniture,
developing craft, designing and screen printing posters
and elaborate window dressings.
Typing letters – badly – with tippex as a mate.
Organising and cleaning, legwork and graft.
Meetings and minutes, fatigue and fallings out.

Christmas Day festivities with the elderly, lonesome and rejected –
with unsold festive foods from supermarkets,
collected in the 'banshee' on Christmas Eve.
Cooking and providing sanctuary amongst the cherubs,
the baubles and the over-cooked sprouts –
then putting on a show for their bemused delight.

And, later, when funds ran short – the amazing Beano Club –
wild cabaret in Walcot Village Hall. Grand pianos and beer.
Scratch theatre, kitsch, created in a day, then performed at night.
Charged with adrenalin, seedy, sweaty, greasepaint glamour
and a wilful, skilful talent, energy and flair.

The London to Brighton Bicycle Ride, with theatre along the route.
And adventure playgrounds, where health and safety
wasn't in our vocabulary. And adventure was real.
But the wild kids survived, swinging on ropes, banging in nails,
an aerial runway and a dirty hand-built pool –
for swimming.

These were times before girls fully understood
the real cost of their freely given sex –
when gender was shifting and love and lust were
frantically jumbled in the sack, with fears of STDs and
unplanned infants. But we did it anyway.

And we grafted, obeyed the boys and learned along the way –
my consciousness emerging, thanks mostly to my female pals.
We started objecting, protesting, raising dissent –
making sure we young women had a voice and our say.

This was a time that had the smell of a rugged kind of freedom.
A jumbled, earthy, blown about time of learning and change,
a time of squats, disobedience and occupation,
a time when you could afford to wander, discover, get lost,
make mistakes unseen and learn from your indiscretions.
A time before everything was recorded in a virtual world, forever.

Bath Arts Workshop – once a ladies' hairdressers –
a place where I learned the ropes of survival, made a lifelong treasured friend,
first heard the word proletariat and first began to understand
my context, my ambition, my commitment to the world.

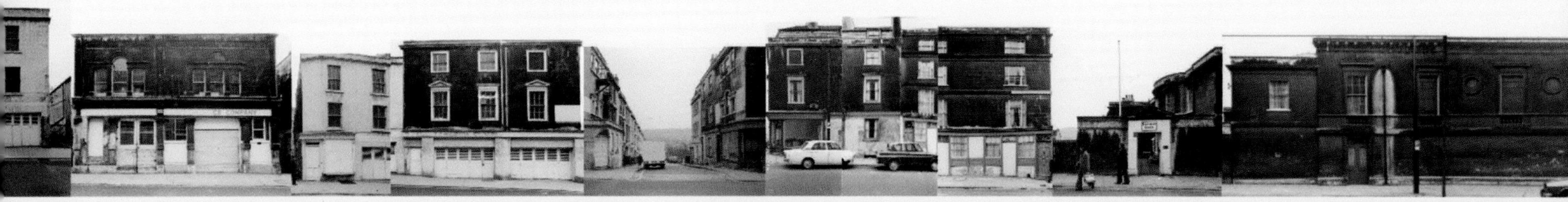

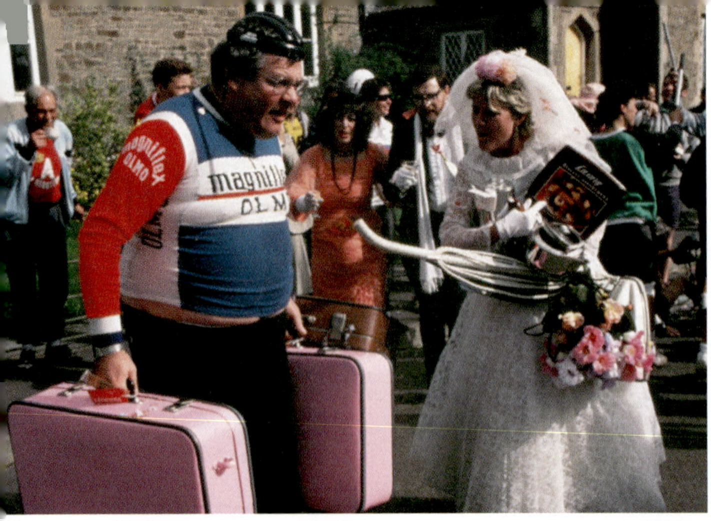
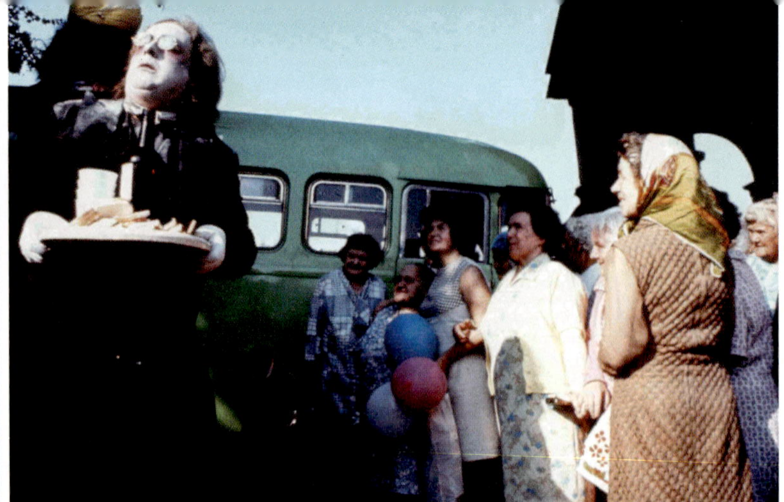
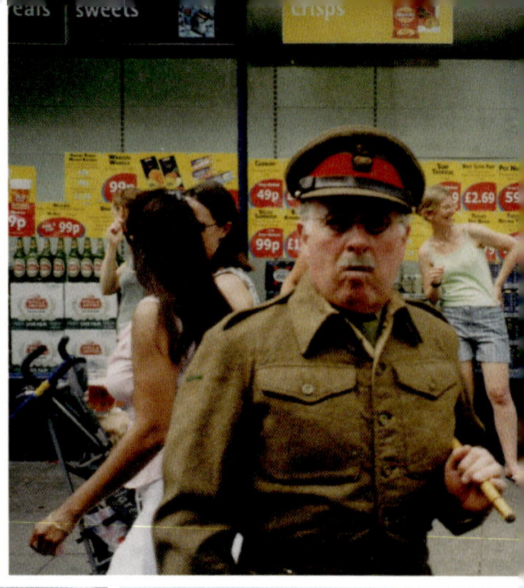
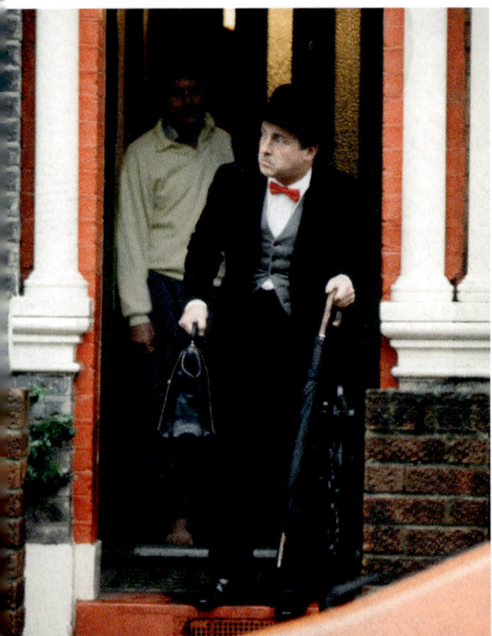
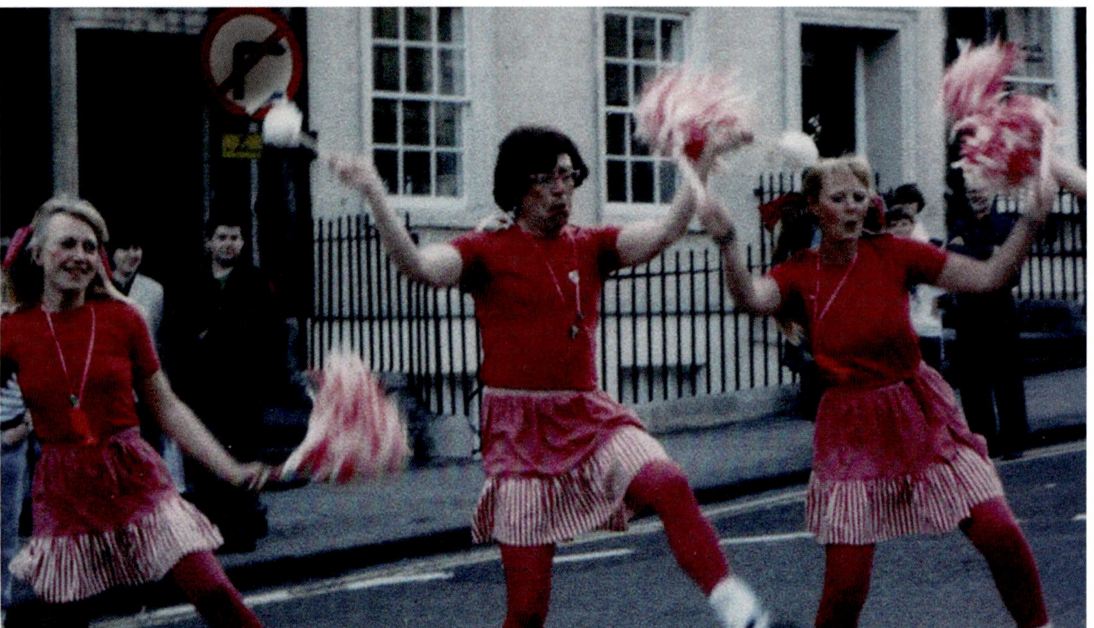

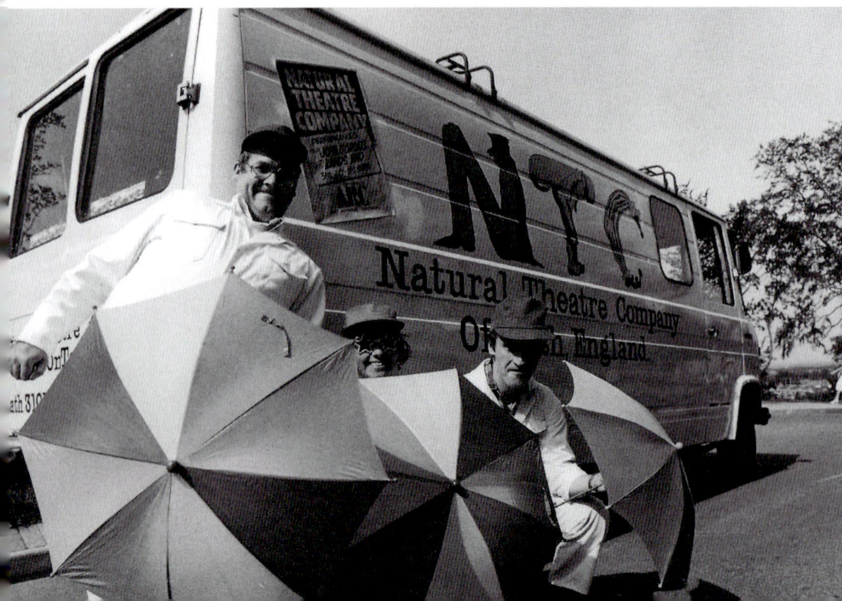
NATIONAL THEATRE COMPANY
NTC
Natural Theatre Company
Of England
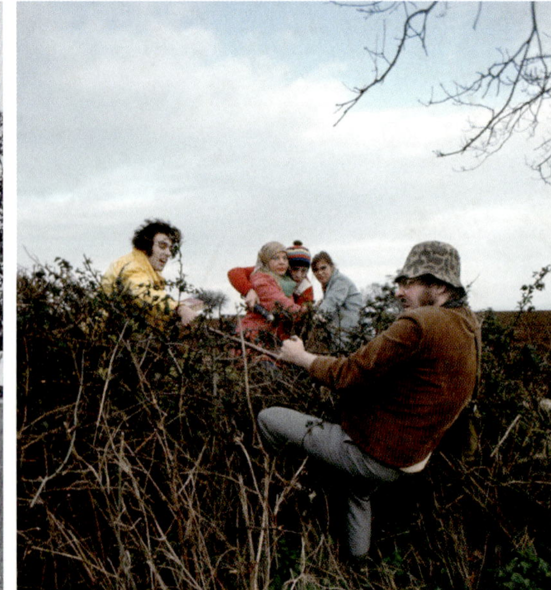
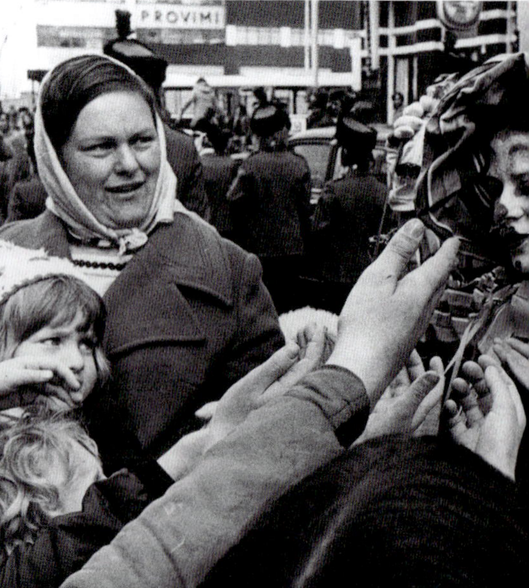

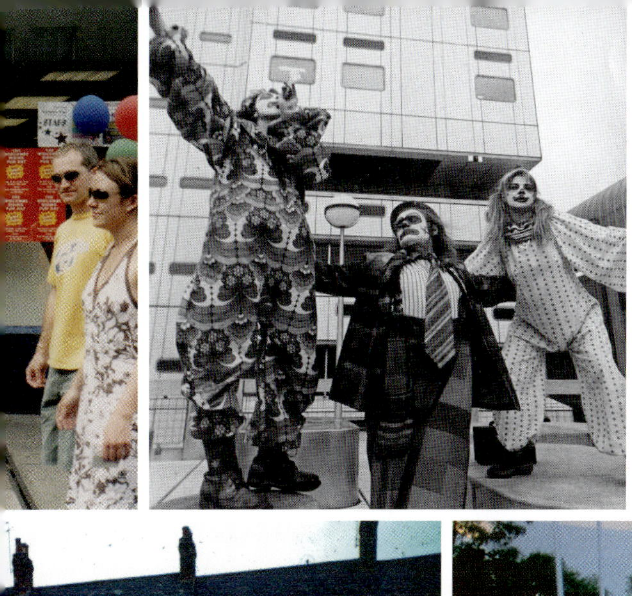
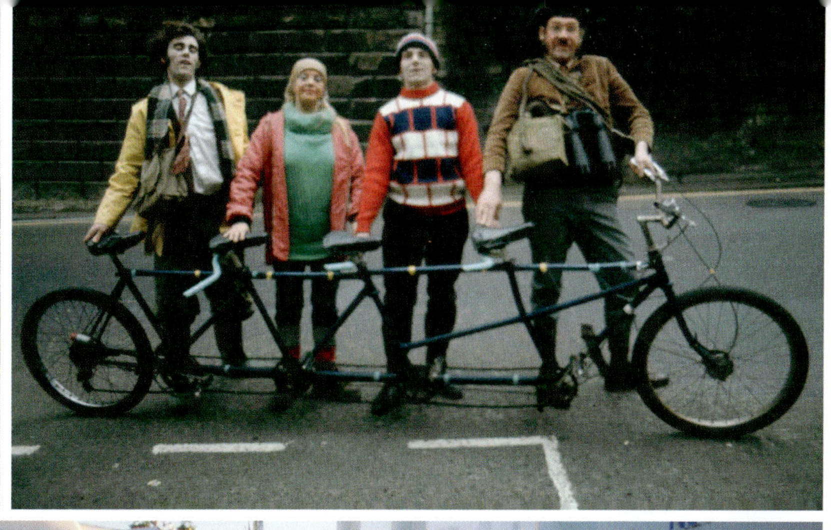
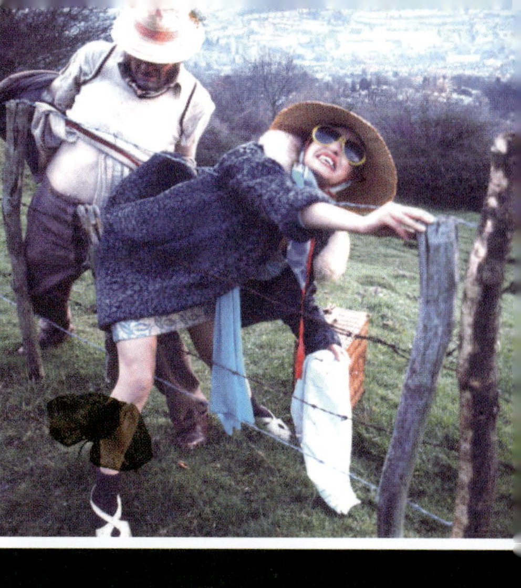
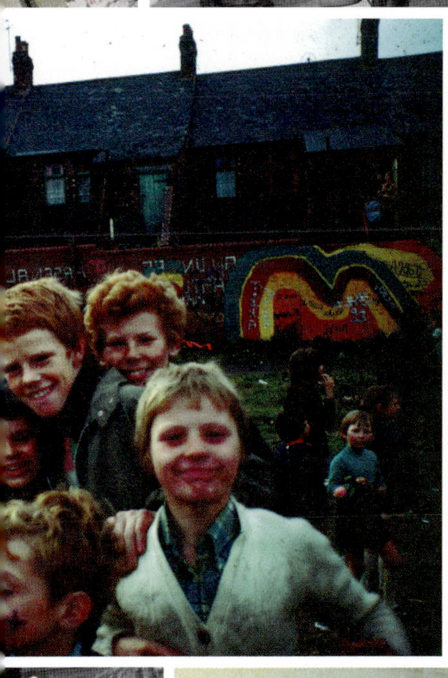
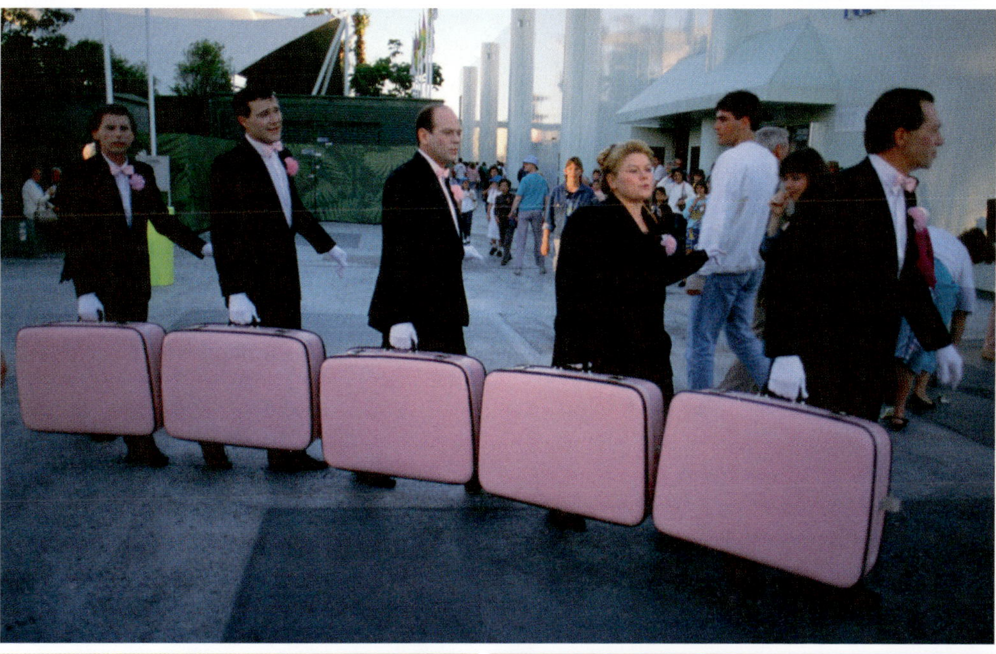
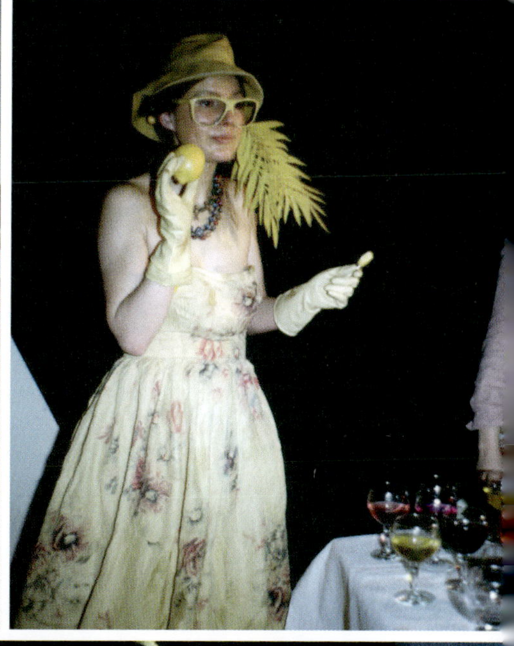
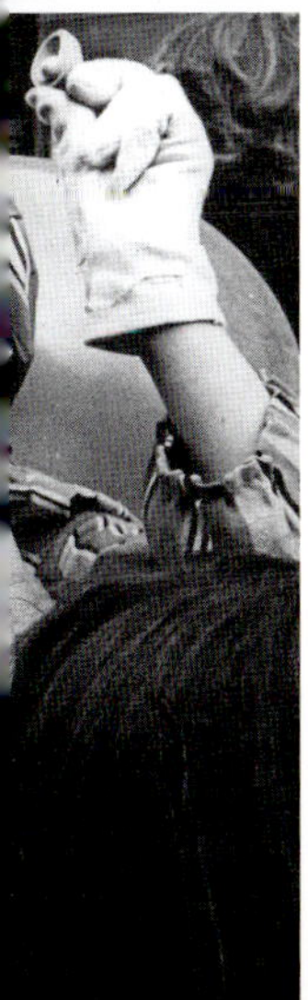
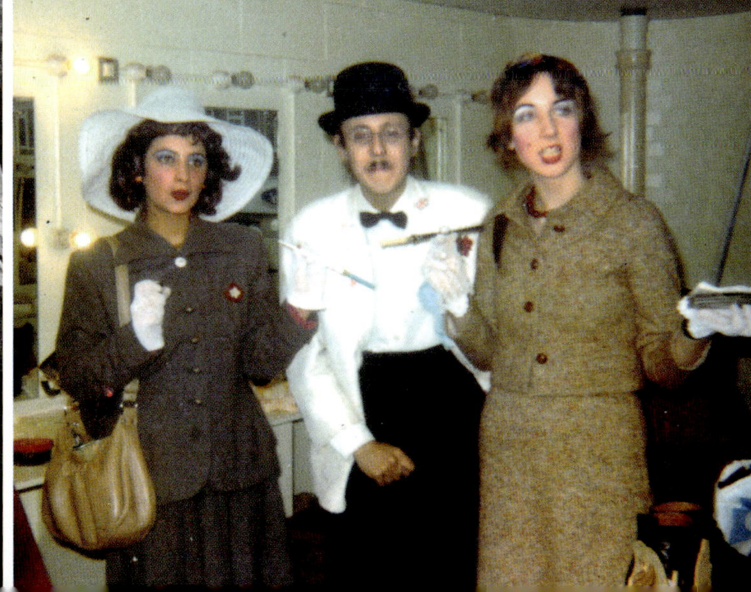
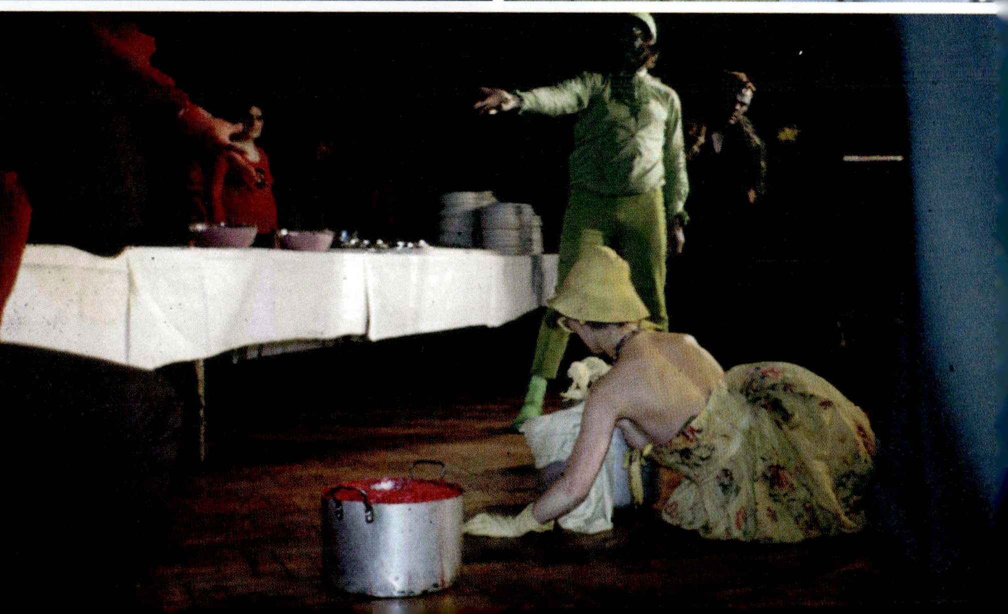

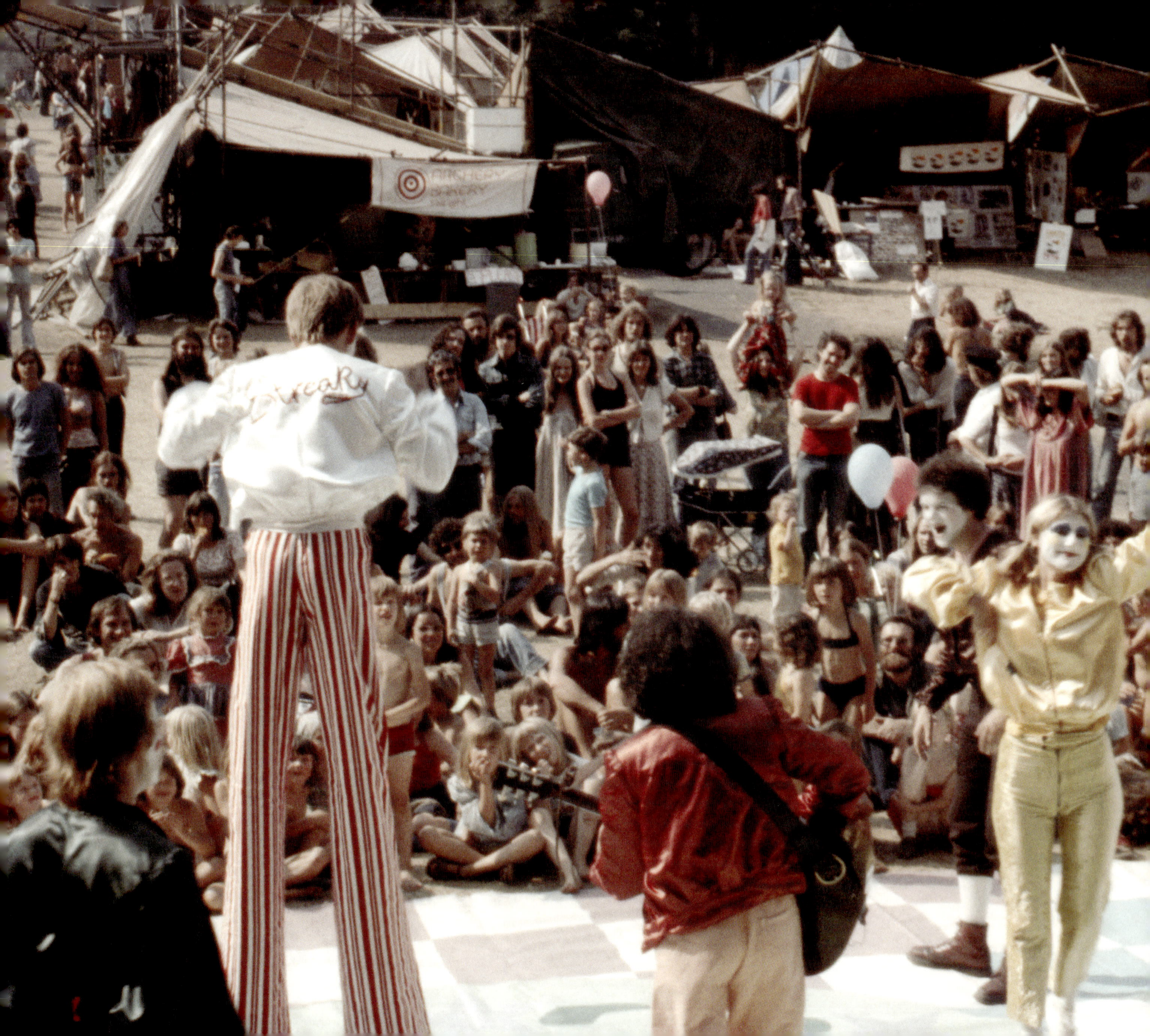

# CHAPTER 9

# WALCOT WAIVES THE RULES 1975-79

**The burial field was resurrected and the community found its strength. Street performers flocked to the festivals and 'paramilitaries' occupied the weir. A musical hippie went straight and there were midnight coups in Walcot Nation.**

**Tory:** By 1975, we had run three big summer festivals, two of which aimed to bridge the gap between the wealthy and the not-so-well-off in Bath, by taking the festival to outlying areas. It was a bold and worthwhile vision, but one that would have required more people and resources to fully bring to fruition. The Walcot festivals built on that experience and focused instead on building connections within our local area. They were more intimate, based mainly on the Walcot burial field, but the objectives were the same: to provide up to eight days of virtually free entertainment for residents and all comers, with strong community involvement throughout. Comtek's exhibitions also came into their own during these years, with community technology meshing seamlessly into the whole.

**Corinne:** In 1976, Bath City Council was motivated to convene a meeting on the future of Walcot Street in relation to the blight under which it had struggled for so many years – BAW's community involvement was (unusually) directly referenced appreciatively here. Many things seemed to be still growing then. Paradoxically perhaps, I see BAW's decision to focus on Walcot as an expansion of sorts, which was only possible because of a geographic contraction.

As ever, we were living the alternative rather than explicitly declaring it, which is probably why it felt so liberating and inclusive. But our human and financial resources were dwindling for community arts work, although the Printshop and truant school carried on into the next decade, and internally the focus was on our expanding theatre work. The broader political climate was also changing and in 1977 we decided to withdraw from running festivals. As it turned out, that decision marked a moment of transformation. A group of Walcotians (artists and performers all) decided to take over. They did some fantastically creative fundraising and organised the last two Walcot Festivals, and eventually Bath Fringe Festival, which is still running annually. The power of collective creativity lives on.

# Walcot Festival 1975

**Corinne:** The first festival, in 1975, was a week-long event in August. The main site was the burial field, with the Walcot Village Hall being used for the first time as a venue for exhibitions, performances, and workshops.[1] The grand opening procession was led by the Mendip Lady, a beautiful vintage steam engine locally owned by Eddie Haygreen. On arrival at the site, it was attached to a steam organ which played now and again throughout the week. Natural Theatre's clown drumming band, the Adventure Playground Fancy Dress Float, Madame Zoro Aster's Unicorn, Lumiere

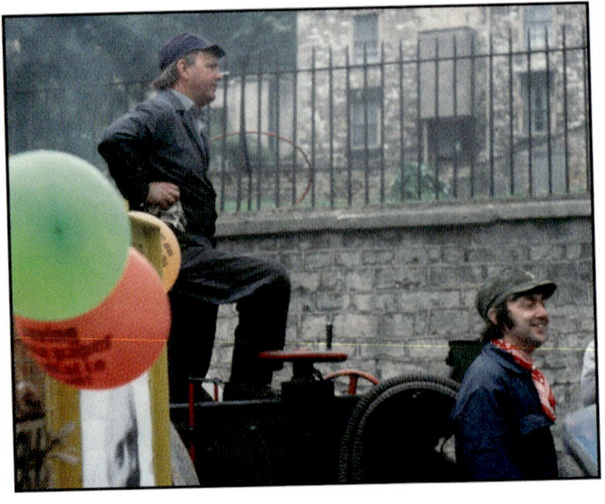

Eddie Haygreen and Mendip Lady

& Son, Professor Crump and The Hat & Feather float were among those who took part. The opening ceremony on the field was presided over by **Dusty** (Springfield) **Lane**, a drag artist and the son of Kitty Sutton who worked in our shop. Throughout the week, we ran our usual slightly anarchic but enjoyable programmes of kids' events, old folks' teas, poetry, film shows, discos, inflatables, puppet, street theatre, sports days and workshops.

Nigel managed to borrow a Rotork Sea Truck, a weird-looking cross between a truck and a flat-bottomed boat, more commonly used for diving and rescue operations. He

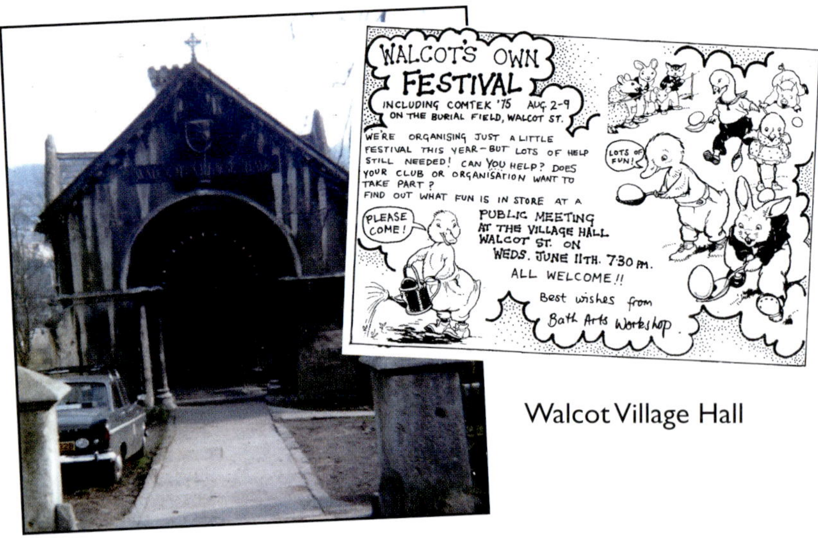



Walcot Village Hall

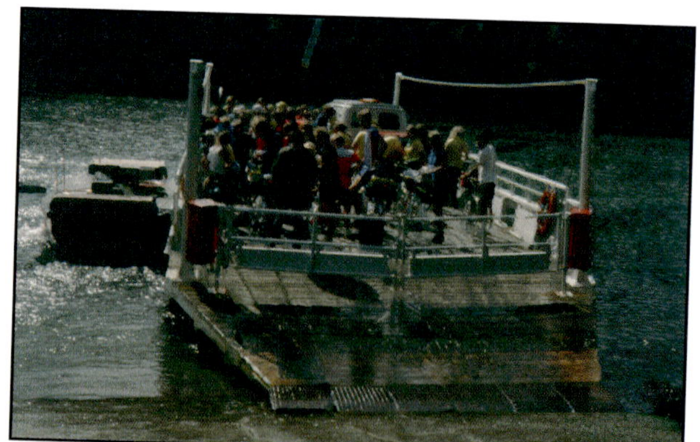

Sea Truck

---

1. See pp 138-9 for information on Comtek's refurbishment of the Village Hall. By 1975, it was managed and run by a committee of BAW members and residents.

served as the captain of a free service that ferried visitors from the city centre to the festival by way of the River Avon.

## Music

That year, for want of a nearby venue, we held rock concerts in St Alphege's Hall in Oldfield Park, with Jess Roden Band headlining at one gig. But smaller bands played throughout the week. Journalist Tony Durham was there for **Comtek 75** and wrote an article about the festival music:

**Tony Durham:** That week things seemed to come into an almost astrological conjunction. But more tangible contributions to the extraordinary atmosphere were made by the site itself – a steep riverside meadow – and the weather, which blazed during the day and went mad with wild thunderstorms on Monday and Friday nights; and of course the music… surely one of the most powerful of all forms of community technology.

There were Reg Meuross and Martyn Raphael, singing and playing guitar by a wood fire in the corner of the field on Wednesday night. Then there were Ace Drummers, with their picturesque collection of African instruments. They drummed as the Parachute Dome was erected, infusing ritual into engineering. They drummed in the dusk on the hillside and people joined in on penny whistles and an old oil drum. They drummed quietly, out of sight behind the tents, and a subliminal pulse-beat throbbed over the site. On Friday night, as basically-clad dancers tested the chapel floor at a disco in the Village Hall, lightning lashed marshmallow pink and baby blue over the sodden gravestones outside… I'm sure the heavens were celebrating not angry. It was so nice and warm, the best protection against the deluge was to stay in your trunks (**Undercurrents 12**, September-October 1975).

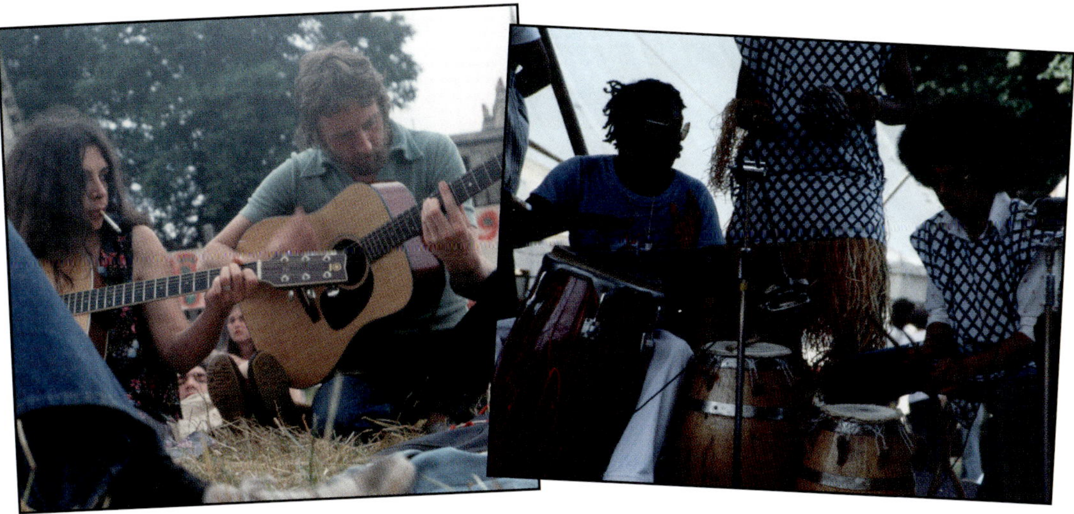

**Bands who played were**

Alberto y Lost Trios Paranoias

Clancy

Cruiser

Global Village Trucking Company

Jess Roden Band

Manifest

Skywhale

Under the Sun

Zeus

And (of course) The Rocky Show

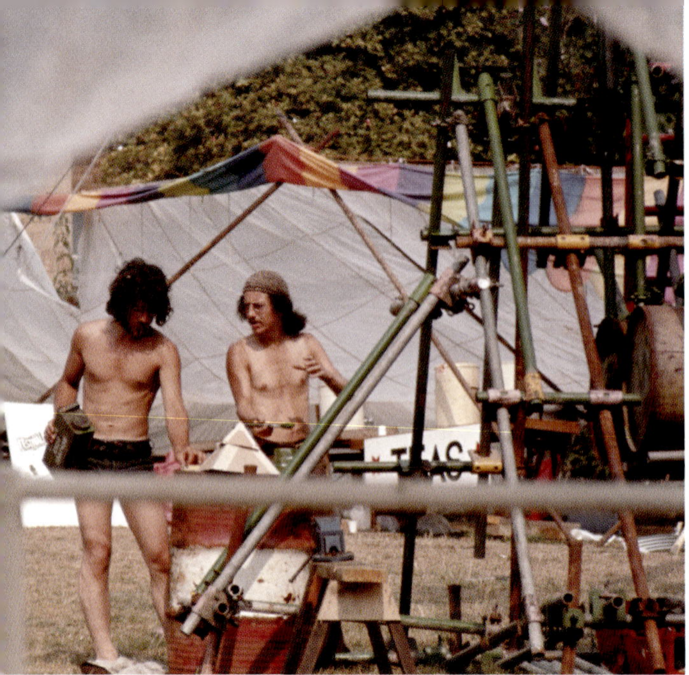

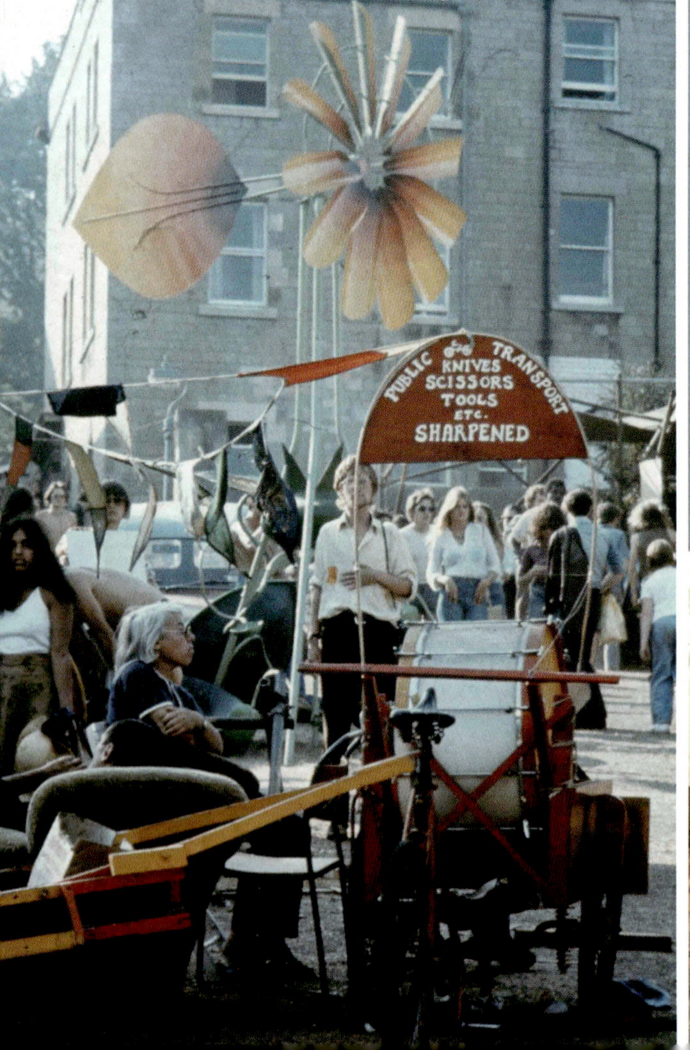

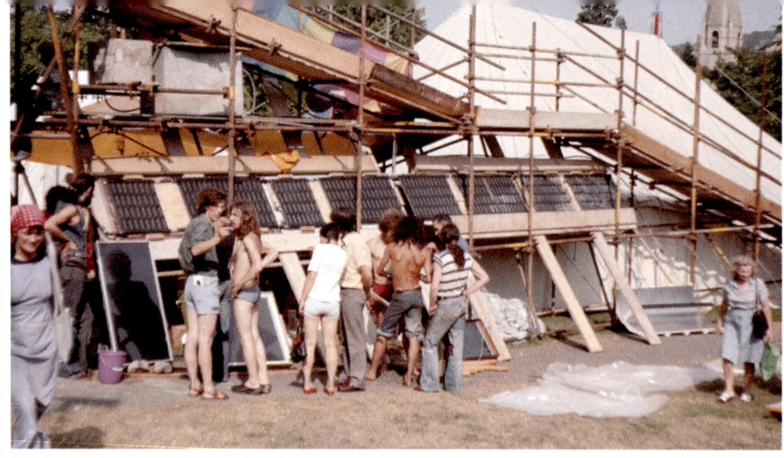

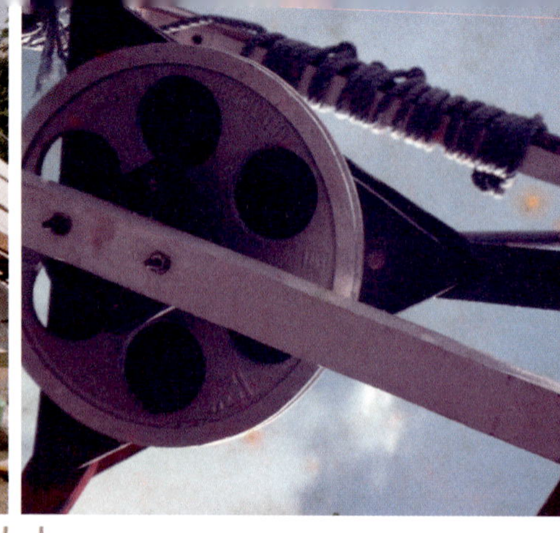

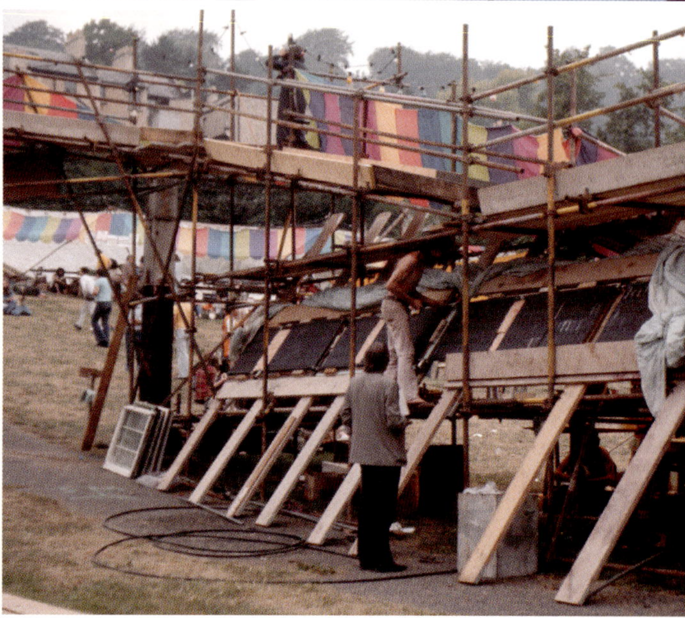

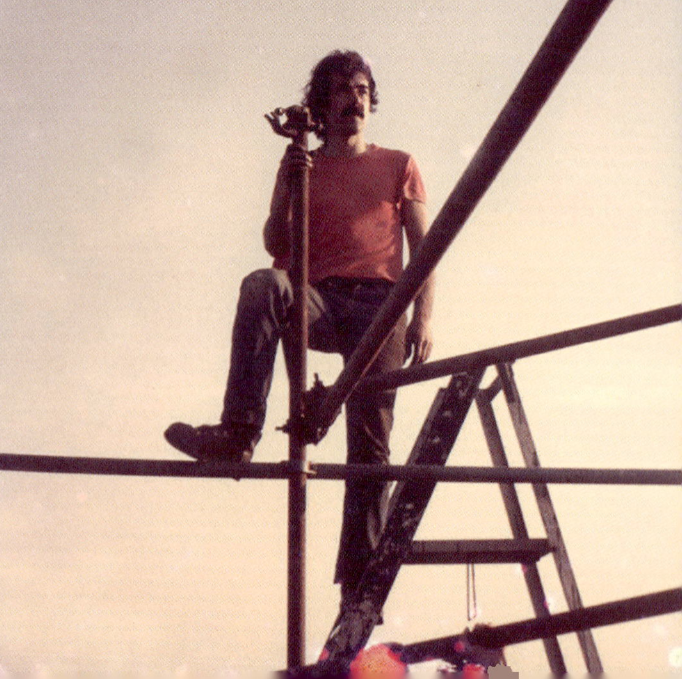

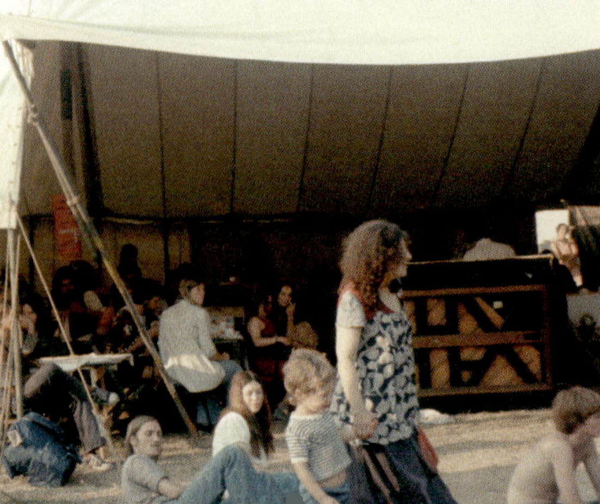

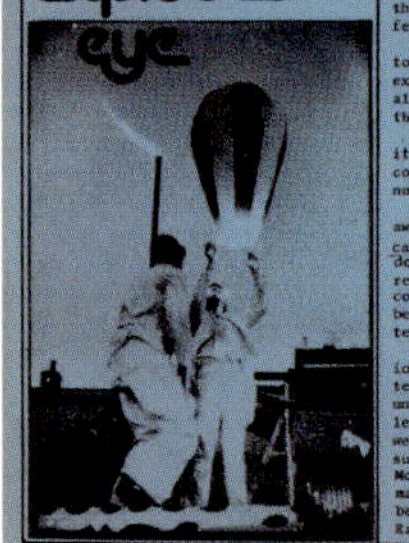



# WALCOT FESTIVAL
## the complete story
### 8 page feature

## start here

Festival of the absurd, always funny, yet with pathos, humility and organization. Always something new, something different, something exciting and always rain.

What's the purpose of a Festival if not to entertain and what better place than the vast, balmy amphitheatre of Bath in which to hold such delights.

This isn't a posh, polite festival, it's an earthy community event, packed with interesting and exciting things to do and see.

From August 2nd to 9th is the WALCOT FESTIVAL. An assortment of music, theatre, films, alternative technology; and down to earth things like kids sports, goats, boat trips, picnics, dances, clowning, bingo, seaside outing; all good fun for the family, granny and toddler alike or for the serious and totally flippant - free to get in (though if you bought a Plain Dealer at the gate it would help), and free to do what you like.

This is the fifth Festival organized by the Bath Arts Workshop, whose philosophy is total participation in the community and, hopefully, participation by the community in itself.

## exploded eye

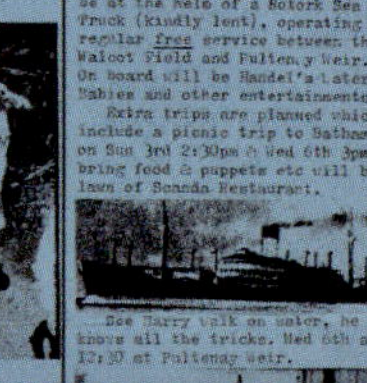

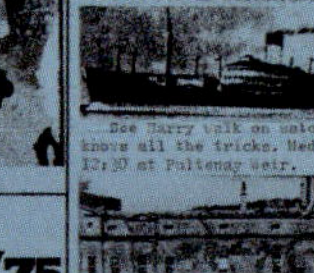

The Captain Fantastics of street and avant garde theatre, who produce strange and beautiful images, noted all across the landscape. Originally from Bath, but now based in London, they will be performing throughout most of the Festival. Don't miss these very enjoyable events - see Walcot Sleeper for details.

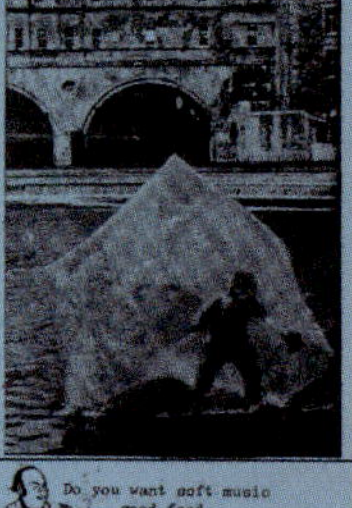

## COMTEK '75

Last year, the "Last Festival" of community arts came to an end with the introduction of a new concept, festivals of community technology.

This was Comtek '74, a coming together of the country's leading exponents of self sufficiency and alternative technology; and it was the first time this had happened.

For AT to be truly alternative, it must be made available to the community at large and this, in a nut shell, is the aim of Comtek.

If the community is made more aware of its own potential for carrying out energy-saving projects, doing its own building work and re-using waste materials through co-operative D.I.Y., then we will begin to achieve a community technology.

COMTEK '75 is the second national exhibition of alternative technology and should provide a unique opportunity for everyone to learn more about the ways in which we can achieve a greater self-sufficiency. Everything starts on Monday Aug 4th, but on Sat Aug 2nd many of those already on site will be going to the Anti-Metrication Rally & Fete at Calne, Wilts.

## sea truck trips

Captain Leash (nee Birdseye) will be at the helm of a Rotork Sea Truck (kindly lent), operating a regular _free_ service between the Walcot Field and Pulteney Weir. On board will be Handel's Later Babies and other entertainments.

Extra trips are planned which include a picnic trip to Bathampton on Sun 3rd 2:30pm & Wed 6th 3pm, bring food & puppets etc will be on lawn of Scanda Restaurant.

See Barry walk on water, he knows all the tricks. Wed 6th at 12:30 at Pulteney Weir.

Do you want soft music
good food
nice atmosphere
pleasant company
good service

## don't try us

try your own

HAT and FEATHER

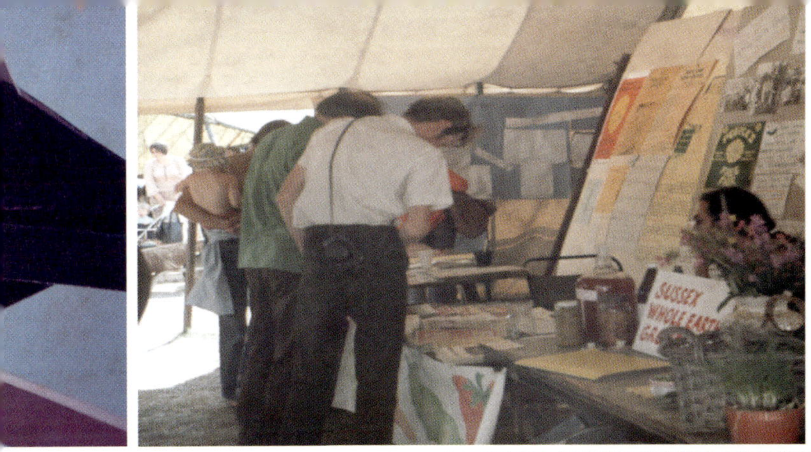

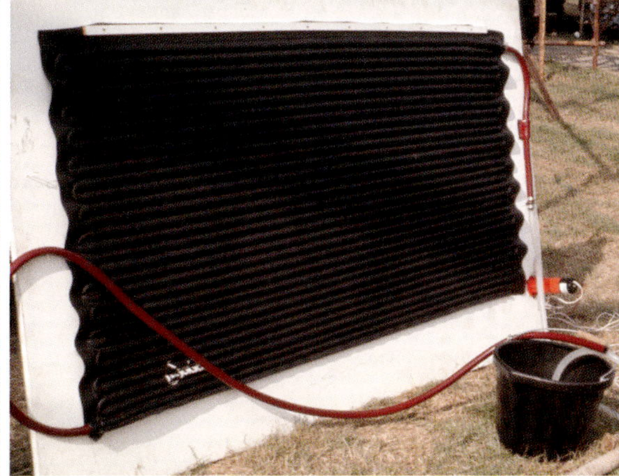

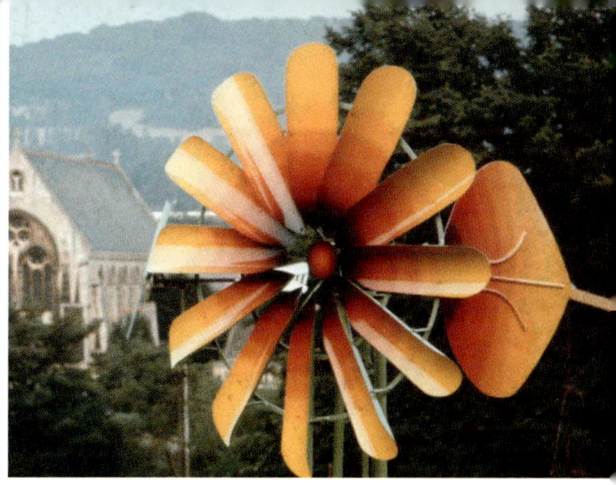

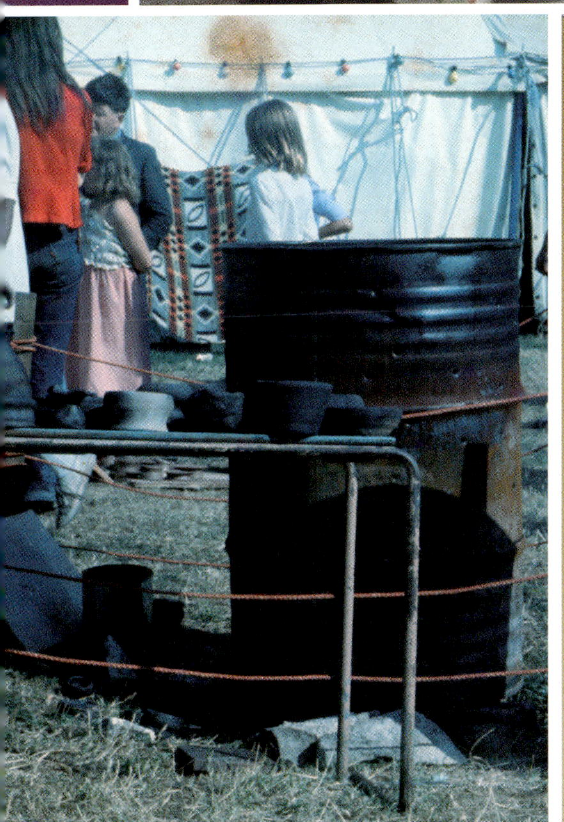

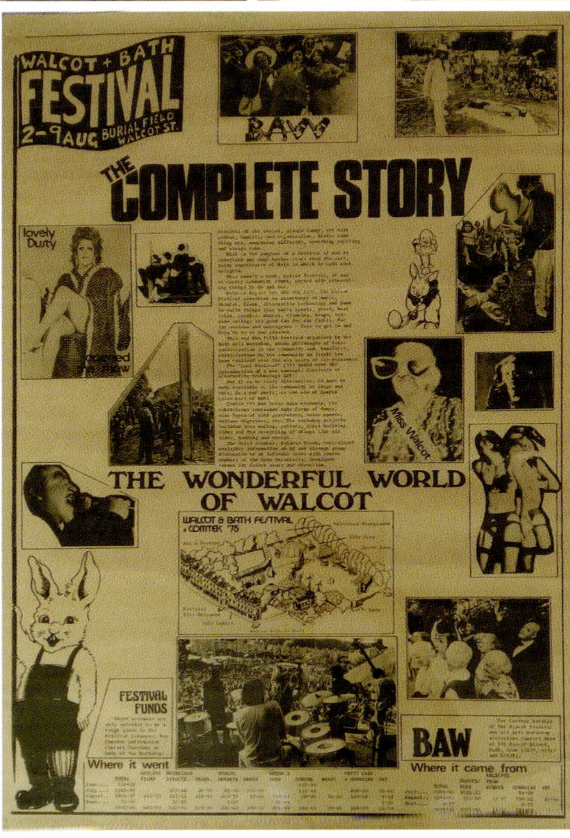

WALCOT + BATH FESTIVAL
2-9 AUG BURIAL FIELD WALCOT ST.
BAW
THE COMPLETE STORY
lovely Dusty
Miss Walcot
THE WONDERFUL WORLD OF WALCOT
WALCOT & BATH FESTIVAL & COMTEK '75
FESTIVAL FUNDS
Where it went
BAW
Where it came from


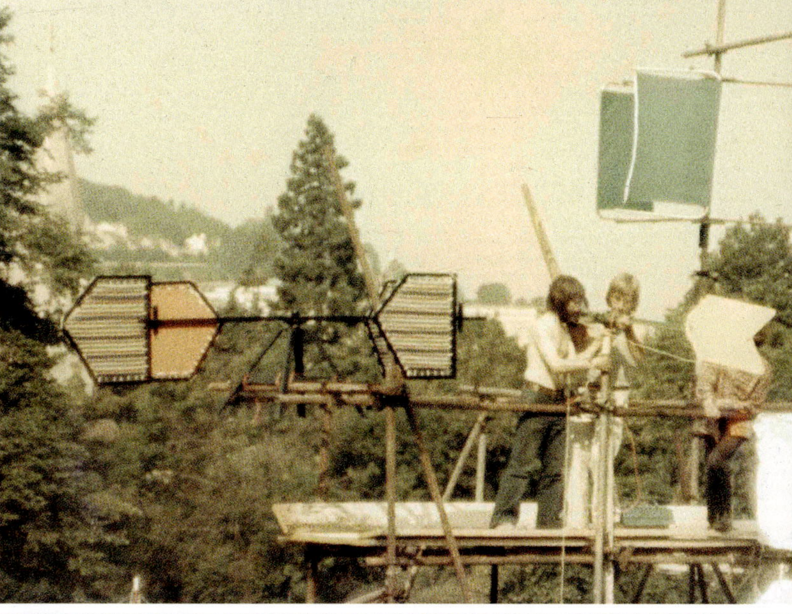

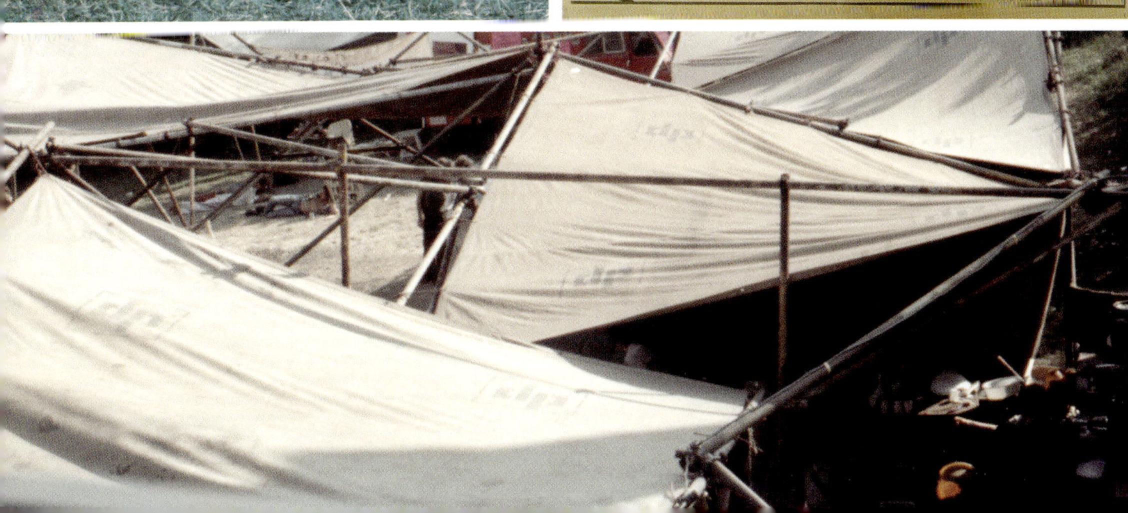

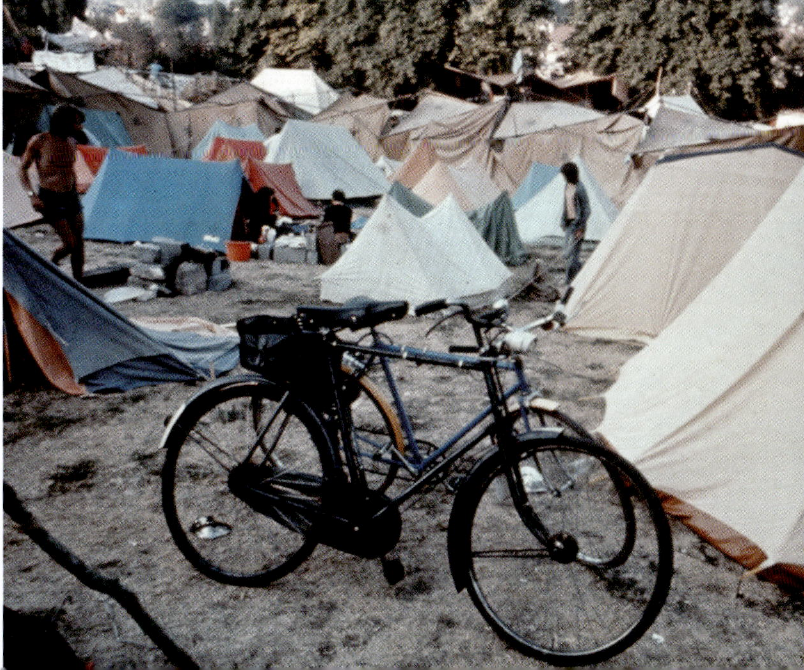

## Inflatables

**Robert Stredder** and his companions brought giant inflatables they made at **Groundwell Farm,** a cooperative near Swindon. He writes: The **Walcot Festival** was always a family-orientated event open to all ages and all creeds and denominations. We became friends for life with the BAW people. The theatre and the art were always mixed in with the second-hand shops, Women's Institute teas, and an atmosphere of anything goes, provided it was amusing and of quality for the Walcot community. Recycling all furniture became part of the shows and the environment.

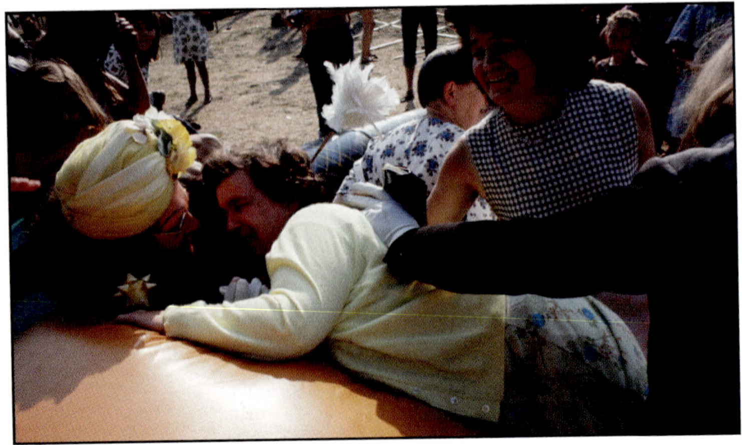

Lady Margaret and friends bouncing gently

too. We often had grannies bouncing gently on the 90-foot caterpillar inflatables, which I made with Richard Vulliamy who designed the adventure playground at Longleat. The Walcot Festival will always go down in my mind as the best street and local community festival of all; and long will the sound of laughter echo over the fields of Walcot.

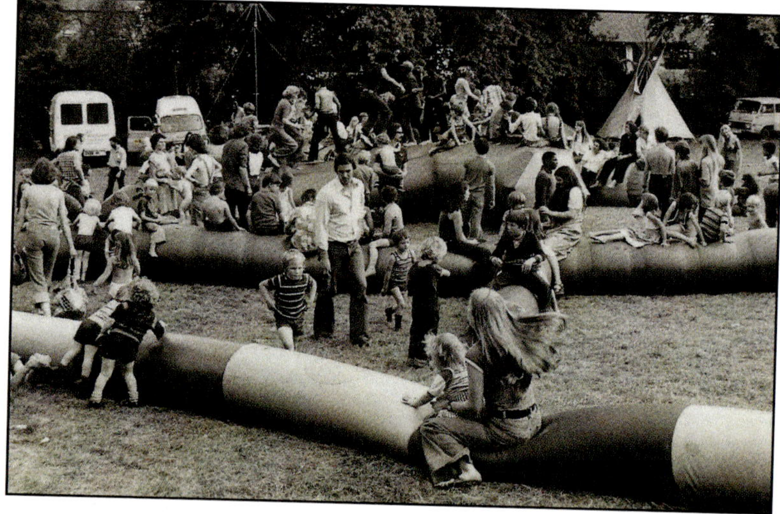

Robert Stredder of Groundwell Farm

We always stopped at The Hat & Feather when we arrived in Bath and had a quick one, which often turned into a slow one if we were late. Anyway, we were rarely late because hundreds of children were waiting for us. They must all be grown up by now with families of their own. Old people liked them,

## Comtek 75 and 76

**Thornton:** From early February 1975, Brian Ford, Nick Moore and I, along with various others, began preparing the exhibition.[2] We set about raising funds, organising pre-publicity and exhibitors, with Brian organising the events programme and the exhibits. During the two weeks before it started, I organised and built most of the walkway, designed and built the big scaffolding stage with its innovative paraboloid sheeting cover, plus setting up the electrics,

---

2. Nick had studied architecture at Kingston Poly before coming to Bath and joining in with Comtek. He later trained to be a stone mason.

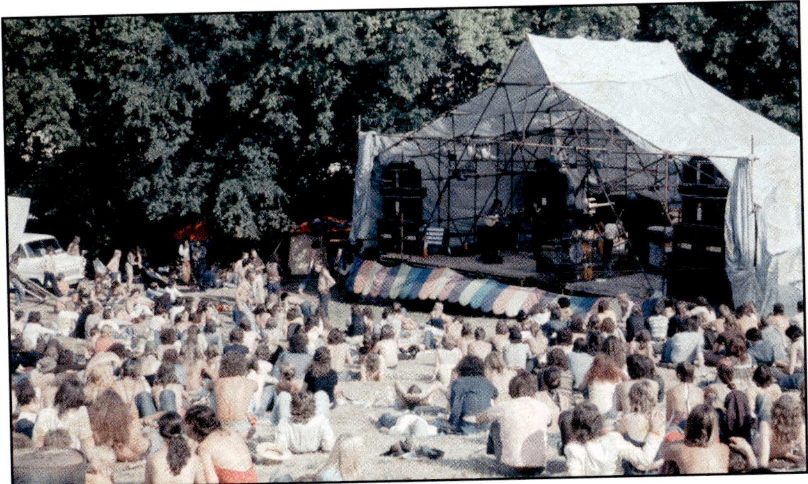

water supply and so on. Rick Knapp and Dave Rappaport were also key to the whole thing and others, too.

**Brian Ford:** Sloping gently towards the river, the burial field formed a natural amphitheatre, with stalls, tents and other structures on the higher ground, and the main stage and other event spaces closer to the river. Our huge elevated walkway snaked down through the site, serving as a platform for a wide range of DIY wind generators, and

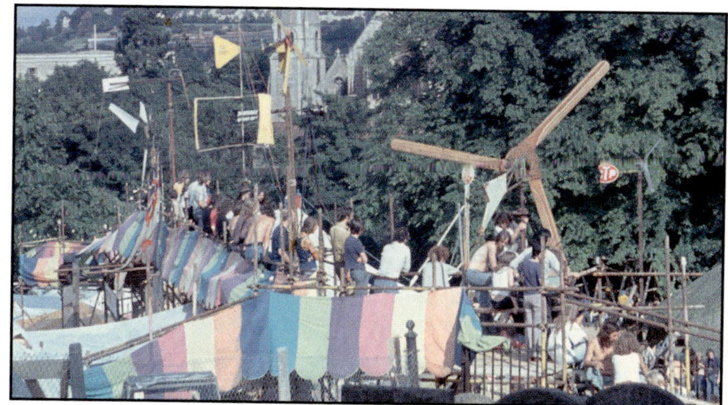

Gantry walkway

a viewing point for festival visitors. The lower sections of the walkway were used to provide support for a large solar water heating system (made from old radiators, car radiator hose and jubilee clips), which was plumbed in and delivered hot water to the main festival kitchen.

**Glyn Davies** (Co-founder of Comtek): The aims of the Comtek exhibitions were threefold: to increase knowledge of community technology; to provide a forum for the exchange of ideas among those already involved; and to serve as a vehicle for communicating these ideas to the local community. The exhibition was framed around a forum, workshops and exhibits.

**Brian Ford:** Domes also featured on the site, where talks and workshops were held. Wonder Construction Co of Cornwall put up an enormous parachute tent for the first time. The framework was made from theatre backdrop slats soaked in oil and bolted together with couplings from Quethiock Smithy. On top was a huge camouflage parachute, whose younger days had been spent dropping tanks.

A parachute dome

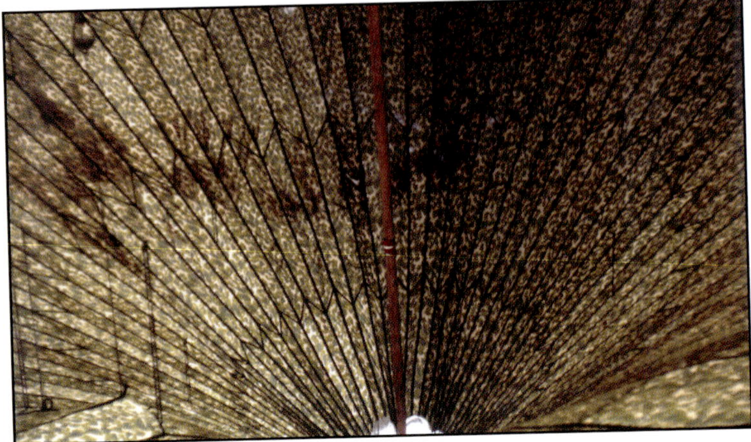

Camouflage dome

The exhibition ran from 2 to 10 August, in a blaze of sunshine (albeit with thunderstorms towards the end of the week). It proved to be a celebration and demonstration of what Graham Caine of Street Farm called 'do-it-yourself sufficiency'. On display were small-scale backyard techniques to harness renewable energy, promote low-impact construction and develop organic gardening, among others. The exhibition thus explored a wide range of social and environmental alternatives to the norms of the day. There were talks, workshops, shows and exhibitions, many of them recorded on film for a *Futures Forum* held at the end of the week. Stalls included food by Bath's own Harvest Wholefoods, recycling by Comtek, and *Undercurrents* alternative science magazine.[3] The budget for the whole thing was about £550.

---

3. Comtek 75 was covered in *Undercurrents 12*, September-October 1975, pp 25-32; and Comtek 76 in *Undercurrents 18*, October-November 1976 pp 6-7. Online versions are available at https://issuu.com/undercurrents

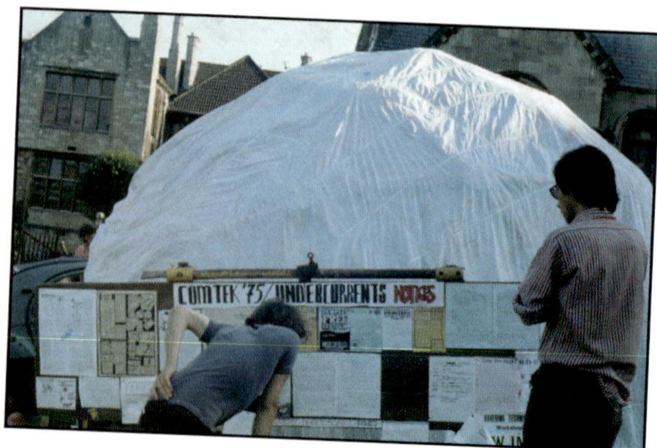



*Undercurrents* magazine stall

**Brian Ford:** We received positive feedback from many participants and visitors, including the Intermediate Technology Development Group, who wanted to organise a similar festival and exhibition of technological alternatives in London, to coincide with the UN Habitat Conference due to take place in Vancouver in the summer of 1976. Nick and I got involved with this project which became the ***People's Habitat Festival,*** which took place in the derelict Surrey Docks in East London. Two of the legacies of this London festival were the construction of a wind pump (designed by

**Workshops at Comtek 75**

Kite making
Bike recycling
Pottery and crafts
Leatherwork
Solar Panels
Video TV
Earth block making
  & building

engineer Bryn Bird) to provide water to allotments in the former dock area, and the start of the Surrey Docks Urban Farm, created by Hilary Peters.

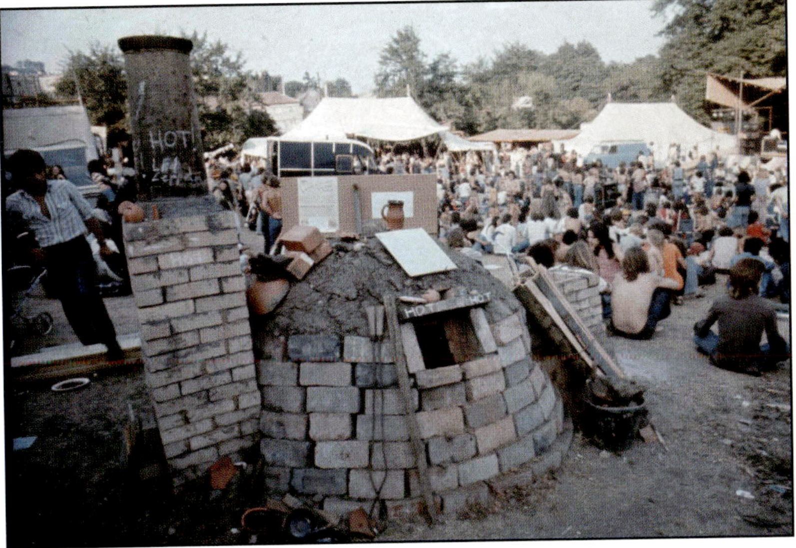

Kiln

**Brian Ford:** The following year, Nick and I ran **Comtek 76** as part of the **Sunshine Festival** during one of the hottest summers on record. Among the gadgetry on display, were a bike-powered grindstone by Public Transport from Hull; a potter's wheel; a do-it-yourself kiln built from old bricks; and a 'dandelion' windmill that later went to a children's playground in Exeter. It followed broadly the same format as the year before, including stalls representing different groups or individuals, a large exhibition tent and more talks and workshops organised within a **Futures Forum** on themes of renewable energy, eco-construction, fish culture, organic food production etc. A packed Village Hall

discussion organised by Land for the People was stunned when someone actually offered to donate a few acres of land in Dorset, in a 'barter' arrangement!

**Terry Pratchett**, at the time a local journalist, wrote: Comtek means community technology, which means more control over the things that shape your life. It gets mixed up with Alternative (AT to its adherents) which on a homely level is concerned with power without pollution. They both mean windmills instead of power stations, small scale instead of huge, consumer-controlled rather than government dictated. Comtek is also a department of that example of anarchy harnessed to practical purposes, the Bath Arts Workshop. *Bath & Wilts Evening Chronicle, 9 August 1975*

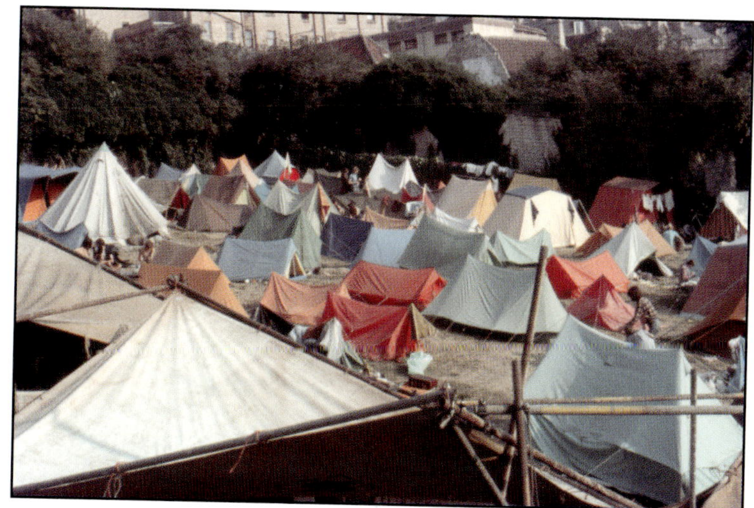

Campsite
Page 202: Site plan

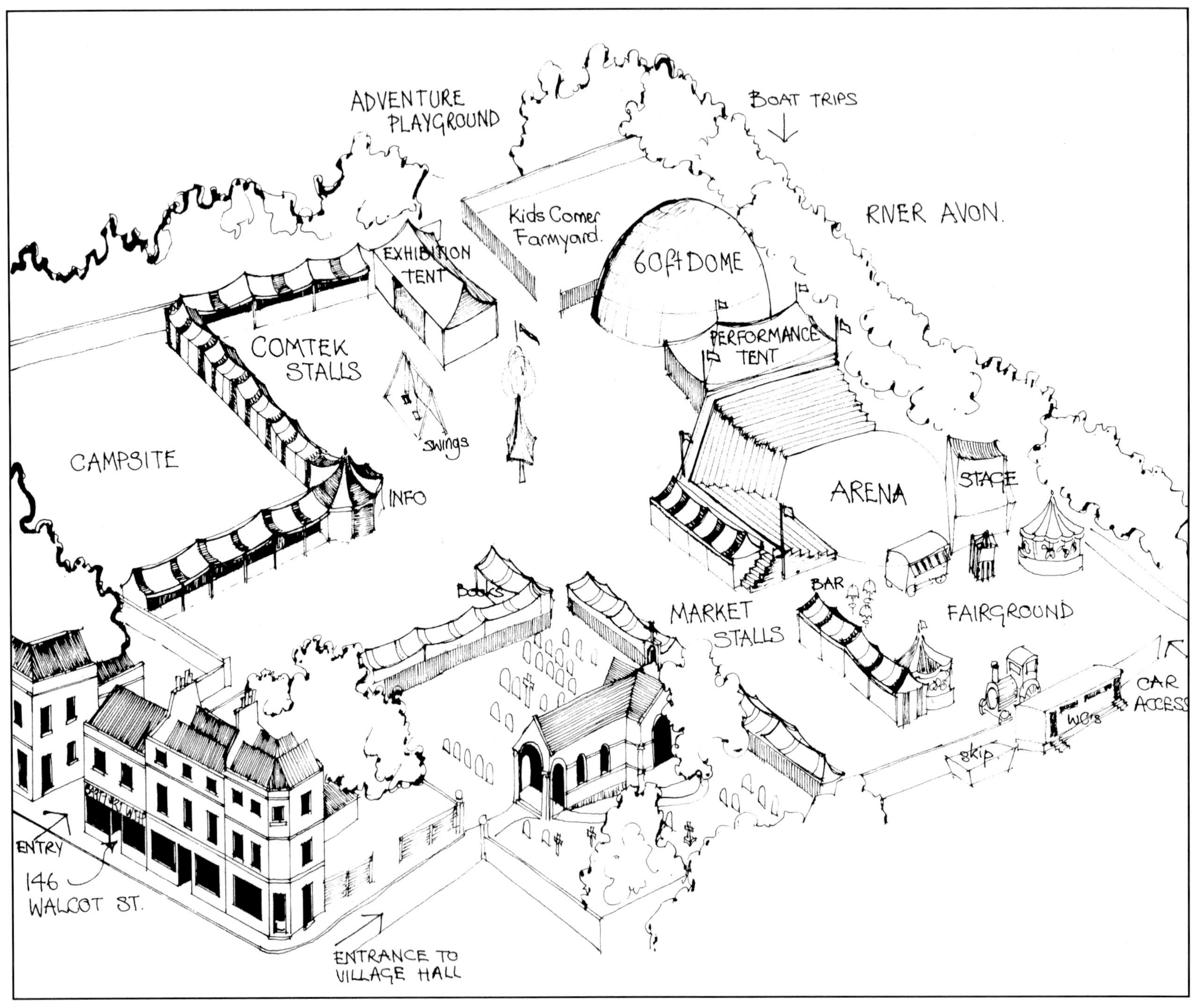
ADVENTURE PLAYGROUND
BOAT TRIPS
Kids Corner Farmyard.
RIVER AVON.
EXHIBITION TENT
60ft DOME
COMTEK STALLS
PERFORMANCE TENT
CAMPSITE
Swings
INFO
ARENA
STAGE
BOOKS
MARKET STALLS
BAR
FAIRGROUND
CAR ACCESS
WC's
skip
ENTRY
146 WALCOT ST.
ENTRANCE TO VILLAGE HALL

# Sunshine Festival 1976

**Corinne:** I was heavily involved in organising and coordinating the *Sunshine Festival*, working closely with Ralph. It was a glorious affair. Despite tempting fate with the title,

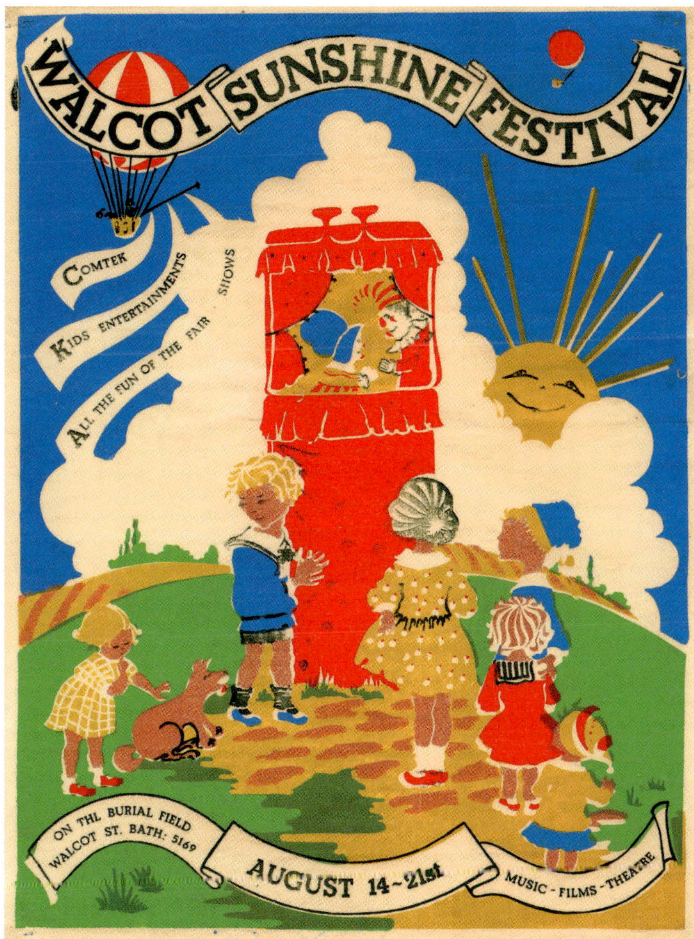



it took place during the hottest driest summer on record. It was almost a relief when the sun set after another day of scorching heat. The yellow marigolds we planted in wooden boxes shrivelled up and turned brown as did the grass on the burial field. The only truly yellow flowers were the giant sunflowers Charlie and Molly had painted into the huge mural on the outside wall of our shop.

Dried up marigolds

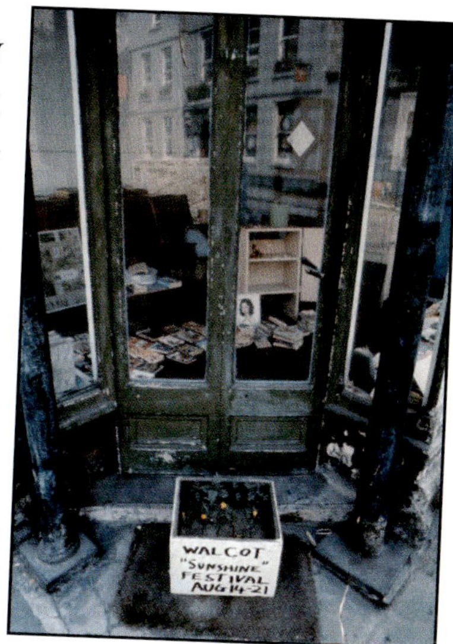



**Charlie Carfrae:** One day in summer 76, my flatmate Molly and I were working at The Hat & Feather when someone asked if I'd like to do a mural for the festival. A few days later, Molly and I found ourselves on a scaffolding tower outside the window of the Workshop shop. I chalked out the sunflowers and we coloured them in

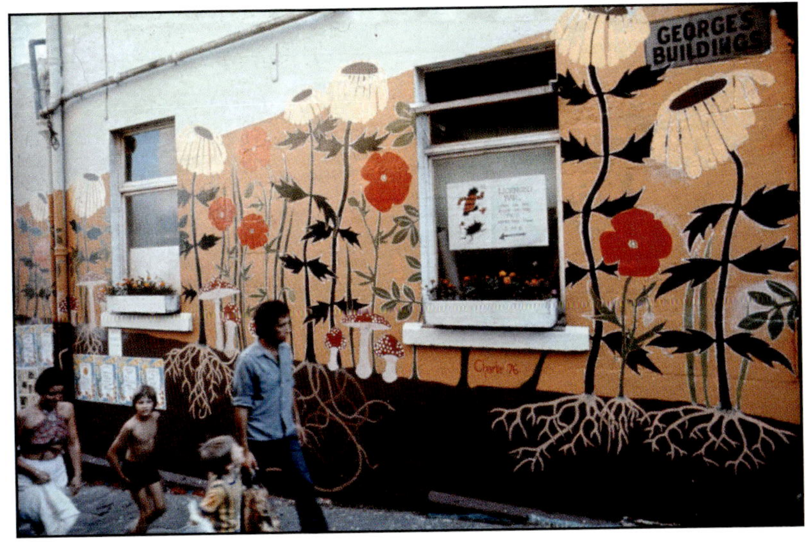



Charlie's mural

with a little help from a young Pete Smith (of Snow Hill Road Show). While painting, we taught each other to harmonise songs, which seemed to excite Brian Popay who recorded us on video. Molly and I were broke so we also did a bit of busking – one fan said we were the new Andrews Sisters.

Next thing we knew, we were to perform at the festival as The Sunshine Sisters… scary! We roped in my brother Jim on guitar (he refused to dress in drag) and Heather Brown on another fiddle. We played two sets during the festival, a gig at The Hat and one at the festival club, Luxury Liner, where Heather's and my hero, Stuart Gordon, was in the audience.

## Street theatre lived on

**John Wood:** There was some brilliant street theatre in the town centre. I still can't walk past Pulteney Weir without remembering the *Northern School of Film Realists* from ***John Bull Puncture Repair Kit***. They were 'filming' their mad version of Jaws, complete with plywood shark and Diz

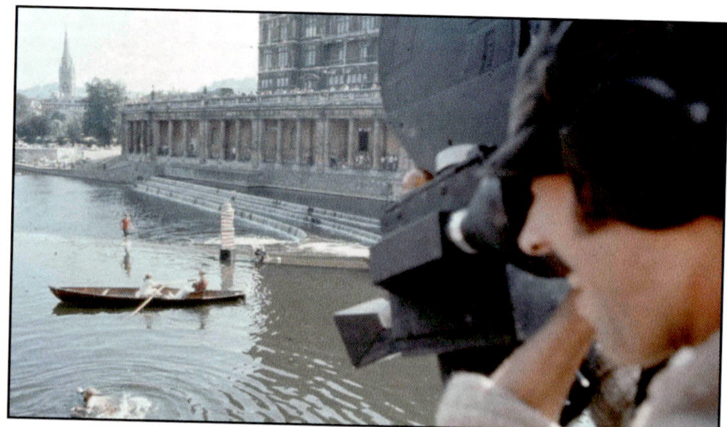

Northern School of Film Realists

Willis jumping into the river with an exploding firework. The 'star', Peter Slim, 'bicycled' into shot, pulled along by the stuntman and followed by his trusty Alsatian. Later, he commandeered a rowing boat and set off across the weir while the stuntman strapped on some shark fins and jumped into the river for a sequence involving an attempted assassination.

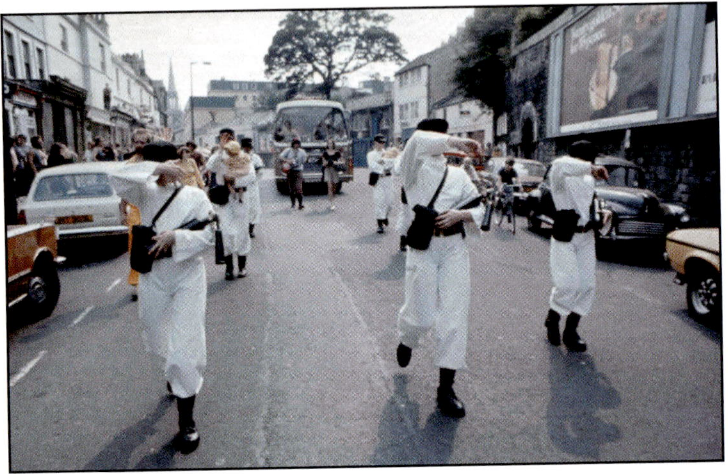

Lumiere & Son lead the procession

**Mick Banks:** Later that week, the weir was the setting for a piece by ***Lumiere & Son.*** David Gale and Hilary Westlake's band of art school misfits had earlier paraded their *Special Forces* through the city centre in white boiler suits and heavy boots, leading the festival procession with fascist precision. There were seven of them in line, carrying a baby, a fire extinguisher, a baby, a fire extinguisher. That evening, they marched onto the concrete apron of the weir's edge and stood there, equidistantly spaced, at attention, for 30 earth-shattering minutes.

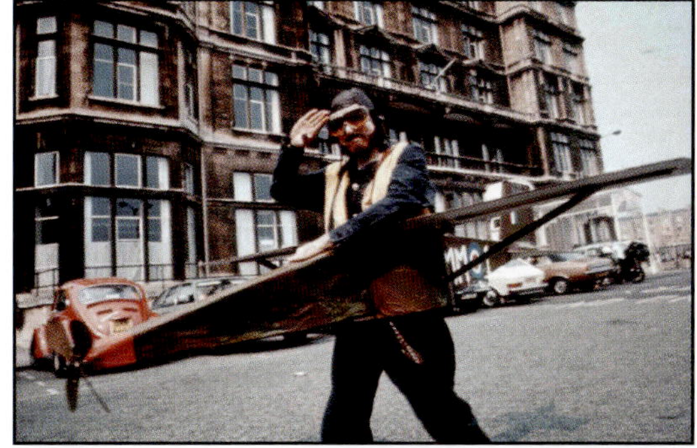

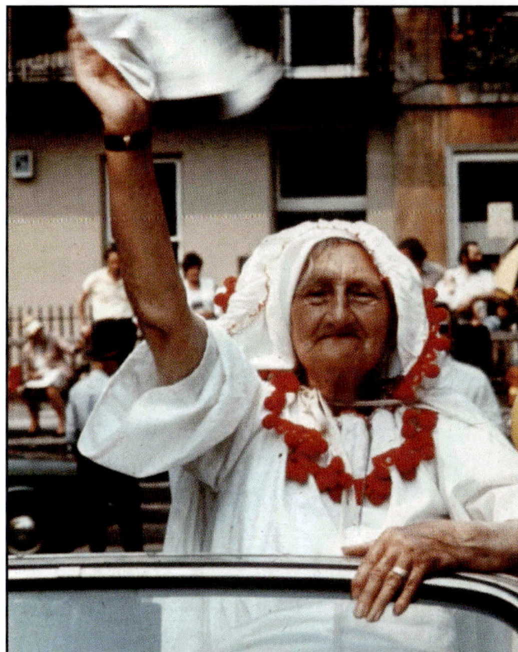

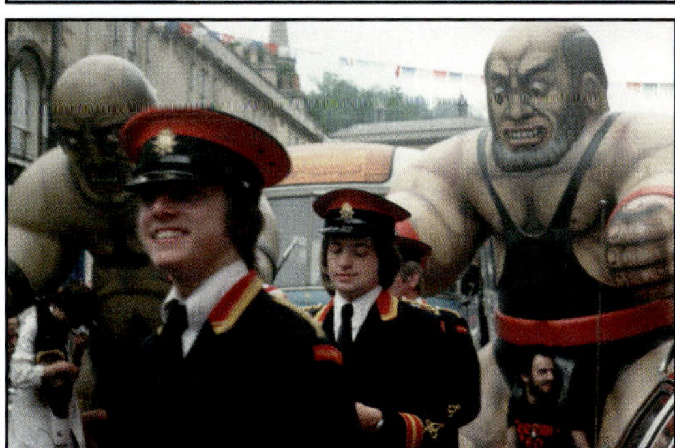

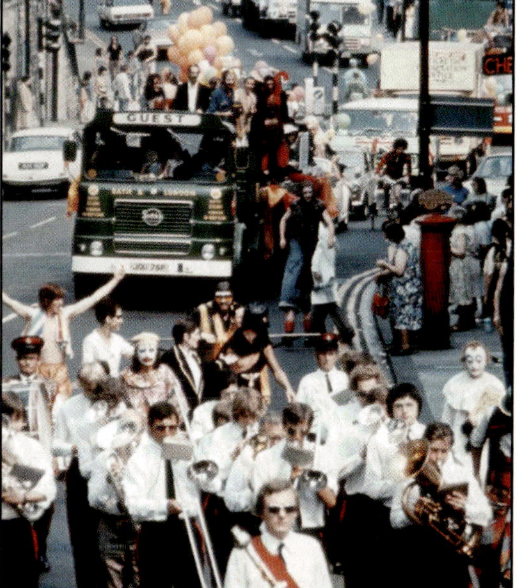

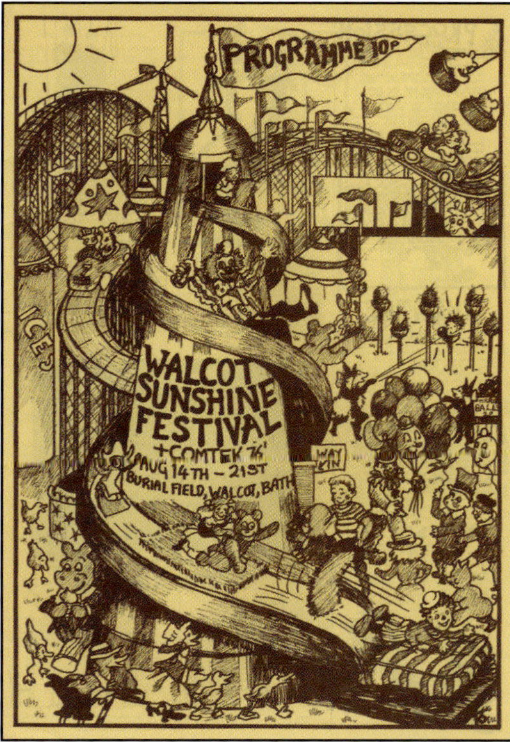



**David Gale:** We made our way onto the weir as the evening light faded and stood upon it for some time in our uniforms of menace. We had stout boots and found that the water was only three inches deep as it ran over the edge; and the stonework beneath was not too treacherous. The cops came and said 'get down' but they couldn't get onto the weir in case they fell in, so they had to hang about until we had thoroughly satisfied our milling public. Then they told us off. We said it was 'art'.

**Corinne:** Meanwhile back at HQ Gerry Pilgrim of *Hesitate & Demonstrate* had turned up unexpectedly to be part of the action. The perfectly poised English lady, she headed off to the Abbey Churchyard and set up a card table on which she laid her curiosities for inspection. In later years, she was accompanied by Janet Goddard. They also performed their signature piece on the burial field: Two meticulously-attired ladies in black stalked each other silently, finally coming face to face in an elegant version of a clown custard pie showdown, although their cream cakes were more reminiscent of a genteel tea party.

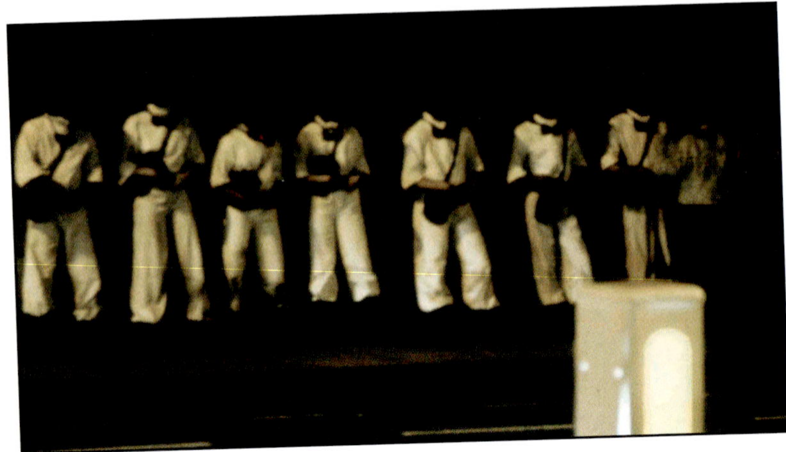

Lumiere & Son Special Forces about
to raid The Hat & Feather

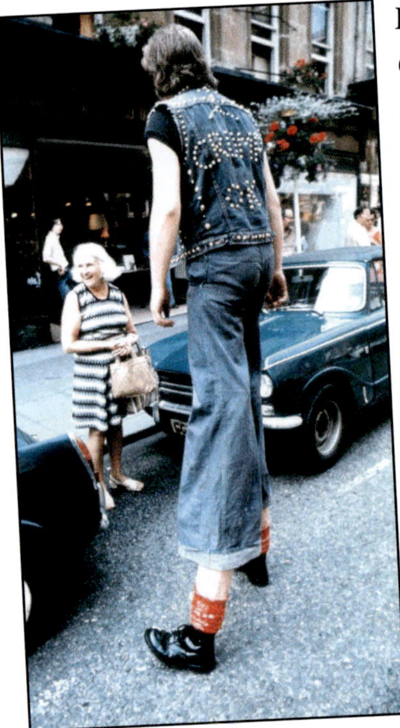

Bovver boy
(Paul Goddard)

**Paul Goddard** (*Professor Crump*) first came to Bath in 1973. He became a good friend and a regular at all our festivals. He writes: One most memorable festival was in 1976. The festival site was awash with 'alternative' outlets and I purchased some hand-made green leather shoes (which never quite fitted) from travelling cobbler, Rob Llewellyn, later known for his role as Kryten in the TV sci-fi sitcom *Red Dwarf*.

Stilts were now a regular feature of my act. I paraded round the streets as a denim-clad 'bovver boy' with Lol Coxhill and Dave Holland providing the music. I hobbled around the festival with tall crutches on giant 'broken' stilts wrapped in white plaster. Little did I know that five years later I'd be on stilts in a West End musical, using skills I'd acquired on a field in Walcot. Bath at that time was an excellent platform to encourage creative theatrical thoughts. Today, I wonder and worry if there are similar situations for emerging artists. It was the 1970s. I was lucky.

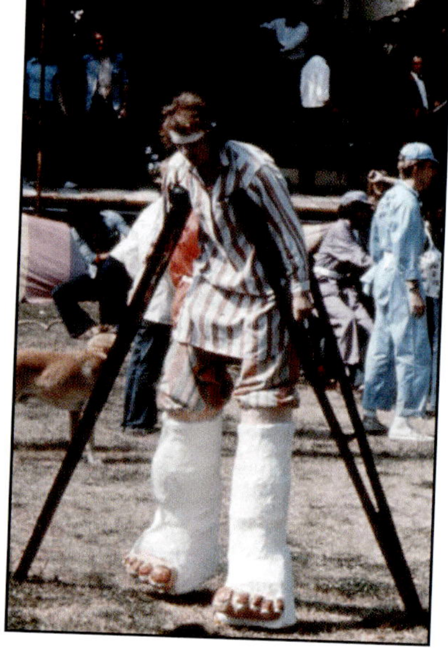

**Corinne:** Even more performers, events and crazy juxtapositions. I could hardly keep track of the extra artists who turned up at the last minute, hoping to perform. We found a slot for most of them in between the Caribbean curries and steel bands, the giant inflatables, dance workshops, outdoor yoga classes, Magic Lantern shows, the adventure playground with a specially-built pool, outings and teas for old people, and the authentic open-air wrestling ring one group erected on the site.

**Phil:** I was working in the East End of London at the time and invited a team of drum majorettes from the Isle of Dogs to come and join the festivities. Their skills were impressive,

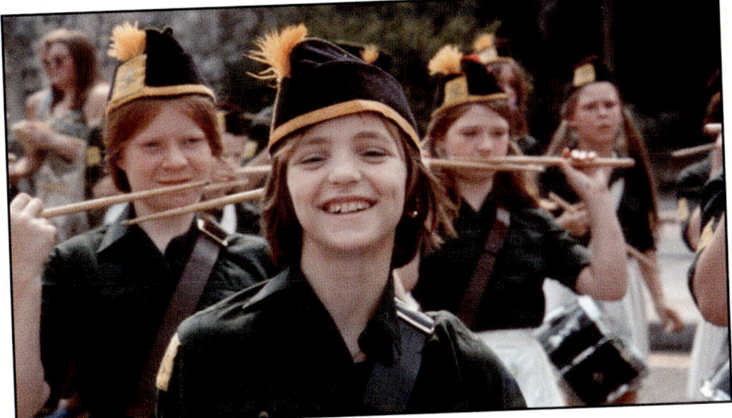

Drum majorettes from the Isle of Dogs

**Corinne:** One day, during a mid-afternoon lull in the programme, Tory and I decided on an impromptu walkabout performance. We raided our costume store and the shop jumble for anything vaguely floaty and psychedelic. I painted a flower over my third eye, donned a wig and grabbed a tambourine. We were ready! Thoroughly turned on and tuned in. We looked so far out there was a danger we might never come back. Ready to spread love, peace and laughter wherever they went, our two hip-chick alter egos set off for the 'free' festival, never to be seen again.

**Corinne:** The festivals were a huge amount of work and took months to organise, but they were the highlight of our year and something we all looked forward to avidly. It was such a social event – there were countless old friends among the regular performers, musicians, engineers and eco-activists who took part. And many of the various former members of BAW who had left to do other things in other places, returned every year to help. We always made new friends too, so it was a hugely inclusive and sociable gathering of broadly like-minded individuals, albeit with some wits capitalising on the situation to spread a lot of gossip and in-jokes.

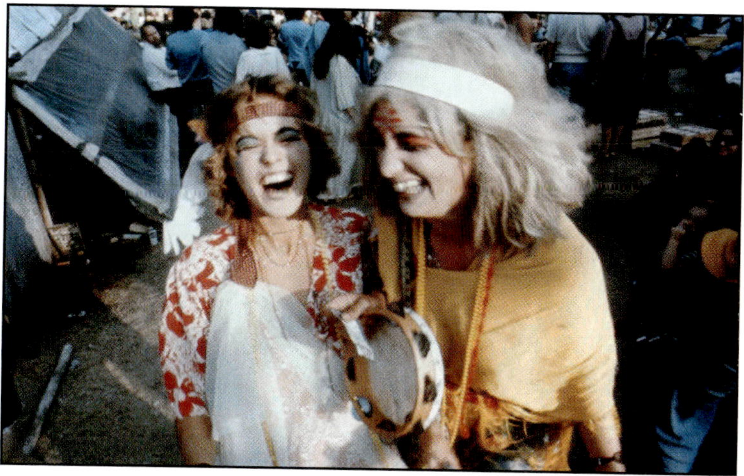

# THE HAT & FEATHER

**Corinne:** The Hat & Feather, at the top of Walcot Street, was our local – 30 seconds from our shop, which was fortuitous as last orders were called at

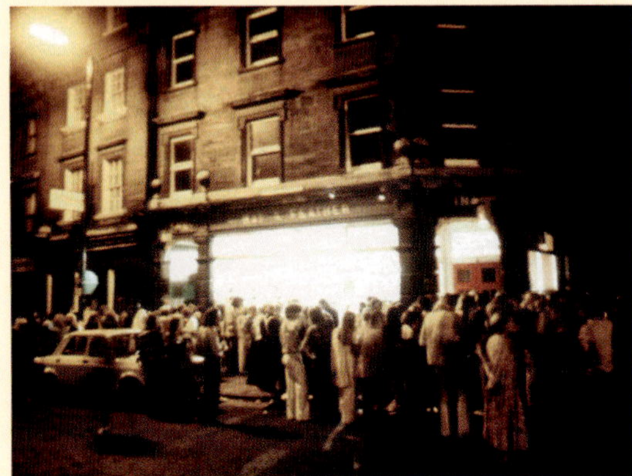

The Hat & Feather overflowing

10.20pm. The landlords, Heriot and Jenny, welcomed us with open arms and became unlikely collaborators and supporters in many weird and wonderful events. Granted their pub was often filled to overflowing – but they gave us the run of the place in a way that most publicans would have baulked at.

**Mitch:** The legendary Hat & Feather was the unofficial Bath Arts Workshop social centre and playground – a crucible of wishing and hoping, planning and dreaming. This was where new ideas and initiatives were fomented amongst the socialising people gathered there.

We put on countless events in the upstairs room – public meetings and theatre workshops (once in the nude) and a variety of theatre and music performances by ourselves and other artists. We staged discos in the bar, and during the festivals the whole place was bulging at the seams with performers and hundreds of spectators spilling out onto the streets at a time when you could still smoke indoors.

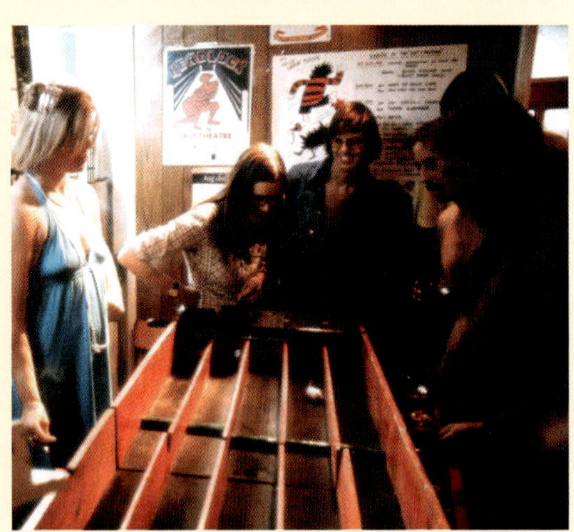

Mouse racing

You might encounter **Landscapes and Living Spaces** (Roland Miller and Shirley Cameron), suggestively eulogising and demonstrating the merits of certain vegetables; Peter Leaborne of **The Lemmings** taking bets on mouse racing (with real mice); **Rob Con** with his painted wooden dog on castors which urinated on unsuspecting customers; or **Ian Hinchcliffe**, the *enfant terrible* of performance art, doing something even more outrageous. Or you might have been the victim of an impromptu raid by **Lumiere & Son's** paramilitary 'Special Forces'.

I often worked behind the bar. It was a welcome source of income in the days before Workshop wages, and Heriot and Jenny usually threw in a hearty meal after the shift. And we always relied on them for licences to serve alcohol at the theatre and music events we put on in venues all over town.

Heriot and Jenny helped us in immeasurable ways, above and beyond the call of duty or capitalism.

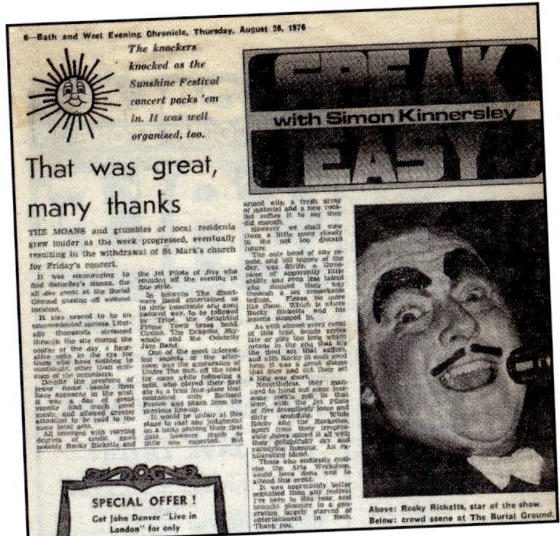



## Rocky plays to a huge crowd

**Corinne:** On the last evening, there was a rock concert on the stage at the bottom of the field. Top of the bill was our own Rocky Ricketts and the Jet Pilots of Jive, featuring (of course) the fabulous Rockettes. Phil Shepherd was the hippy promoter with his mane of red hair who appeared naked onstage to introduce the band to a huge crowd. At the end of the show Vince Pube, Rocky's seedy manager, took to the microphone and announced: *'Well, that's the end of the festival. We won't be organising it next year so you can do it your fucking selves'*. Ralph (Vince himself) describes the fall out: The comments were directed at the audience but it was a powerful sound system so people as far away as Camden Road (high on a hill above the field) heard it and complained. The council was not amused and wrote to inform me that even though they presumed it was all a joke, I could be *'prosecuted for obscenity'*.

## Changing times 1977

**Corinne:** After the previous year's 'obscenity' incident, the council asked us to submit a festival plan in advance. We listed the usual events – a procession, street theatre and a fete on the burial field. A couple of musical events were proposed, along with a pledge to end amplified music by 9pm. The plan ended with a proposal for a concert involving *'one loud awful pop group, swearing and drugs from 3pm to 9pm'*. Comments from councillors were reported in the *Bath Evening Chronicle*. In the end, the **Walcot Jubilee Carnival** was a one-day event in August.

By 1977, the **Natural Theatre Company** had grown and developed considerably and although we were still running lots of community activities, we were also spending more time performing in the UK and Europe. After the Jubilee event we stepped back from organising the festivals, and handed it over to willing Walcotians, although we continued to offer as many resources as we could muster to those who stepped in to do it themselves. The Workshop as a whole was also up against it financially. The 1976 festival budget was £4,600 plus whatever we raised from programme sales and door takes (not much as we kept our prices low).[4] We had nothing like that sum in 1977.

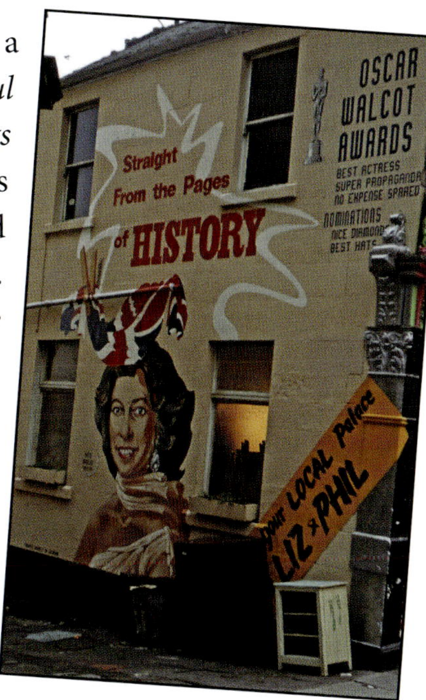



Jubilee mural

---

4. This was made up of £4,000 from the Arts Council and £600 from Bath City Council.

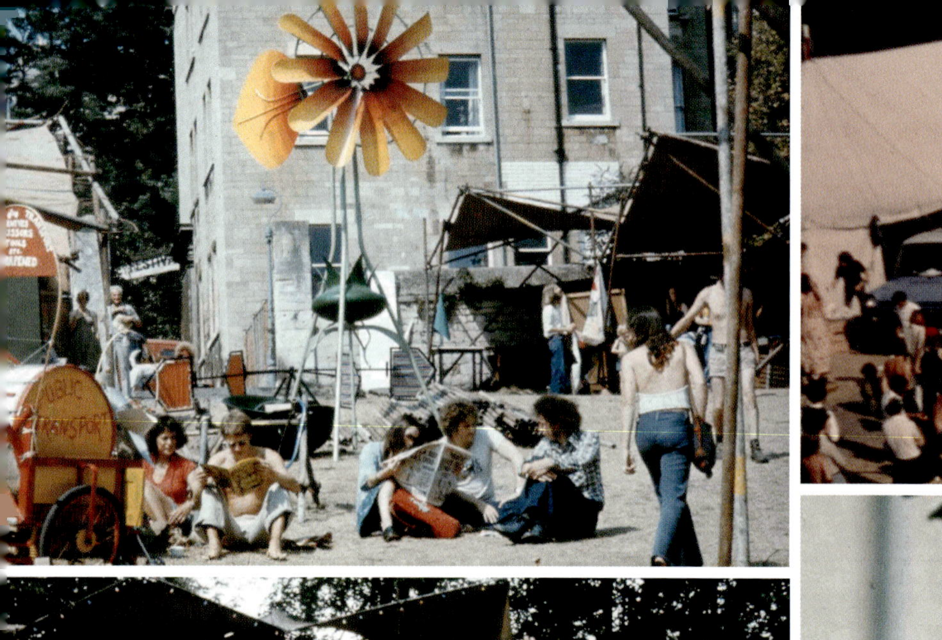
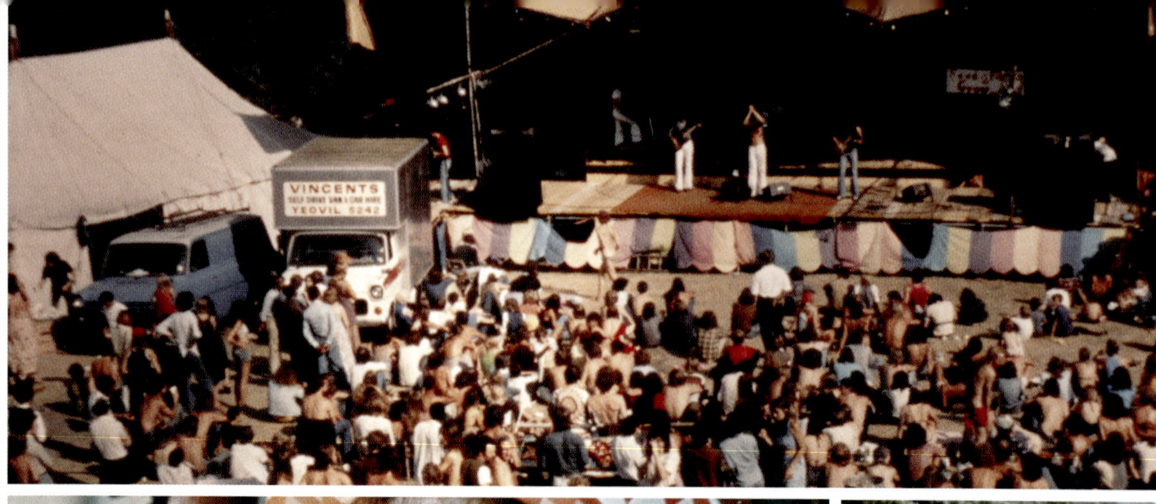
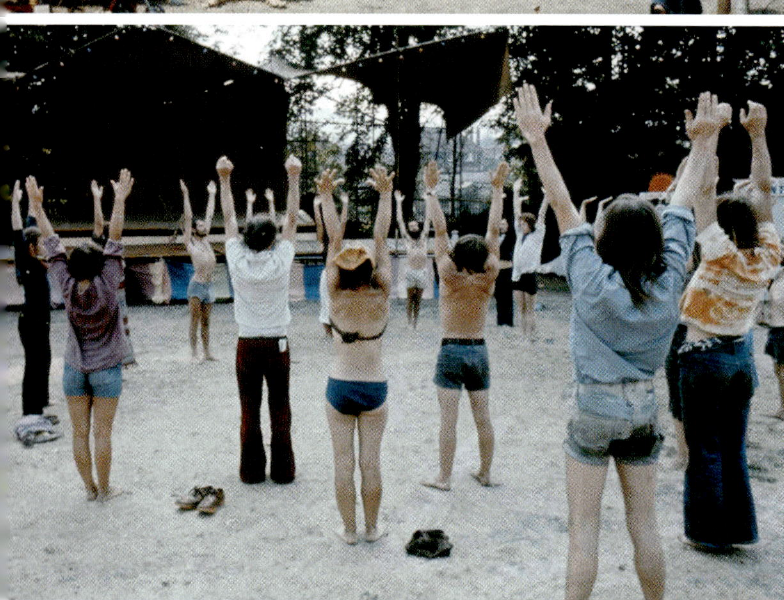
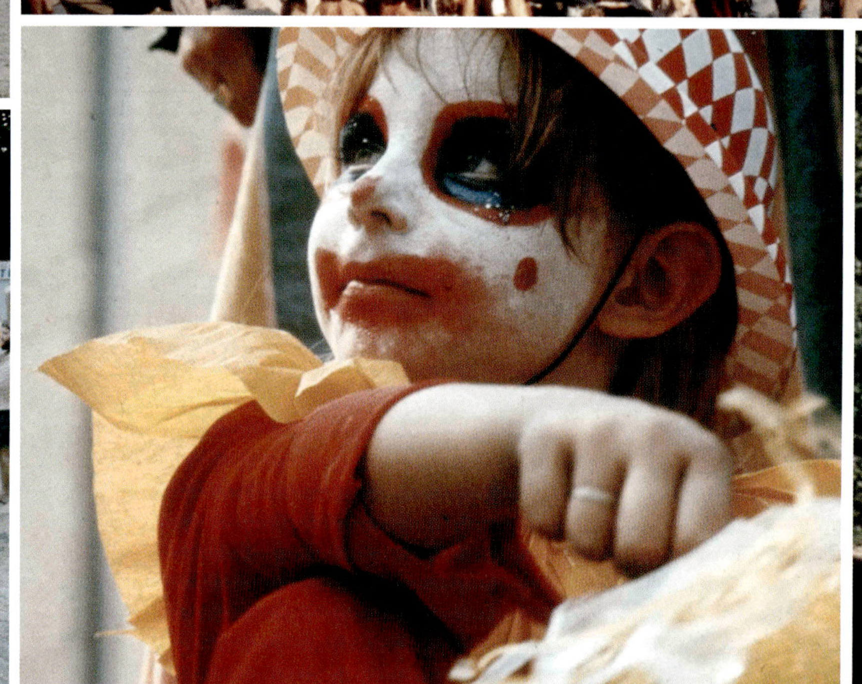
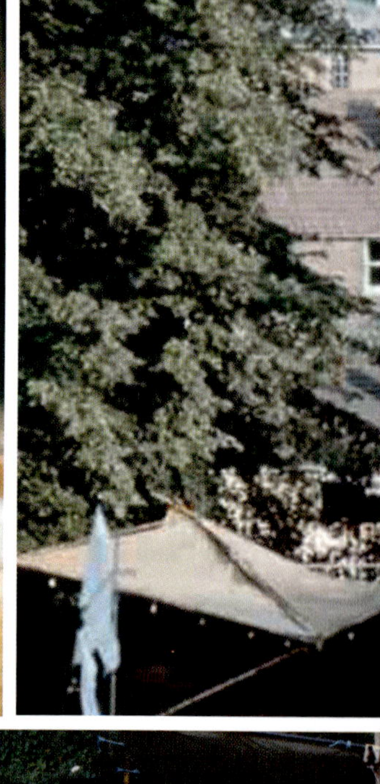
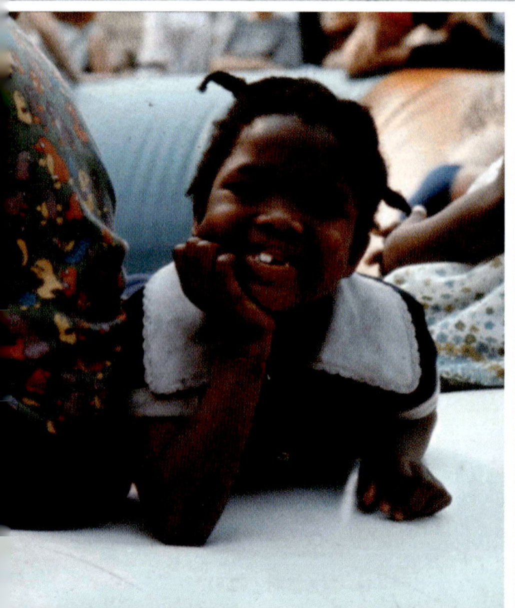
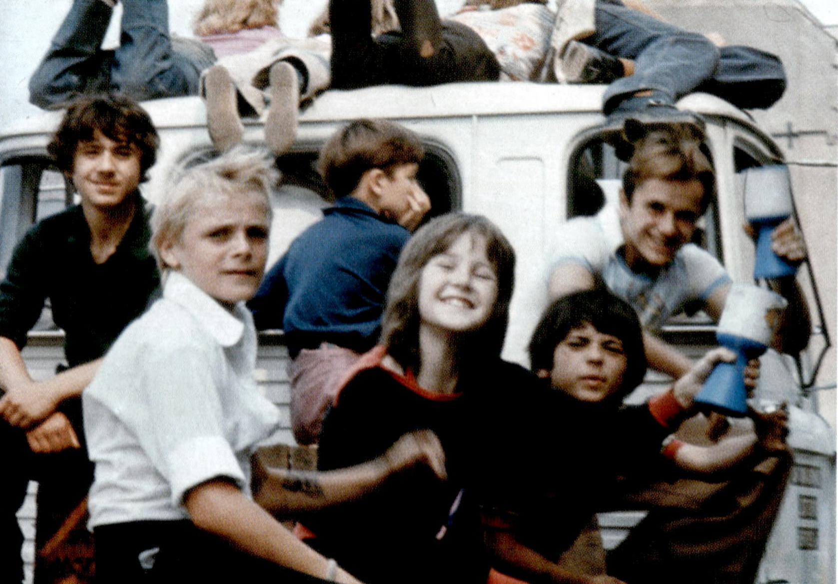
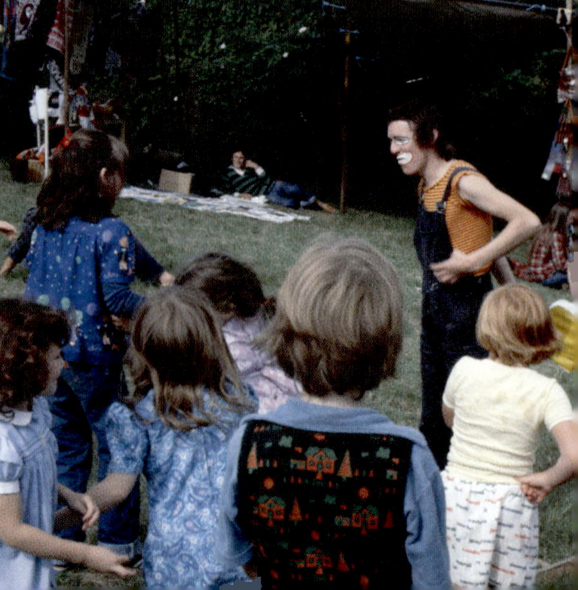

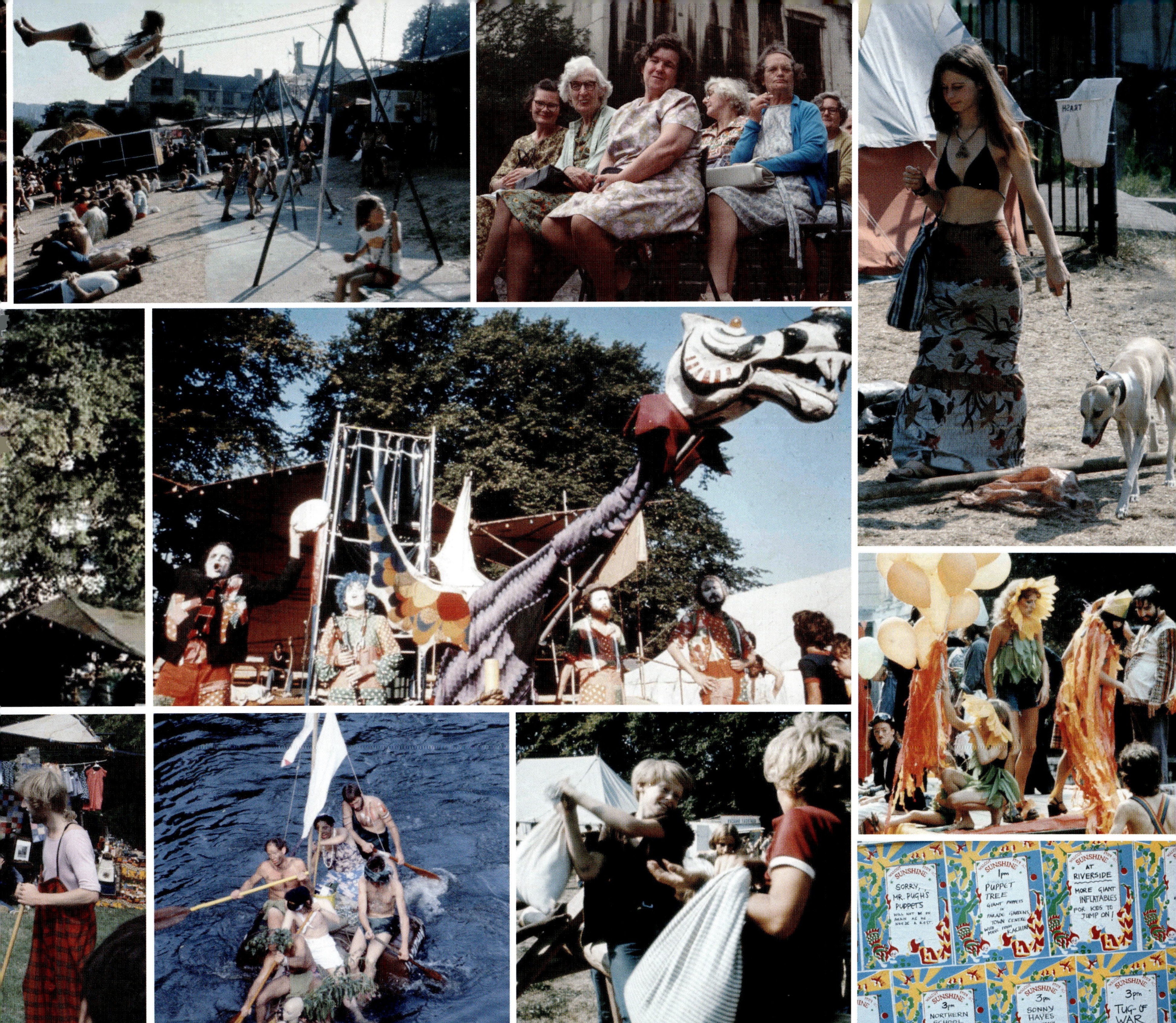
SUNSHINE
SORRY, MR. PUGH'S PUPPETS
WILL NOT BE ON AGAIN AS HE NEEDS A REST.
SUNSHINE
1pm
PUPPET TREE
GIANT PUPPETS IN PARADE GARDENS, TOWN CENTRE WITH MUSIC FROM KACHINA
SUNSHINE
AT RIVERSIDE
MORE GIANT INFLATABLES FOR KIDS TO JUMP ON!
SUNSHINE
3pm
NORTHERN SCHOOL OF FILM REALISTS
FILMING IN
SUNSHINE
3pm
SONNY HAYES
WILL TEACH YOU HOW TO JUGGLE
SUNSHINE
3pm
TUG-OF WAR

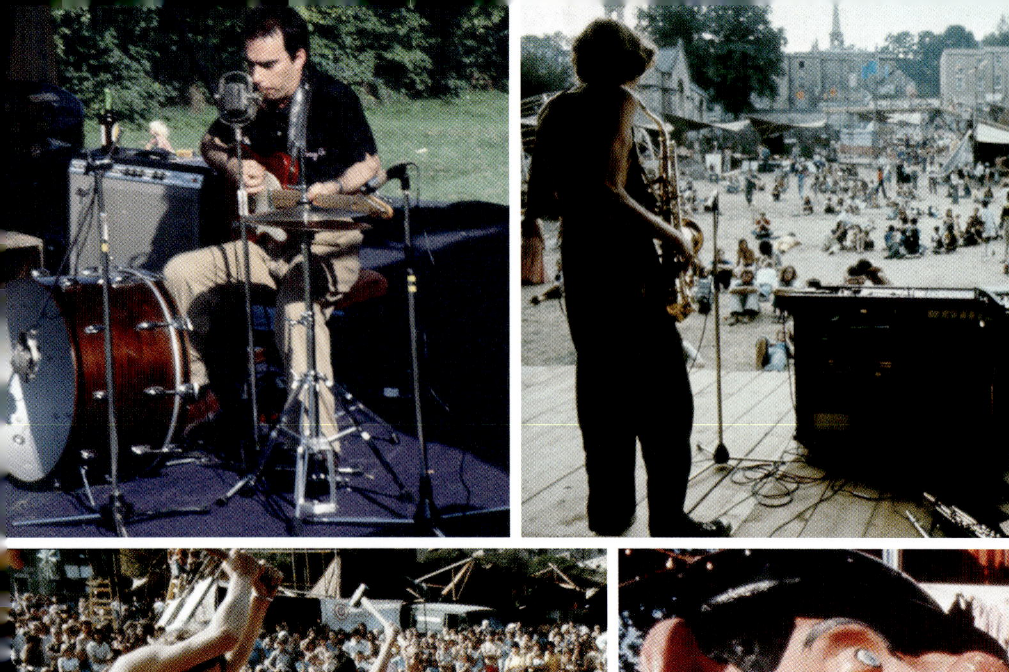
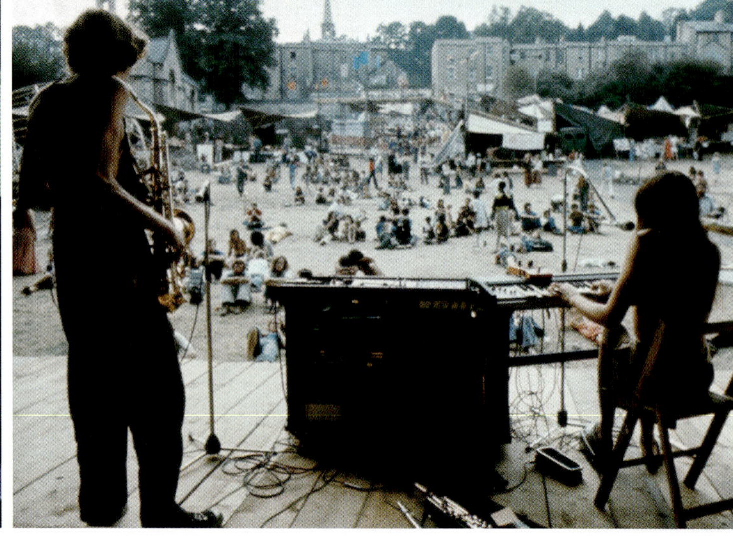
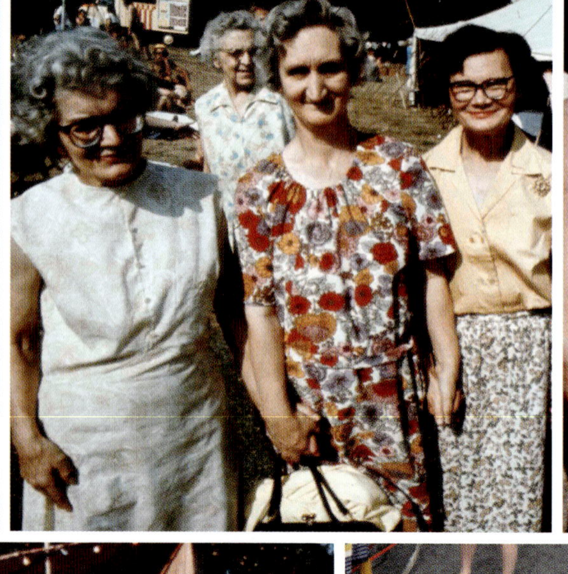
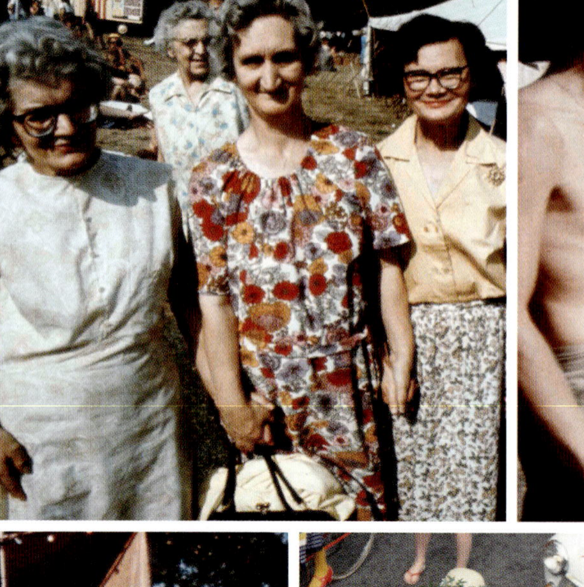
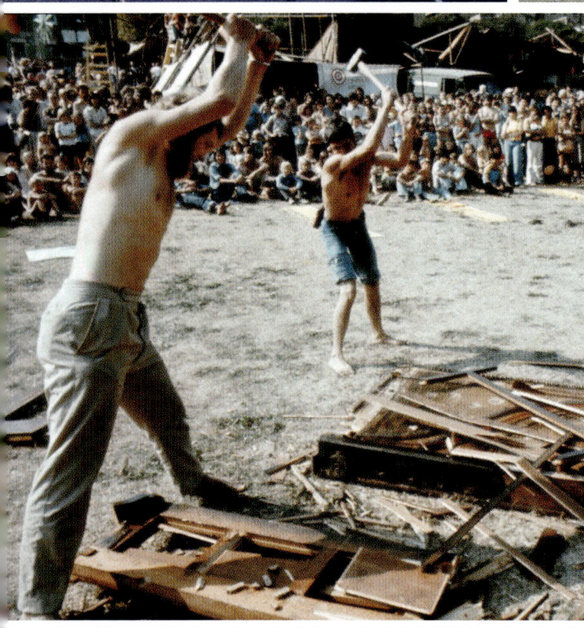
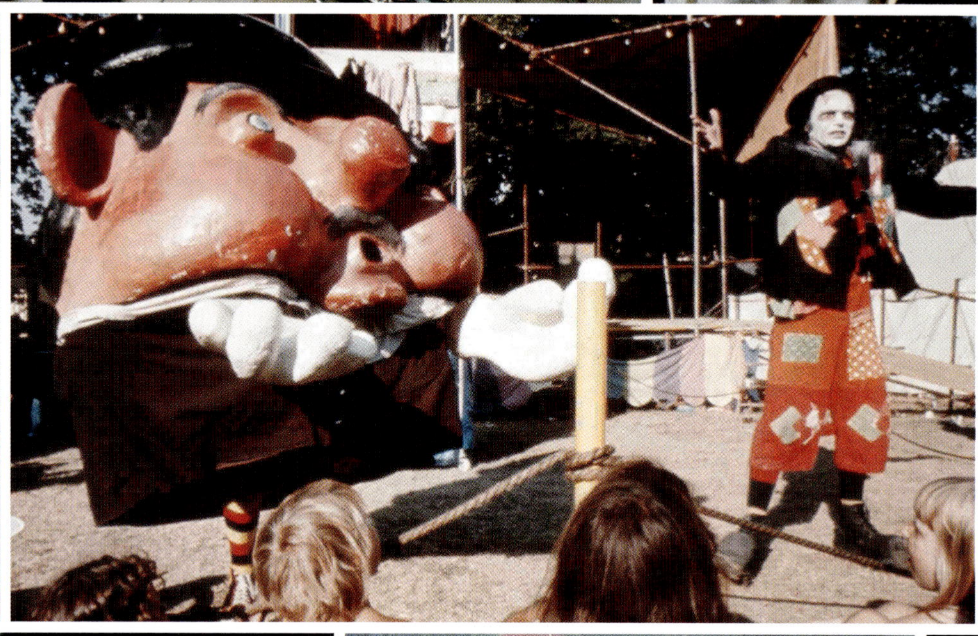
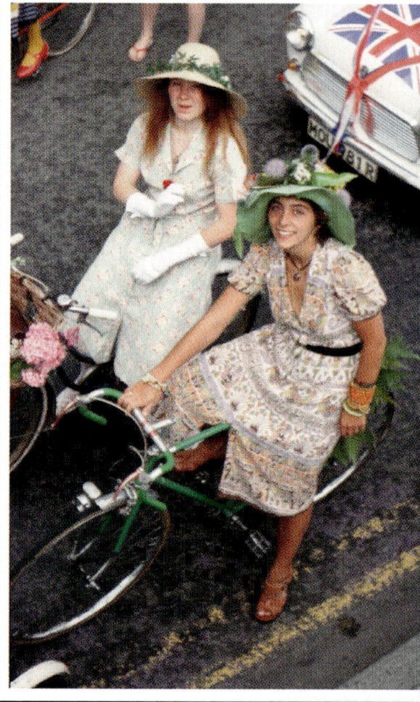
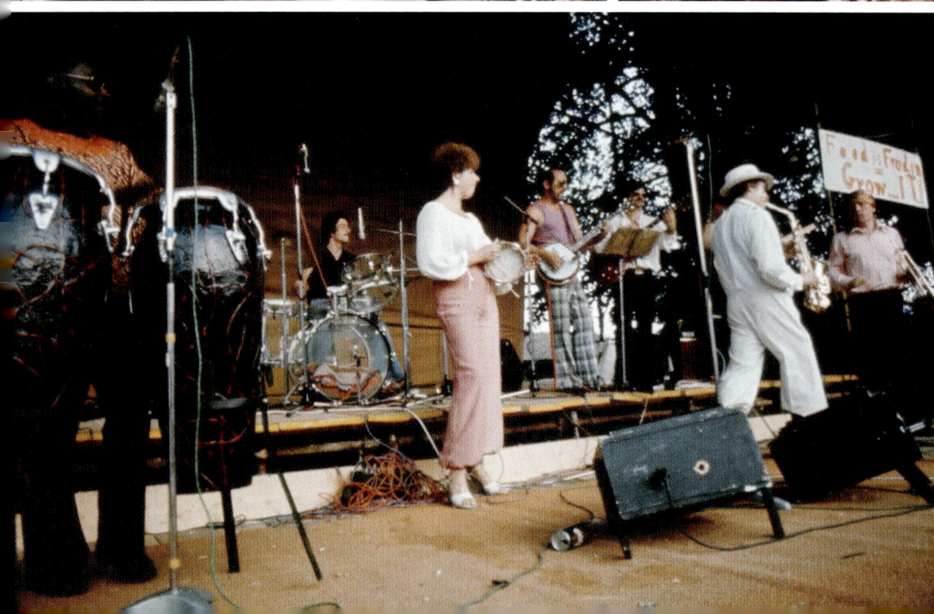


Food is Friday
Grow IT!


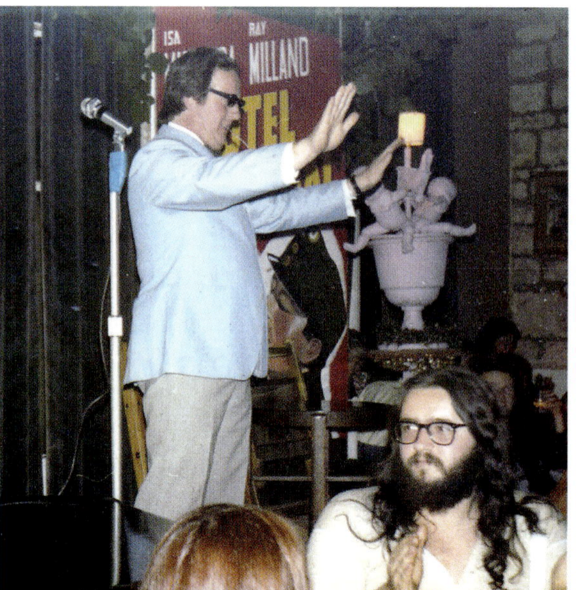


ISA
RAY MILLAND


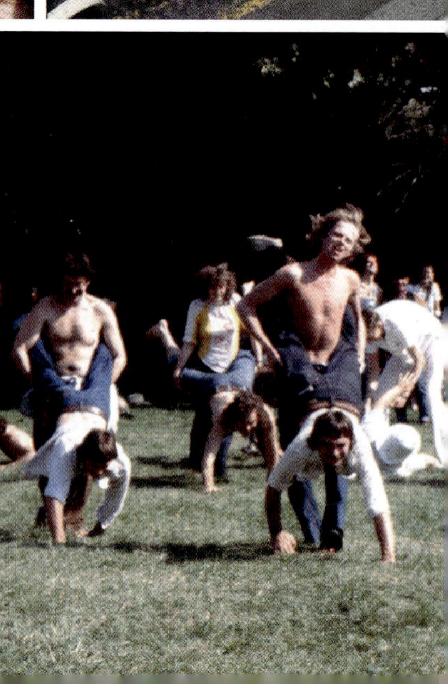

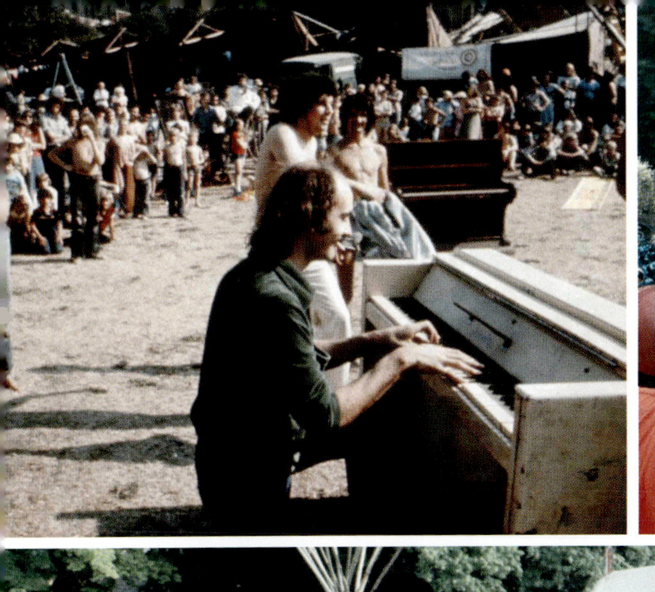
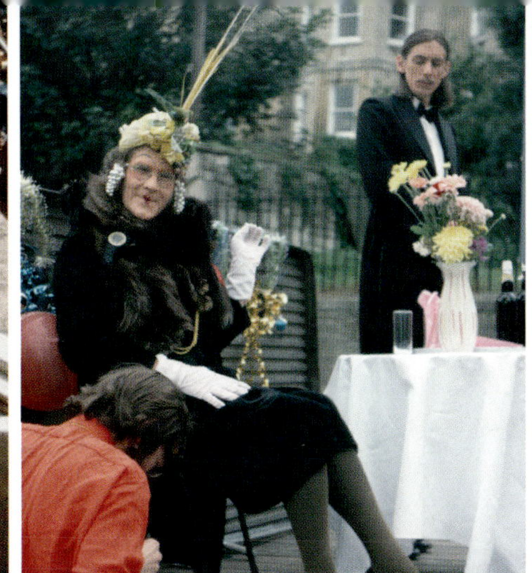
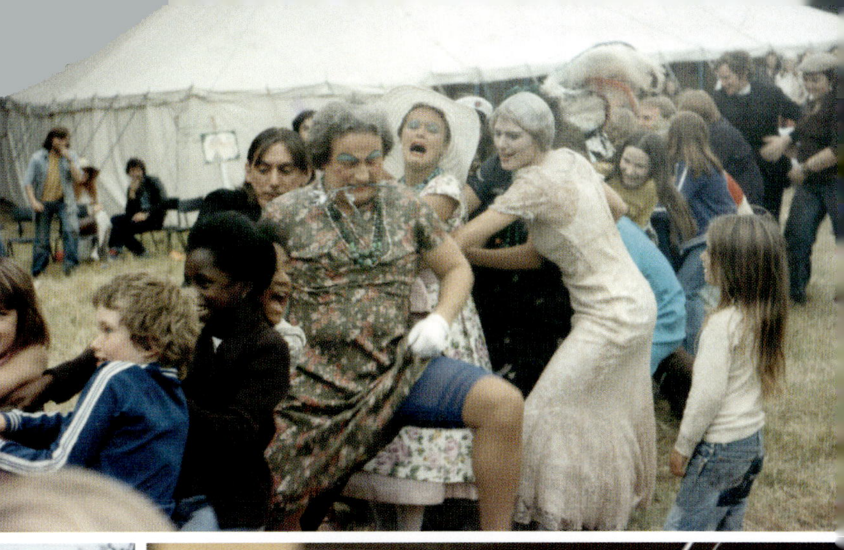
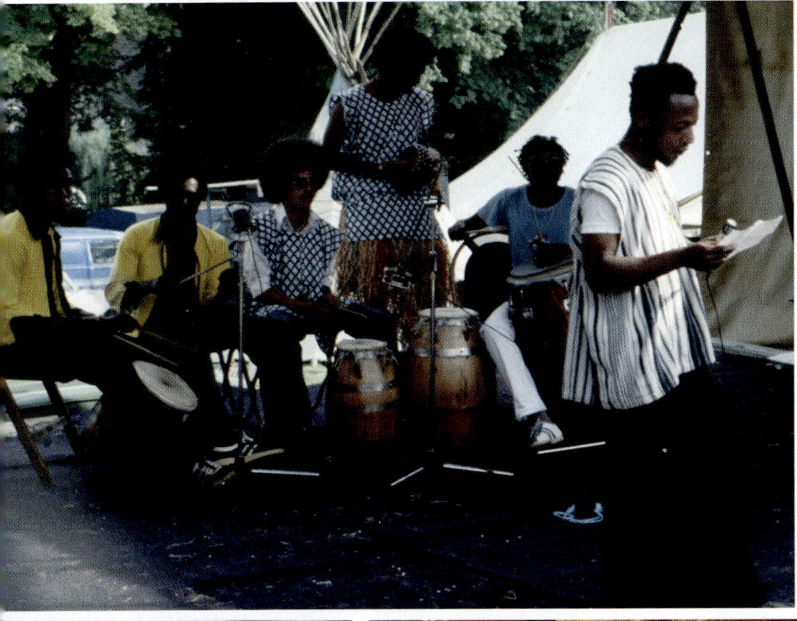
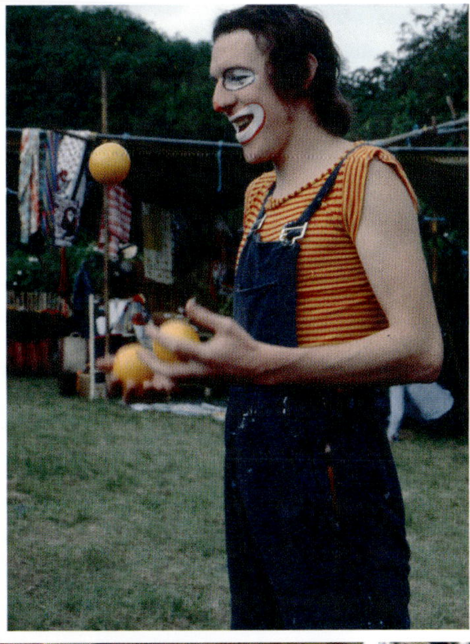
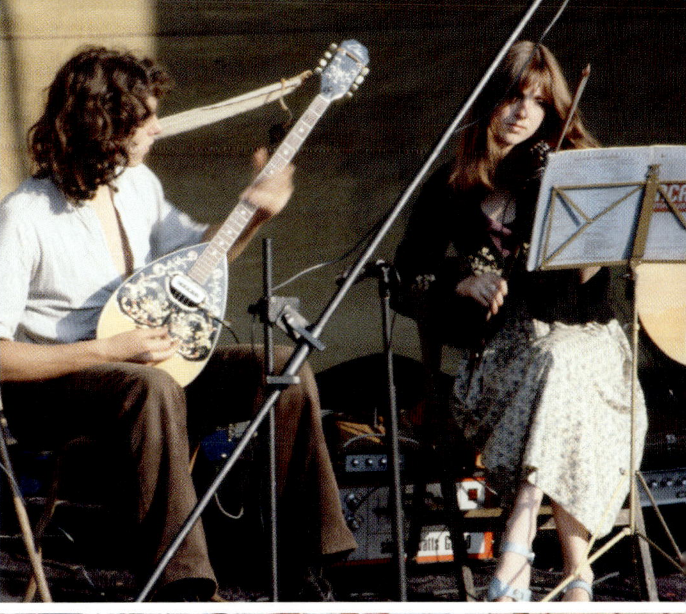
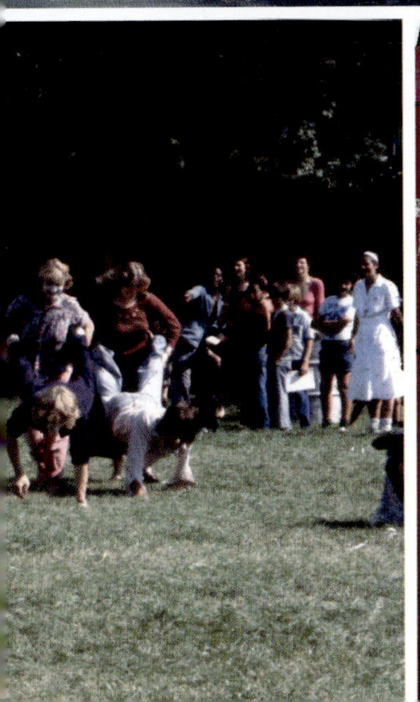
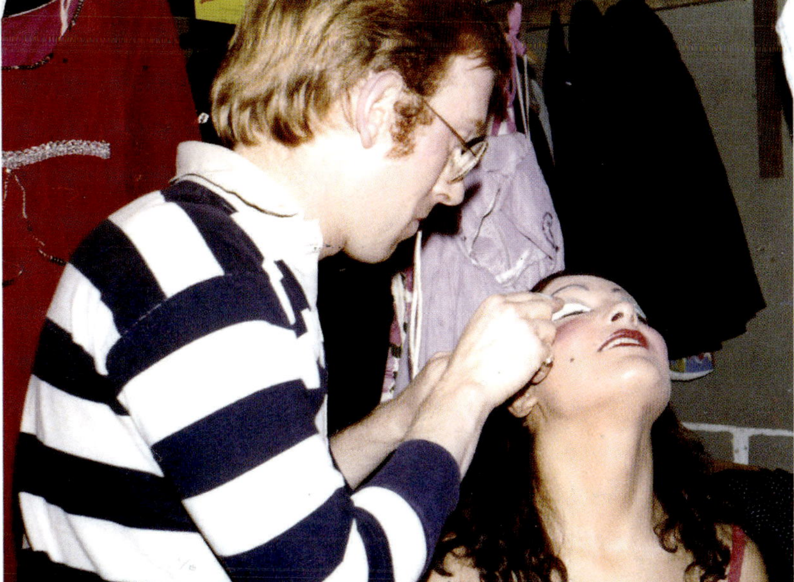
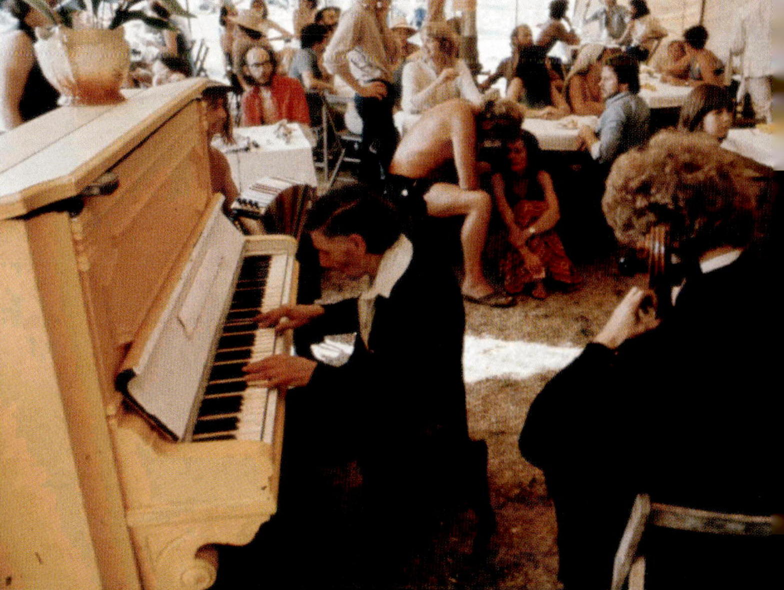

# Beano Club and Festival 1978

**John Wood:** The idea of no more festivals caused consternation in the wider Walcot community. I was devastated that these amazing events wouldn't happen again and called a meeting in the Village Hall to see if anyone was interested in carrying it on. And people were.

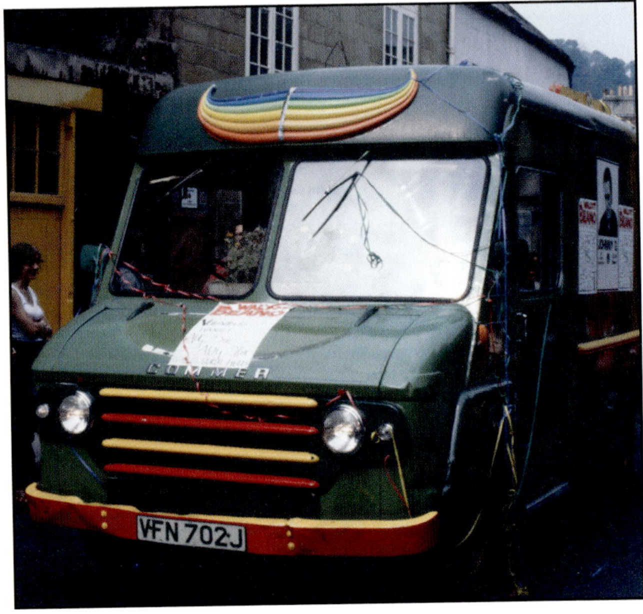

Workshop van, volunteers needed

The hall was full and I spoke passionately about how it was a vital part of our community, a lesson on how to come together to celebrate life, and more along those lines. People were enthused. We would somehow find a way to raise the funds ourselves.

We decided to put on cabaret evenings in the village hall as fundraisers. We'd call it the **Beano Club**, in memory

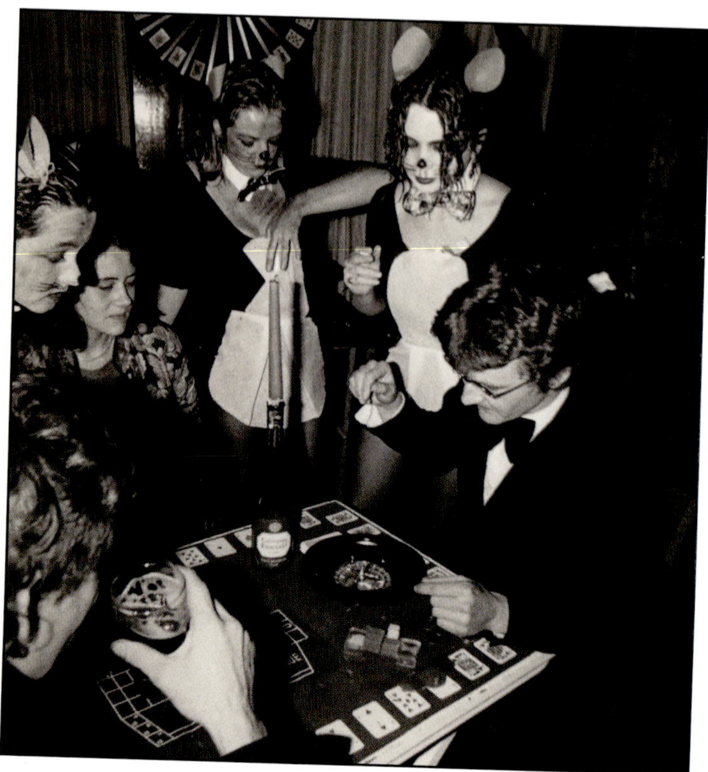

The Rat Girls, Beano Club casino night

of Jam Beano, an old Bath name for a community knees-up. We opened the doors in spring 1978, wondering if anyone would turn up. They did, in droves. The club happened every Saturday night for three months leading up to the Walcot Beano Festival, featuring a musical Beano Combo, led by Chas Ambler on piano. Every week, we came up with an original cabaret starring only the talent and creativity of local people. We held informal discussions in the Workshop shop on Monday, to come up with a theme and take it from there. There were Italian nights, a Policeman's Ball, a wartime austerity night, lots of different things. It never failed.

**Tory:** One act I clearly remember involved Chas Ambler the pianist. He had beautiful dark ringlets that flowed down his back. That night he wore a kaftan and sunglasses – he was an archetypal hippy. He sat down at the piano and began playing *Are you going to San Francisco?* by the Mamas & the Papas, a song we all knew from 1968. As he played, a hairdresser arrived with his kit (unbeknownst to the audience he was a friend). For about ten minutes he cut Chas's hair, his thick locks falling to the ground as he played on and sang. In the end Chas had a short conventional haircut. He stood up and took off his kaftan to reveal a grey suit and tie beneath. Then he simply walked off and left the Village Hall. Not a word was spoken throughout.

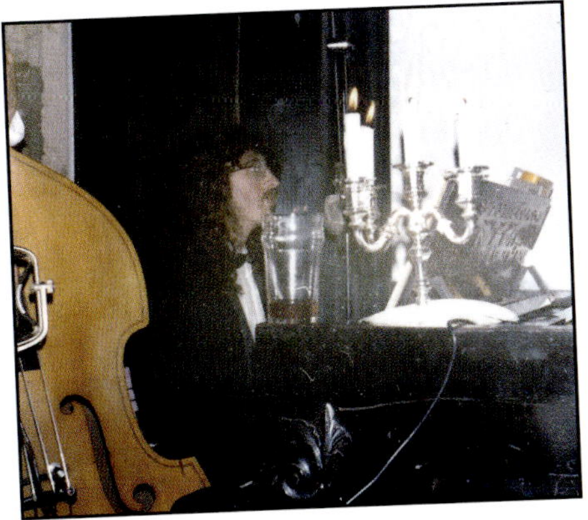

Chas Ambler

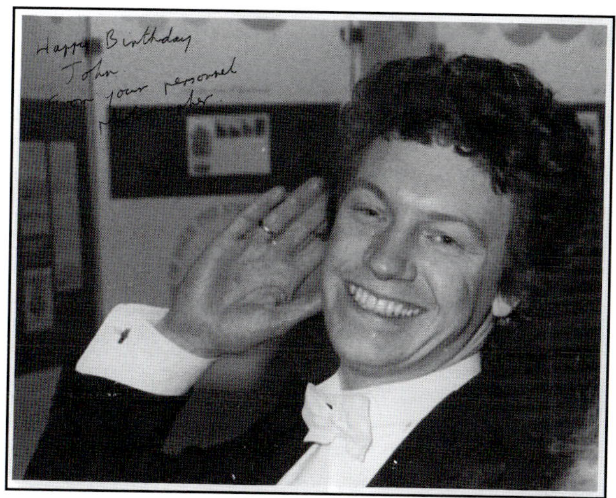

John Wood

**John Wood:** Often there were more people queuing outside than the hall could hold and we had to go to the end of the line to turn people away. No-one was paid. We ran our own bar, charged a reasonable admission and in the end raised about £1,500 – the equivalent of about nine grand today.[5] We ran 32 **Beano Clubs** in those two years. The high point for me was on 16 June 1979, my birthday. I was performing a sketch when Pav Douglas suddenly took off the outer costume of a character he was playing, and said 'John Wood, This is Your Life!' And did the whole works, with a ring binder of stories from my life, and recorded messages from my parents and old friends elsewhere. Everyone was in on it, and I had no inkling. It was one of the nicest things anyone's ever done for me. I was high for days.

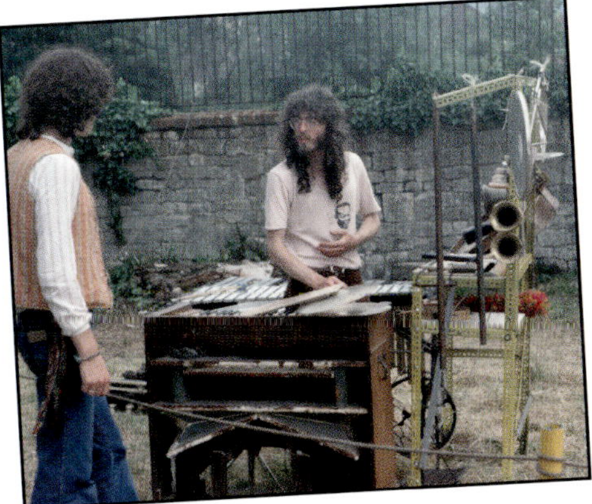

Chas on the field

The **Beano Festival** itself was a success; and on a scale to match the earlier Workshop-run ones. And the finances balanced. We did it entirely ourselves. We were our own Arts Council.

---

5. The Workshop chipped in another £1,500 of their Arts Council grant. Not a lot to run a big festival but we were used to running things on a shoestring, and you could get a lot of shoestring for £3,000.

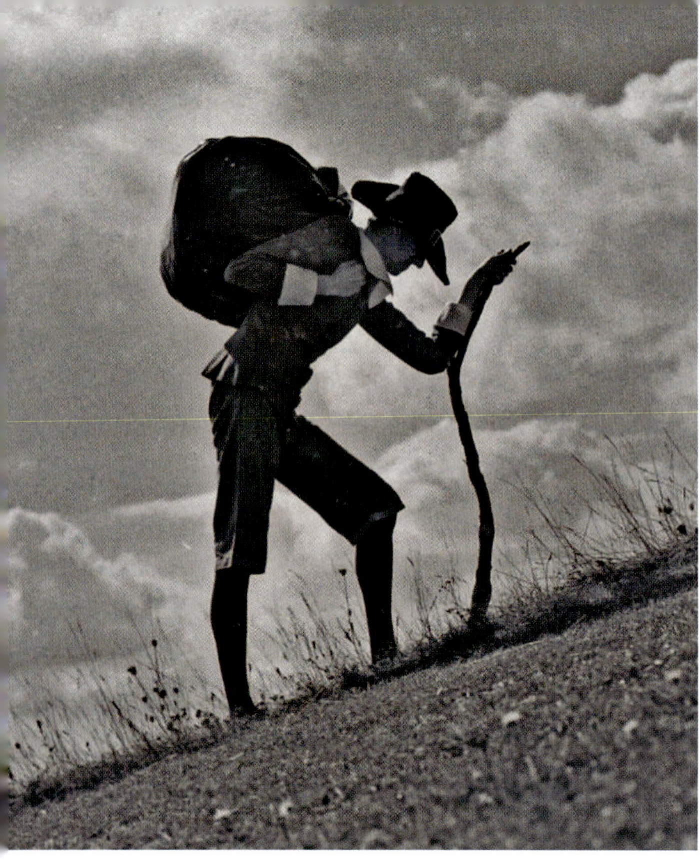



**B**y 1977, Mick Banks of **John Bull Puncture Repair Kit** (aka the 'movie star' Peter Slim) had joined the **Natural Theatre Company**. For the Beano he created a theatrical guided tour of Walcot loosely based on John Bunyan's *The Pilgrim's Progress*.[6]

**Mick** takes up the story: My initial idea was to draw on the novel to create an interactive pilgrimage around the

---

6. *The Pilgrim's Progress* was published in 1678 as a religious allegory; it is famous for the opening line *'As I walked through the wilderness of this world… I dreamed a dream'*.

neighbourhood – to stage Walcot's very own Oberammergau. The story begins in the City of Destruction (Earth) and ends at the gates of the Celestial City (Heaven).

## Cast Notes

**Mick Banks as Phil Grimm.** Startlingly tall with a slight stoop. Ideal for carrying the sins of the world on his back. The costume: elegant, tailored, funereal with a slight flair; topped off with a natty cloak of Puritan grey and an imposing hat.

**Ralph Oswick as Narrator.** A neatly-presented vicar, the Reverend Thomas Cook, megaphone in hand, guiding, shepherding, making religion relevant again. One eye on Heaven, the other on his watch.

**Corinne D'Cruz as Companion.** Jumpered and jodphured, an individualist with her own agenda. A pragmatist, attempting to hitchhike to the Celestial City the logical way – via the London Road and the A38.

**Brian Popay as Mister Worldly Wise.** A Georgian hedonist sporting a wig that – if left unchecked – could fill an entire room.

Finding the route was key. The graveyard outside the Village Hall was the obvious assembly point. Hedgemead Park made a suitably municipal Heaven; but to achieve it the tour must cross a busy main road and work around the hillside. Thomas Street was on the line of march, perfect for Bunyan's Hill of Difficulty, but it was a cul-de-sac. Somehow or other it all fell into place and on The Day of Judgement, 28 August at 3pm, we set out.

From the onset, the show's appeal lay in its agility at crossing time zones. A 20th century vicar introducing a 17th century pilgrim who is then accosted by an 18th century Georgian fop, Mister Worldly Wise, who believes he has found heaven here on earth. Cue the first vignette: A curtain falls to reveal a frenzied crowd of semi-naked wantons in a Walcot Street shop window.

Further along the road, we pause outside The Hat & Feather for a contemporary lesson on abstinence. Geoff,

Below: Fop, left: Phil Grimm

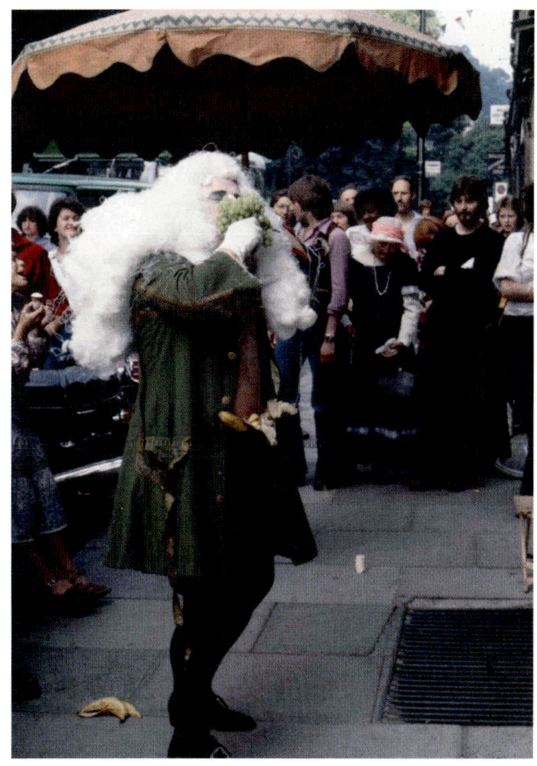

the landlord, throws out the faithful Companion who is looking for Truth in the pub. Having tried hitchhiking, she agrees to join Phil Grimm if she can take her bike. Reverend Cook parts the traffic and we ascend to the safety of the High Pavement. A cherub flies across the London Road with directions for the tour guide. (In an SAS-style covert operation the previous evening, a wire was installed from Nasher's kitchen window over the A4 to a lamppost opposite).

We turn the corner into Thomas Street and begin the steep ascent. We are not alone. David Symington tempts us to linger over afternoon tea, served whilst miraculously levitating halfway up the front of his house. The popular Bathonian housewife Mary Mingeworthy (Chris Peecock) joins us with a month's worth of groceries. Halfway up, a bungee snaps and the trolley careers backwards down the hill with her as an unwilling passenger.

A third of the way in, the piece began to develop gravitas. Passers-by innocently walking their dogs suddenly found

themselves swept along by an ardent band of believers comprised of many adults and a veritable throng of rowdy kids.

We ran out of road at the top of Thomas Street so we re-routed the tour through Lesley Flanagan's house. By the time we emerged onto Lower Hedgemead Road, even the sight of Phil Shepherd brandishing a chainsaw was not going to prevent us entering Paradise. But before we did so, and in a nod to the topicality of the original book, Jennie and her two children are being evicted from their council house.[7]

Guided by the solicitous Sister Louise, we step into the Promised Land, where we meet Rick Knapp as God. A face to face interview with the deity over a steaming cup of ambrosia and a selfie. With Paul Lawrence as the Angel Gabriel, tasked with refreshments and referrals. *'No autographs, please!'*

---

7. The book was written as a social critique whilst Bunyan was imprisoned for religious subversion.

# Walcot Nation 1979

**John Wood:** After the success of the **Beano**, we did it all again in 1979. The four-day independence festival was a triumph, with its notion of **Walcot Nation** as a newly-formed country, complete with passports (the festival programme),

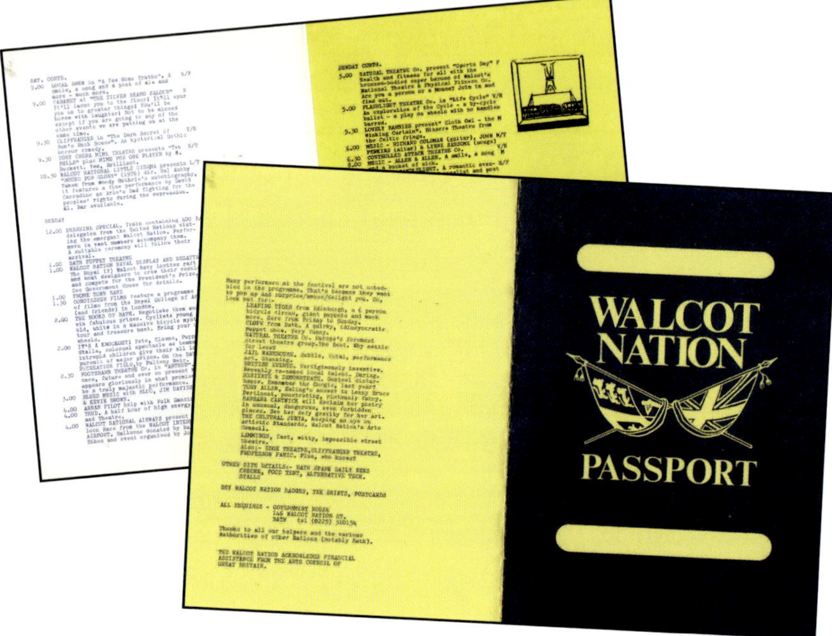

Walcot Nation passports

ministries and institutions; and of course its motto *Walcot Waives the Rules*. Chas composed the national anthem and I co-wrote the lyrics with him. The first time we played it we put the words on a big sheet – we thought people might need coaxing to join in. We did that once. After that everyone knew it by heart.[8]

---

8. The Walcot State Choir, run by Su Hart, is still going today.

## Walcot National Anthem

Across the grey bridges
And down from the crescents
We run to you.

Though many amongst us
Were children and youngsters
Away from you.

Walcot! The council site for car parks
Access roadworks and new hotels.
Walcot! It needs no interference
Or site clearance, hear as we tell:

We shall not be fooled
Walcot waives the rules!

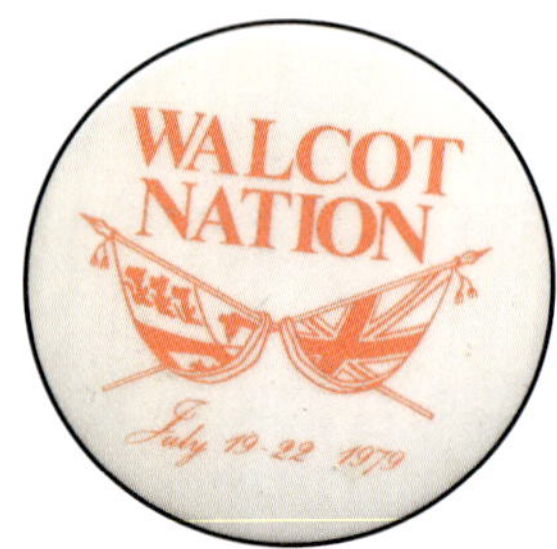

Walcot Nation
badge

**Mick Banks:** During the festival, Walcot declared independence each morning, and there was a *coup d'Etat* at midnight every night when a new government took over. The next day's heads of state arrived by various means of transport: By military truck, on horseback and by high-speed train from Paddington. Rulers included a South American-style dictatorship (myself and Corinne); Brian Popay as a General Patton cigar-chewing US commander on a tank; and Pav Douglas and Jackie Popay as a Shah and his wife. They arrived in pomp and splendour at Bath station, to be met by a brass band and a hastily press-ganged crowd of passengers waiting for their trains along with random well-wishers.

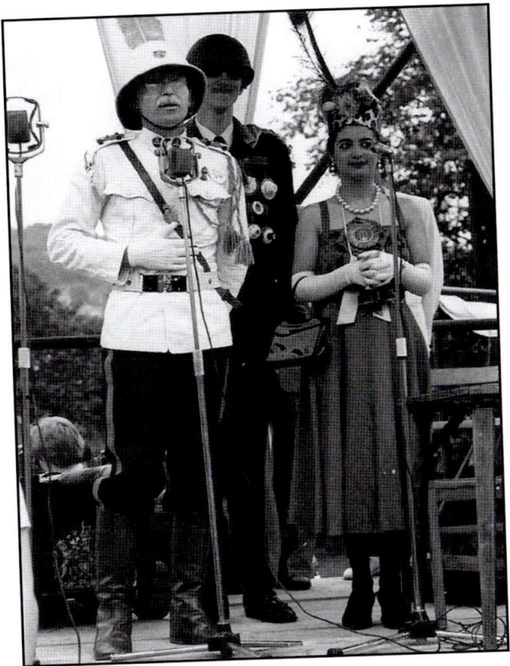

Rulers of South American
dictatorship

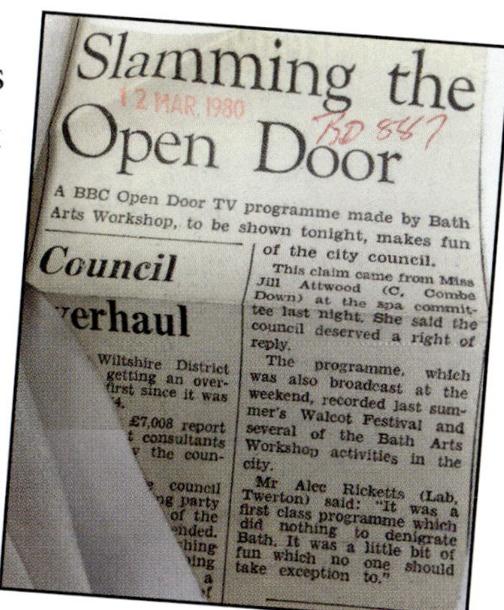

Slamming the
Open Door



A BBC Open Door TV programme made by Bath Arts Workshop, to be shown tonight, makes fun of the city council.

This claim came from Miss Jill Attwood (C. Combe Down) at the spa committee last night. She said the council deserved a right of reply.

The programme, which was also broadcast at the weekend, recorded last summer's Walcot Festival and several of the Bath Arts Workshop activities in the city.

Mr Alec Ricketts (Lab, Twerton) said: "It was a first class programme which did nothing to denigrate Bath. It was a little bit of fun which no one should take exception to."

**Shaun Smith:** I do remember Brian Popay dressed as an army general driving down Walcot Street and arresting those who did not have a Walcot passport. I also have the feeling that he was in an armoured vehicle borrowed from some history museum, but I could be wrong there. (He was!)

**John Wood** adds: Alongside all that were all the usual visiting and local bands, theatre companies and other people turning up in vans and buses and being put up in local houses by friendly Walcotians. For a week, Walcot became the mouse that roared!

**Corinne:** The Workshop later made a TV programme for the BBC's *Open Door* documentary series. It used new and existing footage with help from Paul Nachman (Nasher) of Workshop Films. It was written by John Wood and Ric Jerrom and the whole show was presented through the theatrical lens of the Walcot Nation. It opened with a '*Partly political broadcast on behalf of the Walcot Nation*' in which the Walcot prime minister outlined the events leading up to Walcot's Declaration of Independence. It went on to present the various 'governments', who appeared one after the other along with short clips of all the Workshop's other activities.

When the programme was broadcast in March 1980, it provoked unreasoned fury from one councillor who claimed that it made fun of Bath City Council. According to the *Chronicle* another councillor retorted: '*It was a first class programme which did nothing to denigrate Bath. It was a little bit of fun which no one should take exception to.*'

**Sonny Hayes**, a magician: I first met the jolly pranksters from Natural Theatre at the Melkweg club and culture centre in Amsterdam. Their show was a Rock 'n' Roll epic and ours was comedy magic stuff. There was an instant connection. From there, we played at the Workshop festivals for several years. For the artists and performers involved there was a crucible of interaction and an exchange of ideas that even after all these years I have not seen repeated. At a time when the arts and community are under attack and the festival has fallen. At the going down of the sun and in the morning we shall remember it. We who served shall not forget the Walcot Nation or that Walcot waives the rules!

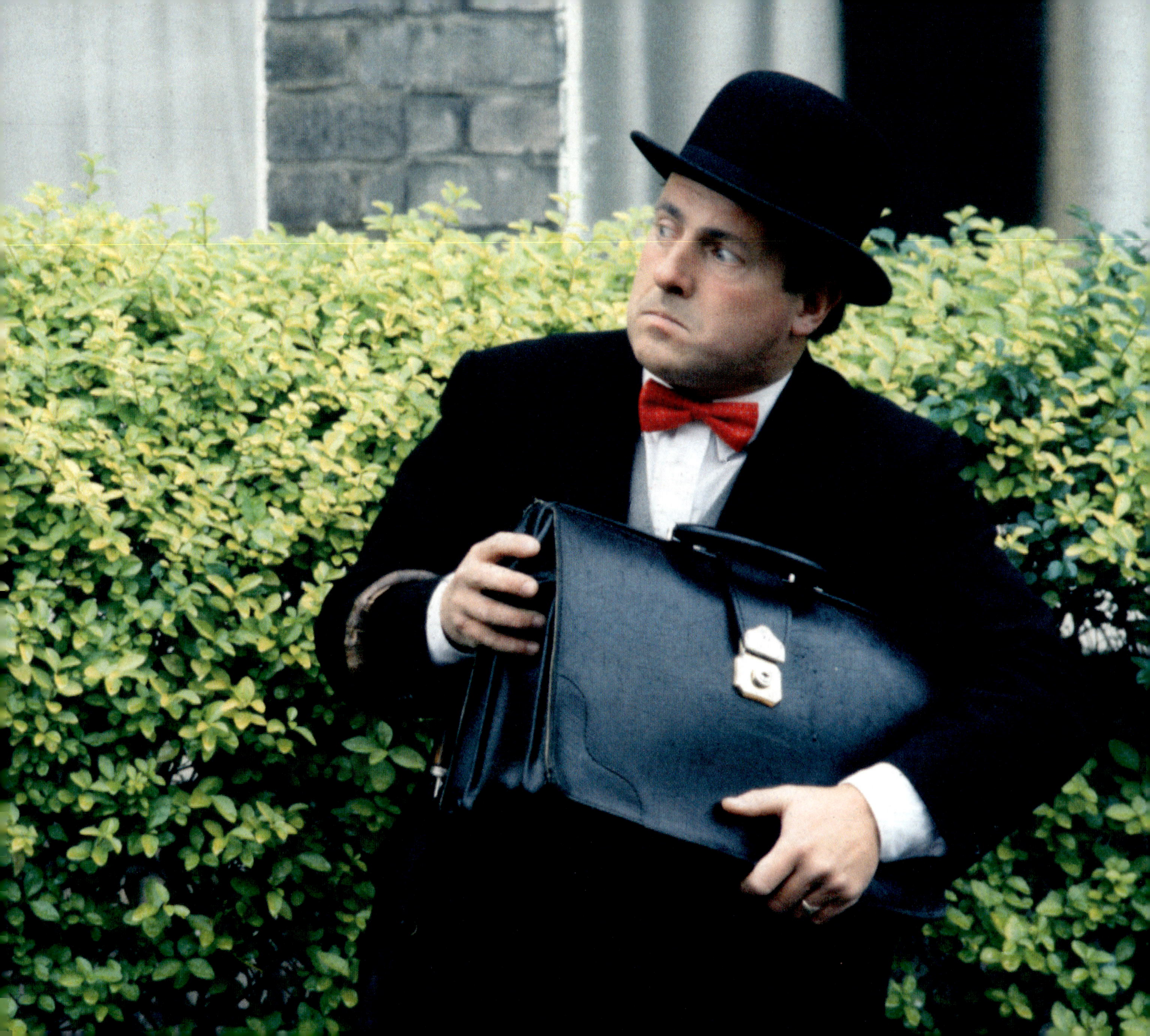

# CHAPTER 10

# ENDING AND NEW BEGINNINGS 1979

**BAW closed but lived on in the Natural Theatre and the Printshop; and community arts took root across the UK. Resource conservation and eco-activism gathered momentum and became essential for planetary survival. A creative flame still burns brightly in Walcot… and the door is ever open for something else to happen.**

**Tory:** As we moved into the second half of the decade, the Arts Workshop and *Natural Theatre Company* (NTC) were thriving but limited by lack of space and funding. The Printshop had found other premises and continued to operate successfully into the early 1980s. Yet of necessity, our community arts and theatre activities were still being run from our cramped shop and office. This challenging situation led to one last attempt to acquire a permanent space for the arts and theatre, a dream we had long held but foregone with our move from the Organ Factory in 1973. Sadly it was not to be and BAW was closed in late 1981.

The Workshop's legacy was nevertheless deep rooted and multifarious. The theatre company moved to new premises in Widcombe, from where it continues to perform in the UK and across the globe. Many former BAW members went on to develop community and performance work across the country and the need for art that is relevant to local communities was recognised by the British arts establishment. Comtek's pioneering forays into community technology were prototypes for many later initiatives and its protagonists contributed to the adoption of greener policies in the UK and beyond. The resource-conserving social enterprises that emerged in the wake of Comtek – notably Walcot Reclamation and John's Bikes – flourished for a couple of decades more, providing useful services and employment for many. And in Walcot, residents, artists, activists, musicians and performers went on to set up a myriad of events and activities, some of which are still going strong today.

## What might have been

**Ralph Oswick:** In early 1977, Corinne and I initiated an ambitious project to take over Ladymead House, a large premises in Walcot Street, and convert it into an arts and performance space. The building was jointly owned by Bath City Council and the St John's Trust, and was at the time a

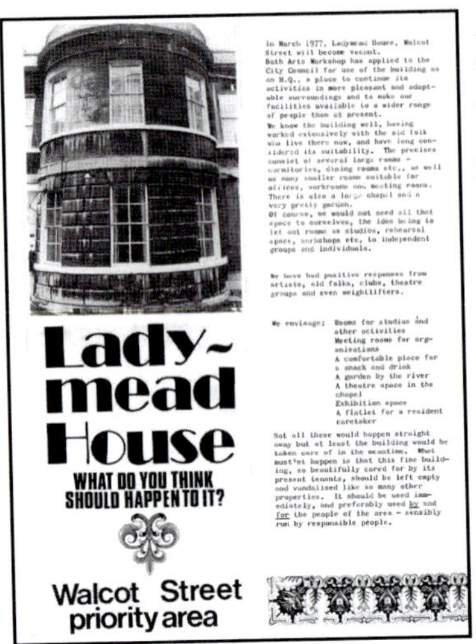



home for mentally vulnerable but active elderly women. It had a riverside garden and a spacious first floor chapel with rose windows, as well as numerous other rooms spread over three floors, and the lease was due for renewal in March.

**Corinne:** We set up a committee of local people and produced a silver brochure setting out our plans, accompanied by detailed and beautiful three-dimensional drawings by architect Glyn Davies showing how the building could be used.[1] We visualised a wonderful multi-purpose venue housing us and other community groups and artists, with a theatre in the chapel, a cafe and a large courtyard garden. Also listed as possible uses were film and video and recording studios, meeting rooms, artists' studios, exhibition and rehearsal spaces and even residential flats for building caretakers. Income would be earned by renting out the spaces, and local artists and organisations were invited to put forward their requests.

**Ralph:** The plans were also laminated onto Formica boards by the delightful Mr Saffrey who had a tablemat factory in the street (typical Walcot), and then they disappeared into the labyrinthine corridors of power at the Guildhall. A councillor later told me, 'We didn't really know what to do with them'.

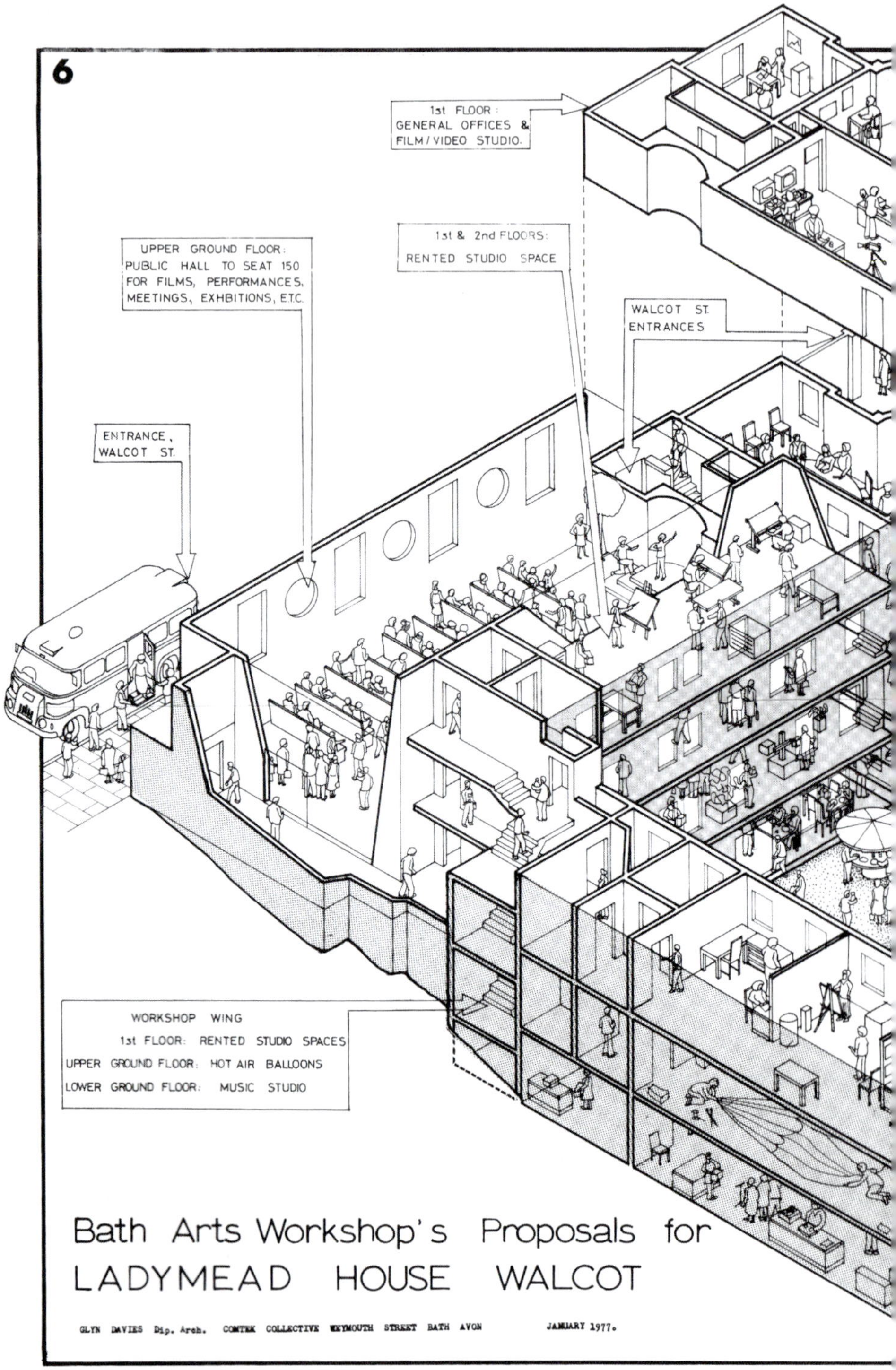

1. The smart, mirror-bound proposal was also submitted to the Queen's Silver Jubilee programme.

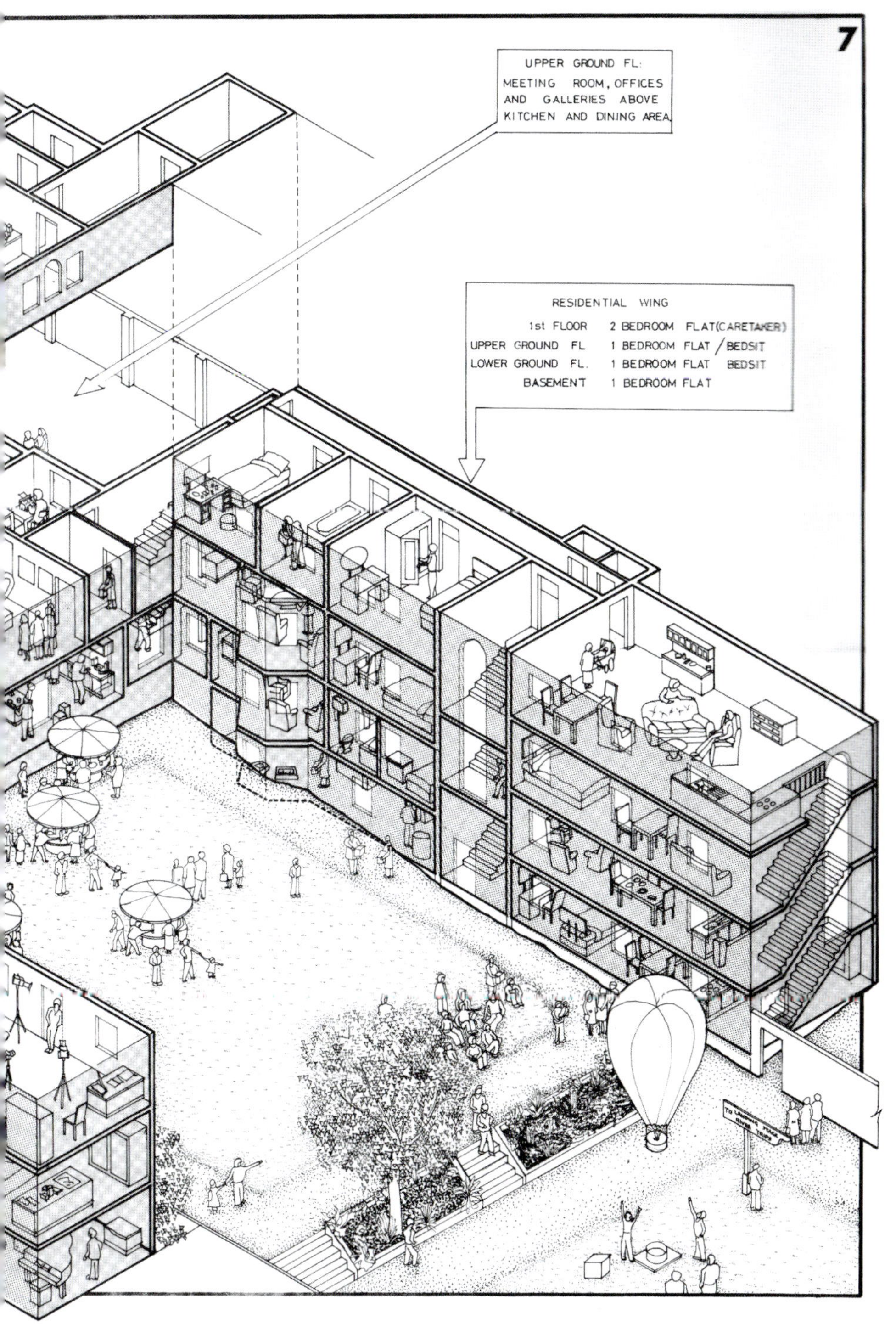


**Ralph:** Phil came back from his job in east London to support us on the day we pitched our proposal to the city council. Sadly, and despite the obvious benefits of a multi-use arts space in Walcot, our proposal was turned down. The building was eventually converted into sheltered accommodation and latterly developed into gated luxury retirement flats. The chapel became a particularly chic open-plan loft style apartment. The Ladymead ladies, who had been among our most enthusiastic supporters, moved to Bristol where they went on to live independent lives in more modern sheltered homes.

## The end of Bath Arts Workshop

**Corinne:** Would Ladymead have been a successful project? It is impossible to say from this standpoint. What is certain is that if we had gone ahead it would have set the future of the Workshop on a different course altogether, and perhaps one that was truer to our original intention – an arts and performance space accessible to all. As it was, the rejection came at a time when a turning point loomed on the horizon. By then the ***Natural Theatre Company*** was travelling further afield, touring nationally and in Europe, winning prizes and receiving rave reviews for its street theatre work.

**Ralph:** Realistically we couldn't continue to run our community arts activities and support summer festivals alongside our expanding theatre work, which had become the main focus of our activities and funding. Some of the more successful local community projects were surviving more or less independently, with some set for permanent

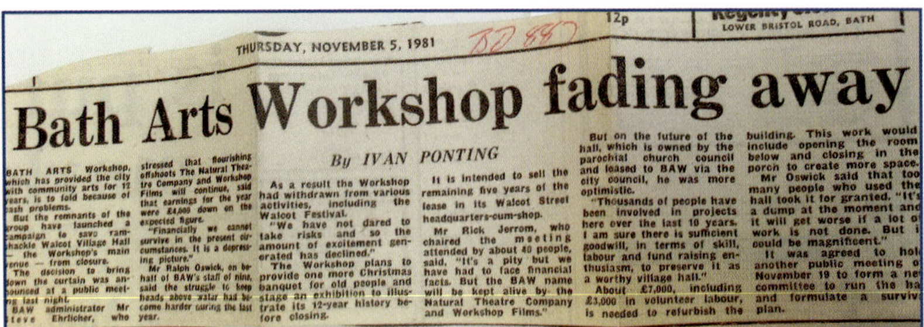

THURSDAY, NOVEMBER 5, 1981

# Bath Arts Workshop fading away

### By IVAN PONTING

BATH ARTS Workshop, which has provided the city with community arts for 12 years, is to fold because of cash problems.

But the remnants of the group have launched a campaign to save ramshackle Walcot Village Hall — the Workshop's main venue — from closure.

The decision to bring down the curtain was announced at a public meeting last night.

BAW administrator Mr Steve Ehrlicher, who stressed that flourishing offshoots The Natural Theatre Company and Workshop Films will continue, said that earnings for the year were £4,000 down on the expected figure.

"Financially we cannot survive in the present circumstances. It is a depressing picture."

Mr Ralph Oswick, on behalf of BAW's staff of nine, said the struggle to keep heads above water had become harder during the last year.

As a result the Workshop had withdrawn from various activities, including the Walcot Festival.

"We have not dared to take risks and so the amount of excitement generated has declined."

The Workshop plans to provide one more Christmas banquet for old people and stage an exhibition to illustrate its 12-year history before closing.

It is intended to sell the remaining five years of the lease in its Walcot Street headquarters-cum-shop.

Mr Rick Jerrom, who chaired the meeting attended by about 40 people, said, "It's a pity but we have had to face financial facts. But the BAW name will be kept alive by the Natural Theatre Company and Workshop Films."

But on the future of the hall, which is owned by the parochial church council and leased to BAW via the city council, he was more optimistic.

"Thousands of people have been involved in projects here over the last 10 years. I am sure there is sufficient goodwill, in terms of skill, labour and fund raising enthusiasm, to preserve it as a worthy village hall."

About £7,000, including £3,000 in volunteer labour, is needed to refurbish the building. This work would include opening the room below and closing in the porch to create more space.

Mr Oswick said that too many people who used the hall took it for granted. "It's a dump at the moment and it will get worse if a lot of work is not done. But it could be magnificent."

It was agreed to hold another public meeting on November 19 to form a new committee to run the hall and formulate a survival plan.

future development. Others were exciting flashes in the pan that stood in their own right. Within the Workshop itself, people had moved on, got jobs and had babies. Of course the need for community arts projects did not disappear and there was much we could have opted to support and develop. But in the end, a combination of all the above resulted in our decision to close the BAW as a public-facing organisation, although its charity status and the basic aims of the original constitution were preserved where possible. The Bath Arts Workshop closed at a public meeting in the Village Hall on Wednesday 4 November 1981.

## How the Naturals survived

**Ralph:** And so the *Natural Theatre Company* moved away from Walcot. We temporarily occupied several premises. They included the attic of the Little Cinema (then only accessible by pulley) and the lower portion of Harvest Wholefood's storage facility. Eventually, we drew up plans for the refurbishment of both the Old Bakery in Twerton and the Harvest warehouse in Widcombe, known as Widcombe Institute, and submitted them to the Lottery Fund. Ours was one of the first ever complete projects to make a successful application and, of the two possibilities, Widcombe Institute was chosen because it had the potential for community involvement. Thus the dream of creating a street theatre factory was achieved, and the NTC became an institution in its own right, having the unique profile of being a world-renowned touring company whilst also linked to its local community in Widcombe. It has since played an important role in the regeneration of that neighbourhood.

> **Jackie Popay:** I have worked with the Natural Theatre Company for 50 years. Touring the world, making people laugh and creating the absurd. At the age of 70 I am still performing and teaching young people to have dreams. Thank you BAW.

**Ralph:** The Naturals grew ever bigger, with up to four street theatre teams and an indoor musical stage tour touring worldwide at any time. The NTC has travelled all over the world, from Chippenham to China and from Keynsham to Kazakhstan (with dozens more in between). In this way, I always believed that the theatre company upheld the original concepts of BAW in almost everything it did. Nearly 50 years later it still does, in the form of accessible arts, an eye for detail, a search for new ways of looking and above all a sense of fun. In addition, many of those concepts will have been preserved in countless other projects across the land in big or small ways. So when I stood up, shaking of hand and quavering of voice in Walcot Village Hall to announce the demise of BAW, I wasn't entirely correct.

# THE MALE GAZE

Phil: To quote Ralph, 'new ways of looking' and 'having fun' were certainly some of the hallmarks of our experiences in the 70s. But what part did gender politics play? Several contributors to this book have spoken eloquently about how it was to be a woman in BAW, and it feels important to say something about how it was to be a man. Notwithstanding our progressive aspirations of the day, and writing with the benefit of hindsight, I have to say that sexist assumptions existed in the Workshop.

Although there were highly capable women involved right from the start, this in itself was not enough to ensure that we achieved genuine gender parity. Helena Kennedy, in her book *Eve Was Framed,* says that *'treating as equal those who are unequal does not produce equality'.* We needed to be talking about *'substantive equality which acknowledges the historic imbalances between men and women'.*[2] But were we having those debates? Certainly, they were touched on sometimes in the so-called 'psychodramas' we organised in the early days, and informally doubtless on many occasions throughout the decade. But as Kennedy also observed, *'It is often the way with discriminatory practice that its victims know full well what is happening whilst those who perpetrate it are oblivious'.* Was it perhaps too easy for us men to remain conveniently unconcerned, to avoid thinking about and unpacking those contradictions? While we embraced the counterculture's confidence that we were building a society that could be free, and what Mark Fisher has described as *'A new humanity, a new seeing, a new thinking, a new loving',* did we significantly underestimate the work we would have to do on ourselves to ensure that this could happen?[3] Despite supporting the Women's Liberation movement of the day, did we men fail to sufficiently heed the core message that *'self-awareness, or naming one's problems, was (necessarily) the first step to radical collective awareness'?* (Ambrose op.cit). I had a lot of learning as well as unlearning to do for sure – it has been a life-long process.

**Brian:** We were all thrown together, almost by accident. For me this was the most exciting and thrilling time of my life. But, politically and sexually naive, I found that the abundance of bright and beautiful young women around me really 'blew my mind'. We had to learn how to get on, how to share, and how to work and live together. Feminist ideas were taking shape and would only later take form and meaning in the pretty rigid male psyches that they were encountering.

---

2. Kennedy, Helena 1993, *Eve Was Framed*, pp. 4 and 14, Vintage Books, London.
3. Ambrose, Darren (ed.) 2018, *Acid Communism (Unfinished Introduction)* in *K-punk, The Collected and Unpublished Writings of Mark Fisher (2004-2016)*, p. 767, Repeater Books, London.

## Eco-activism and reclamation

**Tory:** Meanwhile the skills, services and community technology resources developed by Comtek during the 1970s were transformative both in spirit and in their application to daily life. And their influence has continued to resonate to the present day. Comtek was the first city collective to support communities to harvest wind and solar energy, produce food organically and reuse building materials. Other alternative rural technology and urban architecture groups existed but none with comparable scope. Comtek was thus an early catalyst for a community energy movement that gathered strength throughout the 1980s and 90s and is now significant in moving towards large-scale community-based zero carbon electricity supply. Comtek's architects additionally helped stem the wanton demolition of Bath's 18th century housing. Its campaigns contributed to a national shift in planning policy and recognition of the need to preserve the city's unique architectural heritage. Among other developments, Thornton Kay went on to set up Salvo, which successfully campaigned for the reuse of reclaimed building materials in the UK. Salvo is now part of an EU project to encourage greater reuse of building materials and reduce climate change.

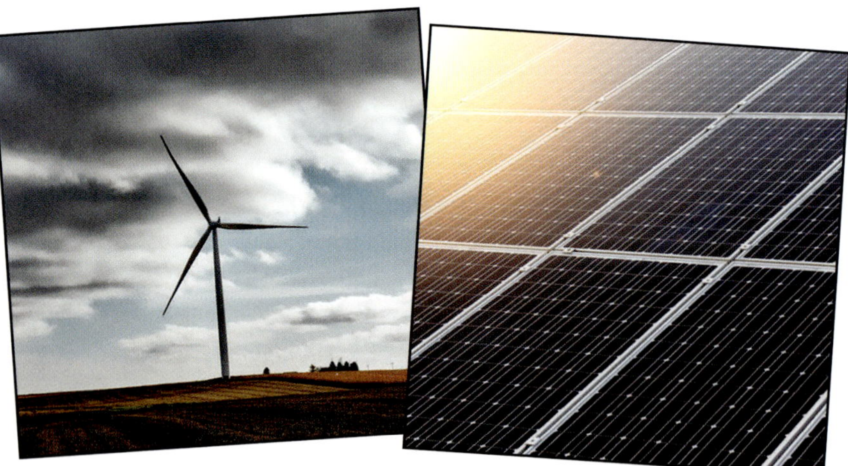

**Rick Knapp:** Walcot Reclamation in its turn pioneered the reclamation and resale of historic building materials retrieved from demolition sites, creating a thriving market for architectural salvage. It also provided workshop space for craftspeople involved in restoring marble, wood, iron and other materials, alongside studios for local artists, thereby serving as a base and a source of income for those who worked there. During the 80s, the business expanded greatly, at one time employing around 30 people, and attracting clients nationally and internationally, a process that was encouraged by profiles in *The World of Interiors* and other style magazines. As the decade went on, the yard continued to be successful, attracting the interest of and a visit by the Prince of Wales! Post millennium, however, interest in the 'old' gradually fell away and the business succumbed to the crash of 2009 after 33 years of activity.

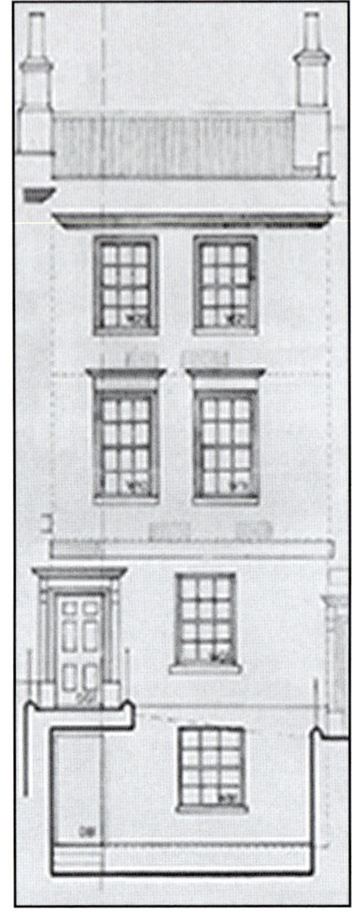

## Bicycle revolution

**Tory:** John Potter first encountered BAW while cooking for the 1973 summer festival and he never looked back. As well as being a regular performer with the **Natural Theatre Company**, and Christmas chef *par excellence,* John went on to play a massive role in promoting cycling locally and nationally. John's Bikes rose from humble beginnings at the Comtek depot to become a flourishing shop in Walcot Street, where it was in business until it closed in 2018.

John and others were among the first to establish large scale charity bike rides via a separate company Bike Events (along with Janie Howard, Margot Richardson and Phil Shepherd). Robert Stredder of **Groundwell Farm** cooperative had set up the first **London to Brighton Bike Ride** in 1975 (with 36 people that year). John joined the ride in 1976, and the following year Bike Events took on organising and running this event. They withdrew some years later but the ride itself

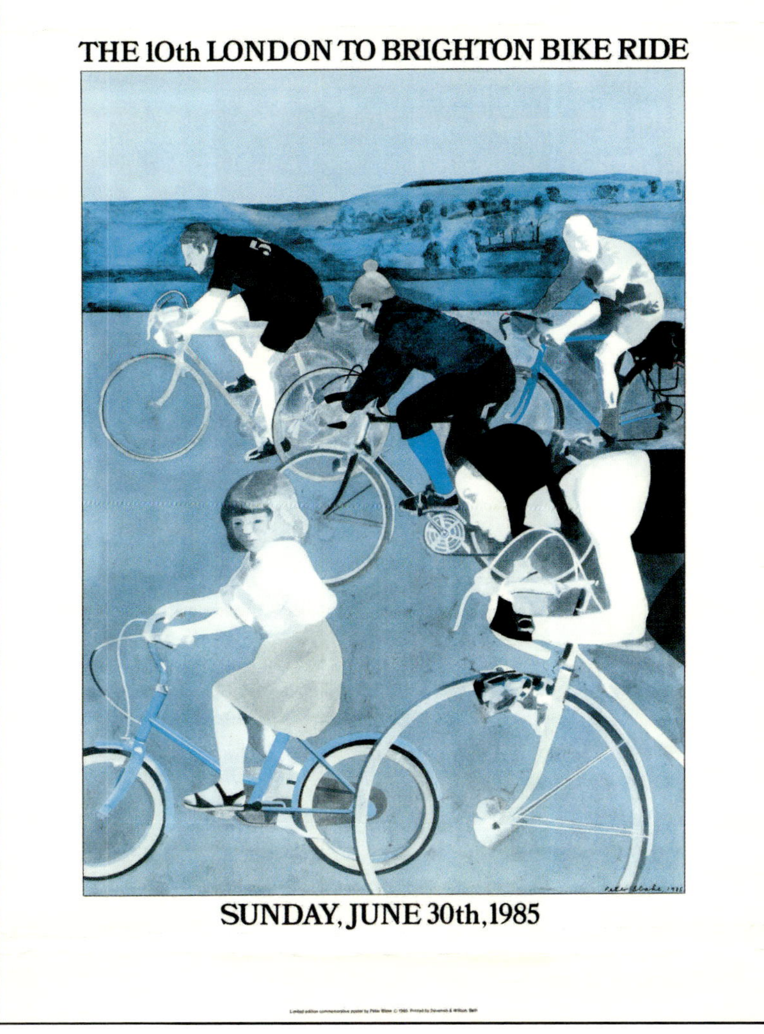



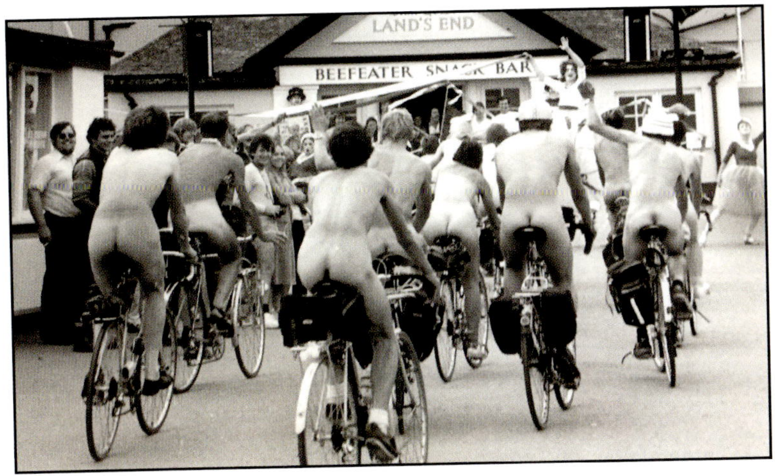

Great British Bike Ride at Land's End

survived. Today, it is the biggest in the world. Some 15,000 cyclists take part annually and it has raised millions of pounds for the British Heart Foundation and other charities.

In the summer of 1982, some 200 cyclists joined the **Great British Bike Ride**, a wild, adventurous journey from John O'Groats to Land's End to fundraise for Friends of the

Earth. Again organised by Bike Events, five more took place over the next decade. (After the first year, it started at Land's End so the prevailing winds were behind the cyclists rather than battering them in the face.) It took two weeks and was a huge operation, involving a complicated route, almost all on minor roads, several vans for tents and luggage and a big field kitchen (Magnus MacDonald was in charge of that). We dug latrines at each campsite and covered them over before leaving the following morning. Ralph and I were *Art on the Run* on the first one, popping up as smart bigots or enthusiastic birdwatchers or some such. At the end of the first ride, a group of cyclists rode naked into Land's End – a tradition that continued thereafter.

Today, there are many sponsored bike rides across the UK and thousands of people cycle to work every day. Cycling is firmly on the political agenda and, although woefully inadequate, some cities have built cycle lanes to promote health and reduce air pollution.

## Walcot, a nation of the mind

**John Wood:** The Workshop's heyday was in its time and of its time, but it was unique and exceptional all the same, and everyone involved in those days knew it. I think it certainly changed things for many of the people who were involved in it, myself included – the musicians, the theatrical folk, the kids on the adventure playground, the cycling tribes, the ones who worked

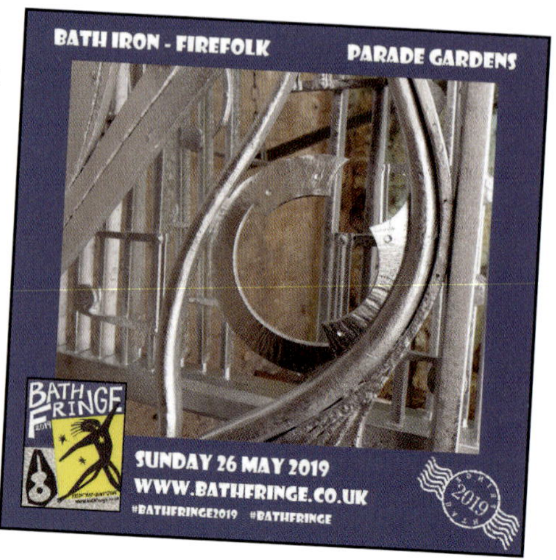


at Comtek and Walcot Reclamation and many others. I think it gave lots of us encouragement to be confident in our abilities and our creativity. And it did foster a community spirit that still lingers. Everything didn't stop dead on 4 November 1981. The Village Hall continued as a venue until the 90s. I organised a final Beano Club there in 1988 for Comic Relief. The churches took over the Workshop's idea of the Christmas dinner, and it's still going.

After the 1980 summer festival, we discussed changing the format and running events as a fringe to the International Music Festival, as in Edinburgh, instead of one big event at a different time of year. And that did happen from 1981, first as a semi-official council funded thing. The council pulled out ten years later but, just as before, Wendy Matthews and others thought it must go on and set out to do it themselves. *Bath Fringe Festival* is still going and Wendy is still there. The Fringe mounted a big Walcot Nation Day event in Walcot Street as part

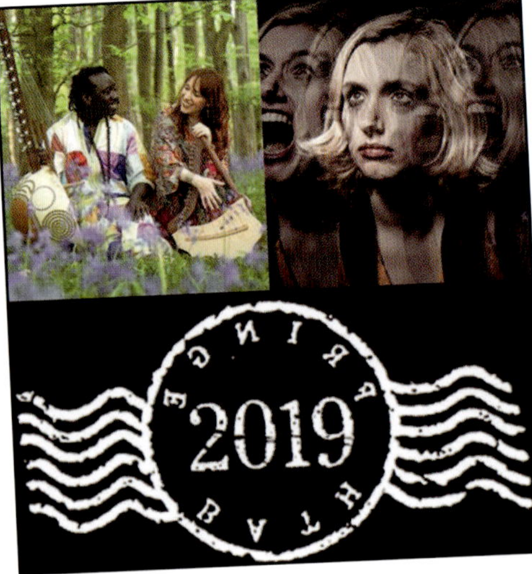

of the 1997 festival and for several years thereafter, with Walcot passports issued once again. In 2013 we, the citizens of Walcot, bought The Bell Inn in a community buy-out when the owner, Ian Wood, decided to sell up. That too is now a cooperative – and as successful as it was in private ownership. Walcot Nationalisation!

### The Bell Inn

**Steve Henwood (of Bath Fringe):** The Bell was a long-established arts/muso hang out in Walcot Street, with a reputation for jazz from trad to modern-ish, under the tutelage of John Bradshaw. Another landlord, Ian Wood, who first rented The Hat & Feather, was also a catalyst here. In a few short years, he had bought The Bell and the Hub nightclub (an artistic mecca itself in its heyday). By then, he was making 3-wheel cycles as Cycles Maximus, initially in the pub's outbuildings. Ian supported and took part in setting up the Bath Fringe, and during the 80s many festival-style Walcot Nation events were run out of and mostly by customers, staff and associates of The Hat and The Bell. The Hat closed in the early 90s but the Bell as a freehold free house remained and retained its strong reputation for free (and independently promoted and funded) music events, with Arts Workshop veterans holding court at the bar, and a variety of endeavours about the place and in the back garden: printing enthusiasts, circus performers, film makers and an Internet Cafe (ahead of the curve there), as well as the Bath Fringe office and store. The sale of the pub to 536 community members was one of the quickest buyouts ever. The Bell is revolutionary in a quieter way than its predecessors, but still a flourishing concern where, we believe, the spirit of Walcot remains strong.

## Community arts legacy

**Phil:** BAW had a 'long tail' indeed, spawning many arts projects and activities. Of course it was not alone. The world of western arts and culture (as well as wider society) was profoundly influenced by the wider counterculture of the 1970s. The emergence of the community arts movement, of which BAW was seen to be a pioneering example, heralded the birth of a more inclusive and collaborative creative landscape. Work generated from these principles has gone on to thrive ever since (albeit intermittently) on streets and housing estates, at festivals and in community venues and theatres across the land. It has been informed by a countercultural generosity of spirit and carries the implicit intention of giving voice to community aspiration, especially to those on the margins of the mainstream.



It's taken many years for arts funding policies to fully recognise the value generated by work of this kind, perhaps because the work itself is grounded in a challenge to the elitism that still holds sway in parts of the establishment and wider society. The flowering of community arts in Bath was particularly potent, facilitated by the confluence

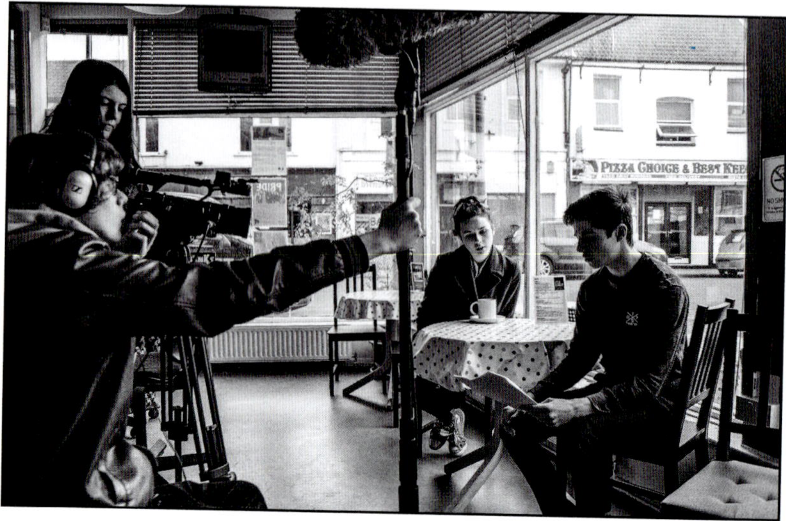

Somerset Film, led by Phil Shepherd, 1995-2020

in a short time of many creative minds and energies in a beautiful city which seemed to naturally lend itself to providing the perfect crucible for a gentle revolution, and which embraced (or at least tolerated) it. [4]

Many BAW-related people went on to further develop work in community and performing arts over the following decades.[5] Among those who did so are Corinne D'Cruz and Mick Banks who founded ***British Events***, a theatre company combining visual humour with sound and pyrotechnic

---

4. Resistance to our work by the then director of South West Arts Association is reflected in correspondence records available at the Victoria and Albert Museum. A more progressive approach to arts funding did eventually occur. Nigel Leach contributed to a meeting of the new Arts Council UK community arts working group in 1975, and was Vice Chair of its first Community Arts Panel from 1976.
5. Brief biographies of the ex-BAW members who created this publication are included at the end of the book.

effects. Mitch and Andy Webster founded ***Original Mixture Theatre*** 'international theatre animation and surrealism of the everyday'. Nigel Leach became arts officer for Yorkshire and Rolande Thomas ran an art gallery alongside his community arts practice before becoming an arts officer for the Welsh Arts Council.

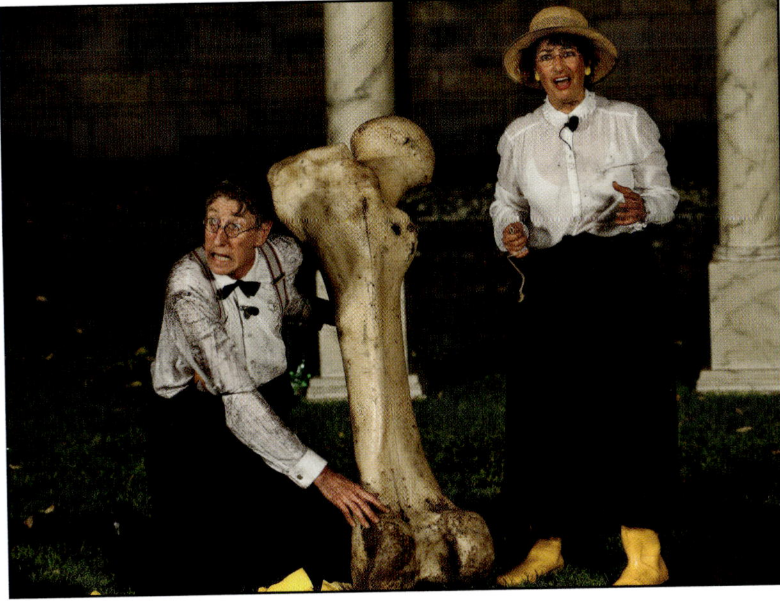

Mick and Corinne

Nicky Millican produced ***Théâtre de Complicité*** in Edinburgh. Ros Rigby (née Birks) co-founded Folkworks in 1988 and became the Performance Programme Director at the Sage Gateshead, being awarded an OBE in 1999. Louise Osborn became a writer, director and teacher in theatre, TV and radio, and was artistic director of ***Theatre Powys*** for twelve years, as well as working in schools and with refugees. Finally, the Mountview Academy of Theatre Arts in Peckham, now runs an MA in 'site-specific performance' – a far cry indeed from our early bold anarchic ventures all those years ago, but nevertheless a recognition of the need for art that is accessible to all.

## Afterword

Bath Arts Workshop was inspired by the counterculture of the 1960s and 70s – a transformative social movement that rejected materialism and deference to established authority across the western world. The counterculture as a whole was anti-war and supported the first strivings for alternative technologies to protect the planet. In the UK, it triggered a questioning of our country's imperialist history – the need to confront the sins of the past and to honestly rethink our ethos and position in the world. It rejected racism and embraced the idea of sexual freedom and equality between men and women.

We in the Workshop interpreted the counterculture in our own unique ways. We were never explicitly political although we certainly challenged (and often flouted) the status quo in order to bring about incremental change. We accommodated people's different views, and often discussed them, but in the end our collective striving for practical action usually prevailed and humour was the glue that held us together. We were committed to conserving the earth's resources and addressing pollution. And at the heart of it all, our conviction that art could be a part of life that touched and transformed everyone for the better.

We shared a yearning to find a place where we could fit in and contribute to a more positive and collaborative world. To quote the historian Theodore Roszak, we were certainly about 'creating opportunities for learning and self-expression'. And like the beat poets, some of us sought to create positive change by building an art that was authentic, that truly reflected the conditions of life – physical, emotional, spiritual – as we lived it. What also brought us together, perhaps unknowingly, was what Allen Ginsberg described as a 'state of emotional and intellectual exhaustion, being open to some other awareness, some deeper perception'. The beat, in his words, of the heart.

Being part of the Workshop helped us to grow personally in ways that might otherwise not have happened. We were a group of people from different backgrounds who gave each other strength and encouragement to live and work differently and strive for social change. Those of us who left travelled off in numerous directions to achieve a multiplicity of ends – from eco-architecture professorships, to setting up schools in Nepal. Many of us have also gone on to lead lives rooted in the performing and creative arts and industries which, despite being the fastest growing part of the UK economy, remain undervalued. This is especially true in the education system, where the arts have been shamefully and short-sightedly marginalised in recent years.

Between us all, we achieved a surprising amount in a short time and our story in its way refutes a narrative that is often recounted of that era – that the 60s revolution achieved

**Phil Shepherd, founder of BAW:** My 1969 letter to Bath City Council proposed making creative opportunities available *to as many people as possible… to provide a valuable contribution to the life of the community and an ideal outlet for local talent'.* We worked hard to make it happen and we were lucky. The social and economic climate was more on our side in the early 70s and, once we'd built momentum, we were able to sustain the energies through most of the later challenges of the decade. This was a project that started with a few of us but grew to be owned and directed by many. It represented a moment of freedom that is resonant today as compassion and resistance return to the fore in the face of global adversity.

little and ended in hedonism, drugs and despair. Our legacy stands. Bath Arts Workshop was a remarkably supportive and generative organisation, sharing a rich spirit of creativity and social enterprise with other community initiatives of the period. Many of the organisations spawned by BAW and Comtek continued for years, providing employment and enriching life in Bath and elsewhere.

We hold true to our belief that creativity can help us envision a different life and that collectively we have the power to realise a freer, more egalitarian world. In the words of the great counterculture novelist Kurt Vonnegut: 'You probably won't win if you try to do things that everyone around you tells you are impossible. But at the same time, it's the only way to go. Give it a go! You might win.'

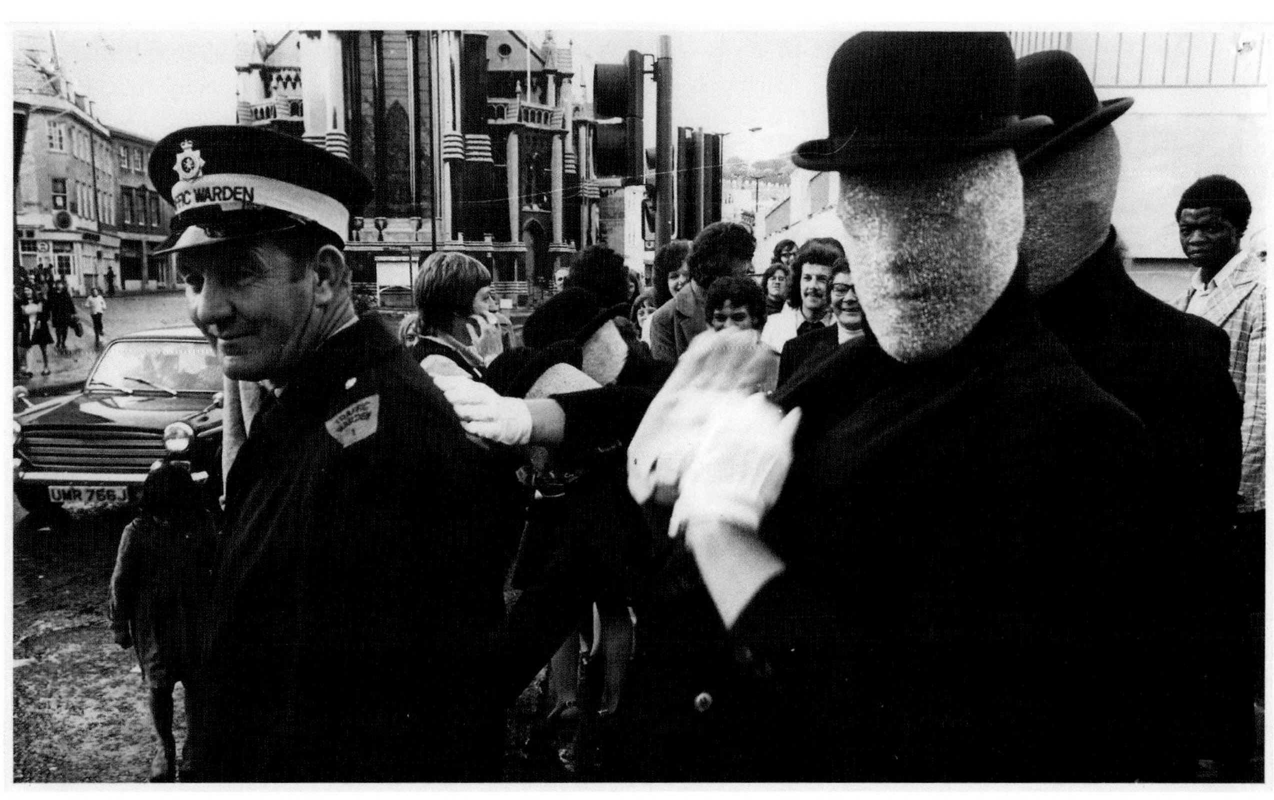

It was 1974. I was 18 when I clambered out of my bedroom window. I met a boy from the village and told him I was leaving home. He gave me a kiss on the cheek, a pound note, and told me to be careful. I walked briskly over the fields until I was standing on the A46. I had very little with me. Only the clothes I stood up in and a small handbag. I felt tough as I was embarking on an adventure which was largely under my control. A friendly lift came quite quickly and I told the driver I was heading to Bath. He left me on the London Road, which I walked along marvelling at the beauty of the architecture. I knew this was a place I would love. I felt good. I was wearing my long, home-made purple paisley skirt, my great grandmother's purple velvet jacket and my blue suede desert boots.

Those boots took me to Walcot Street, where I encountered a brightly painted shop. I had felt like a fish out of water at home with my crazy creative brain!  Now I was beginning to feel something else, a sense of belonging and safety which I had never felt before. I realised this was Bath Arts Workshop and went in. Upstairs, I found several people sitting around a large table covered in books, papers and mugs of tea. They asked me if I had anywhere to stay. I said no, and they directed me to 6 Hanover Street, where Nigel and others lived. They said anyone could stay there if there was room.

My memories of that year in Hanover Street are akin to looking back at a happy childhood. I felt accepted. Without the concern, guidance and foresight of the people at Bath Arts Workshop that day, my stay in Bath might not have been so safe, happy and secure. So, thank you all from the bottom of my heart.

~ Sarah Cashel, on discovering and living in Bath

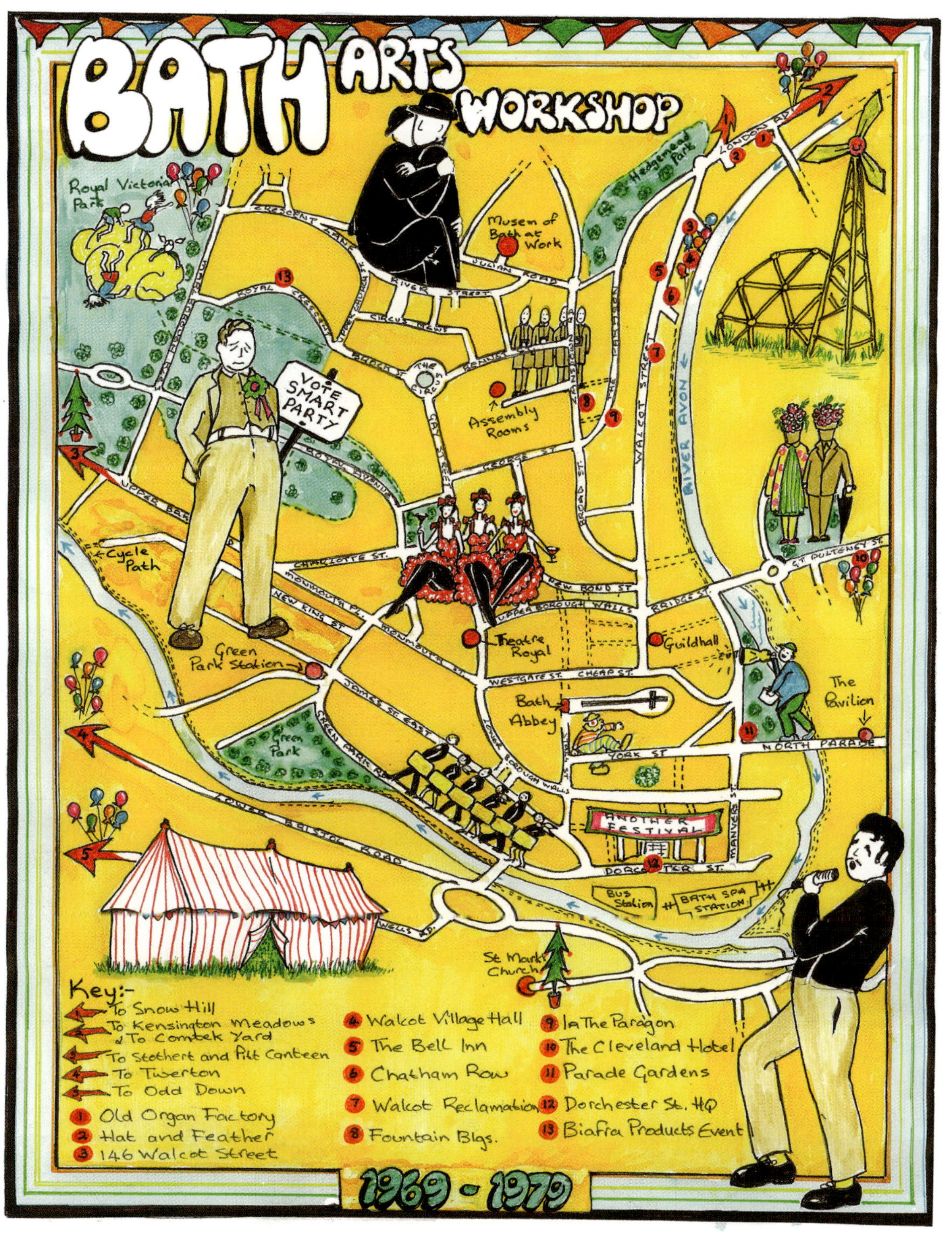

BATH ARTS WORKSHOP
Royal Victoria Park
Musem of Bath at Work
Hedgemead Park
LONDON RD
VOTE SMART PARTY
Assembly Rooms
Cycle Path
Green Park Station
Theatre Royal
Guildhall
The Pavilion
Bath Abbey
ANOTHER FESTIVAL
Bus Station
BATH SPA STATION
St Mark's Church
RIVER AVON
WALCOT STREET
GT PULTENEY ST
NORTH PARADE
NEW BOND ST
WESTGATE ST
CHEAP ST
YORK ST
MANVERS ST
DORCHESTER ST
Green Park
Key:-
To Snow Hill
To Kensington Meadows
To Comdek Yard
To Stothert and Pitt Canteen
To Tiverton
To Odd Down
1  Old Organ Factory
2  Hat and Feather
3  146 Walcot Street
4  Walcot Village Hall
5  The Bell Inn
6  Chatham Row
7  Walcot Reclamation
8  Fountain Blgs.
9  In The Paragon
10  The Cleveland Hotel
11  Parade Gardens
12  Dorchester St. HQ
13  Biafra Products Event
1969 - 1979

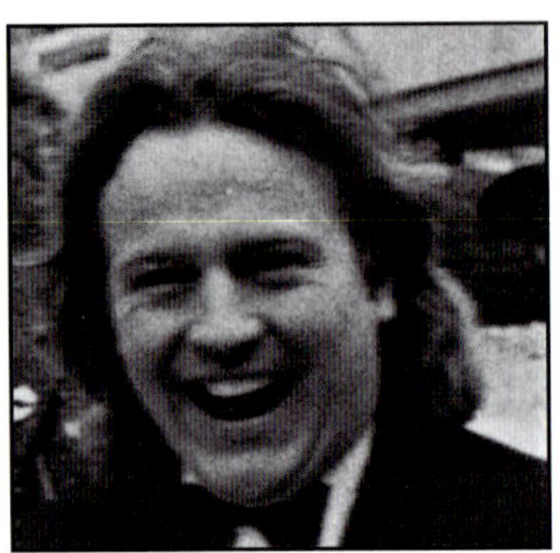

Before BAW, **Brian Popay** studied at Bath Academy of Art and graduated in 1969. He spent the next 40 years mainly with the Workshop and the Natural Theatre Company. He has two children, one aged 45, the other 25 and he lives in Frome. After leaving the Naturals, Brian formed his own performance company, Fine Artistes, in 2009. Despite attending kidney dialysis three times a week, he still finds time to 'keep his hand in' on the performance front.

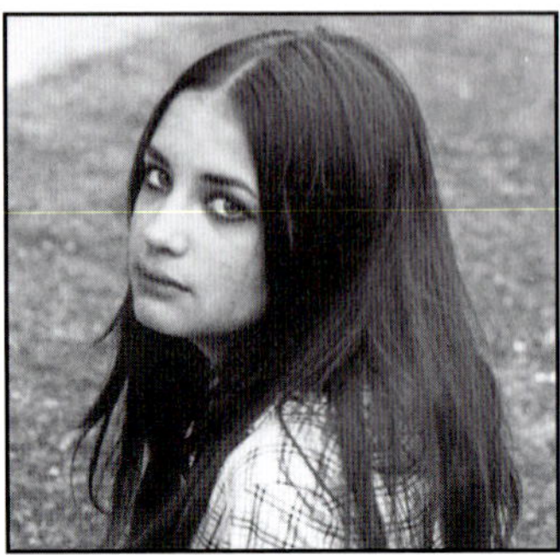

**Corinne D'Cruz** later formed British Events Theatre Company with Mick Banks, an artistic partnership that lives on to this day. Performances are often informed by particular interests and preoccupations, using visual imagery, special effects and humour. Corinne has performed and run teaching projects all over the world, escaping Thatcher's Britain in 1988 to base the company in Germany for 25 years, where she was a founder member of the Federal Association for Theatre in Public Spaces. She continues to believe in the power of the arts to transform reality.

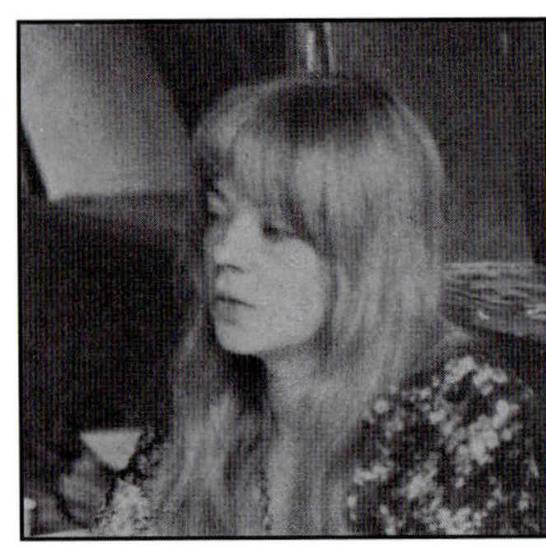

**Jennie Potter-Barrie** worked in a private residential school for severely disturbed boys then went on to mainstream schools to work with children with differing needs. With two jobs and three children she managed to get a first class honours degree in Psychology at the OU, followed by a teaching degree and further special needs qualifications. Jennie feels privileged to have worked with so many courageous children. She has two sons, a daughter, a daughter-in-law and three grandsons – her greatest joy. She is now learning to play guitar, rather badly!

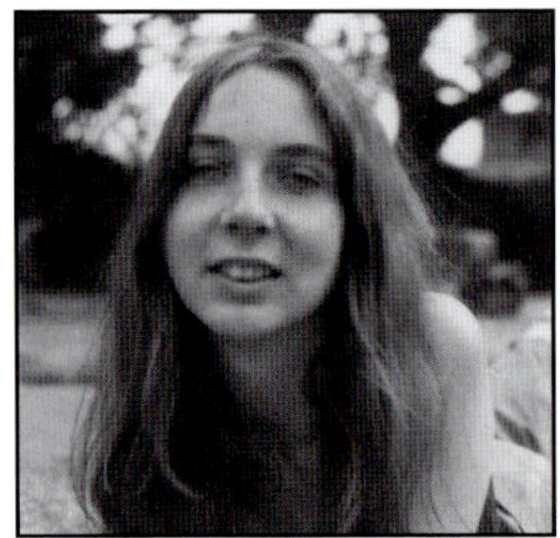

**Penny Dale** studied Fine Art in Exeter, then worked in theatre design and with an alternative technology cooperative. Penny is now a well-known author and illustrator of children's books, with over 30 titles published since 1986. She has produced sessions and workshops in schools, festivals and galleries, as well as collaborating on reading initiatives and group exhibitions. She met her husband at the 1976 Sunshine Festival and they now live in South Wales. They have a daughter and a grandson.

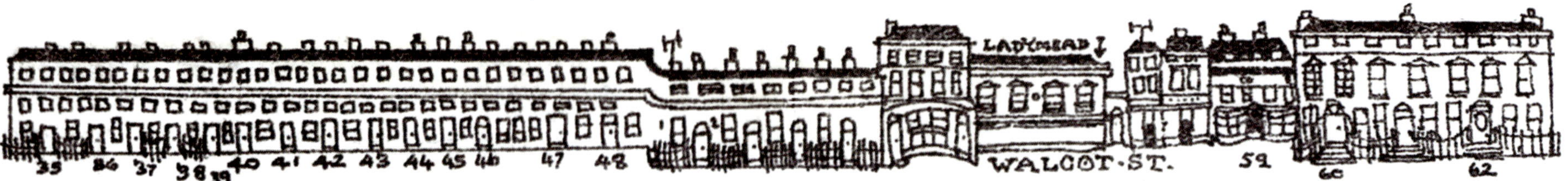

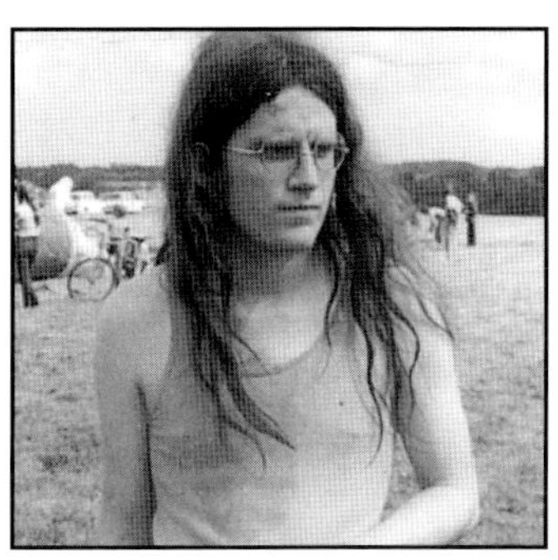

After travelling in South America, **Phil Shepherd** worked in the arts and film in Tower Hamlets, Bristol and New York. He became a Dad in 1985, helped establish the London to Brighton Bike Rides, studied at Bournemouth Film School and worked in documentary production at BBC Children's TV. In 1995, Phil set up an educational charity, Somerset Film, establishing the Engine Room media centre in 2003. Just now he's finishing an OU humanities degree and loving it.

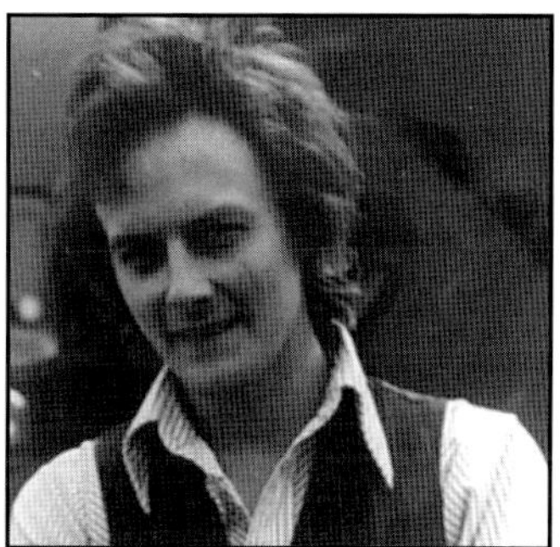

In the 1980s, **Thornton Kay** ran a salvage yard, made a car run on wood, and persuaded the Bath MP and then Environment Minister, Chris Patten, to include reclamation and reuse in the UK planning system. In the 1990s, he co-founded Salvo with Hazel Matravers, moved to France, Ireland and Northumberland and started an annual fair promoting reuse. Salvo now has a global impact helping reduce climate change and is a partner in a major EU project to increase reuse of reclaimed building materials.

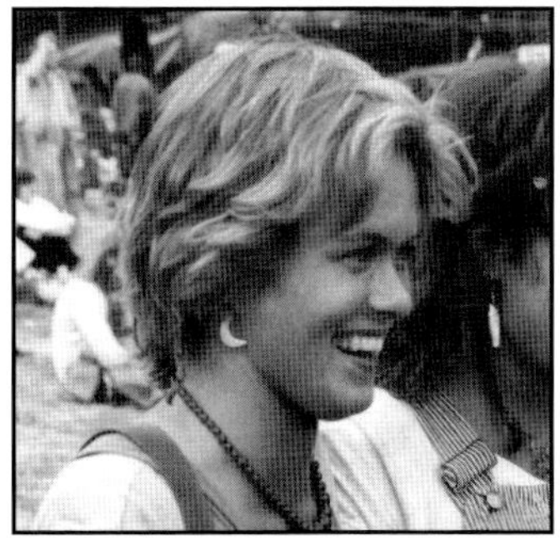

Aged 25, **Victoria (Tory) Forbes Adam** went to university then spent a year in a Mexican town researching for her social anthropology PhD. In the 1980s, she had a research job at Amnesty International's London HQ. Tory went on to spend six years working on human rights and living in Haiti (a country full of artists). She came back to London in 2001 with her daughter and joined an organisation working to end the use of child soldiers. Lately, Tory has been learning about group dynamics and psychotherapy.

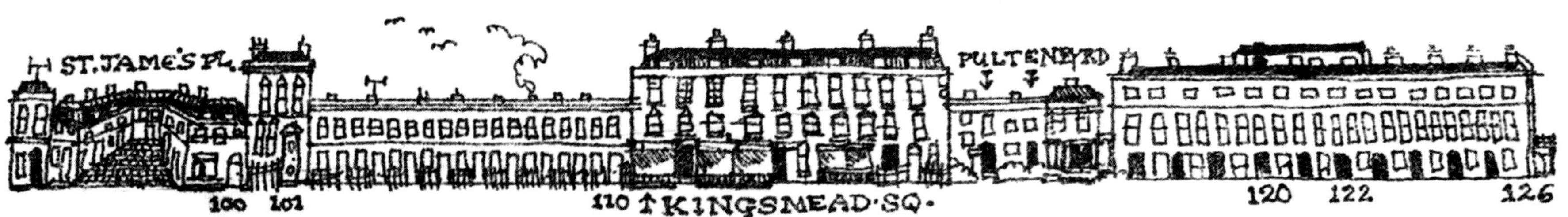

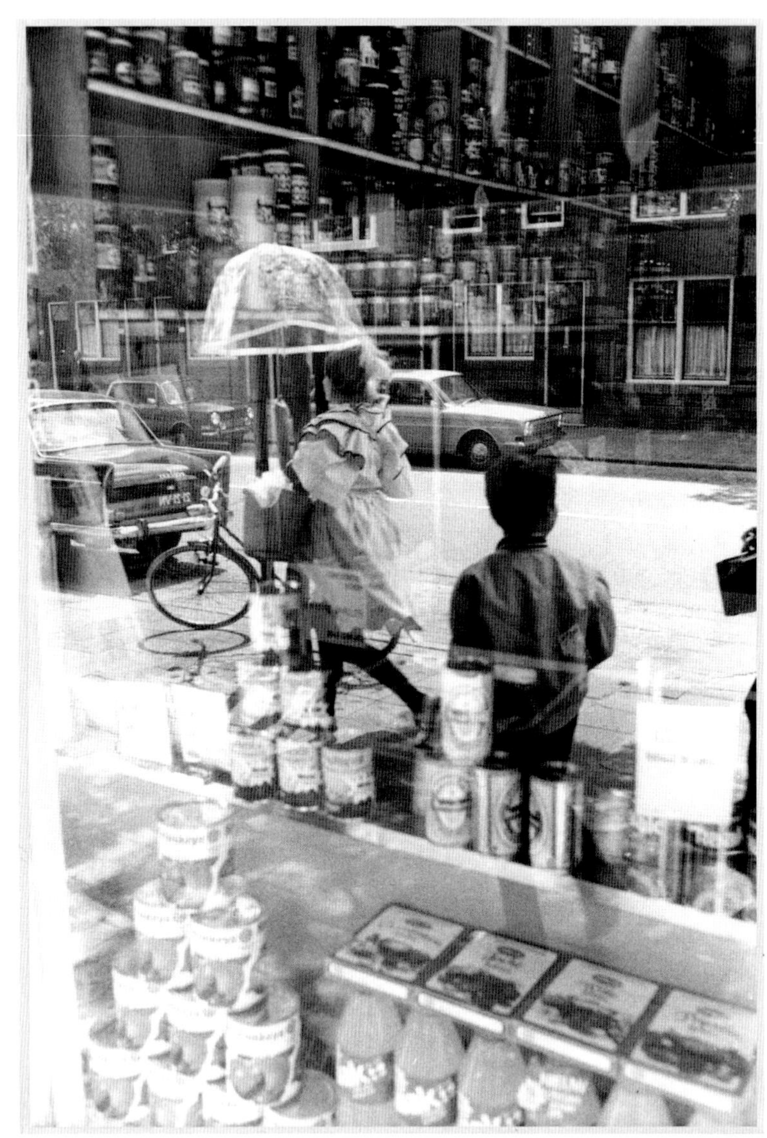

# PHOTO AND ILLUSTRATION CREDITS

## Photos

| | |
|---|---|
| Alistair Campbell | p. 230 Somerset Film |
| R Andre de la Porte | p. 50 Clown with pram |
| Bryan Dale | p. 11 |
| Bernard Farrel | p. 180 weeping brides |
| Dave Dyas | pp. 54, 55, 56, 57, 72, 73, 74 84, 85, 86, 87, 88, 233 |
| Detlev Güthenke | p. 231 British Events at Gütersloh International Theatre Festival |
| Glyn Davies | pp. 37, 96 (solar trumpet), 97, 120, 121, 124, 125, 127 (not bike ride), 128 (dome), 129, 130-131 (not protesters), 132, 134, 135, 136, 137, 138, 139, 140, 141, 146 (shop), 188, 189 |
| Guy Erwood | p. 190 bottom left, NTC van |
| Hans Pattist | p. 176 Clown band, p.181 hermaphrodites |
| Hugh Rayner | pp. 102 (Brian Damage), 108, 111, 216 |
| John Austin | pp. 16, 17, 18, 19, 20, 23, 25, 26, 27, 65 (Rocky and May), 69 |
| Neil Hornick | p. 76 Phantom Captain with May Branch |
| Roger Perry | pp. 36, 39, 44, 45, 48, 49, (included in 50, 51), 53, 102 (Rocky), 104, 112, 149 (Penny and Sarah), 170-171, 173, 238 |
| Vivien McKenzie | p. 176 Clown band, p. 214 Rat Girls |

## Illustrations

| | |
|---|---|
| Carl Willson | p. 84 ticket design |
| Carol Maltby | pp. 218, 219, Festival badges, private collection |
| Glyn Davies | pp. 122-123, 133, 137, 138, 141, 163, 202, 222-223 |
| Jennie Potter-Barrie | pp. 28 (horse) 41, 42, 57, 61, 66, 82, 113, 116, 165, 174, 182, 186 (top left), 235 |
| Louise Ingham | p. 203 Sunshine Festival poster |
| Martin Turner | p. 129 reproduced from *Undercurrents* Magazine 12, October 1975 |
| Penny Dale | pp. 40, 70, 70-71 (poster), 81, 114, 205 (programme) |
| Perry Harris | p. 229 The Bell Inn poster |
| Peter Blake | p. 227 10th London to Brighton Bike Ride poster |
| Ralph Oswick | pp. 28 (map), 29, 64, 66, 71 (programme), 88, 89, 92, 186, 187, 194, 226, 236-237 (buildings listed for demolition) |
| Vic King | p. 71 Theatre Royal ticket stub |

Every effort was made to trace the owners of photos and illustrations, but this was not possible in every case. We are grateful to all those who gave permission to use photos and pictures from their private collections.

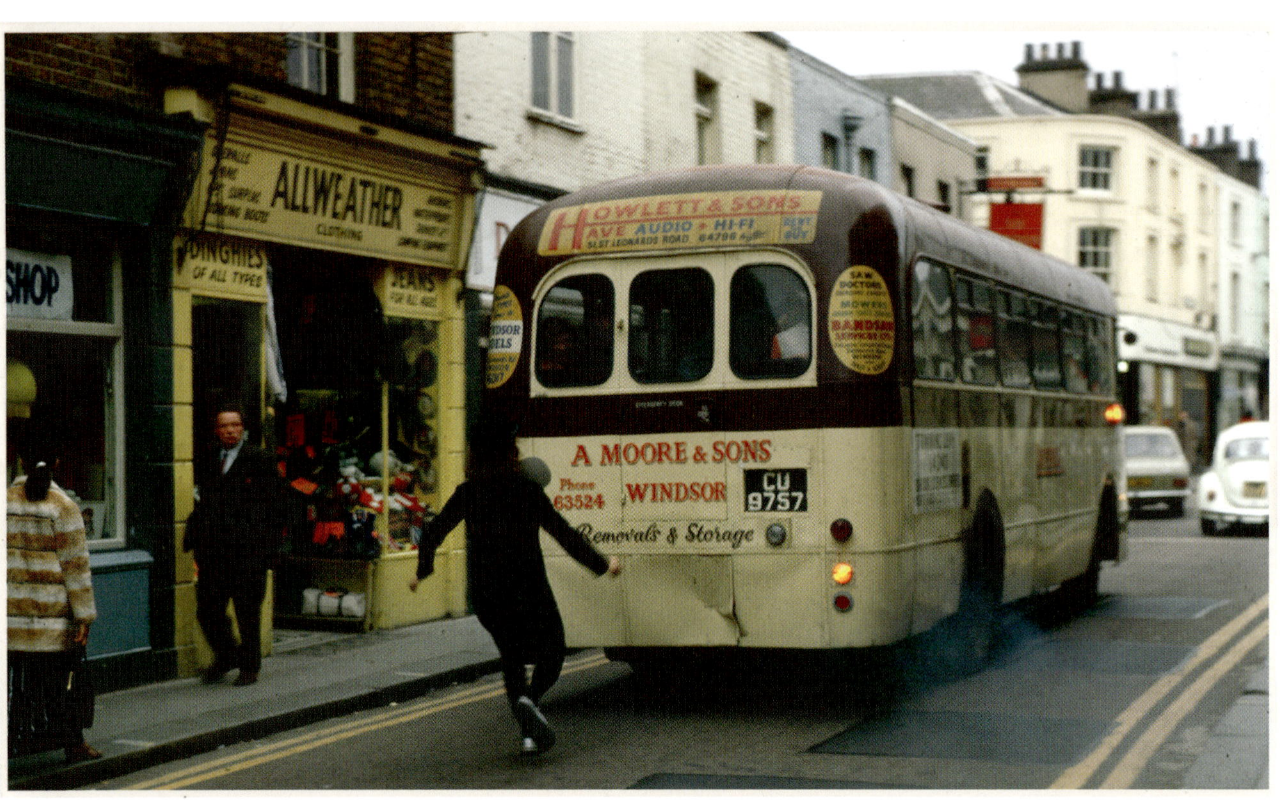
ALLWEATHER
CLOTHING
DINGHIES
OF ALL TYPES
JEANS
FOR ALL AGES
SHOP
HOWLETT & SONS
HAVE AUDIO + HI-FI
RENT
BUY
A MOORE & SONS
WINDSOR
Phone
63524
Removals & Storage
CU
9757